KNOWLEDGE-BASED
SYSTEMS IN
ARTIFICIAL INTELLIGENCE

McGraw-Hill Computer Science Series

McGraw-Hill Advanced Computer Science Series

KNOWLEDGE-BASED SYSTEMS IN ARTIFICIAL INTELLIGENCE

Randall Davis
Massachusetts Institute of Technology

Douglas B. Lenat
Stanford University

McGraw-Hill International Book Company

New York   St. Louis   San Francisco   Auckland   Bogotá   Guatemala
Hamburg   Johannesburg   Lisbon   London   Madrid   Mexico   Montreal   New Delhi
Panama   Paris   San Juan   São Paulo   Singapore   Sydney   Tokyo   Toronto

KNOWLEDGE-BASED SYSTEMS IN ARTIFICIAL INTELLIGENCE

1234567890   KPKP   8987654321

The editors were Diane D. Heiberg and David A. Damstra;
the production supervisor was John Mancia.
The cover was designed by Nicholas Krenitsky.
Kingsport Press, Inc., was printer and binder.

Library of Congress Cataloging in Publication Data

Davis, Randall,
    Knowledge-based systems in artificial intelligence.

    (McGraw-Hill advanced computer science series)
    Bibliography: p.
    Includes index.
        1.   Artificial intelligence—Case studies.
I.   Lenat, Douglas B., joint author.   II.   Title.
III.   Series.
Q335.D38   001 53′5   80-14578

0-07-015557-7

CONTENTS

Appendixes

3 Trace

4 Bibliography

Part 2 Teiresias: Applications of Meta-Level Knowledge

1 Introduction

2 Background

3 Explanation

FOREWORD

As this foreword is being written, the American Association for Artificial Intelligence is about to gather at Stanford to hold its first annual scientific conference. The time of the society's birth is midmorning in the growth of the science of AI, and takes place in a warm and supportive climate. Several hundred scientists from universities and industries, and several dozen of their R&D managers and government program managers attend the birth, amidst a rising tide of interest and activity in the applications of AI to science, engineering, medicine, and defense.

For a science whose very name has been ridiculed by some as a contradiction in terms, it is indeed the best of times. How have we arrived at this happy state?

Artificial intelligence research is that part of computer science that investigates symbolic, nonalgorithmic reasoning processes, and the representation of symbolic knowledge for use in machine inference. Its most fundamental views are as follows: that intelligence can be explained as symbol-manipulating activity; that, as Newell and Simon pointed out in their famous ACM Turing Award lecture (1976), such activity is realizable in a physical symbol system (in particular, by digital computers as universal symbol-manipulating devices); that the various aspects of human intelligence can be modeled by such physical symbol systems; and, as a working hypothesis, and as a long-range goal, that there can be discovered a theory of intelligence general and powerful enough to encompass the phenomena of both human and machine intelligence.

AI research springs from a variety of motives. Some researchers, like Lenat in this book, concerned with the long-range goal, make daring inquiries of abstraction and program construction aimed at providing the conceptual structure for a theory of intelligence. Others, with motives indistinguishable from those of traditional psychology, intentionally constrain their acts of abstraction and construction to fit the demands of the available empirical data on the phenomena of human cognition. By far the largest group of AI researchers emphasizes construction rather than abstraction—the construction of intelligent artifacts that will serve as aids to human activity (e.g., in problem solving, understanding speech and pictures, manufacturing, and so on).

An intelligence artifact that is merely a toy quickly loses its fascination, since it is not complex enough, not rich enough with potentialities, to sustain attention. Along the way from the toy problems of the early years of AI to the complex tasks of today, AI researchers made an important discovery. As with all such insights, it appears in retrospect to be common sense: that the power of an intelligent program to perform its task well depends primarily on the quantity and quality of knowledge it has about that task. This observation arises not only in the work of the artifact builders, but in the work of the psychologists (e.g., the studies of Simon and his colleagues on the nature of "expert" thought in physics and chess playing); in the work of the image understanding researchers; and the work on understanding natural language. It was no accident that Winograd's well known SHRDLU work was followed by years of work by him on KRL, a knowledge-representation language system. It is also not accidental that human specialists, striving for high levels of proficiency in their chosen fields, spend years acquiring the knowledge and skills necessary to support such performance.

Thus, knowledge is seen to be of paramount importance, and AI research has shifted its focus from an inference-based paradigm to a knowledge-based paradigm. Knowledge is viewed as consisting of facts and heuristics. The "facts" constitute a body of information that is widely shared, publicly available, and generally agreed-upon by experts in a field. The "heuristics" are most private, little-discussed rules of good judgment (rules of plausible reasoning, rules of good guessing) that characterize expert-level decision making in a field.

Three major research issues of AI's knowledge-based paradigm are grouped as issues of knowledge representation, knowledge utilization, and knowledge acquisition.

1. Knowledge representation

How shall the knowledge that is necessary for expert-level performance be represented as symbolic data structures for computer use? How can one achieve flexibility in adding and changing knowledge in the development of a knowledge base?

2. Knowledge utilization

What designs are available for the inference procedure to be used by the intelligent artifact? How can one achieve efficient, as well as accurate, performance as the combinatorics of the problem space increase?

3. Knowledge acquisition

How can the knowledge in a field of work be systematically acquired for computer use? How can it be discovered by a program itself acting autonomously? If it is true that the power of an intelligent program is primarily a function of the quality and completeness of the knowledge base, then these are the critical "bottleneck" problems of the knowledge-based paradigm.

The research of Davis and Lenat was nurtured by a laboratory whose primary focus over the past fifteen years has been the development and exploitation of the knowledge-based paradigm. The Stanford Heuristic Programming Project began this adventure in artifact construction and methodological innovation in 1965, with the DENDRAL program. DENDRAL solved problems of structure elucidation in organic chemistry, initially by a knowledge-intensive analysis of physical spectra of the molecules. Its descendent, META-DENDRAL, analyzed sets of spectral data and inferred chemical rules of spectral analysis (created knowledge from data, guided by a few basic principles). META-DENDRAL and Lenat's AM program, described in this book, bear a family resemblance, though AM was done independently and exploits a much richer knowledge structure in its search for plausible mathematical conjectures than META-DENDRAL does in its search for new rules.

The Project's first foray into clinical medicine was the MYCIN effort. MYCIN was a program that performed consultations with physicians about infectious disease diagnosis and antimicrobial therapy. The production rule representation that proved so effective in parts of DENDRAL was adapted to fit the needs of the medical knowledge. Issues in machine-facilitated knowledge acquisition, in the representation of knowledge, and in program control arose from this work on a consultation system, providing the inspiration for Davis' work on the TEIRESIAS program presented in this book.

In the last five years, there has been a flowering of other knowledge-based systems development and software tool building at the Heuristic Programming Project— a complex of artifact building which we refer to as "knowledge engineering" experiments. Here are some examples of past, present, and new experiments. The molecular genetics assistant, MOLGEN, plans experiments in gene cloning that use the recombinant DNA techniques. Along the way to MOLGEN, a knowledge representation system called UNITS was developed. Lenat generalized UNITS and the knowledge structure used in AM to a more powerful representational system. RLL. MYCIN was generalized to EMYCIN, a tool that was used to construct consultation systems in as diverse a pair of fields as structural engineering (SACON) and pulmonary disease diagnosis (PUFF). EMYCIN uses the debugging techniques described by Davis to aid in knowledge base construction. New projects are exploiting knowledge-based system building tools in experimental programs for tutoring students about the contents of complex knowledge bases, for interpreting medical data, for diagnosing computer system failures, and for the layout of very large-scale integrated circuit chips (VLSI).

The work of the Heuristic Programming Project grew out of the basic research in artificial intelligence of the formative years 1955–65 and continues to draw upon and add to the basic research ideas of the field. The original DENDRAL program was built on classic lines of heuristic search, as was the AM program described in this book. The MYCIN and TEIRESIAS programs elaborated basic ideas of backward-chained reasoning. The representational systems UNITS and RLL draw upon the basic research on semantic network structures. For every program we have done, there are such links, and it is a pleasure to watch the science of artificial intelligence cumulate in this way.

Yet the knowledge-based systems research and the knowledge engineering experiments that lead to intelligent systems pose their own special problems. It is to these that we now turn our attention.

Using domain-specific knowledge to obtain expert performance in programs is one of the leading themes of current artificial intelligence research. Both Davis and

Lenat have contributed to the theme in important ways, as we see in this volume.[1] The two parts of the book are reports of separate research projects. Each is clearly organized and written, and thus stands as an excellent description of that piece of work. Even though they can be read and understood separately, the same important themes of knowledge representation, utilization and acquisition are interwoven throughout both.

The computer program that Lenat wrote is called AM. It makes conjectures in number theory that are interesting and plausible. It does not prove them—its task is to suggest them. Because the set of possible theorems is infinite, AM needs considerable knowledge of mathematics to sort out the interesting conjectures from the uninteresting and implausible ones.

The program that Davis wrote is called TEIRESIAS, after the famed seer in Greek literature. It is really a collection of programs whose overall task is to assist a user of a complex program, like MYCIN in (a) understanding the reasoning chain of that program and (b) finding and fixing errors in the knowledge base. It is built around the concept of meta-level knowledge, which it uses to reason about the structure and content of the domain-specific knowledge base.

Both the TEIRESIAS and AM programs are excellent examples of the art of knowledge engineering. These are programs that manipulate and reason about large knowledge bases, and do not merely execute fixed instructions.[2]

REPRESENTATION

Selecting a suitable representation for the domain knowledge is one of the first problems to be encountered in building a knowledge-based system. TEIRESIAS works with domain-specific knowledge encoded in production rules—conditional sentences that describe actions to perform when specified conditions are true. The representation is deliberately simple and uniform to facilitate reading and manipulating the knowledge base. TEIRESIAS is expected to keep track of many of the low-level, syntactic details itself, using explicit models of the knowledge base that it is expected to help explain

---

[1]Historical Note: Both of these pieces of work were done as Ph.D. research projects in the CSD at Stanford. It is interesting that neither Davis nor Lenat began working on these projects until late in their graduate years. Davis had embarked on a project in computer vision, when his long-standing interest in medical computing turned his attention to the medical consultant project we were actively engaged in. He was accepted in medical school about the same time, but decided not to attend. On the strength of the work described here, Davis was awarded a Chaim Weizmann postdoctoral fellowship. Lenat, on the other hand, had embarked on a project in automatic programming—designing computer programs that write other programs—and was concurrently pursuing some ideas in mathematics left over from his days as a graduate student in mathematics. This was the work that blossomed into AM. He found that Stanford would give him a degree for doing what he really wanted to do, and so turned his attention full time to AM. Lenat was awarded the Computers and Thought Award at IJCAI-77, in recognition of the quality and promise of this research.

[2]It is no accident that these, and most other, AI programs are written in LISP. Their complexity demands a rich, interactive editing and debugging environment that is nearly unique to LISP. More fundamentally, however, the reasoning performed by these programs requires removing the distinction between programs and data, which LISP does, in order to treat the rules and heuristics in the knowledge base sometimes as data to be reasoned about and sometimes as code to be executed.

and debug. It is expected as well to monitor strategies (also encoded as production rules) that guide the problem solver to efficient, focused lines of reasoning. These are part of what we call meta-level knowledge: knowledge about the domain knowledge.

In AM, the primary knowledge structure is a hierarchy of concepts and properties (or "slots") of concepts—a knowledge structure that is a near-perfect example of what Minsky calls "frames." In addition, specific production rules and procedures in AM are attached to each concept frame. AM uses framelike structures to encode some of the same kinds of information as Davis puts explicitly in meta-level statements. The statements made about all mathematics concepts in AM are themselves stored in framelike structures, as are the mathematics concepts. For example, AM has the following meta-level knowledge: "A concept is interesting if it is—accidentally—precisely the boundary of some other, interesting concept," and "A concept is not interesting if, after several attempts, only a couple examples are found."

One of the lessons we learned from early AI work on DENDRAL and other knowledge-based systems is that the domain-specific knowledge needed for high performance must not be "hard wired" into the system if that knowledge needs to be changed frequently. In the early days of AI, we were pleased to have a program exhibit approximations to intelligent behavior by "hook or by crook." The knowledge of arithmetic, chess, or chemistry (or whatever domain was used as a testbed) was programmed into the system directly. Then, as we learned how difficult it was to change definitions or extend tables that are distributed throughout the code, we moved to indirect references to concepts, centralizing their definitions in separate functions or data structures and referencing those by name.

It is interesting to note the progress from those primitive ideas about knowledge representation to the ideas used by Davis and Lenat. The advantages of separate, explicit statements of facts and associations are numerous. One of the most interesting ways of looking at TEIRESIAS and AM is to look for the benefits of the separation.

UTILIZATION

Designing a flexible control structure for using knowledge is another major problem in building a knowledge-based system. Accuracy, efficiency and intelligibility are concerns in both AM and TEIRESIAS, and it is interesting for the reader to look for the mechanisms in which these concerns are reflected.

Focus of attention for a problem solver is always an important issue, for it influences many other design decisions concerning knowledge utilization. As in all intelligent systems, in AM and TEIRESIAS the context greatly influences what each system does next. The concept of meta-rules used by TEIRESIAS provides a context-sensitive mechanism for focusing a problem solver's attention along strategic lines. Strategies can be explicitly stated and used in meta-rules. The global strategy in AM is always to work on the most interesting pending problem, but the system is guided by a rich variety of specific heuristics that determine what is interesting and what is not.

In TEIRESIAS, the goals of explaining and modifying the knowledge base—in the context of a particular example—drive the system's behavior. It assumes that a knowledgeable person is interacting with it in order to "debug" the knowledge base used to provide advice on a test case. If the knowledge base is complete and consistent, then the expert will find no fault with the advice. However, if the advice provided is wrong, then TEIRESIAS will explain the reasoning behind the advice in order to isolate the fault, it will help repair the knowledge base, and it will verify the correctness of the updated knowledge base. These tasks are accomplished by different mechanisms, all of which use meta-level knowledge about the knowledge base in response to directions set by the expert during the interaction.

The interpreter in AM is conceptually simpler: pick a task from an agenda and do it. There is considerable intelligence required to pick the "best" task, however, and considerable mathematics knowledge required in order to carry out the tasks. The main idea is to give the system a number of heuristics for extending or combining the prisms and criteria for determining which extensions are more interesting than others. It behaves, then, much as a heuristic search program that explores the space of possible concepts in finite set theory. The heuristics generate plausible moves in the space so that not every possible concept is considered. The evaluation function guides the search to the parts of the space that are most likely to be fruitful. The ordering of tasks is determined by a dynamic measure of "interestingness" attached to each task, which allows the system to select the most interesting task to work on whenever it is momentarily idle. Moreover, the amount of time spent working on the task is controlled by this measure of interestingness, in order to allocate system resources where they are most likely to pay off.

ACQUISITION

Acquisition and maintenance of a large knowledge base is a critical problem for knowledge-based systems. One of the lessons learned from work of the 1960s is that considerable domain-specific knowledge is required for high performance. Generality in problem-solving systems, where it exists, must be found not just in the inference methods but in the methods for constructing and maintaining large, domain-specific knowledge bases. Just putting an initial knowledge base together in a suitable representation is a formidable task. However, in large, open-ended problem areas, such as medicine or mathematics, the task is never-ending. Thus the system builder must be given powerful tools for keeping the knowledge base accurate and current.

TEIRESIAS and AM are elegant examples of two very different methods for coping with expanding knowledge in a domain. Roughly speaking, these are interactive and automatic methods. Although there are other examples of these methods in the AI literature, these are excellent case studies in knowledge cumulation that demonstrate the state of the art.

During knowledge base construction, TEIRESIAS aids the system designer by helping keep track of numerous details about each new item of knowledge added as well as a global plan. TEIRESIAS aids the designer with the details of each item and some of the global interactions among items. One of the key ideas in the implementation of the aids is the idea of meta-level knowledge. Because of its knowledge about the knowledge structures, TEIRESIAS can help the designer fill out those knowledge structures with domain-specific knowledge. The structures remain constant from one domain to another, but they are filled in with different concepts and relations by different designers.

The representation is tied closely to conditional rules, partly because we were experimenting at the time with the strength and limits of production rules. The ideas behind TEIRESIAS, however, apply to any representation.

AM exemplifies a "pure" approach to knowledge cumulation, in which the system is given a small set of primitive facts by a designer and then builds on those facts without further help from the designer. It is not an induction program, primarily, although it does do some generalizing from known instances. Nor does it learn from experience, in the traditional sense of learning programs, because past experience has little influence on future behavior. Instead, it accumulates knowledge by positing interesting extensions to its existing concepts—either new concepts or new relations—and verifying their plausibility.

AM starts with a small number of concepts of finite set theory, and a large number of heuristics about how to extend them and judge their interest. From these the system was able to rediscover the concept of prime numbers and the prime factorization theorem.

SUMMARY

We are pleased to introduce the reader to these fine pieces of work. There are numerous ideas to reflect on, from the details of the implementation to speculation on what these trends will bring to science and mathematics. We believe they offer a glimpse of the future and at the same time offer a better understanding of the power and limits of AI methods.

Bruce G. Buchanan
Edward A. Feigenbaum
Department of Computer Science
Stanford University

Part One

AM: Discovery in Mathematics as Heuristic Search

Indeed, you can build a machine to draw demonstrative conclusions for you, but I think you can never build a machine that will draw plausible inferences.

Pólya
Mathematical Discovery

This part describes a program, called "AM," which models one aspect of elementary mathematics research: developing new concepts under the guidance of a large body of heuristic rules. "Mathematics" is considered as a type of intelligent behavior, not merely as a finished product.

The local heuristics communicate via an agenda mechanism, a global list of tasks for the system to perform and reasons why each task is plausible. A single task might direct AM to define a new concept, or to explore some facet of an existing concept, or to examine some empirical data for regularities, etc. Repeatedly, the program selects from the agenda the task having the best supporting reasons, and then executes it.

Each concept is an active, structured knowledge module. A hundred very incomplete modules are initially provided, each one corresponding to an elementary set-theoretic concept (*e.g.*, union). This provides a definite but immense "space" which AM begins to explore, guided by a corpus of 250 heuristic rules.

1

AM extends its knowledge base, ultimately rediscovering hundreds of common concepts (*e.g.*, numbers) and theorems (*e.g.*, unique factorization).

Chapter 1

Overview

We need a super-mathematics in which the operations are as unknown as the quantities they operate on, and a super-mathematician, who does not know what he is doing when he performs these operations.

Eddington

1–1 FIVE-PAGE SUMMARY OF THE PROJECT

Scientists often face the difficult task of formulating nontrivial research problems which are solvable. In any given branch of science, it is usually easier to tackle a specific given problem than to propose interesting yet manageable new questions to investigate. For example, contrast *solving* the Missionaries and Cannibals problem with the more ill-defined reasoning which led to *inventing* it.

This half of the book is concerned with creative theory formation in mathematics: how to propose interesting new concepts and plausible hypotheses connecting them. The experimental vehicle of my research is a computer program called AM.[1] Initially, AM is given the definitions of 115 simple set-theoretic concepts (like "Delete" or "Equality"). Each concept is represented internally as a

---

[1] The original meaning of this mnemonic has been abandoned. As Exodus states: *I AM that I AM*.

data structure with a couple dozen slots or facets (like "Definition," "Examples," "Worth"). Initially, most facets of most concepts are blank, and AM uses a collection of 250 heuristics—plausible rules of thumb—for guidance, as it tries to fill in those blanks. Some heuristics are used to select which specific facet of which specific concept to explore next, while others are used to actually find some appropriate information about the chosen facet. Other rules prompt AM to notice simple relationships between known concepts, to define promising new concepts to investigate, and to estimate how interesting each concept is.

1–1.1   Detour: Analysis of a Discovery

Before discussing how to *synthesize* a new theory, consider briefly how to *analyze* one, how to construct a plausible chain of reasoning which terminates in a given discovery. One can do this by working backwards, by reducing the creative act to simpler and simpler creative acts. For example, consider the concept of prime numbers. How might one be led to define such a notion? Notice the following plausible strategy:

> "If f is a function which transforms elements of A into elements of B, and B is ordered, then consider just those members of A which are transformed into *extremal* elements of B. This set is an interesting subset of A."

When $f(x)$ means "divisors of x," and the ordering is "by length," this heuristic says to consider those numbers which have a minimal[2] number of factors—that is, the primes. So this rule actually *reduces* our task from "proposing the concept of prime numbers" to the more elementary problems of "discovering ordering-by-length" and "inventing divisors-of."

But suppose we know this general rule: "If f is an interesting function, consider its inverse." It reduces the task of discovering divisors-of to the simpler task of discovering multiplication.[3] Eventually, this task reduces to the discovery of very basic notions, like substitution, set-union, and equality. To explain how a given researcher might have made a given discovery, such an analysis is continued until that inductive task is reduced to "discovering" notions which the researcher already knew, which were his conceptual primitives.

1–1.2   What AM Does: Syntheses of Discoveries

This leads to the paradox that the more original a discovery the more obvious it seems afterwards. The creative act is not an act of creation in the sense of the Old Testament. It does not create something out of nothing; it uncovers, selects, re-shuffles, combines, synthesizes already existing facts, faculties, skills. The more familiar the parts, the more striking the new whole.

Koestler

---

[2] The other extreme, numbers with a *maximal* number of factors, was also proposed by AM as worth investigating. This led AM to many interesting questions.

[3] Plus noticing that multiplication is associative and commutative.

Suppose a large collection of these heuristic strategies has been assembled (*e.g.*, by analyzing a great many discoveries, and writing down new heuristic rules whenever necessary). Instead of using them to *explain* how a given idea might have evolved, one can imagine starting from a basic core of knowledge and "running" the heuristics to *generate* new concepts. We're talking about reversing the process described in the last section: not how to *explain* discoveries, but how to *make* them.

Such syntheses are precisely what AM does. The program consists of a large corpus of primitive mathematical concepts, each with a few associated heuristics.[4] AM's activities all serve to expand AM itself, to enlarge upon a given body of mathematical knowledge. To cope with the enormity of the potential "search space" involved, AM uses its heuristics as judgmental criteria to guide development in the most promising direction. It appears that the process of inventing worthwhile new[5] concepts can be guided successfully using a collection of a few hundred such heuristics.

Each concept is represented as a frame-like data structure with 25 different facets or slots. The types of facets include: Examples, Definitions, Generalizations, Domain/Range, Analogies, Interestingness, and many others. Modular representation of concepts provides a convenient scheme for organizing the heuristics; for example, the following strategy fits into the Examples facet of the Predicate concept: *"If, empirically, 10 times as many elements fail some predicate P, as satisfy it, then some* generalization *(weakened version) of P might be more interesting than P."* AM considers this suggestion after trying to fill in examples of each predicate.[6]

AM is initially given a collection of 115 core concepts, with only a few facets filled in for each concept. Its sole activity is to choose some facet of some concept, and fill in that particular slot. In so doing, new notions will often emerge. Uninteresting ones are forgotten, mildly interesting ones are kept as parts of one facet of one concept, and very interesting ones are granted full concept-module status. Each of these new modules has dozens of blank slots; hence the space of possible actions (blank facets to fill in) grows rapidly. The same heuristics are used both to suggest new directions for investigation and to limit attention: both to sprout and to prune.

1–1.3   Results

The particular mathematical domains in which AM operates depend upon the choice of initial concepts. Currently, AM begins with nothing but a scanty knowledge of concepts which Piaget might describe as *prenumerical*: Sets, substitution, operations, equality, and so on. In particular, AM is not told anything

---

[4] Situation/action rules which function as local "plausible move generators." Some suggest tasks for the system to carry out, some suggest ways of satisfying a given task, etc.

[5] Typically, "new" means new to AM, not to human beings; and "worthwhile" can be judged only with hindsight.

[6] In fact, after AM attempts to find examples of SET-EQUALITY, so few are found that AM decides to generalize that predicate. The result is the creation of a new predicate which means "Has-the-same-length-as"—*i.e.*, a rudimentary precursor to natural numbers.

about proof, single-valued functions, or numbers.

From this primitive basis, AM quickly discovered[7] elementary numerical concepts (corresponding to those we refer to as natural numbers, multiplication, factors, and primes) and wandered around in the domain of elementary number theory. AM was not designed to *prove* anything, but it did *conjecture* many well-known relationships (*e.g.*, the unique factorization theorem).

AM was not able to discover any "new-to-Mankind" mathematics purely on its own, but *has* discovered several interesting notions hitherto unknown to the author. A couple bits of new mathematics have been *inspired* by AM. A synergetic AM–human combination can sometimes produce better research than either could alone.[8] Although most of the concepts AM proposed and developed were already very well known, AM defined some of them in novel ways (*e.g.*, prime pairs were defined by restricting addition to primes; that is, for which primes p, q, r is it possible that $p + q = r$?[9]).

Everything that AM does can be viewed as testing the underlying body of heuristic rules. Gradually, this knowledge becomes better organized, its implications clearer. The resultant body of detailed heuristics may be the germ of a more efficient programme for educating math students than current dogma.[10]

Another benefit of actually constructing AM is that of *experimentation*: one can vary the concepts AM starts with, vary the heuristics available, etc., and study the effects on AM's behavior. Several such experiments were performed. One involved adding a couple dozen new concepts from an entirely new domain: plane geometry. AM busied itself exploring elementary geometric concepts, and was almost as productive there as in its original domain. New concepts were defined, and new conjectures formulated. Other experiments indicated that AM was more robust than anticipated; it withstood many kinds of "de-tuning." Others demonstrated the tremendous impact that a few key concepts (*e.g.*, Equality) had on AM's behavior. Several more experiments and extensions have been planned for the future.

---

[7] "Discovering" a concept means that (1) AM recognized it as a distinguished entity (*e.g.*, by formulating its definition) and also (2) AM decided it was worth investigating (either because of the interesting way it was formed, or because of surprising preliminary empirical results).

[8] This is supported by Gelernter's experiences with his geometry program: while lecturing about how it might prove a certain theorem about isosceles triangles, he came up with a new, cute proof. Similarly, Guard and Eastman noticed an intermediate result of their SAM resolution theorem prover, and wisely interpreted it as a nontrivial result in lattice theory (now known as SAM's lemma).

[9] The answer is that either p or q must be 2, and that the other two primes are a prime pair—*i.e.*, they differ by two.

[10] Currently, an educator takes the very best work any mathematician has ever done, polishes it until its brilliance is blinding, then presents it to the student to induce upon. Many individuals (*e.g.*, Knuth and Polya) have pointed out this blunder. A few (*e.g.*, Papert at MIT, Adams at Stanford, Seely-Brown and Goldstein at Xerox-Parc) are experimenting with more realistic strategies for "teaching" creativity.

1–1.4   Conclusions

AM is forced to judge *a priori* the value of each new concept, to lose interest quickly in concepts which aren't going to develop into anything. Often, such judgments can only be based on hindsight. For similar reasons, AM has difficulty formulating new heuristics which are relevant to the new concepts it creates. Heuristics are often merely compiled hindsight. While AM's "approach" to empirical research may be used in other scientific domains, the main limitation (reliance on hindsight) will probably recur. This prevents AM from progressing indefinitely far on its own.

This ultimate limitation was reached. AM's performance degraded more and more as it progressed further away from its initial base of concepts. Nevertheless, AM demonstrated that selected aspects of creative discovery in elementary mathematics could be adequately represented as a heuristic search process. Actually constructing a computer model of this activity has provided an experimental vehicle for studying the dynamics of plausible empirical inference.

1–2   VIEWING AM AS SOME COMMON PROCESS

This section will provide a few metaphors: some hints for squeezing AM into paradigms with which the reader might be familiar. For example, the existence of heuristics in AM is functionally the same as the presence of domain-specific information in any knowledge-based system.

Consider assumptions, axioms, definitions, and theorems to be syntactic rules for the language that we call Mathematics. Thus theorem-proving, and the whole of textbook mathematics, is a purely syntactic process. Then the heuristic rules used by a mathematician (and by AM) would correspond to the semantic knowledge associated with these more formal methods.

Just as one can upgrade natural-language-understanding by incorporating semantic knowledge, so AM is only as successful as the heuristics it knows.

Four more ways of "viewing" AM as something else will be provided: (*i*) AM as a hill-climber, (*ii*) AM as a heuristic search program, (*iii*) AM as a mathematician, and (*iv*) AM as half a book.

1–2.1   AM as Hill-Climbing

Let's draw an analogy between the process of developing new mathematics and the familiar process of hill-climbing. We may visualize AM as exploring a space using a measuring or "evaluation" function which imparts to it a topography.

Consider AM's core of very simple knowledge. By compounding its known concepts and methods, AM can explore beyond the frontier of this foundation a little wherever it wishes. The incredible variety of alternatives to investigate includes all known mathematics, much trivia, countless dead ends, and so on. The only "successful" paths near the core are the narrow ridges of known mathematics (plus perhaps a few as-yet-undiscovered isolated peaks).

How can AM walk through this immense space with any hope of following the few, slender trails of already-established mathematics (or some equally successful new fields)? AM must do hill-climbing: as new concepts are formed, decide how promising they are, and always explore the currently most-promising new concept. The evaluation function is quite nontrivial, and the work reported in this half of the book may be viewed as an attempt to study and explain and duplicate the judgmental criteria people employ. Preliminary attempts[11] at codifying such "mysterious" emotive forces as intuition, aesthetics, utility, richness, interestingness, relevance. . .indicated that a large but not unmanageable collection of heuristic rules should suffice.

The important visualization to make is that with proper evaluation criteria, AM's planar mass of interrelated concepts is transformed into a three-dimensional relief map: the known lines of development become mountain ranges, soaring above the vast flat plains of trivia and inconsistency below.

Occasionally an isolated hill is discovered near the core;[12] certainly whole ranges lie undiscovered for long periods of time,[13] and the terrain far from the initial core is not yet explored at all.

1–2.2   AM as Heuristic Search

We earlier referred to AM as a kind of "heuristic search" program. That must mean that AM is exploring a particular "space," using some informal evaluation criteria to guide it.

The flavor of search which is used here is that of progressively enlarging a tree. Certain "evaluation-function" heuristics are used to decide which node of the tree to expand next, and other guiding rules are then used to produce from that node a few interesting successor nodes. To do mathematical research well, I claim that it is necessary and sufficient to have good methods for proposing new concepts from existing ones, and for deciding how interesting each "node" (partially-studied concept) is.

AM is initially supplied with a few facts about some simple math concepts. AM then explores mathematics by selectively enlarging that basis. One could say that AM consists of an active body of mathematical concepts, plus enough "wisdom" to use and develop them effectively (for "wisdom," read "heuristics"). Loosely speaking, then, AM is a heuristic search program. To see this more clearly, we must explain what the nodes of AM's search space are, what the successor operators or links are, and what the evaluation function is.

AM's space can be considered to consist of all nodes which are consistent, partially-filled-in concepts. Then a primitive "legal move" for AM would be to (i) enlarge some facet of some concept, or (ii) create a new, partially-complete concept. Consider momentarily the size of this space. If there were no constraint

---

[11] These took the form of informal simulations. Although far from controlled experiments, they indicated the feasibility of attempting to create AM, by yielding an approximate figure for the amount of informal knowledge such a system would need.

[12] For example, Conway's numbers, as described in [Knuth 74].

[13] For example, non-Euclidean geometries weren't thought of until 1848.

on what the new concepts can be, and no informal knowledge for quickly finding entries for a desired facet, a blind "legal-move" program would go nowhere— slowly! One shouldn't even call the activity such a program would be doing "math research."

The heuristic rules are used as little "plausible move generators." They suggest which facet of which concept to enlarge next, and they suggest specific new concepts to create. The only activities which AM will consider doing are those which have been motivated for some specific good[14] reason. A global *agenda of tasks* is maintained, listing all the activities suggested but not yet worked on.

AM has a definite algorithm for rating the nodes of its space. Many heuristics exist merely to estimate the worth of any given concept. Other heuristics use these worth ratings to order the tasks on the global agenda list. Yet AM has no specific goal criteria: it can never "halt," never succeed or fail in any absolute sense. AM goes on forever.[15]

Consider Nilsson's descriptions of depth-first searching and breadth-first searching ([Nilsson 71]). He has us maintain a list of "open" nodes. Repeatedly, he plucks the top one and expands it. In the process, some new nodes may be added to the Open list. In the case of depth-first searching, they are added at the top; the next node to expand is the one most recently created; the Open-list is being used as a push-down stack. For breadth-first search, new nodes are added at the bottom; they aren't expanded until all the older nodes have been; the Open-list is used as a queue. For heuristic search, or "best-first" search, new nodes are evaluated in some numeric way, and then "merged" into the already-sorted list of Open nodes.

This process is very similar to the agenda mechanism AM uses to manage its search. This will be discussed in detail in Chapter 3. Each entry on the agenda consists of three parts: (*i*) a plausible task for AM to do, (*ii*) a list of reasons supporting that task, and (*iii*) a numeric estimate of the overall priority this task should have. When a task is suggested for some reason, it is added to the agenda. A task may be suggested several times, for different reasons. The global priority value assigned to each task is based on the combined value of its reasons. The control structure of AM is simply to select the task with the highest priority, execute it, and select a new one. The agenda mechanism appears to be a very well-suited data structure for managing a "best-first" search process.

Similar control structures were used in LT [Newell, Shaw, & Simon 57], the predictor part of Dendral [Buchanan *et al.* 69], SIMULA-67 [Dahl 68], and KRL [Bobrow & Winograd 77]. The main difference is that in AM, symbolic reasons are used (albeit in trivial token-like ways) to decide whether—and how much—to boost the priority of a task when it is suggested again.

There are several difficulties and anomalies in forcing AM into the heuristic search paradigm. In a typical heuristic search (*e.g.*, Dendral [Feigenbaum *et al.* 71],

---

[14] Of course, AM thinks a reason is "good" if—and only if—it was told that by a heuristic rule; so those rules had better be plausible, preferably the ones actually used by the experts.

[15] Technically, forever is about 100,000 list cells and a couple of cpu hours.

Meta-Dendral [Buchanan *et al.* 72], most game-playing programs [Samuel 67]), a "search space" is defined implicitly by a "legal move generator." Heuristics are present to constrain that generator so that only plausible nodes are produced. The second kind of heuristic search, of which AM is an example, contains no "legal move generator." Instead, AM's heuristics are used as plausible move generators. Those heuristics themselves implicitly define the possible tasks AM might consider, and *all* such tasks should be plausible ones. In the first kind of search, removing a heuristic widens the search space; in AM's kind of search, removing a heuristic *reduces* it.

Another anomaly is that the operators which AM uses to enlarge and explore the space of concepts are themselves mathematical concepts (*e.g.*, some heuristic rules result in the creation of new heuristic rules; "Compose" is both a concept and an operation which results in new concepts). Thus AM should be viewed as a mass of knowledge which enlarges *itself* repeatedly. Typically, computer programs keep the information they "discover" quite separate from the knowledge they use to make discoveries.[16]

Perhaps the greatest difference between AM and typical heuristic search procedures is that AM has no well-defined target concepts or target relationships. Rather, its "goal criterion"—its sole aim—is to maximize the interestingness level of the activities it performs, the priority ratings of the top tasks on the agenda. It doesn't matter precisely which definitions or conjectures AM discovers—or misses—so long as it spends its time on plausible tasks. There is no fixed set of theorems that AM should discover, so AM is not a typical *problem-solver*. There is no fixed set of traps AM should avoid, no small set of legal moves, and no winning/losing behavior, so AM is not a typical *game-player*.

For example, no stigma is attached to the fact that AM never discovered real numbers;[17] it was rather surprising that AM managed to discover *natural* numbers! Even if it hadn't done that, it would have been acceptable[18] if AM had simply gone off and developed ideas in set theory.

1–2.3   AM as a Mathematician

Before diving into the innards of AM, let's take a moment to discuss the totality of the mathematics which AM carried out. Like a contemporary historian summarizing the work of the Babylonian mathematicians, we shan't hesitate to use current terms and criticize by current standards.

---

[16] Of course, this is often because the two kinds of knowledge are very different: For a chess-player, the first kind is "good board positions," and the second is "strategies for making a good move." Theorem-provers are an exception. They produce a new theorem, and then use it (almost like a new operator) in future proofs. A program to learn to play checkers [Samuel 67] has this same flavor, thereby indicating that this "self-help" property can be used in many domains, not simply in mathematics.

[17] There are many "nice" things which AM didn't—and can't—do: *e.g.*, devising *geometric* concepts from its initial simple set-theoretic knowledge. See the discussion of the limitations of AM, Section 7–2.2.

[18] Acceptable to whom? Is there really a domain-invariant criterion for judging the quality of AM's actions? See the discussions in Section 7–1.

AM began its investigations with scanty knowledge of a few set-theoretic concepts (sets, equality of sets, set operations). Most of the obvious set-theory relations (*e.g.*, de Morgan's laws) were eventually uncovered; since AM never fully understood abstract algebra, the statement and verification of each of these was quite obscure. AM never derived a formal notion of infinity, but it naively established conjectures like "a set can never be a member of itself," and procedures for making chains of new sets ("insert a set into itself"). No sophisticated set theory (*e.g.*, diagonalization) was ever done.

After this initial period of exploration, AM decided that "equality" was worth generalizing, and thereby discovered the relation "same-size-as." "Natural numbers" were based on this, and soon most simple arithmetic operations were defined.

Since addition arose as an analog to union, and multiplication as a repeated substitution followed by a generalized kind of unioning,[19] it came as quite a surprise when AM noticed that they were related (namely, $n + n = 2 \times n$). AM later rediscovered multiplication in three other ways: as repeated addition, as the numeric analog of the Cartesian product of sets, and by studying the cardinality of power sets.[20] These operations were defined in different ways, so it was an unexpected (to AM) discovery when they all turned out to be equivalent. These surprises caused AM to give the concept "Times" quite a high Worth rating.

Exponentiation was defined as repeated multiplication. Unfortunately, AM never found any obvious properties of exponentiation, hence lost all interest in it.

Soon after defining multiplication, AM investigated the process of multiplying a number by itself: squaring. The inverse of this turned out to be interesting, and led to the definition of square-root. AM remained content to play around with the concept of *integer*-square-root. Although it isolated the set of numbers which had no square root, AM was never close to discovering rationals, let alone irrationals.

Raising to fourth-powers, and fourth-rooting, were discovered at this time. Perfect squares and perfect fourth-powers were isolated. Many other numeric operations and kinds of numbers were isolated: Odds, Evens, Doubling, Halving, etc. Primitive notions of numeric inequality were defined but AM never even discovered Trichotomy.

The associativity and commutativity of multiplication indicated that it could accept a BAG of numbers as its argument. When AM defined the inverse operation corresponding to Times, this property allowed the definition to be: "any *bag of numbers* (> 1) whose product is x." This was just the notion of factoring a number x. Minimally-factorable numbers turned out to be what we call primes.

---

[19] Take two bags A and B. Replace each element of A by the bag B. Remove one level of parentheses by taking the union of all elements of the transfigured bag A. Then that new bag will have as many elements as the product of the lengths of the two original bags.

[20] The size of the set of all subsets of S is $2^{\|S\|}$. Thus the power set of $A \bigcup B$ has length equal to the *product* of the lengths of the power sets of A and B individually (assuming A and B are disjoint).

Maximally-factorable numbers were also thought to be interesting.

Prime pairs were discovered in a bizarre way: by restricting addition (its arguments and its values) to Primes.[21] AM conjectured the fundamental theorem of arithmetic (unique factorization into primes) and Goldbach's conjecture (every even number greater than 2 is the sum of two primes) in a surprisingly symmetric way. The unary representation of numbers gave way to a representation as a bag of primes (based on unique factorization), but AM never thought of exponential notation.[22] Since the key concepts of remainder, greater-than, gcd, and exponentiation were never mastered, progress in number theory was arrested.

When a new base of *geometric* concepts was added, AM began finding some more general associations. In place of the strict definitions for the equality of lines, angles, and triangles, came new definitions of concepts we refer to as Parallel, Equal-measure, Similar, Congruent, Translation, Rotation, plus many which have no common name (*e.g.*, the relationship of two triangles sharing a common angle). An unexpected geometric interpretation of Goldbach's conjecture was found.[23] Lacking a geometry "model" (an analogic representation like the one Gelernter employed), AM was doomed to failure with respect to proposing only plausible geometric conjectures.

Similar restrictions due to poor "visualization" abilities would crop up in topology. The concepts of continuity, infinity, and measure would have to be fed to AM before it could enter the domains of analysis. More and more drastic changes in its initial base would be required, as the desired domain gets further and further from simple finite set theory and elementary number theory.

1–2.4   AM as Half a Book

Walking home along a deserted street late at night, the reader may imagine himself to feel in the small of his back a cold, hard object; and to hear the words spoken behind him, "Easy now. This is a stick-up. Hand over your money." What does the reader do? He attempts to generate the utterance. He says to himself, now if I were standing behind someone holding a cold, hard object against his back, what would make me say that? What would I mean by it? The reader is advised that he can only arrive at the deep structure of this book, and through the deep structure the semantics, if he attempts to generate the book for himself. The author wishes him luck.

Linderholm

Each chapter is of roughly equal importance, which explains the huge variation

---

[21] That is, consider the set of triples p, q, r, all primes, for which $p + q = r$. Then one of them must be "2," and the other two must therefore form a prime pair.

[22] A tangential note: All of the discoveries mentioned above were made by AM working by itself, with a human being observing its behavior. If the level of sophistication of AM's concepts were higher (or the level of sophistication of its users were lower), then it might be worthwhile to develop a nice user–system interface. The user in that case could—and ought to—work right along with AM as a co-researcher.

[23] Given all angles of a prime number of degrees, $(0, 1, 2, 3, 5, 7, 11, \ldots, 179^\circ)$, then any angle between 0 and 180° can be approximated (to within 1°) as the sum of two of those angles.

in length. Start looking over Chapter 2 right away: it contains a detailed example of what AM does. Since you're reading this sentence now, we'll assume that you want a preview of what's to come in the rest of this document.

Chapter 3 covers the top-level control structure of the system, which is based on the notion of an "agenda" of tasks to perform. In Chapter 4 the low-level control structure is revealed: AM is really guided by a mass of heuristic rules of varying generality. Chapter 5 contains more than you want to know about the representation of knowledge in AM. It contains a diagram showing some of AM's starting concepts, which is worth a look.

Most of the results of the project are presented in Chapter 6. In addition to simply "running" AM, several experiments have been conducted with it. It's awkward to evaluate AM, and therefore Chapter 7 is quite long and detailed.

The appendices provide material which supplements the text. Appendix 1 contains a description of a few of the initial concepts, some examples of how they were coded into Lisp, and a partial list of the concepts AM defined and investigated along the way. Appendix 2 exhibits all 253 heuristics that AM is explicitly provided with. Appendix 3 contains traces of AM in action.

This book—and its readers—must come to grips with a very interdisciplinary problem. For the reader whose background is in Artificial Intelligence, most of the system's actions—the "mathematics" it does—may seem inherently uninteresting. For the mathematician, the word "LISP" signifies nothing beyond a speech impediment (to Artificial Intelligence types it also connotes a programming impediment). As a result, there is a good bit of definition and explanation, and the reader's indulgence is entreated.

Chapter 2

Example: Discovering Prime Numbers

This chapter will present an example of AM in action, an excerpt from the output of AM, as it investigates some concepts. After a brief discussion of AM's control structure in Section 2–1, the reader will be told what the point of this example is—and Section 2–2 explains what it is *not*. Section 2–3 provides a few eleventh-hour hints at decoding the example.

The excerpt itself follows in Section 2–4. It skips the first half of the session, and picks up at a point just after AM has defined the concept "Divisors-of." Soon afterward, AM defines Primes, and begins to find interesting conjectures related to them. The excerpt goes on to show how AM conjectured the fundamental theorem of arithmetic and Goldbach's conjecture. AM derived the notion of partitioning a collection of n objects into smaller bundles, but failed to find any interesting conjectures about that process. Instead, AM was side-tracked into the (probably) fruitless investigation of numbers which can be represented as the sum of two primes in one unique way.

The final section of this chapter will recap this example the way a math historian might report it.

2–1   DISCUSSION OF THE AM PROGRAM

2–1.1   Representation

AM is a program which expands a knowledge base of mathematical concepts. Each concept is stored as a particular kind of data structure, namely as a collection of properties or "facets" of the concept. For example, here is a miniature example of a concept:[1]

NAME: *Prime Numbers*
DEFINITIONS:
       ORIGIN: *Number-of-divisors-of(x) = 2*
       PREDICATE–CALCULUS: $Prime(x) \Leftrightarrow (\forall z)(z \mid x \Rightarrow (z = 1 \otimes z = x))$
       ITERATIVE: *(for $x > 1$):For i from 2 to $\sqrt{x}$, $i \nmid x$*
EXAMPLES: 2, 3, 5, 7, 11, 13, 17
       BOUNDARY: 2, 3
       BOUNDARY–FAILURES: 0, 1
       FAILURES: 12
GENERALIZATIONS: *Nos., Nos. with an even no. of divisors*
SPECIALIZATIONS: *Odd Primes, Prime Pairs, Prime Uniquely–addables*
CONJECS: *Unique factorization, Goldbach's conjec., Extrema of No-of-divisors-of*
INTU'S: *A metaphor to the effect that Primes are the building blocks of all numbers*
ANALOGIES:
       Maximally-divisible numbers are converse extremes of Number-of-divisors-of
       Factor a non-simple group into simple groups
INTEREST: *Conjectures tying Primes to Times, to Divisors-of, to related operations*
WORTH: 800

"Creating a new concept" is a well-defined activity: it involves setting up a new data structure like the one above, and filling in entries for some of its facets or slots. Filling in a particular facet of a particular concept is also quite well-defined, and is accomplished by executing a collection of relevant heuristic rules. This process will be described in great detail in later chapters.

2–1.2   Agenda and Heuristics

An agenda of plausible tasks is maintained by AM. A typical task is "Fill-in examples of Primes." The agenda may contain hundreds of entries such as this one. AM repeatedly selects the top task from the agenda and tries to carry it out. This is the whole control structure! Of course, we must still explain how AM creates plausible new tasks to place on the agenda, how AM decides which task will be the best one to execute next, and how it carries out a task.

---

[1] The right arrow ("$\Rightarrow$") is the symbol for "implies." "Nos." is an abbreviation for "Numbers." The vertical bar "|" is a symbol for the predicate "divides evenly into;" with a slash through it ("$\nmid$") we denote "does not divide evenly into." "$\otimes$" indicates exclusive or, and the symbol "$\forall$" is read "for all."

If the task is "Fill-in new Algorithms for Set-union," then *satisfying* it would mean actually synthesizing some new procedures, some new LISP code capable of forming the union of any two sets. A heuristic rule is *relevant* to a task if and only if executing that rule brings AM closer to satisfying that task. Relevance is determined *a priori* by where the rule is stored. A rule tacked onto the Domain/range facet of the Compose concept would be presumed relevant to the task "Check the Domain/range of Insert∘Delete."

Once a task is chosen from the agenda, AM gathers some heuristic rules which might be relevant to satisfying that task. They are executed, and then AM picks a new task. While a rule is executing, three kinds of actions or effects can occur:

1   Facets of some concepts can get filled in (*e.g.*, examples of primes may actually be found and tacked onto the "Examples" facet of the "Primes" concept). A typical heuristic rule which might have this effect is:

To fill in examples of X, where X is a kind of Y (for some more general concept Y), Check the examples of Y; some of them may be examples of X as well.

For the task of filling in examples of Primes, this rule would have AM notice that Primes is a kind of Number, and therefore look over all the known examples of Number. Some of those would be primes, and would be transferred to the Examples facet of Primes.

2   New concepts may be created (*e.g.*, the concept "primes which are uniquely representable as the sum of two other primes" may be somehow be deemed worth studying). A typical heuristic rule which might result in this new concept is:

If some (but not most) examples of X are also examples of Y (for some concept Y), Create a new concept defined as the intersection of those 2 concepts (X and Y).

Suppose AM has already isolated the concept of being representable as the sum of two primes in only one way (AM actually calls such numbers "Uniquely-prime-addable numbers"). When AM notices that some primes are in this set, the above rule will create a brand new concept, defined as the set of numbers which are both prime and uniquely prime addable.

3   New tasks may be added to the agenda (*e.g.*, the current activity may suggest that the following task is worth considering: "Generalize the concept of prime numbers"). A typical heuristic rule which might have this effect is:

If very few examples of X are found, Then add the following task to the agenda: "Generalize the concept X."

Of course, AM contains a precise meaning for the phrase "very few." When AM looks for primes among examples of already-known kinds of numbers, it will find dozens of non-examples for every example of a prime it uncovers. "Very few" is thus naturally implemented as a statistical confidence level.[2]

The concept of an agenda is certainly not new: schedulers have been around for a long time. But one important feature of AM's agenda scheme *is* a new idea:

---

[2] The ratio of examples found to non-examples stumbled over lies between .001 and .05. Philosophers outraged by this may be somewhat appeased by knowledge that large changes in the precise numbers very rarely alter AM's behavior.

attaching—and using—a list of quasi-symbolic[3] reasons to each task which explain why the task is worth considering, why it's plausible. *It is the responsibility of the heuristic rules to include reasons for any tasks they propose.*[4] For example, let's reconsider the heuristic rule mentioned in (3) above. It really looks more like the following:

> *If very few examples of X are found,*
> *Then add the following task to the agenda: "Generalize the concept X," for the following reason: "X's are quite rare; a slightly less restrictive concept might be more interesting."*

If the same task is proposed by several rules, then several different reasons for it may be present. In addition, one ephemeral reason also exists: "Focus of attention." Any tasks which are similar to the one last executed get "Focus of attention" as a bonus reason. AM uses all these reasons to decide how to rank the tasks on the agenda. The "intelligence" AM exhibits is not so much "what it does," but rather the *order* in which it arranges its agenda.[5] AM uses the list of reasons in another way: Once a task has been selected, the quality of the reasons is used to decide how much time and space the task will be permitted to absorb, before AM quits and moves on to a new task. This whole mechanism will be detailed in Section 3–2.

2–2   WHAT (NOT) TO GET OUT OF THIS EXAMPLE

The purpose of the example which comprises the next subsection is to convey a bit of AM's flavor. After reading through it, the reader should be convinced that AM is *not* a theorem prover, nor is AM *randomly* manipulating entries in a knowledge base, nor is it *exhaustively* manipulating or searching. AM is carefully growing a network of data structures representing mathematical concepts, by repeatedly using heuristics both (a) for guidance in choosing a task to work on next and (b) for providing methods to satisfy the chosen task.

The following points are important but can't be conveyed by any lone example:

1   Although AM appears to have reasonable natural language abilities, this is a typical AI illusion: most of the phrases AM types are mere tokens, and the

---

[3] Each reason is an English sentence. While AM can tell whether two given reasons coincide, it can't actually do any internal processing on them. If this lack of intelligence had proved to be a limiting problem, then more work would have been expended on giving AM some such abilities.
[4] An alternative scheme, perhaps even a bit more human-like, would be to (perhaps only occasionally) allow a burst of poorly-motivated tasks to be proposed, and then use some pruning criteria to weed out the obvious losers. During this time, AM could type out to the user (who otherwise would be closely monitoring its activities) a cute anthropomorphic phrase like "I'm now sitting back and puffing on my pipe, lost in contemplation."
[5] For example, alternating a randomly-chosen task and the "best" task (the one AM chose to do) only slows the system down by a factor of 2, yet it totally destroys its credibility as a rational researcher (as judged by the human user of AM). This is one conclusion of experiment 4 (see Section 5–4).

syntax which the user must obey is unnaturally constrained. For the sake of clarity, I have "touched up" some of the wording, indentation, syntax, etc., of what AM actually outputs, but left the spirit of each phrase intact. As the reader becomes more familiar with AM, future examples can be "unretouched." If it is desired, the reader may glance at Appendix 3–2, which shows some actual listings of AM in action.

2   The reader should be skeptical of the generality of the program; is the knowledge base "just right" (*i.e.*, finely tuned to elicit this one chain of behaviors)? The answer is "*No.*"[6] The whole point of this project is to show that a relatively small set of general heuristics can guide a nontrivial discovery process. Each activity, each task, was proposed by some heuristic rule (like "look for extreme cases of X") which was used time and time again, in many situations. It was not considered fair to insert heuristic guidance which could "guide" only in a single situation.

This kind of generality can't be shown convincingly in one example. Nevertheless, even within this small excerpt, the same line of development which leads to decomposing numbers (using $Times^{-1}$), thereby discovering unique factorization, also leads to decomposing numbers (using Add^{-1}), thereby discovering Goldbach's conjecture. The same heuristic which caused AM to expect that unique factorization would be useful, also caused AM to suspect that Goldbach's conjecture would be useless.

Let me reemphasize that the point of this example is *not* the specific mathematical concepts, nor the particular chains of plausible reasoning AM produces, nor the few flashy conjectures AM spouts, but rather an illustration of the *kinds* of things AM does.

2–3   DECIPHERING THE EXAMPLE

Recall that, in general, each task on the agenda will have several reasons attached to it. In the example excerpt, the reasons for each task are printed just after the task is chosen and before it is executed.

AM numbers its activities sequentially. Each time a new task is chosen, a counter is incremented. The first task in the example excerpt is labelled <u>Task 65</u>, meaning that the example skips the first 64 tasks which AM selects and carries out. The reason simply is that the development of simple concepts related to divisibility will probably be more intelligible and palatable to the reader than AM's early ramblings in finite set theory.

In the example itself, several irrelevant tasks have been excised.[7] About half of those omitted tasks were interesting in themselves, but all of them were

---

[6] The *design* of AM was finely tuned so that the answer to this question would be "No." Ponder that one!

[7] This is fair, despite the results of Experiment 5 (see Section 5–3.5) because the remaining tasks clump together in twos, threes, etc; they are uninterrupted lines of research (for example, Tasks 65–67) separated by very large gaps (for example, the jump from Task 68 to 79).

tangential or unrelated to the development shown. The reader can tell by the global task numbering how many were skipped. For example, notice that the excerpt jumps from Task 67 to Task 79.

To help gauge AM's abilities, the reader may be interested to know that AM defined "Natural Numbers" during Task 32, and "Times" was defined during Task 122. AM started with no knowledge of numbers, and only scanty knowledge of sets and set-operations. Task 2, *e.g.*, was to fill in examples of Sets.

The concepts that AM talks about are self-explanatory—by and large. The following are some nonstandard concepts (whenever there is a conflict between "computer science jargon" and "math jargon," I have opted for the latter; *e.g.*, all "functions" are necessarily single-valued for each member of their domain):

BAG   is a kind of list structure, a bunch of elements which are unordered, but one in which multiple copies of the same element are permitted. One may visualize a paper bag filled with cardboard letters. Technically, we shall say that a set is *not* considered to be a bag. A bag is denoted by enclosure within parentheses, just as sets are within braces. So the bag containing X and four Y's might be written (X Y Y Y Y), and would be considered indistinguishable from the bag (Y Y Y X Y).

Number   will mean (typically) a positive integer.

Times^{-1}   is a particular relation. For any number x, Times$^{-1}(x)$ is a set of bags. Each bag contains some numbers which, when multiplied together, equal x. For example, Times$^{-1}(18) = \{(18)\ (2\ 9)\ (2\ 3\ 3)\ (3\ 6)\}$. Checking, we see that multiplying the numbers in the bag (2 3 3) together, we do get $2 \times 2 \times 3 = 18$. Times$^{-1}(x)$ contains all possible such bags (containing natural numbers > 1).

Add^{-1}   is a relation analogous to Times^{-1}. For any number x, Add$^{-1}(x)$ is also a set of bags. Each bag contains a bunch of numbers which, when added together, equal x. For example, Add$^{-1}(4) = \{(4)\ (1\ 1\ 1\ 1)\ (1\ 1\ 2)\ (1\ 3)\ (2\ 2)\}$. Add$^{-1}(x)$ contains all possible such bags (containing numbers > 0); it finds all possible *partitions* of x.

Divisors-of   is a more standard relation. For any number x, Divisors-of(x) is the set of all positive numbers which divide evenly into x. For example, Divisors-of(18) $= \{1\ 2\ 3\ 6\ 9\ 18\}$.

2–4   THE EXAMPLE ITSELF

AM is an *interactive* computer program. It prints out phrases indicating what it is doing at each moment, and a human being, referred to as the *User*, watches AM's activities. At any moment, the user can interrupt AM to ask questions or re-direct its energies. In the excerpt, the user never re-directs AM, although he or she does occasionally ask AM to rename some concept and to explain its behavior (*e.g.*, just after *Task 106*). For the benefit of the reader, I have prefaced all the user's comments by "USER:," and italicized my *post hoc* annotations.

Task 65

Filling in examples of the following concept: "Divisors-of." 3 Reasons:
    (1) No known examples for Divisors-of so far.
    (2) Times, which is related to Divisors-of, is now very interesting.
    (3) Focus of attention: AM recently defined Divisors-of.
26 examples found, in 9.2 seconds. *e.g.*: Divisors-of(6) = {1 2 3 6}.

Task 66

Considering numbers which have very small sets of Divisors-of (*i.e.*, very few divisors).
2 Reasons:
    (1) Worthwhile to look for extreme cases.
    (2) Focus of attention: AM recently worked on Divisors-of.
Filling in examples of numbers with 0 divisors. 0 examples found, in 4.0 seconds.
Conjecture: no numbers have 0 divisors.
Filling in examples of numbers with 1 divisors. 1 examples found, in 4.0 seconds.
e.g.: Divisors-of(1) = {1}. Conjecture: 1 is the only number with 1 divisor.

Filling in examples of numbers with 2 divisors. 24 examples found, in 4.0 seconds.
e.g.: Divisors-of(13)={1 13}. No obvious conjecture. This kind of number merits
more study. Creating a new concept: "Numbers-with-2-divisors."

> AM *had previously derived the notion of singleton, doubleton, etc. Above,*
> AM *was actually defining the set of numbers which gets mapped into a*
> *doubleton of numbers by the operation Divisors-of. I took the liberty of*
> *translating this into the above form, which uses the numeral "2."*

Filling in examples of numbers with 3 divisors. 11 examples found, in 4.0 seconds.
e.g.: Divisors-of(49) = {1 7 49}. All numbers with 3 divisors are also Squares. This kind
of number merits more study. Creating a new concept: "Numbers-with-3-divisors."

> *How did* AM *notice that conjecture? t took a random example of Numbers-*
> *with-3-divisors, say, 49. Then it asked what other known concepts "49" was*
> *an example of. The two answers were: Odd-numbers and Perfect-squares.*
> AM *then tested these conjectures on the other ten examples just found.*
> *The only surviving conjecture was that all numbers-with-3-divisors are also*
> *perfect-squares.*

Task 67

Considering the square-roots of Numbers-with-3-divisors. 2 Reasons:
    (1) Numbers-with-3-divisors are unexpectedly also perfect Squares.
    (2) Focus of attention: AM recently worked on Numbers-with-3-divisors.
All square-roots of Numbers-with-3-divisors seem to be Numbers-with-2-divisors.
e.g., Divisors-of(Square-root(169)) = Divisors-of(13) = {1 13}.
Formulating the converse to this statement. Empirically, it seems to be true. The
square of each Number-with-2-divisors seems to be a Number-with-3-divisors. This
is very unusual. It is not plausibly a coincidence. (Chance of coincidence is <.001)
Boosting interestingness factor of the concepts involved: Interestingness factor of
"Divisors-of" raised from 300 to 400. Interestingness factor of "Numbers-with-2-
divisors" raised from 100 to 600. Interestingness factor of "Numbers-with-3-divisors"
raised from 200 to 700.

USER: Call the set of numbers with 2 divisors "Primes."

Task 68

Considering the squares of Numbers-with-3-divisors. 2 Reasons:
  (1) Squares of Numbers-with-2-divisors were interesting.
  (2) Focus of attention: AM recently worked on Numbers-with-3-divisors.

⋮

This gap in the sequencing—from Task 68 to Task 79—eliminates some tangential and boring tasks. See page 19 for an explanation.

⋮

Task 79

Examining Times$^{-1}(x)$, looking for patterns involving its values. 2 Reasons:
  (1) Times^{-1} is related to the newly-interesting concept "Divisors-of."
  (2) Many examples of Times^{-1} are known, to induce from.
Looking specifically at Times$^{-1}(12)$, which is $\{(12)(2\,6)(2\,2\,3)(3\,4)\}$. 13 conjectures proposed, after 2.0 seconds. e.g., "Times$^{-1}(x)$ always contains a bag containing only even numbers." Testing the conjectures on other examples of Times^{-1}.
5 false conjectures deal with even numbers. AM will at some time consider the restriction of Times^{-1} to even numbers.
Only 2 out of the 13 conjectures are verified for all 26 known examples of Times^{-1}:
Conjecture 1: Times$^{-1}(x)$ always contains a singleton bag. e.g., Times$^{-1}(12)$, which is $\{(12)(2\,6)(2\,2\,3)(3\,4)\}$, contains (12). e.g., Times$^{-1}13)$, which is $\{(13)\}$, contains (13).
Creating a new concept, "Single-times." Single-times is a relation from Numbers to Bags-of-numbers. Single-times(x) is all bags in Times$^{-1}(x)$ which are singletons. e.g., Single-times(12) = $\{(12)\}$. e.g., Single-times(13) = $\{(13)\}$.
Conjecture 2: Times$^{-1}(x)$ always contains a bag containing only primes.
e.g., Times$^{-1}(12)$, which is $\{(12)(2\,6)(2\,2\,3)(3\,4)\}$, contains (2\,2\,3). e.g., Times$^{-1}(13)$, which is $\{(13)\}$, contains (13).
Creating a new concept, "Prime-times." Prime-times is a relation from Numbers to Bags-of-numbers. Prime-times(x) is all bags in Times$^{-1}(x)$ which contain only primes. e.g., Prime-times(12) = $\{(2\,3\,3)\}$. e.g., Prime-times(13) = $\{(13)\}$.

Task 80

Considering the concept "Prime-times."
2 Reasons:
    (1) Conjecs about Prime-times will tell much about Primes and Times^{-1}.
    (2) Focus of attention: AM recently defined Prime-times.
Looking specifically at Prime-times(48), which is {(2 2 2 2 3)}. 4 conjectures proposed,
after .6 seconds. e.g., "x is never inside any member of Prime-times(x)." Testing
them on other examples of Prime-times.
Only 1 out of the 4 conjectures are verified for all 23 known examples of Prime-times:
Conjecture 1: Prime-times(x) is always a singleton set. That is, Prime-times is a
function, not just a relation. e.g., Prime-times(48), which is { (2 2 2 2 3) }, is a
singleton set. e.g., Prime-times(47), which is { (47) }, is a singleton set. This holds for
all 17 known examples of Prime-times. (Chance of coincidence is .0001) This fails for
2 of the boundary cases (extreme numbers): 0 and 1. Conjecture is amended: Each
number $>$1 is the product of a unique bag of primes. I suspect that this conjecture
may be very useful.

> *How did AM know this? One of the (unfortunately few!) meta-heuristics in
> AM said the following: "When using the 'look at the inverse of extreme items
> under the operation f' rule, Tack the following note onto the Interest facet
> of the new concept which is created: 'Conjectures involving this concept and
> f (or f^{-1}) are natural, interesting, and probably useful.'" Now the concept
> PRIMES was defined using the 'extrema' heuristic rule, with f=Divisors-of.
> When PRIMES was first created, the meta-rule we just presented tacked the
> following note onto Primes.Interest: "Conjectures involving Primes and divi-
> sion (or multiplication) are natural, interesting, and probably useful." Thus
> the unique factorization conjecture triggers this feature, whereas Goldbach's
> conjecture wouldn't.*

USER: Call this conjecture "Unique factorization conjecture."

      ⋮

> *To show that AM isn't really always right on the mark, the next sequence of
> tasks includes a crime of omission (ignoring the concept of Partitions) and
> a false start (worrying about numbers which can be represented as the sum
> of two primes in precisely one way). Notice the skip here; 3 tasks have been
> omitted.*

Task 84

Examining $Add^{-1}(x)$, looking for patterns involving its values.

2 Reasons: (1) Add^{-1} is analogous to the newly-interesting concept "$Times^{-1}$."
     (2) Many examples of Add^{-1} are known, to induce from.

Looking specifically at $Add^{-1}(6)$, which is { (1 1 1 1 1 1) (1 1 1 1 2) (1 1 1 3) (1 1 2 2) (1 1 4) (1 2 3) (1 5) (2 2 2) (2 4) (3 3) (6)}. 17 conjectures proposed, after 3.9 seconds. e.g., "$Add^{-1}(x)$ always contains a bag of primes." Testing them on other examples of Add^{-1}. Only 11 out of the 17 conjectures are verified for all 19 known examples of Add^{-1}: 3 out of the 11 conjectures were false until amended.

Conjecture 1: $Add^{-1}(x)$ never contains a singleton bag.

Conjecture 2: $Add^{-1}(x)$ always contains a bag of size 2 (also called a "pair" or a "doubleton"). e.g., $Add^{-1}(6)$ contains (1 5), (2 4), and (3 3). e.g., $Add^{-1}(4)$ contains (1 3), and (2 2).

Creating a new concept, "Pair-add." Pair-add is a relation from Numbers to Pairs-of-numbers. Pair-add(x) is all bags in $Add^{-1}(x)$ which are doubletons (*i.e.*, of size 2). e.g., Pair-add(12)={ (1 11) (2 10) (3 9) (4 8) (5 7) (6 6) }. e.g., Pair-add(4)={ (1 3) (2 2) }.

Conjecture 3: $Add^{-1}(x)$ always contains a bag containing only 1's.

$$\vdots$$

Conjecture 10: $Add^{-1}(x)$ always contains a pair of primes. This conjecture is false. Conjecture is amended: "$Add^{-1}(x)$ usually (but not always) contains a pair of primes." e.g., $Add^{-1}(10)$ contains (3 7), and (5 5). e.g., $Add^{-1}(4)$ contains (2 2). e.g., $Add^{-1}(11)$ does not contain a pair of primes.

Creating a new concept, "Prime-add." Prime-add is a relation from Numbers to Pairs-of-numbers. Prime-add(x) is all bags in $Add^{-1}(x)$ which are pairs of primes. e.g., Prime-add(12)={ (5 7) }. e.g., Prime-add(10)={ (3 7) (5 5) }. e.g., Prime-add(11) = { }

$$\vdots$$

Task 106

Considering the set of numbers for which Prime-add is defined (has non-empty value). 1 Reason:

     (1) Prime-add often has non-empty value. Worth isolating that case.

Warning: no task on the agenda has an interestingness value above 200!!!

Creating a new concept "Prime-addable." Prime-addable is a kind of Number. x is Prime-addable iff Prime-add(x) is non-empty. Will spend 5.0 seconds filling in examples of Prime-addable. 18 examples found. Here are some of them: 4 5 6 7 8 9 10 12 13 14 17 16 18. Empirically, all even numbers are also in this set (ignoring boundary cases: 0 2 4 6). So conjectured. Danger: must examine boundary cases: the numbers 0, 2, 4, and 6. Two exceptions noticed. The only exceptions are the smallest boundary cases: 0, 2. Conjecture is amended: All even numbers $>$2 are the sum of two primes.

Warning: I expect this conjecture will be cute but useless.

USER: Why?

Because the concept of "Primes" originally arose as extreme cases of Divisors-of. The more closely an operation F is related to the concept Divisors-of, the more natural will be any conjecture involving both that operation F and Primes. *e.g.*, conjectures involving both Primes and Times will be natural and useful. But this conjecture, which involves Primes and Add^{-1}, will be cute but useless, since the relation "Add^{-1}" is unrelated to the relation "Divisors-of."

End of explanation.

USER: Call this conjecture "Goldbach's conjecture."

Task 107

Considering the set of numbers for which the relation Prime-add is single-valued.
3 Reasons:
    (1) Prime-add often has singleton value. Worth isolating that case.
    (2) Restricted to this set, Prime-add would be a function.
    (3) Focus of attention: AM recently worked on Prime-add.
Creating a new concept "Uniquely-prime-addable." "Uniquely-prime-addable" is a
kind of Number. x is Uniquely-prime-addable iff Prime-add(x) is a singleton. Will
spend 10.0 seconds filling in examples of Uniquely-prime-addable. 11 examples found.
Here are some of them: 4 5 7 8 9 12 13. No obvious conjecture derived empirically.

Will forget "Uniquely-prime-addable numbers," if no Ties found in near future.

2–5   RECAPPING THE EXAMPLE

Let's once again eavesdrop on a mathematician, who is describing to a colleague
what AM did:

This example was preceded by the momentous discoveries of multiplication
and division. Several interesting properties of these operations were noticed. The
first task illustrated (_Task 65_) involves exploring. the concept of "divisors of a
number" (meaning all positive integers which divide evenly into the given number).
After tiring of finding examples of this relation, AM investigates extreme cases:
that is, it wonders which numbers have very few or very many divisors.

AM thus discovers Primes in a curious way. Numbers with 0 or 1 divisor are
essentially nonexistent, so they're not found to be interesting. AM notices that
numbers with 3 divisors always seem to be squares of numbers with 2 divisors
(primes). This raises the interestingness of several concepts, including primes.
Soon (_Task 79_), another conjecture involving primes is noticed: Many numbers
seem to factor into primes. This causes a new relation to be defined, which
associates to a number x, all prime factorizations of x. The first question AM
asks about this relation is "is it a function?" This question is the full statement of
the unique factorization conjecture: the fundamental theorem of arithmetic. AM
recognized the value of this relationship, and assigned it a high interestingness
rating.

In a similar manner, though with lower hopes, it noticed some more relationships involving primes, including Goldbach's conjecture. AM quite correctly
predicted that this would turn out to be cute but of no future use mathematically.

The last activity mentioned (_Task 107_) shows AM examining a rather nonstandard concept: "numbers which can be written as the sum of a pair of primes,
in only one way." These are termed "uniquely-prime-addable" numbers. It was
mildly unfortunate that AM gave up on this concept before noticing that $p + 2$ is
uniquely-prime-addable, for any prime number p, and that in fact these are the
only odd uniquely-prime-addable numbers. The session was repeated once, with
a human user telling AM explicitly to continue studying this concept. AM did
in fact construct "Uniquely-prime-addable-odd-numbers," and then notice this
relationship. Here we see an example of unstable equilibrium: if pushed slightly
this way, AM will get very interested and spend a lot of time working on this kind

of number. Since it doesn't have all the sophistication (*i.e.*, compiled hindsight) that we have, it can't know instantly whether what it's doing will be fruitless.

Chapter 3

Agenda

'Objectively' given, 'important' problems may arise [in math]. But even then the mathematician is essentially free to take it or leave it and turn to something else, while an 'important' problem in [any other science] is usually a conflict, a contradiction, which 'must' be resolved. The mathematician has a wide choice of which way to turn, and he enjoys a very considerable freedom in what he does.

von Neumann

Section 3–1 will give the reader a feeling for the immensity of AM's search space. This is the "problem." The next section will give the top-level "solution": the flow of control is governed by a job-list, an agenda of plausible tasks. Section 3–3 will present some details of this global control scheme. Chapter 4 deals with the way AM's heuristics operate; this could be viewed as the "low-level" or *local* control structure of AM.

3–1 AM'S SEARCH

To develop mathematics, one must always labor to substitute ideas for calculations.

Dirichlet

Let's first spend a paragraph reviewing how concepts are stored. AM contains a collection of data structures, called *concepts*. Each concept is meant to coincide intuitively with one mathematical idea (*e.g.*, Sets, Union, Trichotomy). As such, a concept has several aspects or parts, called *facets* (*e.g.*, Examples, Definitions, Domain/range, Worth). If you wish to think of a concept as a "frame," then its facets are "slots" to be filled in. Each facet of a concept will either be totally blank, or else will contain a bunch of *entries*. For example, the Algorithms facet of the concept Union may point to several equivalent LISP functions, each of which can be used to form the union of two sets.[1] Even the "heuristic rules" are merely entries on the appropriate kind of facet (*e.g.*, the entries on the Interest facet of the Structure concept are rules for judging the interestingness of Structures).[2]

At any moment, AM contains a couple hundred concepts, each of which has only *some* of its facets filled in. AM starts with 115 concepts, and grows to about 300 concepts before running out of time/space. Most facets of most concepts are totally blank. AM's basic activity is to select some facet of some concept, and then try to fill in some entries for that slot.[3] Thus the primitive kind of *task* for AM is to deal with a particular facet/concept pair. A typical task looks like this:

> Check the entries on the "Domain/range" facet of the "Bag-Insert" concept

If the average concept has ten or twenty blank facets, and there are a couple hundred concepts, then clearly there will be about $20 \times 200 = 4000$ "fill-in" type tasks for AM to work on at any given moment. If several hundred facets have recently been filled in, there will be that many "check-entries" type tasks available. Executing a task happens to take around ten or twenty cpu seconds, so over the course of a few hours only a small percentage of these tasks can ever be executed.[4]

Since most of these tasks will never be explored, what will make AM appear smart—or stupid—are its choices of which task to pick at each moment.[5] So it's worth AM spending a nontrivial amount of time deciding which task to execute next. On the other hand, it had better not be *too* much time, since a task does

---

[1] The reasons for having multiple algorithms is that sometimes AM will want one that is fast, sometimes AM will be more concerned with economizing on storage, sometimes AM will want to "analyze" an algorithm. For these reasons it must be a very unoptimized function.

[2] A typical such rule is: "*A structure is very interesting if all its elements are mildly interesting in precisely the same way.*"

[3] This is not quite complete. In addition to filling in entries for a given facet/concept pair, AM may wish to check it, split it up, reorganize it, etc.

[4] The precise "18 seconds average" figure is not important. All heuristic-search programs suffer this same handicap: as the depth to which they've searched increases, the percentage of nodes (at or above that level) which have been examined *decreases* exponentially (assuming the branching factor b is strictly larger than unity).

[5] This is true of all heuristic search programs. The branchier the search, the more it applies.

take only a dozen seconds.[6]

One question that must be answered is: What percentage of AM's legal moves (at any typical moment) would be considered intelligent choices, and what percentage would be irrational? The answer comes from empirical results. The percentages vary wildly depending on the previous few tasks. Sometimes, AM will be obviously "in the middle" of a sequence of tasks, and only one or two of the legal tasks would seem plausible. Other times, AM has just completed an investigation by running into dead-ends, and there may be hundreds of tasks it could choose and not be criticized. The median case would perhaps permit about six of the legal tasks to be judged reasonable.

It is important for AM to locate one of these currently-plausible tasks, but it's not worth spending much time deciding which of *them* to work on next. AM still faces a huge search: find one of the six winners out of a few thousand candidates.

Its choice of tasks is made even more important due to the 10-second "cycle time"—the time to investigate/execute one task. A human user is watching, and ten seconds is a nontrivial amount of time to a person. The user can therefore observe, perceive, and analyze each and every task that AM selects. Even just a few bizarre choices will greatly lower the user's opinion of AM's intelligence. The trace of AM's actions is what counts, not its final results. So AM can't draw much of its apparent intelligence from the *speed* of the computer.

Chess-playing programs have had to face the dilemma of the trade-off between "intelligence" (foresight, inference, processing, etc.) and total number of board situations examined. In chess, the characteristics of current-day machines, language power *vs.* speed, and (to some extent) the limitations of our understanding of how to be sophisticated, have to date unfortunately still favored fast, nearly-blind[7] search. Although machine speed and LISP slowness may allow blind search to win over symbolic inference for *shallow* searches, it can't provide any more than a constant speed-up factor for an exponential search. Inference is slowly gaining on brute force,[8] and must someday triumph.

Since the number of "legal moves" for AM at any moment is in the thousands, it is unrealistic to consider "systematically"[9] walking through the entire space that AM can reach. In AM's problem domain, there is so much "freedom" that symbolic inference finally *can* win over the "simple but fast" exploration strategy.[10]

---

[6] The answer is that AM spends this "deciding" time not just before a task is *picked*, but rather each time a task is added to the agenda. A little under 1 cpu second is spent, on the average, to place the task properly on the agenda, to assign it a meaningful numeric priority value. So "action time" is roughly one order of magnitude larger than "deciding time."

[7] That is, using a very simple static evaluation function.

[8] For example, see Berliner[74]. There, searching is used mainly to verify plausible moves (a convergent process), not to discover them (a bushier search).

[9] For example, exhaustively, or using $\alpha\beta$ minimaxing, etc.

[10] This is the author's opinion, partially supported by the results of AM. Paul Cohen disagrees, feeling that machine speed should be the key to an automated mathematician's success.

3–2   CONSTRAINING AM'S SEARCH

There exist too many combinations to consider all combinations of existing entities; the creative mind must only propose those of potential interest.

Poincaré

A great deal of heuristic knowledge is required to constrain the necessary processing effectively, to zero in on a good task to tackle next. This is done in two stages:

   1   A list of plausible facet/concept pairs is maintained. Nothing can get onto this list unless there is some reason why filling in (or checking) that facet of that concept would be worthwhile.
   2   All the plausible tasks on this "job list" are ranked by the number and strength of the different reasons supporting them. Thus the facet/concept pairs near the top of the list will all be very promising tasks to work on.

   The first of these constraints is akin to replacing a *legal* move generator by a *plausible* move generator. The second kind of constraint is akin to using a heuristic evaluation function to select the best move from among the plausible ones. [11]

   The job-list or *agenda* is a data structure which is a natural way to store the results of these procedures. It is a list of all the plausible tasks which have been generated, and it is kept ordered by the numeric estimate of how worthwhile each task is. A typical entry on the agenda might look like this:

Fill in the EXAMPLES facet of the PRIMES concept
            ||
            ||
            || *Reasons for filling in this facet*
            ||
            ⇓
   1. No examples of primes are known so far.
   2. Focus of attention: AM just defined Primes.
            ||
            ||
            || *Overall value of these reasons*
            ||
            ⇓
           250

   While the top task is being executed, some new tasks might get proposed and merged into the agenda. Also, some new concepts might get created, and this, too, would generate a flurry of new tasks.

---

[11] Past AI programs (*e.g.*, [Samuel 67]) have indicated that constraining generation (stage 1, above) is more important than sophisticated ordering of the resultant candidates (stage 2). This was confirmed by the experiments performed on AM.

After AM stops filling in entries for the facet specified in the chosen task, it removes that task from the agenda, and moves on to work on whichever task is the highest-rated at that time.

The reader probably has a dozen good questions in mind at this point (*e.g.*, How do the reasons get rated? How do the tasks get proposed? What happens after a task is selected?). The next section should answer most of these. Some more judgmental ones (How dare you propose a numeric calculus of plausible reasoning! If you slightly de-tune all those numbers, does the system's performance fall apart?) will be answered in Chapter 7.

3–3   THE AGENDA

Creative energy is used mainly to ask the right question.

Halmos

3–3.1   Why an Agenda?

This subsection provides motivation for the following one, by arguing that a job-list scheme is a natural mechanism to use to manage the task-selection problem AM faces.

Recall that AM must zero in on one of the best few tasks to perform next, and it repeatedly makes this choice. At each moment, there might be thousands of directions to explore (plausible tasks to consider).

If all the legal tasks were written out, and reasons were thought up to support each one, then perhaps we could order them by the strength of those reasons, and thereby settle on the "best" task to work on next. In order to appear "smart" to the human user, AM should *never* execute a task having no reasons attached.

For the moment, assume some magical function exists, which provides a numeric rating, a priority value, for any given task. The function looks at a given facet/concept pair, examines all the associated reasons supporting that task, and computes an estimate of how worthwhile it would be for AM to spend some time now working on that facet of that concept.

So AM will maintain a list of those legal tasks which have some good reasons tacked onto them, which justify why each task should be executed, why it is plausible. At least implicitly, AM has a numeric rating for each task.

Give or take a few features, this notion of a job-list is the one which AM uses. It is also called an *agenda*.[12] "A task on the agenda" is the same as "a job on the job-list" is the same as "a facet/concept pair which has been proposed" is the same as "an active node in the search space." Henceforth, I'll use the following all interchangeably: task, facet/concept pair, node, job.[13]

---

[12] Borrowed from Kaplan's term for the job-list present in KRL0 (see Bobrow & Winograd[77]). For an earlier general discussion of agendas, see Knuth[68].

[13] Each of these terms will conjure up a slightly different image: a "job" is something to do, a "node" is an item in a search space, "facet/concept pair" reminds you of the format of a task.

The flavor of agenda-list used here is analogous to the control structure of HEARSAY-II [Lesser *et al.* 75]. Vast numbers of tasks are proposed and added to the job-list. Occasionally, when some new data arrive, some task is repositioned.

3–3.2   Details of the Agenda Scheme

At each moment, AM has many plausible tasks (hundreds or even thousands) which have been suggested for some good reason or other, but haven't been carried out yet. Each task is at the level of working on a certain facet of a certain concept: filling it in, checking it, etc. Recall that each task also has tacked onto it a list of symbolic reasons explaining why the task is worth doing.

In addition, a number (between 0 and 1000) is attached *to each reason*, representing some absolute measure of the value of that reason (at the moment). One global formula[14] combines all the reasons' values into a single priority value for the task as a whole. This overall rating is taken to indicate how worthwhile it would be for AM to bother executing that task, how interesting the task would probably turn out to be. The "intelligence" of AM's selection of task is thus seen to depend on this one formula. Yet experiments show that its precise form is not important. We conclude that the "intelligence" has been pushed down into the careful assigning of reasons (and *their* values) for each proposed task.

A typical entry on the agenda might look like this:

```
TASK: Fill-in examples of Sets
PRIORITY: 300
REASONS:
    100: No known examples for Sets so far.
    100: Failed to fillin examples of Set-union, for lack of examples of Sets
    200: Focus of attention: AM recently worked on the concept of Set-union
```

Notice the similarity of this to the initial few lines which AM types just after it selects a job to work on.

The priority value of a task serves a dual purpose: first, it is used to determine which task on the agenda is the most promising one to work on next. Second, once a task has been chosen, that task's priority value then is used as an estimate of how much time and space it deserves. The sample task above might rate 20 cpu seconds and 200 list cells. When either of these resources is used up, AM terminates work on the task, and proceeds to pick a new one. These two limits will be referred to henceforth as *time/space quanta* which are allocated to the chosen task. Whenever several techniques exist for satisfying some task, the remaining time/space quanta are divided evenly among those alternatives; *i.e.*, each method is tried for a small time. This policy of parceling out time and space quanta is called "activation energy" in [Hewitt 76] and called "resource-limited processes" in [Norman & Bobrow 75]. In the case of filling in examples of sets,

---

[14] Here is that formula: $Worth(J) = \|\sqrt{\Sigma R_i^2}\| \times (0.2 \times Worth(A) + 0.3 \times Worth(F) + 0.5 \times Worth(C))$, where J = job to be judged = (Act A, Facet F, Concept C), and $\{R_i\}$ are the ratings of the reasons supporting J. For the sample job pictured in the box below, A=FillIn, F=Examples, C=Sets, $\{R_i\} = \{100, 100, 200\}$. The formula will be repeated—and explained—in Section 4–3.

the space quantum (200 cells) will be used up quickly (long before the 20 seconds expire).

There are two big questions now:

- Exactly how is a task proposed and ranked?
   How is a plausible new task first formulated?
   How do the supporting reasons for the task get assigned?
   How does each reason get assigned an absolute numeric rating?
   Does a task's priority value change? When and how?
- How does AM execute a task, once it's chosen?
   Exactly what can be done during a task's execution?

The next chapter will deal with both of these questions.

Chapter 4

Heuristics

Assume that somehow AM has selected a particular task from the agenda—say, "Fill-in Examples of Primes." What precisely does AM do in order to execute the task? How are examples of primes filled in?

The answer can be compactly stated as follows:

AM selects relevant heuristics, and executes them.

This really just splits our original question into two new ones: (i) How are the relevant heuristics selected, and (ii) What does it mean for heuristics to be executed (e.g., how does executing a heuristic rule help to fill in examples of primes?).

These two topics (in reverse order) are the two major subjects of this chapter. Although several examples of heuristics will be given, the complete list is relegated to Appendix 2.[1]

The first section explains what heuristic rules look like (their "syntax," as it were). The next three sections illustrate how they can be executed to achieve their desired results (their "semantics").

Section 4–5 explains where the rules are stored and how they are accessed at the appropriate times.

---

[1] There they are condensed and phrased in English. The reader wishing to see examples of the heuristics as they actually were coded in LISP should glance at Appendix 3.2.

Finally, the initial body of heuristics is analyzed. The informal knowledge they contain is categorized and described. Unintentionally, the distribution of heuristics among the concepts is quite nonhomogeneous; this too is described in Section 4-6.

4-1   SYNTAX OF THE HEURISTICS

Let's start by seeing what a heuristic rule looks like. In general (see [Davis & King 75] for historical references to production rules), it will have the form

     If <*situational fluent*>

     Then <*actions*>

As an illustration, here is a heuristic rule, relevant when checking examples of anything:

If the current task is to Check Examples of any concept X,

    and (for some Y) Y is a generalization of X,

    and Y has at least 10 examples,

    and all examples of Y are also examples of X,

Then print the following conjecture: " X is really no more specialized than Y,"

    and add it to the Examples facet of the concept named "Conjectures,"

    and add the following task to the agenda: "Check examples of Y", for the reason:

    "Just as Y was no more general than X, one-of Generalizations(Y) may turn out to

    be no more general than Y," with a rating for that reason computed as the average

    of ‖Examples(Generalizations(Y))‖, ‖Examples(Y)‖, and Priority(Current task).

As with production rules, and formal grammatical rules, each of AM's heuristic rules has a left-hand side and a right-hand side. On the left is a test to see whether the rule is applicable, and on the right is a list of actions to take if the rule applies. The left-hand side will also be called the IF-part, the predicate, the preconditions, left side, or the situational fluent of the rule. The right-hand side will sometimes be referred to as the THEN-part, the response, the right side, or the actions part of the rule.

4-1.1   Syntax of the Left-Hand Side

The situational fluent (left-hand side) is a LISP predicate, a function which always returns True or False (in LISP, it actually returns either the atom T or the atom NIL). This predicate may investigate facets of any concept (often merely to see whether they are empty or not), use the results of recent tests and behaviors (*e.g.*, to see how much cpu time AM spent trying to work on a certain task), etc.

The left side is a conjunction of the form $P_1 \wedge P_2 \wedge \ldots$. All the conjuncts, except the very first one, are arbitrary LISP predicates. They are constrained only to obey two commandments:

Be quick!   (return either True or False in under 0.1 cpu seconds)

Have no side effects!   (destroying or creating list structures or Lisp functions, resetting global variables)

Here are some sample conjuncts that might appear inside a left-hand side (but *not* as the very first conjunct):

- *More than half of the current task's time quantum is already exhausted,...*
- *There are some known examples of Structures,...*
- *Some generalization of the current concept (the concept mentioned as part of the current task) has an empty Examples facet,...*
- *The space quantum of the current task is gone, but its time allocation is less than 10% used up,...*
- *A task recently selected had the form* "Restructure facet F of concept X", *where F is any facet, and X is the current concept,...*
- *The user has used this system at least once before,...*
- *It's Tuesday,...*

The very first conjunct of each left-hand side is special. Its syntax is highly constrained. It specifies the domain of applicability of the rule, by naming a particular facet of a particular concept to which this rule is relevant.

AM uses this first conjunct as a fast "pre-precondition," so that the only rules whose left-hand sides get evaluated are already known to be somewhat relevant to the task at hand. In fact, AM physically attaches each rule to the facet and concept mentioned in its first conjunct.[2]

Here are two typical examples of allowable first conjuncts:

- *The current task (the one last selected from the agenda) is of the form* "Check the Domain/range facet of concept X", *where X is any operation*
- *The current task is of the form* "Fillin the examples facet of the Primes concept"

These are the only guidelines which the left-hand side of a heuristic rule must satisfy. Any LISP predicate which satisfies these constraints is a syntactically valid left-hand side for a heuristic rule. It turned out later that this excessive freedom made it difficult for AM to inspect and analyze and synthesize its own heuristics; such a need was not foreseen at the time AM was designed.

Because of this freedom, there is not much more to say about the left-hand sides of rules. As you encounter heuristics in the next few sections, you should notice the (unfortunate) variety of conjuncts which may occur as part of their left-hand sides.

4–1.2   Syntax of the Right-Hand Side

"Running" the left-hand side means evaluating the series of conjoined little predicates there, to see if they all return True. If so, we say that the rule "triggers." In that case, the right-hand side is "run," which means executing

---

[2] Sometimes, I will mention where a certain rule is attached; in that case, I can omit explicit mention of the first conjunct. Conversely, if I include that conjunct, I needn't tell you where the rule is stored.

all the actions specified there. A single heuristic rule may have a list of several actions as its right-hand side. The actions are executed in order, and we then say the rule has finished running.

Only the right-hand side of a heuristic rule is permitted to have side effects. The right side of a rule is a series of little LISP functions, each of which is called an *action*.

Semantically, each action performs some processing which is appropriate in some way to the kinds of situations in which the left-hand side would have triggered. The final value that the action function returns is irrelevant.

Syntactically, there is only one constraint which each function or "action" must satisfy: Each action has one of the following 3 side-effects, and no other side-effects:

- It suggests a new task for the agenda.
- It causes a new concept to be created.
- It adds (or deletes) a certain entry to a particular facet of a particular concept.

To repeat: the right side of a rule contains a list of actions, each of which is one of the above three types. A single rule might thus result in the creation of several new concepts, the addition of many new tasks to the agenda, and the filling in of some facets of some already existing concepts. These three kinds of actions will now be discussed in the following three sections.

4–2   HEURISTICS SUGGEST NEW TASKS

This section discusses the "proposing a new task" kind of action. Here is the basic idea in a nutshell: The left-hand side of a rule triggers. Scattered among the "things to do" in its right-hand side are some suggestions for future tasks. These new tasks are then simply added to the agenda list.

4–2.1   An Illustration: "Fill in Generalizations of Equality"

If a new task is suggested by a heuristic rule, then that rule must specify how to assemble the new task, how to get reasons for it, and how to evaluate those reasons. For example, here is a typical heuristic rule which proposes a new task to add to the agenda. It says to generalize a predicate if it is very rarely[3] satisfied:

If the current task was (Fill-in examples of X),

---

[3] The most suspicious part of the situational fluent (the IF-part) is the number ".05." Where did it come from? Hint: if all humans had f fingers per hand, h hands, t toes per foot, and F feet, this would probably be $1/(fh+tF)$. Seriously, one can change this value (to .01 or to .25) with virtually no change in AM's behavior. This is the conclusion of experiment 3 (see Section 6.2.3). Such empirical justification is one important reason for actually writing and running large programs like AM.

> *and X is a predicate,*
> *and more than 100 items are known in the domain of X,*
> *and at least 10 cpu seconds were spent trying to randomly instantiate X,*
> *and the ratio of successes/failures is both >0 and less than .05*
> *Then add the following task to the agenda:* (Fill-in generalizations of X),
> *for the following reason:*
> *"X is rarely satisfied; a less restrictive concept might be more interesting."*
> *This reason's rating is computed as three times the ratio of nonexamples/examples found.*

Even this is one full step above the actual LISP implementation, where "X is a predicate" would be coded as "(MEMBER X (EXAMPLES PREDICATE))." The function EXAMPLES(X) rummages about looking for already-existing examples of X. Also, the LISP code contains information for normalizing all the numbers produced, so that they will lie in the range 0–1000.

Let's examine an instance of where this rule was used. At some point, AM chose the task "Fillin examples of List-equality." One of the ways it filled in examples of this predicate was to run it on pairs of randomly chosen lists, and observe whether the result was True or False.[4] Say that 244 random pairs of lists were tried, and only twice was this predicate satisfied. Sometime later, the IF part of the above heuristic is examined. All the conditions are met, so it "triggers." For example, the "ratio of successes to failures" is just 2/242, which is clearly greater than zero and less than 0.05. So the right-hand side (THEN-part) of the above rule is executed. The right-hand side initiates only one action: the task "Fillin generalizations of List-equality" is added to the agenda, tagged with the reason "List-equality is rarely satisfied; a slightly less restrictive concept might be more interesting," and that reason is assigned a numeric rating of $3 \times (242/2) = 363$.

Notice that the heuristic rule above supplied a little function to compute the value of the reason. That formula was: "three times the ratio of nonexamples/examples found."[5] Functions of this type, to compute the rating for a reason, satisfy the same two constraints as the left-hand side did: the function must be very fast and it must have no side effects. The "intelligence" that AM exhibits in selecting which task to work on ultimately depends on the accuracy of these local rule evaluation formulae. Each one is so specialized that it is "easy" for it to give a valid result; the range of situations it must judge is quite narrow. Note that these little formulae were handwritten, individually, by the author. AM wasn't able to create new little reason-rating formulae.

The reason-rating function is evaluated at the moment the job is suggested, and only the numeric result is remembered, not the original function. In other words, we tack on a list of reasons and associated numbers, for each job on the

---

[4] The True ones became examples of List-equality, and the pairs of lists which didn't satisfy this predicate became known as non-examples (failures, foibles, etc.). A heuristic similar to this "random instantiation" one is illustrated in Section 4–3.8.

[5] In actuality, this would be checked to ensure that the result lies between 0 and 1000.

agenda. The agenda *doesn't* maintain copies of the reason-rating functions which gave those numbers. This simplification is used merely to save the system some space and time.

Let's turn now from the reason-rating formulae to the reasons themselves. Each reason supporting a newly suggested job is simply an English sentence (an opaque string, a token). AM cannot do much intelligent processing on these reasons. AM is not allowed to inspect parts of it, parse it, transform it, etc. The most AM can do is compare two such tokens for equality. Of course, it is not to hard to imagine this capability extended to permit AM to syntactically analyze such strings, or to trivially compute some sort of "difference" between two given reasons.[6] Each reason is assumed to have some semantic impact on the user, and is kept around partly for that purpose.

Each reason for task τ has a numeric rating (a number between 0 and 1000) assigned to it locally by the heuristic rule which proposed τ for that reason. One global formula then combines all the reasons' ratings into one single priority value for the task.

4–2.2   The Ratings Game

In general, a task on the agenda list will have several reasons in support of it. Each reason consists of an English phrase and a numeric rating. How can a task have more than one reason? There are two contributing factors: (*i*) A single heuristic rule can have several reasons in support of a job it suggests, and (*ii*) When a rule suggests a "new" task, that very same task may already exist on the agenda, with quite distinct reasons tacked on there. In that case, the new reason(s) are added to the already-known ones.

One global formula looks at all the ratings for the reasons, and combines them into a single priority value for the task as a whole. Below is that formula, in all its gory detail:

$$Worth(J) = \|\sqrt{\Sigma R_i^2}\| \times (.2 \cdot Worth(A) + .3 \cdot Worth(F) + .5 \cdot Worth(C))$$

(where J = job to be judged = (Act A, Facet F, Concept C) and $\{R_i\}$ are the ratings of the reasons supporting J).

For example, consider the job J = (Check examples of Primes). The act A would be "Check," which has a numeric worth of 100. The facet F would be "Examples," which has a numeric worth of 700. The concept C would be "Primes," which at the moment might have a Worth of 800. Say there were four reasons, having values 200, 300, 200, and 500. The double lines "$\|...\|$" indicate normalization, which means that the final value of the square-root must be between 0 and 1, which is done by dividing the result of the Square-root by 1000 and then truncating to 1.0 if the result exceeds unity.

---

[6] It is in fact trivial to *imagine* it. Of course *doing* it is quite a bit less trivial. In fact, it probably is the toughest of all the "open research problems" I'll propose.

In this case, we first compute $\sqrt{200^2 + 300^2 + 200^2 + 500^2} = \sqrt{420,000}$, which is about 648. After normalization, this becomes 0.648. The expression in large parentheses in the formula is actually computed as the dot-product of two vectors, namely, (Worth(A), Worth(F), Worth(C)) and (.2 .3 .5); in this case it is the dot-product of (100 700 800) and (.2 .3 .5), which yields 630. This is multiplied by the normalized Square-root value, 0.648, and we end up with a final priority rating of 408.

The four reasons each have a fairly low priority, and the total priority of the task is therefore not great. It is, however, higher than any single reason multiplied by 0.648. This is because there are many *distinct* reasons supporting it. The global formula uniting these reasons' values does not simply take the largest of them (ignoring the rest), nor does it simply add them up.

The above formula was intended originally as a first pass, an *ad hoc* guess, which I expected I'd have to modify later. Since it has worked successfully, I have not messed with it. There is no reason behind it, no justification for taking dot-products of vectors, etc. I concluded, and recent experiments tend to confirm, that the particular form of the formula is unimportant; only some general characteristics need be present:

- The priority value of a task is a monotone increasing function of each of its reasons' ratings. If a new supporting reason is found, the task's value is increased. The better that new reason, the bigger the increase.
- If an already-known supporting reason is re-proposed, the value of the task is *not* increased (at least, it's not increased very much). Like humans, AM is fooled whenever the same reason reappears in disguised form.
- The priority of a task involving concept C should be a monotone increasing function of the overall worth of C. Two similar tasks dealing with two different concepts, each supported by the same list of reasons and reason ratings, should be ordered by the worth of those two concepts.

I believe that all these criteria are absolutely essential to good behavior of the system. Several of the experiments discussed later bear on this question (see Section 6–2). Note that the messy formula does incorporate all three of these constraints. In addition, there are a few features of that formula which, while probably not necessary or even desirable, the reader should be informed of explicitly:

- The task's value does not depend on the order in which the reasons were discovered. This is not true psychologically of people, but it is a feature of the particular priority-estimating formula initially selected.
- Two reasons are either considered identical or unrelated. No attempt is made to reduce the priority value because several of the reasons are overlapping semantically or even just syntactically. This, too, is no doubt a mistake.
- There is no need to keep around all the individual reasons' rating numbers. The addition of a new reason will demand only the knowledge of the *number* of other reasons, and the old priority value of the task.

- A task with no reasons gets an absolute zero rating. As new reasons are added, the priority slowly increases toward an absolute maximum which is dependent upon the overall worth of the concept and facet involved.

There is one topic of passing interest which should be covered here. Each possible Act A (*e.g.*, Fillin, Check, Apply) and each possible facet F (*e.g.*, Examples, Definition, Name(s)) are assigned a fixed numeric value (by hand, by the author). These values are used inside the formula on the last page, where it says "Worth(A)" and "Worth(F)." They are fairly resistant to change, but certain orderings should be maintained for best results. For example, "Examples" should be rated higher than "Specializations," or else AM may whirl away on a cycle of specialization long after the concept has been constrained into vacuousness. As for the Acts, their precise values turned out to be even less important than the Facets'.

Now that we've seen how to compute this priority value for any given task, let's not forget what it's used for. The overall rating has two functions:

1   These ratings determine which task to execute next. This is not an ironclad policy: In reality, AM prints out the top few tasks, and the user has the option of interrupting and directing AM to work on one of those other tasks instead of the very top one.

2   Once a task is chosen, its rating determines how much time and space AM will expend on it before quitting and moving on to a new task. The precise formulae are unimportant. Roughly, the 0–1000 rating is divided by ten to determine how much time to allow, in cpu seconds. The rating is divided by two to determine how much space to allow, in list cells.

4–3   HEURISTICS CREATE NEW CONCEPTS

Recall that a heuristic rule's actions are of three types:

- Suggest new tasks and add them to the agenda.
- Create a new concept.
- Fill in some entries for a facet of a concept.

This section discusses the second activity.

Here is the basic idea: Scattered among the "things to do" in the right-hand side of a rule are some requests to create specific new concepts. For each such request, the heuristic rule must specify how to construct it. At least, the rule must specify ways of assembling enough facets of the new concept to distinguish it from all the other known concepts. Typically, the rule will explain how to fill in the Definition of—or an Algorithm for—the new concept. After executing these instructions, the new concept will "exist," and a few of its facets will be filled in, and a few new jobs will probably exist on the agenda, indicating that AM might want to fill in certain other facets of this new concept in the near future.

4–3.1   An Illustration: Discovering Primes

Here is a heuristic rule that results in a new concept being created:

If the current task was (Fill-in examples of F),
   and F is an operation from domain space A into range space B,
   and more than 100 items are known examples of A (in the domain of F),
   and more than 10 range items (in B) were found by applying F to these domain items,
   and at least 1 of these range items is a distinguished member (esp: extremum)[7] of B,

Then (for each such distinguished member 'b'∈B) create the following new concept:

Name: F^{-1}-of-b
Definition: $\lambda(x)(F(x) = b)$
Generalization: A
Worth: $Average\big(Worth(A), Worth(F), Worth(B), Worth(b),$
$\qquad\qquad 100 \times max(10, \|Examples(B)\|)\big)$
Interest: *Any conjecture involving both this concept and either F or F^{-1}*

In case the user asks, the reason for doing this is: "Worthwhile investigating those A's which have an unusual F-value, namely, those whose F-value is b"

and the total amount of time to spend right now on all of these new concepts is computed as:

   Half the remaining cpu time in the current task's time quantum.

and the total amount of space to spend right now on each of these new concepts is computed as:

   90% of the remaining space quantum for the current task.

Heuristics for the new concept are quite hard to fill in. This was one of AM's most serious limitations, in fact (see Chapter 7). Above, we see a trivial kind of "heuristic schema" or template, which gets instantiated to provide one new, specialized heuristic about the new concept. That new heuristic tells how to judge the interestingness of any conjecture which crops up involving this new concept. As new conjectures get proposed, they are evaluated by calling on a set of heuristics including this one.

   Although some examples of F^{-1}-of-b might be easily obtained (or already known) at the moment of its creation, the above rule doesn't specifically tell AM how to fill in that facet. The very last line of the heuristic indicates that a few cpu seconds may be spent on just this sort of activity: filling in facets of the new concept which, though not explicitly mentioned in the rule, are easy to fill in now. Any facet f which didn't get filled in "right now" will probably cause

---

[7] This is handled as follows: AM takes the given list of range items. It eliminates any which are not interesting (according to Interests(B)) or extreme (an entry on B.Exs-Bdy, the boundary examples of B). Finally, all those extreme range items are moved to the front of this list. AM begins walking down this list, creating new concepts according to the rule. Sooner or later, a timer (or a storage-space watcher) will terminate this costly activity. Only the frontmost few range items on the list will have generated new concepts. So "especially" really just means priority consideration.

a new task to be added to the agenda, of the form: "Fillin facet f of concept F^{-1}-of-b." Eventually, AM would choose that task, and spend a large quantum of time working on that single facet.

Now let's look at an instance of when this heuristic was used. At one point, AM was working on the task "Fill-in examples of Divisors-of."

This heuristic's IF-part was triggered because: Divisors-of is an operation (from Numbers to Sets of numbers), and far more than 100 different numbers are known, and more than 10 different sets of factors were found altogether, and some of them were distinguished by being extreme kinds of sets: empty-sets, singletons, doubletons and tripletons.

After its left side triggered, the right side of the heuristic rule was executed. Namely, four new concepts were created immediately. Here is one of them:

> Name: *Divisors-of^{-1}-of-Doubleton*
> Definition: $\lambda(x)$ (*Divisors-of(x) is a Doubleton*)
> Generalization: *Numbers*
> Worth: *100*
> Interest: *Any conjecture involving both this concept and either Divisors-of or Times*

This is a concept representing a certain class of numbers, in fact the numbers we call *primes*. The heuristic resets a certain variable, so that in case the user interrupts and asks Why?, AM responds: *'This concept was created because it's worthwhile investigating those numbers which have an extreme divisors-of value; in this case, numbers which have only two divisors."*

AM was willing to spend half the remaining quantum of time allotted to the task "Fillin examples of Divisors-of" on these four new concepts.[8]

The heuristic rule is applicable to any operation, not just numeric ones. For example, when AM was filling in examples of Set-Intersection, it was noticed that some pairs of sets were mapped into the extreme kind of set Empty-set. The above rule then had AM define the concept of *Disjointness*: pairs of sets having empty intersection.

4–3.2   The Theory of Creating New Concepts

All the heuristic rule must do is to fill in enough facets so that the new concept is distinguished from all the others, so that it is "defined" clearly. Should AM pause and fill in lots of facets at that time? After all, several pieces of information are trivial to obtain at this moment, but may be hard to reconstruct later (*e.g.,*

---

[8] Some trivial details: One-eighth of the remaining time is spent on each of these four concepts: Numbers-with-0-divisors, Numbers-with-1-divisor, Numbers-with-2-divisors, Numbers-with-3-divisors. The original time/space limits were in reality about 25 cpu seconds and 800 list cells, and at the moment this heuristic was called, only about 10 seconds and 600 cells remained, so the concept Primes was allotted only 1.2 cpu seconds to "get off the ground." This was no problem, as it used far less than that. The heuristic rule states that each of the four new concepts may use up to 90% of the remaining space allocation (540 out of 600 cells), and Primes needed only a fraction of that initially.

the reason why C was created). On the other hand, filling in anything without a good reason is a bad idea (it uses up time and space, and it won't dazzle the user as a brilliant choice of activity).

So the universal motto of AM is to fill in facets of a new concept if—and only if—that filling-in activity will be much easier at that moment than later on.

In almost all cases, the following facets[9] will be specified explicitly in the heuristic rule, and thus will get filled in right away: Definitions, Algorithms, Domain/range, Worth, plus a tie to some related concept (*e.g.*, if the new concept is a generalization of Equality, then we can trivially fill in an entry on its Specializations facet: "Equality.")

On the other hand, the following facets will *not* be trivial to fill in: Conjectures, Examples, Generalizations, Specializations, and Interestingness. For example, filling in the Specializations facet of a new concept may involve creating some new concepts; finding some entries for its Conjectures facet may involve a great deal of experimenting; finding some Examples of it may involve twisting its definition around or searching. None of these is easier to do at time of creation than any other time, so it's deferred until some reason for doing it exists.

For each such "time-consuming" facet F, of the new concept C, one new task gets added to the agenda, of the form "Fill in entries for facet F of concept C," with reasons of the form "Because C was just created," and also "No entries exist so far on C.F."[10] Most of the tasks generated this way will have low priority ratings, and may stay near the bottom of the agenda until/unless they are re-suggested for a new reason.

Using the Primes example, from the last subsection, we see that a new task like "Fillin specializations of Primes" was suggested with a low rating, and "Fillin examples of Primes" was suggested with a mediocre[11] rating. The ratings of these tasks increase later on, when the same tasks are re-proposed for new reasons.

4–3.3   Another Illustration: Squaring a Number

Let's take another simple (though not atypical) illustration of how new concepts get created.

Assume that AM has recently discovered the concept of multiplication, which it calls "TIMES," and AM decides that it is very interesting. A heuristic rule exists which says:[12]

---

[9] The reader may wish to glance ahead to Section 5–2, to note the full range of facets that any concept may possess: what their names are and the kind of information that is stored in each.

[10] C.F is an abbreviation for facet F of concept C.

[11] Not as low a rating as the task just mentioned. Why? Each possible facet has a worth rating which is fixed once and for all. As an illustration, we mention that the facet Examples is rated much higher than Specializations. Why is this? Because looking for examples of a concept is often a good expenditure of time, producing the raw data on which empirical induction thrives. On the other hand, each specialization of the new concept C would itself be a brand new concept. So filling in entries for the Specializations facet would be a very explosive process.

[12] By glancing back at the Primes example, in Section 2–4.3.1, you can imagine what this rule actually looked like. There is nothing to be gained by stretching it out in all its glory, hence I've taken the liberty condensing it, inserting pronouns, etc.

If a newly-interesting operation F(x,y) takes a pair of N's as arguments,
Then create a new concept, a specialization of F, called F-Itself, taking just one N as
argument, defined as F(x,x), with initial worth Worth(F).

In the case of F = TIMES, we see that F takes a pair of numbers as its arguments, so the heuristic rule would have AM create a new concept called TIMES-Itself, defined as TIMES-Itself(x) = TIMES(x,x). That is, create the new concept which is the operation of *squaring a number.*

What would AM do in this situation? The global list of concepts would be enlarged to include the new atom "TIMES-Itself," and the facets of this new concept would begin to be filled in. The following facets would get filled in almost instantly:

>   NAME: *TIMES-Itself*
>   DEFINITIONS:
>   ORIGIN: $\lambda(x, y)(TIMES. DEFN(x, x, y))$
>   ALGORITHMS: $\lambda(x)(TIMES. ALG(x, x))$
>   DOMAIN/RANGE: *Number* $\Rightarrow$ *Number*
>   GENERALIZATIONS: *TIMES*
>   WORTH: *600*

The name, definition, domain/range, generalizations, and worth are specified explicitly by the heuristic rule.

The lambda expression stored under the definition facet is an executable LISP predicate, which accepts two arguments and then tests them to see whether the second one is equal to TIMES-Itself of the first argument. It performs this test by calling upon the predicate stored under the definition facet of the TIMES concept. Thus TIMES-Itself.Defn(4,16) will call on TIMES.Defn(4,4,16), and return whatever value *that* predicate returns (in this case, it returns True, since 4×4 does equal 16).

A trivial transformation.of this definition provides an algorithm for computing this operation. The algorithm says to call on the Algorithms facet of the concept TIMES. Thus TIMES-Itself.Alg(4) is computed by calling on TIMES.Alg(4,4) and returning *that* value (namely, 16).

The worth of TIMES was 600 at the moment TIMES-Itself was created, and this becomes the worth of TIMES-Itself.

TIMES-Itself is by definition a specialization of TIMES, so the SPECIALIZATIONS facet of TIMES is incremented to point to this new concept. Likewise, the GENERALIZATIONS facet of TIMES-Itself points to TIMES.

Note how easy it was to fill in these facets now, but how difficult it might be later on, "out of context." By way of contrast, the task of filling in *Specializations* of TIMES-Itself will be no harder later on than it is right now, so we may as well defer it until there's a good reason for it. This task will probably be added to the agenda with so low a priority that AM will never get around to it, unless some new reasons for it emerge.

The task "Fill-in examples of TIMES-Itself" is probably worthwhile doing soon, but again it won't be any harder to do at a later time than it is right now.

So it is not done at the moment; rather, it is added to the agenda (with a fairly high priority).

Incidentally, the reader may be interested to know that the next few tasks AM selected (in reality) were to create the inverse of this operation (*i.e.*, integer square-root), and then to create a new kind of number, the ones which can be produced by squaring (*i.e.*, perfect squares). Perfect squares were deemed worth having around because Integer-square-root is *defined* precisely on that set of integers.

4–4 HEURISTICS FILL IN ENTRIES FOR A FACET

The last two sections dealt with how a heuristic rule is able to propose new tasks and create new concepts. This section will illustrate how a rule can find some entries for a specific facet of a specific concept.

4–4.1 An Illustration: "Fill in Examples of Set-union"

Typically, the facet/concept involved will be the one mentioned in the current task which was chosen from the agenda. If the task "Fillin Examples of Set-union" were plucked from the agenda, then the "relevant" heuristics would be those useful for filling in entries for the Examples facet of the Set-union concept.

Here's one such relevant heuristic, attached to the concept Activity:

If the current task is to fill in examples of the activity[13] *F,*

One way to get them is to run F on randomly chosen examples of the domain of F. Of course, in the LISP implementation, this situation-action rule is not coded quite so neatly. It would be more faithfully translated as follows:

If CURRENT-TASK matches (FILLIN EXAMPLES F⇐anything)),
   and F isa Activity,
Then carry out the following procedure:
   1. Find the domain of F, and call it D;
   2. Find examples of D, and call them E;
   3. Find an algorithm to compute F, and call it A;
   4. Repeatedly:
      4a. Choose any member of E, and call it E1.
      4b. Run A on E1, and call the result X.
      4c. Check whether <E1,X> satisfies the definition of F.
      4d. If so, then add <E1 ⇒ X> to the Examples facet of F.
      4e. If not, then add <E1 ⇒ X> to the Non-examples facet of F.

When the current task is "Fillin examples of Set-union," the left-hand side of the rule is satisfied, so the right-hand side is run.

Step (1) says to locate the domain of Set-union. The facet labelled Domain/-Range, on the Set-union concept, contains the entry (SET SET ⇒ SET), which

---

[13] "Activity" is a general concept which includes operations, predicates, relations, functions, etc.

indicates that the domain is a pair of sets. That is, Set-union is an operation which accepts (as its arguments) a pair of sets, and returns (as its value) some new set.

Since the domain elements are sets, step (2) says to locate examples of sets. The facet labelled Examples, on the Sets concept, points to a list of about 30 different sets. This includes {Z}, {A,B,C,D,E}, {}, {A,{{B}}},...

Step (3) involves nothing more than accessing some randomly chosen entry on the Algorithms facet of Set-union. One such entry is a recursive LISP function of two arguments, which halts when the first argument is the empty set, and otherwise pulls an element out of that set and SET-INSERT's it into the second argument, and then recurs on the new values of the two sets. For convenience, we'll refer to this algorithm as UNION.

We then enter the loop of Step (4). Step (4a) has us choose one pair of our examples of sets, say the first two {Z} and {A,B,C,D,E}. Step (4b) has us run UNION on these two sets. The result is {A,B,C,D,E,Z}. Step (4c) has us grab an entry from the Definitions facet of Set-union, and run it. A typical definition is this formal one:

λ (S1 S2 S3)
   (AND
      (For all x in S1, x is in S3)
      (For all x in S2, x is in S3)
      (For all x in S3, x is in S1 or x is in S2)
)

It is run on the three arguments S1={Z}, S2={A,B,C,D,E}, S3={A,B,C,D,E,Z}. Since it returns "True," we proceed to Step (4d). The construct <{Z}, {A,B,C,D,E} ⇒ {A,B,C,D,E,Z}> is added to Set-union.Examples.

At this stage, control returns to the beginning of the Step (4) loop. A new pair of sets is chosen, and so on.

But when would this loop stop? Recall that each task has a time and a space allotment (based on its priority value). If there are many different rules all claiming to be relevant to the current task, then each one is allocated a small fraction of those time/space quanta. When either of these resources is exhausted, AM would break away at a "clean" point (just after finishing a cycle of the Step (4) loop) and would move on to a new heuristic rule for filling in examples of Set-union.

This concludes the demonstration that a heuristic rule really can be executed to produce the kinds of entities requested by the current task.

4–4.2   Heuristics Propose New Conjectures

We saw in the sample excerpt (Chapter 2) that AM occasionally notices some unexpected relationship, and formulates it into a precise conjecture. Below is an example of how this is done. As you might guess from the placement of this subsection, the mechanism is our old friend the heuristic rule which fills in entries for certain facets.

In fact, a conjecture evolves through four stages:

1   A heuristic rule looks for a particular kind of relationship. This will typically be of the form "X is a Generalization of Y," or "X is an example of Y," or "X is the same as Y," or "F1.Defn(X,Y)."[14]

2   Once found, the relationship is checked, using supporting contacts. A great deal of empirical evidence must favor it, and any contradictory evidence must be "explained away" somehow.

3   Now it is believed, and AM prints it out to the user. It is added as a new entry to the Conjecs facet of both concepts X and Y. It is also added as an entry to the Examples facet of the Conjecture concept.

4   Eventually, AM will get around to the task "Check Examples of Conjecture," or to the task "Check Conjecs of X." If AM had any concepts for proving conjectures, they would then be invoked. In the current LISP implementation, these are absent. Nevertheless, several "checks" are performed: (i) see if any new empirical evidence (pro or con) has appeared recently; (ii) see if this conjecture can be strengthened; (iii) check it for extreme cases, and modify it if necessary; and (iv) modify the worth ratings of the concepts involved in the conjecture.

The left-hand side of such a heuristic rule will be longer and more complex than most other kinds, but the basic activities of the right-hand side will still be filling in an entry for a particular facet.

The entries filled in will include: (i) a new example of Conjectures, (ii) a new entry for the Conjec facet of each concept involved in the conjecture, (iii) if we're claiming that concept X is a generalization of concept Y, then "X" would be added to the Generalizations facet of Y, and "Y" added to the Specializations facet of X, (iv) if X is an Example of Y, "X" is added to the Examples facet of Y, and "Y" is added to the ISA facet of X.

The right-hand side may also involve adding new tasks to the agenda, creating new concepts, and modifying entries of particular facets of particular concepts. As is true of all heuristic rules, both sides of this type of conjecture-perceiving rule may run any little functions they want to: any functions which are quick and have no side effects (*e.g.*, FOR-ALL tests, PRINT functions, accesses to a specified facet of some concept).

4–4.3   An Illustration: "All Primes Except 2 Are Odd"

As an illustration, here is a heuristic rule, relevant when checking examples of any concept:

If the current task is to Check Examples of X,
   and (Forsome Y) Y is a generalization of X,
   and Y has at least 10 examples,
   and all examples of Y (ignoring boundary cases) are also examples of X,
Then print the following conjecture: X is really no more specialized than Y,

---

[14] This says that F1(X)=Y, where F1 is an active concept AM knows about.

and add it to the Examples facet of Conjectures,

and if the user asks, inform the user that the evidence for this was that all $\|Examples(Y)\|$ *Y's (ignoring boundary examples of Y's) turned out to be X's as well,*

and Check the truth of this conjecture on boundary examples of Y,

and add "X" to the Generalizations facet of Y,

and add "Y" to the Specializations facet of X,

and (if there is an entry in the Generalizations facet of Y) add the following task to the agenda "Check examples of Y", for the reason: "Just as Y was no more general than X, one-of Generalizations(Y) may turn out to be no more general than Y," with a rating for that reason computed as: $.4 \cdot \|Examples(Generalizations(Y))\| + .3 \cdot \|Examples(Y)\| + .3 \cdot Priority(Current \; task).$

Let's take a particular instance where this rule would be useful. Say the current task is "Check examples of Odd-primes." The left-hand side of the rule is run, and is satisfied when the generalization Y is the concept "Primes." Let's see why this is satisfied.

One of entries of the Generalization facet of Odd-primes is "Primes." AM grabs hold of the 30 examples of primes (located on the Examples facet of Primes), and removes the ones which are tagged as boundary examples ("2" and "3"). A definition of Odd-prime numbers is obtained (Definitions facet of Odd-primes), and it is run on each remaining example of primes (5, 7, 11, 13, 17, ...). Sure enough, they all satisfy the definition. So all primes (ignoring boundary cases) appear to be odd. The left-hand side of the rule is satisfied.

At this point, the user sees a message of the form "Odd-primes is really no more specialized than Primes." If the user interrupts and asks about it, AM responds that the evidence for this was that all 30 primes (ignoring boundary examples of primes) turned out to be Odd-primes.

Of the boundary examples (the numbers 2 and 3), only the integer "2" fails to be an odd-prime, so the the user is notified of the finalized conjecture: "All primes (other than '2') are also odd-primes." This is added as an entry on the Examples facet of the concept named 'Conjectures.'

Before beginning all this, the Generalizations facet of Odd-primes pointed to Primes. Now, this rule has us add "Primes" as an entry on the Specializations facet of Odd-primes. Thus Primes is both a generalization and a specialization of Odd-primes (to within a single stray exception), and AM will be able to treat these two concepts as if they were merged together. They are still kept separate, however, in case AM ever needs to know precisely what the difference between them is, or in case later evidence shows the conjecture to be false.[15]

The final action of the right-hand side of this rule is to propose a new task (if there exist some generalizations of the concept Y, which in our case is "Primes"). So AM accesses the Generalizations facet of Primes, which is "(Numbers)." A

---

[15] When space is exhausted, one emergency measure AM takes is to destructively coalesce a pair of concepts X,Y where X is both a generalization of and a specialization of Y, even if there are a couple "boundary" exceptions.

new task is therefore added to the agenda: "Check examples of Primes," with an associated reason: "Just as Primes was no more general than Odd-primes, so Numbers may turn out to be no more general than Primes." The reason is rated according to the formula given in the rule; say it gets the value 500.

To make this example a little more interesting, let's suppose that the task "Check examples of Primes" already existed on the agenda, but for the reason "Many examples of Primes have been found, but never checked," with a rating for the reason of 100, and for the task as a whole of 200. The global task-rating formula then assigns the task a new overall priority of 600, because of the new, fairly good reason supporting it.

When that task is eventually chosen, the heuristic rule pictured above (at the beginning of this subsection) will trigger and will be run again, with X=Primes and Y=Numbers. That is, AM will be considering whether (almost) all numbers are primes. The left-hand side of the heuristic rule will quickly fail, since, *e.g.*, "6" is an example of Numbers which does not satisfy the definition of Primes.

4–4.4 Another Illustration: Discovering Unique Factorization

Below is a heuristic rule which is a key agent in the process of "noticing" the fundamental theorem of arithmetic.[16]

> *If F(a) is unexpectedly a BB,*
> *Then maybe (∀x) F(x) is a BB.*

Below, the same rule is given in more detail. The first conjunct on the IF-part of the heuristic rule indicates that it's relevant to checking examples of any given operation F. A typical example is selected at random, say $F(x)=y$. Then y is examined, to see if it satisfies any more stringent properties than those specified in the Domain/range facet of F. That is, the Domain/range facet of F contains an entry of the form $A \Rightarrow B$; so if x is an A, then all we are guaranteed about y is that it is an example of a B. But now, this heuristic is asking if y isn't really an example of a much more specialized concept than B. If it is (say it's an example of a BB), then the rest of the examples of F are examined to see if they too satisfy this same property. If all examples appear to map from domain set A into range set BB (where BB is much more restricted than the set B specified originally in the Domain/range facet of F), then a new conjecture is made: the Domain/range of F is really $A \Rightarrow BB$, not $A \Rightarrow B$. Here is that rule, in crisper notation:

> *If the current task is to Check Examples of the operation F,*
> *and F is an operation from domain A into range B,*
> *and F has at least 10 examples,*
> *and a typical one of these examples is "$<x \Rightarrow y>$" (so x∈A and y∈ B),*
> *and (Forsome Specialization BB of B), y is a BB.*
> *and all examples of F (ignoring boundary cases) turn out to be BB's,*
> *Then print the following conjecture: "F(a) is always a BB, not simply a B,"*

---

[16] The unique factorization conjecture: any positive integer *n* can be represented as the product of prime numbers in precisely one way (to within reorderings of those prime factors). Thus 28 = 2x2x7, and we don't distinguish between the factorization (2 2 7) and (2 7 2).

and add it to the Examples facet of Conjectures concept,

and add "$<A \Rightarrow BB>$" as a new entry to the Domain/range facet of F, replacing
"$<A \Rightarrow B>$,"

and if the user asks, respond that the evidence for this was that all ||Examples(F)||
examples of F (ignoring boundary examples) turned out to be BB's,

and check the truth of this conjecture by running F on boundary examples of A.

Let's see how this rule was used in one instance. In Task 79 in the sample
excerpt in Chapter 2, AM defined the concept Prime-times, which was a function
transforming any number n into the set of all factorizations of n into primes. For
example, Prime-times(12)={(2 2 3)}, Prime-times(13)={(13)}. The domain of
F=Prime-times was the concept Numbers. The range was Sets. More precisely,
the range was Sets-of-Bags-of-Numbers, but AM didn't know that concept at
that time.

The above heuristic rule was applicable. F was Prime-times, A was Numbers,
and B was Sets. There were far more than 10 known examples of Prime-times
in action. A typical example was this one: $<21 \Rightarrow \{(3,7)\}>$. The rule now
asked that $\{(3,7)\}$ be fed to each specialization of Sets, to see if it satisfied any of
their definitions. The Specializations facet of Sets was accessed, and each concept
pointed to was run (its definition was run) on the argument "$\{(3,7)\}$." It turned
out that Singleton and Set-of-doubletons were the only two specializations of Sets
satisfied by this example. At this moment, AM had narrowed down the potential
conjectures to these two:

- *Prime-times(x) is always a singleton set.*
- *Prime-times(x) is always a set of doubletons.*

Each example of Prime-times was examined, until one was found to refute each
conjecture (for example, $<8 \Rightarrow \{(2,2,2)\}>$ destroys conjecture 2). But no example
was able to disprove conjecture 1. So the heuristic rule plunged forward, and
printed out to the user "A new conjecture: Prime-times(n) is always a singleton-
set, not simply a set." The entry $<Numbers \Rightarrow Singleton-sets>$ was added to the
Domain/range facet of Prime-times, replacing the old entry $<Numbers \Rightarrow Sets>$.

Let's digress for a moment to discuss the robustness of the system. What if
this heuristic were to be excised? Could AM still propose unique factorization?
The answer is yes, there are other ways to notice it. If AM has the concept of
a Function,[17] then a heuristic rule like the one in the previous subsection will
cause AM to ask if Prime-times is not merely a Relation, but also a Function.

The past few sections should have convinced the reader that isolated heuristic
rules really can do all kinds of things: propose new tasks, create new concepts, fill
in entries for specific facets (goal-driven), and look for conjectures (data-driven

---

[17] A single-valued relation. That is, for any domain element x, F(x) contains precisely
one member. It is never empty (*i.e.*, undefined), nor is it ever larger than a singleton (*i.e.*,
multiple-valued).

empirical induction). The rules appear to be fairly general[18] —though that must be later verified empirically. They are redundant in a pleasing way; some of the most "important," well-known, and interesting conjectures can (apparently) be derived in many ways. Again, we must justify this experimentally.

4–5 GATHERING RELEVANT HEURISTICS

Each concept has facets which (may) contain some heuristics. Some of these are for filling in, some for checking, some for deciding interestingness,[19] some for noticing new conjectures, etc.

AM contains hundreds of these heuristics. In order to save time (and to make AM more rational), each heuristic should be tried only in situations where it might apply, where it makes sense, in its "domain of applicability."

4–5.1 Domain of Applicability

How is AM able to zero in on the relevant heuristic rules, once a task has been selected from the agenda?

The secret is that each heuristic rule is stored somewhere *a propos* to its "domain of applicability." This "proper place" is determined by the first conjunct in the left-hand side of the rule. What does this mean? Consider this heuristic:

If the current task is to fill in examples of the operation F,   ⇐ ═ ═ ═ ═
  and some examples of the domain of F are known,
Then one way to get examples of F is to run F on randomly chosen examples of the domain of F.

This is a reasonable thing to try—but only in certain situations. Should it be tried when the current task is to check the Worth facet of the Sets concept? No, it would be irrational. Of course, even if it were tried then, the left-hand side would fail very quickly. Yet *some* cpu time would have been used, and if the user were watching, his or her opinion of AM would decrease.[20]

That particular heuristic has a precise domain of applicability: AM should use it whenever the current task is to fill in examples of an operation, and only in those kinds of situations.

---

[18] That is, applicable in many situations. It would be worse than useless if a rule existed which could lead to a single discovery like "Fibonacci series" but never lead to any other discoveries. The reasons for demanding generality are not only "fairness," but the insights which occur when it is observed that several disparate concepts were all motivated by the same general principle (*e.g.*, "looking for the inverse image of extrema").

[19] The reader has already seen several heuristics useful for filling in and checking facets; here is one for judging interestingness: an entry on the Interest facet of Compose says that a composition AoB is more interesting if the range of B *equals* the domain of A, rather than if they only *partially* overlap.

[20] This notion of worrying about a human user who is observing AM run in real time may appear to be quite language- and machine-dependent. An increase in speed of a couple orders of magnitude would radically alter the qualitative appearance of AM. In Chapter 7, however, the reader will grasp how difficult it is to objectively rate a system like AM. For that reason, all measures of judgment must be respected. Also, to the actual human being using the system this really is one of the more important measures.

The key observation is that a heuristic typically applies to *all examples of a particular concept C*. In the case we were considering, C=Operation. Intuitively, we'd like to tack that heuristic onto the Examples facet of the concept Operation, so it would only "come to mind" (*i.e.*, be used) in appropriate situations. This is precisely where the heuristic rule *is* stored.

Initially, the author identified the proper concept C and facet F for each heuristic H which AM possessed, and tacked H onto C.F.[21] This was all preparation, completed long before AM started up. Each heuristic was tacked onto the facet which uniquely indicates its domain of applicability. The first conjunct of the IF-part of each heuristic indicates where it is stored and where it is applicable. Notice the arrow ($\Longleftarrow$===) pointing to that conjunct above.[22]

While AM is running, it will choose a task dealing with, say, facet F of concept C. AM must quickly locate the heuristic rules which are relevant to satisfying that chosen task. AM simply locates all concepts which claim C as an example. If the current task were "Check the Domain/range of Union∘Union,"[23] then C would be Union∘Union. Which concepts claim C as an example? They include Compose-with-Self, Composition, Operation, Active, Any-concept, and Anything. AM then collects the heuristics tacked onto facet F (in this case, F is Domain/range) of each of those concepts. All such heuristics will be relevant. In the current case, some relevant heuristics might be garnered from the Domain/range facet of the concept Operation. Any heuristic which can deal with the Domain/range facet of *any* operation can certainly deal with Union∘Union's Domain/range. A typical rule on Operation.Domain/range.Check[24] would be this one:

If a Dom/ran entry of F is of the form $<D\ D\ D...D \Rightarrow R>$,
    and R is a generalization of D,
Then test whether the range might not be simply D.

Suppose one entry on Union∘Union.Dom/ran was "<Nonempty-sets Nonempty-sets Nonempty-sets $\Rightarrow$ Sets>." Then this last heuristic rule would be relevant, and would have AM ask the plausible question: Is the union of three nonempty sets always nonempty? The answer is empirically affirmative, so AM modifies that Domain/range entry for Union∘Union. AM would ask the same question for Intersect∘Intersect. Although the answer then would be "*No*," it's still a rational inquiry. If AM called on this heuristic rule when the current task were "Fillin specializations of Bags," it would clearly be an irrational act. The domain of applicability of the rule is clear, and is precisely fitted to the slot where the rule is stored (tacked onto Operation.Domain/range).

To recap the basic idea: when dealing with a task "Do act A on facet F of concept C," AM must locate all the concepts X claiming C as an example. AM

---

[21] Recall that C.F is an abbreviation for facet F of concept C.

[22] In the LISP implementation, these first conjuncts are omitted, since the *placement* of a heuristic serves the same purpose as if it had some "pre-preconditions" (like these first conjuncts) to determine relevance quickly.

[23] This operation is defined as: $Union \circ Union(x, y, z) =_{df} (x \bigcup y) \bigcup z$. It accepts three sets as arguments, and returns a new set as its value.

[24] The "Check" subfacet of the "Domain/range" facet of the "Operation" concept.

then gathers the heuristics tacked onto X.F.A, for each such general concept X. All of them—and only they—are relevant to satisfying that task.

So the whole problem of locating relevant heuristics has been reduced to the problem of efficiently finding all concepts of which C is an example (for any given concept C). This process is called *"rippling away from C in the ISA direction,"* and forms the subject of the next subsection.

4–5.2 Rippling

Given a concept C, how can AM find all the concepts which claim C as an example?

The most obvious scheme is to store this information explicitly. So the Examples facet of C would point to all known examples of C, and the Isa facet of C would point to all known concepts claiming C as one of their examples. Why not just do this?[25] Because one can substitute a modest amount of processing time (via chasing links around) for the vast amount of storage space that would be needed to have "everything point to everything."

Each facet contains only enough pointers so that the entire graph of Exs/Isa and Spec/Genl links could be *reconstructed* if needed. Since "Genl" is a transitive relation, AM can compute that Numbers is a generalization of Mersenne-primes, if the facet Mersenne-primes.Genl contains the entry "Odd-primes," and Odd-primes.Genl contains a pointer to "Primes," and Primes.Genl points to "Numbers." This kind of *"rippling"* activity is used to efficiently locate all concepts related to a given one X. In particular, AM knows how to "ripple upward in the Isa direction," and quickly[26] locate all concepts which claim X as one of their examples.

It turns out that AM cannot simply call for X.Isa, then the Isa facets of those concepts, etc., because Isa is not transitive.[27] For the interested reader, the algorithm AM uses to collect Isa's of X is given below:[28]

1 *All generalizations of the given concept X are located. AM accesses X.Genl, then the Genl facets of those concepts, etc.*
2 *The "Isa" facet of each of those concepts is accessed.*
3 *AM locates all generalizations of these newly found higher-level concepts. This is the list of all known concepts which claim X as one of their examples.*

In regular form, one might express this rippling recipe more compactly as:
$Isas(x) =_{df} Genl^*(Isa(Genl^*(x)))$.

---

[25] This is the implementation chosen by several projects, *e.g.* MOLGEN [Stefik 78].

[26] With about 200 known concepts, with each Isa facet and each Genl facet pointing to about 3 other concepts, about 25 links will be traced along in order to locate about a dozen final concepts, each of which claims the given one as an example. This whole rippling process, tracing 25 linkages, uses less than .01 cpu seconds, in compiled Interlisp, on a KI-10 type PDP-10.

[27] If x isa y, and y isa z, then x is (generally) *NOT* a z. This is due to the intransitivity of "member-of." Generalization is transitive, on the other hand, because "subset-of" is transitive.

[28] For the *very* interested reader, it is explained in great detail in the permanently archived file RIPPLE[dis,dbl] at SAIL. Copies are available from the author.

4–5.3   Ordering the Relevant Heuristics

Now that all these relevant heuristics have been assembled, in what order should AM execute them?[29] It is important to note that the heuristics tacked onto very general concepts will be applicable frequently, yet will not be very powerful. For example, here is a typical heuristic rule which is tacked onto the Examples facet of the very general concept Any-concept:

> *If the current task is to fill in examples of any concept X,*
> *Then one way to get them is to symbolically instantiate[30] a definition of X.*

It takes a tremendous amount of inference to squeeze a couple awkward examples of IntersectoIntersect out of that concept's definition. Much time could be wasted doing so.[31]

Just as general heuristics are weak but often relevant, specific heuristics are powerful but rarely relevant. Consider this heuristic rule, which is attached to the very specific concept Compose-with-Self:

> *If the current task is to fill in examples of the composition FoF,*
> *Then include any fixed-points of F.*

For example, since Intersect(ϕ,X) equals ϕ, so must IntersectoIntersect(ϕ,X,Y).[32] Assuming that such examples exist already on Intersect.Examples, this heuristic will fill in a few examples of IntersectoIntersect with essentially no processing required. Of course the domain of applicability of this heuristic is minuscule.

As we expected, the narrower its domain of applicability, the more powerful and efficient a heuristic is, and the less frequently it's useful. Thus in any given situation, where AM has gathered many heuristic rules, it will probably be best to execute the most specific ones first, and execute the most general ones last.

Below are summarized the three main points that make up AM's scheme for finding relevant heuristics in a "natural" way and then using them:

- Each heuristic is tacked onto the most general concept for which it applies: it is given as large a domain of applicability as possible. This will maximize its generality, but leave its power untouched. This brings it closer to the "ideal" tradeoff point between these two quantities.

---

[29] The discussion below assumes that the heuristics don't interact with each other; *i.e.*, that each one may act independently of all others (they are not "strongly coupled"). The validity of this simplification is tested empirically (see Chapter 6) and discussed theoretically (see Chapter 7) later.

[30] "Symbolic instantiation" is a euphemism for a bag of tricks which transform a declarative definition of a concept into particular entities satisfying that definition. The only constraint on the tricks is that they not actually *run* the definition. One such trick might be: if the definition is recursive, merely find some entity that satisfies the base step. AM's symbolic instantiation tricks are too hand-crafted to be of great interest, hence this will not be covered any more deeply here. The interested reader is directed to the pioneering work by Lombardi & Raphael[64], or the more recent literature on these techniques applied to automatic program verification (*e.g.*, [Moore 75], [Balzer 78]).

[31] Incidentally, this illustrates why no single heuristic should be allowed to monopolize the processing of any one task.

[32] ϕ (read "phi") is another name for the empty set, also written {}. This last sentence thus says that since {} $\bigcap$ X = {}, then ({} $\bigcap$ X) $\bigcap$ Y must also equal {}.

• When the current task deals with concept C, AM ripples away from C and quickly locates all the concepts of which C is an example. Each of them will contain heuristics relevant to dealing with C.

• AM then applies those heuristics in order of increasing generality. You may wonder how AM orders the heuristics by generality. It turns out that the rippling process automatically gathers heuristics in order of increasing generality. In the LISP system, each rule is therefore executed as soon as it's found. So AM nevers wastes time gathering heuristics it won't have time to execute.

4–6 AM'S STARTING HEURISTICS

This section will briefly characterize the collection of 242 heuristic rules which AM was originally given. A complete listing of those rules is found in Appendix 2; the rule numbers below refer to the numbering given in that appendix.

4–6.1 Heuristics Grouped by the Knowledge They Embody

Many heuristics embody the belief that mathematics is an empirical inquiry. That is, one approach to discovery is simply to perform experiments, observe the results, thereby gather statistically significant amounts of data, induce from that data some new conjectures or new concepts worth isolating, and then repeat this whole process again. Some of the rules which capture this spirit are numbers 21, 43–57, 91, 136–139, 146–148, 153–154, 212–216, 225, and 241. As one might expect, most of these are "Suggest" type rules. They indicate plausible moves for AM to make, promising new tasks to try, new concepts worth studying. Almost all the rest are "Fillin" type rules, providing empirical methods to find entries for a specified facet.

Another large set of heuristics is used to embody—or to modify—what can be called "focus of attention." When should AM keep on the same track, and when not? The first rules expressing varying nuances of this idea are numbers 1–5. The last such rules are numbers 209–216. Some of these rules are akin to goal-setting mechanisms (*e.g.*, rule 141). In addition, many of the "Interest" type rules have some relation to keeping AM interested in recently chosen concepts (or: in concepts related to them, *e.g.*, by Analogy, by Genl/Spec, by Isa/Exs,...).

The remaining "Interest" rules are generally some echoing of the following notion: X is interesting if F(X) has an unexpected (interesting) value. For example, in rule 26, "F(X)" is just "Generalizations of X." In slightly more detail, the principal characteristics of interestingness are

• *Symmetry (e.g., in an expanding analogy)*
• *Coincidence (e.g., in a concept being rediscovered often)*
• *Appropriateness (e.g., in choosing an operation H so that GoH will have nicer Domain/Range characteristics than G itself did)*
• *Recency (see the previous paragraph on focus of attention)*
• *Individuality (e.g., the first entity observed which satisfies some property)*

- *Usefulness (e.g., there are many conjectures involving it)*
- *Association (i.e., the given concept is related to an interesting one)*

One group of heuristic rules embeds syntactic tricks for generalizing definitions (Lisp predicates), specializing them, instantiating them, symbolically evaluating them, inverting them, rudimentarily analyzing them, etc. For example, see rules 31 and 89. Some rules serve other syntactic functions, like ensuring that various limits aren't exceeded (*e.g.*, rule 15), that the format for each facet is adhered to (*e.g.*, rule 16), that the entries on each facet are used as they are meant to be (*e.g.*, rules 9 and 59), etc. Many of the "Check" type heuristics fall into this category.

Finally, AM possesses a mass of miscellaneous rules which evade categorization. See, *e.g.*, rules 185 and 236. These range from genuine math heuristics (rules which lead to discovery frequently) to simple data management hacks.

4–6.2   Heuristics Grouped by How Specific They Are

Another dimension of distribution of heuristics, aside from the above *functional* one, is simply that of how high up in the Genl/Spec tree they are located. The table below summarizes how the rules were distributed in that tree:

LEVEL	e.g.	# Con's	# w/Heur	# Heurs	Avg	Avg w/Heur	# Fillin	# Sugg	# Check	# Int
0	Anything	1	1	10	10.0	10.0	0	5	0	5
1	Any-Concept	1	1	110	110.0	110.0	39	30	20	21
2	Active	2	2	24	12.0	12.0	7	10	4	3
3	Operation	6	3	31	5.2	10.3	11	3	3	14
≥4	Union	100	11	63	0.6	5.7	26	15	8	16

Here is a key to the column headings:

LEVEL: *How far down the Genl/Spec tree of concepts we are looking.*

e.g.: *A sample concept at that level.*

Con's: *The total number of concepts at that level.*

w/Heur: *How many of them have some heuristics.*

Heurs: *The total number of heuristics attached to concepts at that level.*

Avg: *The mean number of heuristics per concept, at that level.*

Avg w/Heur: *(# Heurs) / (# w. Heurs)*

Fillin: *Total number of "Fillin" type heuristics at that level.*

Sugg: *Total number of "Suggest" type heuristics at that level.*

Check: *Total number of "Check" type heuristics at that level.*

Int: *Total number of "Interestingness" type heuristics at that level.*

As the table shows, the heuristic rules are *not* distributed uniformly, homogeneously, among all the initial concepts. The extent of this skewing was not realized by the author until the above table was constructed. A surprising proportion of rules are attached to the very general concepts. The top 10% of the concepts contain 73% of all the heuristics. One notable exception is the "Interest" type heuristics: they seem more evenly distributed throughout the tree of initial concepts. This tends to suggest that future work on providing "meta-heuristics" should concentrate on how to automatically synthesize those Interest heuristics for newly created concepts.

Chapter 5

Concepts

This chapter contains material about AM's anatomy: the knowledge AM starts with, and how that knowledge is represented.

5–1 MOTIVATION AND OVERVIEW

Each concept consists merely of a bundle of facets. The facets represent the different aspects of each concept, the kinds of questions one might want to ask about the concept:

- How valuable is this concept?
- What is its definition?
- If it's an operation, what is legally in its domain?
- What are some generalizations of this concept?
- How can you separate the interesting instances of this concept from the dull ones?

Since each concept represents a mathematical entity, the kinds of questions one might ask are fairly constant from concept to concept. This set of questions might change somewhat for a new domain of concept.

One "natural" representation for a concept in LISP is as a set of attribute/value pairs. That is, each concept is maintained as an atom with a property list. The *names* of the properties (Worth, Definitions, Domain/range, Generalizations, Interestingness, etc.) correspond to the questions above, and the *value* stored under property F of atom C is simply the value of the F-facet of the C-concept. This value can also be viewed as the answer which expert C would give, if asked question F. Or, it can be viewed as the contents of slot F of frame C.

5–1.1   A Glimpse of a Typical Concept

As an example, here is a stylized rendition of the SETS concept. This is a concept which is meant to correspond to the notion of a set of elements. For example, according to the concept shown below, "Singleton" is one entry on the Specializations facet of Sets—*i.e.*, singletons are specific kinds of sets.

    Name(s): *Set, Class, Collection*
    Definitions:
        Recursive: λ *(S) [S={} or Set.Definition (Remove(Any-member(S),S))]*
        Recursive quick: λ *(S) [S={} or Set.Definition (CDR(S))]*
        Quick: λ *(S) [Match S with {...}]*
    Specializations: *Empty-set, Nonempty-set, Set-of-structures, Singleton*
    Generalizations: *Unordered-structure, No-multiple-elements-structure*
    Examples:
        Typical: $\{\{\}\}, \{A\}, \{A,B\}, \{3\}$
        Barely: $\{\}, \{A,B,\{C,\{\{\{A,C,(3,3,3,9), <4,1,A,\{B\},A>\}\}\}\}\}$
        Not-quite: $\{A,A\}, (), \{B,A\}$
        Foible: $<4,1,A,1>$
    Conjec's: *All unordered-structures are sets.*
    Intu's:
        Geometric: *Venn diagram.*[1]
    Analogues: *Bag, List, Oset*
    Worth: *600*
    View:
        Predicate: $\lambda(P)\{x \in Domain(P) \mid P(x)\}$
        Structure: $\lambda(S)$ *Enclose-in-braces(Sort(Remove-multiple-elements(S)))*
    Suggest: *If P is an interesting predicate over X, consider* $\{x \in X \mid P(x)\}$.
    In-domain-of: *Union, Intersection, Set-difference, Set-equality, Subset, Member*
        In-range-of: *Union, Intersection, Set-difference, Satisfying*

To decipher the Definitions facet, there are a few things you must know. An expression of the form "(λ (x) E)" is called a Lambda expression after Church,[2] and may be considered an executable procedure. It accepts one argument, binds the variable "x" to the value of that argument, and then evaluates "E" (which is probably some expression involving the variable x). For example, "(λ (x) (x+5))"

---

[1] See Venn[89] or Skemp[71].
[2] Before and during Church, it's called a function. See [Church 41].

is a function which adds 5 to any number; if given the argument 3, this lambda expression will return the value 8.

The second thing you must know is that facet F of concept C will occasionally be abbreviated as C.F. In those cases where F is "executable," the notation C.F will refer to applying the corresponding function. So the first entry in the Definitions facet is recursive because it contains an embedded call on the function Set.Definition. Notice that we are implying that the *name* of that lambda expression itself is "Set.Definition."

There are some unusual implications of this: since there are three separate but equivalent definitions, AM may choose whichever one it wants when it recurs. AM can choose one via a random selection scheme, or always try to recur into the same definition as it was just in, or perhaps suit its choice to the form of the argument at the moment.

For example, one definition might be great for arguments of size 10 or less, but slow for bigger ones, and another definition might be mediocre for all size arguments; then AM should use the mediocre definition over and over again, until the argument becomes small enough, and from then on recur only into the fast definition. Although AM embodies this "smart" scheme, the little comments necessary to see how it does so have be excised from the version shown above; this will be detailed later in this chapter, in Section 5-2.8.

All concepts possess executable definitions, though not necessarily effective ones. They each have a LISP predicate, but that predicate is not guaranteed to terminate. Notice that the definitions for Sets are all definitions of finite sets.

5-1.2   The Main Constraint: Fixed Set of Facets

One important constraint on the representation is that the set of facets be fixed for all the concepts. An additional constraint is that this set of facets not grow, that it be fixed once and for all. So there is one unchanging, universal list of two dozen types of facets. Every facet of every concept *must* have one of those standard names. All concepts which have some examples must store them as entries on a facet called Examples; they can't call them Instances, or Cases, or G00037's. This constraint is known as the "Beings constraint,"[3] and has three important consequences:

1   OUTLINE: First, it provides a nice, distributed, universal framework on which to display all that is known about a given concept. AM can instantly tell what facets are not yet filled in for any given concept, and this will in turn suggest new tasks to perform. In other words, this constraint helps define the "space" which AM must explore, and makes it obvious what parts of each concept have and have not yet been investigated.

2   STRUCTURE: The constraint specifies that there be a *set* of facets, not just one. This set was made large enough that all the efficiency advantages of a "structured" representation are preserved (unlike totally uniform representations,

---

[3] See [Lenat 75b]. Historically, each concept module was called a "BEING."

e.g., pure production systems with simple memories as data structures, or predicate calculus).

3   UNIFORMITY: When AM wishes a piece of information, it must ask a concept a "question"—*i.e.*, mention a particular facet by name. The benefit of the Beings constraint is that there is a fixed, small repertoire of questions it may ask, hence there will be no long searching, no misunderstandings. This is the same advantage that always accrues when everyone uses a common language.

We shall illustrate the last two advantages by using the Sets concept pictured above. How does AM handle a task of this form: "Check examples of Sets"? AM accesses the Examples facet of the Sets concept, and obtains a bunch of items which are all probably sets. If any isn't a set, AM would like to make it one, if that involves nothing difficult. AM locates all the generalizations of Sets,[4] and comes up with the list <Sets, Unordered-structures, No-multiple-elements-structures, Structures, Objects, Any-concept, Anything>. Next, the "Check" facet of each of these is examined, and all its heuristics are collected. For example, the Check facet of the No-multiple-elements-structures concept contains the following entry: "Eliminate multiple occurrences of each element" (of course this is present not as an English sentence but rather as a little LISP function). So even though Sets has no entries for its Check facet, several little functions will be gathered up by the rippling process. Each potential set would be subjected to all those checks, and might be modified or discarded as a result.

There is enough "structure" around to keep the heuristic rules relevant to this task isolated from very irrelevant rules, and there is enough "uniformity" to make finding those rules very easy.

The same rippling would be done to find predicates which tell whether a set is interesting or dull. For example, one entry on the Interestingness facet of the Structure concept says that a structure is interesting if all pairs of members satisfy the same rare predicate $P(x,y)$ [for any such P]. So a set, all pairs of whose members satisfy "Equality," would be considered interesting. In fact, every Singleton is an interesting *Structure* for just that reason. A singleton might be an interesting *Anything* because it takes only a few characters to type it out (thereby satisfying a criterion on Anything.Interest).

To locate all the specializations of Sets, the rippling would go in the opposite direction. For example, one of the entries on the Specializations facet of Sets is Set-of-structures; one of *its* Specialization entries is Set-of-sets. So this latter concept will be caught in the net when rippling away from Sets in the Specializations direction.

If AM wants lots of examples of sets, it has only to ripple in the Specializations direction, gathering Examples of each concept it encounters. Examples of Sets-of-sets (like this one: $\{\{A\}, \{\{C, D\}\}\}$) will be caught in this way, as will examples of Sets-of-numbers (like this one: $\{1,4,5\}$), because two specializations of Sets

---

[4] By "rippling" upward from Sets, in the Genl direction.

are Sets-of-Sets and Sets-of-Numbers.[5]

In addition to the three main reasons for keeping the set of facets the same for all the concepts (see previous page), we claimed there were also reasons for keeping that set fixed once and for all. Why not dynamically enlarge it? To add a new facet, its value has to be filled in for lots of concepts. How could AM develop the huge body of heuristics needed to guide such filling-in and checking activities? Also, the number of facets is small to begin with because people don't seem to use more than a few tens of such "properties" in classifying knowledge about a concept.[6] If the viability of AM seemed to depend on this ability, I would have worked on it. AM got along fine without being able to enlarge its set of facets, so no time was ever spent on that problem. I leave it as a challenging, ambitious "open research problem."

5–1.3   BEINGs Representation of Knowledge

Before discussing each facet in detail, let's interject a brief historic digression, to explain the origins of this modular representation scheme.

The ideas arose in an automatic programming context, while working out a solution to the problem of constructing a computer system capable of synthesizing a simple concept-discrimination program (similar to [Winston 70]). The scenario envisioned was one of mutual cooperation among a group of a hundred or so experts (some or all of which may be computer modules), each a specialist in some minute detail of coding, concept formation, debugging, communicating, etc. Each expert was modeled by one module, one BEING. Each BEING had the same kinds of slots (parts, facets), and each slot was interpreted as a *question* which that BEING could answer. The community of experts carried on a round-table discussion of a programming task which was specified by a human user. Eventually, by cooperating and answering each other's questions, they hammered out the program the user desired. See Lenat[75b] for details.

The final system, called PUP6, did actually synthesize several large LISP programs, including many variants of the concept-learning program. This is described in detail in [Lenat 75a]. Unfortunately, PUP6 had virtually no natural language ability and was therefore unusable by an untrained human. Its modal output was "*Eh?* " The search for a new problem domain where this communication difficulty wouldn't be so severe led to consideration of elementary mathematics.

The other main defect of PUP6 was its narrowness, the small range of "target" programs which could be synthesized. PUP6 had been designed with just one target in mind, and almost all it could do was to hit that target. The second constraint on the new task domain was then one of having a non-specific target, a very broad or diffuse goal. This pointed to an automated researcher, rather than to a problem-solver.

---

[5] We are assuming that AM has run for some time, and already discovered Numbers, and already defined Sets-of-Numbers.

[6] This data is gathered from introspection by myself and a few others, and should probably be tested by performing some psychological experiments.

The two constraints then were (i) elementary math, because of communication ease, and (ii) self-guided exploration, because of the danger of too specific a goal. Together, they directed the author to an investigation which ultimately resulted in the AM project.

5-2 FACETS

How *is* each concept represented? Without claiming that this is the "best" or preferred scheme, this section will treat in detail AM's representation of this knowledge.

We have seen that the representation of a concept can loosely be described as a collection of facet/value pairs, where the facets are drawn from a fixed set of about 25 total possible facets.

The facets break down into three categories:

- Facets which relate this concept C to some other one(s): Generalizations, Specializations, Examples, Isa's, In-domain-of, In-range-of, Views, Intu's, Analogies, Conjec's.
- Facets which contain information intensive to this concept C itself: Definitions, Algorithms, Domain/range, Worth, Interest.
- Sub-facets, containing heuristics, which can be tacked onto facets from either group above. These include: Suggest, Fillin, Check (and might be extended to include Justification, Origin, and other fields).

Some facets come in several flavors (*e.g.*, there are really four separate facets—not just one—which point to Examples: boundary, typical, just-barely-failing, foibles).

This section will cover each facet in turn. Let's begin by listing each of them. For a change of pace, we'll show a typical question that each might answer about concept C:[7]

Name: What shall we call C when communicating with the user?

Generalizations: Which other concepts have less restrictive definitions than C?

Specializations: Which concepts have C's definition plus some additional constraints?

Examples: What are some things that satisfy C's definition?

Isa's: Which concepts' definitions does C itself satisfy?[8]

In-domain-of: Which operations can be performed on C's?

In-range-of: Which operations result in values which are C's?

Views: How can we view some other kind of entity as if it were a C?

Intu's: What is an abstract, analogic representation for C?

---

[7] In this discussion, "C" represents the name of the concept whose facet is being discussed, and may be read "the given concept."

[8] Notice that C will therefore be an Example of each member of Isa's(C).

Analogies: Are there similar (though formally unrelated) concepts?

Conjec's: What are some potential theorems involving C?

Definitions: How can we tell if x is an example of C?

Algorithms: How can we execute the operation C on a given argument?

Domain/range: What kinds of arguments can operation C be executed on? What kinds of values will it return?

Worth: How valuable is C? (overall, aesthetic, utility, etc.)

Interestingness: What special features make a C especially interesting?

In addition, each facet F of concept C can possess a few little subfacets which contain heuristics for dealing with that facet of C's:

C.F.Fillin: How can entries on C.F be filled in? These heuristics get called on when the current task is "Fillin facet F of concept X", where X is a C.

C.F.Check: How can potential entries on C.F be checked and patched up?

C.F.Suggest: If AM gets bogged down, what are some new tasks (related to C.F) it might consider?

5–2.1   Generalizations/Specializations

Generalization makes possible conscious, controlled, and accurate accommodation of one's existing schemas, not only in response to the demands for assimilation of new situations as they are encountered, but ahead of these demands, seeking or creating new examples to fit the enlarged concept.

Skemp

We say concept A *"is a generalization of"* concept B iff every example of B is an example of A. Equivalently, this is true iff the definition of B can be phrased as "λ (x) [A.Defn(x) *and* P(x)];" that is, for x to satisfy B's definition, it must satisfy A's definition plus some additional predicate P. The Generalizations facet of concept C will be abbreviated as C.Genl.

C.Genl does not contain *all* generalizations of C; rather, just the "immediate" ones. More formally, if A is a generalization of B, and B of C, then C.Genl will *not*[9] contain a pointer to A. Instead, C.Genl will point to B, and B.Genl will point to A.

Here are the recursive equations which permit a search process to quickly find all generalizations or specializations of a given concept X:

$$Generalizations(X) =_{df} Genl^*(X) =_{df} \{X\} \bigcup Generalizations(X.Genl)$$
$$Specializations(X) =_{df} Spec^*(X) =_{df} \{X\} \bigcup Specializations(X.Spec)$$

For the reader's convenience, here are the similar equations, presented elsewhere in the text, for finding all examples of—and Isa's of—X:

$$Examples(X) =_{df} Spec^*(Exs(Spec^*(X)))$$
$$Isa's(X) =_{df} Genl^*(Isa(Genl^*(X)))$$

---

[9] The reason for these strange constraints is so that the total number of links can be minimized. There is no harm if a few redundant ones sneak in. In fact, frequently used paths are granted the status of single links, as we shall soon see.

The *format* of the Generalizations facet is quite simple: it is a list of concept names. The Generalizations facet for Odd-primes might be:

(Odd-numbers Primes)

We've been talking about both Specializations and Generalizations as if they were very similar to each other. It's time to make that more explicit:

Specializations are the converse of Generalizations. The format is the same, and (hopefully) A is an entry on B's Specializations facet iff B is an entry on A's Generalizations facet.

The uses of these two facets are many:

- AM can sometimes establish independently that A is both a generalization and a specialization of B; in that case, AM would like to recognize that fact easily, so it can conjecture that A and B specify equivalent concepts. Such coincidences are easily detected as *cycles* in the graph of all Genl (or Spec) relations known to AM. In these cases, AM may physically merge A and B (and all the other concepts in the cycle) into one concept.

- Sometimes, AM wants to assemble a list of all specializations (or generalizations) of X, so that it can test whether some statement which is just barely true (or false) for X will hold for any of those specializations of X.

- Sometimes, the list of generalizations is used to assemble a list of Isa's; similarly, the list of specializations helps assemble a list of examples.

- A common and crucial use of the list of generalizations is to locate all the heuristic rules which are relevant to a given concept. Typically, the relevant rules are those tacked onto Isa's of that concept, and the list of Isa's is built up from the list of generalizations of that concept.

- To incorporate new knowledge. If AM learns, conjectures, etc. that A is a specialization of B, then all the machinery (all the theorems, algorithms, etc.) for B become available for working with A.

Here is a little trick that deserves a couple paragraphs of its own. AM stores the answers to common questions (like "What are *all* the specializations of Operation?") explicitly, by intentionally permitting redundant links to be maintained. If two requests arrive closely in time, to test whether A is a generalization of B, then the result is stored by adding "A" as an entry on the Generalizations facet of B, and adding "B" as a new entry on the Specializations facet of A. The slight extra space is more than recompensed in cpu time saved. Computer scientists will perceive the analogy between this redundant storage (to save later recomputation) and the well-known hardware technique of *caching*.

If the result were False (A turned out not to be a generalization of B) then the links specify that finding explicitly, so that the next request does not generate a long search again. Such failures are recorded on two additional facets: Genl-not and Spec-not. Since *most* concept pairs A/B are related by Spec-not and by Genl-not, the only entries which get recorded here are the ones which were frequently called for by AM. If space ever gets tight, all such redundant links can be discarded with no permanent damage done.

These two "shadow" facets (Genl-not and Spec-not) are not useful or interesting in their own right. If AM ever wished to know all the concepts which are *not* generalizations of C, the fastest way would be to take the set-difference of {all concepts} and Generalizations(C). Since they are quite incomplete, Genl-not and Spec-not are used more like a cache memory: they save time whenever they are applicable, and don't really cost much when they aren't applicable.

5–2.2 Examples/Isa's

Usually, to show that a definition implies no contradiction, we proceed by example, we try to make an example of a thing satisfying the definition. We wish to define a notion A, and we say that, by definition, an A is anything for which certain postulates are true. If we can demonstrate directly that all these postulates are true of a certain object B, the definition will be justified; the object B will be an example of an A.

Poincaré

Following Poincaré, we say "*concept A is an example of concept B*" iff A satisfies B's definition.[10] Equivalently, we say that "*A Isa B.*" It would be legal (in that situation) for "A" to be an entry on B.Exs (the Examples facet of concept B) and for "B" to be an entry on A.Isa (the Isa's facet of concept A).

The Examples facet of C does not contain *all* examples of C; rather, it contains just the "immediate" ones. The Examples facet of Numbers will not contain "11" since it is contained in the Examples facet of Odd-primes. A "rippling" procedure is used to acquire a list of all examples of a given concept. The basic equation is:

$$Examples(X) =_{df} Specializations(Exs(Specializations(X)))$$

where Exs(x) is the contents of the Examples facet of x. Examples(x) represents the final list of all known items which satisfy the definition of X. Examples(x) thus must include Exs(x). Specializations(x) = $Spec^*(x)$; that is, all members of x.Spec, all members of *their* Spec facet, etc. Note the similarity of this to the formula for Isa's(x), given on the last page.

As with Generalizations/Specializations, the reasons behind the incomplete pointer structure is simply to save space, and to minimize the difficulty of updating the graph structure whenever new links are found. Suppose a new Mersenne prime is computed. Wouldn't it be nice simply to add a single entry to the Exs facet of Mersenne-primes, rather than to have to update the Exs pointers from a dozen concepts? There is no harm if a few redundant links sneak in.

---

[10] What does this mean? B.Defn is a Lisp predicate, a Lambda expression. If it is fed A as its argument, and it returns True, we say that A is a B, or that A satisfies B's definition. If B.Defn returns NIL, we say that A is not a B, or that A fails B's definition. If B.Defn runs out of time before returning a T/NIL value, there is no definite statement of this form we can make.

"Isa's" is the converse of "Examples." The format is the same, and (if A and B are both concepts) A is an entry on B.Isa iff B is an entry on A.Exs. In other words, A is a member of Examples(B) iff B is a member of Isa's(A).

The *uses* of the Exs/Isa's facets are similar to those for Genl/Spec (see previous subsection), but their formats are quite a bit more complicated (at the implementation level). There are really a cluster of different facets all related to Examples:

- TYPICAL: This is a list of average examples. Care must be taken to include a wide spectrum of allowable kinds of examples. For "Sets," these would include sets of varying size, nesting, complexity, type of elements, etc.
- BOUNDARY: Items which just barely pass the definition of this concept. This might include items which satisfy the base step of a recursive definition, or items which were intuitively believed to be *non*-examples of the concept. For "Sets," this might include the empty set.
- BOUNDARY-NOT: Items which just barely fail the definition. This might include an item which had to be slightly modified during checking, like {A,B,A} becoming {A,B}.
- FOIBLES: Total failures. Items which are completely against the grain of this concept. For "Sets," this might include the operation "Compose."
- NOT: This is the "cache" trick used to store the answers to frequently-asked questions. If AM frequently wants to know whether X is an example of Y, and the answer is *No*, then much time can be saved by adding X as an entry to the Exs-not facet of Y.

An individual item on these facets may just be a concept name, or it may be more complicated. In the case of an operation, it is an item of the form $<a_1 a_2 \ldots \Rightarrow v>$; *i.e.*, actual arguments a_i and the value v returned. In the case of objects, it is an object of that form (*e.g.*, Sets.Exs might contain $\{k, r\}$ as one entry).

Here is a more detailed illustration. Consider the Examples facet of Set-union. It might appear thus:

TYPICAL: $\{A\} \cup \{A,B\} \Rightarrow \{A,B\}$;
    $\{A,B\} \cup \{A,B\} \Rightarrow \{A,B\}$;
    $\{A,<3,4,3>,\{A,B\}\} \cup \{3,A\} \Rightarrow \{A,<3,4,3>,\{A,B\},3\}$.
BOUNDARY: $\{\} \cup X \Rightarrow X$[11]
BOUNDARY-NOT: $\{A,B\} \cup \{A,C\} \Rightarrow \{A,B,A,C\}$;
    $\{A,B,C,D\} \cup \{E,F,G,H,I,J\} \Rightarrow \{A,B,C,E,F,G,H,I,J\}$
FOIBLES: $<2,A,2>$
NOT: *no entries*

---

[11] Actually, AM is not quite smart enough to use the variable X as shown in the boundary examples. It would simply store a few instances of this general rule, plus have an entry of the form <Equivalent: Identity(X) and Set-union(X,{})> on the Exs facet of Conjectures. Notice that because of the asymmetric way Set-union was defined, only one lopsided boundary example was found. If another definition were supplied, the converse kind of boundary examples would be found.

The format for Isa's are much simpler: there are only two kinds of links, and they're each merely a list of concept names. Here is the Isa facet of Set-union:

Isa: (Operation[12] Domain=Range-op)
Isa-NOT: (Structure Composition Predicate)

At some time, some rule asked whether Set-union *Isa* Composition. As a result, the negative response was recorded by adding "Composition" to the Isa-not facet of Set-union, and adding "Set-union" to the Exs-not subfacet of the Examples facet of the concept Composition (indicating that Set-union was definitely not an example of Composition, yet there was no reason to consider it a foible).

5–2.3   In-domain-of/In-range-of

We shall say that A is in the domain of B (written "A In-dom-of B") iff:

- A and B are concepts.
- B Isa Operation.
- A is equal to (or at least a specialization of) one of the domain components of the operation B. That is, B can be executed using any example of A as one of its arguments.

Although it can be recomputed very easily, we may wish to record the fact that A In-dom-of B by adding the entry "B" to the In-dom-of facet of A. AM may even wish to add this new entry to the Domain/range facet of B (where A is a specialization of the jth domain component of B):
$$<D_1\,D_2\ldots D_{j-1}\,A\,D_{j+1}\ldots D_i \;\Rightarrow\; R>.$$

The semantic content of "In-dom-of" is: what can be done to any example of a given concept C? Given an example of concept C, what operations can be run on that thing? *e.g.,* "Primes In-dom-of Squaring" tells us that we can apply the operation Squaring to any particular prime number we wish.

Let us now turn from "In-dom-of" to the related facet "In-ran-of." We say that concept A is in the range of B iff B is an Activity and A is (a specialization of) the range of B.

For example, Odd-perfect-squares is In-ran-of Squaring, since (*i*) Squaring is an operation, hence an Activity, and (*ii*) one of its Domain/range entries is <Numbers $\Rightarrow$ Perf-squares>, and Perf-squares is a generalization of Odd-perfect-squares.[13]

Here is what the In-ran-of facet of Odd-perfect-squares might look like:

(Squaring Add TIMES Maximum Minimum Cubing)

Each of these operations will—at least sometimes—produce an odd perfect square as its result.

Semantically, the In-ran-of relation between A and B means that one might be able to produce examples of A by running operation B. Aha! This is a potential

---

[12] This entry is redundant.
[13] Why? Because Generalizations(Odd-perfect-squares) is the set of concepts {Odd-numbers Perf-squares Numbers Objects Any-concept Anything}, hence contains Perf-squares.

mechanism for finding examples of a concept A. All you need do is get hold of In-ran-of(A), and run each of those operations. Even more expeditious is to examine the Examples facets of each of those operations, for already-run examples whose values should be tested using A.Defn, to see if they are examples of A's. AM relies on this in times of high motivation; it is too "blind" a method to use heavily all the time.

This facet is also useful for generating situations to investigate. Suppose that the Domain/range facet of Doubling contains only one entry: $<$ Numbers $\Rightarrow$ Numbers $>$. Then syntactically, Odd-numbers is in the range of Doubling. Eventually a heuristic rule may have AM spend some time looking for an example of Doubling, where the result was an odd number. If none is quickly found, AM conjectures that it *never* will be found. Since one definition of Odd-number(x) is "Number(x) and Not(Even-number(x))," the only non-odd numbers are even numbers. So AM will increment the Domain/range facet of Doubling with the entry $<$Numbers $\Rightarrow$ Even-numbers$>$, and remove the old entry. Thus Odd-numbers will no longer be In-dom-of Doubling. AM can of course chance upon this conjecture in a more positive way, by noticing that all known examples of Doubling have results which are examples of Even-numbers.[14]

A more productive result is suggested by examining the cases where Odd-perfect-squares are the result of cubing. The smallest such odd numbers are 1, 729, and 15625. In general, these numbers are all those of the form $(2n + 1)^6$ How could AM notice such an awkward relationship?

The general question to ask, when A In-ran-of B, is "What is the set of domain items whose values (under the operation B) are A's?" In case the answer is "All" or "None," some special modifications can be made to the Domain/range facets and In-dom-of, In-ran-of facets of various concepts, and a new conjecture can be printed. In other cases, a new concept might get created, representing precisely the set of all arguments to B which yield values in A. If you will, this is the inverse image of A, under operation B. In the case of B a predicate, this might be the set of all arguments which satisfy the predicate.

In the case of B=Cubing and A=Odd-perfect-squares, the heuristic mentioned above will have AM create a new concept: the inverse image of Odd-perfect-squares under the operation of Cubing. That is, find numbers whose cubes are Odd-perfect-squares. It is quickly noticed that such numbers are precisely the set of Odd-perfect-squares themselves! So The Domain/range facet of Cubing might get this new entry: $<$Odd-perfect-squares $\Rightarrow$ Odd-perfect-squares$>$. But not all squares can be reached by cubing, only a few of them can. AM will notice this, and the new range would then be isolated and might be renamed by the user "Perfect-sixth-powers." Note that all this was brought on by examining the In-ran-of facet of Odd-perfect-squares. "Cubing" was just one of the seven entries there. There are six more stories to tell in this tiny nook of AM's activities.

How exactly does AM go about gathering the In-ran-of and In-dom-of lists?

---

[14] This positive approach is in fact the way AM noticed this particular relationship.

[6] Wrong. That was an exponent, not a footnote!

Given a concept C, AM can scan down the global tree of operations (the Exs and Spec links below the concept 'Active'). For if C is not In-dom-of F, it certainly won't be In-dom-of any specialization of F. Similarly, if it can't *legally* be produced by F, it won't be produced by any specialization of F: if you can't get x using Doubling you'll never get it by Doubling-perfect-numbers. So AM simply ripples around, as usual. The precise code for this algorithm is of little interest. There are not that many operations, and it is inexpensive to tell whether X is a specialization of a given concept, so even an exhaustive search wouldn't be prohibitive. Finally, recall that such a search is not done all the time. It will be done initially, perhaps, but after that the In-dom-of and In-ran-of networks will only need slight updating now and then.

5–2.4   Views

Often, two concepts A and B will not be equivalent, yet there will be a "natural" bijection between one and (a subset of) the other.

For example, consider a finite set S of atoms, and consider the set of all its subsets, 2^S, also called the *power set* of S, $\mathcal{P}(S)$. Now S is a member of, but not a *subset* of, 2^S (e.g., if S$=\{x, y, \dots\}$, then x is not a member of 2^S). On the other hand, we can identify or view S as a subset by the mapping $v \to \{v\}$. Then S is associated with the following subset of 2^S: $\{\{x\}, \{y\}, \dots\}$. Why would we want to do this? Well, it shows that S is identified with a *proper* subset of 2^S, and indicates that S has a lower cardinality (remember: all sets are finite).

As another example, most of us would agree that the set $\{x, \{y\}, z\}$ can be associated with the following bag: $(x, \{y\}, z)$. Each of them can be viewed as the other. Sometimes such a viewing is not perfectly natural, or isn't really a bijection: how could the bag (2, 2, 3) be viewed as a set? Is $\{2, 3\}$ better or worse than $\{2, \{2\}, 3\}$?

The View facet of a concept C describes how to view instances of another concept D as if they were C's. For example, this entry on the View facet of Sets explains how to view any given structure as if it were a Set:

Structure: λ *(x) Enclose-in-braces(Sort(Remove-multiple-elements(x)))*

If given the list <z,a,c,a>, this little program would remove multiple elements (leaving <z,a,c>), sort the structure (making it <a,c,z>), and replace the "<...>" by "{...}," leaving the final value as {a,c,z}. Note that this transformation is not 1–1 (injective); the list <a,c,z> would get transformed into this same set. On the other hand, it may be more useful than transforming the original list into {z,{a,{c,{a}}}} which retains the ordering and multiple element information. Both of those transformations may be present as entries on the View facet of Sets.

As it turns out, the View facet of Sets actually contains only the following information:

Structure: λ *(x) Enclose-in-braces(x)*

Thus the Viewing will produce entities which are not quite sets. Eventually, AM will get around to executing a task of the form "Check Examples of Sets," and at that time the error will be corrected. One generalization of Sets is No-multiple-elements-structures, and one of its entries under Examples.Check says to remove all multiple elements. Similarly, Unordered-structures is a generalization of Sets, and one of its Examples.Check subfacet entries says to sort the structure. If either of these alters the structure, the old structure is added to the Boundary-not subfacet (the 'Just-barely-miss' kind) of Examples facet of Sets.

The syntax of the View facet of a concept C is a list of entries; each entry specifies the name of a concept, X, and a little program P. If it is desired to view an instance of X as if it were a C, then program P is run on that X; the result is (hopefully) a C. The programs P are opaque to AM; they must have no side effects and be quick.

Here is an entry on the View facet of Singleton:

Anything: λ *(x) Set-insert(x, ϕ)*

In other words, to view anything as a singleton set, just insert it into the empty set. Note that this is also one way to view *anything* as a set.

As you've no doubt guessed, there is a general formula explaining this:

$$Views(X) =_{df} View(Specializations(X))$$

Thus, to find all the ways of viewing something as a C, AM ripples away from C in the Spec direction, gathering all the View facets along the way. All of their entries are valid entries for C.View as well.

In addition to these built-in ways of using the Views facets, some special uses are made in individual heuristic rules. Here is a heuristic rule which employs the Viewing facets of relevant concepts in order to find some examples of a given concept C:

> IF *the current task is to Fill-in Examples of C,*
>   *and C has some entries on its View facet,*
>   *and one of those entries <X,P> indicates a concept X which has some known Examples,*
> THEN *run the associated program P on each member of Examples(X),*
>   *and add the following task to the agenda: "Check Examples of C," for the following reason: "Some very risky techniques were used to find examples of C," and that reason's rating is computed as: Average(Worth(X), || the examples of C found in this manner||).*

Say the task selected from the agenda was "Fill-in Examples of Sets." We saw that one entry on Sets.View was Structure: λ(x) Enclose-in-braces(x). Thus it is of the form <X,P>, with X=Structure. The above heuristic rule will trigger if any examples of Structures are known. The rule will then use the View facet of Sets to find some examples of Sets. So AM will go off, gathering all the examples of structures. Since Lists is a Specialization of Structure, the computation of Examples(Structures) will eventually ripple downwards and ask for Examples of Lists. If the Examples facet of Lists contains the entry <z,a,c,a,a>, then this will be retrieved as one of the members of Examples(Structure). The heuristic rule takes each such member in turn, and feeds it to Set.View's little program P. In this case, the program replaces the list brackets with set braces, thus converting $<z,a,c,a,a>$ to $\{z,a,c,a,a\}$.

In this manner, all the existing structures will be converted into sets, to provide examples of sets. After all such conversions take place, a great number of potential examples of Sets will exist. The final action of the right side of the above heuristic rule is to add the new task "Check examples of Sets" to the agenda. When this gets selected, all the "slightly wrong" examples will be fixed up. For example, $\{z,a,c,a,a\}$ will be converted to $\{a,c,z\}$.

If any reliance is made on those unchecked examples, there is the danger of incorrectly rejecting a valid conjecture. This is not too serious, since the very first such reliance will boost the priority of the task "Check examples of Sets," and it would then probably be the very next task chosen.

5–2.5   Intuitions

The mathematician does not work like a machine; we cannot overemphasize the fundamental role played in his research by a special intuition (frequently wrong), which is not common-sense, but rather a divination of the regular behavior he expects of mathematical beings.

Bourbaki

This facet turned out to be a "dud," and was later excised from all the concepts. It will be described below anyway, for the benefit of future researchers. Feel free to skip directly to the next subsection.

The initial idea was to have a set of a few (3–10) large, global, opaque LISP functions. Each of these functions would be termed an "Intuition" and would have some suggestive name like "Jigsaw-puzzle," "See-saw," "Archery," etc. Each function would somehow model the particular activity implied by its name. There would be a multitude of parameters which could be specified by the "caller" as if they were the arguments of the function. The function would then work to fill in values for any unspecified parameters. That's all the function does. The caller would also have to specify which parameters were to be considered as the "results" of the function.

For the See-saw, the caller might provide the weight of the left-hand side sitter, and the final position of the See-saw, and ask for the weight of the right-hand sitter. The function would then compute that weight (as any random number greater/less-than the left-hand weight, depending on the desired tilt of the board). Or, the caller might specify the two weights and ask for the final position.

The See-saw function is an expert on this subject; it has efficient code for computing any values which can be computed, and for randomly instantiating any variables which may take on any value (*e.g.*, the first names of the people doing the sitting). When an individual call is made on this function, the caller is not told how the final values of the variables were computed, only what those values end up as.

So the Intuitions were to be experimental laboratories for AM, wherein it could get some (simulated) real-world empirical data. If the seesaw were the Intuition for ">," and "weight" corresponded to "Numbers," then several relationships might be visualized intuitively (like the antisymmetry of ">").

This is a nice idea, but in practice the only relationships derived in this way were the ones that were thought up while trying to encode the Intuition functions. This shameful behavior led to the excision of the Intuitions facets completely from the system.

As another example, suppose AM is considering composing two relations R and S. If they have no common Intuition reference, then perhaps they're not meaningfully composable. If they do both tie into the same Intuition function, then perhaps that function can tell us something about the composition.

This is a nice idea, but in practice very few prunings were accomplished this way, and no unanticipated combinations were fused.

Each Intuition entry is like a "way in" to one of the few global scenarios. It can be characterized as follows:

- One of the salient features of these entries—and of the scenarios—is that AM is absolutely forbidden to look inside them, to try to analyze them. They are *opaque*. Most Intuition functions use numbers and arithmetic, and it would be pointless to say that AM discovered such concepts if it had access to those algorithms all along.
- The second characteristic of an Intuition is that it be *fallible*. As with human intuition, there is no guarantee that what is suggested will be verified even empirically, let alone formally. Not only does this make the programming of Intuition functions easier, it was meant to provide a degree of "fairness" to them. AM wasn't cheating quite as much if the See-saw function was only antisymmetric 90% of the time.
- Nevertheless, the intuitions are very *suggestive*. Many conjectures can be proposed only via Intuitions. Some analogies (see the next subsection) can also be suggested via common intuitions.

After they were coded and running, I decided that the intuition functions were unfair; they contained some major discoveries "built-in" to them. They had the power to propose otherwise obscure new concepts and potential relationships. They contributed nothing other than what was originally programmed into them; *they were not synergetic*. Due to this dubious character of the contributions by AM's few Intuition functions, they were removed from the system. All the examples and all the discoveries listed in this document were made without their assistance.

We shall now drop this de-implemented idea. I think there is some real opportunity for research here. For the benefit of any future researchers in this area, let me point to the excellent discussion of analogic representations in [Sloman 71].

5–2.6   Analogies

The whole idea of analogy is that 'Effects', viewed as a function of situation, is a continuous function.

Poincaré

As with Views and Intuitions, this facet is useful for shifting between one part of the universe and another. Views dealt with transformations between two specific concepts; Intuitions dealt with transformations between a bunch of concepts and a large standard scenario which was carefully hand-crafted in advance. In contrast, this facet deals with transforming between a list of concepts and another list of concepts.

Analogies operate on a much grander scale than Views. Rather than simply transforming a few isolated items, they initiate the creation of many new concepts. Unlike Intuitions, they are not limited in scope beforehand, nor are they opaque. They are dynamically proposed.

The concept of "prime numbers" is *analogous* to the notion of "simple groups." While not isomorphic, you might guess at a few relationships involving simple groups just by my telling you this fact: simple groups are to groups what primes are to numbers.[15]

Let's take three elementary examples, involving very fundamental concepts:

- AM was told how to *View* a set as if it were a bag.
- AM was told it could *Intuit* the relation "$\geq$" as the predetermined "See-saw" function.
- AM, by itself, once *Analogized* that these two lists correspond:

<Bags, Same-length, Operations $\mathcal{F}_i$ on&into Bags>
<Bags-of-T's, Equality, Those $\mathcal{F}_i$ restricted to Bags-of-T's>

The concept of a bag, all of whose elements are "T"'s, is the unary representation of *numbers* discovered by AM. When the above analogy (third one) is first proposed, there are many known Bag-operations,[16] but there are as yet no numeric operations.[17] This triggers one of AM's heuristic rules, which spurs AM on to finding the analogues of specific Bag-operations. That is, what special properties do the bag-operations have when their domains and/or ranges are restricted from Bags to Bags-of-T's (i.e, Numbers). In this way, in fact, AM discovers Addition (by restricting Bag-union to the Domain/range <Bags-of-T's Bags-of-T's $\Rightarrow$ Bags-of-T's>), plus many other nice arithmetic functions.

---

[15] If a group is not simple, it can be factored. Unfortunately, the factorization of a group into simple groups is not unique. Another analogizing contact: For each prime p, we can associate the cyclic group of order p, which is of course simple. AM never came up with the concept of simple groups; this is just an illustration for the reader.

[16] That is, all entries on In-dom-of(Bag) and In-ran-of(Bag); a few of these are: Bag-insert, Bag-union, Bag-intersection.

[17] Examples of Operation whose Domain/range contains "Number".

Well, if it leads to the discovery of Addition, that analogy is certainly worth having. How would an analogy like that be proposed? As the reader might expect by now, the mechanism is simply some heuristic rule adding it as an entry to the Analogies facet of a certain concept. For example:

> IF the current task has just created a canonical specialization C2 of concept C1, with respect to operations F1 and F2, [i.e., two members of C2 satisfy F1 iff they satisfy F2],
> THEN add the following entry to the Analogies facet of C2:
> <C1, F1, Operations-on-and-into(C1)>
> <C2, F2, Those operations restricted to C2's>

After generalizing "Equality" into the operation "Same-length," AM seeks to find a canonical[18] representation for Bags. That is, AM seeks a canonizing function f, such that (for any two bags x,y) $Same-length(x,y) \Leftrightarrow Equal(f(x),f(y))$. Then the range of f would delineate the set of "canonical" Bags. AM finds such an f and such a set of canonical bags: the operation f involves replacing each element of a bag by "T," and the canonical bags are those whose elements are all T's. In this case, the above rule triggers, with C1=Bags, C2=Bags-of-T's, F1=Same-length, F2=Equality, and the analogy which is produced is the one shown as the third example above.

The Analogy facets are not implemented in full generality in the existing LISP version of AM, and for that reason I shall refrain from delving deeper into their format. Since good research has already been done on reasoning by analogy,[19] I did not view it as a central feature of my work. Very little space will be devoted to it in this document.

An important type of analogy which was untapped by AM was that between heuristics. If two situations were similar, then conceivably the heuristics useful in one situation might be useful (or have useful analogues) in the new situation. Perhaps this is a viable way of enlarging the known heuristics. Such "meta-level" activities were kept to a minimum throughout AM, and this proved to be a serious limitation.

Let me stress that the failure of the Intuitions facets to be nontrivial was due to the lack of spontaneity which they possessed. Analogies facets were useful and "fair" since their uses were not predetermined by the author.

5–2.7   Conjec's

The "Conjec" facet of a concept C is a list of relationships which involve C. There are several uses for C.Conjec:

- ⊚ Store awkwardly phrased conjectures: this wasn't really useful, since

---

[18] A natural, standard form. All bags differing in only "unimportant" ways should be transformed into the same canonical form. Two bags B1 and B2 which have the same length should get transformed into the same canonical bag.

[19] An excellent discussion of reasoning by analogy is found in [Pólya 54]. Some early work on emulating this was reported in [Evans 68]; a more recent thesis on this topic is [Kling 71].

most conjectures fell out naturally as simple relationships, expressible, *e.g.*, as a single Genl arc, or a single Isa arc.

    • Store flimsy conjectures: apparent relationships worth remembering but not quite believed yet.

    • Hold heuristics which notice and check conjectures.

    • Obviate the need for many nearly indistinguishable concepts: Collapse the entire essence of a concept like "Odd-primes" into one or two relationships involving "Primes;" then discard "Odd-primes."

    • Untangling paradoxes: a historic record, to facilitate backtracking in case of catastrophe, which (luckily!) wasn't ever needed.

    • Improve existing algorithms (*e.g.*, once you know primes are odd, hunt only through odd numbers), improve testing procedures, representations, etc.

    • Display AM's most impressive observed relationships in a form which is easily inspected by the user.

The syntax of this facet is simply a list of conjectures, where each conjecture has the form of a relationship: (R a b c...d). R is the name of a known operation (in which case, abc... are its arguments and we claim that d is its value). For instance, "*(Same-size Insert(S,S) S False)*" is a conjecture that inserting a set into itself will always give you a set of a different length. This conjecture happens to be true for finite sets.

5–2.8 Definitions

A typical way to distinguish a concept from all others is to provide a "definition" for it.[20] Almost every concept had some entries initially supplied on its "Definitions" facet. The format of this facet is a list of entries, each one describing a separate definition. A single entry will have the following parts:

    • Descriptors: Recursive/Linear/Iterative, Quick/Slow, Opaque/Transparent, Once-only/Early/Late, Destructive/Nondestructive.

    • Relators: Reducing to the definition of concept X, Same as Y except..., Specialized version of Z, Using the definition of W, etc.

    • Predicate: A small, executable piece of LISP code, to tell if any given item is an example of this concept.

The semantics of this are that the predicate or "code" part of the entry (*i*) must be faithfully described by the Descriptors, and (*ii*) must be related to other concepts just as the Relators claim.

Here is a typical entry from the Definitions facet of the Set-union concept:

    Descriptors: *Slow, Recursive, Transparent*

---

[20] As EPAM studies showed [Feigenbaum 63], one can never be sure that this definition will specify the concept uniquely for all time. In the distant future, some new concept may differ in ways thought to be ignorable at the present time.

Relators: *Uses the algorithm for Set-insert, Uses the definition of Empty-set, Uses the definition of Set-equal, Uses the algorithm for Some-member, Uses the algorithm for Set-delete, Uses the definition of Set-union*

Code: λ *(A B C)*
    IF *Empty-set. Defn(A)*
    THEN *Set-equal. Defn(B,C)*
    ELSE
        X ← Some-member. Alg(A)[21]
        A ← Set-delete. Alg(X,A)
        B ← Set-insert. Alg(X,B)
        Set-union. Defn(A,B,C)

Let me stress that this is just one entry from one facet of one concept.

This particular definition is not very efficient, but it is described as Transparent. That means it is very well suited to analysis and modification by AM itself. Suppose some heuristic rule wants to generalize this definition. It can peer inside it, and, *e.g.*, replace the base step call on Set-equal, by a call on a generalization of Set-equal (say "Same-length"[22]).

How could *different* definitions help here? Suppose there were a definition which first checked to see if the three arguments were Set-equal to each other, and if so then it instantly returned T as the value of the definition predicate; otherwise, it recurred into Set-union.Defn again. This might be a good algorithm to try at the very beginning, but if the Equality test fails, we don't want to keep recurring into this definition. This algorithm should thus have a Descriptor labeling it ONCE-ONLY EARLY.

There are three purposes to having Descriptors and Relators hanging around:

1   For the benefit of the user. AM appears more intelligent because it can *describe* the kind of definition it is using—and why.

2   For the sake of efficiency. When all AM wants to do is to evaluate Set-union(A,B), it's best just to grab a *fast* definition. When trying to generalize Set-union, it's more appropriate to modify a very clean, transparent definition—even if it is a slow one.

3   For the benefit of the heuristic rules. Often, a left- or right-hand side will ask about a certain kind of definition. For example, *"If a transparent definition of X exists, then try to specialize X"*.

Let me pull back the curtain a little further, and expose the actual implementation of these ideas in AM. The secrets about to be revealed will not be acknowledged anywhere else in this document. They may, however, be of interest to future researchers. Each concept may have a cluster of Definition

---

[21] The notation "X ← Some-member.Alg(A)" means that any one algorithm for the concept Some-member should be accessed, and then it should be run on the argument A. The result, which will be an element of A, is to be assigned the name "X." The effect is to bind the variable X to some member of set A.

[22] For disjoint sets, the new definition would specify the operation which we call "addition."

facets, just as it can have several kinds of Examples facets. These include three types: Necessary and sufficient definitions, necessary definitions, and sufficient definitions. These three types have the usual mathematical meanings. All that has been alluded to before (and after this subsection) is the necc&suff type of definition (x is an example of C *if and only if* x satisfies C.Def/necc&suff). Often, however, there will be a much quicker sufficient definition (x satisfies C.Def/suf, *only if* x is certainly a C). Similarly, entries on C.Def/nec are useful for quickly checking that x is *not* an example of C (to check this, it suffices to verify that x *fails* to satisfy a necessary definition of C).

So given the task of deciding whether or not x is an example of C, we have many alternatives:

1   If x is a concept, see if C is a member of x.Isa (if so, then x is an example of C).
2   Try to locate x within C.Exs. (depending upon the flavor of subfacet on which x is found, this may show that x is or is not an example of C).
3   If x is a concept, ripple to collect Isa's(x), and see if C is a member of Isa's(x).
4   If there is a fast sufficent definition of C, see if x satisfies it.
5   If there is a fast necessary definition of C, see if x fails it (if so, then x is *not* an example of C).
6   If there is a necessary and sufficient definition of C, see whether or not x satisfies that definition (this may show that x is or is not an example of C).
7   Try to locate x within C.Exs. (depending upon the flavor of subfacet on which x is found, this may show that x is or is not an example of C).
8   Recur: check to see if x is an example of any specialization of C.
9   Recur: check to see if x is *not* an example of some generalization of C (if so, then x is *not* an example of C).

In fact, there is a LISP function, IS-EXAMPLE, which performs those nine steps in that order. At each moment, there is a timer set, so even if there is a necessary and sufficient definition hanging around, it might run out of time before settling the issue one way or the other. Each time the function recurs, the timer is granted a smaller and smaller quantum, until finally it has too little to bother recurring anymore. There is a potential overlap of activity: to see if x is an example of C, the function might ask whether x is or is not an example of a particular generalization of C (step 9, above); to test *that*, AM might get to step 6, and again ask if x is an example of C. Even though the timer would eventually terminate this fiasco (and even though the true answer might be found despite this wasted effort) it is not overly smart of AM to fall into this loop. Therefore, a stack is maintained, of all concepts whose definitions the IS-EXAMPLE function tried to test on argument x. As the function recurs, it adds the current value of C to that stack; this value gets removed when the recursion pops back to this level, when that recursive call "returns" a value.

5–2.9　Algorithms

Earlier, we said that each concept can have any facets from the universal fixed set of 25 facets. This is not strictly true. Sometimes, a whole class of concepts will possess a certain type of facet which no others may meaningfully have. That is, there will be a *domain of applicability* for the facet, just as we defined such domains of applicability for heuristics. For example, consider the "Domain/range" facet. It is meaningful only to "operations."

Let's view this in a more general light. For each facet f, the only concepts which can have entries for facet f are examples of some particular concept *Dscr*(f). *Dscr*(f) is the domain of applicability of facet f. If C is any concept which is not an example of *Dscr*(f), then it can never meaningfully possess any entries for that facet f. For almost all facets f, *Dscr*(f) is "Any-concept." Thus any concept can possess almost any facet. For example, *Dscr*(Defn)="Any-concept," so any concept may have definitions. But *Dscr*(Domain/range)="Operation." So only operations can have Domain/range facets.

Similarly, *Dscr*(Algorithms)="Actives." This facet is the subject of this section. The Algorithms facet is present for all—but only for—Actives (predicates, relations, and operations).

The representation is, just as with Definitions, a list of entries, each one describing a separate algorithm, and each one having three parts: Descriptors, Relators, Program. Instead of a LISP predicate, however, the Algorithms facets possess a LISP function (an executable piece of code whose value will in general be other than True/False).

All the details about understanding the descriptors and relators are embedded in the fine structure of the heuristic rules. A left-hand side may test whether a certain kind of algorithm exists for a given concept. A right-hand side which fills in a new algorithm must also worry about filling in the appropriate descriptors and relators. As with newly created concepts, such information is trivial to fill in at the time of creation, but becomes much harder after the fact.

Here is a typical heuristic rule which results in a new entry being added to the Algorithms facet of the newly created concept named Compose-Set-Intersect&-Set-Intersect: [23]

IF the task is to Fillin Algorithms for F,
　　and F is an example of Composition
　　and F has a definition of the form $F =_{df} G \circ H$,
　　and F has no transparent, nonrecursive algorithm,
THEN add a new entry to the Algorithms facet of F,
　　with Descriptors: Transparent, Non-recursive
　　with Relators: Reducing to G.Alg and H.Alg, Using the Definition of $<$G.Domain$>$
　　with Program:
　　　　$\lambda(\| < G.Domain > \|, \| < H.Domain > \| - 1, X)$
　　　　(SETQ X (H.Alg $\| <$G.Domain$>\|$))

---

[23] The operation "$\cap \circ \cap$" takes three sets and intersects them.

> *(AND*
>   *(<G.Domain>.Defn X)*
>   *(G.Alg X || <H.Domain>|| − 1))*

The intent of the little program which gets created is to apply the first operator, check that the result is in the domain of the second, and then apply the second operator. The expression $|| < G.Domain > ||$ means find a Domain/range entry for G, count how many domain components there are, and form a list that long from randomly chosen variable names *(u,v,w,x,y,z)*.

For the case mentioned above, F = Compose-Set-Intersect&Set-Intersect, G = Set-Intersect, and H = Set-Intersect. The domain of G is a pair of Sets, so $|| < G.Domain > ||$ is a list of 2 variables, say *"(u v)."* Similarly, $|| < H.Domain > || − 1$ is a list of 1 variable, say *"(w)."* Putting all this together, we see that the new definition entry created for Compose-Set-Intersect&Set-Intersect would look like this:

> Descriptors: *Non-Recursive, Transparent*
> Relators: *Reducing to Set-Intersect.Alg, Using the definition of Sets*
> Code: λ *(u,v,w,X)*
>   *(SETQ X (Set-Intersect.Alg u v))*
>   *(AND*
>   *(Sets.Defn X)*
>   *(Set-Intersect.Alg X w)*

At times, AM will be capable of producing only a slow algorithm for some new concept C. For example, $\text{TIMES}^{-1}(x)$ was originally defined by AM as a blind, exhaustive search for bags of numbers whose product is x. As AM uses that algorithm more and more, AM records how slow it is. Eventually, a task is selected of the form "Fillin new algorithms for C", with the two reasons being that the existing algorithms are all too slow, and they are used frequently. At this point, AM should draw on a body of rules which take a declarative definition and transform it into an efficient algorithm, or which take an inefficient algorithm and speed it up. Doing a good job on just those rules would be a mammoth undertaking, and the author decided to omit them. The reader who wishes to know more about rules for creating and improving LISP algorithms is directed to [Darlington and Burstall 73]. A more general discussion of the principles involved can be found in [Simon 72].

5–2.10   Domain/range

Another facet possessed only by active concepts is Domain/range. The syntax of this facet is quite simple. It is a list of entries, each of the form $< D_1 D_2 \ldots \Rightarrow R >$, where there can be any number of D_i's preceding the arrow, and R and all the D_i's are the names of concepts. Semantically, this entry means that the active concept may be run on a list of arguments where the first one is an example of D_1, the second an example of D_2, etc., and in that case will return a value guaranteed to be an example of R. In other words, the concept may be considered a relation on the Cartesian product $D_1 \times D_2 \times \cdots \times R$. We shall say that the *domain* of the concept is $D_1 \times D_2 \times \cdots$, and that its *range* is R. Each D_i is called a *component* of the domain.

For example, here is what the Domain/range facet of TIMES might look like:

{

    < *Numbers Numbers* $\Rightarrow$ *Numbers* >

    < *Odd-numbers Odd-numbers* $\Rightarrow$ *Odd-numbers* >

    < *Even-Numbers Even-Numbers* $\Rightarrow$ *Even-numbers* >

    < *Odd-numbers Even-Numbers* $\Rightarrow$ *Even-Numbers* >

    < *Perf-Squares Perf-Squares* $\Rightarrow$ *Perf-Squares* >

    < *Bags-of-Numbers* $\Rightarrow$ *Numbers* >

}

The Domain/range part is useful for pruning away absurd compositions, and for syntactically suggesting compositions and "coalescings." Let's see what this means.

Suppose some rule sometime tried to compose TIMES∘Set-union. A rule tacked onto Compose says to ensure that the range of Set-union at least intersects (and preferably is *equal* to) some component of the domain of TIMES. But there are no entities which are both sets and numbers; ergo this fails almost instantaneously.

The claim was also made that Domain/range facets help propose plausible coalescings. By "*coalescing*" an operation, we mean defining a new one, which differs from the original one in that a couple of the arguments must now coincide. For example, coalescing TIMES(x,y) results in the new operation F(x) defined as TIMES(x,x). Syntactically, we can coalesce a pair of domain components of the Domain/range facet of an operation if those two domain components are equal, or if one of them is a specialization of the other, or even if they merely intersect. In the case of one related to the other by specialization, the more specialized concept will replace both of them, In case of merely intersecting, an extra test will have to be inserted into the definition of the new coalesced operation.

Given this Domain/range entry for Set-insert: < Anything Sets $\Rightarrow$ Sets >, we see that it is ripe for coalescing. Since Sets is a specialization of Anything, the new operation F(x), which is defined as Set-insert(x,x), will have a Domain/range entry of the form < Sets $\Rightarrow$ Sets >. That is, the specialized concept Sets will replace both of the old domain elements (Anything and Sets). F(x) takes a set x and inserts it into itself. Thus $F(\{a, b\}) = \{a, b, \{a, b\}\}$. In fact, this new operation F is very exciting because it always seems to give a new, larger set than the one you feed in as the argument.

We have seen how the Domain/range facets can prune away meaningless coalescings, as well as meaningless compositions. Any proposed composition or coalescing will at least be syntactically meaningful. If all compositions are proposed only for at least one good semantic reason, then those passing the Domain/range test, and hence those which ultimately get created, will all be valuable new concepts. Since almost all coalescings are semantically interesting, *any* of them which have a valid Domain/range entry will get created and probably will be interesting.

This facet is occasionally used to suggest conjectures to investigate. For example, a heuristic rule says that if the Domain/range entries have the form $<DDD\ldots \Rightarrow genl(D)^{24}>$, then it's worthwhile seeing whether the value of this operation doesn't really always lie inside D itself. This is used right after the Bags$\Leftrightarrow$Numbers analogy is found, in the following way. One of the Bag-operations known already is Bag-union. The analogy causes AM to consider a new operation, with the same algorithm as Bag-union, but restricted to Bags-of-T's (numbers in unary representation). The Domain/range facet of this new, restricted mutation of Bag-union contains only this entry: $<$Bags-of-T's Bags-of-T's $\Rightarrow$ Bags$>$. Since Bags is a generalization of Bags-of-T's, the heuristic mentioned above triggers, and AM sees whether or not the union of two Bags-of-T's is always a bag containing only T's. It appears to be so, even in extreme cases, so the old Domain/range entry is replaced by this new one: $<$Bags-of-T's Bags-of-T's $\Rightarrow$ Bags-of-T's$>$. When the user asks AM to call these bags-of-T's "numbers," this entry becomes $<$Numbers Numbers $\Rightarrow$ Numbers$>$. In modern terms, then, the conjecture suggested was that the sum of two numbers is always a number.

To sum up this last ability in fancy language, we might say that one mechanism for proposing conjectures is the prejudicial belief in the unlikelihood of asymmetry. In this case, it is asymmetry in the parts of a Domain/range entry that draws attention. Such conjecturing can be done by any action part of any heuristic rule; the Conjec facet entries don't have a monopoly on initiating this type of activity.

5–2.11   Worth

How can we represent the worth of each concept? Here are some possible suggestions:

1   The most intelligent (but most difficult) solution is "totally symbolic; ' that is, an individualized description of the good and bad points of the concept; when it is useful, when misleading, etc.

2   A simpler solution would be to "standardize" the above symbolic description once and for all, fixing a universal list of questions. So each concept would have to answer the questions on this list (How good are you at motivating new concepts?, How costly is your definition to execute?,...). The answers might each be symbolic (*e.g.*, arbitrary English phrases.)

3   To simplify this scheme even more, we can assume that the answers to each question will be numeric-valued functions (*i.e.*, LISP code which can be evaluated to yield a number between 0 and 1000). The vector of numbers produced by *Evaluating* all these functions will then be easy to manipulate (*e.g.*, using dot-product, vector-product, vector-addition, etc.), and the functions themselves may be inspected for semantic content. Nevertheless, much content is lost in passing from symbolic phrases to small LISP functions.

4   A slight simplification of the above would be to just store the vector of numbers answering the fixed set of questions; *i.e.*, don't bother storing a bunch

---

24 *"Genl(D)"* means: any generalization of concept D.

of programs which compute them dynamically.

    5   Even simpler would be to try to assign a single "worthwhileness" number to each concept, in lieu of the vector of numbers. Simple arithmetic operations could manipulate Worth values then. In some cases, this linear ordering seems reasonable ("primes" really are better than "palindromes.") Yet in many cases we find concepts which are too different to be so easily compared (*e.g.*, "numbers" and "angles").

    6   The least intelligent solution is none at all: each concept is considered equally worthwhile as any other concept. This threatens to be combinatorial dynamite.

As we progress along the intelligent $====\Rightarrow$ trivial dimension, we find that the schemes get easier and easier to code, the Worth values get easier and easier to deal with, but the amount of reliable knowledge packed into them decreases.

    Initially, scheme #3 above was chosen for AM: a vector of numeric-valued procedural answers to a fixed set of questions. Here are those questions, the components of the Worth vectors for each concept:

- Overall aesthetic worth.
- Overall utility. Combination of usefulness, ubiquity.
- Age. How many cycles since this concept was created?
- Life-span. Can this concept be forgotten yet?
- Cost. How much cpu time has been spent on this concept, since its creation?

Notice that in general no constant number can answer one of these questions once and for all (consider, *e.g.*, Life-span). Each 'answer' had to be a numeric-valued LISP function.

    A few questions which crop up often are not present on this list, since they can be answered trivially using standard LISP functions (*e.g.*, "How much space does concept C use up?" can be found by calling the function "COUNT" on the property-list of the LISP atom "C").

    Another kind of question, which was anticipated and did in fact come up frequently, is of the form "How good are the entries on facet F of this concept?," for various values of F. Since there are a couple dozen kinds of facets, this would mean adding a couple dozen more questions to the list. The line must be drawn somewhere. If too much of AM's time is drained by evaluating where it is already, it can never progress.

    The heuristic rules are responsible for initially setting up the various entries on the Worth facets of new concepts, and for periodically altering those entries for *all* concepts, and for delving into those entries when required.

    Recent experiments[25] have shown that there was little change in behavior when each vector of functions was replaced by a single numeric function (actually,

---

[25] See Experiment 1, which is described in subsection 6-2.2.

the sum of the values of the components of the "old" vector of functions). There wasn't even too much change when this was replaced by a constant. There *was* a noticeable degradation (but no collapse) when all the concepts' Worth numbers were set equal to each other initially.

For the purposes of this document, then (except for this page and the discussion of Experiment 1), we may as well assume that each concept has a single number (between 0 and 1000) attached as its overall "Worth" rating. This number is set[26] and referenced and updated by heuristic rules. Experiment 1 can be considered as showing that a more sophisticated Worth scheme is not necessary for the particular kinds of behaviors that AM exhibits.

5–2.12   Interest

Now that we know how how to judge the overall worth of the concept "Composition," let's turn to the question of how interesting some specific composition is. Unfortunately, the Worth facet really has nothing to say about that problem. The Worth of the concept "Compose" has little effect on how interesting a particular composition is: "CountoDivisors-of" is very interesting, and "InsertoMember"[27] is less so. The Worth facets of *those* concepts will say something about their overall value. And yet there is some knowledge, some "features" which would make any composition which possessed them more interesting than a composition which lacked them:

- Are the domain and range of the composition equal to each other?
- Are interesting properties of each component of the composition preserved?
- Are undesirable properties lost (*i.e.*, *not* true about the composition)?
- Is the new composition equivalent to some already-known operation?

These hints about "features to look for" belong tacked onto the Composition concept, since they modify all compositions. Where and how can this be done?

For this purpose each concept—including "Composition"—can have entries on its "*Interest*" facet. It contains a bunch of features which (if true) would make any particular example of the current concept interesting.

The format for the Interest facet is as follows:

```
< Conflict-matrix
    <Feature₁, Value₁, Reason₁, Used₁>
    <Feature₂, Value₂, Reason₂, Used₂>

       ⋮

    <Featureₖ, Valueₖ, Reasonₖ, Usedₖ>
  >
```

This is the format of the facet itself, not of each entry. The conflict-matrix is special and will be discussed below. Each Feature/Value/Reason/Used quadruple will be termed an "entry" on the Interest facet.

---

[26] The author initially sets this value for the 115 initial concepts. Heuristic rules set it for each concept created by AM.

[27] INSERToMEMBER(x,y,z) is defined to be: if x∈y, then insert 'T' into z, else insert 'NIL' into z.

Each "Feature$_i$" is a LISP predicate, indicating whether or not some interesting property is satisfied. The corresponding "Value$_i$" is a numeric function for computing just how valuable this feature is. The "Reason$_i$" is a token (usually an English phrase) which is tacked along and moved around, and can be inspected by the user. The "Used$_i$" subpart is a list of all the concepts whose definitions are known to incorporate[28] this feature; all examples of such concepts will then automatically satisfy this Feature$_i$.

For example, here is one entry from the Interest facet of Compose:

FEATURE: *Domain(Arg1)=Range(Arg2)*
VALUE: $.4 + .4 \cdot Worth(Domain(Arg1)) + .2 \cdot Priority(currenttask)$
REASON: *"The composition of Arg1 and Arg2 will map from C back into C"*
USED: *Compose-with-self-Domain=Range-operation, Interesting-compose-4*

Just as with Isa's and Generalizations, we can make a general statement about Interest features:

> Any feature tacked onto the Interest facet of any member of Isa's(C), also applies to C.

That is, X.Interest is relevant to C iff C is an example of X. For example, any feature which makes an operation interesting, also makes a composition interesting.

So we'd like to define the function Interests(C) as the union of the Interest features found tacked onto any member of Isa's(C).[29] But some of these might have already been conjoined to a definition, to form the concept C (or a generalization of C). So all C's will trivially (by definition) satisfy such features. The USED subparts can be employed to find such features. In fact, the final value of Interests(C) is Interest(Isa's(C)) *minus* all the features whose USED subparts pointed to any member of Isa's(C).

This covers the purpose of each subpart of each entry on a typical Interest facet. Now we're ready to motivate the presence of the Conflict-matrices.

Often, AM will specialize a concept by conjoining onto its definition some features which would make any example of the concept interesting. So *any* example of this new specialized concept is thus guaranteed to be an *interesting* example of the old concept. Sometimes, however, a pair of features are exclusive: both of them can never be satisfied simultaneously. For example, a composition can be interesting if its domain and range coincide, but it can also be interesting if its range is much more interesting than its domain. Clearly, these two Interestingness features can't both be true ("x=y" and "x much more interesting than y" can't occur simultaneously). If AM didn't have some systematic way to realize this, however, it might create a new concept, called Interesting-composition, defined as any composition satisfying both of those features. But then this concept will

---

[28] Not *satisfy* the feature. Thus the general concept Domain=Range-op *incorporates* the feature "range(x) is one component of domain(x)" as just one of the conjuncts in its definition. On the other hand, Set-union *satisfies* the feature, since its range, Sets, really is one component of its domain.

[29] Recall that the formula for this is Isa's(C) = Generalizations(Isa(Generalizations(C))).

be vacuous: *no* operation can possibly satisfy that over-constrained definition; this new concept will have no examples; it is the null concept; it is trivially forgettable. Merely to think of it is a blot on AM's claim to rationality. This is where the Conflict-matrix fits in.

The "Conflict-matrix" is specified to prevent many such trivial combinations from eating up a lot of AM's time. If there are K features present for the Interest facet of the concept, then its conflict-matrix will be a $K \times K$ matrix. In row i, column j of this matrix is a letter or symbol, indicating the relationship between features i and j:

E *Exclusive of each other:*   They both can't be true at the same time.
Implies: If feature i holds, then feature j must hold.
Implied by: If feature j holds, then so does feature i.
= *Equal:*   Feature i holds precisely when feature j holds.
U *Unrelated:*   As far as known, there is no connection between them.

These little relations are utilized by some of the heuristic rules. Here is one such rule. Its purpose is to create a new, specialized form of concept C, if many examples of C were previously found very quickly.

IF *Current-task is (Fillin Specializations of C)*
  and $\|C.Examples\| > 30$
  and Time-spent-on-C-so-far < 3 *cpu seconds,*
  and Interests(C) is not null,
THEN *create a new concept named Interesting-C,*
  Defined as the conjunction of C.Defn and the highest-valued member of Interests(C) which is U *(unrelated) to any feature USED in the definition of C.*
  and add the following task to the agenda: Fillin examples of Interesting-C, with value computed as the Value subpart of the chosen feature, for this reason: "Any example of Interesting-C is automatically an interesting example of C."
  and add "Interesting-C" to the USED subpart of the entry where that feature was originally plucked from.

5–2.13   Suggest

This section describes a space-saving "trick" and a "fix-up" to undo some potentially serious side-effects of that trick. AM maintains two numeric threshholds: Do-threshhold and a lower one, Be-threshhold.

When a new task is proposed, if its global priority is below Be-threshhold, then it won't even be entered on the agenda. This value is set so low that any task having even one mediocre reason will make it onto the agenda.

After a task is finished executing, the top-rated one from the agenda is selected to work on next. If its priority rating is below Do-threshhold, however, it is put back on the agenda, and AM complains that no task on the agenda is very interesting at the moment. AM then spends a minute or so looking around for new tasks, re-evaluating the priorities of the tasks on the agenda already, etc.

One way to find new tasks (and new reasons for already-existing tasks) is to evaluate the *"Suggest"* facets of all the concepts in the system. More precisely, each Suggest facet contains some heuristics, encoded into LISP functions. Each function accepts a number N as an argument (representing the minimum tolerable priority value for a new task), and the function returns as its output a list of new tasks. These are then merged into the agenda, if desired.

Semantically, each function is one heuristic rule for suggesting a new task which might be very plausible, promising, and *a propos* at the current time. For example, here is one entry from the Suggest facet of Any-concept:

> *IF there are no examples for concept C filled in so far,*
> *THEN consider the task "Fillin examples of C," for the following reason: "No examples of C filled in so far," whose value is half of Worth(C). If that value is below arg1, then forget it; otherwise, try to add to to the agenda.*

The argument "arg1" is that low numeric value, N, supplied to the Suggest facet.

This entry alone will produce a multitude of potential tasks; for concepts whose Worth numbers are high, or for which a task is already on the agenda to fill in their examples, these suggested tasks will be remembered; most of the other ones will typically be forgotten.

One use of this facet is thus to "beef up" the agenda whenever AM is discontented with all the tasks thereon. At such a time, AM may call on all the Suggest facets in the system, and a large volume of new tasks will be added to the agenda. Many of them will exist there already, but for different reasons, so many old tasks' priority values will rise. After this period of suggesting is over, the agenda's highest-ranking task will hopefully have a higher value than any did before. Also at this time, the Be-threshhold and Do-threshhold numbers are reduced. So there are two reasons why the top task may now be rated higher than Do-threshhold. If it isn't, then the threshholds are lowered again, and again all the Sugg facets are triggered (this time with a lower N value).

Both threshholds are raised slightly every time AM succeeds in picking and executing a task. So they follow a pattern of slow increase, followed by a sudden decrement, followed by another slow increase, etc. This was intended to mimic a human's increasing expectations while progressing. It also is suggestive of the way a human strains mentally when an obstacle to that progress appears; if the straining doesn't produce a brilliant new insight, he grudgingly is willing to reduce his expectations, and perhaps resume some "old path" abandoned earlier.

5–2.14   Fill/Check

To doubt everything doesn't suffice; one must know why he doubts.

Poincaré

There is one more level of structure to AM's representation of a concept than the simple "properties on a property-list" image. Each concept consists of a bunch of facets; each facet follows the format layed down for it (and described in the preceding several subsections). Yet each facet of each concept can have two additional "subfacets" (little slots that are hung onto any desired slot) named *Fillin* and *Check*.

The "Fillin" field of facet F of concept C is abbreviated C.F.Fillin. The format of that subfield is a list of heuristic rules, encoded into LISP functions. Semantically, each rule in C.F.Fillin should be relevant to filling in entries for facet F of any concept which is a C. This substructure is an implementation answer to the question of where to place certain heuristic rules.

As an illustration, let me describe a typical rule which is found on Compose.Examples.Fillin. According to the last paragraph, this must be useful for filling in examples of any operation which is a composition. The rule says that if the composition A∘B is formed from two very time-consuming operations A and B, then it's worth trying to find some examples of A∘B by symbolic means; in this case, scan the examples of A and of B, for some pair of examples x→y (example of B) and y→z (example of A). Then posit that x→z is an example of A∘B.

As another illustration, let me describe a typical rule which is found on Compose.Conjec.Fillin. It says that one potential conjecture about a given composition A∘B is that it is unchanged from A (or from B). This happens often enough that it's worth examining each time a new composition is made. This rule applies precisely to the task of filling in conjectures about particular compositions.

Let's take yet a third illustration. The subfacet Any-Concept.Examples.Fill-in is quite large; it contains all the known methods for filling in examples of C (when all we know is that C is a concept). Here are a few of those techniques:[30]

- Instantiate C.Defn.
- Search the examples facets of all the concepts on Generalizations(C) for examples of C.
- Run some of the concepts named in In-ran-of(C)[31] and collect the resultant values.

Any-Concept.Examples.Check is large for similar reasons. A typical entry there says to examine each verified example of C: if it is also an example of a specialization of C, then it must be removed from C.Examples and inserted[32] into the Examples facet of that specialized concept.

Here is one typical entry from Operation.Domain/range.Check:

---

[30] The interested reader will find them all listed in Appendix 2–2.37.

[31] That is, operations whose range is C.

[32] Conditionally. Since each concept is of finite worth, it is allotted a finite amount of space. A random number is generated to decide whether or not to actually insert this example into the Examples facet of the specialization of C. The more that specialized concept is "exceeding its quota," the narrower the range that the random number must fall into to have that new item inserted. The probability is never precisely 1 or 0.

IF a Domain/range entry has the form (D D D. . . ⇒ R),
   and all the D's are equal, and R is a generalization of D,
THEN it's worth seeing whether (D D D. . . ⇒ D) is consistent with all known
examples of the operation.
If there are no known examples, add a task to the agenda requesting they be filled
in.
If there are examples, and (DDD. . . ⇒ D) is consistent, add it to the Domain/range
facet of this operation.
If there are some contradicting examples, create a new concept which is defined as
this operation restricted to (D D D. . . ⇒ D).

Note that this "Checking" rule doesn't just passively check the designated facet; it actively "fixes up" faulty entries, adds new tasks, creates new concepts, etc. All the check rules are very aggressive in this way. For example, one entry on No-multiple-elements-structure.Examples.Check will actually remove any multiple occurrences of an element from a structure.

The set Checks(C.F) of all relevant rules for checking facet F of concept C is obtained as (Isa's(C)).F.Check. That is, look for the Check subfacet of the F facet of all the concepts on Isa's(C)). Similarly, Fillins(C.F) is the union of the Fillin subfacets of the F facets of all the concepts on Isa's(C).

When AM chooses a task like "Fillin examples of Primes," its first action is to compute Fillins(Primes.Exs). It does this by asking for Isa's(Primes); that is, a list of all concepts of which Primes is an example. This list is: <Objects Any-concept Anything>. So the relevant heuristics are gathered from Objects.Exs.Fillin, etc. This list of heuristics is then executed, in order (last executed are the heuristics attached to Anything.Exs.Fillin).

5–2.15 Other Facets Which Were Considered

Most facets (like "Definitions") were anticipated from the very beginning planning of AM, and proved just as useful as expected. Others (like "Intuitions") were also expected to be very important, yet were a serious disappointment. Still others (like "Suggest") were unplanned and grumblingly acknowledged as necessary for the particular LISP program that bears the name AM. Finally, we turn to a few facets which were initially planned, and yet which were adjudged useless around the time that AM was coded. They were therefore never really a part of the LISP program AM, although they figured in its proposal. Let me list them, and explain why each one was dropped.

- UN-INTERESTINGNESS. This was to be similar to the Interest facet. It would contain entries of the form feature/value/reason, where the feature would be a *bad* (dull, trivializing, undesirable, uninteresting) property that an entity (a concept or a task) might possess. If it did, then the value component would return a negative number as its contribution to the worth/priority of that entity. This sounded plausible, but turned out to be useless in practice: (*i*) There were very few features one could point to which explicitly indicated when something was boring; (*ii*) Often, a conjunction of many such features would make the entity seem unusual, hence interesting; (*iii*) Most entities were viewed as very mediocre unless/until specific reasons to the contrary, and in those cases the presence a few boring properties would be outshadowed by the few non-boring ones. In a sea of mediocrity, there is little need to separate the boring from the very boring.

- JUSTIFICATION. For conjectures which were not yet believed with certainty, this part would contain all the known evidence supporting them. This would hopefully be convincing, if the user (or a concept) ever wanted to know. In cases of contradictions arising somehow, this facet was to keep hold of the threads that could be untangled to resolve those paradoxes. As described earlier, this duty could naturally be assumed by the Conjecs facet of each concept. The other intended role for this facet was to hold sketches of the proofs of theorems. Unfortunately, the intended concepts for Proof and Absolute truth were never implemented, and thus most of the heuristic rules which would have interacted with this facet are absent from AM. It simply was never needed.

- RECOGNITION. Originally, it was assumed that the location of relevant concepts and their heuristics would be much more like a free-for-all (pandemonium) than an orderly rippling process. As with the original use of BEINGs,[33] the expectation was that each concept would have to "shout out" its relevance whenever the activities triggered some recognition predicate inside that concept. Such predicates were to be stored in this facet. But it quickly became apparent that the triggering predicates which were the left-hand sides of the heuristic rules were quick enough to obviate the need for preprocessing them too heavily. Also, the only rules relevant to a given activity on concept C always seemed to be attainable by rippling in a certain direction away from C. This varied with the activity, and a relatively small table could be written, to specify which direction to ripple in (for any given desired activity). We see that for "Fill-in examples of...," the direction to ripple in is "Generalizations," to locate relevant heuristic rules. For "Judge interest of..." the direction is also Generalizations. For "Access specializations of," the direction is Specializations, etc. The only important point here is that the Recognition facet was no longer needed.

5–3 AM'S STARTING CONCEPTS

The first subsection presents a diagram of the top-level (general) concepts AM started with, with the lines indicating the Generalizations/Specializations kinds of relationships (single line links) and a few Examples/Isa's links (triple vertical lines). Several specific concepts have been omitted from that picture. All the concepts initially fed to AM are then listed alphabetically and described. Finally, in Section 2–5.2.3, we discuss the choice of starting concepts.

---

[33] Interacting knowledge modules, each module simulating a different expert at a round-table meeting. See [Lenat 75b].

5–3.1 Diagram of Initial Concepts

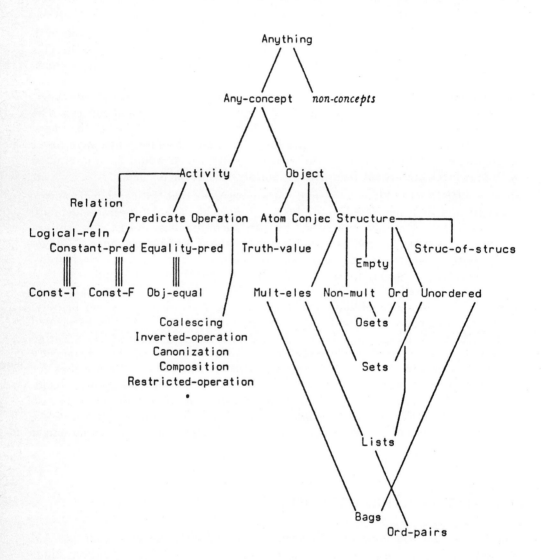

The diagram above represents the "topmost" concepts which AM had initially, shown connected via Specialization links (single lines) and Examples links (triple lines). The only concepts not diagrammed are the 47 *examples* of the concept Operation.

Also, we should note that many entities exist in the system which are not themselves concepts. For example, the number "3," though it be an *example* of many concepts, is not itself a concept. All entities which are concepts are present on the list called CONCEPTS, and they all have property lists (with facet names as the properties). In hindsight, this somewhat arbitrary scheme is regrettable. A more aesthetic designer might have come up with a more uniform system of representation than AM's.

5–3.2   Summary of Initial Concepts

Since the precise set of concepts is not central to the design of AM, or the quality of behaviors of AM, it is not worth detailing here. On the other hand, a cursory familiarity with the concepts' names and definitions should aid the reader in building up an understanding of what AM has done. For that reason, the concepts will now be briefly described, in alphabetical order.

ACTIVITY represents something that can be "performed." All Actives—and *only* Actives—have Domain/range facets and Algorithms facets.

ALL-BUT-FIRST-ELEMENT is an operation which takes an ordered structure and removes the first element from it. It is similar in spirit to the Lisp function "CDR."

ALL-BUT-LAST-ELEMENT takes an ordered structure and removes its last element.

ANY-CONCEPT is useful because it holds all the very general tactics for filling in and checking each facet. The definition of Any-concept is "λ (x) xϵCONCEPTS", where "CONCEPTS" is AM's global list of entities known to be concepts. Initially, this list contains the hundred or so concepts which AM starts with (*e.g.*, all those diagrammed on the preceding page).

ANYTHING is defined as "λ (x) T"; *i.e.*, a predicate which will *always* return true. Notice that the singleton $\{a\}$ is an example of Anything, but (since it's not on the list CONCEPTS) it is not an example of Any-concept.

ATOM contains data about all primitive, indivisible objects (identifiers, constants, variables).

BAG is a type of structure. It is unordered, and multiple occurrences of the same element are permitted. They are isomorphic to the concept known as 'multiset', except that we stipulate that sets are *not* bags.

BAG-DELETE is an operation which takes two arguments, x and B. Although x can be anything, B must be a bag. The procedure is to remove one occurrence of x from B.

BAG-DIFF is an operation which takes two bags B,C. It repeatedly picks a member of C, and removes it (one occurrence of it) from both B and C. This continues until C is empty.

BAG-INSERT is an operation which adds (another occurrence of) x into bag B.

BAG-INTERSECT takes two bags B,C, and creates a new bag D. An item occurs in D the *minimum* number of times it occurs in either B or C.

BAG-UNION takes bag C and dumps all its elements into bag B.

CANONIZE is both an example of and a specialization of "Operation." It accepts two predicates P1 and P2 as arguments, both defined over some domain

A×A, where P1 is a generalization of P2. Canonize then tries to produce a "standard representation" for elements of A, in the following way. It creates an operation f from A into A, satisfying: *P1(x,y) iff P2(f(x),f(y))*. Then any item of the form f(x) is called a canonical member of A. The set of such canonical-A's is worth naming, and it is worth investigating the restrictions of various operations' domains and ranges to this set of canonical-A's.[34] "Canonize" contains lots of information relevant to creating such functions f (given P1 and P2). Thus Canonize is an example of the concept Operation. Canonize also contains information relevant to dealing with any and all such f's. So Canonize is a specialization of Operation.

COALESCE admits the same duality.[35] This very useful operation takes as its argument any operation F(a,b,c,d...), locates two domain components which intersect (preferably, which are equal; say the second and third), and then creates a new operation G defined as G(a,b,d...) $=_{df}$ F(a,b,b,d...). That is, F is called upon with a pair of arguments equal to each other. If F were Times, then G would be Squaring. If F were Set-insert, then G would be the operation of inserting a set S into itself.

COMPOSITION involves taking two operations A and B, and applying them in sequence: A∘B(x) $=_{df}$ A(B(x)). This concept deals with (*i*) the activity of creating new compositions, given a pair of operations; (*ii*) all the operations which were created in this fashion. That is why this concept is both a specialization of ánd an example of Operation.

CONJECTURES are a kind of object. This concept knows about—and can store—conjectures. When proof techniques are inserted into AM, this tiny twig of the tree of concepts will grow to giant proportions.

CONSTANT-PREDICATE is a predicate which can afford to have a very liberal domain: it always ignores its arguments and just returns the same logical value all the time.

DELETE is an operation which contains all the information common to all flavors of removing an element from a structure (regardless of the type of structure which is being attenuated). When called upon to actually perform a deletion, this concept determines the type of structure and then calls the appropriate specialized delete concept (*e.g.*, Bag-delete).

DIFFERENCE is another general operation, which accepts two structures, determines their type (*e.g.*, Bags), and then calls the appropriate specialized version of difference (*e.g.*, Bag-diff).

EMPTY-strucTURE contains data relevant to structures with no members.

FIRST-ELEMENT is an operation which takes an ordered structure and returns the first element. It is like the Lisp function 'CAR'.

IDENTITY is just what it claims to be. It takes one argument and returns

---

[34] That is, take an operation which used to have "A" as one of its domain components or as its range, and try to create a new operation with essentially the same definition but whose Domain/range says "Canonical-A" instead of "A."

[35] Both a specialization of Operation and an example of Operation.

it immediately. The main purpose of knowing about this boring transformation is just in case some new concept turns out unexpectedly to be equivalent to it.

INSERT takes an item x and a structure S, determines S's type, and calls the appropriate flavor of specialized Insertion concept. The general INSERT concept contains any information common to all of those insertion concepts.

INTERSECT is an operation which computes the intersection of any two structures. It, too, has a separate specialization for Bags, Sets, Osets, and Lists.

INVERT-AN-OPERATION is a very active concept. It can invert any given operation. If $F:X \rightarrow Y$ is an operation, then its inverse will be abbreviated F^{-1}, and $F^{-1}(y)$ is defined as all the x's in X for which $F(x)=y$. The domain and range of F^{-1} are thus the range and domain of F.

INVERTED-OP contains information specific to operations which were created as the inverses of more primitive ones.

LAST-ELEMENT takes an ordered structure and returns its final member.

LIST is a type of structure. It is ordered, and multiple occurrences of the same element are permitted. Lists are also called vectors, tuples, and obags (for "ordered bags").

LIST-DELETE is an operation which takes two arguments, x and B. Although x can be anything, B must be a list. The procedure is to remove the first occurrence of x from B.

LIST-DIFF is an operation which takes two lists B,C. It repeatedly picks a member of C, and removes it (the first remaining occurrence of it) from both B and C. This continues until there are no more members in C.

LIST-INSERT is an operation which adds (another occurrence of) x onto the front of list B. It is like the Lisp function 'CONS'.

LIST-INTERSECT takes two lists B,C, and creates a new list D. An item occurs in D the *minimum* number of times it occurs in either B or C. D is arranged in order as (a sublist of) list B.

LIST-UNION takes list C glues it onto the end of list B. It's like 'APPEND' in Lisp.

LOGICAL-RELATION contains knowledge about Boolean combinations: disjunction, conjunction, implication, etc.

MULTIPLE-ELEMENTS-strucTURES are a specialized kind of Structure. They permit the same atom to occur more than once as a member. (*e.g.*, Bags and Lists)

NO-MULTIPLE-ELEMENTS-strucTURES are a specialization of Structure. They permit the same atom to occur only once as a member. (*e.g.*, Sets and Osets)

NONEMPTY-strucTURES are a specialization of Structure also. They contain data about all structures which have some members.

OBJECT is a general, static concept. Objects are like the subjects and direct objects in sentences, while the Actives are like the verbs.[36]

OBJECT-EQUALITY is a predicate. It takes a pair of objects, and returns

---

[36] As in English, a particular Activity can sometimes itself be the subject.

True if (i) they are identical, or (ii) they are structures, and each corresponding pair of members satisfies Object-Equality. Often we'll call this 'Equal', and denote it as '$=$'.

OPERATIONS are Actives which take arguments and return a value. While a predicate examines its arguments and returns either True or False, an operation examines *its* arguments and returns any number of values, of varying types. Assuming that the arguments lay in the domain of the operation (as specified by some entry on its Domain/range facet), then every value returned must lie within its range (as specified by that same Domain/range entry).

ORDERED-PAIR is a kind of List. It has just two 'slots', however: a front and a rear element.

ORDERED-strucTURE is a specialized type of Structure. It includes all structures for which the order of insertion of two members can make a difference in whether the structures are equal or not. Ordered-structures are those for which it makes sense to talk about a front and a rear, a first element and a last element.

OSET is a type of structure. It is ordered, and multiple occurrences of the same element are not permitted. The short-term-memory of Newell's PSG [Newell 73] is an Oset, as is a cafeteria line. Not much use was found for this concept by AM.

OSET-DELETE removes x from oset B (if x was in B).

OSET-DIFF is an operation which takes two osets B,C. It removes each member of C from B.

OSET-INSERT is an operation which adds x to the front of oset B. If x was in B previously, it is simply moved to the front of B.

OSET-INTERSECT takes two osets B,C, and removes from B any items which are *not* in C as well. B thus 'induces' the ordering on the resultant oset.

OSET-UNION takes oset C, removes any elements in B already, then glues what's left of C onto the rear of B.

PARALLEL-JOIN is an operation which takes a kind of structure and an operation H. It creates a new operation F, whose domain is that type of structure. For any such structure S, F(S) is computed by appending together H(x) for each member x of S.

PARALLEL-JOIN2 is a similar operation. It creates an operation F with two structural arguments. F(S,L) is computed by appending the values of H(x,L), as x runs through the elements of S.[37]

PARALLEL-REPLACE is an operation used to synthesize new substitution operations. It takes a structural type and an operation H as its arguments, and creates a new operation F. F(S) is computed by simply replacing each member x of S by the value of F(x). The operation produced is very much like the Lisp function MAPCAR.

PARALLEL-REPLACE2 is a slightly more general operation. It creates F,

---

[37] Here, the args to PARALLEL-JOIN2 are two types of structures SS and LL, and an operation H whose range is also a structural type DD. Then a new operation is created, with domain SS×LL and range DD.

where F(S,L) is computed by replacing each x∈S by F(x,L).

PREDICATES are actives which examine their arguments and then return T or NIL (True or False). It is only due to the capriciousness of AM's initial design that predicates are kept distinct from operations. Of course, each example of an operation can be viewed as if it were a predicate; if F:A→B is any operation from A to B, then we can consider F a relation on $A \times B$, that is a subset of $A \times B$, and from there pass to viewing F as a (characteristic) predicate F:A×B→ {T,F}. Similarly, any predicate on $A \times \ldots \times B \times C$ may be considered an operation (a multivalued, not-always-defined function) from $A \times \ldots \times B$ into C. There are no unary predicates. If there were one, say P:A→ $\{T, F\}$, then that predicate would essentially be a new way to view a certain subset of A; the predicate would then be transformed into $\{a\epsilon A \mid P(a)\}$, made into a new concept, tagged as a specialization of A, and its definition would be "λ $(a)(A.Defn(a) \wedge P(a))$."

PROJECTION1 is a simple operation. It is defined as "λ (x y) x." Notice that Identity is just a specialized restriction of Proj1. Proj1(Me,You)=Me.

PROJECTION2 is a similar operation. Proj2(Me,You)=You.

RELATION is any Active which has been encapsulated into a set of ordered pairs. This concept bridges the gap between active and static concepts.

REPEAT is an operation for generating new operations by repeating old ones. Given as its argument a structural type $\mathcal{S}$ and an existing operation H (with domain and range of the form $\mathcal{S} \times \mathcal{S} \Rightarrow \mathcal{S}$), Repeat($\mathcal{S}$,H) synthesizes a brand new operation F. The Domain/range of F is just that of H. F(S) is computed by repeating TEMP←H(x,TEMP) for each element x of S. TEMP is initialized as some member (preferably the first element) of S.

REPEAT2 is similar, but requires that H take three arguments, and it creates a new operation F, where F(S,L) is computable by repeatedly doing TEMP←H(x,TEMP,L).

RESTRICT is an operation which turns out new operations. Given as an argument some operation (or predicate) F, RESTRICT would synthesize a new operation which would have the same definition as F, but would have its domain and/or range curtailed.

REVERSE-ORDERED-PAIR transforms the ordered pair $< x, y >$ into $< y, x >$.

SET is a type of structure. It is unordered, and multiple occurrences of the same element are not permitted.

SET-DELETE is an operation which takes two arguments, x and B. Although x can be anything, B must be a set. The procedure is to remove x from B (if x was in B), then return the resultant value of B.

SET-DIFF is an operation which takes two sets B,C. It removes each member of C from B.

SET-INSERT is an operation which adds x to set B.

SET-INTERSECT removes from set B any items which are *not* in set C, too.

SET-UNION dumps into B all the members of C which weren't in there already.

STRUCTURE, the antithesis of ATOM, is inherently divisible. A structure is something that has members, that can be broken into pieces. There are two questions one can ask about any kind of structure: Is it ordered or not? Can there be multiple occurrences of the same element in it or not? There are four sets of answers to these two questions, and each of the four specifies a well-known kind of structure (Sets, Lists, Osets, Bags).

STRUCTURE-OF-STRUCTURES is a specialization of Structure, representing those structures all of whose *members* are themselves structures.

TRUTH-VALUE is a specialized kind of atomic object. Its only examples are True and False. This concept is the range set for all predicates.

UNION is a general kind of joining operation. It takes two structures and combines them. Four separate variants of this concept are given to AM initially (*e.g.*, Set-union).

UNORDERED-STRUCTURE is a specialized type of Structure. It includes all structures for which the order of insertion of two members never makes any difference in whether the structures are equal or not. Unordered-structures cannot be said to have a front or a rear, a first element or a last element.

5–3.3   Rationale behind Choice of Concepts

A necessary part of realizing AM was to choose a particular set of starting concepts. But how should such a choice be made?

My first impulse was to gather a *complete* set of concepts. That is, a basis which would be sufficient to derive all mathematics. The longer I studied this, the larger the estimated size of this basis grew. It immediately became clear that this would never fit in 256k.[38] One philosophical problem here is that future mathematics may be inspired by some real-world phenomena which haven't even been observed yet. Aliens visiting Earth might have a different mathematics from ours, since their collective life experiences could be quite different from ours.

Scrapping the idea of a sufficient basis, what about a necessary one? That is, a basis which would be *minimal* in the following sense: if you ever removed a concept from that basis, it could never be rediscovered. In isolated cases, one can tell when a basis is *not* minimal: if it contains both addition and multiplication, then it is too rich, since the latter can be derived from the former.[39] And yet, the same problem about "absoluteness" cropped up: how can anyone claim that the discovery of X can *never* be made from a given starting point? Until recently, mathematicians didn't realize how natural it was to derive numbers and arithmetic from set theory (a task which AM does, by the way).[40] So 50 years ago the concepts of set theory and number theory would both have been undisputedly placed into a "minimal" basis. There are thus no absolute conceptual primitives; each culture (perhaps even each individual) possesses its own basis.

---

[38] This is the size of the core memory of the computer I had at my disposal.

[39] By AM, and by any mathematician. As Don Cohen points out, if the researcher lacked the proper discovery methods, then he or she might never derive Times from Plus.

[40] The "new math" is trying to get young children to do this as well; unfortunately, no one showed the elementary-school teachers the underlying harmony, and the results have been saddening.

Since I couldn't give AM a minimal basis, nor a complete one, I decided AM might as well have a *nice* one. Although it can never be minimal, it should nevertheless be made very small (order of magnitude: 100 concepts). Although it can never be complete, it should suffice for rediscovering much of already-known mathematics. Finally, it should be *rational*, by which I mean that there should be a simple rule for deciding which concepts do and don't belong in that basis.

The concepts AM starts with are meant to be those possessed by young children (age 4, say). This explains some omissions of concepts which would otherwise be considered fundamental: (*i*) Proof and techniques for proof/disproof; (*ii*) Abstract properties of relations, like associativity, single-valued, onto; (*iii*) Cardinality, arithmetic; (*iv*) Infinity, continuity, limits. The interested reader should see [Piaget 55] or [Copeland 70].

Because my programming time and the PDP-10's memory space were both quite small, only a small percentage of these 'pre-numerical' concepts could be included. Some unjustified omissions are: (*i*) visual operations, like rotation, coloration; (*ii*) Games, rules, procedures, strategies, tactics; (*iii*) Geometric notions, *e.g.*, outside and between.

AM is not supposed to be a model of a child, however. It was never my intention (and it would be much too hard for me) to try to emulate a human child's whimsical imagination and emotive drives. And AM is not ripe for "teaching," as are children.[41] Also, though it possesses a child's ignorance of most concepts, AM is given a large body of sophisticated "adult" heuristics. So perhaps a more faithful image is that of Ramanujan, a brilliant modern mathematician who received a very poor education, and was forced to rederive much of known number theory all by himself. Incidentally, Ramanujan never did master the concept of formal proof.

There is no formal justification for the particular set of starting concepts. They are all reasonably primitive (sets, composition), and lie several levels "below" the ones which AM managed to ultimately derive (prime factorization, square-root). It might be valuable to attempt a similar automated math discoverer, which began with a very different set of concepts (*e.g.*, start it out as an expert in lattice theory, possessing all known concepts thereof). The converse kind of experiments are to vary the initial base of concepts, and observe the effects on AM's behavior. A few experiments of that form are described in Section 6–2.

---

[41] Learning psychologists might label AM as neo-behavioristic and cognitivistic. See [LeFrancois 72].

Chapter 6

Results

Now we have seen that mathematical work is not simply mechanical, that it could not be done by a machine, however perfect. It is not merely a question of applying rules, of making the most combinations possible according to certain fixed laws. The combinations so obtained would be exceedingly numerous, useless, and cumbersome. The true work of the inventor consists in choosing among these combinations so as to eliminate the useless ones or rather to avoid the trouble of making them, and the rules which must guide this choice are extremely fine and delicate. It is almost impossible to state them precisely; they are felt rather than formulated. Under these conditions, how imagine a sieve capable of applying them mechanically?

Poincaré

6-1   WHAT AM DID

AM is both a mathematician of sorts, and a big computer program.

•   By granting AM more anthropomorphic qualities than it deserves, we can describe its progress through elementary mathematics. It rediscovered many well-known concepts, a couple interesting but not-generally-known ones, and several concepts which were hitherto unknown and should have stayed that way. Section 1–5 recapped what AM did, much as a historian might critically evaluate

Euler's work. Instead of repeating any of this descriptive prose here, we now provide a very brief listing of what AM did in a single good run, task by task. These task-by-task listings are not complete listings of every task AM ever attempted in any of its many runs, but rather a trace of a single, better-than-average run of the program.[1] The reader may wish to consult the brief alphabetized glossary of concept names in the previous chapter. Following this linear trace of AM's behavior is a more appropriate representation of what it did: namely, a two-dimensional graph of that same behavior as seen in "concept-space."

⊙ By under-estimating AM's sophistication, one can demand answers to the typical questions to ask about a computer program: how big is it, how much cpu time does it use, what language it's coded in, etc. These are found in the third subsection (6–1.3).

6–1.1   Linear Task-by-Task Summary of a Good Run

1. Fill in examples of Compose. Failed, but suggested next task:
2. Fill in examples of Set-union. Also failed, but suggested:
3. Fill in examples of Sets. Many found (*e.g.*, by instantiating Set.Defn) and then more derived from those examples (*e.g.*, by running Union.Alg).
4. Fill in specializations of Sets (because it was very easy to find examples of Sets). Creation of new concepts. One, INT-Sets, is related to "Singletons." Another, "BI-Sets," is all nests of braces (no atomic elements).
5. Fill in examples of INT-Sets. This indirectly led to a rise in the worth of Equal.
6. Check all examples of INT-Sets. All were confirmed. AM defines the set of Nonempty INT-Sets; this is renamed "Singletons" by the user.
7. Check all examples of Sets. To check a couple conjectures, AM will soon look for Bags and Osets.
8. Fill in examples of Bags.
9. Fill in specializations of Bags. Created INT-Bags (contain just one kind of element), and BI-Bags (nests of parentheses).
10. Fill in examples of Osets.
11. Check examples of Osets.
12. Fill in examples of Lists.
13. Check examples of Lists.
14. Fill in examples of All-but-first.
15. Fill in examples of All-but-last.
16. Fill in specializations of All-but-last. Failed.
17. Fill in examples of List-union.
18. Fill in examples of Proj1.
19. Check examples of All-but-first.
20. Check examples of All-but-last.

[1] In fact, it is perhaps the best overall run. It occurred in two stages (due to space problems; unimportant). In this particular run, AM misses the few "very best" discoveries it ever made, since the runs they occurred in went in somewhat different directions. It also omits some of the more boring tasks: see, *e.g.*, the description of task number 33.

21. Fill in examples of Proj2.

22. Fill in examples of Empty-structures. 4 found.

23. Fill in generalizations of Empty-structures. Failed.

24. Check examples of List-union.

25. Check examples of Bags. Defined Singleton-bags.

26. Fill in examples of Bag-union.

27. Check examples of Proj2.

28. Fill in examples of Set-union.

29. Check examples of Set-union. Define $\lambda(x,y)\ x\bigcup y = x$, later called Superset.

30. Fill in examples of Bag-insert.

31. Check examples of Bag-insert. Range is really Nonempty bags. Isolate the results of insertion restricted to Singletons: call them Doubleton-bags.

32. Fill in examples of Bag-intersect.

33. Fill in examples of Set-insert.

34. Check examples of Set-insert. Range is always Nonempty sets. Define λ (x,S) Set-insert(x,S)=S; *i.e.*, set membership. Define Doubleton sets.

35. Fill in examples of Bag-delete.

36. Fill in examples of Bag-difference.

37. Check examples of Bag-intersect. Define $\lambda(x,y)\ x\bigcap y = ()$; *i.e.* disjoint bags.

38. Fill in examples of Set-intersect.

39. Check examples of Set-intersect. Define $\lambda(x,y)\ x\bigcap y = x$; *i.e.*, subset. Also define disjoint sets: $\lambda(x,y)\ x\bigcap y = \{\}$.

40. Fill in examples of List-intersect.

41. Fill in examples of Equal. Very difficult to find examples; this led to:

42. Fill in generalizations of Equal. Define "Same-size," "Equal-CARs," and some losers.

43. Fill in examples of Same-size.

44. Apply an Algorithm for Canonize to the args Same-size and Equal. AM eventually synthesizes the canonizing function "Size." AM defines the set of canonical structures: bags of T's; this later gets renamed as "Numbers."

45. Restrict the Domain/range of Bag-union. A new operation is defined, Number-union, with Domain/range entry <Number Number $\Rightarrow$ Bag>.

46. Fill in examples of Number-union. Many found.

47. Check the Domain/range of Number-union. Range is 'Number'. This operation is renamed "Add2."

48. Restrict the Domain/range of Bag-intersect to Numbers. Renamed "Minimum."

49. Restrict the Domain/range of Bag-delete to Numbers. Renamed "SUB1."

50. Restrict the Domain/range of Bag-insert to Numbers. AM calls the new operation "Number-insert." Its Domain/range entry is <Anything Number $\Rightarrow$ Bag>.

51. Check the Domain/range of Number-insert. This doesn't lead anywhere.

52. Restrict the Domain/range of Bag-difference to Numbers. This becomes "Subtract."

53. Fill in examples of Subtract. This leads to defining the relation LEQ ($\leq$).[2]

54. Fill in examples of LEQ. Many found.

55. Check examples of LEQ.

56. Apply algorithm of Coalesce to LEQ. LEQ(x,x) is Constant-True.

57. Fill in examples of Parallel-join2. Included is Parallel-join2(Bags,Bags,Proj2), which is renamed "TIMES," and Parallel-join2(Structures,Structures,Proj1), a generalized Union operation renamed "G-Union," and a bunch of losers.

58. –69. Fill in and check examples of the operations just created.

70. Fill in examples of Coalesce. Created: Self-Compose, Self-Insert, Self-Delete, Self-Add, Self-Times, Self-Union, etc. Also: Coa-repeat2, Coa-join2, etc.

71. Fill in examples of Self-Delete. Many found.

72. Check examples of Self-Delete. Self-Delete is just Identity-op.

73. Fill in examples of Self-member. No positive examples found.

74. Check examples of Self-member. Self-member is just Constant-False.

75. Fill in examples of Self-Add. Many found. User renames this "Doubling."

76. Check examples of Coalesce. Confirmed.

77. Check examples of Add2. Confirmed.

78. Fill in examples of Self-Times. Many found. Renamed "Squaring" by the user.

79. Fill in examples of Self-Compose. Defined Squaring∘Squaring. Created Add∘Add (two versions: Add2_1 which is $\lambda(x, y, z)(x+y)+z$, and Add2_2 which is $x+(y+z)$). Similarly, two versions of Times∘Times and of Compose∘Compose.

80. Fill in examples of Add2_1 (*i.e.*, $(x + y) + z$). Many are found.

81. Fill in examples of Add2_2 (i.e, $x + (y + z)$). Again many are found.

82. Check examples of Squaring. Confirmed.

83. Check examples of Add2_2. Add2_1 and Add2_2 appear equivalent. But first:

84. Check examples of Add2_1. Add2_1 and Add2_2 still appear equivalent. Merge them. So the proper argument for a generalized "Add" operation is a Bag.

85. Apply algorithm for Invert to argument 'Add'. Define Inv-add(x) as the set of all bags of numbers (>0) whose sum is x. Also denoted $\text{Add}^{-1}(x)$.

86. Fill in examples of TIMES2_1. (xy)z. Many are found.

87. Fill in examples of TIMES2_2. x(yz). Again many are found.

88. Check examples of TIMES2_2. TIMES2_1 and TIMES2_2 may be equivalent.

89. Check examples of TIMES2_1. TIMES2_1 and TIMES2_2 still appear equivalent. Merge them. So the proper argument for a generalized "TIMES" operation is a Bag. Set up an analogy between TIMES and ADD, because of this fact.

90. Apply algorithm for Invert to argument 'TIMES'. Define Inv-TIMES(x) as the set of all bags of numbers (>1) whose product is x. Also denoted TIMES^{-1}. Analogic to Inv-Add.

91. Fill in examples of Parallel-replace2. Included are Parallel-replace2(Bags,Bags,Proj2) (called MR2-BBP2), and many losers.

92. –107. Fill in and check examples of the operations just created.

108. Fill in examples of Compose. So easy that AM creates Int-Compose.

---

[2] If a larger number is "subtracted" from a smaller, the result is zero. AM explicitly defines the set of ordered pairs of numbers having zero "difference." $<$x,y$>$ is in that set iff x is less than or equal to y.

109. Fill in examples of Int-Compose. The two chosen operations G,H must be such that range(H) is a component (subset) of domain(G), and range(G) is a component of domain(H); both G and H must be interesting. Create G-Union∘MR2-BBP2,[3] Insert∘Delete, Times∘Squaring, etc.

110. –127. Fill in and check examples of the compositions just created. Notice that G-Union∘MR2-BBP2 is just TIMES.

128. Fill in examples of Coa-repeat2. Among them: Coa-repeat2(Bags-of-Numbers, Add2) [*multiplication again!*], Coa-repeat2(Bags-of-Numbers, Times) [*exponentiation*], Coa-repeat2(Structures, Proj1) [*CAR*], Coa-repeat2(Structures, Proj2) [*Last-element-of*], etc.

129. Check the examples of Coa-repeat2. All confirmed.

130. Apply algorithms for Invert to 'Doubling'. The result is called "Halving" by the user. AM then defines "Evens."

131. Fill in examples of Self-Insert.

132. Check examples of Self-Insert. Nothing special found.

133. Fill in examples of Coa-repeat2-Add2.

134. Check examples of Coa-repeat2-Add2. It's the same as TIMES.

135. Apply algorithm for Invert to argument 'Squaring'. Define "Square-root."

136. Fill in examples of Square-root. Some found, but very inefficiently.

137. Fill in new algorithms for Square-root. Had to ask user for a good one.

138. Check examples of Square-root. Define the set of numbers "Perfect-squares."

139. Fill in examples of Coa-repeat2-Times. This is exponentiation.

140. Check examples of Coa-repeat2-Times. Nothing special noticed, unfortunately.

141. Fill in examples of Inv-TIMES. Many found, but inefficiently.

142. Fill in new algorithms for Inv-TIMES. Obtained opaquely from the user.

143. Check examples of Inv-TIMES. This task suggests the next one:

144. Compose G-Union with Inv-TIMES. Good Domain/range. Renamed "Divisors."

145. Fill in examples of Divisors. Many found, but not very efficiently.

146. Fill in new algorithms for Divisors. Obtained from the user.

147. Fill in examples of Perfect-squares. Many found.

148. Fill in specializations of TIMES. Times1(x) $=_{df}$ $1 \cdot x$, Times2(x) $=_{df}$ $2 \cdot x$, Times-sq is TIMES with its domain restricted to bags of perfect squares, Times-ev takes only even arguments, Times-to-evens requires that the result be even, Times-to-sq, $\cdots$

149. Check examples of Divisors. Define 0-Div, 1-Div, 2-Div, and 3-Div, the sets of numbers whose Divisors value is the empty set, a singleton, a doubleton, and a tripleton, respectively.

150. Fill in examples of 1-Div. Only one example found: "1." Lower 1-Div.Worth.

151. Fill in examples of 0-Div. None found. Lower the worth of this concept.

152. Fill in examples of 2-Div. A nice number of examples are found. Raise 2-Div.Worth.

153. Check examples of 2-Div. All confirmed, but no pattern noticed.

154. Fill in examples of 3-Div. A nice number found.

155. Check examples of 3-Div. All confirmed. All are perfect squares.

156. Restrict Square-root to numbers which are in 3-Div. Call this Root3.

---

[3] An alternate derivation of the operation of multiplication.

157. Fill in examples of Root3. Many found.

158. Check examples of Root3. All confirmed. All are in 2-Div. Raise their worths.

159. Restrict Squaring to 2-divs. Call the result Square2.

160. Fill in examples of Square2. Many found.

161. Check the range of Square2. Always 3-Divs. Conjecture: x has 2 divisors iff x^2 has 3 divisors.

162. Restrict Squaring to 3-Divs. Call the result Square3.

163. Restrict Square-rooting to 2-Divs. Call the result Root2.

164. Fill in examples of Square3. Many found.

165. Compose Divisors-of and Square3. Call the result Div-Sq3.

166. Fill in examples of Div-Sq3. Many found.

167. Check examples of Div-Sq3. All such examples are Same-size.

168. –175. More confirmations and explorations of the above conjecture. Gradually, all its ramifications lead to dead-ends (as far as AM is concerned).

176. Fill in examples of Root2. None found. Conjecture that there are none.

177. Check examples of Inv-TIMES. Inv-TIMES always contains a singleton bag, and always contains a bag of primes.

178. Restrict the range of Inv-TIMES to bags of primes. Call this Prime-Times.

179. Restrict the range of Inv-TIMES to singletons. Called Single-Times.

180. Fill in examples of Prime-times. Many found.

181. Check examples of Prime-times. Always a singleton set. User renames this conjecture *The unique factorization theorem.*

182. Fill in examples of Single-TIMES. Many found.

183. Check examples of Single-TIMES. Always a singleton set. Single-TIMES is actually the same as Bag-insert!

184. Fill in examples of Self-set-union. Many found.

185. Check examples of Self-set-union. This operation is same as Identity.

186. Fill in examples of Self-bag-union. Many found.

187. Check examples of Self-bag-union. Confirmed. Nothing interesting noticed.

188. Fill in examples of Inv-ADD.

189. Check examples of Inv-ADD. Hordes of boring conjectures, so:

190. Restrict the domain of Inv-ADD to primes (Inv-Add-primes), to evens (Inv-Add-evens), to squares, etc.

191. Fill in examples of Inv-add-primes. Many found.

192. Check examples of Inv-add-primes. Confirmed, but nothing special noticed.

193. Fill in examples of Inv-add-evens. Many found.

194. Check examples of Inv-add-evens. Always contains a bag of primes.

195. Restrict the range of Inv-Add-evens to bags of primes. Called Prime-ADD.

196. Restrict the range of Inv-ADD to singletons. Call that new operation Single-ADD.

197. Fill in examples of Prime-ADD. Many found.

198. Check examples of Prime-ADD. Always a nonempty set (of bags of primes). User renames this conjecture *Goldbach's conjecture.*

199. Fill in examples of Single-ADD. Many found.

200. Check examples of Single-ADD. Always a singleton set. This operation is the same as Bag-insert and Single-TIMES.

201. Restrict the range of Prime-ADD to singletons, by analogy to Prime-TIMES.[4] Call the new operation Prime-ADD-SING.

202. Fill in examples of Prime-ADD-SING. Many found.

203. Check examples of Prime-ADD-SING. Nothing special noticed.

204. Fill in examples of Times-sq.[5] Many examples found.

205. Check Domain/range of Times-sq. Is the range actually Perfect-squares? Yes!

206. Fill in examples of Times1. Recall that $\text{Times1}(x) =_{df} \text{TIMES}(1,x) = 1 \cdot x = x$.

207. Check examples of Times1. Apparently just a restriction of Identity.

208. Check examples of Times-sq. Confirmed.

209. Fill in examples of Times0.

210. Fill in examples of Times2.

211. Check examples of Times2. Apparently the same as Doubling. That is, $x + x = 2 \cdot x$. Very important. By analogy, define $\text{Ad2}(x)$ as $x+2$.

212. Fill in examples of Ad2.

213. Check examples of Ad2. Nothing interesting noticed.

214. Fill in specializations of Add. Among those created are: Add0 (x+0), Add1, Add3, ADD-sq (addition restricted to perfect squares), Add-ev (sum of even numbers), Add-pr (sum of primes), etc.

215. Check examples of Times0. The value always seems to be 0.

216. Fill in examples of Times-ev.[6] Many examples found.

217. Check examples of Times-ev. Apparently all the results are Evens.

218. Fill in examples of Times-to-ev.[7] Many found.

219. Fill in examples of Times-to-sq. Only a few found.

220. Check examples of Times-to-sq. All arguments always seem to be squares. Conjec: Times-to-sq is really the same as Times-sq. Merge the two. This is a false conjecture, but did AM no harm.

221. Check examples of Times-to-ev. The domain always contains an even number.

222. Fill in examples of Self-Union.

223. Check examples of Self-Union.

224. Fill in examples of SubSet.

225. Check example of SubSet.

226. Fill in examples of SuperSet.

227. Check examples of SuperSet. Conjec: Subset(x,y) iff Superset(y,x). Important.

228. Fill in examples of Compose∘Compose-1. AM creates some explosive combination (e.g., (Compose∘Compose)∘(Compose∘Compose)∘(Compose∘Compose)), some poor ones (e.g., Square∘Count∘ADD^{-1}), and even a few—very few—winners (e.g., SUB1∘Count∘Self-Insert, which is later recognized to coincide with Count).

229. Check examples of Compose∘Compose-1.

---

[4] In this case, AM is asking which numbers are uniquely representable as the sum of two primes.

[5] Recall that this is just TIMES restricted to operate on perfect squares.

[6] Recall that Times-ev is just like TIMES restricted to operating on even numbers.

[7] That is, consider bags of numbers which multiply to give an even number.

230. Fill in examples of Compose∘Compose-2.[8] AM recreates many of the previous tasks' operations.

231. Check examples of Compose∘Compose-2. Nothing noticed yet.[9]

232. –252. Fill in and check examples of the losing compositions just created.

253. Fill in examples of Add-sq (*i.e.*, sum of squares).

254. Check Domain/range entries of Add-sq. The range is not always perfect squares. Define Add-sq-sq(x,y), which is True iff x and y are perfect squares and their sum is a perfect square as well.

255. Fill in examples of Add-pr; *i.e.*, addition of primes.

256. Check Domain/range entries of Add-pr. AM defines the set of pairs of primes whose sum is also a prime. This is a bizarre derivation of prime pairs.

6–1.2   Two-Dimensional Behavior Graph

On the next two pages is a graph of the same "best run" which AM executed. The nodes are concepts, and the links are actions which AM performed. Labels on the links indicate when each action was taken, so the reader may observe how AM jumped around. It should also be easy to perceive from the graph which paths of development were abandoned, which concepts ignored, and which ones concentrated upon. These are precisely the features of AM's behavior which are awkward to infer from a simple linear trace (as in the previous section).

In more detail, here is how to read the graph: Each node is a concept. To save space, these names are often highly abbreviated. For example, "x0" is used in place of "TIMES-0."

Each concept name is surrounded by from zero to four numbers:

$$318 \qquad 288$$
$$\text{WIDGETING}$$
$$310 \qquad 291$$

The upper right number indicates the task number (see last section) during which examples of this concept were filled in. The lower right number tells when they were checked. The upper left number indicates when the Domain/range facet of that concept was modified. Finally, the lower left number is the task number during which some new Algorithms for that concept were obtained. A number in parentheses indicates that the task with that number was a total failure.

Because of the limited space, it was decided that if a concept were ever renamed by the user, then only that newer, mnemonic name would be given in the diagram. Thus there is an arrow from "Coalesce" to "Square," an operation originally called "Self-Times" by AM.

Sometimes, a concept will have under it a note of the form ≡ GROK. This simply means that AM eventually discovered that the concept was equivalent to the already-known concept "GROK," and probably forgot about this one (merged it into the one it already knew about). The "trail" of discovery may pick up

---

[8] Recall that the difference between this operation and the last one is merely in the order of the composing: Fo(GoH) versus (FoG)oH.

[9] Later on, AM will use these new operations to discover the associativity of Compose.

again at that preexisting concept. A node written as =GROK means that the concept was really the same as "GROK," but AM never investigated it enough to notice this.

The arrows indicate the creation of new concepts. Thus an arrow leading to concept "Widgeting" indicates how that concept was created. An arrow directed away from Widgeting points to a concept created as, *e.g.*, a specialization or an example of Widgeting. No arrowheads are in practice necessary: all arrows are directed *downward*.

The arrows may be labeled, indicating precisely what they represent (*e.g.*, composition, restriction) and what the task number was when they occurred. For space reasons, the following convention has proven necessary: if an arrow emanating from C is unnumbered, it is assumed to have occurred at the same time as the arrow to its immediate left which also points from C; if all the arrows emanating from C have no number, than all their times of occurrence are assumed to be the *lower right*[10] number of C. Finally, if C has no lower right number, the arrow is assumed to have the value of the upper right number of C.

An unlabeled arrow is assumed to be an act of Specialization or the creation of an Example.[11] Labels, when they do occur, are given in capitals and small letters; concept names (nodes) are by contrast in all capitals. All the numbers correspond to those given to the tasks in the task-by-task traces presented in the last section.

The first part of this graph (presented below) contains static structural (and ultimately numerical) concepts which were studied by AM:

STRUCTURES

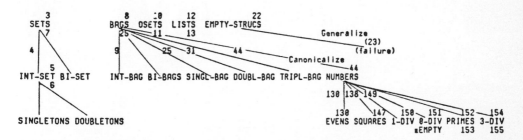

The rest of the graph (presented on the next page) deals with activities which were investigated:

---

[10] This is often true because many concepts are created while checking examples of some known concept.

[11] It should be clear in each context which is happening. If not, refer to the short trace in the preceding section, and look up the appropriate task number.

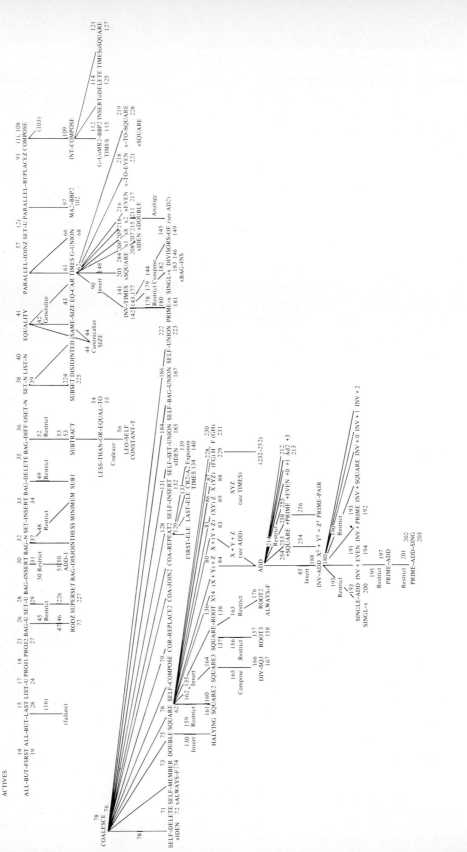

6-1.3 AM as a Computer Program

When viewed as a large LISP program, there is very little of interest about AM. There are the usual battery of customized functions (*e.g.*, a conditional PRINT function), the storage hacks (special emergency garbage collection routines, which know which facets are expendible), the time hacks (omnisciently arrange clauses in a conjunction so that the one most likely to fail will come first), and the bugs (if the user renames a concept while it's the current one being worked on, there is a 5% chance of AM entering an infinite loop).

Below are listed a few parameters of the system, although I doubt that they hold any theoretical significance. The reader may be curious about how big AM is, how long it takes to execute, etc.

Machine: SUMEX, PDP-10, KI-10 uniprocessor, 256k core memory.

Language: Interlisp, January 1975 release, which occupies 140k of the total 256k, but which provides a surplus "shadow space" of 256k additional words available for holding compiled code.

AM support code: 200 compiled (not block-compiled) utility routines, control routines, etc. They occupy roughly 100k, but all are pushed into the shadow space.

AM itself: 115 concepts, each occupying about .7k (about two typed pages, when Pretty-printed with indentation). Facet/entries stored as property/value on the property list of atoms whose names are concepts' names.[12] Each concept has about 8 facets filled in.

Heuristics are tacked onto the facets of the concepts. The more general the concept, the more heuristic rules it has attached to it.[13] "Any-concept" has 121 rules; "Active concept" has 24; "Coalesce" has 7; "Set-Insertion" has none. There are 250 heuristic rules in all, divided into four flavors (Fillin, Check, Suggest, Interestingness). Although the mean number of rules is therefore only about 2.2 (*i.e.*, less than 1 of each flavor) per concept, the standard deviation of this is a whopping 127.4. The average number of heuristics (of a given flavor) encountered rippling upward from a randomly-chosen concept C (along the network of generalization links) is about 35, even though the mean path length is only about 4.[14]

The total number of jobs executed in a typical run (from scratch) is about 200. The run ends because of space problems, but AM's performance begins to degrade near the end anyway.

"Final" state of AM: 300 concepts, each occupying about 1k. Many are swapped out onto disk. Number of winning concepts discovered: 25 (estimated).

---

[12] Snazzy feature: Executable entries on facets (*e.g.*, an entry on Union.Alg) are stored uncompiled until the first time they are actually called on, at which time they are compiled and then executed.

[13] This was not done consciously, and may or may not hold some theoretical significance.

[14] If the heuristics were homogeneously distributed among the concepts, the number of heuristics (of a given type) along a typical path of length 4 would only be about 2, not 35. If all the heuristics were tacked onto Anything and Any-concept, the number encountered in any path would be 75, not 35.

Number of acceptable concepts defined: 100 (est.).[15] Number of losing concepts unfortunately worked on: 60 (est.). The original 115 concepts have grown to an average size of 2k. Each concept has about 11 facets filled in.

About 30 seconds of cpu time were allocated to each task, on the average, but the task typically used only about 18 seconds before quitting. Total CPU time for a run is about 1 hour. Total cpu time consumed by this research project was about 500 cpu hours.

Real time: about 1 minute per task, 2 hours per run. The idea for AM was formulated in the fall of 1974, and AM was coded in the summer of 1975. Total time consumed by this project to date has been about 2600 man-hours: 700 for planning, 500 for coding, 600 for modifying and debugging and experimenting, 700 for writing the thesis, and 100 for editing it into book form.

AM was working by itself: it received no help from the user, and all its concepts' Intuitions facets had been removed.

6–2   EXPERIMENTS WITH AM

One valuable aspect of AM is that it is amenable to many kind of interesting experiments. Although AM is too *ad hoc* for numerical results to have much significance, the qualitative results perhaps do have some valid things to say about research in elementary mathematics, about automating research, and at least about the efficacy of various parts of AM's design.

This section will explain what it means to perform an experiment on AM, what kinds of experiments are imaginable, which of those are feasible, and finally will describe the many experiments which were performed on AM.

By modifying AM in various ways, its behavior can be altered, and the *quality* of its behavior will change as well. As a drastic example, one experiment involved forcing AM to select the next task to work on *randomly* from the agenda, not the top task each time. Needless to say, the performance was very different from usual.

By careful planning, each experiment can tell us something new about AM: how valuable a certain piece of it is, how robust a certain scheme really is, etc. The results of these experiments would then have something to contribute to a discussion of the "real intelligence" of AM (*e.g.*, what features were superfluous), and contribute to the design of the "next" AM-like system. Generalizing from those results, one might suggest some hypotheses about the larger task of automated math research.

Let's cover the different *kinds* of experiments one could perform on AM:

1   Remove individual concept modules, and/or individual heuristic rules. Then examine how AM's performance is degraded. AM should operate even if most of its heuristic rules and most of its concept modules were excised. If the remaining fragment of AM is too small, however, it may not be able to

---

[15] For a list of "winners" and "acceptables," see the final section in Appendix 1.

find anything interesting to do. In fact, this situation was actually encountered experimentally, when the first few partially complete concepts were inserted. If only a little bit of AM is removed, the remainder will in fact keep operating without this "uninteresting collapse." The converse situation should also hold: although still functional with any concept module unplugged, AM's performance *should* be noticeably degraded. That is, while not indispensable, each concept should nontrivially help the others. The same holds for each individual heuristic rule. When a piece of AM is removed, which concepts does AM then "miss" discovering? Is the removed concept/heuristic later discovered anyway by those which are left in AM? This should indicate the importance of each kind of concept and rule with which AM starts.

    2   Vary the relative weights given to features by the criteria which judge aesthetics, interestingness, worth, utility, etc. See how important each factor is in directing AM along successful routes. In other words, vary the little numbers in the formulae (both the global priority-assigning formula and the local reason-rating ones inside heuristic rules). One important result will be some idea of the robustness or "toughness" of the numeric weighting factors. If the system easily collapses, it was too finely tuned initially.

    3   Add several new concept modules (including new heuristics relevant to them) and see if AM can work in some unanticipated field of mathematics (like graph theory or calculus or plane geometry). Do earlier achievements—concepts and conjectures AM synthesized already—have any impact in the new domain? Are some specialized heuristics from the first domain totally wrong here? Do all the old general heuristics still hold here? Are they sufficient, or are some "general" heuristics needed here which weren't needed before? Does AM "slow down" as more and more concepts get introduced?

    4   Try to have AM develop nonmathematical theories (like elementary physics, or program verification). This might require limiting AM's freedom to "ignore a given body of data and move on to something more interesting." The exploration of very non-formalizable fields (*e.g.*, politics) might require much more than a small augmentation of AM's base of concepts. For some such domains, the "Intuitions" scheme, which had to be abandoned for math, might prove valid and valuable.

    5   Add several new concepts dealing with proof, and of course add all the associated heuristic rules. Such rules would advise AM on the fine points of using various techniques of proof/disproof: when to use them, what to try next based on why the last attempt failed, etc. See if the *kinds* of discoveries AM makes are increased.

    Several experiments (of types 1, 2, and 3 above) were set up and performed on AM. We're now ready to examine each of them in detail. The following points are covered for each experiment:

    1   How was it thought of?

    2   What will be gained by it? What would be the implications of the various possible outcomes?

    3   How was the experiment set up? What preparations/modifications had to be made? How much time (man-hours) did it take?

4   What happened? How did AM's behavior change? Was this expected? Analysis.

5   What was learned from this experiment? Can we conclude anything which suggests new experiments (*e.g.*, use a better machine, a new domain) or which bears on a more general problem that AM faced (*e.g.*, a new way to teach math, a new idea about doing math research)?

6–2.1   Must the Worth numbers be finely tuned?

Each of the 115 initial concepts has supplied to it (by the author) a number between 0 and 1000, stored as its Worth facet, which is supposed to represent the overall value of the concept. "Compose" has a higher initial Worth than "Structure-delete," which is higher than "Equality".[16]

Frequently, the priority of a task involving C depends on the overall Worth of C. How sensitive is AM's behavior to the initial settings of the Worth facets? How finely tuned must these initial Worth values be?

This experiment was thought of because of the "brittleness" of many other AI systems, the amount of fine tuning needed to elicit coherent behavior. For example, see the discussion of limitations of PUP6, in Lenat[75b]. The author believed that AM was very resilient in this regard, and that a demonstration of that fact would increase credibility in the power of the ideas which AM embodies.

To test this, a simple experiment was performed. Just before starting AM, the mean value of all concepts' Worth values was computed. It turned out to be roughly 200. Then each concept had its Worth reset to the value 200.[17] This was done "by hand," by the author, in a matter of seconds. AM was then started and run as if there were nothing amiss, and its behavior was watched carefully.

What happened? By and large, the same major discoveries were made—and missed—as usual, in the same order as usual. But whereas AM proceeded fairly smoothly before, with little superfluous activity, it now wandered quite blindly for long periods of time, especially at the very beginning. Once AM "hooked into" a line of productive development, it followed it just as always, with no noticeable additional wanderings. As one of these lines of developments died out, AM would wander around again, until the next one was begun.

It took roughly three times as long for each major discovery to occur as normal. This "delay" got shorter and shorter as AM developed further. In each case, the tasks preceding the discovery and following it were pretty much the same as normal; only the tasks "between" two periods of development were different—and much more numerous.

The reader may be interested to learn that the Worth values of many of the concepts—and most of the new concepts—ended up very close to the same values that they achieved in the original run. Overrated concepts were investigated and

---

[16] As AM progresses, it notices something interesting about Equality every now and then, and pushes its Worth value upwards.

[17] The initial spread of values had previously been from 100 to 600.

proved boring; underrated concepts had to wait longer for their chances, but then quickly proved interesting and had their Worth facets boosted.

The conclusion I draw from this change in behavior is that the Worth facets are useful for making blind decisions—where AM must choose based only on the overall worths of the various concepts in its repertoire. Whenever a specific reason existed, it was far more influential than the "erroneous" Worth values. The close, blind, random decisions occur between long bursts of specific-reason-driven periods of creative work.[18]

The general answer, then, is *No*, the initial settings of the Worth values are not crucial. Guessing reasonable initial values for them is merely a time-saving device. This suggests an interesting research problem: what impact does the *quality* of initial starting values have on humans? Give several bright undergraduate math majors the same set of objects and operators to play with, but tell some of them (*i*) nothing, and some of them (*ii*) a certain few pieces of the system are very promising, then (*iii*) emphasize a different subset of the objects and operators. How does "misinformation" impede the humans? How about no information? Have them give verbal protocols about where they are focussing their attention, and why.

Albeit at a nontrivial cost, the Worth facets did manage to correct themselves by the end of a long[19] run. What would happen if the Worth facets of those 115 concepts were not only initialized to 200, but were held fixed at 200 for the duration of the run?

In this case, the delay still subsided with time. That is, AM still got more and more "back to normal" as it progressed onward. The reason is because AM's later work dealt with concepts like Primes, Square-root, etc., which were so far removed from the initial base of concepts that the initial concepts' Worths were of little consequence.

Even more drastically, we could force all the Worth facets of all concepts— even newly created ones—to be kept at the value 200 forever. In this case, AM's behavior doesn't completely disintegrate, but that delay factor actually increases with time: apparently, AM begins to suffer from the exponential growth of "things to do" as its repertoire of concepts grows linearly. Its purposiveness, its directionality depends on "focus of attention" more and more, and if that feature is removed, AM loses much of its rationality. A factor of 5 delay doesn't sound that bad "efficiency-wise," but the actual apparent behavior of AM is as staccato bursts of development, followed by wild leaps to unrelated concepts. AM no longer can "permanently" record its interest in a certain concept.

So we conclude that the Worth facets are (*i*) not finely tuned, yet (*ii*) provide important global information about the relative values of concepts. If the Worth facets are completely disabled, the rationality of AM's behavior hangs on the slender thread of "focus of attention."

---

[18] Incidentally, GPS behaved just this same way. See, *e.g.*, Newell&Simon[72].

[19] A couple cpu hours, about a thousand tasks total selected from the agenda.

6-2.2   How Finely Tuned is the Agenda?

The top few candidates on the agenda always appear to be reasonable (to me). If I work with the system, guiding it, I can cause it to make a few discoveries it wouldn't otherwise make, and I can cause it to make its typical ones much faster (by about a factor of two). Thus the *very* top task is not always the best.

If AM randomly selects one of the top 20 or so tasks on the agenda each time, what will happen to its behavior? Will it disintegrate, slow down by a factor of ten, slow down slightly, etc.

This experiment required only a few seconds to set up, but demanded a familiarity with the LISP functions which make up AM's control structure. At a certain point, AM asks for Best-task(Agenda). Typically, the LISP function Best-task is defined as CAR—*i.e.*, pick the first member from the list of tasks. What I did was to redefine Best-task as a function which randomly selected n from the set $\{1, 2, \cdots, 20\}$, and then returned the nth member of the job-list.

If you watch the top job on the agenda, it will take about 10 cycles until AM chooses it. And yet there are many good, interesting, worthwhile jobs sprinkled among the top 20 on the agenda, so AM's performance is cut by merely a factor of three, as far as cpu time per given major discovery. Part of this better-than-20 behavior is due to the fact that the eighteenth best task had a much lower priority rating than the top few; hence it was allocated much less cpu time for its quantum than the top task would have received. Whether it succeeded or failed, it used up very little time. Since AM was frequently working on a low-value task, it was unwilling to spend much time or space on it. So the mean time allotted per task fell to about 15 seconds (from the typical 30 secs). Thus, the "losers" were dealt with quickly, so the detriment to cpu-time performance was softened.

To carry this investigation further, another experiment was carried out. AM was forced to alternate between choosing the top task on the agenda, and a randomly chosen one. Although its rate of discovery was cut by less than half, its behavior was almost as distasteful to the user as in the last (always-random) experiment.

Conclusion: Selecting (on the average) the tenth-best candidate impedes progress by a factor of less than ten (about a factor of three), but it dramatically degrades the "sensibleness" of AM's behavior, the continuity of its actions. Humans place a big value on absolute sensibleness, and believe that doing something silly 50% of the time is *much* worse than half as productive as always doing the next most logical task.

Corollary: Having 20 multi-processors simultaneously execute the top 20 jobs will increase the rate of "big" discoveries, but not by a full factor of twenty—more like a factor of three.

Another experiment in this same vein was done, one which was designed to be far more crippling to AM. Be-threshhold was held at 0 always, so *any* task which ever got proposed was kept forever on the agenda, no matter how low its priority. The Best-task function was modified so it randomly selected any member of the list of jobs. As a final insult, the Worth facets of all the concepts were initialized to 200 before starting AM.

Result: Many "explosive" tasks were chosen, and the number of new concepts increased rapidly. As expected, most of these were real "losers." There seemed no rationality to AM's sequence of actions, and it was quite boring to watch it floundering so. The typical length of the agenda was about 500, and AM's performance was "slowed" by at least a couple orders of magnitude. A more subjective measure of its "intelligence" would say that it totally collapsed under this random scheme.

Conclusion: Having an unlimited number of processors simultaneously execute all the jobs on the agenda would increase the rate at which AM made big discoveries, at an ever-accelerating pace (since the length of the agenda would grow exponentially).

Having a uniprocessor *simulate* such parallel processing would be a losing idea, however. The truly "intelligent" behavior AM exhibits is its plausible sequencing of tasks.

6–2.3   How Valuable is Tacking Reasons onto Each Task?

Let's dig inside the agenda scheme now. One idea I've repeatedly emphasized is the attaching of reasons to the tasks on the agenda, and using those reasons and their ratings to compute the overall priority value assigned to each task. An experiment was done to ascertain the amount of intelligence that was emanating from that idea.

The global formula assigning a priority value to each job was modified. We let it still be a function of the reasons for the job, but we "trivialized" it: the priority of a job was computed as simply the number of reasons it has (normalized by multiplying by 100, and cut-off if over 1000).

This raised the new question of what to do if several jobs all have the same priority. In that case, I had AM execute them in stack-order (most recent job tackled first).[20]

Result: I secretly expected that this wouldn't make too much difference on AM's apparent level of directionality, but such was definitely not the case. While AM started by doing tasks which were far more interesting and daring than usual (*e.g.*, filling in various Coalescings right away), it soon became obvious that AM was being swayed by hitherto trivial coding decisions. Whole classes of tasks—like Checking Examples of C—were never chosen, because they only had one or two reasons supporting them. Previously, one or two good reasons were sufficient. Now, tasks with several poor reasons were rising to the top and being worked on. Even the LIFO (stack) policy for resolving ties didn't keep AM's attention focussed.

Conclusion: Unless a conscious effort is made to ensure that each reason really will carry roughly an equal amount of semantic impact (charge, weight), it is not acceptable merely to choose tasks on the basis of how many reasons they

---

[20] Why? Because (*i*) it sounds right intuitively to me, (*ii*) this is akin to human focus of attention, and mainly because (*iii*) this is what AM did anyway, with no extra modification.

possess. Even in those constricted equal-weight cases, the similarities between reasons supporting a task should be taken into account.

6–2.4   What If Certain Concepts Are Eliminated or Added?

Feeling in a reckless mood one day, I eliminated the concept "Equality" from AM to see what it would then do. Equality was a key concept, because AM discovered Numbers via the technique of generalizing the relation "Equality" (exact equality of 2 given structures, at all internal levels). What would happen if we eliminate this path? Will AM rederive Equality? Will it get to Cardinality via another route? Will it do some set-theoretic things?

Result: Rather disappointing. AM never did rederive Equality or Cardinality. It spent its time thrashing about with various flavors of data-structures (unordered *vs.* ordered, multiple-elements allowed or not, etc.), deriving large quantities of boring results about them. Very many composings and coalescings were done, but no exciting new operations were produced.

A kinder type of experiment would be to *add* a few concepts. One such experiment was done: the addition of Cartesian-product. This operation, named C-PROD, accepts two sets as arguments and returns a third set as its value: the Cartesian product of the first two.

Result: The only significant change in AM's behavior was that TIMES was discovered first as the restriction of C-PROD to Canonical-Bags. When it soon was rediscovered in a few other guises, its Worth was even higher than usual. AM spent even more time exploring concepts concerned with it, and deviated much less for quite a long time.

Synthesis of the above experiments: It appears that AM may really be more specialized than expected; AM may be able to forge ahead only along one or two main lines of development—at least if we demand it make very interesting, well-known discoveries quite frequently. Removing certain key concepts can be disastrous. On the other hand, adding some carefully chosen new ones can greatly enhance AM's directionality (hence its apparent intelligence).

Conclusion: In its current state, AM is thus seen to be *minimally competent:* if any knowledge is removed, it appears much less intelligent; if any is added, it appears slightly smarter.

Suggestion for future research: A hypothesis, which should be tested experimentally, is that the importance of the presence of each individual concept decreases as the number of—and *depth* of—the synthesized concepts increases. That is, any excision would eventually "heal over," given enough time. The failure of AM to verify this may be due to the relatively small amount of development in toto (an hour of cpu time, a couple hundred new concepts, a few levels deeper than the starting ones).

6–2.5   Can AM Work in a New Domain: Plane Geometry?

A true strategy should be domain-independent.

Adams

As McDermott points out [McDermott 76], just labelling a bunch of heuristics "Operation heuristics" doesn't suddenly make them relevant to any operation; all it does is give that impression to a human who looks at the code (or a description of it). Since the author hoped that the labelling really was fair, an experiment was done to test this. Such an experiment would be a key determiner of how general AM is.

How might one demonstrate that the "Operation" heuristics really could be useful or dealing with any operation, not just the ones already in AM's initial base of concepts?

One way would be to pick a new domain, and see how many old heuristics contribute to—and how many new heuristics have to be added to elicit—some sophisticated behavior in that domain. Of course, some new primitive concepts would have to be introduced (defined) to AM.

Only one experiment of this type was attempted. The author added a new base of concepts to the ones already in AM. Included were: Point, Line, Angle, Triangle, Equality of points/lines/angles/triangles. These simple plane geometry notions were sufficiently removed from set-theoretic ones that those preexisting specific concepts would be totally irrelevant; on the other hand, the general concepts—the ones with the heuristics attached—would still be just as relevant: Any-concept, Operation, Predicate, Structure, etc.

For each new geometric concept, the only facet filled in was its Definition. For the new predicates and operators, their Domain/range entries were also supplied. No new heuristics were added to AM.

Result: Fairly good behavior. AM was able to find examples of all the concepts defined, and to use the character of the results of those examples searches to determine intelligent courses of action. AM derived congruence and similarity of triangles, and several other well-known simple concepts. An unusual result was the repeated derivation of the idea of "timberline." This is a predicate on two triangles: Timberline(T1,T2) iff T1 and T2 have a common angle, and the side opposite that angle in the two triangles are parallel:

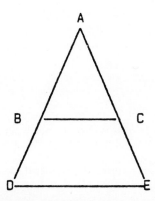

Timberline(ABC,ADE)

Since AM kept rederiving this in new ways, it seems surprising that there is no very common name for the concept. It could be that AM is using techniques which humans don't—at least, for geometry.

The only new bit of knowledge that came out of this experiment was a "use" for Goldbach's conjecture: any angle ($0\text{--}180°$) can be built up (to within $1°$) as the sum of two angles of prime degrees ($<180°$). This result is admittedly esoteric at best, but is nonetheless worth reporting.

The total effort expended on this experiment was: a few months of subconscious processing, ten hours of designing the base of concepts to insert, ten hours inserting and debugging them. The whole task took about two days of real time.

The conclusion to be drawn is that heuristics really can be generally useful; their attachment to general-sounding concepts is not an illusion.[21] The implication of this is that AM can be grown incrementally, domain by domain. Adding expertise in a new domain requires only the introduction of concepts local to that domain; all the very general concepts—and their heuristics—already exist and can be used with no change.

The author feels that this result can be generalized: AM can be expanded in scope, even to nonmathematical fields of endeavor. In each field, however, the rankings of the various heuristics[22] may shift slightly. As the domain gets further away from mathematics, various heuristics are important which were ignorable before (*e.g.,* those dealing with ethics), and some pure math research-oriented heuristics become less applicable ("giving up and moving on to another topic" is not an acceptable response to the 15-puzzle, nor to a hostage situation).

Well, it sounds as if we've shifted our orientation from "Results" to a subjective evaluation of those results. Let's start a new chapter to legitimize this type of commentary.

---

[21] Or it's a very good illusion! But note: If this phenomenon is repeatable and useful, then (like Newtonian mechanics) it won't pragmatically matter whether it's only an approximation to reality.

[22] The numeric values that should be returned by the local ratings formulae which are attached to the heuristic rules.

Chapter 7

Evaluating AM

All mathematicians are wrong at times.

Maxwell

This chapter contains discussions "meta" to AM itself. First comes an essay about judging the performance of a system like AM. This is a very hard task, since AM has no "goal." Even using current mathematical standards, should AM be judged on what it produced, or the quality of the path which led to those results, or the difference between what it started with and what it finally derived?

Section 7-2 then deals with the capabilities and limitations of AM:

- What concepts can be elicited from AM now? With a little tuning/tiny additions?
- What are some notable omissions in AM's behavior? Can the user elicit these?
- What could probably be done within a couple months of modifications?
- Aside from a total change of domain, what kinds of activities does AM lack (*e.g.*, proof capabilities)? Are any discoveries (*e.g.*, analytic function theory) clearly beyond its design limitations?

Finally, all the conclusions will be gathered, and a short summary of this project's "contribution to knowledge" will be indulged in.

7-1 JUDGING PERFORMANCE

One may view AM's activity as a progression from an initial core of knowledge to a more sophisticated body of concepts and their facets. Then each of the following is a reasonable way to measure success, to "judge" AM:

1   By AM's ultimate achievements. Examine the list of concepts and methods AM developed. Did AM ever discover anything interesting yet unknown to the user?[1] Anything new to humanity?

2   By the character of the difference between the initial and final states. Progressing from set theory to number theory is much more impressive than progressing from two-dimensional geometry to three-dimensional geometry.

3   By the quality of the route AM took to accomplish these advances: How clever, how circuitous, how many of the detours were quickly identified as such and abandoned?

4   By the character of the User–System interactions: How important is the user's guidance? How closely must AM be guided? What happens if the user doesn't say anything ever? When he or she does want to say something, is there an easy way to express that to AM, and does AM respond well to it? Given a reasonable kick in the right direction, can AM develop the mini-theories which the user intended, or at least something equally interesting?

5   By its intuitive heuristic powers: Does AM believe in "reasonable" conjectures? How accurately does AM estimate the difficulty of tasks it is considering? Does AM tie together (*e.g.*, as analogous) concepts which are formally unrelated yet which benefit from such a tie?

6   By the results of the experiments on the system (described in Section 6–2). How "tuned" is the Worth numbering scheme? The task priority rating scheme? How fragile is the set of initial concepts and heuristic rules? How domain-specific are those heuristics really? The set of facets?

7   By the very fact that the kinds of experiments outlined in Section 6–2 can easily be "set up" and performed on AM. Regardless of the experiments' outcomes, the features of AM which allow them to be carried out at all are worthy of note.

8   By the implications of this project. What can AM suggest about educating young mathematicians (and scientists in general)? What can AM say about doing math? About empirical research in general?

9   By the number of new avenues for research and experimentation it opens up. What new projects can we propose?

10   By comparison to other, similar systems.

---

[1] The "user" is a human who works with AM interactively, giving it hints, commands, questions, etc. Notice that by "new" we mean new to the user, not new to humanity. This might occur if the user were a child, and AM discovered some elementary facts of arithmetic. This is not really so provincial: mathematicians take "new" to mean new to Mankind, not new in the Universe. I feel philosophy slipping in, so this footnote is terminated.

For each of these ten measuring criteria, a subsection will now be provided. Other measures of judging performance exist,[2] of course, but haven't been applied to AM.

7–1.1 AM's Ultimate Discoveries

Two of the ideas which AM proposed were totally new and unexpected:[3]

- Consider numbers with an abnormally high number of divisors. If $d(n)$ represents the number of divisors of n,[4] then AM defines the set of "maximally-divisible numbers" to be $\{n \epsilon N \mid (\forall m < n)\, d(m) < d(n)\}$. By factoring each such number into primes, AM noticed a regularity in them. The author then developed a "mini-theory" about these numbers. It later turned out that Ramanujan had already proposed that very same definition (in 1915), and had found that same regularity. His results only partially overlap those of AM and the author, however, and his methods are radically different.
- AM found a cute geometric application of Goldbach's conjecture. Given a set of all angles of prime degree, from 0 to 180°,[5] then any angle between 0 and 180° can be approximated to within 1° by adding a pair of angles from this prime set. In fact, it is hard to find smaller sets than this one which approximate any angle to that accuracy.

By and large, the other concepts which AM developed were either already-known, or real losers. For example, AM composed Set-insert with the predicate Equality. The result was an operation Insert∘Equal(x,y,z), which first tested whether x was Equal to y or not. The value of this was either True or False. Next, this T/F value was inserted into z. For example, Insert∘Equal({1,2},{3,4},{5,6}) = {False,5,6}. The first two arguments are not equal, so the atom 'False' was inserted into the third. Although hitherto "unknown," this operation would clearly be better off left in that status.

Another kind of loser occurred whenever AM entered upon some "regular" behavior. For example, if it decided that Compose was interesting, it might try to create some examples of compositions. It could do this by picking two operations and composing them. What better operations to pick than Compose and Compose! Thus Compose∘Compose would be born. By composing that with itself, an even

---

[2] For example, Ken Colby sent transcripts of a session with PARRY to various psychiatrists, and had them evaluate each interaction along several dimensions. The same kind of survey could be done for AM. A quite separate measure of AM would be to wait and see how many future articles in the field refer to this work (and in what light!).

[3] Note that these are "ultimate discoveries" only in the sense of what has been done at the time of writing this book. For one of AM's ideas to be "new," it should be previously unknown to both the author and the user. Why? If the author knew about it, then the heuristics he provided AM with might unconsciously encode a path to that knowledge. If the user knew about that idea, his (or her or its) guidance might unconsciously help AM to derive it. An even more stringent interpretation would be that the idea be hitherto unknown to the collective written record of Mathematics.

[4] For example, $d(12) = \text{Size}(\{1,2,3,4,6,12\}) = 6$.

[5] Included are $0°$ and $1°$, as well as the "typical" primes $2°$, $3°$, $5°$, $7°$, $11°, \ldots, 179°$.

more monstrous operation is spawned: Compose∘Compose∘Compose∘Compose. Since AM actually uses the word "Compose" instead of that little infix circle, the PNAME of the data structure it creates is horrendous. Its use is almost nonexistent: it must take 5 operations as arguments, and it returns a new operation which is the composition of those five.

An analogous danger which exists is for AM to be content conjecturing a stream of very similar relationships (*e.g.*, the multiplication table). In all such cases, AM must have meta-rules which pull it up out of such whirlpools, to perceive a higher generalization of its previous sequence of related activities.

In summary, then, we may say that AM produced a few winning ideas new to the author, a couple of which were new to the world. Several additional "new" concepts were created which both AM and the user agreed were better forgotten.

7–1.2   The Magnitude of AM's Progress

Even with men of genius, with whom the birth rate of hypotheses is very high, it only just manages to exceed the death rate.

W. H. George

We can ask the following kind of question: how many "levels" did AM ascend? This is a fuzzy notion, but basically we shall say that a new level is reached when a valuable new bunch of connected concepts are defined in terms of concepts at a lower level.

For example, AM started out knowing about sets and set operations. When it progressed to numbers and arithmetic, that was one big step up to a new level. When it zeroed in on primes, unique-factorization, and divisibility, it had moved up another level.

When fed simple geometry concepts, AM moved up one level when it defined some generalizations of the equality of geometric figures (parallel lines, congruent and similar triangles, angles equal in measure) and their invariants (rotations, translations, reflections).

The above few examples are unfortunately exhaustive: that just about sums up the major advances AM made. Its progress was halted not so much by cpu time and space, as by a paucity of meta-knowledge: heuristic rules for filling in new heuristic rules. Thus AM's successes are finite, and its failures infinite, along this dimension.

A more charitable view might compare AM to a human who was forced to start from set theory, with AM's sparse abilities. In that sense, perhaps, AM would rate quite well. The "unfair" advantage it had was the presence of many heuristics which themselves were gleaned from mathematicians: *i.e.*, they are like compiled hindsight. A major purpose of mathematics education in the university is to instill these heuristics into the minds of the students.

AM is thus characterized as possessing heuristics which are powerful enough to take it a few "levels" away from the kind of knowledge it began with, but *only* a few levels. The limiting factors are (*i*) the heuristic rules AM begins with, and more specifically (*ii*) the expertise in recognizing and compiling new heuristics, and more generally (*iii*) a lack of real-world situations to draw upon for analogies, intuitions, and applications.

7–1.3   The Quality of AM's Route

Thinking is not measured by what is produced, but rather is a property of the way something is done.

Hamming

No matter what its achievements were, or the magnitude of its advancement from initial knowledge, AM could[6] still be judged "unintelligent" if, *e.g.*, it were exploring vast numbers of absurd avenues for each worthwhile one it found. The quality of the route AM followed is thus quite significant.

Of the two hundred new concepts it defined, about 130 were acceptable—in the sense that one can defend AM's reasoning in at least exploring them; in the sense that a human mathematician might have considered them. Of these "winners," about two dozen were significant—that is, useful, catalytic, well-known by human mathematicians, etc. Unfortunately, the sixty or seventy concepts which were losers were *real* losers: the set of even primes, the set of numbers with only one divisor, etc.

Once again we must observe that the quality of the route is a function of the quality of the heuristics. If there are many clever little rules, then the steps AM takes will often seem clever and sophisticated. If the rules superimpose nicely, joining together to collectively buttress some specific activity, then their effectiveness may surprise—and surpass—their creator.

Such moments of great insight (*i.e.*, where AM's reasoning surpassed mine) did occur, although rarely. Both of AM's "big discoveries" started by its examining concepts I felt weren't really interesting. For example, I didn't like AM spending so much time worrying about numbers with many divisors; I "knew" that the converse concept of primes was infinitely more valuable. And yet AM saw no reason to give up on maximally-divisible numbers; it had several good reasons for continuing that inquiry (they were the converse to primes which had already proved interesting, their frequency within the integers was neither very high nor very low nor very regular, their definition was simple, they were extremals of the interesting operation "Divisors-of," etc., etc.). Similarly, I "knew" that Goldbach's conjecture was useless, so I was unhappy that AM was bothering to try to apply it in the domain of geometry. In both cases, AM's reasons for its actions were unassailable, and in fact it did discover some interesting new ideas both times.

---

[6] Not necessarily *would* be so judged. Humans may very well consider an incredible number of silly ideas before the right pair of "hooked atoms" collide into a sensible thought, which is then considered in full consciousness. If, like humans, AM was capable of doing this processing in a sufficiently brief period of real time, it would not reflect ill on its evaluation. Of course, this may simply be the *definition* of "sufficiently brief."

Sometimes AM's behavior was displeasing, even though it wasn't "erring." Occasionally it was simultaneously developing two mini-theories (say primes and maximally-divisibles). Then it might pick a task or two dealing with one of these topics, then a task or two dealing with the other topic, etc. The task picked at each moment would be the one with the highest priority value. As a theory is developed, the interestingness of its associated tasks go up and down; there may be doldrums for a bit, just before falling into the track that will lead to the discovery of a valuable relationship. During these temporary lags, the interest value of tasks related to the other theory's concepts will appear to have a higher priority value: *i.e.*, better reasons supporting it. So AM would then skip over to one of *those* concepts, develop it until *its* doldrums, then return to the first one, etc. Most humans found this behavior unpalatable[7] because AM had no compunction about skipping from one topic to another. Humans have to retune their minds to do this skipping, and therefore treat it much more seriously. For that reason, AM was given an extra mobile reason to use for certain tasks on its agenda: "focus of attention." Any task with the same kind of topic as the ones just executed are given this extra reason, and it raises their priority values a little. This was enough sometimes to keep AM working on a certain mini-theory when it otherwise would have skipped somewhere else.

The above "defect" is a cute little kind of behavior AM exhibited which was non-human but not clearly "wrong." There were *genuine* bad moments also, of course. For example, AM became very excited[8] when the conjunction of "empty-set" and other concepts kept being equal to empty-set. AM kept repeating conjunctions of this form, rather than stepping back and generalizing this data into a (phenomenological) conjecture. Similar blind looping behavior occurred when AM kept composing Compose with itself, over and over. In general, one could say that "regular" behavior of any kind signals a probable fiasco. A heuristic rule to this effect halted most of these disgraceful antics. This rule had to be careful, since it was almost the antithesis of the "focus of attention" idea mentioned in the preceding paragraph. Together, those two rules seem to say that you should continue on with the kind of thing you were just doing, but not for *too* long a time.

AM has very few heuristics for deciding that something was *uninteresting*, that work on it should halt for a long time. Rather, AM simply won't have anything positive to say about that concept, and other concepts are explored instead, essentially by default. Each concept has a worth component which corresponded to its right to life (its right to occupy storage in core). This number slowly declines with time, and is raised whenever something interesting happens with that concept. If it ever falls below a certain threshhold, and if space is

---

[7] Although it might be the "best" from a dynamic management point of view, it probably would be wrong in the long run. Major advances really do have lulls in their development.

[8] Please excuse this anthropomorphism. Technically, we may say that the priority value of the best job on the agenda is the "level of excitement" of AM. 700 or higher is called "excitement," on a scale of 0-1000.

exhausted,[9] then the concept is forgotten: its list cells are garbage collected, and all references to it are erased, save those which will keep it from being re-created. This again is not purposeful forgetting, but rather by default; not because X is seen as a dead-end, but simply because other concepts seem so much more interesting for a long time.

Thus AM did not develop the sixty "losers" very much: they ended up with an average of only 1.5 tasks relevant to them ever having been chosen. The "winners" averaged about twice as many tasks, which helped fill them out more. Also, the worth ratings of the losers ended up far below those of the winners in all but two cases.

The final aspect of this important dimension of evaluation is the quality of the reasons AM used to support each task it chose to work on. The *Zeitgeist* of having expert systems possess self-explanatory capabilities is reflected in both the systems described in this book. AM's English phrases corresponded quite nicely to the "real" reasons a human might give to justify why something was worth trying, and the ordering of the tasks on the agenda was rarely far off from the one that I would have picked myself.

7–1.4 The Character of the User-System Interactions

AM is not a "user-oriented" system. There were many nice human-interaction features in the original grandiose proposal for AM which never got off the drawing board. At the heart of these features were two assumptions:

- The user must understand AM, and AM must likewise have a good model of the particular human using AM. The only time either should initiate a message is when their model of the other is not what they want that model to be. In that case, the message should be specifically designed to fix that discrepancy.[10]

- Each kind of message which is to pass between AM and its user should have its own appropriate language. Thus there should be a terse comment language, whereby the user can note reactions to what AM is doing, a questioning language for either party to get/give reasons to the other, a picture language for communicating certain relationships, etc.

Neither of these ideas ever made it into the LISP code that is now AM, although they are certainly not prohibited in any way by AM's design.

As one might expect, the reason for this atrophy is simply because very little guidance from the user was needed by AM. In fact, all the discoveries, cpu time quotes, etc., mentioned in this document are taken from totally unguided runs by AM. If the user guides as well as she can, then about a factor of 2 or 3 speedup is possible. Of course, this assumes that the user is dragging AM directly along a line of development that is known to be successful. The user's "reasons" at each

---

[9] No concepts were forgotten in this way until near the end of AM's runs, when AM would usually collapse from several causes including lack of space.

[10] This idea was motivated by a lecture given in 1975 by Terry Winograd.

step are based essentially on hindsight. Thus this is not at all "fair." If AM ever becomes more user-oriented, it would be nice to let children (say 6–12 years old) experiment with it, to observe them working with it in domains unfamiliar to either of them.[11]

The user can "kick" AM in one direction or another, *e.g.*, by interrupting and telling AM that Sets are more interesting than Numbers. Even in that particular case, AM fails to develop any higher-level set concepts (diagonalization, infinite sets, etc.) and simply wallows around in finite set theory (de Morgan's laws, associativity of Union, etc.). When geometric concepts are input, and AM is kicked in *that* direction, much nicer results are obtained. See the report on the Geometry experiment, in section 6–2.5.

There is one important result to observe: the very best examples of AM in action were brought to full fruition only by a human developer. That is, AM thought of a couple great concepts, but couldn't develop them well on its own. A human (the author) then took them and worked on them by hand, and interesting results were achieved. These results could be told to AM, who could then go off and look for new concepts to investigate. This interaction is of course at a much lower frequency than the kind of rapidfire question/answering talked about above. Yet it seems that such synergy may be the ultimate mode of AM-like systems: creative *assistants* to experts.

7–1.5   AM's Intuitive Powers

Intuitive conviction surpasses logic as the brilliance of the sun surpasses the pale light of the moon.

Kline

Let me hasten to mention that the word "intuitive" in this subsection's title is not related to the (currently non-existent) "Intuitions" facets of the concepts. What is meant is the totality of plausible reasoning which AM engages in: empirical induction, generalization, specialization, maintaining reasons for jobs on the agenda list, creation of analogies between bunches of concepts, etc.

AM only considers conjectures which have been explicitly suggested: either by empirical evidence, by analogy, or (de-implemented now) by Intuition facets. Once a conjecture has been formulated, it is tested in all ways possible: new experimental evidence is sought (especially extreme cases), it is examined formally[12] to see if it follows from already-known conjectures, etc.

Because of this grounding in plausibility, the only conjectures the user ever sees (the ones AM is testing) are quite believable. If they turn out to be false,

---

[11] Starred (*) exercise for the reader: carry out such a project on a statistically significant sample of children, wait thirty years, and observe the incidence of mathematicians and scientists in general, compared to the national averages. Within whatever occupation they've chosen, rate their creativity and productivity.

[12] Currently, this is done in trivial ways. An open problem, which is under attack now, is to add more powerful formal reasoning abilities to AM.

both the user and AM are surprised. For example, both AM and the user were disappointed when nothing came out of the concept of Uniquely-prime-addable numbers (positive integers which can be represented as the sum of two primes in precisely one way). Several conjectures were proposed via analogy with unique prime factorization, but none of them held experimentally. Each of them seemed worth investigating, to both the user and the system. It is still not known whether there is anything interesting about that concept or not.

AM's estimates of the value of each task it attempts were often far off from what hindsight proved their true values to be. Yet this was not so different from the situation a real researcher faces, and it made little difference on the discoveries and failures of the system. AM occasionally mismanaged its resources due to errors in these estimates. To correct for such erroneous prejudgments, heuristic rules were permitted to dynamically alter the time/space quanta for the current task. If some interesting new result turned up, then some extra resources would be allotted. If certain heuristics failed, they could reduce the time limits, so not as much total cpu time would be wasted on this loser.

Some poor analogies were considered, like the one between bags and singleton-bags. The ramifications of this analogy were painfully trivial.[13]

7–1.6   Experiments on AM

The experiments described in Section 6–2 provide some results relevant to the overall value of the AM system. The reader should consult that section for details; neither the experiments nor their results will be repeated here. A few conclusions will be summarized:

The worth-numbering scheme for the concepts is fairly robust: even when all the concepts's worths are initialized at the same value, the performance of AM doesn't collapse, although it is noticeably degraded.

Certain mutilations of the priority-value scheme for tasks on the agenda will cripple AM, but it can resist most of the small changes tried in various experiments.

Sometimes, removing just a single concept (*e.g.*, Equality) was enough to block AM from discovering some valuable concepts it otherwise got (in this case, Numbers). This makes AM's behavior sound very fragile, like a slender chain of advancement. But on the other hand, many concepts (*e.g.*, TIMES, Timberline, Primes[14]) were discovered in several independent ways. If AM's behavior *is* a chain, it is multiply-stranded (except for a few weak spots, like "Numbers").

---

[13] The bag-operations, applied to singletons, did not produce singletons as their result: $(x) \bigcup (y)$ is (x,y) which is not a singleton. Whether a bag-operation did produce a singleton bag or not depended only on the equality or inequality of the two arguments. There were many tiny conjectures proposed which merely re-echoed this general conclusion.

[14] Primes was discovered independently as follows: all numbers (>0) were seen to be representable as the sum of smaller numbers; Add was known to be analogous to TIMES; But not all numbers (>1) appeared to be representable as the *product* of two smaller ones; Rule number 166 triggered (see Appendix 2), and AM defined the set of exceptions: the set of numbers which could not be expressed as the product of two smaller ones; *i.e.*, the primes.

The heuristics are specific to their stated domain of applicability. Thus when working in geometry, the Operation heuristics were just as useful as they were when AM worked in elementary set theory or number theory. The set of facets seemed adequate for those domains, too. The Intuition facet, which was rejected as a valid source of information about sets and numbers, might have been more acceptable in geometry (*e.g.*, something similar to Gelernter's model of a geometric situation).

7–1.7   How to Perform Experiments on AM

The very fact that the kinds of experiments mentioned in the last section (and described in detail in Section 6–2) can be "set up" and performed on AM, reflects an important quality of the AM program.

Most of those experiments took only a matter of minutes to set up, only a few tiny modifications to AM. For example, the one where all the Worth ratings were initialized to the same value was done by evaluating the single LISP expression:

(MAPC CONCEPTS '(λ (c) (PUT c 'Worth 200)))

Similarly, here is how AM was modified to treat all tasks as if they had equal value: the function Pick-task has a statement of the form

(SETQ Current-task (First-member-of Agenda))

All that was necessary was to replace the call on the function "First-member-of" by the function "Random-member-of."

Even the most sophisticated experiment, the introduction of a new bunch of concepts—those dealing with geometric notions like Between, Angle, Line—took only a day of conscious work to set up.

Of course *running* the experiment involves the expenditure of hours of cpu time.

There are certain experiments one can't easily perform on AM: removing all its heuristics, for example. Most heuristic search programs would then wallow around, displaying just how big their search space really was. But AM would just sit there, since it would have nothing plausible to do. AM's heuristics are *plausible move generators*, not *implausible move constrainers*.

Many other experiments, while cute and easy to set up, are quite costly in terms of cpu time. For example, the class of experiments of the form: "remove heuristics x, y, and z, and observe the resultant affect on AM's behavior." This observation would entail running AM for an hour or two of cpu time! Considering the number of subsets of heuristics, not all these questions are going to get answered in our universe's lifetime. Considering the small probable payoff from any one such experiment, very few should actually be attempted.

One nice experiment would be to monitor the contribution each heuristic is making. That is, record each time it is used and record the final outcome of its activation (which may be several cycles later). Unfortunately, AM's heuristics are not all coded as separate Lisp entities, which one could then "trace." Rather, they are often interwoven with each other into large program pieces. So this experiment can't be easily set up and run on AM.

Even those experiments which can be run, can be set up only by someone familiar with the LISP code of AM. It would be quite hard to modify AM so that the untrained user could easily perform these experiments. Essentially, that would demand that AM have a deep understanding of its own structure. This is of course desirable, fascinating, challenging, but wasn't part of the design of AM.[15]

7–1.8   Future Implications of this Project

One harsh measure of AM would be to demand what possible applications it will have. This really means (*i*) the uses for the AM system, (*ii*) the uses for the ideas of how to create such systems, (*iii*) conclusions about math and science one can draw from experiments with AM.

Here are some of these implications, both real and potential: applications.>

1   New tools for computer scientists who want to create large knowledge-based systems to emulate some creative human activity.

    1a   The modular representation of knowledge that AM uses might prove to be effective in any knowledge-based system. Division of a global problem into a multitude of small chunks, each of them of the form of setting up one quite local "expert" on some concept, is a nice way to make a hard task more managable. Conceivably, each needed expert could be filled in by a human who really is an expert on that topic. Then the global abilities of the system would be able to rely on quite sophisticated local criteria. Fixing a set of facets once and for all permits effective inter-module communication.

    1b   Some ideas may carry over unchanged into many fields of human creativity, wherever local guiding rules exist. These include: (a) ideas about heuristics having domains of applicability, (b) the policy of tacking them onto the most general knowledge source (concept, module) they are relevant to, (c) the rippling scheme to locate relevant knowledge, etc.

2   A body of heuristics which can be built upon by others.

    2a   Most of the particular heuristic judgmental criteria for interestingness, utility, etc., might be valid in developing theorizers in other sciences. Recall that each rule has its domain of applicability; many of the heuristics in AM are quite general.

    2b   Just within the small domain in which AM already works, this base of heuristics might be enlarged through contact with various mathematicians. If they are willing to introspect and add some of their "rules" to AM's existing base, it might gradually grow more and more powerful.

    2c   Carrying this last point to the limit of possibility, one might imagine the program possessing more heuristics than any single human. Of course, AM as it stands now is missing so much of the "human element," the life experiences that a mathematician draws upon continually for inspiration, that merely amassing more

---

[15] A general suggestion for future research projects in this area: such systems should be designed in a way which facilitates a poorly trained user not only *using* the system but *experimenting* on it.

heuristics won't automatically push it to the level of a super-human intelligence. Another far-out scenario is that of the great mathematicians of each generation pouring their individual heuristics into an AM-like system. After a few generations have come and gone, running that program could be a valuable way to bring about "interactions" between people who were not contemporaries.

3 New and better strategies for math educators.

3a Since the key to AM's success seems to be its heuristics, and not the particular concepts it knows, the whole orientation of mathematics education should perhaps be modified, to provide experiences for the student which will build up these rules in his mind. Learning a new theorem is worth much less than learning a new heuristic which lets you discover new theorems.[13] I am far from the first to urge such a revision (see, *e.g.*, Koestler[67], p.265, or see Papert[72]).

3b If the repertoire of intuition (simulated real-world scenarios) were sufficient for AM to develop elementary concepts of math, then educators should ensure that children (4-6 years old) are thoroughly exposed to those scenarios. Such activities would include seesaws, slides, piling marbles into pans of a balance scale, comparing the heights of towers built out of cubical blocks, solving a jigsaw puzzle, etc. Unfortunately, AM failed to show the value of these few scenarios. This was a potential application which was not confirmed.

3c One use for AM itself would be as a "fun" teaching tool. If a very nice user interface is constructed, AM could serve as a model for, say, college freshmen with no math research experience. They could watch AM, see the kinds of things it does, play with it, and perhaps get a real flavor for (and get turned on by) doing math research. A vast number of brilliant minds are too turned off by high-school drilling and college calculus to stick around long enough to find out how exciting—and different—research math is compared with textbook math.

4 Further experiments on AM might tell us something about how the theory formation task changes as a theory grows in sophistication. For example, can the same methods which lead AM from premathematical concepts to arithmetic also lead AM from number systems up to abstract algebra? Or are a new set of heuristic rules or extra concepts required? My guess is that a few of each are lacking currently, but *only* a few. There is a great deal of disagreement about this subject among mathematicians. By tracing along the development of mathematics, one might categorize discoveries by how easy they would be for an AM-like system to find. Sometimes, a discovery required the invention of a brand new heuristic rule, which would clearly be beyond AM as currently designed. Sometimes, discovery is based on the lucky random combination of existing concepts, for no good *a priori* reason. It would be instructive to find out how often this is necessarily the case: how often *can't* a mathematical discovery be motivated and "explained" using heuristic rules of the kind AM possesses?

5 An unanticipated result was the creation of new-to-humanity math (both directly and by defining new, interesting concepts to investigate by hand). The amount of new bits of mathematics developed to date is minuscule.

---

[16] Usually. One kind of exception is the following: the ability to take a powerful theorem, and extract from it a new, powerful heuristic. AM cannot do this, but it may turn out that this mechanism is quite crucial for humans' obtaining new heuristics. This is another open research problem.

5a   As described in (2c) above, AM might absorb heuristics from several individuals and thereby integrate their particular insights. This might eventually result in new mathematics being discovered.

5b   An even more exciting prospect, which never materialized, was that AM would find a new redivision of existing concepts, an alternate formulation of some established theory, much like Hamiltonian mechanics is an alternate unification of the data which led to Newtonian mechanics. The only rudimentary behavior along these lines was when AM occasionally derived a familiar concept in an abnormal way (*e.g.*, TIMES was derived in four ways; Prime pairs were noticed by restricting Addition to primes).

7–1.9   Open Problems: Suggestions for Future Research

While AM can and should stand as a complete research project, part of its value will stem from whatever future studies are sparked by it. Of course the "evaluation" of AM along this dimension must wait for years, but even at the present time several such open problems come to mind:

* Devise Meta-heuristics, rules capable of operating on and synthesizing new heuristic rules. AM has shown the solution of this problem to be both nontrivial and indispensable. AM's progress ground to a halt because fresh, powerful heuristics were never produced. The next point suggests that the same need for new rules exists in mathematics as a whole:

* Examine the history of mathematics, and gradually build up a list of the heuristic rules used. Does the following thesis have any validity: "*The development of mathematics is essentially the development of new heuristics.*" That is, can we "factor out" all the discoveries reachable by the set of heuristics available (known) to the mathematicians at some time in history, and then explain each new big discovery as requiring the synthesis of a brand new heuristic? For example, Bolyai and Lobachevsky did this a century ago when they decided that counter-intuitive systems might still be consistent and interesting. Non-Euclidean geometry resulted, and no mathematician today would think twice about using the heuristic they developed. Einstein invented a new heuristic more recently, when he dared to consider that counter-intuitive systems might actually have physical reality.[17] What was once a bold new method is now a standard tool in theoretical physics.

* In a far less dramatic vein, a hard open problem is that of building up a body of rules for symbolically instantiating a definition (a LISP predicate). These rules may be structured hierarchically, so that rules specific to operating on "operations whose domain and range are equal" may be gathered. Is this set finite and managable; *i.e.*, does some sort of "closure" occur after a few hundred (thousand?) such rules are assembled?

---

[17] As Courant says, "When Einstein tried to reduce the notion of 'simultaneous events occurring at different places' to observable phenomena, when he unmasked as a metaphysical prejudice the belief that this concept must have a scientific meaning in itself, he had found the key to his theory of relativity."

- More generally, we can ask for the expansion of all the heuristic rules, of all categories. This may be done by eliciting them from mathematicians, or automatically by the application of very sophisticated meta-heuristics. Some categories of rules include: how to generalize/specialize definitions, how to find examples of a given concept, how to optimize LISP algorithms.

- Experiments can be done on AM. A few have been performed already, many more are proposed in Section 6–2, and no doubt some additional ones have already occurred to the reader.

- Extend the analysis already begun of the set of heuristics AM possesses. One reason for such an analysis would be to achieve a better understanding of the contribution of the heuristics. In some sense, the heuristics and the choice of starting concepts "encode" the discoveries which AM makes, and the way it makes them. A better understanding of that encoding may lead to new ideas for AM and for future AM-like systems. More generally, we know very little about "the space of heuristics;" the time may be ripe for research in this area.

- Rewrite AM. In Chapter 1, it was pointed out that there are two common species of heuristic search programs. One type has a legal move generator, and heuristics to constrain it. The second type, including AM, has only a set of heuristics, and they act as plausible move generators. Since AM seemed to create new concepts, propose new conjectures, and formulate new tasks in a very few distinct ways, it might very well be feasible to find a purely syntactic "legal move generator" for AM, and to convert each existing heuristic into a form of constraint. In that case, one could, *e.g.*, remove all the heuristics and still see a meaningful (if explosive) activity proceed. There might be a few surprises down that path.

- A more tractible project, a subset of the former one, would be to recode just the conjecture-finding heuristics as constraints on a new, purely syntactic "legal conjecture generator." A simple Generate-and-Test paradigm would be used to synthesize and examine large numbers of conjectures. Again, removing all the heuristics would be a worthwhile experiment.

- At the reaches of feasability, one can imagine trying to extend AM into more and more fields, into less-formalizable domains. International politics has already been suggested as a very hard future applications area

- Abstracting that last point, try to build up a set of criteria which make a domain ripe for automating (*e.g.*, it possesses a strong theory, it is knowledge-rich (many heuristics exist), the performance of the professionals/experts is much better than that of the typical practitioners, the new discoveries in that field all fall into a small variety of syntactic formats,...?). Initially, this study might help humans build better and more appropriate scientific discovery programs. Someday, it might even permit the creation of an automatic-theory-formation-program-writer.

- The interaction between AM and the user is minimal and painful. Is there a more effective language for communication? Should several languages exist, depending on the type of message to be sent (pictures, control characters, a subset of natural language, induction from examples, etc.)? Can AM's output be raised in sophistication by introducing an internal model of the user and the user's state of knowledge at each moment? Perhaps AM should also contain models of several known *groups* of users (mathematicians, computer scientists, students)—say, stored as concepts in a specialization/generalization hierarchy.

- Human protocol studies may be appropriate, to test out the model of mathematical research which AM puts forward. Are the sequences of actions similar? Are the mistakes analogous? Do the pauses which the humans emit *quantitatively* correspond to AM's periods of gathering and running "Suggest" heuristics?
- Can the idea of Intuition functions be developed into a useful mechanism? If not, how else might real-world experiences be made available to an automated researcher to draw upon (for analogies, to base new theories upon)? Could one interface physical effectors and receptors and quite literally allow the program to "play around in the real world" for his analogies?
- Most of the "future implications" discussed in the last section suggest future activities (*e.g.*, new educational experiments and techniques).
- Most of the "limiting assumptions" discussed in a later section (7–2.4) can be tackled with today's techniques (plus a great deal of effort). Thus each of them counts as an open problem for research.
- Perform an information-theoretic analysis on AM. What is the value of each heuristic? the new information content of each new conjecture?
- If you're interested in natural language, the very hard problem exists of giving AM (or a similar system) the ability to really do inferential processing on the *reasons* attached to tasks on the agenda. Instead of just being able to test for equality of two reasons, it would be much more intelligent to be able to infer the kind of relationship between any two reasons; if they overlap semantically, we'd like to be able to compute precisely how that should that effect the overall rating for the task; etc.
- Modify the control structure of AM, as follows. Allow mini-goals to exist, and supply new rules for setting them up (plausible goal generators) and altering those goals, plus some new rules and algorithms for satisfying them. The modification I have in mind would result in new tasks being proposed because of certain current goals, and existing tasks would be reordered so as to raise the chance of satisfying some important goal. Finally, the human watching AM would be able to observe the rationality (hopefully) of the goals which were set. The simple "Focus of Attention" mechanism already in AM is a tiny step in this goal-oriented direction. Note that this proposal itself demonstrates that AM is not inherently opposed to a goal-directed control structure. Rather, AM simply possesses only a partial set of mechanisms for complete reasoning about its domain.

7–1.10   Comparison to Other Systems

One popular way to judge a system is to compare it to other, similar systems, and/or to others' proposed criteria for such systems. There is no other project (known to the author) having the same objective: automated math research.[18] Many somewhat related efforts have been reported in the literature and will be mentioned here.

Several projects have been undertaken which overlap small pieces of the AM system and in addition concentrate deeply upon some area *not* present in

---

[18] In [Atkin & Birch 1971], *e.g.*, we find no mention of the computer except as a number cruncher.

AM. For example, the CLET system [Badre 73] worked on learning the decimal addition algorithm[19] but the "*mathematics discovery*" aspects of that system were neither emphasized nor worth emphasizing; it was an interesting natural language communication study. The same comment applies to several related studies by IMSSS.[20]

Boyer and Moore's theorem-prover [Boyer&Moore 75] embodies some of the spirit of AM (*e.g.*, generalizing the definition of a LISP function), but its motivations are quite different, its knowledge base is minimal, and its methods purely formal.[21] The same comments apply to the SAM program [Guard 69], in which a resolution theorem-prover is set to work on unsolved problems in lattice theory.

Among the attempts to incorporate heuristic knowledge into a theorem prover, we should also mention [Wang 60], [Pitrat 70], [Bledsoe 71], and [Brotz 74]. How did AM differ from these "heuristic theorem-provers"? The goal-driven control structure of these systems is a real but only minor difference from AM's control structure (*e.g.*, AM's "focus of attention" is a rudimentary step in that direction). The fact that their overall activity is typically labelled as deductive is also not a fundamental distinction (since constructing a proof is usually in practice quite *inductive*).[22] Even the character of the inference processes are analogous: The provers typically contain a couple binary inference rules, like Modus Ponens, which are relatively risky to apply but can yield big results; AM's few "binary" operators have the same characteristics: Compose, Canonize, Logically-combine (disjoin and conjoin). The main distinction is that *the theorem provers each incorporate only a handful of heuristics*. The reason for this, in turn, is the paucity of good heuristics which exist for the very general task environment in which they operate: domain-independent (asemantic) predicate calculus theorem proving. The need for additional guidance was recognized by these researchers. For example, see [Wang 60], p. 3 and p. 17. Or as Bledsoe says:[23]

> There is a real difference between *doing* some mathematics and *being* a math-
> ematician. The difference is principally one of judgment: in the selection of a
> problem (theorem to be proved); in determining its relevance;... It is precisely
> in these areas that machine provers have been so lacking. This kind of judgment
> has to be supplied by the user... Thus a crucial part of the resolution proof is
> the *selection* of the reference theorems by the *human* user; the human, by this one
> action, usually employs more skill than that used by the computer in the proof.

---

[19] Given the addition table up to 10 + 10, plus an English text description of what it means to carry, how and when to carry, etc., actually write a program capable of adding two 3-digit numbers.

[20] See [Smith 74a], for example.

[21] This is not meant as criticism; considering the goals of those researchers, and the age of that system, their work is quite significant.

[22] See [Lakatos 76] for a marvelous discussion of the continual spiral of criticism and improvement, as the mathematics community zeros in toward a proof, uncovers a refutation, finds a new proof of a slightly modified conjecture, and so on.

[23] [Bledsoe 71], p. 73.

Many researchers have constructed programs which pioneered some of the techniques AM uses. [Gelernter 63] reports the use of prototypical examples as analogic models to guide search in geometry, and [Bundy 73] employs models of "sticks" to help his program work with natural numbers. The single heuristic of analogy was studied in [Evans 68] and [Kling 71]. Brotz's program, [Brotz 74], uses this to propose useful lemmata.

Theory formation systems in *any* field have been few. Meta-Dendral [Buchanan 74] represents perhaps the best of these. Its task is to unify a body of mass spectral data (examples of "proper" identifications of spectra) into a small body of rules for making identifications. Thus even this system is given a fixed task, a fixed set of data to find regularities within. AM, however, must find its own data, and take the responsibility for managing its own time, for not looking too long at worthless data.[24] There has been much written about scientific theory formation (*e.g.*, [Hempel 52]), but very little of it is specific enough to be of immediate *operational* use to AI researchers. A couple pointers to excellent discussions of this sort are: [Fogel 66], [Simon 73], and [Buchanan 75]. Also worth noting is a discussion near the end of [Amarel 69], in which "formation" and "modelling" problems are treated:

> The problem of model finding is related to the following general question raised by Schutzenberger [in discussion at the Conference on Intelligence and Intelligent Systems, Athens, Ga., 1967]: *"What do we want to do with intelligent systems that relates to the work of mathematicians?."* So far all we have done in this general area is to emulate some of the reasonably simple activities of mathematicians, which is finding consequences from given assumptions, reasoning, proving theorems. A certain amount of work of this type was already done in the propositional and predicate calculi, as well as in some other mathematical systems. But this is only one aspect of the work that goes on in mathematics.
>
> Another very important aspect is the one of finding general properties of structures, finding analogies, similarities, isomorphisms, and so on. This is the type of activity that is extremely important for our understanding of model-finding mechanisms. Work in this area is more difficult than theorem-proving. The problem here is that of *theorem finding*.

AM is one of the first attempts to construct a "theorem-finding" program. As Amarel noted, it may be possible to learn from such programs how to tackle the general task of automating scientific research.

Besides "math systems," and "creative thinking systems," and "theory formation systems," we should at least discuss others' thoughts on the issue of algorithmically doing math research. Some individuals feel it is not so far-fetched to imagine automating mathematical research (*e.g.*, Paul Cohen). Others

---

[24] Another way of looking at that: Meta-Dendral has a fixed set of templates for rules which it wishes to find, and a fixed vocabulary of mass spectral concepts which can be plugged into those templates. AM also has only a few stock formats for conjectures, but it selectively enlarges its vocabulary of math concepts.

(*e.g.*, Pólya) would probably disagree. The presence of a high-speed, general-purpose symbol manipulator in our midst now makes investigation of that question possible.

There has been very little published thought about discovery in mathematics from an algorithmic point of view; even clear thinkers like Pólya and Poincaré treat mathematical ability as a sacred, almost mystic quality, tied to the unconscious. The writings of philosophers and psychologists invariably attempt to examine human performance and belief, which are far more manageable than creativity *in vitro*. Belief formulae in inductive logic[25] invariably fall back upon how well they fit human measurements. The abilities of a computer and a brain are too distinct to consider blindly working for results (let alone algorithms!) one possesses which match those of the other.

7–2   CAPABILITIES AND LIMITATIONS OF AM

The first two subsections contain a general discussion of what AM can and can't do. Later subsections deal with powers and limitations inherent in using an agenda scheme, in fixing the domain of AM, and in picking one specific model of math research to build AM upon. The AM program exists only because a great many simplifying assumptions were tolerated; these are discussed in Section 7–2.6. Finally, some speculation is made about the ultimate powers and weaknesses of any systems which are designed very much like AM.

7–2.1   Current Abilities

What fields has AM worked in so far? AM is now able to explore a small bit of the theory of sets, data types, numbers, and plane geometry. It by no means has been fed—nor has it rediscovered—a large fraction of what is known in any of those fields. It might be more accurate to be humble and restate those domains as: elementary finite set theory, trivial observations about four kinds of data types, arithmetic and elementary divisibility theory, and simple relationships between lines, angles, and triangles. So a sophisticated concept in each domain—which was discovered by AM—might be:

- de Morgan's laws.
- The fact that Delete∘Insert[26] never alters Bags or Lists.
- Unique factorization.
- Similar triangles.

Can AM work in a new field, like politics? AM can work in a new elementary, formalized domain, if it is fed a supplemental base of conceptual primitives for

---

[25] For example, see [Hintikka 62], [Pietarinin 72]. The latter also contains a good summary of Carnap's λ, α formalization.

[26] Take an item x, insert it into (the front of) structure B, then delete one (the first) occurrence of x from B.

that domain. To work in plane geometry, it sufficed to give AM about twenty new primitive concepts, each with a few parts filled in. Other domains which AM could work in include elementary mechanics, game-playing, and programming. The more informal (non-internally-formalizable) the desired field, the less of AM that is relevant. Perhaps an AM-like system could be built for a constrained, precise political task.[27] Disclaimer: Even for a very small domain, the amount of common-sense knowledge such a system would need is staggering. It is unfortunate to provide such a trivial answer to such an important question, but there is no easy way to answer it more fully until years of additional research are performed.

Can AM discover X? Why didn't it do Y? It is difficult to predict whether AM will (without modifications) ever make a specific given discovery. Although its capabilities are small, its limitations are hazy. What makes the matter even worse is that, given a concept C which AM missed discovering, there is probably a reasonable heuristic rule which is missing from AM, which would enable that discovery. One danger of this "debugging" is that a rule will be added which only leads to that one desired discovery, and isn't good for anything else. In that case, the new heuristic rule would simply be an *encoding* of a specific bit of mathematics which AM would then appear to discover using general methods. This must be avoided at all costs, *even at the cost of intentionally giving up a certain discovery.* If the needed rule is general—it has many applications and leads to many interesting results—then it really was an oversight not to include it in AM. Although I believe that there are not too many such omissions still within the small realm AM explores, there is no objective way to demonstrate that, except by further long tests with AM.

In what ways are new concepts created? Although the answer to this is accurately given in Section 4–3 (namely, this is mainly the jurisdiction of the right sides of heuristic rules), and although I dislike the simple-minded way it makes AM sound, the list below does characterize the major ways in which new concepts get born:

- Fill in examples of a concept (*e.g.*, by instantiating or running its definition).
- Create a generalization of a given concept (*e.g.*, by weakening its definition).
- Create a specialization of a given concept (*e.g.*, by restricting its domain/range).
- Compose two operations f,g, thereby creating a new one h. [Define $h(x) =_{df} f(g(x))$].
- Coalesce an operation f into a new one g. [Define $g(x) =_{df} f(x,x)$].
- Permute the order of the arguments of an operation. [Define $g(x,y) =_{df} f(y,x)$].

---

[27] For example, such a politics-oriented AM-like system might conceive the notion of a group of political entities which view themselves as quite disparate, but which are viewed from the outside as a single unit: *e.g.*, "the Arabs," "the American Indians." Conjectures about this concept might include its reputation as a poor combatant (and why). Many of the same facets AM uses would carry over to represent concepts in that new domain.

- Invert an operation [g(x)=y iff f(y)=x] (*e.g.*, from Squaring, create Square-rooting).
- Canonize one predicate P1 with respect to a more general one P2 [create a new concept f, an operation, such that: P2(x,y) iff P1(f(x),f(y))].
- Create a new operation g, which is the repeated application of an existing operation f.
- The usual logical combinations of existing concepts x,y: $x \wedge y$, $x \vee y$, $\neg x$, ..., etc.

Below is a similar list, giving the primary ways in which AM formulates new conjectures:

- Notice that concept C1 is really an example of concept C2.
- Notice that concept C1 is really a specialization (or: generalization) of C2.
- Notice that C1 is equal to C2; or: *almost always* equal.
- Notice that C1 and C2 are related by some known concept.
- Check and update the domain/range of an existing operation.
- If two concepts are analogous, extend the analogy to their conjectures as well.

7–2.2   Current Limitations

Below are several shortcomings of AM, which hurt its behavior but are not believed to be inherent limitations of its design. They are presented in order of decreasing severity.

Perhaps the most serious limitation on AM's current behavior arose from the lack of constraints on left sides of heuristic rules. It turned out that this excessive freedom made it difficult for AM to inspect and analyze and synthesize its own heuristics; such a need was not foreseen at the time AM was designed. It was thought that the power to manipulate heuristic rules was an ability which the author must have, but which the system wouldn't require. As it turned out, AM did successfully develop new concepts several levels deeper than the ones it started with. But as the new concepts got further and further away from those initial ones, they had fewer and fewer specific heuristics filled in (since they had to be filled in by AM itself). Gradually, AM found itself relying on heuristics which were very general compared to the concepts it was dealing with (*e.g.*, forced to use heuristics about Objects when dealing with Numbers). Heuristics for dealing with heuristics do exist, and their number could be increased. This is not an easy job: finding a new meta-heuristic is a tough process. Heuristics are rarely more than compiled hindsight; hence it's difficult to create new ones "before the fact." Our current research is based on the hypothesis that heuristics can be discovered and reasoned about in much the same way that mathematical operations can. What this means is recoding each of AM's heuristics as a full-fledged concept. This would enable the heuristics to work on each other, as well as on concepts corresponding to mathematical entities.

AM has no notion of proof, proof techniques, formal validity, heuristics for finding counterexamples, etc. Thus it never really establishes any conjecture formally. This could be partially remedied by adding about 25 new concepts (and their 100 new associated heuristics) dealing with such topics. The needed concepts have been outlined on paper, but not yet coded. It would probably require a few hundred hours to code and debug them. [Lakatos 76] demonstrates the value of proof as an instrument of discovery: As one spirals in from conjecture to theorem, along the path of repeated criticism and improvement, one often finds motivation for modifying concepts' definitions, or for defining new, promising ones.

The user interface is quite primitive, and this again could be dramatically improved with just a couple hundred hours' work. AM's explanation system is almost nonexistent: the user must ask a question quickly, or AM will have already destroyed the information needed to construct an answer. A clean record of recent system history and a nice scheme for tracking down reasons for modifying old rules and adding new ones dynamically does not exist at the level which is found, *e.g.*, in MYCIN [See part I of this book]. There is no trivial way to have the system print out its heuristics in a format which is intelligible to the untrained user.

An important type of analogy which was untapped by AM was that between heuristics. If two situations were similar, conceivably the heuristics useful in one situation might be useful (or have useful analogues) in the new situation (see [Koppelman 75]). Perhaps this is a viable way of enlarging the known heuristics. Such "meta-level" activities were kept to a minimum throughout AM, and this proved to be a serious limitation.

The idea of "Intuitions" facets was a flop. Intuitions were meant to model reality, at least little pieces of it, so that AM could perform (simulate) physical experiments, and observe the results. The major problem here was that *so* little of the world was modelled that the only relationships derivable were those foreseen by the author. This lack of generality was unacceptable, and the intuitions were completely excised. The original idea might lead somewhere if it were developed fully.

7–2.3 Limitations of the Agenda Scheme

Currently, it is difficult to include heuristics which interact with one another in any significant way. The whole fibre of the Agenda scheme assumes perfect independence of heuristics. The global formula used to rate tasks on the agenda assumes perfect superposition of reasons: there are no "cross-terms." Is this assumption always valid? Unfortunately *no*, not even for the limited domain AM has explored. Sometimes, two reasons are very similar: "Examples of Sets would permit finding examples of Union" and "Examples of Sets would permit finding examples of Intersection." In that case, their two ratings shouldn't cause such a big increase in the overall priority value of the task "Fillin examples of Sets." There are a few other minor limitations of the current Agenda scheme:

1 Sometimes, a heuristic rule will want to *dissuade* the system from some

activity; so occasionally we'd like a *negative* numeric contribution to a task's priority value.

2   AM discards the formula which produced a reason's rating, and keeps around only the numeric result of that formula; but many of those formulae involve time-dependent quantities (*e.g.*, the number of entries on a particular facet of a particular concept).

3   Better than a single priority value for each task would be for AM to maintain a vector of numbers, or, better still, symbolic descriptions.

4   The agenda list should really be an agenda *tree* (maybe an agenda *Heap*), since the ordering of tasks is really just partial, not total. The utility of this is extremely high if multiprocessor technology is available to run the program on.

7–2.4   Limiting Assumptions

AM only "got off the ground" because a number of sweeping assumptions were made, pertaining to what could be ignored, how a complex process could be adequately simulated, etc. Now that AM *is* running, however, those same simplifications crop up as limitations to the system's behavior. Each of the following points is a "convenient falsehood." Although the reader has already been told about some of these, it's worth listing them all together here:

- The only communication necessary from AM to the user is keeping the user informed of what AM is doing. No natural language ability is required by AM; simple template instantiation is sufficient.
- The only communication from the user to AM is an occasional interrupt, when the user wishes to provide some guidance or to pose a query. Both of these can be stereotyped and passed easily through a very narrow channel.[28]
- Each heuristic has a well-defined domain of applicability, which can be specified just by giving the name of a single concept.
- If concept C1 is more specialized than C2, then C1's heuristics will be more powerful and should be executed before C2's (whenever both concepts' heuristics are relevant).
- If h1 and h2 are two heuristics attached to concept C, then it is not necessary to spend any time ordering them.
- Heuristics superimpose perfectly; they never interact strongly with each other.
- The reasons supporting a task can be mere tokens; it suffices to be able to inspect them for equality. They need not follow a constrained syntax. The value of a reason is adequately characterized by a unidimensional numeric rating.
- The reasons supporting a task superimpose perfectly; they never interact with each other.
- Supporting reasons—and their ratings—never change with time, with one exception: the ephemeron "Focus of attention."

---

[28] For example, a set of escape characters, so ↑ *W* means *"Why did you do that?,"* ↑ *U* means *"Uninteresting! Go on to something else,"* etc.

- It doesn't matter in what order the supporting reasons for a task were added.
- There is no need for negative or inhibitory reasons, which would decrease the priority value of a task.
- At any moment, the top few tasks on the agenda are not coupled strongly; it is not necessary to expend extra processing time to carefully order them.
- The tasks on the agenda are completely independent of each other, in the sense of one task "enabling" or "waking-up" another.
- Mathematics research has a clean, simple model (see Section 7–3.5) which indicates that it is a search process governed by a large collection of heuristic rules.
- Elementary mathematics is such that valuable new concepts will be discovered fairly regularly.
- The worth of each new concept can be estimated easily, after just a brief investigation.
- Contradictions will arise extremely infrequently, and it is not disastrous to ignore them when they do occur. The same indifference applies to the danger of believing in false conjectures.
- When doing theory formation in elementary mathematics, proof and formal reasoning are dispensable.
- Even as more knowledge is obtained, the set of facets need never change.
- For any piece of knowledge sought or obtained, there is precisely one facet of one existing[29] concept where that knowledge ought to be stored, and it is easy to determine that proper location.
- Even as more concepts are defined, the body of heuristics need not grow much.
- Any common-sense knowledge required by AM is automatically present within the heuristic rules. So, *e.g.*, no special spatial visualization abilities are needed.

It is worth repeating here that the above assumptions are all clearly false. Yet none of them was too damaging to AM's behavior, and their combined presence made the creation of AM feasible.

7–2.5   Choice of Domain

The genesis of mathematical creation is a problem which should intensely interest the psychologist. It is the activity in which the human mind seems to take least from the outside world, in which it acts or seems to act only of itself and on itself, so that in studying the procedure of mathematical thought we may hope to reach what is most essential in man's mind.

Poincaré

Here are some questions this subsection will address:

---

[29] The only allowable exception is that a new piece of information might require the creation of a brand new concept, and then require storage somewhere on that concept.

- What are the inherent limitations—and advantages—in fixing a domain for AM to work in?
- What characteristics are favorable to automating research in any given domain?
- What are the specific reasons for and against elementary finite set theory as the chosen starting domain?

Research in various domains of science and math proceeds slightly differently. For example, psychology is interested in explaining people, not in creating new kinds of people. Math is not interested in individual entities so much as in new kinds of entities. There are ethical restrictions on physicians which prevent certain experiments from being done. Political experiments rarely permit backtracking, etc. Each field has its own peculiarities.

If we want a system to work in many domains, we have to sacrifice some power.[30] Within a given field of knowledge (like math), the finer the category we limit ourselves to, the more specific are the heuristics which become available. So it was reasonable to make this first attempt limited to one narrow domain.

This brings up the choice of domain. What should it be? As the DENDRAL project illustrated so clearly,[31] choice of subject domain is quite important when studying how researchers discover and develop their theories. Mathematics was chosen as the domain of this investigation, because:

1   In doing math research, one needn't cope with the uncertainties and fallibility of testing equipment; that is, there are no uncertainties in the data (compared to, *e.g.*, molecular structure inference from mass spectrograms).

2   Reliance on experts' introspections is one of the most powerful techniques for codifying the judgmental criteria necessary to do effective work in a field; I personally have had enough training in elementary mathematics so that I didn't have to rely completely on external sources for guidance in formulating such heuristic rules. Also, several excellent sources were available [Pólya, Skemp, Hadamard, Kershner, etc.].

3   The more formal a science is, the easier it is to automate. For a machine to carry out research in psychology would require more knowledge about human information processing than now is known, because psychology deals with entities as complex as you and I. Also, in a formal science, the *languages* to communicate information can be simple even though the *messages* themselves be sophisticated.

4   Since mathematics can deal with any conceivable constructs, a researcher there is not limited to explaining observed data. Related to this is the freedom to investigate—or to give up on—whatever the researcher wants to. There is no single discovery which is the "goal," no given problem to solve, no right or wrong behavior.

---

[30] This is assuming a system of a given fixed size. If this restriction isn't present, then a reasonable "general-purpose" system could be built as several systems linked by one giant switch.

[31] See [Feigenbaum et. al. 71]. In that case, the choice of subject was enabled by [Lederberg 64].

5   Unlike "simpler" fields, such as propositional logic, there is an abundance of heuristic rules available for the picking.

The limitations of math as a domain are closely intertwined with its advantages. Having no ties to real-world data can be viewed as a limitation, as can having no clear goal. There is always the danger that AM will give up on each theory as soon as the first tough obstacle crops up.

Since math (and in particular geometry and number theory) has been worked on for millenia by some of the greatest minds from many different cultures, it is unlikely that a small effort like AM would make any new inroads, have any startling insights. In that respect, Dendral's space was much less explored. Of course math—even at the elementary level that AM explored it—still has undiscovered gems (*e.g.*, the recent unearthing of Conway's numbers [Knuth 74]).

One point of agreement between Weizenbaum and Lederberg[32] is that AI can succeed in automating an activity only when a "strong theory" of that activity exists. AM is built on a detailed model of how humans do math research. In the next subsection, we'll discuss the model of math research that AM assumes.

7–2.6   Limitations of the Model of Math Research

Weizenbaum does point to projects in mathematics and chemistry where computers have shown their potential for assisting human scientists in solving problems. He correctly points out that these successes are based on the existence of "strong theories" about their subject matter.

Lederberg

AM, like anything else in this world, is constrained by a mass of assumptions. Most of these are "compiled" or interwoven into the very fabric of AM, hence can't be tested by experiments on AM. Some of these were just discussed a few pages ago, in Section 7–2.4.

Another body of assumptions exists. AM is built around a particular model of how mathematicians actually go about doing their research. This model was derived from introspection, but can be supported by quotes from Pólya, Kershner, Hadamard, Saaty, Skemp, and many others. No attempt will be made to justify any of these premises. Here is a simplified summary of that information processing model for math theory formation:

MODEL OF MATH RESEARCH

1   The order in which a math textbook presents a theory is almost the exact opposite of the order in which it was actually discovered and developed. In a text, new definitions are stated with little or no motivation, and they turn out to be

---

[32] See the quote at the front of the next subsection. It is from [Lederberg 76], a review of [Weizenbaum 76].

just the ones needed to state the next big theorem, whose proof then magically appears. In contrast, a mathematician doing research will examine some already-known concepts, perhaps trying to find some regularity in experimental data involving them. The patterns the mathematician notices become the conjectures that must be investigated further, and these relationships directly motivate the defining of new terms.

    2   Each step the researcher takes while developing a new theory involves choosing from a large set of "legal" alternatives—that is, searching. The key to keeping this from becoming a blind, explosive search is the proper use of evaluation criteria. Each mathematician uses his or her own personal heuristics to choose the "best" alternative available at each moment—the one most plausible.

    3   Non-formal criteria (aesthetic interestingness, inductive inference from empirical evidence, analogy, and utility) are much more important than formal deductive methods in developing mathematically worthwhile theories, and in avoiding barren diversions.

    4   Progress in *any* field of mathematics demands much non-formal heuristic expertise in *many* different "nearby" mathematical fields. So a broad, universal core of knowledge must be mastered before any single theory can meaningfully be developed.

    5   It is sufficient (and pragmatically necessary) to have and use a large set of informal heuristic rules. These rules direct the researcher's next activities, depending on the current situation. These rules can be assumed to superimpose ideally: the combined effect of several rules is just the sum of the individual effects.

    6   The necessary heuristic rules are virtually the same in all branches of mathematics, and at all levels of sophistication. Each specialized field will have some of its own heuristics; those are normally much more powerful than the general-purpose heuristics.

    7   For true understanding, the researcher should grasp[33] each concept in several ways: declaratively, abstractly, operationally, knowing when it is relevant, and as a bunch of examples.

    8   Common metaphysical assumptions about nature and science: Nature is fair, uniform, and regular. Coincidences have meaning. Statistical considerations are valid when looking at mathematical data. Simplicity and symmetry and synergy are the rule, not the exception.

7–2.7   Ultimate Powers and Weaknesses

Consider now *any* system which is consistent with the preceding model of math research, and whose orientation is to discover and develop new (to the system) mathematical theories. This includes AM itself, but might also include a bright high-school senior who has been taught a large body of heuristic rules.

    What can such systems ultimately achieve? What are their ultimate limits? Answers to ultimate questions are hard to come by experimentally, so this discussion will be quite philosophical, speculative, and short. The model of math

---

[33] Have access to, relate to, store, be able to manipulate, be able to answer questions about...

research hinges around the use of heuristic rules for guidance at all levels of behavior. It is questionable whether or not all known mathematics could evolve smoothly in this way. As a first order fixup, we've mentioned the need to provide good meta-heuristics, to keep enlarging the set of heuristics. If this is not enough (if meta-meta-...-heuristics are needed), then the model is a poor one and has some inherent limitations.[34] If some discoveries can only be made non-rationally (by random chance, by Gestalt, etc.) then any such system would be incapable of finding those concepts.

Turning aside from math, what about systems whose design—as a computer program—is similar to AM?[35] Building such systems will be "fun," and perhaps will result in new discoveries in other fields. Eventually, scientists (at least in a few very hard domains) may relegate more and more of their "hack" research duties to AM-like systems. The ultimate limitations will be those arising from incorrect (*e.g.*, partial) models of the activities the system must perform. The systems themselves may help improve these models: experiments that are performed on the systems are actually tests of the underlying model; the results might cause revisions to be made in the model, then in the system, and the whole cycle would begin again.

7-3 CONCLUSIONS

Before quitting, let's summarize what's worth remembering about this research project.

- It is a demonstration that a few hundred general heuristic rules suffice to guide an automated math researcher as it explores and expands a large but incomplete knowledge base of math concepts. AM serves as a living existence proof that creative research can be effectively modelled as heuristic search.
- The book also introduces a control structure based upon an agenda of small research tasks, each with a list of supporting reasons attached.
- The main limitation of AM was its inability to synthesize powerful new heuristics for the new concepts it defined.
- The main successes were the few novel ideas it came up with, the ease with which a new task domain was fed to the system, and—most importantly—the overall rational sequences of behavior AM exhibited.
- The greatest long-range importance of AM may well lie in the body of heuristics assembled, either as the seed for a huge base of experts' heuristics, or as a new orientation for mathematics education.

---

[34] If Ptolemy had had access to a digital computer, all his data could have been made to fit (to any desired accuracy), just by computing epi-cycles, epi-epi-cycles,... to the needed number of epi's. We in AI must constantly be on guard against that error.

[35] Having an agenda of tasks with reasons and reason-ratings combining to form a global priority for each task, having units/modules/frames/Beings/Actors/scripts/concepts which have parts/slots/aspects/facets, etc. Heuristic rules are tacked onto relevant concepts, and are executed to produce new concepts, new tasks, new facet entries.

Concepts

1-1 LISP REPRESENTATION

Two of AM's initial concepts are presented in detail, "Compose" and "Osets" (composition of relations, and ordered sets). The entries in each of their facets are displayed: We provide (*i*) the LISP expressions which were actually stored there in the AM program, and (*ii*) an English, Lambda calculus, and math notation condensation of all the knowledge initially supplied to AM about that facet of that concept.

If there is any unmentioned facet for a concept, then it started out blank. Many of the facets of the original concepts were left blank *intentionally*, knowing that AM would be able to fill them in as well. After all, if you can fill in examples of any new concept, you ought to be able to fill in examples of Compositions!

1-1.1 The 'Compose' Concept

ENGN [1] (COMPOSE Compose Composition (Afterwards))
   Anglicised condensation:

   Name(s): Compose, Composition, sometimes: afterwards.

DEFN   (TYPE NEC&SUFF PC DECLARATIVE SLOW *(FOREACH X IN (DO-*

---

[1] This is short for "English name," and is the facet called "Name(s)" everywhere else in this book.

MAIN BA2) RETURN (APPLYB² BA1 ALGS (APPLYB BA2 ALGS X]

DEFN-SUFF [[TYPE SUFFICIENT NONRECURSIVE QUICK
(AND (ISA BA1 'ACTIVE)
(ISA BA2 'ACTIVE)
(ISA BA3 'ACTIVE)
(ARE-EQUIV BA3 (ALREADY-COMPOSED³ BA1 BA2]

[TYPE SUFFICIENT QUASIRECURSIVE SLOW
(ARE-EQUIV BA3
(APPLYB 'COMPOSE 'ALGS BA1 BA2]⁴

[TYPE SUFFICIENT QUASIRECURSIVE QUICK
(EQUAL BA3
(APPLYB 'COMPOSE 'ALGS BA1 BA2]]
Anglicised condensation:

> Definitions:
> Declarative slow: $\lambda\,(A,B,C)\;\forall\,x,\,C(x) = A(B(x))$
> Sufficient Nonrecursive Quick: $\lambda\,(A,B,C)C$ has the Name '$A \circ B$'.
> Sufficient, Slow: Are-equivalent(C,Compose.Algs(A,B)).
> Sufficient, Quick: C=Compose.Algs(A,B).

D-R [5]

((OPERATION ACTIVE OPERATION)
(RELATION RELATION RELATION)
(PREDICATE ACTIVE PREDICATE)
(ACTIVE ACTIVE ACTIVE))

DOMAIN-RANGE–FILLIN1
(PROGN (ARGS-ASA COMPOSE F1 F2) (CADAR (CON-MERGE-ARGS⁶ F1 F2)))

DOMAIN-RANGE–FILLIN1–EXS
[PROGN (ARGS-ASA COMPOSE F1 F2)
[SETQ RAN1 (LAST (ANY1OF (GETB F1 'D-R] (* RAN1 is the range of F1)
[SETQ DOM1 (ALL-BUT-LAST (ANY1OF (GETB F1 'D-R]
[SETQ RAN2 (LAST (ANY1OF (GETB F2 'D-R] (* RAN2 is the range of F2)
[SETQ DOM2 (ALL-BUT-LAST (ANY1OF (GETB F2 'D-R]
[SETQ X (MAXIMAL RAN2 DOM1 'FRAC-OVERLAP]
(NCONC1 (LSUBST DOM2 for X in DOM1) RAN1]

---

[2] The function "APPLYB" indicates that a concept's facet is to be accessed and then executed. (APPLYB C F x y...) means: access an entry on facet F of concept C, and then run it on the arguments x,y,...

[3] This LISP function checks to see whether the two operations have been composed before.

[4] The arguments to Compose.Defn (and to Compose.Algs as well) are called BA1, BA2,... Thus we would write each definition of Compose as "λ (BA1 BA2 BA3) ..."

[5] "D-R" is short for "Domain-Range."

[6] This is a LISP function, opaque to AM, which analyzes the Domain/range facets of the two operations F1 and F2, and sees how (if at all) the range of F1 can be made to overlap the domain of F2. Note that F2 is applied *after* F1.

Anglicised condensation:

> Domain/range:
>   <Active Active ⇒ Active>
>   <Operation Active ⇒ Operation>
>   <Predicate Active ⇒ Predicate>
>   <Relation Relation ⇒ Relation>
> Fillin: 2 *(out of a total of 9)* heuristics.
>   In Appendix 2, these are heuristics numbers 23 and 189.

ALGS ((TYPE QUASIRECURSIVE INDIRECT CASES
      [PROGN
        (COND
          ((NULL BA1)
            (APPLYB 'COMPOSE
              'ALGS
              (RAND-MEMB (EXS ACTIVE))
              BA2 BA3 BA4))[7]
      & [8]
          ((ALREADY-COMPOSED BA1 BA2)
            (* Note: this sets GTEMP12)
            GTEMP12)
          ((AND BA1 BA2 (IS-CON[9] *BA1)*
            (IS-CON BA2)
            (ISA BA1 'ACTIVE)
            (ISA BA2 'ACTIVE)
            (SETQ GTEMP11 (CON-MERGE-ARGS BA1 BA2 GTEMP12)))
          (* GTEMP12 is now the name of the new composition)
          (CREATEB[10] *GTEMP12)*
          [SETQ GUP1 (COND ((ISAG CS-B 'COMPOSE) CS-B) (T 'COMPOSE]
          (* GUP1 is now the KIND of concept which GTEMP12 is to be an example of. This
          will usually be "COMPOSE" or some variant of it.)
          [INCRB[11] *GTEMP12 'DEFN*
          (LIST TYPE 'APPLICATION 'OF GUP1
            (APPEND (LIST 'APPLYB (Q[12] *COMPOSE) (Q ALGS) (KWOTE BA1)*
                (KWOTE BA2))
              (FIRSTN (LENGTH (CAAR GTEMP11)) BA-LIST]
          (* Another way to fill in an entry for GTEMP12.Defn)
          (COND
            ([SETQ GTEMP308 (CAR (SOME (EXS COMPOSE)

---

[7] Note what this clause says: if Compose.Algs is ever called with its first argument missing, randomly select an Active to use as that constituent of the composition.

[8] Similar to last case: takes care of missing second argument. The ampersand, "&," indicates an omission from this listing.

[9] An abbreviation for (APPLYB 'ANY-CONCEPT 'DEFN BA1); *i.e.*, test whether BA1 is a bona fide concept or not.

[10] CREATEB is a function which sets up a new blank data structure for a new concept.

[11] The function call (INCRB C F X) means: add entry X to the F facet of concept C.

[12] The LISP function "Q" is like a double quote; after one evaluation (Q X) returns 'X; after one more evaluation, 'X returns X; after a final evaluation, we get the VALUE of X.

```
(FUNCTION (LAMBDA (C)
    (MEMBER (LASTELE (GETB GTEMP12 'DEFN))
        (GETB (LASTELE C) 'DEFN]
(FORGET-CONCEPT GTEMP12)
(CPRIN1S 8 GTEMP12 turned-out to be equivalent to GTEMP308 DCR)¹³
GTEMP308)
(T (INCRB GUP1 'EXS (NCONC1 (GEARGS GUP1) GTEMP12))
[SOME (RIPPLE GUP1 'GENL)
    (FUNCTION (LAMBDA (G)
        (SOME (GETB G 'D-R)
            (FUNCTION (LAMBDA (D)
                (AND (ISA BA1 (CAR D))
                (ISA BA2 (CADR D))
                (INCRB GTEMP12 'UP¹⁴ (CADDR D))
                (INCRB (CADDR D) 'EXS·GTEMP12]
(* This last INCRB says that if an operation f maps onto range C, and we apply
f and get a new Being, then that Being ISA C)¹⁵
    (INCRB GTEMP12 'IN-RAN-OF GUP1)
    (INCRB BA2 'IN-DOM-OF GUP1)
    (INCRB BA1 'IN-DOM-OF GUP1)
    (* Now see if the composition GTEMP12 shares any ISA's entries with either
constituent operation: BA1 or BA2)¹⁶
[MAPC [INTERSECTION (SET-DIFF
            [UNION (GETB BA1 'UP) (GETB BA2 'UP]
            (GETB GTEMP12 'UP]
    (FUNCTION (LAMBDA (Z)
        (COND
            ((DEFN Z GTEMP12)
            (INCRB Z 'EXS GTEMP12)
            (INCRB GTEMP12 'UP Z]
    (COND
        [(GETB GTEMP12 'UP)
        (SETB GTEMP12 'GUP (COPY (GETB GTEMP12 'UP]
        (T (INCRB GTEMP12 'UP 'OPERATION)
        (INCRB 'OPERATION 'EXS GTEMP12)))
    & (* A similar search now for GENL/SPEC of the composition)
    (SETB GTEMP12 'D-R (CAR GTEMP11))
    (INCRB GTEMP12 'ALGS
        (LIST TYPE 'NONRECURSIVE 'APPLICATION 'OF GUP1 (CADR GTEMP11)))
    & (* Code for synthesizing a Defn entry for GTEMP12)
    (SETB GTEMP12 'WORTH
    (MAP2CAR (GETB BA1 'WORTH) (GETB BA2 'WORTH)
```

¹³ A conditional print statement. If the verbosity level is high enough (>8), this message is typed out to the user.

¹⁴ The ISA's facet is called "UP" in the LISP program.

¹⁵ This is a streamlined, specialized version of the more general heuristic rule number 180.

¹⁶ This next MAPC is thus the LISP encoding of heuristic rule number 101.

```
                TIMES1000))
            (GS-CHECK¹⁷ GTEMP12]]))]
```

Anglicised condensation:

> Algorithms:
>> Distributed: use the heuristics attached to Compose to guide
>> the filling in of various facets of the new composition.
>> (The heuristics referred to are shown in Appendix 2.21.)
>> Fillin: 5 *(out of a total of 9)* heuristics.
>> Check: 1 heuristic *(out of a total of 2).*

UP   (OPERATION)

Anglicised condensation:

> Isa's: Operation

WORTH   (300)

Anglicised condensation:

> Worth: 300

INT¹⁸

```
    [(IMATRIX (1 2 3) (4 5))
    (COND [(INTERSECTION (MAPAPPEND (GETB BA2 D-R) 'LAST)
               (MAPAPPEND (GETB BA1 D-R) 'ALL-BUT-LAST))
       300
       (IDIFF 400 (ITIMES 100 (IPLUS (LENGTH (GETB BA1 D-R))
               (LENGTH (GETB BA2 D-R]
       (REASON (* Range-of-op2 is 1 component of Domain-of-op1)))
    (COND [[MEMB [CAR (LAST (CAR (GETB BA2 D-R]
           (ALL-BUT-LAST (CAR (GETB BA1 D-R]
       400
       (IDIFF 1000 (ITIMES 100 (LENGTH (CAR (GETB BA1 D-R]
       (REASON (* In canonical interpretation, Range-of-op2 is a component of Domain of
       op1)))
    (COND [(INTERSECTION (GETB CS-B TIES)
           (UNION (GETB BA1 TIES)(GETB BA2 TIES)))
       100
       (ITIMES 100 [LENGTH (INTERSECTION (GETB CS-B TIES)
               (UNION (GETB BA1 TIES)(GETB BA2 TIES)])
       (REASON (* This composition preserves some good properties of its constituents))])
    (COND [(SET-DIFFERENCE (GETB CS-B TIES)
           (UNION (GETB BA1 TIES)(GETB BA2 TIES)))
       100
       (ITIMES 100 [LENGTH (SET-DIFFERENCE (GETB CS-B TIES)
```

---

¹⁷ This is a general-purpose·function for testing that there is no hidden cycle in the Generalization network, that no two concepts are both generalizations and specializations of each other, unless they are tagged as being equivalent to each other.

¹⁸ Note that although the Fillin and Suggest heuristics are blended into the relevant facets (*e.g.*, into the Algorithms for COMPOSE), the INTERESTINGNESS type heuristics are kept separate, in this facet ("INT").

```
            (UNION (GETB BA1 TIES)(GETB BA2 TIES])
      (REASON (* This composition has some new props, not true of either constituent))])
  (COND [(OR (GREATERP (GETB BA1 WORTH) 500))
        (GREATERP (GETB BA2 WORTH) 500)))
      300
      (IQUOTIENT (ITIMES (GETB BA1 WORTH)(GETB BA2 WORTH))
        1000)
      (REASON (* Op1 and/or Op2 are very interesting themselves))])
  (COND [[IS-ONE-OF [CAR (LAST (CAR (GETB BA2 D-R]
        (ALL-BUT-LAST (CAR (GETB BA1 D-R]
      350
      (IDIFF [ITIMES 100 (IDIFF
        [LENGTH (CAR (GETB BA1 D-R]
        (LENGTH (RIPPLE [IS-ONE-OF
                [SETQ TMP4 (CAR (LAST (GETB BA2 D-R]
                (ALL-BUT-LAST (CAR (GETB BA1 D-R]
            'GENL]
        (ITIMES 50 (LENGTH (RIPPLE TMP4 'GENL]
      (REASON (* In canonical interpretation, Range-of-op2 is a specialization of a component
        of Domain-of-op1)))
  (COND [[MEMB [CAR (LAST (CAR (GETB BA1 D-R]
        (ALL-BUT-LAST (CAR (GETB BA2 D-R]
      450
      (IPLUS 300 (COND ([MEMB [CAR (LAST (CAR (GETB BA1 D-R]
            (ALL-BUT-LAST (CAR (GETB BA1 D-R]
          10)
          (T 250))
        (COND ([MEMB [CAR (LAST (CAR (GETB BA2 D-R]
            (ALL-BUT-LAST (CAR (GETB BA2 D-R]
          11)
          (T 250))
        (ITIMES 70 (LENGTH (RIPPLE [CAR (LAST (CAR (GETB BA1 D-R] 'GENL]
      (REASON (* In canonical interpretation,
        Range-of-op1 is one component of Domain-of-op2))
&
  (COND [[ISA [CAR (LAST (CAR (GETB BA1 D-R]
        (ALL-BUT-LAST (CAR (GETB BA2 D-R]
      250
      (IPLUS 50 (COND ([ISA [CAR (LAST (CAR (GETB BA1 D-R]
            (ALL-BUT-LAST (CAR (GETB BA1 D-R]
          10)
          (T 100))
        (COND ([ISA [CAR (LAST (CAR (GETB BA2 D-R]
            (ALL-BUT-LAST (CAR (GETB BA2 D-R]
          11)
          (T 100))
        (ITIMES 50 (LENGTH (RIPPLE [CAR (LAST (CAR (GETB BA1 D-R] 'GENL]
      (REASON (* Range-of-op1 is a specialization of a component of Domain-of-op2]
```

Anglicised condensation:

> Interest: 11 heuristics.
> (Shown in English in Appendix 2.25)

1–1.2 The 'Osets' Concept

Here is the actual property list of the data-structure corresponding to the Osets concept, at the time AM is started:

ENGN (OSET Oset Oset-structure OSET-STRUC, Ordered-set (Set))

DEFN (TYPE NEC&SUFF RECURSIVE TRANSPARENT
    [COND
      ((EQUAL BA1 (OSET)) T)
      (T (APPLYB 'OSET 'DEFN (APPLYB 'OSET-DELETE 'ALGS
           (APPLYB 'SOME-MEMB 'ALGS BA1)
           BA1])
    (TYPE NEC&SUFF RECURSIVE QUICK
    [COND
      ((EQUAL BA1 '(OSET)) T)
      ((CDDR BA1) (APPLYB 'OSET 'DEFN (RPLACD BA1 (CDDR BA1)))
      (T NIL])
    (TYPE NEC&SUFF NONRECURSIVE QUICK
    (MATCH BA1 WITH ('OSET ←← ANY)))

GENL (ORD-STRUC NO-MULT-ELES-STRUC)

WORTH (400)

IN-DOM-OF (OSET-JOIN OSET-INTERSECT OSET-DIFF OSET-INSERT OSET-DELETE)

IN-RAN-OF (OSET-JOIN OSET-INTERSECT OSET-DIFF OSET-INSERT OSET-DELETE)

VIEW (STRUCTURE (RPLACA BA1 'OSET))

Compare this with the following Anglicised condensation:

> Name(s): Oset, Oset-structure, Ordered-set, sometimes: Set.
> Definitions:
>   Recursive: λ (S) (S=[ ] or
>   Oset.Definition(Oset-Delete.Alg(Member.Alg(S),S)))
>   Recursive quick: λ (S) (S=[ ] or Oset.Definition (CDR(S)))
>   Quick: λ (S) (Match S with [...])
>   Generalizations: Ordered-Struc., No-multiple-elements-Struc.
>   Worth: 400
>   In-domain-of: Oset-union, Oset-intersect, Oset-difference,
>   Oset-insert, Oset-delete
>   In-range-of: Oset-union, Oset-intersect, Oset-difference,
>   Oset-insert, Oset-delete
>   View: To view any structure as a Oset, do:
>   λ (x) Enclose-in-square-brackets(x)

1–2   CONCEPTS CREATED BY AM

The list below is not meant as an exhaustive catalogue, but rather merely to suggest the breadth of AM's syntheses. The concepts are listed in the order in which they were defined (see Section 6–2.3). In place of the (usually-awkward) name chosen by AM, I have given either the standard math/English name for the concept, or else a short description of what it is.

Sets with less than 2 elements (singletons and empty sets).
Sets with no atomic elements (nests of braces).
Singleton sets.
Bags containing (multiple occurrences of) just one kind of element.
Superset (contains).
Doubleton bags and sets.
Set-membership.
Disjoint bags.
Subset.
Disjoint sets.
Singleton osets.
Same-length (same number of elements).
Same number of left parentheses, plus identical leftmost atoms.
Count (find the number of elements of a given structure).
Numbers (unary representation).
Add.
Minimum.
SUB1 (λ (x) x-1).
Insert x into a given Bag-of-T's (almost ADD1, but not quite).
Subtract (except: if x<y, then the result of x-y will be zero[19]).
Less than or equal to.
Times.
Union of a *bag* of structures.
& (the ampersand represents the creation of several real losers.)
Compose a given operation Ḟ with itself (form F∘F).
Insert structure S into itself.
Try to delete structure S from itself (a loser).
Double (add 'x' to itself).
Subtract 'x' from itself (as an operation, this is a real zero[20]).
Square (TIMES(x,x)).
Union structure S with itself.
Coalesced-replace2: replace each element s of S by F(s,s).
Coalesced-join2: append together F(s,s), for each member s∈ S.
Coa-repeat2: create a new op which takes a structure S, an operation F, and
      repeats F(s,t,S) all along S.
Compose three operations: λ(F,G,H) F∘(G∘H).
Compose three operations: λ(F,G,H) (F∘G)∘H.
& (lots of losing compositions created, *e.g.*, Self-insert∘Set-union.)

---

[19] This is "natural-number subtract," in the same spirit of naming as we find for "Integer division."

[20] A Natural zero?

ADD^{-1}(x): all ways of representing x as the sum of positive numbers.

$\{G \circ H \mid H(G(H(x)))$ is always defined (wherever H is), and G and H are interesting$\}$.

Insert$\circ$Delete.

Delete$\circ$Insert.

Size$\circ$ADD^{-1}. (λ (n) The number of ways to partition n)

Cubing

&

Exponentiation.

Halving (in natual numbers only; thus Halving(15)=7).

Even numbers.

Integer square-root.

Perfect squares.

Divisors-of.

Numbers-with-0-divisors.

Numbers-with-$\ominus$1-divisor.

Primes (Numbers-with-2-divisors).

Squares of primes (Numbers-with-3-divisors).

Squares of squares of primes.

Square-roots of primes (a loser).

TIMES^{-1}(x): all ways of representing x as the product of a bunch of numbers (>1).

All ways of representing x as the product of just one number (a trivial notion).

All ways of representing x as the product of primes.

All ways of representing x as the sum of primes.

All ways of representing x as the sum of two primes.

Numbers uniquely representable as the sum of two primes.

Products of squares.

Multiplication by 1.

Multiplication by 0.

Multiplication by 2.

Addition of 0.

Addition of 1.

Addition of 2.

Product of even numbers.

Sum of squares.

Sum of even numbers.

& (losers: various compositions of 3 operations.)

Pairs of perfect squares whose sum is also a perfect square ($x^2 + y^2 = z^2$).

Prime pairs (p, p+2 are prime).

$\vdots$

1–3   MAXIMALLY-DIVISIBLE NUMBERS

I then adopt a different point of view [from Dirichlet, Wigert, and other mathematicians who have studied d(n)]. I define a highly composite number as a number whose number of divisors exceeds that of all its predecessors.

Ramanujan

This part of the "Concepts" appendix discusses a discovery motivated by AM: a new little bit of mathematics.

Just as AM defined and studied "primeness" (natural numbers having as few divisors as possible), it also defined and studied the converse kind of numbers: those which possess an abnormally *large* number of divisors. The AM program made the following definition of what we shall call the set M of maximally-divisible numbers:

$$M = \{x \in \mathcal{N}^+ \mid (\forall\, y < x)\; (d(y) < d(x))\}$$

where $d(n)$ is the number of divisors of n,[21] $\mathcal{N}^+$ is the set of positive integers, and the vertical bar "|" is read "such that."

In words, this says that M is the set of all positive integers satisfying the property that every smaller number has fewer divisors. That is, we throw into the set M a number x if (and only if) it has more divisors than any smaller number. So 1 gets thrown in (the smallest number with 1 divisor), 2 (having 2 divisors), 4 (3 divisors, namely 1, 2, and 4), 6 (4 divisors), 12 (6 divisors), etc. Another way to specify M is as the set containing (for all n) the smallest number having at least n divisors.[22]

One of the questions at the heart of our study is "Given d, what is the smallest number with at least d divisors?"

How can we even start on this question? The most powerful tool we have is the following combinatorially-proved theorem:

If we write n as $2^{a_1} 3^{a_2} 5^{a_3} \cdots p_k^{a_k}$, Then

$$d(n) = (a_1 + 1) \cdot (a_2 + 1) \cdots (a_k + 1). \qquad (T1)$$

Our central question could be answered if we could somehow invert this formula into one which expressed n as a function of d, and then found the minima of that function $n(d)$. Coupled with the knowledge that each number can be factored uniquely into prime factors, T1 provides a closed-form way of manipulating $d(n)$. That is, n is really a function of the sequence of exponents when written as $2^{a_1} 3^{a_2} \cdots$, so we can consider $n = n(a_1, a_2, \ldots)$. Then T1 is really a way of expressing $d(n) = d(a_1, a_2, \ldots)$.

After AM collected a fair amount of empirical data, some relationships were conjectured. The following one was proven by Knuth, using the technique of Lagrange multipliers:

If the a_i were *real* numbers, then the minimal value of n (for a given value of d) will occur whenever

$$(\forall\, i, j = 1, 2, \ldots k)\; \frac{(a_i + 1)}{(a_j + 1)} = \frac{\log(p_j)}{\log(p_i)}. \qquad (T2)$$

This is really a set of $k - 1$ equations in the k different variables $a_1, \ldots, a_k$. Using (as our k^{th} equation) the formula for d which T1 provides, we can solve this system of equations for each a_i in terms only of d. The resulting formulae are:

$$(\forall\, i \leq k)\; a_i + 1 = \frac{\left(d \cdot \log(2) \cdot \log(3) \cdots \log(p_k)\right)^{1/k}}{\log(p_i)} \qquad (T3)$$

---

[21] For example, $d(12) = \|\{1, 2, 3, 4, 6, 12\}\| = 6$.

[22] Notice that we are *not* going to include "the smallest number with *precisely* 5 divisors," since this number (which happens to be 2^4 or 16) is bigger than 12 (which has 6 divisors). So no number in M has precisely five divisors.

For example: consider $d = 1344$. The largest that k can be without T3 calling for $a_k < 0.5$ is $k = 7$. For this d and k, T3 predicts exponents 5.9, 3.3, 2.0, 1.4, 1.0, 0.9, and 0.7. Rounding this off, we get 6, 3, 2, 1, 1, 1, 1. Next we compute $2^6 3^3 5^2 7^1 11^1 13^1 17^1$. This is 735,134,400. T1 tells us that this has in fact precisely 1344 divisors. Exhaustive search tells us that no smaller n has that many divisors. Incidentally, the ideal value for n (using real exponents a_i) is 603,696,064. Notice that it is close to, and less than, the smallest integer having at least 1344 divisors.

$n = 2^8 3^5 5^3 7^2 11^2 13^1 17^1 19^1 23^1 29^1 31^1 37^1 41^1 43^1 47^1 53^1$ is another such "rounded-exponent" number. The progression of its exponents+1 (9 6 4 3 3 2 2 2 2 2 2 2 2 2 2 2) is about as close as one can get to satisfying the "logarithm" constraint. By that I mean that 9/6 is close to $\log(3)/\log(2)$; that 2/2 is close to $\log(47)/\log(43)$, etc. Changing any exponent by plus or minus 1 would make those ratios worse than they are. This number n is about 25 billion, and has about 4 million divisors. The AM conjecture is that there is no smaller number with that many divisors. Incidentally, the average number in the neighborhood of n has about $2^{\log \log n}$ divisors (about 9 divisors, for numbers near 25 billion).

Very recently, the author was directed to the work of Srinivasa Ramanujan Aiyangar. This Indian mathematician was essentially self-taught. Receiving little formal education, he had almost no contact with Western number theory. Yet he became interested in number theoretic issues, and re-derived much of that field all by himself. In that way, he is perhaps the closest human analogue to AM: he had ability, techniques, background knowledge, and he was left to explore and redevelop much elementary mathematics on his own. Let me quote from G. H. Hardy's final[23] sketch of this genius:

> The limitations of his knowledge were as startling as its profundity... Here was a man who...had found the dominant terms of many of the most famous problems in the analytic theory of numbers, and yet...his ideas of mathematical proof were of the most shadowy description. All his results, new or old, right or wrong, had been arrived at by...intuition and induction from numerical examples.

It was exciting to learn that Ramanujan had also defined the very same set M, which he called *highly-composite* numbers. His great interest in them has been almost unique[24] within mathematics circles—until AM was led to consider them. In an article published in 1915, Ramanujan derives the relationship: $a_i \cdot \log(p_i) = constant$, which he says holds approximately, for values of i which are much smaller than k. He establishes this using inequalities (and using the distribution of prime numbers $\pi(x)$). Thus it has a different flavor from the similar relationship (T2) derived using calculus. Also, Ramanujan at this point went off on quite a different path from AM: he defined a specialization of this concept, which he called "*superior highly-composite numbers*," and investigated them in detail. Neither AM nor the author had the sophistication to make that definition and to find the results which Ramanujan subsequently uncovered about superior highly-composite numbers.

---

[23] Taken from Ramanujan's obituary notice, 1921. Found in the preface to [Ramanujan 27].

[24] Recently, Paul Erdos has been studying these highly-composite numbers.

Heuristics

Infallible rules of discovery leading to the solution of all possible mathematical problems would be more desirable than the philosophers' stone, vainly sought by the alchemists. Such rules would work magic; but there is no such thing as magic. To find unfailing rules applicable to all sorts of problems is an old philosophical dream; but this dream will never be more than a dream.

Pólya

To the extent that a professor of music at a conservatoire can assist his students in becoming familiar with the patterns of harmony and rhythm, and with how they combine, it must be possible to assist students in becoming sensitive to patterns of reasoning and how they combine. The analogy is not far-fetched at all.

Dijkstra

This appendix lists all the heuristics with which AM is initially provided. They are organized by concept, most general concepts first. Within a concept, they are organized into four groups:

- Fillin: rules for filling in new entries on various facets.
- Check: rules for patching up existing entries on various facets.
- Suggest: rules which propose new tasks to break AM out of stagnant loops.
- Interest: criteria for estimating the interestingness of various entities.

Each heuristic is presented in English translation. Whenever there is a very tricky, non-obvious, or brilliant translation of some English clause into LISP, a brief note will follow about how that is coded. Also given (usually) are some example(s) of its use, and its overall importance. Concepts which have no heuristics are not present in this appendix.

All the heuristics in this appendix were used by AM; in addition, many heuristics were planned on paper but never coded (*e.g.*, those dealing with proof techniques, those dealing with the drives and rewards of generalized message senders/receivers), and whole classes of rules were coded but never used by AM during any of its runs (*e.g.*, how to deal with contradictions, how to deal with Intu's facets). Such superfluous rules will not be included here. They would raise the total number of heuristic rules from 242 to about 500.

The rule numbering in this appendix is referred to occasionally elsewhere. The total number of rules coded in AM is actually higher, since many rules are present but never used, and since many rules listed with one number here are really *several* rules in LISP (*e.g.*, see rules 35 and 188).

1. *If entity X is an example of concept C, and X satisfies some features on C.Int,*
Then X is interesting, and C's Interestingness features will indicate a numeric rating for X.

This is practically the *definiton* of the Int facet. Below is a much more unusual rule:

2. *If entity X is an example of concept C, and X satisfies absolutely none of the features on C.Int, and X is just about the only C which doesn't satisfy something,*
Then X is interesting because of its unusual boringness.

Since most singletons are interesting because all pairs of their elements are Equal, the above rule says it would be interesting actually to find a singleton for which not all pairs of its members were equal. While it would be interesting, AM has very little chance of finding such a critter.

2–1   HEURISTICS DEALING WITH ANY-CONCEPT

This concept has a huge number of heuristics. For that reason, I have partitioned off—both here and in AM itself[1] —the heuristics which apply to each kind of facet.

2–1.1   Heuristics for Any Facet of Any-Concept

The first set of heuristics we'll look at is very general, applying to no particular facet exclusively.

Any-concept . Fillin

3. *When trying to fill in facet F of concept C, for any C and F,*
If C is analogous to concept X, and X.F has some entries,
Then try to construct the analogs of those entries, and see if they are really valid entries for C.F.

---

[1] Thus the LISP program has a separate concept called "Examples-of-any-concept," another concept called "Definitions-of-any-concept," etc.

Recall that "C.F" is shorthand for "facet F of concept C." This rule simply says that if an analogy exists between two concepts C and X, then it may be strong enough to map entries on X.F into entries for C.F. Note that F can be any given facet. There is an analogy between Sets and Bags, and AM uses the above rule to turn the extreme example of Sets—the empty set—into the extreme kind of bag.

Any-concept . Suggest

4. If the F facet of concept X is blank,
Then consider trying to fill it in.

The above ultra-weak rule will result in a new task being added to the agenda, for every blank facet of every concept. It is more of a legal move generator than a plausible move proposer. The rating of each such task will depend on the Worth of the concept X and the overall worth of the type F facet, but in all cases will be *very small*. The "emptiness" of a facet is always a valid reason for trying to fill it in, but never an *a priori* important reason. So the net effect of the rule is to slightly bias AM toward working on blank—rather than non-blank—facets.

5. While trying to fill in facet F of concept C, for any C and F, if C is known to be similar to some other concept D, except for difference d,
Then try to fill in C.F by selecting items from D.F for which d is nonexistent.

This rule is made more specific when F is actually known, and hence the format of d is actually determined. For example, if C=Reverse-at-all-levels, F=examples, then (at one particular moment) a note is found on the Conjecs facet of concept C which says that C is just like the concept D=Reverse-top-level, except C also recurs on the nonatomic elements of its arguments, whereas D doesn't. Thus d is made null by choosing examples of D for which there are no nonatomic elements. So an example like "Reverse-top-level($<$a b c$>$)=$<$c b a$>$" will be selected and will lead to the proposed example "Reverse-at-all-levels($<$a b c$>$)=$<$c b a$>$", which is in fact valid.

6. After dealing with concept C,
Slightly, temporarily boost the priority value of each existing task which involves an Active concept whose domain or range is C.

This is done efficiently using the In-dom-of and In-ran-of facets of C. A typical usage was after checking the just-filled-in examples of Bags, when AM slightly boosted the rating of filling in examples of Bag-union, and this task just barely squeaked through as the next one to be chosen. Note that the rule reinforced that task twice, since both domain and range of Bag-union are bags.

Any-concept . Check

7. When checking facet F of concept C, (for any F and C,)
Prune away at the entries there until the facet's size is reduced to the size which C merits.

The algorithm for doing this is as follows: The Worth of C is multiplied by the overall worth of facet type F. This is normalized in two ways, yielding the maximum amount of list cells that C.F may occupy, and also yielding the maximum number of separate entries to keep around on C.F. If either limit is being exceeded, then an entry is plucked at random (but weighted to favor selection from the rear of the facet) and excised. This repeats as long as C.F is oversized. As space grows tight, the normalization weights decline, so each concept's allocation is reduced.

8. *When checking facet F of concept C,*
Eliminate redundant entries.

Although it might conceivably mean something for an entry to occur twice, this was never desirable for the set of facets which each AM concept possessed.

Any-concept . Interest

The interest features apply to tell how interesting a concept is, and are rarely subdivided by relevant facet. That is, most of the reasons that Any concept might be interesting will be given below.

9. *A concept X is interesting if X.Conjecs contains some interesting entries.*

10. *A concept is interesting if its boundary accidentally coincides with another, well-known, interesting concept.*

The boundary of a concept means the items which just barely fall into (or just barely miss satisfying) the definition of that concept. Thus the boundary of Primes might include 1,2,3,4. If the boundary of Even numbers includes numbers differing by at most 1 from an even number, then clearly their boundary is *all* numbers. Thus it coincides with the already-known concept Numbers, and this makes Even-nos more interesting. This expresses the property we intuitively understand as: no number is very far from an even number.

11. *A concept is interesting if its boundary accidentally coincides with the boundary of another, very different, interesting concept.*

Thus, for example, Primes and Numbers are both a little more interesting since the extreme cases of numbers are all boundary cases of primes. Even numbers and Odd numbers both have the same boundary, namely Numbers. This is a tie between them, and slightly raises AM's interest in both concepts.

12. *A concept is interesting if it is—accidentally—precisely the boundary of some other, interesting concept.*

In the case mentioned for the above rule, Numbers is raised in interest because it turns out to be the boundary for even and odd numbers.

13. *A concept is boring if, after several attempts, only a couple examples are found.*

Another rule indicates, in such situations, that the concept may be forgotten and replaced by some conjecture.

14. *Concept C is interesting if some normally-inefficient operation F can be efficiently performed on C's.*

Thus it is very fast to perform Insert of items into lists because (*i*) no pre-existence checking need be done (as with sets and osets), and (*ii*) no ordered merging need be done (as with bags). So "Lists" is an interesting concept for that reason, according to the above rule.

15. *Concept C is interesting if each example of C accidentally seems to satisfy the otherwise-rarely satisfied predicate P, or (equivalently) if there is an unusual conjecture involving C.*

This is almost a primitive affirmation of interestingness.

16. *Concept C is interesting if C is closely related to the very interesting concept X.*

This is interestingness by association. AM was interested in Divisors-of because it was closely related to TIMES, which had proven to be a very interesting concept.

17. *Concept C is interesting if there is an analogy in which C corresponds to Y, and the analogs of the Interest features of Y indicate that C is interesting.*

This might have been a very useful rule, if only there had been more decent analogies floating around the system. As it was, the rule was rarely used to advantage. It essentially says that the analogs of Interest criteria are themselves (probably) valid criteria.

18. *A concept C is interesting if one of its generalizations or specializations turns out to be unexpectedly very interesting.*

"Unexpected" means that the interesting property hadn't already been observed for C. If C is interesting in some way, and then one of its generalizations is seen to be interesting in exactly the same way, then that is "expected." It's almost more interesting if the second concept unexpectedly *lacks* some fundamental property about C. At least in that case AM might learn something about what gives C that property. In fact, AM has this rule:

19. *If concept C possesses some very interesting property lacked by one of its specializations S,*
Then both C and S become slightly more interesting.

In the LISP program, this is closely linked with rule 18.

20. *If a concept C is rederived in a new way, that makes it more interesting.*
If concepts C1 and C2 turn out to be equivalent concepts, then merge them. The combined concept is now more interesting than either of its predecessors.

The two conditionals above are really the same rule, so they aren't given separate numbers. C1 and C2 might be conjectured equivalent because their examples coincide, each is a generalization of the other, their definitions can be formally shown to be equivalent, etc. This rule is similar in spirit to rule number 101.

2–1.2 Heuristics for the Examples Facets of Any-concept

The following heuristics are used for dealing with the many kinds of examples facets which a concept can possess: non-examples, boundary examples, Isa links, etc.

```
Any-concept . Examples . Fillin
```

21. *To fill in examples of X, where X is a kind of Y (for some more general concept Y),*
Inspect the examples of Y; some of them may be examples of X as well.
The further removed Y is from X, the less cost-effective this rule is.

For the task of filling in Empty-structures, AM knows that concept is a specialization of Structures, so it looks over all the then-known examples of Structures. Sure enough, a few of them are empty (satisfy Empty-structures.Defn). Similarly, for the task of filling in examples of Primes, this rule would have AM notice that Primes is a kind of Number, and therefore look over all the known examples of Number. It would not be cost-effective to look for primes by testing each example of Anything, and the third and final clause in the above rule recognizes that fact.

22. To fill in non-examples of concept X,
Search the specializations of X. Look at all their non-examples. Some of them may turn out to be non-examples of X as well.

This rule is the counterpart of the last one, but for non-examples. As expected, this was less useful than the preceding positive rule.

23. If the current task is to fill in examples of any concept X,
Then one way to get them is to symbolically instantiate a definition of X.

That rule simply says to use some known tricks, some hacks, to wring examples from a declarative definition. One trick AM knows about is to plug already-known examples of X into the recursive step of a definition. Another trick is simply to try to instantiate the base step of a recursive definition. Another trick is to take a definition of the form "λ (x) x isa P, and *sub-expression*>," work on instantiating just the *sub-expression*, and then pop back up and see which of those items are P's.

24. If the current task is to fill in non-examples of concept X,
Then one fast way to get them is to pick any random item, any example of Anything, and check that it fails X.Defn.

This is an affirmation that for any concept X, most things in the universe will probably not be X's. This rule was almost never used to good advantage: non-examples of a concept X were never sought unless there was some reason to expect that they might not exist. In those cases, the presumption of the above rule was wrong, and it failed. That is, the rule succeeded iff it was not needed.[2]

25. To fill in examples of concept X,
If X.View tells how to view a Z as if it were an X, and some examples of Z are known,
Then just run X.View on those examples, and check that the results really are X's.

Thus examples of osets were found by viewing other known examples of structures (*e.g.*, examples of sets) as if they were osets.

26. To fill in examples of concept X,
Find an operation whose range is X,[3] and find examples of that operation being applied.

To fill in examples of Even-nos, this rule might have AM notice the operation 'Double'. Any example of Double will contain an example of an even number as its value: *e.g.*, $<3{\Rightarrow}6>$ contains the even number 6.

27. If the current task is to fill in examples of concept X,
One bizarre way is to specialize X, adding a strong constraint to X.Defn, and then look for examples of that new specialization.

Like the classical "insane heuristic,"[4] this sounds crazy but works embarrassingly often. If I ask you to find numbers having a prime number of divisors, the rate at which you find them will probably be lower than if I'd asked you to find numbers with precisely 2 divisors. The *variety* of examples will suffer, of course. The converse of this heuristic—for non-examples—was deemed too unaesthetic to feed to AM.

---

[2] Catch-22?

[3] Or at least *intersects* X. Use the In-ran-of facets and the rippling mechanism to find such an operation.

[4] A harder task might be easier to do. A stronger theorem might be easier to prove. This is called "The Inventor's Paradox," on page 121 of [Pólya 57].

28. *To fill in examples of X,*
One inefficient method is to examine random examples of Anything, checking each by running X.Defn to see if it is an X. Slightly better is to ripple outward from X in all directions, testing all the examples of the concepts encountered.

This is blind generate-and-test, and was (luckily) not needed much by AM.

29. *To find more examples of X (or: to find an extreme example of X), when a nice big example is known, and X has a recursive definition,*
Try to plug the known example into the definition and produce a simpler one. Repeat this until an example is produced which satisfies the base-step predicate of the definition. That entity is then an extreme (boundary) example of X.

For example, AM had a definition of a set as
"Set.Defn $=_{df}$ λ (S) S=={} or Set.Defn(Remove-random-element(S))." When AM found the big example $\{A, B, \{\{C\}, D\}, \{\{\{E\}\}\}, F\}$ by some other means, it used the above rule and the recursive definition to turn this into $\{A, B, \{\{\{E\}\}\}, F\}$ by removing the randomly-chosen third element. $\{A, B, F\}$ was produced next, followed by $\{B, F\}$ and $\{F\}$. After that, $\{\}$ was produced and the rule relinquished control.

30. *To find examples of X, when X has a recursive definition,*
One method with low success rate but high payoff is to try to invert that definition, thereby creating a procedure for generating new examples.

Using the previous example, AM was able to turn the recursive definition of a set into the program "Insert-any-random-item(S)," which turns any set into a (usually different and larger) new set. Since the rules which AM uses to do these transformations are very special-purpose, they are not worth detailing here. This is one very manageable open problem, where someone might spend some months and create a decent body of definition-inversion rules. A typical rule AM has says:

"Any phrase matching *'Removing an x and ensuring that P(x)'* can be inverted and turned into this one: *'Finding any random x for which P(x) holds, then inserting x'.*"

The class of definitions which can be inverted using AM's existing rules is quite small; whenever AM needed to be able to invert another particular definition, the author simply supplied whatever rules would be required.

31. *While filling in examples of C,*
if two constructs x and y are found which are very similar yet only one of which is an example of the concept C,
Then one is a boundary example of C, and the other is a boundary non-example,
and it's worth creating more boundary examples and boundary non-examples by slowly transforming x and y into each other.

Thus when AM notices that $\{a\}$ and $\{a, b, a\}$ are similar yet not both sets, it creates $\{a, b\}$, $\{b, a\}$, $\{a, a\}$ and sees which are and are not examples of sets. In this way, some boundary items (both examples and non-examples) are created. The rules for this slow transformation are again special purpose. They examine the difference between the items x and y, and suggest operators (*e.g.*, Deletion) which will reduce that difference. This GPS-like strategy has been well studied by others, and its inferior implementation inside AM will not be detailed.

32. *If the main task now is to fill in examples of concept C,*
Consider all the examples of "first cousins" of C. Some of them might be examples of
C as well.

By "first cousins," we mean all direct specializations of all direct generalizations of a concept, or vice versa. That is, going up once along a Genl link, and then down once along a Spec link (or going down one link and then up one link).

33. *If the main task now is to fill in boundary (non-)examples of concept C,*
Consider all the boundary (non-)examples of "first cousins" of C. Some of them might
lie on the boundary of C as well.

If they turn out not to be boundary examples, they can be recorded as boundary non-examples, and vice versa.

34. *To fill in Isa's links of concept X, (that is, to find a list of concepts of which X is*
an example),
Just ripple down the tree of concepts, applying a definition of each concept. Whenever
a definition fails, don't waste time trying any of its specializations. The Isa's of X are
then all the concepts tried whose definitions passed X.

When a new concept is created, *e.g.*, a new composition, this rule can ascertain the most specific Isa links that can be attached to it. Another use for this rule would be: If the Isa link network ever got fouled up (contained paradoxes), this rule could be used to straighten everything out (with a logarithmic expenditure of time).

Any-concept . Examples . Suggest

35. *If some (but not most) examples of X are also examples of Y (for some concept Y),*
and some (but not most) examples of Y are also examples of X,
Then create a new concept defined as the intersection of those two concepts ($X \cap Y$).
This will be a specialization of both concepts.

If you happen to notice that some primes are palindromic, this rule would suggest creating a brand new concept, defined as the set of numbers which are both palindromic and prime. AM never actually noticed this, since it represented all numbers in unary. If pushed, AM will define Palindrome(n) to mean that the sequence of exponents of prime factors is symmetric; thus $2^3 3^8 5^1 7^1 11^8 13^3$ is palindromic in AM's sense because the sequence of its exponents (3 8 1 1 8 3) is unchanged upon reversal. In this sense, the only Prime palindromes are the primes themselves (or: just "2," depending upon the precise definition).

36. *If very few examples of X are found,*
Then add the following task to the agenda: "Generalize the concept X," for the following
reason: "X's are quite rare; a slightly less restrictive concept might be more interesting."

Of course, AM contains a precise meaning for the phrase "very few." When AM looks for primes among examples of already-known kinds of numbers, it will find dozens of non-examples for every example of a prime it uncovers. "Very few" is thus naturally implemented as a statistical confidence level. AM uses this rule when very few examples of Equality are found readily.

37. *If very many examples of X are found in a short period of time,*
Then try to create a new, specialized version of X.

This is similar to the preceding rule. Since numbers are easy to find, this might cause us to look for certain more interesting subclasses of numbers to study.

38. *If there are no known examples for the interesting concept X,*
Then consider spending some time looking for such examples.

I've heard of a math student who defined a set of number which had quite marvelous properties. After the 20th incredible theorem about them he'd proved, someone noticed that the set was empty. The danger of unwittingly dealing with a vacuous concept is even worse for a machine than for a human mathematician. The above rule explicitly prevents that.

39. *If the totality of examples of concept C is too small to be interesting,*
Then consider these reactions: (i) generalize C; (ii) forget C completely; (iii) replace C by one conjecture.

This is a good example of when a task like "Fill in generalizations of Numbers-with-1-divisors" might get proposed with a high-priority reason. The class of entities which C encompasses is simply too small, too trivial to be worth maintaining a separate concept. When C is numbers-with-1-divisor, C is really just another disguise for the singleton set {1}. The above rule might cause a new task to be added to the agenda, Fill in generalizations of Numbers-with-1-divisor. When that task is executed, AM might create the concept Numbers-with-odd-no-of-divisors, Numbers-with-prime-number-of-divisors, etc. Besides generalizing that concept, the above rule gives AM two other alternatives. AM may simply obliterate the nearly-vacuous concept, perhaps leaving around just the statement "*1 is the only number with one divisor.*" That conjecture might be tacked onto the Conjecs facet of Divisors-of. The actual rule will specify criteria for deciding which of the three alternatives to try. In fact, AM really starts all three activities: a task will always be created and added to the agenda (to generalize C), the vacuous concept will be tagged as "forgettable," and AM will attempt to formulate a conjecture (the only items satisfying C.Defn are C.Exs).

40. *If the totality of examples of concept C is too large to be interesting,*
Then consider these three possible reactions: (i) specialize C; (ii) forget C completely; (iii) replace C by one conjecture.

This is analogous to the preceding rule, but is used far less frequently. One common use is when a disjunction of two concepts has been formed which is accidentally large or already-known (*e.g.*, "Evens $\bigcup$ Odds" would be replaced by a conjecture).

41. *After filling in examples of C, if some examples were found,*
Look at all the operations which can be applied to C's (that is, access C.In-dom-of), find those which are interesting but which have no known examples, and suggest that AM fill in examples for them, because some items are now known which are in their domain, namely C.Exs.

This rule had AM fill in examples of Set-insertion, as soon as some examples of Sets had been found.

42. *After filling in examples of C, if some examples were found,*
Consider the task of Checking the examples facet of concept C.

This was very frequently used during AM's runs.

43. *After checking examples of C, if many examples remain,*
Consider the task of "Filling in some Conjecs for C."

This was used often by AM. After checking the examples of C, AM would try to empirically formulate some interesting conjecture about C.

44. *After successfully filling in non-examples of X, if no examples exist,*
If AM has not recently tried to find examples of X, then it should do so.
If AM has recently tried and failed to find examples, consider the conjecture that X is vacuous, empty, null, always-False. Consider generalizing X.

45. *After trying in vain to find some non-examples of X, if many examples exist,*
Consider the conjecture that X is universal, always-True. Consider specializing X.

46. *After successfully filling in examples of X, if no non-examples exist,*
If AM has not recently tried to find non-examples of X, then it should consider doing so.
If AM has recently tried and failed to find non-examples, consider the conjecture that X is universal, always-True. Consider specializing X.

47. *After trying in vain to find some examples of X,*
If many non-examples exist,
Consider the conjecture that X is vacuous, null, empty, always-False. Consider generalizing X.

Any-concept . Examples . Check

48. *If the current task is to Check Examples of concept X,*
and (Forsome Y) Y is a generalization of X with many examples,
and all examples of Y (ignoring boundary cases) are also examples of X,
Then conjecture that X is really no more specialized than Y,
and Check the truth of this conjecture on boundary examples of Y,
and see whether Y might itself turn out to be no more specialized than one of its generalizations.

This rule caused AM, while checking examples of odd-primes, to conjecture that all primes were odd-primes.

49. *If the current task is to Check Examples of concept X,*
and (Forsome Y) Y is a specialization of X,
and all examples of X (ignoring boundary cases) are also examples of Y,
Then conjecture that X is really no more general than Y,
and Check the truth of this conjecture on boundary examples of X,
and see whether Y might itself turn out to be no more general than one of its specializations.

This rule is analogous to the preceding one for generalizations.

50. *When checking boundary examples of a concept C,*
ensure that every scrap of C.Defn has been used.

It is often the tiny details in the definition that determine the precise boundary. Thus we must look carefully to see whether Primes allows 1 as an example or not. A definition like "numbers divisible only by 1 and themselves" includes 1, but this definition doesn't: "numbers having precisely 2 divisors." In the LISP program, this rule contains several hacks (tricks) for checking that the definition has been stretched to the fullest. For example: if the definition is of the form "all x in X such that...," then pay careful attention to the boundary of X. That is, take the time to access X.Boundary-exs and X.Boundary-non-exs, and check them against C.Defn.

51. *When checking examples of C,*
Ensure that each example satisfies C.Defn, and each non-example fails it. The precise member of C.Defn to use can be chosen depending on the example.

As described earlier in the text, definitions can have descriptors which indicate what kinds of arguments they might be best for, their overall speed, etc.

52. *When checking examples of C,*
If an entry e is rejected (i.e., it is seen to be not an example of C after all), then remove e from C.Exs and consider inserting it on the Boundary non-examples facet of C.

There is a complicated[5] algorithm for deciding whether to forget e entirely or to keep it around as a close but not close enough kind of example.

53. *When checking examples of C,*
After an entry e has been verified as a bona fide example of C,
Check whether e is also a valid example of some direct specialization of C.
If it is, then remove it from C.Exs, and consider adding it to the examples facet of that specialization, and suggest the task of Checking examples of that specialization.

54. *When checking examples of C,*
If an entry e is rejected,
Then check whether e is nevertheless a valid example of some generalization of C.
If it is, consider adding it to that concept's boundary-examples facet, and consider adding it to the boundary non-examples facet of C.

This is similar to the preceding rule.

55. *When checking non-examples of C, including boundary non-examples,*
Ensure that each one fails a definition of C. Otherwise, transfer it to the boundary examples facet of C.

56. *When checking non-examples of C, including boundary non-examples,*
After an entry e has been verified as a bona fide non-example of C,
Check whether e is also a non-example of some direct generalization of C.
If it is, then remove it from C.Non-Exs, and consider adding it to the non-examples facet of that generalization, and suggest the task of Checking examples of that generalization.

57. *When checking (boundary) non-examples of C,*
If an entry e is rejected, that is if it turns out to be an example of C after all,
Then check whether e is nevertheless a non-example of some specialization of C.
If it is, consider adding it to that concept's boundary non-examples facet.

This is similar to the preceding rule.

---

[5] Not necessarily sophisticated. First, AM accesses the Worth of C. From this it determines how many boundary non-examples C deserves to keep around (and how many total list cells it merits). AM compares these quotas with the current number of (and size of) entries already listed on C.bdy-non-exs. The degree of need of another entry there then sets the "odds" for insertion versus forgetting. Finally a random number is computed, and the odds determine what range it must lie in for e to be remembered.

2–1.3　Heuristics for the Conjecs Facet of Any-concept

Any-concept . Conjecs . Fillin

When the task is to look around and find conjectures dealing with concept C, the following general rules may be useful.

58. *If there is an analogy from X to C, and a nice item in X.Conjecs, formulate and test the analogous conjecture for C.*

Since an analogy is not much more than a set of substitutions, formulating the "analogous conjecture" is almost a purely syntactic transformation.

59. *Examine C.Exs for regularities.*

What mysteries are lurking in the LISP code for *this* rule, you ask? Nothing but a few special-purpose hacks and a few ultra-general hacks. Here is a slightly more specific rule for you seekers:

60. *Look at C.Exs. Pick one element at random. Write down statements true about that example e. Include a list of all concepts of which it is an example, all Interests features it satisfies, etc.*
Then check each conjecture on this list against all other known examples of C. If any example (except a boundary example) of C violates a conjecture, discard it.
Take all the surviving conjectures, and eliminate any which trivially follow from other ones.

This is a common way AM uses: induce a conjecture from one example and test it on all the rest. A more sophisticated approach might be to induce it by using a few examples simultaneously, but I haven't thought of any nontrivial way to do that. The careful reader will perceive that most of the conjectures AM will derive using this heuristic will be of the form "X is unexpectedly a specialization of Y," or "X is unexpectedly an example of Y," etc. Indeed, most of AM's conjectures are really that simple syntactically.

61. *Formulate a parameterized conjecture, a "template," which gets slowly specialized or instantiated into a definite conjecture.*

AM has only a few trivial methods for doing this (*e.g.*, introduce a variable initially and find the constant value to plug in there later). As usual, they will be omitted here, and the author encourages some research in this area, to turn out a decent set of general rules for accomplishing this hypothesis template instantiation. The best effort to date along these lines, in one specific sophisticated scientific field, is that of META-DENDRAL [Buchanan].

Any-concept . Conjecs . Check

62. *If a universal conjecture (For all X's, . : .) is contradicted by empirical data, gather the data together and try to find a regularity in those exceptions.*
If this succeeds, give the exceptions a name N (if they aren't already a concept), and rephrase the conjecture (For all X's which are not N's. . .). Consider making X - N a new concept.

Again note how "active" this little checking rule can be. It can patch up nearly-true conjectures, examine data, define new concepts, etc.

63. After verifying a conjecture for concept C,
See if it also holds for related concepts (e.g., a generalization of C).

There are of course bookeeping details not explicitly shown above, which are present in the LISP program. For example, if conjecture X is true for all specializations of C, then it must be added to C.Conjecs and removed from the Conjecs facets of each specialization of C.

```
Any-concept . Conjecs . Suggest
```

64. If X is probably related to Y, but no definite connection is known,
It's worthwhile looking for a specific conjecture tying X and Y together.

How might AM know that X and Y are only *probably* related? X and Y may play the same role in an analogy (*e.g.*, the singleton bag "(T)" and "any typical singleton bag" share many properties), or they may both be specializations of the same concept Z (*e.g.*, two kinds of numbers), or they may both have been created in the same unusual way (*e.g.*, Plus and Times and Exponentiation all can be created by *repeating* another operation).

```
Any-concept . Conjecs . Interest
```

65. A conjecture about X is interesting if X is very interesting.

66. A nonconstructive existence conjecture is interesting.

Thus the unique factorization theorem is judged to be interesting because it merely guarantees that some factoring will be into primes. If you give an algorithm for that factoring, then the theorem actually loses its mystique and (according to this rule) some of its value. But it increases in value due to the next rule.

67. A constructive existence conjecture is interesting if it is frequently used.

68. A conjecture C about X is interesting if the origin and the verification of C for each specialization of X was quite independent of each other, and preceded C's being noticed applicable to all X's.

This would be even more striking if *proof* techniques were known, and each specialized case had a separate kind of proof. Many number theory results are like this, where there exists a general proof only for numbers bigger than 317, say, and all smaller numbers are simply checked individually to make sure they satisfy the conjecture. Category theory is built upon practically nothing but this heuristic.

2–1.4   Heuristics for the Analogies Facet of Any-concept

```
Any-concept . Analogies . Fillin
```

69. To fill in conjectures involving concept C, where C is analogous to D,
Consider the analogue of each conjecture involving D.

70. If the current task involves a specific analogy, and the request is to find more conjectures,
Then consider the analog of each interesting conjecture about any concept involved centrally in the analogy.

That is, this rule suggests applying the preceding rule to each concept which is central to the given analogy. The result is a flood of new conjectures. There is a tradeoff (explicitly taken into account in the LISP version of this rule) between how interesting a conjecture has to be, and how centrally a concept has to fit into the analogy, in order to determine what resources AM should be willing to expend to find the analogous conjecture. Note that this is not a general suggestion of what to do, but a specific strategy for enlarging the analogy itself. If the new conjecture is verified, then not only would it be entered under some Conjecs facet, but it would also go to enlarging the data structure which represents the analogy.

71. *Let the analogy suggest how to specialize and generalize each concept into what is at least the analog of a known, very interesting concept.*

Like the last rule, this one simply says to use the analogy itself as the "reason" for exploring certain new entities, in this case new concepts. When the Bags↔Numbers analogy is made, AM notices that Singleton bags and Empty bags are two interesting, extreme specializations of Bags. The above rule then allows AM to construct and study what we know and love as the numbers one and zero. The analogy is flawed because there is only one "one," although there are many different singleton bags. But just as singletons and empty bags have special properties under bag operations, so do 0,1 under numeric operations. This was one case where an analogy paid off handsomely.

72. *If it is desired to have an analogy between concepts X and Y, then look for two already-known analogies between X↔Z and Z↔Y, for any Z.*
If found, compose the two analogies and see if the resultant analogy makes sense.

Since the analogies are really just substitutions, composing them has a familiar, precise meaning. This rule was not used by AM during its "good run," due to the paucity of analogies. The user can push AM into creating more of them, and ultimately using this rule. A chain from X↔Z↔Y↔X can be found which presents a new, bizarre analogy from X to itself.

```
Any-concept . Analogies . Suggest
```

73. *If an analogy is strong, and one concept has a very interesting universal conjecture C (For all x in B...), but the analog conjecture Ć is false,*
Then it's worth constructing the set of items in B́ for which the conjecture holds. It's perhaps even more interesting to isolate the set of exceptional elements.

With the Add↔Times analogy, it's true that all numbers $n > 1$ can be represented as the sum of two other numbers (each of them smaller than n), but it is *not* true that all numbers (with just a couple exceptions) can be represented as the product of other (hence smaller) numbers. The above rule has AM define the set of numbers which can/can't be so represented. These are just the composite numbers and the set of primes. This second way of encountering primes was very unexpected—both by AM and by the author. It expresses the deep fact that one difference between Add and Times is the presence of primes only for multiplication. At the time of its discovery, AM didn't appreciate this fully of course.

74. *If space is tight, and no use of the analogy has ever been made, and it is very old, and it takes up a lot of space,*
Then it is permissible to forget it without a trace.

75. *If two valuable conjectures are syntactically identical, and can be made identical by a simple substitution, then tentatively consider the analogy which is that very substitution.*

The associative/commutative property of Add and Times causes them to be tied together in an analogy, because of this rule.

76. *If an analogy is very interesting and very complete,*
Then spend some time refining it, looking for small exceptions. If none are found, see whether the two situations are genuinely isomorphic.

77. *If concepts X and Y are analogous, look for analogies between their specializations, or between their generalizations.*

This rule is not used much by AM, although the author thought it would be.

| Any-concept . Analogies . Interest |

78. *An analogy which has no discrepancies whatsoever is not as interesting as a slightly flawed analogy.*

79. *An analogy is interesting if it associates (for the first time) two concepts which are each unusually fully filled out (having many conjectures, many examples, many interest features, etc.).*

2–1.5   Heuristics for the Genl/Spec Facets of Any-concept

| Any-concept . Genl/Spec . Fillin |

80. *To fill in specializations of X, if it was very easy to find examples of X,*
Grab some features which would indicate than an X was interesting (some entries from X.Interest, or more remote Interest predicates garnered by rippling), and conjoin them onto the definition of X, thereby creating a new concept.

Here's one instance where the above rule was used: It was so easy for AM to produce examples of sets that it decided to specialize that concept. The above rule then plucked the interestingness feature "*all pairs of members satisfy the same rare predicate*" and conjoined it to the old definition of Sets. The new concept, Interesting-sets, included all singletons (because all pairs of members drawn from a singleton satisfy the predicate Equal) and empty sets.

81. *To fill in generalizations of concept X,*
Take the definition $\mathfrak{D}$, and replace it by a generalization of $\mathfrak{D}$. If $\mathfrak{D}$ is a concept, use $\mathfrak{D}$.Genl; if $\mathfrak{D}$ is a conjunction, then remove a conjunct or generalize[6] a conjunct; if $\mathfrak{D}$ is a disjunction, then add a disjunct or generalize a disjunct; if $\mathfrak{D}$ is negated, then specialize the negate; if $\mathfrak{D}$ is an example of Δ, then replace $\mathfrak{D}$ by "any example of Δ"; if $\mathfrak{D}$ satisfies any property P, then replace $\mathfrak{D}$ by "anything satisfying P"; if $\mathfrak{D}$ is a constant,[7] then replace $\mathfrak{D}$ by a new variable (or an existing one) which could assume value $\mathfrak{D}$; if $\mathfrak{D}$ is a variable, then enlarge its scope of possible bindings.

---

[6] That is, recur.
[7] Of course it's unlikely that a concept is defined simply as a constant, but the preceding footnote shows that this little program can be entered recursively, being fed a sub-expression of the definition.

This rule contains a bag of tricks for generalizing any LISP predicate, the definition of any concept. They are all *syntactic* tricks, however.

82. *To fill in generalizations of concept X, If some conjecture exists about "all X's and Y's" or "in X or Y," for some other concept Y,*
Create a new concept, a generalization of both X and Y, defined as their disjunction.

This rule contains another trick for generalizing any concept, although it is more meaningful, more semantic than the previous rule's tricks. Many theorems are true about numbers with 1 or 2 divisors, so this might be one reasonable way to generalize Numbers-with-1-divisor into a new useful[8] concept.

83. *To fill in generalizations of concept X,*
If other generalizations G1, G2 of X exist but are too general,
Create a new concept, a generalization of X and a specialization of both G1 and G2, defined as the conjunction of G1 and G2's definitions.

Thus when AM generalizes Reverse-all-levels into Reverse-top-level and Reverse-first-element, the above rule causes AM to create a new operation, which reverses the top level and which reverses the CAR[9] of the original list. While not particularly useful, the reader should observe that it is midway in generality between the original Reverse function and the first two generalizations.

84. *To fill in specializations of concept X,*
Take the definition $\mathfrak{D}$ of X, and replace it by a specialization of $\mathfrak{D}$. If $\mathfrak{D}$ is a concept, use $\mathfrak{D}$.Genl; if $\mathfrak{D}$ is a disjunction, then remove a disjunct or specialize a disjunct; if $\mathfrak{D}$ is a conjunction, then add a conjunct or specialize a conjunct; if $\mathfrak{D}$ is negated, then generalize the negate; if $\mathfrak{D}$ is "any example of Δ," then replace $\mathfrak{D}$ by a particular example of Δ; if $\mathfrak{D}$ is "anything satisfying $\mathfrak{P}$," then replace $\mathfrak{D}$ by a particular satisfier of $\mathfrak{P}$; if $\mathfrak{D}$ is a variable, then replace it by a well-chosen constant or restrict its scope.

This rule contains a bag of tricks for specializing any LISP predicate, the definition of any concept. They are all *syntactic* tricks, however. Note that the Lisp code for this rule will typically call itself (recur) in order to specialize small pieces of the original definition.

85. *To fill in specializations of concept X, If some conjecture exists about "all X's which are also Y's" or "in X and Y," for some other concept Y,*
Create a new concept, a specialization of both X and Y, defined as their conjunction.

This rule contains another trick for specializing any concept, although it is more meaningful, more semantic than the previous rule's tricks. Many theorems about primes contain the condition "$p>2$;" *i.e.*, they are really true about primes which are odd. So this might be one reasonable way to specialize Primes into a new concept: by conjoining the definitions of Primes and Odd-numbers, into the new concept Odd-primes. Here's another usage of this rule: If AM had originally defined Primes to include '1', then the frequency of conjectures where 1 was an exception would trigger this rule to define Primes more normally ($p \geq 2$).

86. *To fill in specializations of concept X,*
If other specializations S1, S2 of X exist but are too restrictive to be interesting,

---

[8] At least, several theorems will be stated more concisely using this new concept: Numbers with 1 or 2 divisors.
[9] Also the CAR of the CAR, etc., until a non-list is encountered.

Create a new concept, a specialization of X and a generalization of both S1 and S2,
defined as the disjunction of S1 and S2's definitions.

87. To fill in generalizations of concept X, when a recursive definition of X exists,
If the definition contains two conjoined recursive calls, replace them by a disjunction
or eliminate one call entirely.
If there is only one recursive call, disjoin a second call, this one on a different destructive
function applied to the original argument. If the original destructive function is one of
{CAR, CDR}, then let the new one be the other member of that pair.

AM uses the first part of this rule to turn Equal-lists into two variants of Same-length-as. The second part, while surprisingly unused, could work on this definition of *MEMBER:* "λ *(x,L) LISTP(L) and:* [x=CAR(L) or MEMBER(x,CDR(L))]", which is just "membership at the top level of," or "ε," and transform it into this one of *MEM*, which represents membership at any depth: "λ *(x,L) LISTP*[10] *(L) and:* [x=CAR(L) or *MEM(x,CDR(L)) or MEM(x,CAR(L))]*". The rule noticed a recursive call on CDR(L), and simply disjoined a recursive call on CAR(L).

88. To fill in specializations of concept X, when a recursive definition of C exists,
If the definition contains two disjoined recursive calls, replace them by a conjunction
or eliminate one call entirely.
If there is only one recursive call, conjoin a second on another destructive function
applied to the original argument. Often the two recursions will be on the CAR and the
CDR of the original argument to the predicate which is the definition for X.

This is closely related to the preceding rule. Just as it turned the concept of 'element of' into the more general one of 'membership at any depth', the above rule can specialize the definition of *MEMBER* into this one, called *AMEM:* "λ *(x,L) LISTP(L)* *and:* [x=CAR(L) or: [AMEM(x,CDR(L)) and AMEM(x,CAR(L))]]".[11]

89. To fill in specializations of concept X,
Find, within a definition of X (at even parity of NOT's), an expression of the form 'For
some x in X, P(x)", and replace it either by 'For all x in X, P(x)," or by P(x_0).

Thus "sets, all pairs of whose members satisfy *some* interesting predicate" gets specialized into "sets, all pairs of whose members satisfy Equality." The same rule, with "even parity" replaced by "odd parity," is useful for *generalizing* a definition. This rule is really 4 separate rules, in the LISP program. The same rule, with the transformations going in the opposite direction, is also used for generalizing. The same rule, with the transformations reversed and the parity reversed, is used for specializing a definition. Here is that doubly-switched rule:

90. To fill in specializations of concept X,
Find within a definition of X (at odd parity of NOT's) an expression of the form 'For
all x in X, P(x)", and replace it either by 'For some x in X, P(x)," or by P(x_0). Or replace
'P(c)", where c is a constant, by 'For some x in C, P(x)" where C is a concept of which
c is one example.

---

[10] The Interlisp function LISTP(L) tests whether or not L is a (nonnull) list.

[11] This operation is almost impossible to explain verbally. AMEM(x,L) means that x is an element of L, and for each member M of L before the x, M is an ordered structure and x is an element of M, and for each member N of M before the x which is inside M,... etc. For example, <[x] [< <x a b> <x> x d e> <x f> x g h] [<x i> x j] x k [l] m>.

91. *When creating in a specialization S of concept C,*
Note that S.Genl should contain C, and that C.Spec should contain S.

The analogous rule exists, in which all spec and genl are switched.

Any-concept . Genl/Spec . Suggest

---

92. *After creating a new specialization S of concept C,*
Explicitly look for ties between S and other known specializations of C.

For example, after AM defines the new concept of Numbers-with-3-divisors, it looks around for ties between that kind of number and other kinds of numbers.

93. *After creating a new generalization G of concept C,*
Explicitly look for ties between G and other close generalizations of C.

For example, AM defined the predicates Same-size-CARs and Same-size-CDRs[12] as two new generalizations of Equality. The above rule then suggested that AM explicitly try to find some connection between these two new predicates. Although *AM* failed, Don Knuth (using a similar heuristic, perhaps?) also looked for a connection, and found one: it turns out that the two predicates are both ways of defining the relation we intuitively understand as "having the same length as."

94. *After creating a new specialization S of concept C,*
Consider looking for examples of S.

This has to be said explicitly, because all too often a concept is specialized into vacuousness.

95. *After creating a new generalization G of concept C,*
Consider looking for non-examples of G.

This has to be said explicitly, because all too often a concept is generalized into vacuous universality. This rule is less useful to AM than the preceding one.

96. *If concept C possesses some very interesting property lacked by one of its specializations S,*
Then considering creating a concept intermediate in specialization between C and S, and see whether that possesses the property.

This rule will trigger whenever a new generalization or specialization is created.

97. *If concept S is now very interesting, and S was created as a specialization of some earlier concept C,*
Give extra consideration to specializing S, and to specializing concept C again (but in different ways than ever before).

The next rule is the analog of the preceding one. They incorporate tiny bits of the strategies of hill-climbing and learning from one's successes.

98. *If concept G is now very interesting, and G was created as a generalization of some earlier concept C,*
Give extra consideration to generalizing G, and to generalizing C in other ways.

---

[12] Two lists satisfy Same-size-CDRs iff they have the same number of members. Two lists satisfy Same-size-CARs iff (when written out in standard LISP notation) they have the same number of initial left parentheses and also have the same first identifier following that last initial left parenthesis.

The analogous rules exist, for concepts that have become so boring they've just been discarded:

99. *If concept X proved to be a dead-end, and X was created as a generalization of (specialization of) some earlier concept C,*
Give less consideration to generalizing (specializing) X, and to generalizing (specializing) C in other ways in the future.

> **Any-concept . Genl/Spec . Check**

100. *When checking a generalization G of concept C,*
Specifically test to ensure that G is not equivalent to C.
The easiest way is to examine the non-examples (especially boundary non-examples) of C, and look for one satisfying G; or examine the examples of G (especially boundary) and look for one failing to satisfy C.
If they appear to be the same concept, look carefully at G. Are there any specializations of G whose examples have never been filled in? If so, then by all means suggest looking for such concepts' examples before concluding that G and C are really equivalent.
If they are the same, then replace one by a conjecture.
If they are different, make sure that some boundary non-example of C (which is an example of G) is explicitly stored for C.

This rule makes sure that AM is not deluding itself. When AM generalizes Numbers-with-1-divisor into Numbers-which-equal-their-no-of-divisors, it still hasn't gotten past the singleton set {1}. The conjecture in this case would be "*The only number which equals its own number of divisors is 1.*" Typically, when a generalization G of C turns out to be equivalent to C, there is theorem lurking around, of the form "All G's also satisfy this property...," where the property is the "extra" constraint present in C's definition but absent from G's. This rule also was used when AM had just found some examples of Sets. AM almost believed that all Unordered-Structures were also Sets, but the last main clause of the rule had AM notice that Bags is a specialization of Unordered-structures, and that the latter concept had never had any of its examples filled in. As a result, AM printed out this message: "Almost concluded that Unordered-structures are also always Sets. But will wait until examples of Bags are found. Perhaps some Bags will not be Sets." In fact, examples of Bags are soon found, and they aren't sets.

101. *When checking a specialization S of concept C,*
Specifically test to ensure that S is not equivalent to C.
If they are the same, then replace one by a conjecture.
If they are different, make sure that some boundary example of C (which is not an example of S) is explicitly stored for C.

This rule is similar to the preceding one. If adding a new constraint P to the definition doesn't change the concept C, then there is probably a theorem there of the form "All C's also satisfy constraint P."

102. *When checking a specialization S of a specialization X of a concept C,*
if there exist other specs. of specs. of C,
then ensure that none of them are the same as S. This is especially worthwhile if the specializing operators in each case were the same but reversed in order.

Thus we can add a constraint to C and collapse the first two arguments, or we can collapse the arguments and add the constraint; either way, we get to the same very specialized new concept. The above rule helps detect those accidental duplicates. *e.g.*, Coalesced- Dom=Ran- Compositions are really the same as Dom=Ran- Coalesced-Compositions, and this rule would suspect that they might be.

103. *When checking the Genl or Spec facet entries for concept C,*
ensure that C.Genl and C.Spec have no common member Z. If they do, then conjecture that C and Z are actually equivalent.

In fact, this rule actually ensures that Generalizations(C) does not intersect Specializations(C). If it does, a whole "cycle" of concepts exists which can be collapsed into one single concept. See also rule 122, below.

Any-concept . Genl/Spec . Interest

104. *A generalization of X is interesting if all the previously-known boundary non-examples are now boundary examples of the concept.*

A check is included here to ensure that the new concept was not simply defined as the closure of the old one.

105. *A specialization of X is interesting if all the previously-known boundary examples are now boundary non-examples of the new specialized concept.*

A check is included here to ensure that the new concept was not simply defined as the interior of the old one.

106. *If C_1 is a generalization of C_2, which is a generalization of C_3,..., which is a generalization of C_j, and it has just been learned that C_j is a generalization of C_1,*
Then all the concepts C_1,...,C_j are equivalent, and can be merged, and the combined concept will be much more interesting than any single one, and the interestingness of the new composite concept increases rapidly with j.

The Lisp code has the new interest value be computed as the maximum value of the old concepts, plus a bonus which increases like the square of j. This is similar to rule number 222. A rule just like the preceding one exists, with 'Specialization' substituted everywhere for 'Generalization'. Thus a closed loop of Spec links constitutes a demonstration that all the concepts in that loop are equivalent. These rules were used more frequently than expected.

2–1.6   Heuristics for the View Facet of Any-concept

Any-concept . View . Fillin

107. *To fill in View facet entries for X,*
Find an interesting operation F whose range is X,
and indicate that any member of Domain(F) can be viewed as an X just by running F on it.

While trying to fill in the View facet of Even-nos, AM used this rule. It located the operation Doubling, whose domain is Numbers and whose range is Even-nos. Then the rule created a new entry: "to view any number as if it were an even number, double it." This is a twisted affirmation of the standard correspondence between natural numbers and even natural numbers.

2–1.7   Heuristics for the In-dom/ran-of Facets of Any-concept

Any-concept . In-dom-of/In-ran-of . Fillin

108. *To fill in entries for the In-dom-of facet of concept X,*
Ripple down the tree of concepts, starting at Active, to empirically determine which active concepts can be run on X's.

This can usually be decided by inspecting the Domain/range facets of the Active concepts. Occasionally, AM must actually try to run an active $\mathcal{F}$ on sample X's, to see whether it fails or returns a value.[13]

109. *To fill in the In-ran-of facet of concept X,*
Ripple down the tree of concepts, starting at Active, to empirically determine which active concepts can be run to yield X's.

This can usually be decided by inspecting the Domain/range facets of the Active concepts. Occasionally, AM inspects known examples of some Active concept, to see if any of the results are X's.

110. *While filling in entries for the In-dom-of facet of X,*
Look especially carefully for Operations which transform examples and non-examples into each other;
This is even better if the operation pushes boundary exs/non-exs 'across the boundary'.

This was used to note that Insert and Delete had a lot to do with the concept of Singleton.

2–1.8   Heuristics for the Definition Facet of Any-concept

Any-concept . Defn . Suggest

111. *If there are no known definitions for concept X,*
Then it is crucial that AM spend some time looking for such definitions.

This situation might occur if only an Algorithm is present for some concept. In that case, the above rule would suggest a new, high-priority task, and AM would then twist the algorithm into a (probably very inefficient) definition. A much more serious situation would occur if a concept were specified only by its Intuition entries (created, *e.g.*, by modifying another concept's intuitions). In that case, rapidly formulating a precise definition would be a necessity. Of course, this need never arose, since all the intuitions were deleted.

Any-concept . Defn . Check

112. *When checking the Definition facet of concept C,*
ensure that each member of C.Exs satisfies all definitions present, and each non-example fails all definitions. If there is one dissenting definition, modify it, and move the offending example to the boundary.

---

[13] One key feature of Lisp which permits this to be done is the Errorset feature.

There is little real "checking" that can be done to a definition, aside from internal consistency: If there exist several suposedly-equivalent definitions, then AM can at least ensure they agree on the known examples and non-examples of the concept. If the Intuitions facets were permitted, then each definition could be checked for intuitive appeal (*i.e.*, consistency with some Intuition).

113. *When checking the Definition facet of concept C,*
Try to find and eliminate any redundant constraints, try to find and eliminate any circularity, check that any recursion will terminate.

Here are the other few tricks that AM knows for "checking" a definition. For each clause in the rule above, AM has a very limited ability to detect and patch up "bugs" of that sort. Checking that recursion will terminate, for example, is done by examining the argument to the recursive call, and verifying that it contains (at some level before the original argument) an application of a LISP function on Destructive-LISP-functions-list. There is no intelligent inference that is going on here, and for that reason the process is not even mentioned within the body of this document.

2–2   HEURISTICS DEALING WITH ANY ACTIVE CONCEPT

All the rules below are applicable to tasks which involve operations, predicates, relations, functions, etc. In short, they apply to all the concepts AM knows about which involve *doing* something, which involve action.

‖ Active . Fillin ‖

114. *If the current task is to fill in examples of the activity F,*
One way to get them is to run F on randomly chosen examples of the domain of F.

Thus, to find examples of Equality, AM repeatedly executed Equality.Alg on randomly chosen pairs of objects. AM found examples of Compositions by actually picking a pair of operations at random and trying to compose them. Of course, most such "unmotivated" compositions turned out to be uninteresting.

115. *While filling in examples of the activity F, by running F.Algs on random arguments from F.Domain,*
It is worth the effort to specifically include extreme or boundary examples of the domain of F, among the arguments on which F.Algs is run.

116. *To fill in a Domain entry for active concept F,*
Run F on various entities, rippling down the tree of concepts, to determine empirically where F seems to be defined.

This may shock the reader, as it sounds dumb and explosive, but the concepts are arranged in a tree (using Genl links), so the search is really quite fast. Although this rule is rarely used, it always seems to give surprisingly good results.

117. *To fill in generalizations of active F,*
Consider just extending F, by enlarging its domain. Revise F.Defn as little as possible.

Although Equality is initially only for structures, AM extends it (using the same definition, actually) to a predicate over all pairs of entities.

118. *To fill in specializations of active F,*
Consider just restricting F, by shrinking its domain. Check F.Defn to see if some optimization is possible.

119. *After an algorithm is known for F, if AM wants a better one,*
AM is permitted to ask the user to provide a fast but opaque algorithm for F.

This was used a few times, especially for inverse functions. A nontrivial open-ended research problem (*)[14] is to collect a body of rules which transform an inefficient algorithm into a computationally acceptable one.

120. *If the current task is to fill in boundary (non-)examples of the activity F,*
One way to get them is to run F on randomly chosen boundary examples and (with proper safeguards) boundary non-examples of the domain of F.

Proper safeguards are required to ensure that F.Algs doesn't loop or cause an error when fed a slightly-wrong (slightly-illegal) argument. In LISP, a timer and an ERRORSET suffice as crude safeguards.

121. *If the current task is to fill in (boundary) non-examples of the activity F,*
One low-interest way to get them is to run F on randomly chosen examples of its domain, and then replace the value obtained by some other (very similar) value. Also, be sure to check that the resultant i/o pair doesn't accidentally satisfy F.Defn.

The parentheses in the above rule mean that it is really two rules: for *boundary* non-examples, just change the final value slightly. For *typical* non-examples, change the result significantly. If you read the words inside in the parentheses in the IF part, then read the words inside the parentheses in the THEN part as well; or else *omit* them in both cases.

Active . Check

122. *When checking an algorithm for active F,*
run that algorithm and ensure that the input/output satisfy F.Defn.

123. *When checking a definition $\mathfrak{D}$ for active concept F,*
Run one of its algorithms and ensure that the input/output satisfy $\mathfrak{D}$.

This is the converse of the preceding rule. They simply say that the definition and algorithm facets must be mutually consistent.

124. *While checking examples or boundary examples of the active concept F,*
Ensure that each input/output pair is consistent with F.Dom/range.

If the domain/range entry is $<D_1 D_2 \ldots D_k \Rightarrow R>$, and the i/o pair is $<d_1 d_2 \ldots d_k , r>$, then each component d_i of the input must be an example of the corresponding D_i, and the output r must be an example of R.

125. *When checking examples of the active concept F,*
If any argument(s) to F were concepts, tag their In-domain-of facets with "F."
If any values produced by F are concepts, tag their In-range-of facets with "F."

For example, Restrict(Union) produced Add, at one time in AM's history. Then the above rule caused "Restrict" to be inserted as a new entry on Union.In-dom-of and also on Add.In-ran-of.

---

[14] Following Knuth, we shall reserve a star (*) for those problems which are quite difficult, which should take the reader roughly three full lifetimes to master. Readers not believing in reincarnation should therefore skip such problems.

Active . Suggest

126. *If there are no known algorithms for active concept F,*
Then AM should spend some time looking for such algorithms.

This situation might occur if only a Definition is present for some operation. In that case, the above rule would suggest a new, high-priority task, and AM would then twist the definition into a (probably very inefficient) algorithm. The rule below is similar, for the Domain/range facet:

127. *If the Domain/range facet of active concept F is blank,*
Then AM should spend some time looking for specifications of F's domain and range.

128. *If a Domain of active concept F is encountered frequently, either within conjectures or as the domain or range of other operations and predicates,*
Then define that Domain as a separate concept, and raise the Worth of F slightly.

The "Domain" here refers to the sequence of components, whose Cartesian product is what is normally referred to in mathematics as the *domain* of the operation. This led to the definition of "Anything $\times$ Structures," which is the domain of several Insertion and Deletion operations, Membership testing predicates, etc.

129. *It is worthwhile to explicitly calculate the value of F for all distinguished (extreme, boundary, interesting) members of and subsets of its domain.*

130. *If some domain component of F has a very interesting specialization,*
Then consider restricting F (along that component) to that smaller domain.

Note that these last couple rules deal with the image of interesting domain items. The next rule deals with the inverse image (pre-image) of unusual range items. We saw earlier in this document (Chapter 2) how this rule led to the definition of Prime numbers.

131. *If the range of F contains interesting items, or an interesting specialization,*
Then it is worthwhile to consider their inverse image under F.

132. *When trying to fill in new Algorithms for Active concept F,*
Try to transform any conjectures about F into (pieces of) new algorithms.

This is one place where a sophisticated body of transformation rules might be inserted. Others are working on this problem [Burstall & Darlington 75], and AM only contains a few simple tricks for turning conjectures into procedures. For example, "All primes are odd, except '2' ," is transformed into a more efficient search for primes: a separate test for x=2, followed by a search through only Odd-numbers.

133. *After trying in vain to fill in examples of active concept F,*
Locate the domain of F, and suggest that AM try to fill in examples for each component of that domain.

Thus after failing to find examples for Set-union, AM was told to find examples of Sets, because that could have let the previous task succeed. There is no recursion here: after the sets are found, AM will not automatically go back to finding examples of Set-union. In practice, that task was eventually proposed and chosen again, and succeeded this time.

134. *After working on an Active concept F,*
Give a slight, ephemeral boost to tasks involving Domain(F): give a moderate size boost
to each task which asks to fill in examples of that domain/range component, and give
a very tiny boost to each other task mentioning such a concept.

This is both a supplement to the more general "focus of attention" rule, and a
nontrivial heuristic for finding valuable new tasks. It is the partial converse of rule 72.

Active . Interest

135. *An active concept F is interesting if there are other operations with the same*
domain as F, and if they are (on the average) fairly interesting. If the other operations'
domain is only similar, then they must be very interesting and have some valuable
conjectures tied to them, if they are to be allowed to push up F's interestingness rating.

The value of having the same domain/range is the ability to compose with them.
If the domain/range is only similar, then AM can hope for analogies or for partial
compositions.

136. *An active concept is interesting if it was recently created.*

This is a slight extra boost given to each new operation, predicate, etc. This bonus
decays rapidly with time, and thus so will the overall worth of the concept, unless some
interesting property is encountered quickly.

137. *An active concept is interesting if its domain is very interesting.*

An important common case of this rule is when the domain is interesting because
all its members are equal to each other. The corresponding statement about *ranges* does
exist, but only operations can be said to have a specific range (not, *e.g.* Predicates).
Therefore, the "range" rule is listed under Operation.Interest, as rule number 111.

2–3   HEURISTICS DEALING WITH ANY PREDICATE

Each of these heuristics can be assumed to be prefaced by a clause of the form "*If the*
current task is to deal with concept X, where X isa Predicate,...." This will be repeated
below, for each rule.

Predicate . Fillin

138. *If the current task was (Fill-in examples of X),*
and X is a predicate,
and more than 100 items are known in the domain of X,
and at least 10 cpu seconds were spent trying to randomly instantiate X,
and the ratio of successes/failures is both >0 and less than .05

Then add the following task to the agenda: (Fill-in generalizations of X), for the following
reason:
"X is rarely satisfied; a slightly less restrictive concept might be more interesting."
This reason's rating is computed as three times the ratio of nonexamples/examples
found.

This rule says to generalize a predicate if it rarely succeeds (rarely returns T). One use for this was when Equality was found to be quite rare; the resultant generalizations did indeed turn out to be more valuable (namely, "numbers"). A similar use was found for predicates which tested for identical equality of two angles, of two triangles, and of two lines. Their generalizations were also valuable (congruence, similarity, parallel, equal-measure). Most rules in this appendix are not presented with the same level of detail as the preceding one, as the reader has no doubt observed.

139. *To fill in Domain/range entries for predicate P,*
P can operate on the domain of any specialization of P,
P can operate on any specialization of the domain of P,
P can operate on some restriction of the domain of any generalization of P,
P may be able to operate on some enlargement of its current domain,
The range of P will necessarily be the doubleton set {T,F},
P is guaranteed return T if any of its specializations do, and F if any of its generalizations do.

This contains a compiled version of what we mean when we say that one predicate is a generalization or specialization of another. Viewed as relations, as subsets of a Cartesian product of spaces, this notion of general/special is just that of superset/subset. The last line of the rule is meant to indicate that adding new constraints onto P can only make it return True less frequently, while relaxing P's definition can only make it return True more often.

Predicate . Suggest

140. *If all the values of Active concept ℱ happen to be Truth-values, and ℱ is not known to be a predicate,*
Then conjecture that ℱ is in fact a predicate.

This rule is placed on the Suggest facet because, if placed anywhere else on this concept, it could only be seen as relevant by AM if AM already knew that ℱ were a predicate. On the other hand, the rule can't be placed, *e.g.*, on Active.Fillin, since just forgetting (deleting) this "Predicate" concept should be enough to delete all references to predicates anywhere in the system.

Predicate . Interest

141. *A predicate 𝒫 is interesting if its domain is Any-concept (the collection of all known concepts). This is especially true if there is a significant positive correlation (theoretical or empirical) between concepts' worths and their 𝒫-values.*

This very high level heuristic wasn't used by AM during its "good" run (the one chronicled in Section 6–2.1).

2–4   HEURISTICS DEALING WITH ANY OPERATION

Operation . Fillin

142. *To fill in examples of operation F (with domain A and range B),*
when many examples α of A are already known,
and F maps some of those examples α into distinguished members (esp: extrema) b of
B,
Then (for each such distinguished member "b"ϵ B) study $F^{-1}(b)$ as a new concept. That
is, isolate those members of A whose F-value is the unusual item bϵB.

This rule says to investigate the inverse image of an unusual item b, under the interesting operation f. When b=2 and f=number-of-divisors-of, this rule leads to the definition of *prime numbers*. When b=ϕ[15] and f=Intersection, the rule led to the discovery of the concept of *disjointness of sets*.

143. *To fill in Domain/range entries for operation F,*
F can operate on the domain of any specialization of F,
F can operate on the specialization of the domain of any specialization of F (including
F itself),
F can operate on some restriction of the domain of any generalization of F, at least on
its current domain and perhaps even on a bigger space,
F may be able to operate on some generalization of (some component(s) of) its current
domain,
F can only (and will always) produce values lying in the range of each generalization
of F,
F can—with the proper arguments—produce values lying in the range of any particular
specialization of F.

There are only a few changes between this rule and the corresponding one for Predicates. Recall that Operations can be multi-valued, and those values are not limited to the set {T,F}.

144. *To fill in Domain/range entries for operation F, when some exist already,*
Take an entry of the form $<D_1 \, D_2 \ldots D_n \Rightarrow R>$ and see if $D_i \times R$ is meaningful for
some i (especially: i=n).
If so, then remove D_i from the left side of the entry, and replace R by $D_i \times R$, and
modify the definition of F.

In LISP, "meaningful" is coded as: either $D_i \times R$ is equivalent to an already-known concept, or else it is found in at least two interesting conjectures. This is probably an instance of what McDermott calls natural stupidity.[16] This rule is tagged as being explosive, and is not used very often by AM.

145. *To fill in a Range entry for operation F,*
Run F on various domain examples, especially boundary examples, to collect examples
of the range. Then ripple down the tree of concepts to determine empirically where F
seems to be sending its values.

This may shock the reader, as it sounds dumb and explosive, but the concepts are arranged in a tree (using Genl links), so the search is really quite fast. Although this rule is rarely used, it always seems to give surprisingly good results.

---

[15] The empty set, phi, NIL, {}.

[16] See [McDermott 76] for natural stupidity. He criticizes the use of very intelligent-sounding names for otherwise-simple program modules. But consider "*Homo sapiens*," which means "wise man." Now *there's* a misleading label...

146. *If operation F has just been applied, and has yielded a new concept C as its result,*
Then carefully examine F.Dom/range to try to find out what C.Isa should be. C.Isa
will be all legal entries listed as values of the range of F.

When F=Compose, say AM has just created C=Empty∘Insert.[17] What is C?
It is a concept, of course, but what else? By examining the Domain/range facet of
Compose, AM finds the entry <Active Active ⇒ Active>. Aha! So C must be an
Active. But AM also finds the entry <Predicate Active ⇒ Predicate>. Since "Empty"
is a predicate, the final composition C must also be a predicate. So C.Isa would be filled
in with "Predicate." AM thus used the above rule to determine that Empty∘Insert was
a predicate. Even if this rule were excised, AM could still determine that fact, painfully,
by noticing that all the values were truth-values.

147. *If operation F has just been applied to $A_1, A_2, \ldots$, and has yielded a new concept*
C as its result,
Then add F to C.In-ran-of; add F to the In-dom-of facet of all the A_i's which are
concepts; add $<A_1\ldots \Rightarrow C>$ to F.Exs.

There is some overlap here with earlier rules, but there is no theoretical or practical
difficulty with such redundancy.

148. *When filling in examples of operation F, if F takes some existing concepts A_1,*
$A_2, \ldots$ and (may) produce a new concept,
Then only consider, as potential A_i's, those concepts which already have some examples.
Prefer the A_i's to be interesting, to have a high worth rating, to have some interesting
conjectures about them, to have several examples and several non-examples, etc.

The danger here is of, *e.g.*, Composing two operations which turn out to be vacuous,
or of Conjoining an empty concept onto another, or of proliferating variants of a boring
concept, etc.

Operation . Check

Below are rules used to check existing entries on various facets of operations.

149. *To check the domain/range entries on the operation F,*
IF a domain/range entry has the form (D D D... ⇒ R),
and all the D's are equal, and R is a generalization of D (or, with less enthusiasm: if R
and D have a significant overlap),
THEN it's worth seeing whether (D D D... ⇒ D) is consistent with all known examples
of the operation:
If there are no known examples, add a task to the agenda requesting they be filled in.
If there are examples, and (D D D... ⇒ D) is consistent, add it to the Domain/range
facet of this operation.
If there are some contradicting examples, create a new concept which is defined as this
operation restricted to (D D D... ⇒ D).

When AM restricts Bag-union to numbers (bags of T's), the new operation has a
Domain/range entry of the form (Numbers Numbers ⇒ Bag). The above rule has AM
investigate whether the range specification mightn't also be narrowed down to Number.

---

[17] That is, insert x into a structure S and then see if S is empty. This leads AM to realize
that inserting can never result in an empty structure.

In this case it is a great help. The rule often fails, of course: the sum of two primes is rarely a prime, the Cartesian product of two lists-of-atoms is not a list-of-atoms, etc. Since this rule is almost instantaneous to execute, it's cost-effective overall.

150. *When checking the domain/range entries on the operation F,*
IF a domain/range entry has the form (D D D... ⇒ R),
and all the D's are equal, and R is a specialization of D,
THEN it's worth inserting (D D D... ⇒ D) as a new entry on F.Dom/ran, even though that is redundant.

This shows that symmetry and aesthetics are sometimes preferable to absolute optimization. That's why we program in Lisp, instead of machine language. On the other hand, this rule wasn't really that useful to AM. Now, by analogy,...?

151. *When checking the Domain/range entries for operation F,*
Ensure that the boundary items in the range can actually be reached by F. If not, see whether the range is really just some known specialization of F.

This rule is a typical checking rule. Note that it is active, not passive: it might alter the Domain/range facet of F, if it finds an error there.

152. *When checking examples of the operation F, for each such example,*
If the value returned by F is a concept C, add 'F' to C.In-range-of.

Operation . Suggest

153. *Whenever the domain of operation F has changed,*
check whether the range has also changed. Often the range will change analogously to the domain, where the operation itself is the Analogy.

154. *After working on Operation F,*
Give a slight, ephemeral boost to tasks involving Range(F).

This wll be a moderate size boost for each task which asks to fill in examples of that range concept, and a very tiny boost for each other task mentioning such a concept. This is both a supplement to the more general "focus of attention" rule, and a nontrivial heuristic for finding valuable new tasks. It is an extension of rule number 99, and a partial converse to rule 88.

Operation . Interest

155. *An operation F is interesting if there are other operations with the same domain and range, and if they are (on the average) fairly interesting.*

156. *An operation F is interesting if it is the first operation connecting its domain concept to its range concept, and if those domain/range components are themselves valuable concepts, and there is no analogy between them, and there are some interesting conjectures involving the domain of F.*

The above two rules say that F can be valuable becuase it's similar to other, already-liked operations, or because it is totally different from any known operation. Although these two criteria are nonintersecting, their union represents only a small fraction of the operations that get created: typically, *neither* rule will trigger.

157. *An operation F is interesting if its range is very interesting.*

Range here refers to the concept in which all results of F must lie. It is the R in the domain/range facet entry $<D \Rightarrow R>$ for concept F. The corresponding rule for "domains" is applicable to any Active, not just to Operations, hence is listed under Active.Interest, as rule number 22.

158. *An operation F is interesting if the values of F satisfy some unusual property which is not (in general) satisfied by the arguments to F.*

Thus doubling is interesting because it always returns an even number. This is one case where the interesting property can be deduced trivially just by looking at the domain and range of the operation: Numbers$\Rightarrow$Even-nos.

159. *An operation is interesting if its values are interesting.*

This can mean that each value is interesting (*e.g.,* Compose is well-received because it produces many new, valuable concepts as its values). Or, it can mean that the operations' values, gathered together into one big set, are interesting as a set. Unlike the preceding rule, this one has no mention whatsoever of the domain items, the arguments to the operation. This rule was used to good advantage frequently by AM. For example, Factorings of numbers are interesting because (using rule 122) for all x, Factorings(x) is interesting in exactly the same way. Namely, Factorings(x), viewed as a set, always contains precisely one item which has a certain interesting property (see rule 225). Namely, all its members are primes (see rule 122 again). This explains one way in which AM noticed that all numbers seem to factor uniquely into primes.

160. *An operation is interesting if its values are interesting, ignoring the images of boundary items from the domain.*

That is, if the image of the domain—minus its boundary—is interesting.

161. *An operation is interesting if its values on the boundary items from the domain are very interesting. Ignore the non-boundary parts of the domain.*

That is, if the image of the boundary of the domain is interesting.

162. *An operation is interesting if it leaves intact any interesting properties of its argument(s). This is even better if it eliminates some undesirable properties, or adds some new, desirable ones.*

Thus a new, specialized kind of Insertion operation is interesting if, even though it stuffs more items into a structure, the nice properties of the structure remain. The operation "Merge" is interesting for this very reason: it inserts items into an alphabetized list, yet it doesn't destroy that interesting property of the list.

163. *An operation is interesting if its domain and range are equal. If there is more than one domain component, then at least one of them should equal the range. The more components which are equal to the range, the better.*

Thus "Insertion" qualifies here, since its domain/range entry is $<$Anything Structures $\Rightarrow$ Structures$>$. But "Union" is even better, since *both* domain components equal the range, namely Structures.

164. *An operation is mildly interesting if its range is related somehow (e.g. specialization of) to one or more components of its range. The more the better.*

A weakened form of the preceding rule.

165. *If the result of applying operation F is a new concept C,*
Then the interestingness of F is weakly tied to that of C.

If the new concept C becomes very valuable, then F will rise slightly in interest. If C is so bad it gets forgotten, F will not be regarded quite as highly. When Canonize scores big its first time used, it rises in interest. This caused AM to form poorly-motivated canonizations, which led to dismal results, which gradually lowered the rating of Canonize to where it was originally.

2–5 HEURISTICS DEALING WITH ANY COMPOSITION

Composition . Fillin

166. *To fill in algorithms for operation F, where F is a composition G∘H,*
One algorithm is: apply H and then apply G to the result.

Of course this rule is not much more than the definition of what it means to compose two operations.

167. *To fill in Domain/range entries for operation F, where F is a composition G∘H,*
Tentatively assume that the domain is Domain(H), and range is Range(G). More precisely, the domain will be the result of substituting Domain(H) for Range(H) wherever Range(H) appears (or: just once) in Domain(G).

Thus for F=Divides∘Count, where Divides:<Number,Number $\Rightarrow$ {T,F}>, and Count:<Bag $\Rightarrow$ Number>, the above rule would say that the domain/range entries for F are gotten by substituting "Bag" for "Number" once or twice in Domain(Divides). The possible entries for F.Dom/range are thus: <Bag,Bag $\Rightarrow$ {T,F}>, <Number,Bag $\Rightarrow$ {T,F}>, and <Bag,Number $\Rightarrow$ {T,F}>.

168. *To fill in Domain/range entries for operation F, where F is a composition G∘H,*
But Range(H) does not occur as a component of Domain(G),
The range of F is still Range(G), but the domain of F is computed as follows: Ascertain the component X of Domain(G) having the biggest (fractional) overlap with Range(H). Then substitute Domain(H) for X in Domain(G). The result is the value to be used for Domain(F).

This rule is a second-order correction to the previous one. If there is no absolute equality, then a large intersection will suffice. Notice that F may no longer be defined on all of its domain, even if G and H are. If identical equality is taken as the maximum possible overlap between two concepts, then this rule can be used to replace the preceding one completely.

169. *When trying to fill in the Isa entries for a composition F=G∘H,*
Examine G.Isa and H.Isa, and especially their intersection. Some of those concepts may also claim F as an example. Run their definition facet to see.

To see how this is encoded into LISP, see Appendix Section 1–2.

170. *When trying to fill in the Genl or Spec entries for a composition F=G∘H,*
Examine the corresponding facet on G and on H.

This rule is similar to the preceding one, but wasn't as useful or as reliable.

171. *A satisfactory initial guess at the Worth value of composition F=G∘H is*

$$\sqrt{G.Worth^2 + H.Worth^2}.$$

172. *To fill in examples of F, where F=GoH, and both G and H are time-consuming, but where many examples of both G and H exist,*
Seek an example x⇒y of H, and an example y⇒z of G, and then return x⇒z as a probable example of F.

Above, "seek" is done in a tight, efficent manner. The examples x⇒y of H are hashed into an array, based on the values y of each one. Then the arguments of the examples of G are hashed to see if they occur in this array. Those that do will generate an example of the new composition.

173. *To fill in examples of F, where F=GoH, and G is time-consuming, but many examples of G exist, and it is not known whether H is time-consuming or not,*
Spend a moment trying to access or trivially fill in examples of H.
If this succeeds, apply the preceding rule.
If this fails, then formally propose that AM fill in examples of H, with priority equal to that of the current task, for these two reasons: (i) if examples of H existed, then AM could have used the heuristic preceding this one, to fill in examples of F, and (ii) it is dangerous to spend a long time dealing with GoH before any examples at all of H are known.

This rule is, of course, tightly coupled to the preceding one. The same rule exists for the case where just H is time-consuming, instead of G.

174. *When trying to fill in Conjecs about a composition F=GoH,*
Consider that F may be the same as G (or the same as H).

It was somewhat depressing that this "stupid" heuristic turned out to be valuable, perhaps even necessary for AM's top performance.

Composition . Check

175. *Check that FoG is really not the same as F, or the same as G. Spend some time checking whether FoG is equivalent to any already-known active concept.*

This happens often enough to make it worth stating explicitly. Often, for example, F will not even bother looking at the result of G! For example,
$$\text{Proj2oSquare}(x,y) = \text{Proj2}(\text{Square}(x),y) = y = \text{Proj2}(x,y).$$

176. *When checking the Algorithms entries for a composition F=GoH,*
If range(H) is not wholly contained in the domain of G,
then the algorithm must contain a "legality" check, ensuring that H(x) is a valid member of the domain of G.

Composition . Suggest

177. *Given an interesting operation $F:A^n \Rightarrow A$,*
consider composing F with itself.

This may result in more than one new operation. From F=division, for example, we get the two operations (x/y)/z and x/(y/z). AM quickly realizes that such variants are really equivalent, and (if prodded) eventually realizes that F(F(x,y),z)=F(x,F(y,z)) is a common situation (which we call associativity of F).

178. *If the newly-formed domain of the composition F=GoH contains more than one occurrence of the concept D, and this isn't true of G or H,*
Then consider creating a new operation, a specialization of F, by Coalescing the domain/range of F, by eliminating one of the D components.

Thus when InsertoDelete is formed, the old Domain/range entries were both of the form <Anything Structure ⇒ Structure>. The newly-created entry for InsertoDelete was <Anything Anything Structure ⇒ Structure>; *i.e.*, take x, delete it from S, then insert y into S. The above rule had AM turn this into a new operation, with domain/range <Anything Structure ⇒ Structure>, which deleted x from S and the inserted the very same x back into S.

Composition . Interest

179. *A composition F=GoH is interesting if G and H are very interesting.*

180. *A composition F=GoH is interesting if F has an interesting property not possessed by either G or H.*

181. *A composition F=GoH is interesting if F has most of the interesting properties which are possessed by either G or H. This is slightly reduced if both G and H possess the property.*

182. *A composition F=GoH is interesting if F lacks any undesirable properties true of G or H. This is greatly increased if both G and H possess the bad property, unless G and H are very closely related to each other (e.g., H=G, or H=G⁻¹).*

The numeric impact of each of these rules was guessed at initially, and has never needed tuning. Here is an area where experimentation might prove interesting.

183. *A composition F=GoH is interesting if F maps interesting subsets of domain(H) into interesting subsets of range(G).*
F is to be judged even more interesting if the image was not thought to be interesting until after it was explicitly isolated and studied because of part 1 of this very rule.

Here, an "interesting" subset of domain(H) is one so judged by Interests(domain(H)). A completely different set of criteria will be used to judge the interestingness of the resultant image under F. Namely, for that purpose, AM will ask for range(G).Interest, and ripple outwards to look for related interest features.

184. *A composition F=GoH is interesting if F⁻¹ maps interesting subsets of range(G) into interesting subsets of domain(F).*
This is even better if the preimage wasn't hitherto realized as interesting.

This is the converse of the preceding rule. Again, "interesting" is judged by two different sets of criteria.

185. *A composition F=GoH is interesting if F maps interesting elements of domain(H) into interesting subsets of range(G).*

186. *A composition F=GoH is interesting if F⁻¹ maps interesting elements of range(G) into interesting subsets of domain(F).*
This is even better if the subset is only now seen to be interesting.

This is the analogue of an earlier rule, but for individual items rather than for whole subsets of the domain and range of F.

187. *A composition F=G∘H is interesting if range(H) is equal to, not just intersects, one component of domain(G).*

188. *A composition F=G∘H is mildly interesting if range(H) is a specialization of one component of domain(G).*

This is a weakened version of the preceding feature. Such a composition is interesting because it is guaranteed to always be applicable. If Range(H) merely intersects a domain component of G, then there must be an extra check, after computing H(x), to ensure it lies within the legal domain of G, before trying to run G on that new entity H(x).

189. *A composition F=G∘H is more interesting if range(G) is equal to a domain component of H.*

This is over and above the slight boost given to the composition because it is an operation whose domain and range coincide (see rule 211).

2–6   HEURISTICS DEALING WITH ANY INSERTIONS

Insertion . Check

190. *When checking an example of any kind of insertion of x into S,*
Ensure that x is a member of S.

The only types of insertions known to AM are unconditional insertions, so this rule is valid. It is useful for ensuring that a particular new operation really is an insertion-operation after all!

2–7   HEURISTICS DEALING WITH THE OPERATION COALESCE

Coalesce . Fillin

191. *When coalescing F(a,b,c,...), whose domain/range is <A B C... ⇒ R>,*
A good choice of two domain components to coalesce is a pair of identically equal ones. Barring that, choose a pair related by specialization (eliminate the more general one). Barring that, choose a pair with a common specialization S, and replace both by S.

Thus to coalesce the operation "InsertoDelete" (which takes two items and a structure, deletes the first argument from the structure and then inserts the second argument), AM examines its Domain/range entry: <Anything Anything Structure ⇒ Structure>. Although it would be legal to collapse the second and third arguments, the above rule says it makes more sense in general to collapse the first and second. In fact, in that case, AM gets an operation which tells it something about multiple elements structures.

192. *When filling in Algorithms for a coalesced version G of active concept F,*
One natural algorithm is simply to call on F.Algs, with two arguments the same.

Of course the two identical arguments are those which have been decided to be merged. This will be decided before the definition and algorithm facets are filled in. Thus a natural algorithm for Square is to call on TIMES.Alg(x,x). The following rule is similar:

193. When filling in Definitions for a coalesced version G of active concept F,
One natural Definition is simply to call on F.Defn, with two arguments the same.

194. When filling in the Worth of a new coalesced version of F,
A suitable value is 0.9·(Worth of F) + 0.1·(Worth of Coalesce).

This is a compromise between (*i*) the knowledge that the new operation will probably be less interesting than F, and (*ii*) the knowledge that it may lead to even more valuable new concepts (*e.g.*, its inverse may be more interesting than F's). The formula also incorporates a small factor which is based on the overall value of coalescings which AM has done so far in the run.

Coalesce . Check

195. If G and H are each two coalescings away from F, for any F,
Then check that G and H aren't really the same, by writing their definitions out in terms of F.Defn.

Thus if R(a,b,c) is really F(a,b,a,c), and S(a,b,c) is really F(a,b,c,c), and R and S get coalesced again, into G(a,b) which is R(a,b,a) and into H(a,b) which is S(a,b,a), then both G and H are really F(a,b,a,a). The order of coalescing is unimportant. This is a boost to the more general impetus for checking this sort of thing, rule 22. This rule is faster, containing a special-purpose program for untangling argument-calls rapidly. If the concept of Coalesce is excised from the system, one can easily imagine it being re-derived by a more general "coincidence" strategy, but how will these specific, high-powered, tightly-coded heuristics ever get discovered and tacked onto the Coalesce concept? This is an instance of the main meta-level research problem proposed earlier in the book (Chapter 7).

Coalesce . Suggest

196. If a newly-interesting active concept F(x,y) takes a pair of N's as arguments,
Then create a new concept, a specialization of F, called F-Itself, taking just one N as argument, defined as F(x,x), with initial worth Worth(F).
If AM has never coalesced F before, this gets a slight bonus value.
If AM has coalesced F before, say into S, then modify this suggestion's value according to the current worth of S.
The lower the system's interest-threshhold is, the more attactive this suggestion becomes.

AM used this rule to coalesce many active concepts. Times(x,x) is what we know as squaring; Equality(x,x) turned out to be the constant predicate True; Intersect(x,x) turned out to be the identity operator; Compose(f,f) was an interesting "iteration" operator;[18] etc. This rule is really a bundle of little meta-rules modifying one suggestion: the suggestion that AM coalesce F. The very last part of the above rule indicates that if the system is desperate, this is the least distasteful way to "take a chance" on a high-payoff high-risk course of action. It is more sane than, *e.g.*, randomly composing two operations until a nice new one is created.

---

[18] For example, Compose(Compose,Compose) is an operator which takes 3 operations f,g,h and forms "f∘g∘h;" *i.e.*, their joint composition.

197. *If concept F takes only one argument,*
Then it is not worthwhile to try to coalesce it.

This rule was of little help cpu-timewise, since even if AM tried to coalesce such an active concept, it would fail almost instantaneously. The rule did help make AM appear smarter, however.

2–8   HEURISTICS DEALING WITH THE OPERATION CANONIZE

Canonize . Fillin

198. *If the task is to Canonize predicates P1 and P2 (over $A \times A$),[19] and the difference between a definition of P1 and definition of P2 is just that P2 performs some extra check that P1 doesn't,*
Then F should convert any $a \epsilon A$ into a member of A which automatically satisfies that extra constraint.

Thus when P1=Same-length, P2=Equality, A=Lists, the extra constraint that P2 satisfies is just that it recurs in the CAR direction: the CARs of the two arguments must also satisfy P2. P1 doesn't have such a requirement. The above rule then has AM seek out a way to guarantee that the CARs will always satisfy Equality. A special hand-crafted piece of knowledge tells AM that since "T=T" is an example of Equality, one solution is for all the CARs to be the atom T. Then the operation F must contain a procedure for converting each member of a structure to the atom "T." Thus (A C {Z A B} Q Q) would be converted to (T T T T T). This rule is a specialized, "compiled" version of the idea expressed in rule number 101.

199. *If the task is to Canonize P1 and P2 over $A \times A$, trying to synthesize F, where A=Structure,*
Then perhaps there is a distinguished type of structure B which the argument to F should always be converted into. In that case, consider P1 and P2 as two predicates over $B \times B$.

This special-purpose rule is used to guide a series of experiments, to determine whether P1 is affected by adding multiple copies of existing elements into its arguments, and whether its value is affected by rearranging some of its arguments' elements. In the case of P1=Same-size, the answers are: multiple elements do make a difference, but rearrangement doesn't. So the canonical type of structure for F=Size must be one which is Mult-eles-allowed and also one which is Unordered. Namely, a Bag. Thus F is modified so that it first converts its argument to a Bag. Then Equality and Same-size are viewed as taking a pair of Bags, and Size is viewed as taking one Bag and giving back a canonical bag.

200. *After F is created from P1 and P2, as Canonize(P1,P2),*
an acceptable value for the worth of F is the maximum of the worths of P1 and P2.

In the actual Lisp code, an extra small term is added which takes into account the overall value of all the Canonizations which AM has recently produced.

---

[19] That is, find a function F such that P1(x,y) iff P2(F(x),F(y)).

201. *If the current task has just created a canonical specialization B of concept A, with respect to predicates P1 and P2, [i.e., two members of B satisfy P1 iff they satisfy P2],*
Then add the following entry to the Analogies facet of B:

$A \leftrightarrow B$

$P1 \leftrightarrow P2$

Operations-on-and-into(A) $\leftrightarrow$ Those operations restricted to B's

This rather incoherent rule says that it's worth taking the trouble to study the behavior of each operation when it is restricted to working on standard or "canonical" items. Moreover, some of the old relationships may carry over—or at least have analogues—in this restricted world. When numbers are discovered as canonical bags, all the bag operations are restricted to work on only canonical bags, and they startlingly turn into what we know and love as numeric operations. Many of the old bag-theoretic relationships have numeric analogues. Thus we knew that the bag-difference of x and x was the empty bag; this is still true for x a canonical bag, but we would word it as "x minus x is zero." This is because the restriction of Bag-difference to canonical bags (bags of T's) is precisely the operation we call subtraction.

202. *When Canonize works on P1, P2 (two predicates), and produces an operation, F, Both predicates must share a common Domain, of the form $A \times A$ for some concept A, and the new operation F can have $<A \Rightarrow A>$ as one of its Domain/range entries.*
If a canonical specialization (say "B") of A is defined, then the domain/range of F can actually be tightened to $<A \Rightarrow B>$, and it is also worth explicitly storing the redundant entry $<B \Rightarrow B>$.

203. *In the same situation as the last rule,*
One conjecture is that P1 and P2 are equal, when restricted to working on pairs of B's [i.e., pairs of Canonical A's, A's which are in F(A), range items for F, items x which are the image F(a) of some a∈ A].

After canonizing Equal and Same-size into the new operation Length, AM conjectures that two canonical bags are equal iff they have the same size.

Canonize . Suggest

204. *When Canonize works on P1, P2, both predicates over $A \times A$, and produces an operation $F:A \rightarrow A$,*
It is worth defining and studying the image F(A); i.e., the totality of A's which are canonical, already in standard form. When this new concept Canonical-A is defined, suggest the task "Fillin Dom/range entries for Canonical-A."

Thus AM studied Canonical-Bags, which turned out to be isomorphic to the natural numbers. What we've called "Canonical-A" in this rule, we've referred to simply as "B" in earlier Canonizing rules.

205. *If P1 is a very interesting predicate over $A \times A$, for some interesting concept A, Then look over P1.Spec for some other predicate P2 which is also over $A \times A$, and which has some interesting properties P1 lacks. For each such predicate P2, consider applying Canonize(P1,P2).*

206. *After producing F as Canonize(P1,P2) [both predicates over $A \times A$], and after defining Canonical-A,*
It is worth restricting operations in In-dom-of(A) to Canonical-A. Some new properties may emerge.

Thus after defining Canonical-Bags, AM looked at Bags.In-dom-of. In that list was the operation "Bag-union." So AM considered the restriction of Bag-union to Canonical-bags. Instead of Bag-union mapping two bags into a new bag, this new operation took two canonical-bags and mapped them into a new bag. AM later noticed that this new bag was itself always canonical. Thus was born the operation we call "Addition."

207. *After Canonical-A is produced,*
It is marginally worth trying to restrict operations in In-range-of(A) to map into Canonical-A.

This gives an added boost to picking Union to restrict, since it is in both Bags.In-dom-of and Bags.In-ran-of. This rule is much harder to implement, since it demands that the range be restricted. There are just a few special-purpose tricks AM knows to do this. Restricting the domain is, by comparison, much cleaner. AM simply creates a new concept with the same definition, but with a more restricted domain/range facet. For restricting the range, AM must insert into the definition a check to ensure that the final result is inside Canonical-A, not just in A. This leads to a very inefficient definition.

208. *After Canonical-A is produced,*
It is worthwhile to consider filling in examples (especially boundary) of that new concept.

This is above and beyond the slight push which rule 111 gives that task.

2–9   HEURISTICS DEALING WITH THE OPERATION SUBSTITUTE

Note that substitution operations are produced via the initial concepts called Parallel-replace and Parallel-replace2. The following rules are tacked on there.

Parallel-replace . Suggest

209. *If two different variables are used to represent the same entity,[20] then substitute one for the other.*
This is very important if the two occurrences are within the same entry on some facet of a single concept, and less so otherwise.
The dominant variable should be the one typed out previously to the user; barring that, the older usage; barring that, the one closest to the letter "a" in the alphabet.

This heuristic was used less often—and proved less impressive—than was originally anticipated by the author. Since most concepts were begotten from older ones, they always assumed the same variable namings, hence there were very few mismatches. A special test was needed to explicitly check for "x=y" occurring as a conjunct somewhere, in which case we removed it and substituted y for x throughout the conjunction.

210. *If two expressions (especially: two conjectures) are structurally similar, and appear to differ by a certain substitution,*
Then if the substitution is permissible we have just arrived at the same expression in various ways, and tag it as such;

---

[20] When we say that x and y represent the same entity, what we really mean is that they have the same domain of identity (*e.g.*, $\forall\, x\epsilon$ Bags) and they are equally free (there is a precise logical definition of all this, but there is little point to presenting it here).

But if the substitution is not seen to be tautologous, then a new analogy is born. Associate the constituent parts of both expressions. This is made interesting if there are several concepts involved which are assigned new analogues.

The similar statements of the associativity of Add and Times led to this rule's identifying them as analogous. If AM had been more sophisticated, it might have eventually formulated some abstract algebra concepts like "semigroup" from such analogies.

2–10 HEURISTICS DEALING WITH THE OPERATION RESTRICT

Restrict . Fillin

211. *When filling in definitions (algorithms) for a restriction R of the active concept F, One entry can simply be a call on F.Defn (F.Algs).*

Thus one definition of Addition will always be as a call on the old, general operation "Bag-union." Of course one major reason for restricting the domain/range of an activity is that it can be performed using a faster algorithm! So the above rule was used frequently if not dramatically.

212. *When creating a restriction R of the active concept F, Note that R.Genl should contain F, and that F.Spec should contain R.*

213. *When creating in a restriction R of the active concept F, by restricting the domain or range to some specialization S of its previous value C, A viable initial guess for R.Worth is F.Worth, augmented by the difference in worth between S and C. Hopefully, S.Worth is bigger than C.Worth!*

2–11 HEURISTICS DEALING WITH THE OPERATION INVERT

Invert . Fillin

214. *When filling in definitions for an Inverse F^{-1} of the active concept F, One "Sufficient Defn" entry can simply be a blind search through the examples of F.*

If we already knew that $4 \Rightarrow 16$ is an example of Square, then AM can use the above rule to quickly notice that Square-Inverse.Defn(16,4) is true. This is almost the "essence" of inverting an operation, of course.

Invert . Suggest

215. *After creating an inverted form F^{-1} of some operation F, If the only definition and algorithm entries are the "obvious" inefficient ones, Then consider the task: "Fill in algorithms for F^{-1}," because the old blind search is just too awful to tolerate.*

2–12   HEURISTICS DEALING WITH LOGICAL COMBINATIONS

Eventually, there may be separate concepts for each kind of logical connective. For the moment, all Boolean operators are lumped together here. Their definition is too trivial for a "Fillin" heuristic to be useful, and even "Check" heuristics are almost pointless.

Logical-combine . Check

216. *The user may sometimes say "Conjunction" when "Repeating" is really meant.*

Logical-combine . Suggest

217. *If there is something interesting to say about entities satisfying the disjunction (conjunction) of two concepts' definitions,*
Then consider creating a new concept defined as that logical combination of the two concepts' definitions.

218. *Given an implication,*
Try to weaken the left side as much as possible without destroying the validity of the whole implication. Similarly, try to strengthen the right side of the implication.

Logical-combine . Interest

219. *A disjunction (conjunction) is interesting if there is a conjecture which is very interesting yet which cannot be made about any one disjunct (conjunct).*

    In other words, their logical combination implies more than any consituent.

220. *An implication is interesting if the right side is more interesting than the left side.*

221. *An implication is interesting if the right side is interesting, yet unexpected, based only on assuming the left side.*

2–13   HEURISTICS DEALING WITH STRUCTURES

Structure . Fillin

222. *To fill in examples of a kind of structure S,*
Start with an empty S, pluck any other member of Examples(Structure), and transfer members one at a time from the random structure into the embryonic S. Finally, check that the resultant S really satisfies S.Defn.

    This is useful, e.g., to convert examples of lists into examples of sets.

223. *To fill in specializations of a kind of structure,*
add a new constraint that each member must satisfy, or a constraint on all pairs of members, or a constraint on all pairs of distinct members, or a constraint which the structure as a whole must satisfy. Such a constraint is often merely a stipulation of being an example of an X, for some interesting concept X.

    Thus AM *might specialize Bags into Bags-of-primes, or into Bags-of-distinct-primes, or into Bags-containing-a-prime.*

Structure . Interest

224. *Structure S is mildly interesting if all members of S satisfy the interesting predicate P, or (equivalently) if they are all accidentally examples of the interesting concept C, or (similarly) if all pairs of members of S satisfy the interesting binary predicate P, etc. Also: a kind of structure is interesting if it appears that each instance of such a structure satisfies the above condition (for a fixed P or C).*

Thus a singleton is interesting because all pairs of members satisfy Equal. The concept "Singletons" is interesting because each singleton is mildly interesting in just that same way. Similarly, AM defines the concept of a bag containing only primes, because the above rule says it might be interesting.

225. *A structure is mildly interesting if one member is very interesting. Even better: exactly one member.*
Also: a kind of structure is interesting if each instance satisfies the above condition in the same way.

Thus the values of ADD^{-1} are interesting because they always contain precisely one bag which is a Singleton.

2–14 HEURISTICS DEALING WITH ORDERED-STRUCTURES

Ordered-struc . Fillin

226. *To fill in some new examples of the ordered structure S, when some already exist, Pick an existing example and randomly permute its members.*

227. *To fill in specializations of a kind of ordered structure,*
add a new constraint that each pair of adjacent members must satisfy, or a constraint on all ordered pairs of members in the order they appear in the structure. Such a constraint is often merely a stipulation of being an example of an X, for some interesting concept X.

Thus Lists-of-numbers might be specialized into Sorted-lists-of-numbers, assuming AM has discovered "$\leq$" and assuming it is chosen as the "constraint" relationship between adjacent members of the list.

Ordered-struc . Check

228. *If the structure is to be accessed sequentially until some condition is met, and if the precise ordering is superfluous,*
Then keep the structure ordered by frequency of use, the most useful element first.

This is a simple data-structure management trick. If you have several rules to use in a certain situation, and rule R is one which usually succeeds, then put R first in the list of rules to try. Similarly, in a pattern-matcher, try first the test most likely to detect non-matching arguments.

229. *If structure S is always to be maintained in alphanumeric order,*
Then AM can[21] actually maintain it as an unordered structure, if desired.

Luckily this heavily implementation-dependent rule was never needed by AM.

---

[21] Due to the current LISP implementation of data-structures.

Ordered-struc . Interest

230. *An ordered structure S is interesting if each adjacent pair of members of S satisfies predicate P (for some rare, interesting P).*

When AM discovers the relation "$\leq$," it immediately thinks that any *sorted* list of numbers is more interesting, due to the above rule.

2–15   HEURISTICS DEALING WITH UNORDERED-STRUCTURES

Unord-struc . Check

231. *To check an example of an unordered structure,*
Ensure that it is in alphanumerically-sorted order. If not, then Sort it.

All unordered objects are maintained in lexicographic order, so that two of them can be tested for equality using the LISP function EQUAL. Because of this convention, any two structures can therefore be tested for equality using this fast list-structure comparator.

2–16   HEURISTICS DEALING WITH MULTIPLE-ELE-STRUCTURES

Mult-ele-struc . Fillin

232. *To fill in some new examples of the structure S, where S is a structure admitting multiple occurrences of the same element, when some examples already exist,*
Pick an existing example and randomly change the multiplicity with which various members occur within the structure.

2–17   HEURISTICS DEALING WITH SETS

Sets . Suggest

233. *If P is a very interesting predicate over X,*
Then study these two sets: the members of X for which P holds, and the ones for which P fails.

While we humans know that this partitions X into two pieces, AM is never explicitly told this. It would occasionally be surprised to discover that the union of two such complements "accidentally" coincided with X. Incidentally, this rule is really the key linkage between predicates and sets; it is close to the entry on Set.View which tells how to view any predicate as a set.

Sets . Interest

234. *A set S is interesting if, for some interesting predicate P, whose domain is X,*
S accidentally appears to be related strongly to $\{x \epsilon\, X \mid P(x)\}$, i.e., to those members of X satisfying P.

To the surprise of the author, this rule was not at all important to AM's behavior.

Appendix Three

Trace

Here is the way that the AM program begins—an unadulterated trace of AM in action—except that the human user's typing is italicised.

The careful reader will notice several small anomalies in this transcript: For one thing, the task numbering here is not precisely the same as in the rest of this document. A task is called a "Cand," and the agenda is called "CANDS." Only some of the reasons are printed out, and they are not as "chatty" as the reasons in, *e.g.*, Chapter 2's example trace. The user has asked AM to type out the top three tasks on the agenda at each "cycle." In a better hardware environment, the user could dynamically watch the top hundred tasks bubbling around on one side of a CRT screen. To interrupt AM, the user types CONTROL-I. At that moment there is a very limited syntax of questions he or she may ask. See the line marked "(ξ)" on page 206.

An approximate level of familiarity of the user with the AM program is maintained by AM, as a numeric variable. Initially, its value is determined by the number of times the human user has used AM in the past.[1] It gradually changes in value as a single session proceeds. Many print statements use this variable to determine the necessary level of detail to type. The level of detail needed for clarity should not be confused with the level of verbosity of output that is desired. Should the user see every function call, or the results of each task, or just monitor the overall character of what AM is doing? A separate variable is maintained for this verbosity indication. Finally, another

---

[1] I shall resist the temptation to call this a simple "user model," even in a footnote.

partially independent dimension is the amount of control the user wishes to have on AM. Must he approve each move AM makes, occasionally redirect AM, be able to ask questions? Another variable indicates the level of user control in effect at the moment.

Entering AM's main loop now.

No Cand on CANDS is good enuf.
Do-thresh reduced from 500 to 333
Must find new candidates and merge them into CANDS.

The top 3 Cands are:
      1: Fill in some examples of Set-struc-intersect
      2: Fill in some examples of Set-struc-join
      3: Fill in some examples of Coalesce

  I choose first Cand. OK? *yes.*

The reason for considering this Cand is: (We have no examples for SET-STRUC-INTERSECT yet)

Beginning 1st cycle.

Failed. Tried to fill in new examples of SET-STRUC-INTERSECT.

<At this moment, the user hit control-I and interrupted AM.>

?: (W, I, E, M, N, ?, Q) ?   ⇐===== (ξ)

Here are more detailed explanations of your options:
W Why: AM gives Ed the explanation behind its last printed message.
I Interest: Ed can modify the interest ratings of concepts and Candidates.
E Evaluate: Ed types in an expression and AM runs EVAL on it.
M Message: What was the last message that AM did NOT type out because the verbosity was too low?
N Name: Rename some concept to whatever you want to call it.
Q Quit: resume execution.
In general, AM will automatically resume execution after answering one query. You must hit ⇑I again to interrupt.

?: *W*
 Why: (No examples of SET-STRUC-INTERSECT were found; there is no reason to even consider specializing it further)

This Cand used 11.159 cpu seconds.

The top 3 Cands are:
      1: Fill in some examples of Set-struc
      2: Fill in some examples of Coalesce
      3: Fill in some examples of Nonempty-struc

  I choose first Cand. OK? *yes.*

The 2 reasons for considering this Cand are:
(Active-exs specifically asked for some examples of SET-STRUC , while trying to Fill in some Set-struc-intersect examples)
(We have no examples for SET-STRUC yet)

Beginning 2nd cycle.

Creating new Being, similar to SET-STRUC, named INT-SET-STRUC, but restricted so as to make it more interesting.
An INT-SET-STRUC is any SET-STRUC for which (Each pair of elements satisfies the same interesting predicate P (for some P)).

Filled in examples of SET-STRUC.

0 examples existed originally on SET-STRUC.

11 potential new entries were just proposed.

Eliminating duplicates, the newly constructed examples are:

(CLASS)

(CLASS DOUG CORDELL BRUCE)

(CLASS R0-7 R1-7 R2-7 R3-7 R4-7 R5-7 R6-7 R7-7)

(CLASS A)

(CLASS B)

(CLASS A B)

(CLASS 0 D F I M)

After eliminating duplicate and already-known entries, AM finds that only 7 new, distinct examples of SET-STRUC had to be added.

Do-thresh raised from 332 to 346 because this last Cand succeeded, so we raise our hopes—and our standards—temporarily.

This Cand used 23.743 cpu seconds.

The top 3 Cands are:

     1: Fill in some examples of Int-set-struc

     2: Fill in some examples of Coalesce

     3: Check all examples of Set-struc

I choose first Cand. OK? *yes.*

The reason for considering this Cand is:- (Any example of INT-SET-STRUC is automatically an interesting example of SET-STRUC)

Beginning 3rd cycle.

Won't try to create a restricted interesting version of INT-SET-STRUC.

Filled in examples of INT-SET-STRUC.

0 examples existed originally on INT-SET-STRUC.

13 potential new entries were just proposed.

Eliminating duplicates, the newly constructed examples are:

(CLASS)

(CLASS A)

(CLASS B)

After eliminating duplicate and already-known entries, AM finds that only 3 new, distinct examples of INT-SET-STRUC had to be added.

Do-thresh raised from 346 to 358.

This Cand used 11.881 cpu seconds.

The top 3 Cands are:

     1: Fill in some examples of Obj-equal

     2: Check all examples of Int-set-struc

     3: Check all examples of Set-struc

I choose first Cand. OK? *yes.*

The reason for considering this Cand is:- (We have no examples for OBJ-EQUAL yet)

Beginning 4th cycle.

Record of attempts to find examples:- An ex (sought) is: ((CLASS A),(CLASS A) → T) +- -+- -+- -+- - - - - - - - - -+- - - - - +- - -

Found 6 examples (and 151 non-exs), in 11.644 secs.

Ratio of exs to non-exs is too low (6 / 151); Exs are too sparse. AM will, at some future time, try to generalize OBJ-EQUAL.

Won't try to create a restricted interesting version of OBJ-EQUAL.

Filled in examples of OBJ-EQUAL.
   0 examples existed originally on OBJ-EQUAL.
   6 potential new entries were just proposed.
Eliminating duplicates, the newly constructed examples are:
   ((CLASS A) (CLASS A) → T)
   ((CLASS O D F I M) (CLASS O D F I M) → T)
   (FALSE FALSE → T)
After eliminating duplicate and already-known entries, AM finds that only 3 new, distinct examples of OBJ-EQUAL had to be added.

Do-thresh raised from 358 to 359.

This Cand used 17.886 cpu seconds.

No Cand on CANDS is good enuf.
Do-thresh reduced from 359 to 239
Must find new candidates and merge them into CANDS.

The top 3 Cands are:
      1: Fill in some examples of Set-struc-intersect
      2: Check all examples of Int-set-struc
      3: Fill in some generalizations of Obj-equal

   I choose first Cand. OK? *yes*.

The reason for considering this Cand is: (We have no examples for SET-STRUC-INTERSECT yet)

AM recently tried this same Cand, so let's skip it now.

The top 3 Cands are:
      1: Check all examples of Int-set-struc
      2: Fill in some generalizations of Obj-equal
      3: Check all examples of Set-struc

   I choose first Cand. OK? *yes*.

The reason for considering this Cand is: (Some new , unchecked examples of INT-SET-STRUC have recently been added)

                     Beginning 5th cycle.

AM is forgetting the entire SUGG facet of the INT-SET-STRUC concept.
   Because: (No sense using this suggestion more than once).

Checked examples of INT-SET-STRUC and all entries were confirmed

This Cand used 11.362 cpu seconds.

The top 3 Cands are:
      1: Check all examples of Set-struc
      2: Fill in some generalizations of Obj-equal
      3: Fill in some examples of Coalesce

   I choose first Cand. OK? *yes*.

The reason for considering this Cand is: (Some new , unchecked examples of SET-STRUC have recently been added)

                     Beginning 6th cycle.

Based on empirical experiments, AM believes that SET-STRUC may really be no more specialized than UNORD-OBJ.

Closer inspection reveals that the evidence for this was quite flimsy. AM will wait until some examples of any of these have been found: (BAG-STRUC), and then see if they truly also are SET-STRUC's.

Based on empirical experiments, AM believes that SET-STRUC may really be no more specialized than NONMULT-STRUC.

Closer inspection reveals that the evidence for this was quite flimsy. AM will wait until some examples of any of these have been found: (OSET-STRUC), and then see if they truly also are SET-STRUC's.

Checked examples of SET-STRUC.
    5 entries were there initially.
    1 small modifications had to be made.
    5 entries are present now.

This Cand used 8.008 cpu seconds.

The top 3 Cands are:
        1: Fill in some examples of Bag-struc
        2: Fill in some examples of Oset-struc
        3: Fill in some generalizations of Obj-equal

    I choose first Cand. OK? *yes*.

The reason for considering this Cand is: (We have no examples for BAG-STRUC yet)
                        Beginning 7th cycle.

Filled in examples of BAG-STRUC.
    0 examples existed originally on BAG-STRUC.
    19 potential new entries were just proposed.
Eliminating duplicates, the newly constructed examples are:
    (BAG)
    (BAG A)
    (BAG B)
    (BAG A B)
    (BAG A A)
    (BAG A A B)
    (BAG 0 D F I M)
    (BAG A B (BAG B) (CLASS))
    (BAG BRUCE CORDELL DOUG)
    (BAG R0-7 R1-7 R2-7 R3-7 R4-7 R5-7 R6-7 R7-7)
After eliminating duplicate and already-known entries, AM finds that only 10 new, distinct examples of BAG-STRUC had to be added.

Do-thresh raised from 239 to 264.

This Cand used 17.692 cpu seconds.

The top 3 Cands are:
        1: Fill in some generalizations of Obj-equal
        2: Fill in some examples of Oset-struc
        3: Fill in some examples of Coalesce

    I choose first Cand. OK? *yes*.

The reason is: (The ratio of examples to non-examples of OBJ-EQUAL is too low ; OBJ-EQUAL is too specialized , too narrow)
                        Beginning 8th cycle.

Considering genlizing a recursive defn of OBJ-EQUAL
    Will try to remove a conjunct.
    2 possible conjuncts to choose from.
    AM generalizes OBJ-EQUAL into the new concept GENL-OBJ-EQUAL, by not recursing on the CAR of each arg.
        i.e., GENL-OBJ-EQUAL will not have a recursive check like this one, which is present in OBJ-EQUAL:

```
(APPLYB
    (QUOTE OBJ-EQUAL)
    (QUOTE DEFN)
    (CAR BA1)
    (CAR BA2))
```

AM generalizes OBJ-EQUAL into the new concept GENL-OBJ-EQUAL-1, by not recursing on the CDR of each arg.

    i.e., GENL-OBJ-EQUAL-1 will not have a recursive check like this one, which is present in OBJ-EQUAL:

```
(APPLYB
    (QUOTE OBJ-EQUAL)
    (QUOTE DEFN)
    (CDR BA1)
    (CDR BA2))
```

If any of (GENL-OBJ-EQUAL GENL-OBJ-EQUAL-1) ever seems to be too specialized, AM will consider disjoining it with other members of that set.

Filled in generalizations of OBJ-EQUAL.
    0 generalizations existed originally on OBJ-EQUAL.
    2 potential new entries were just proposed.
Eliminating duplicates, the newly constructed generalizations are:
    GENL-OBJ-EQUAL
    GENL-OBJ-EQUAL-1
After eliminating duplicate and already-known entries, AM finds that all 2 new, distinct generalizations of OBJ-EQUAL had to be added.

Do-thresh raised from 264 to 335.

This Cand used 6.667 cpu seconds.

The top 3 Cands are:
        1: Fill in some examples of Genl-obj-equal-1
        2: Fill in some examples of Genl-obj-equal
        3: Fill in some examplls of Oset-struc

    I choose first Cand. OK? *yes*.

The reason is: (The generalization GENL-OBJ-EQUAL-1 of OBJ-EQUAL is relatively new and has no exs of its own yet , excepting those of OBJ-EQUAL)

                    Beginning 9th cycle.

?: *N*
Rename which existing concept? *GENL-OBJ-EQUAL*
What is its new name? *SAME-SIZE*
Done.

Record of attempts to find examples:
- An ex (sought) is: ((VECTOR BAG) (VECTOR B (BAG B) (CLASS) A))+- - - -
-++ -+- - -+- - - - - - -++-+- -++-+- - - - - - - - - - -++- - - - - -+-
-+- - - - - - - -+- - - - - - - - - -+-+- - - - - - - - -++- -+- - - - - - - - - - -
- - - - - - -++- - - - - -+-+- - - -+

Found 26 examples (and 105 non-exs), in 8.037 secs.
A nice ratio of exs/non-exs was encountered for GENL-OBJ-EQUAL-1
Won't try to create a restricted interesting version of GENL-OBJ-EQUAL-1.

Filled in examples of GENL-OBJ-EQUAL-1.
    0 examples existed originally on GENL-OBJ-EQUAL-1.
    26 potential new entries were just proposed.
Eliminating duplicates, the newly constructed examples are:
    ((VECTOR BAG) (VECTOR B (BAG B) (CLASS) A) → T)

((OSET O D F I M) (OSET O D F I M) → T)
((BAG) (BAG DON ED) → T)
((OSET D M I F 0) (OSET D M I F 0) → T)
((PAIR DOUG BRUCE) (PAIR DOUG BRUCE) → T)
((VECTOR BAG) (VECTOR D M I F 0) → T)
((VECTOR B) (VECTOR D M I F 0) → T)
((BAG B) (BAG B) → T)
((VECTOR D M I F 0) (VECTOR A A B) → T)
((BAG A) (BAG A B) → T)
((VECTOR) (VECTOR B (BAG B) (CLASS) A) → T)
((OSET BRUCE DON) (OSET B A) → T)
((PAIR COMPOSE-EXS COMPOSE-EXS) (PAIR LIST-STRUC-INTERSECT AN-YB-SPEC) → T)
((OSET R2-1 R2-2 R2-3 R2-4 R2-5 R2-6 R3-1 R3-2 R3-3 R3-4 R3-5 R3-6 R4-1 R4-2 R4-3 R4-4 R4-5 R4-6 R5-1 R5-2 R5-3 R5-4 R5-5 R5-6 R6-1 R6-2 R6-3 R6-4 R6-5 R6-6) (OSET O D F I M) → T)
((OSET A B (BAG B) (CLASS)) (OSET B (BAG B) (CLASS) A) → T)
((OSET O D F I M) (OSET B) → T)
((VECTOR A A) (VECTOR A B) → T)
((OSET DON ED) (OSET BAG) → T)
((BAG A A B) (BAG) → T)
((OSET B) (OSET BRUCE DON) → T)
((CLASS DON ED) (CLASS A) → T)
((PAIR LIST-STRUC-INSERT CANONIZE) (PAIR LIST-STRUC-INTERSECT AN-YB-SPEC) → T)
((VECTOR) (VECTOR BAG) → T)
((OSET A) (OSET D M I F 0) → T)
((VECTOR BAG) (VECTOR BAG) → T)

After eliminating duplicate and already-known entries, AM finds that only 25 new, distinct examples of GENL-OBJ-EQUAL-1 had to be added.

Do-thresh raised from 335 to 367.

This Cand used 29.095 cpu seconds.

The top 3 Cands are:
        1: Fill in some examples of Same-size
        2: Check all examples of Genl-obj-equal-1
        3: Fill in some examples of Coalesce

    I choose first Cand. OK? *yes*.

The 2 reasons are:
(Interestingness of SAME-SIZE has changed recently)
(The generalization SAME-SIZE of OBJ-EQUAL is relatively new and has no exs of its own yet , excepting those of OBJ-EQUAL)

                              Beginning 10th cycle.

Record of attempts to find examples:
- An ex (sought) is: ((VECTOR A) (OSET B))+-- - -+-- -+- - - - - - - - +-- - - -
+++++-- - - - - - - - +-+-- - -+- +- - - - - -+-- - - - - -+- -+- - +- - - +- -
+- - - - - - - - -+-+- - - - - - - - - -+-- - -+- - - -+- - - - +- - -+-- - - - - - -
- - - - - - - -+

Found 26 examples (and 102 non-exs), in 8.032 secs.
A nice ratio of exs/non-exs was encountered for SAME-SIZE
Won't try to create a restricted interesting version of SAME-SIZE.

Filled in examples of SAME-SIZE.
        0 examples existed originally on SAME-SIZE.

36 potential new entries were just proposed.

Eliminating duplicates, the newly constructed examples are:

((OSET 0 D F I M) (OSET 0 D F I M) → T)

((OSET D M I F 0) (OSET D M I F 0) → T)

((PAIR DOUG BRUCE) (PAIR DOUG BRUCE) → T)

((BAG B) (BAG B) → T)

((OSET BRUCE DON) (OSET B A) → T)

((PAIR COMPOSE-EXS COMPOSE-EXS) (PAIR LIST-STRUC-INTERSECT ANY-B-SPEC) → T)

((OSET A B (BAG B) (CLASS)) (OSET B (BAG B) (CLASS) A) → T)

((VECTOR A A) (VECTOR A B) → T)

((PAIR LIST-STRUC-INSERT CANONIZE) (PAIR LIST-STRUC-INTERSECT AN-YB-SPEC) → T)

((VECTOR BAG) (VECTOR BAG) → T)

((VECTOR A) (OSET B) → T)

((BAG A B) (OSET B A) → T)

((CLASS 0 D F I M) (BAG 0 D F I M) → T)

((VECTOR B) (BAG A) → T)

((PAIR LIST-STRUC-INTERSECT ANYB-SPEC) (PAIR DOUG BRUCE) → T)

((OSET DON ED) (PAIR LIST-STRUC-INTERSECT ANYB-SPEC) → T)

((BAG 0 D F I M) (VECTOR D M I F 0) → T)

((VECTOR B) (BAG B) → T)

((OSET BAG) (OSET A) → T)

((VECTOR A A) (BAG A A) → T)

((CLASS A) (VECTOR BAG) → T)

((CLASS A B) (OSET A B) → T)

((PAIR COMPOSE-EXS COMPOSE-EXS) (OSET DON ED) → T)

((VECTOR A) (OSET A) → T)

((OSET BAG) (CLASS A) → T)

((OSET A) (CLASS A) → T)

((OSET B) (OSET A) → T)

((BAG 0 D F I M) (OSET 0 D F I M) → T)

((OSET DON ED) (OSET ED CORDELL) → T)

((OSET ED CORDELL) (OSET B A) → T)

((OSET A) (BAG B) → T).

((OSET B A) (OSET A B) → T)

((VECTOR B A) (OSET ED CORDELL) → T)

((OSET A) (VECTOR BAG) → T)

((OSET B A) (OSET DON ED) → T)

After eliminating duplicate and already-known entries, AM finds that only 35 new, distinct examples of SAME-SIZE had to be added.

Do-thresh raised from 367 to 406.

This Cand used 21.725 cpu seconds.

The top 3 Cands are:

     1: Check all examples of Same-size

     2: Check all examples of Genl-obj-equal-1

     3: Check all things which just barely miss being examples of Same-size

I choose first Cand. OK? *yes*.

The reason is: (Some new , unchecked examples of SAME-SIZE have recently been added)

Beginning 11st cycle.

Checked examples of SAME-SIZE.
>   35 entries were there initially.
>   1 had to be completely discarded.
>   4 had to be transferred elsewhere.
>   30 entries are present now.

Do-thresh raised from 406 to 421.

This Cand used 6.917 cpu seconds.

The top 3 Cands are:
>   1: Check all examples of Genl-obj-equal-1
>   2: Check all things which just barely miss being examples of Same-size
>   3: Fill in some examples of Coalesce

>   I choose first Cand. OK? *yes.*

The reason is: (Some new , unchecked examples of GENL-OBJ-EQUAL-1 have recently been added)

Beginning 12nd cycle.

Checked examples of GENL-OBJ-EQUAL-1.
>   25 entries were there initially.
>   1 had to be completely discarded.
>   4 had to be transferred elsewhere.
>   20 entries are present now.

This Cand used 4.711 cpu seconds.

No Cand on CANDS is good enuf.
Do-thresh reduced from 421 to 333
Must find new candidates and merge them into CANDS.

The top 3 Cands are:
>   1: Canonize these 2 arguments: Genl-obj-equal-1 and Obj-equal
>   2: Canonize these 2 arguments: Same-size and Obj-equal
>   3: Fill in some examples of Coalesce

>   I choose first Cand. OK? *yes.*

The reason is: (It would be nice to find a canonical (with respect to Genl-obj-equal-1 and Obj-equal) representation C for any Object X ; that is ,
>   (GENL-OBJ-EQUAL-1 x y) iff
>   (OBJ-EQUAL (C x) (C y)) .
>   )

Beginning 13rd cycle.

Experiments indicate that GENL-OBJ-EQUAL-1 is affected by the varying the type of structure of its arguments.

GENL-OBJ-EQUAL-1 doesn't look at any elements of OBJECT except possibly the car of the structure which denotes its type, so AM replaces the tail of OBJECT by a canonical distinguished tail, say NIL.

Succeeded!

Some conjectures that AM considers believable:

>   OBJ-EQUAL, restricted to canonical OBJECT's, is indistinguishable from GENL-OBJ-EQUAL-1.
>   There is a powerful analogy between
>   GENL-OBJ-EQUAL-1.................OBJ-EQUAL
>   OBJECT...........................CANONICAL-OBJECT
>   operators on and into   those operators restricted to
>   OBJECT.......................CANONICAL-OBJECT
>   statements involving these.......statements involving these

Do-thresh raised from 333 to 341.

This Cand used 9.02 cpu seconds.

The top 3 Cands are:
     1: Fill in some examples of Canonical-object
     2: Restrict the following: Genl-obj-equal-1 Canonical-object Domain
     3: Canonize these 2 arguments: Same-size and Obj-equal

  I choose first Cand. OK? *yes.*

The reason is: (Any example of CANONICAL-OBJECT is a canonical example of OBJECT)

Beginning 14th cycle.

AM will now try to produce examples of CANONICAL-OBJECT by running the following operations:
    (CANONIZE-GENL-OBJ-EQUAL-1&OBJ-EQUAL).
Won't try to create a restricted interesting version of CANONICAL-OBJECT.

Filled in examples of CANONICAL-OBJECT.
    0 examples existed originally on CANONICAL-OBJECT.
    165 potential new entries were just proposed.
Eliminating duplicates, the newly constructed examples are:
    (VECTOR)
    (BAG)
    (CLASS)
    (OSET)
    FALSE
    T
    TRUE
    (PAIR)
    (T)
    (NIL)
    (TRUE)
    (FALSE)
After eliminating duplicate and already-known entries, AM finds that only 12 new, distinct examples of CANONICAL-OBJECT had to be added.

Do-thresh raised from 341 to 391.

This Cand used 23.827 cpu seconds.

The top 3 Cands are:
     1: Restrict the following: Genl-obj-equal-1 Canonical-object Domain
     2: Canonize these 2 arguments: Same-size and Obj-equal
     3: Fill in examples of Coalesce

  I choose first Cand. OK? *yes.*

The reason is: (GENL-OBJ-EQUAL-1 was one of the predicates which defined the new concept CANONICAL-OBJECT , so it is worth considering the restriction of GENL-OBJ-EQUAL-1 to that subset of OBJECT 's)

Beginning 15th cycle.

Succeeded!

Do-thresh raised from 391 to 431.

This Cand used 3.562 cpu seconds.

The top 3 Cands are:
>   1: Canonize these 2 arguments: Same-size and Obj-equal
>   2: Fill in some examples of Coalesce
>   3: Restrict the following: Obj-equal Canonical-object Domain

   I choose first Cand. OK? *yes*.

The reason is: (It would be nice to find a canonical (with respect to Same-size and Obj-equal) representation C for any Object X ; that is ,
>   (SAME-SIZE x y) iff
>   (OBJ-EQUAL (C x) (C y)) .
>   )

Beginning 16th cycle.

Experiments indicate that SAME-SIZE is not affected by varying the type of structure of its arguments.

Experiments indicate that SAME-SIZE is not affected by reordering elements of its structural arguments.
>   So any canonical arguments can be Bags and Sets.

Experiments indicate that SAME-SIZE is affected by the presence of multiple elements in its structural arguments.
>   So any canonical arguments can be Bags and Lists.

SAME-SIZE doesn't look at the specific elements in OBJECT, like OBJ-EQUAL does, so AM can replace them all by a single distinguished element, say T.

Succeeded!

Some conjectures that AM considers believable:
>   OBJ-EQUAL, restricted to canonical BAG-STRUC's, is indistinguishable from SAME-SIZE.
>   There is a powerful analogy between
>   SAME-SIZE........................OBJ-EQUAL
>   BAG-STRUC........................CANONICAL-BAG-STRUC
>   operators on and into   those operators restricted to
>   BAG-STRUC.................. CANONICAL-BAG-STRUC
>   statements involving these.......statements involving these

Do-thresh raised from 431 to. 457.

This Cand used 17.297 cpu seconds.

The top 3 Cands are:
>   1: Fill in some examples of Canonical-bag-struc
>   2: Restrict the following: Same-size Canonical-bag-struc Domain
>   3: Restrict the following: Bag-struc-join Canonical-bag-struc Domain

   I choose first Cand. OK? *yes*.

The reason is: (Any example of CANONICAL-BAG-STRUC is a canonical example of BAG-STRUC)

Beginning 17th cycle.

AM will now try to produce examples of CANONICAL-BAG-STRUC by running the following operations:
>   (CANONIZE-SAME-SIZE&OBJ-EQUAL).

Filled in examples of CANONICAL-BAG-STRUC.
>   0 examples existed originally on CANONICAL-BAG-STRUC.
>   211 potential new entries were just proposed.
Eliminating duplicates, the newly constructed examples are:
>   (BAG)

```
(BAG T T)
(BAG T T T)
(BAG T)
(BAG T T T T T)
(BAG T T T T)
(BAG T T T T T T T T T T T T T T T T T T T T T T T T T T T T T T T T T)
```

After eliminating duplicate and already-known entries, AM finds that only 7 new, distinct examples of CANONICAL-BAG-STRUC had to be added.

Do-thresh raised from 457 to 478.

This Cand used 35.918 cpu seconds.

The top 3 Cands are:
        1: Restrict the following: Same-size Canonical-bag-struc Domain
        2: Restrict the following: Bag-struc-join Canonical-bag-struc Domain
        3: Restrict the following: Obj-equal Canonical-object Domain

    I choose first Cand. OK? *yes.*

The reason is: (SAME-SIZE was one of the predicates which defined the new concept CANONICAL-BAG-STRUC , so it is worth considering the restriction of SAME-SIZE to that subset of BAG-STRUC 's)

                        Beginning 18th cycle.

Succeeded!

Do-thresh raised from 478 to 495.

This Cand used 3.311 cpu seconds.

?: *N*
Rename which existing concept? *CANONICAL-BAG-STRUC*
What is its new name? *NUMBER*
Done.

?: (W, I, E, M, N, ?, Q) *N*
Rename which existing concept? *CANONIZE-SAME-SIZE&OBJ-EQUAL*
What is its new name? *SIZE*
Done.

The top 3 Cands are:
        1: Check all examples of Number
        2: Restrict the following: Obj-equal Canonical-object Domain
        3: Check all examples of Canonical-object

    I choose first Cand. OK? *yes.*

The 2 reasons are:
(Interestingness of NUMBER has changed recently)
(Some new , unchecked examples of NUMBER have recently been added)
                        Beginning 19th cycle.

Checked examples of NUMBER and all entries were confirmed

This Cand used 1.909 cpu seconds.

The top 3 Cands are:
        1: Check all examples of Canonical-object
        2: Check all things which just barely miss being examples of Number
        3: Restrict the following: Bag-struc-join Number Domain

    I choose first Cand. OK? *yes.*

The reason is: (Some new , unchecked examples of CANONICAL-OBJECT have recently been added)

Beginning 20th cycle.

CANONICAL-OBJECT has 7 examples which occupy 11 list cells, but is not interesting enough to warrant taking up that much space; so about 2 will be selected at random and forgotten.

Checked examples of CANONICAL-OBJECT.

    12 entries were there initially.

    10 were never confirmed or rejected.

    2 had to be completely discarded.

    5 entries are present now.

This Cand used 16. 626 cpu seconds.

No Cand on CANDS is good enuf.

Do-thresh reduced from 495 to 340

Must find new candidates and merge them into CANDS.

The top 3 Cands are:

       1: Fill in some examples of Size

       2: Fill in some examples of Coalesce

       3: Restrict the following: Bag-struc-join Number Domain

    I choose first Cand. OK? *yes.*

The reason is: (We have no examples for SIZE yet)

Beginning 21st cycle.

Record of attempts to find examples:

An ex (sought) is: (BAG T T)-+-
+-+-+-+

Found 26 examples (and 0 non-exs), in .996 secs.

A nice ratio of exs/non-exs was encountered for SIZE

Won't try to create a restricted interesting version of SIZE.

Filled in examples of SIZE.

    13 examples existed originally on SIZE.

    26 potential new entries were just proposed.

Eliminating duplicates, the newly constructed examples are:

    ((BAG T T) → (BAG T T))

    ((BAG T T T T T) → (BAG T T T T T))

    ((BAG B) → (BAG T))

    ((BAG A A) → (BAG T T))

    ((BAG T T T) → (BAG T T T))

    ((BAG T T T T) → (BAG T T T T))

    ((BAG A B) → (BAG T T))

    ((BAG R2-1 R2-2 R2-3 R2-4 R2-5 R2-6 R3-1 R3-2 R3-3 R3-4 R3-5 R3-6 R4-1 R4-2 R4-3 R4-4 R4-5 R4-6 R5-1 R5-2 R5-3 R5-4 R5-5 R5-6 R6-1 R6-2 R6-3 R6-4 R6-5 R6-6) → (BAG T T T T T T T T T T T T T T T T T T T T T T T T T T T T T T))

    ((BAG A A B) → (BAG T T T))

    ((BAG 0 D F I M) → (BAG T T T T T))

    ((BAG A) → (BAG T))

    ((BAG T T T T T T T T T T T T T T T T T T T T T T T T T T T T T T T T) → (BAG T T T T T T T T T T T T T T T T T T T T T T T T T T T T T T T T))

    ((BAG DON ED) → (BAG T T))

    ((BAG A B (BAG B) → (CLASS)) (BAG T T T T))

    ((BAG A B) → (BAG T T))

After eliminating duplicate and already-known entries, AM finds that only 14 new, distinct examples of SIZE had to be added.

Do-thresh raised from 340 to 414.

This Cand used 9.2 cpu seconds.

Bibliography

Of all the articles, books, and memos which were read as background for AM, I have selected those which had some impact on that work (or at least, on this book). While numerous, they form a far from comprehensive list of publications dealing with automated theory formation, with AI in general, and with how mathematicians do research.

Adams, James L., *Conceptual Blockbusting*, W. H. Freeman and Co., San Francisco, 1974.

Amarel, Saul, *On Representations and Modelling in Problem Solving and On Future Directions for Intelligent Systems*, RCA Labs Scientific Report No. 2, Princeton, N.J., 1967.

Atkin, A. O. L., and B. J. Birch, eds., "Computers in Number Theory," *Proceedings of the 1969 SRCA Oxford Symposium*, Academic Press, New York, 1971.

Badre, Nagib A., *Computer Learning From English Text*, Memorandum No. ERL–M372, Electronics Research Laboratory, UCB, December 20, 1972. Also summarized in *CLET—A Computer Program that Learns Arithmetic from an Elementary Textbook*, IBM Research Report RC 4235, February 21, 1973.

Berliner, H., *Chess as Problem Solving: The Development of a Tactics Analyzer*, Carnegie-Mellon University Computer Science Department Thesis, March, 1974.

Beth, E. W., and J. Piaget, *Mathematical Epistemology and Psychology*, Gordon and Breach, New York, 1966.

Beveridge, W. I., *The Art of Scientific Investigation*, Vintage Books, N. Y., 1950.

Biermann, A. W., "Approaches to Automatic Programming," in *Advances in Computers*, v. 15, Academic Press, 1976.

Black, M., *Margins of Precision*, Cornell University Press, Ithaca, New York, 1970.

Blalock, H. M., *Theory Construction*, Prentice-Hall, Englewood Cliffs, N. J., 1969.

Bledsoe, W. W., "Splitting and Reduction Heuristics in Automatic Theorem Proving," Artificial Intelligence 2, 1971, pp. 55–77.

Bledsoe, W. W., and Bruell, Peter, "A Man-Machine Theorem-Proving System," Artificial Intelligence 5, 1974, 51–72.

Bobrow, D., and A. Collins, editors, *Representation and Understanding*, Academic Press, S. F., 1975.

Bobrow, D., and D. Norman, *Some Principles of Memory Schemata*, XEROX PARC Memo CSL 75–4, Palo Alto, July, 1975.

Bobrow, D. G., and T. Winograd, "An Overview of KRL, A Knowledge Representation Language," Journal of Cognitive Science, Vol. 1, No 1, January 1977.

Bourbaki, N., "The Architechture of Mathematics," American Mathematics Monthly, v. 57, pp. 221–232, Published by the MAA, Albany, N. Y., 1950.

Boyer, R. S., and J. S. Moore, "Proving Theorems about LISP Functions," JACM, v. 22, No. 1, January, 1975, pp. 129–144.

Brotz, D. K., *Embedding Heuristic Problem Solving Methods in a Mechanical Theorem Prover*, Ph.D. dissertation published as Stanford Computer Science Report STAN-CS-74-443, August, 1974.

Bruijn, N. G. de, *AUTOMATH, a language for mathematics*, Les Presses de L'Universite de Montreal, Montreal, 1973.

Buchanan, B. G., G. Sutherland, and E. Feigenbaum, *Heuristic Dendral: A Program for Generating Explanatory Hypotheses in Organic Chemistry*, in (Meltzer and Michie, eds.) *Machine Intelligence 4*, American Elsevier Pub., N. Y., 1969, pp. 209-254.

Buchanan, B. G., E. Feigenbaum, and Sridharan, *Heuristic Theory Formation*, *Machine Intelligence 7*, 1972, pp. 267-290.

Buchanan, B. G., *Scientific Theory Formation by Computer*, NATO Advanced Study Institute on Computer Oriented Learning Processes, Bonas, France, 1974.

Buchanan, Bruce G., *Applications of Artificial Intelligence to Scientific Reasoning*, Second USA-Japan Computer Conference, Tokyo, August 26-28. Published by AFIPS and IPSJ, Tokyo, 1975, pp. 189-194.

Bundy, A., *Doing Arithmetic with Diagrams*, 3rd International Joint Conference on Artificial Intelligence (3rd IJCAI), Stanford, 1973, pp. 130-138.

Burstall, R., and J. Darlington, *A Transformation System for Developing Recursive Programs*, University of Edinburgh AI Research Report, March, 1976.

Church, A., *The calculi of Lambda-conversion*, Princeton University Press, Princeton, 1941.

Cohen, P. J., *Set Theory and the Continuum Hypothesis*, W.A.Benjamin, Inc., New York, 1966.

Colby, K. M., "Simulations of belief systems", in [Schank and Colby 73].

Copeland, R. W., *How Children Learn Mathematics*, The MacMillan Company,

London, 1970.

Courant, R., and H. Robins, *What is Mathematics?*, Oxford University Press, New York, 1941.

Dahl, O., et. al., *SIMULA-67: A Common Base Language*, Norwegian Computing Center Publication No. S-2, Oslo, 1968.

Darlington, J., and R. Burstall, *A System Which Automatically Improves Programs*, 3rd IJCAI, 1973, pp. 479-485.

Davis, R., and J. King, *An Overview of Production Systems*, Stanford AI Lab Memo 271, October, 1975.

Dijkstra, E. W., *A Discipline of Programming*, Prentice-Hall, Inc., Englewood Cliffs, N.J., 1976.

Eddington, Sir A. S., *New Pathways in Science*, Macmillan Co., N. Y., 1935.

Engelman, C., *MATHLAB: A Program for On-Line Assistance in Symbolic Computation*, in Proceedings of the FJCC, v. 2, Spartan Books, 1965.

Engelman, C., *MATHLAB '68*, in IFIP, Edinburgh, 1968.

Evans, T. G., *A Program for the Solution of Geometric-Analogy Intelligence Test Questions*, in [Minsky 68], pp. 271-353.

Eynden, C. V., *Number Theory: An Introduction to Proof*, International Textbook Company, Scranton, Pennsylvania, 1970.

Feigenbaum, E. A., *EPAM: The Simulation of Verbal Learning Behavior*, in [Feigenbaum & Feldman 63], Part 2, Section 2, pp. 297-309.

Feigenbaum, E. A., and J. Feldman, editors, *Computers and Thought*, McGraw-Hill Book Company, New York, New York, 1963.

Feigenbaum, E., B. Buchanan, and J. Lederberg, *On Generality and Problem Solving: A Case Study Using The DENDRAL Program*, in (Meltzer and Michie, eds.) *Machine Intelligence 6*, 1971, pp 165-190.

Fogel, L., A. Owens, and M. Walsh, *Artificial Intelligence Through Simulated Evolution*, John Wiley & Sons, Inc., N. Y., 1966.

Fuller, R. B., *Synergetics*, Macmillan Co., N. Y., 1975.

Gardner, M., *Mathematical Games*, Scientific American [numerous columns, including especially: February, 1975.]

Gelernter, H., *Realization of a Geometry-Theorem Proving Machine*, in [Feigenbaum & Feldman 63], Part 1, Section 3, pages 134-152.

Goldstein, I., *Elementary Geometry Theorem Proving*, MIT AI Memo 280, April, 1973.

Goodstein, R. L., *Fundamental Concepts of Mathematics*, Pergamon Press, New York, 1962.

Green, C. C., R. Waldinger, D. Barstow, R. Elschlager, D. Lenat, B. McCune, D. Shaw, and L. Steinberg, *Progress Report on Program-Understanding Systems*, Memo AIM-240, CS Report STAN-CS-74-444, Artificial Intelligence Laboratory, Stanford University, August, 1974.

Guard, J. R., Eastman et al., *Semi-Automated Mathematics*, JACM 16, January, 1969, pp. 49-62.

Hadamard, J., *The Psychology of Invention in the Mathematical Field*, Dover Publications, New York, 1945.

Halmos, P. R., *Innovation in Mathematics*, in [Kline 68]. Originally in Scientific American, September, 1958.

Hardy, G. H., and E. M. Wright, *An Introduction to the Theory of Numbers*, Oxford U. Press, London, 1938. (Fourth edition, 1960)

Hayes-Roth, F., and V. R. Lesser, *Focus of Attention in a Distributed Speech Understanding System*, Computer Science Dept. Memo, Carnegie-Mellon University, Pittsburgh, Pa., January 12, 1976.

Hempel, C. G., *Fundamentals of Concept Formation in Empirical Science*, University of Chicago Press, Chicago, 1952.

Hewitt, C., *A Universal Modular ACTOR Formalism for Artificial Intelligence*, Third International Joint Conference on Artificial Intelligence, 1973, pp. 235-245.

Hewitt, C., *Viewing Control Structures as Patterns of Passing Messages*, MIT AI Lab Working Paper 92, April, 1976.

Hilpinen, R., *Rules of Acceptance and Inductive Logic*, Acta Philosophica Fennica, Fasc. 22, North-Holland Publishing Company, Amsterdam, 1968.

Hintikka, J., *Knowledge and Belief*, Cornell U. Press, Ithaca, N. Y., 1962.

Hintikka, J., and P. Suppes, editors, *Aspects of Inductive Logic*, North-Holland Publishing Company, Amsterdam, 1966.

Iberall, A. S., *Toward a General Science of Viable Systems*, McGraw-Hill Book Co., N. Y. 1972.

Kershner, R. B., and L. R. Wilcox, *The Anatomy of Mathematics*, The Ronald Press Company, New York, 1950.

Kline, M. (ed), *Mathematics in the Modern World: Readings from Scientific American*, W.H.Freeman and Co., San Francisco, 1968.

Kling, R. E., *Reasoning by Analogy with Applications to Heuristic Problem Solving: A Case Study*, Stanford Artificial Intelligence Project Memo AIM-147, CS Department report CS-216, August, 1971.

Knuth, D. E., *Fundamental Algorithms*, v. 1 of *The Art of Computer Programming*, Addison-Wesley Publishing Company, Menlo Park, 1968.

Knuth, D. E., *Surreal Numbers*, Addison-Wesley Publishing Company, Reading, Mass., 1974.

Knuth, D. E., *Ancient Babylonian Algorithms*, CACM 15, July, 1972, pp. 671-677.

Koestler, A., *The Act of Creation*, New York, Dell Pub., 1967.

Koppelman, E., "Progress in Mathematics", in the proceedings of the Workshop on the Historical Development of Modern Mathematics, July, 1975.

Lamon, W. E., *Learning and the Nature of Mathematiccs*, Science Research Associates, Palo Alto, 1972.

Lederberg, J., *DENDRAL-64: A System for Computer Construction, Enumeraion, and Notation of Organic Molecules as Tree Structures and Cyclic Graphs*, Parts I-V of the Interim Report to NASA, 1964.

Lederberg, J.; Review of [Weizenbaum 76], originally intended for the New York Times. This can be obtained as file WEIZEN.LED[pub,jmc]@SAIL, archived in 1976.

Lefrancois, G. R., *Psychological Theories and Human Learning*, Wadsworth Publishing, Belmont, Ca., 1972.

Lenat, D., *Synthesis of Large Programs from Specific Dialogues*, Proceedings of the International Symposium on Proving and Improving Programs, Le Chesnay, France, July, 1975a.

Lenat, D., *BEINGs: Knowledge as Interacting Experts*, 4th IJCAI, Tbilisi, Georgian SSR, USSR, 1975b.

Lenat, D., *The Ubiquity of Discovery: The 5IJCAI Computers and Thought*

Lecture, Proceedings of the Fifth International Joint Conference on Artificial Intellience, Cambridge, 1977.

Lesser, V., R.D. Fennell, L. D. Erman, and D. R. Reddy, *Organization of the Hearsay-II Speech Understanding System*, in IEEE Transactions on Acoustics, Speech, and Signal Processing, v. ASSP-23, 1975, pp. 11-23.

Linderholm, C. E., *Mathematics Made Difficult*, World Publishing Co., N. Y. 1972.

Lombardi, L.A., and B. Raphael, *LISP as the language for an incremental computer*, in (E. C. Berkeley and D. G. Bobrow, eds.) *The Programming Language LISP: Its Operation and Applications*, Information International Inc., 1964.

McDermott, D., *Artificial Intelligence Meets Natural Stupidity*, in Sigart Newsletter, No. 57, April, 1976, pp. 4-9.

Martin, W., and R. Fateman, *The MACSYMA System*, in (S. Petrick, ed.) Second Symposium on Symbolic and Algebraic Manipulation, ACM SIGSAM, N. Y. (conference was held in Los Angeles), 1971, pp. 59-75.

Minsky, M., editor, *Semantic Information Processing*, The MIT Press, Cambridge, Massachusetts, 1968.

Minsky, M., *Frames*, in [Winston 75].

Mirsky, L., *Studies in Pure Mathematics*, Academic Press, New York, 1971.

Moore, J S., *Introducing Iteration into the Pure LISP Theorem Prover*, XEROX PARC report CSL-74-3, Palo Alto, 1975.

Moore, J. and A. Newell, "How can MERLIN understand?," in (Gregg, ed.) *Knowledge and Cognition*, Lawrence Erlbaum Associates, 1973.

Moore, R. C., *D-SCRIPT: A Computational Theory of Descriptions*, MIT AI Memo 278, February, 1973.

Neumann, J. von, *The Mathematician*, in R.B. Heywood (ed), *The Works of the Mind*, U. Chicago Press, pp. 180-196, 1947.

Nevins, Arthur J., *A Human Oriented Logic for Automatic Theorem Proving*, MIT AI Memo 268, October, 1972.

Nevins, Arthur J., *Plane Geometry Theorem Proving Using Forward Chaining*, Artificial Intelligence 6, Spring 1975, pp. 1-23.

Newell, A. *Heuristic Programming: Ill-Structured Problems*, in (A. Aronofsky, ed.) *Progress in Operations Research III*, John Wiley and Sons, 1969.

Newell, A., *Production Systems: Models of Control Structures*, May, 1973 CMU Report, also published in (W.G. Chase, ed.) *Visual Information Processing*, N. Y.: Academic Press, Chapter 10, pp. 463-526.

Newell, A., J. Shaw, and H. Simon, *Empirical Explorations of the Logic Theory Machine: A Case Study in Heuristics*, RAND Corp. Report P-951, March, 1957.

Newell, A., and H. Simon, *Human Problem Solving*, Prentice-Hall, Englewood Cliffs, New Jersey, 1972.

Newell, A. and H. Simon, *Computer Science as Empirical Inquiry: Symbols and Search*, the 1975 ACM Turing Award Lecture, printed in CACM 19, No. 3, March, 1976, pp. 113-126.

Nilsson, N. J., *Problem-solving Methods in Artificial Intelligence*, McGraw-Hill Book Company, New York, New York, 1971

Norman, D., and D. Bobrow, *On Data-limited and Resource-limited Processes*, Journal of Cognitive Psychology, v. 7, 1975, pp. 44-64.

Norman, D., and D. Rumelhart, *Explorations in Cognition*, W. H. Freeman &

Co., S.F., 1975.

Ore, O., *Number Theory and its History*, McGraw-Hill, New York, 1948.

Papert, S., *Teaching Children to be Mathematicians Versus Teaching About Mathematics*, in the International Journal of Mathematical Education in Science and Technology, v. 3, No. 3, July-September, 1972, pp. 249-262.

Piaget, J., *The Language and Thought of the Child*, The World Publishing Co., N. Y., 1955.

Pietarinen, J., *Lawlikeness, Analogy, and Inductive Logic*, North-Holland, Amsterdam, published as v. 26 of the series Acta Philosophica Fennica (J. Hintikka, ed.), 1972.

Pitrat, J., *Heuristic Interest of using Metatheorems*, Symposium on Automatic Demonstration, Springer-Verlag, 1970.

Poincaré, H., *The Foundations of Science: Science and Hypothesis, The Value of Science, Science and Method*, The Science Press, New York, 1929.

Pólya, G., *Mathematics and Plausible Reasoning*, Princeton University Press, Princeton, Vol. 1, 1954; Vol. 2, 1954.

Pólya, G., *How To Solve It*, Second Edition, Doubleday Anchor Books, Garden City, New York, 1957.

Pólya, G., *Mathematical Discovery*, John Wiley & Sons, New York, Vol. 1, 1962; Vol. 2, 1965.

Ramanujan, S. A., *Collected Papers*, (Hardy, Aiyar, and Wilson, eds.), Chelsea Publishing Company, N. Y., 1927.

Rulifson, J., J. Derksen, and R. Waldinger, *QA4: A Procedural Calculus for Intuitive Reasoning*, SRI Project 8721, Technical Note 73, Artificial Intelligence Center, SRI, Menlo Park, California, November, 1972.

Saaty, T. L., and F. J. Weyl, editors, *The Spirit and the Uses of the Mathematical Sciences*, McGraw-Hill Book Company, New York, 1969.

Samuel, A., *Some Studies in Machine Learning Using the Game of Checkers II. Recent Progress*, in the IBM Journal of Research and Development, vol. 11, no. 6, pp. 610-617, November, 1967.

Schank, R. and K. Colby, *Computer Models of Thought and Language.*, W. H. Freeman, 1973.

Schminke, C. W., and W. R. Arnold, editors, *Mathematics is a Verb*, The Dryden Press, Hinsdale, Illinois, 1971.

Simon, H. A., *The Heuristic Compiler*, in [Simon & Siklossy 72], Part 1, Chapter 1, pp. 9-43, 1972.

Simon, H. A., *Does Scientific Discovery Have a Logic?*, Philosophy of Science, v. 40, No. 4, December, 1973, pp. 471-480.

Simon, H. A., and L. Siklossy, editors, *Representation and Meaning: Experiments with Information Processing Systems*, Prentice-Hall Inc., Englewood Cliffs, N.J., 1972.

Skemp, R. R., *The Psychology of Learning Mathematics*, Penguin Books, Ltd., Middlesex, England, 1971.

Sloman, A., *Interactions Between Philosophy and Artificial Intelligence: The Role of Intuition and Non-Logical Reasoning in Intelligence*, Artificial Intelligence 2, 1971, pp. 209-225.

Smith, N. W., *A Question-Answering System for Elementary Mathematics*, Stanford Institute for Mathematical Studies in the Social Sciences (IMSSS), Technical Report 227, April 19, 1974.

Spivak, M., *Calculus on Manifolds*, W.A.Benjamin, Inc., N. Y. 1965.

Stein, S. K., *Mathematics: The Man-Made Universe: An Introduction to the Spirit of Mathematics*, Second Edition, W. H. Freeman and Company, San Francisco, 1969.

Teitelman, W., *INTERLISP Reference Manual*, XEROX PARC, 1974.

Tullock, G., *The Organization of Inquiry*, Duke U. Press, Durham, N. C., 1966.

Venn, J., *The Principles of Empirical or Inductive Logic*, MacMillan and Co., London, 1889.

Waismann, F., *Introduction to Mathematical Thinking*, Frederick Ungar Publishing Co., New York, 1951.

Wang, H., *Toward Mechanical Mathematics*, IBM Journal of Research and Development, v. 4, Number 1, January, 1960, pp. 2-22.

Weizenbaum, J., *Computer Power and Human Reason*, W. H. Freeman, S.F., 1976.

Wickelgren, W. A., *How to Solve Problems: Elements of a Theory of Problems and Problem Solving*, W. H. Freeman and Co., Sanf Francisco, 1974.

Wilder, R. L., *Evolution of Mathematical Concepts*, John Wiley & Sons, Inc., N. Y., 1968.

Winograd, T., *Understanding Natural Language*, Academic Press, Inc., New York, New York, 1972.

Winston, P., *Learning Structural Descriptions from Examples*, Ph.D. thesis, Dept. of Electrical Engineering, TR-76, Project MAC, TR-231, MIT AI Lab, September, 1970.

Winston, P., editor, *New Progress in Artificial Intelligence*, MIT AI Lab Memo AI-TR-310, June, 1974.

Winston, P., editor, *The Psychology of Computer Vision*, McGraw Hill, N. Y. 1975.

Wittner, G. E., *The Structure of Mathematics*, Xerox College Publishing, Lexington, Mass., 1972.

Part Two

Teiresias: Applications of Meta-Level Knowledge

The creation and management of large knowledge bases has become a central problem of artificial intelligence research. This has occurred largely as a result of two recent trends: an emphasis on the use of large stores of domain specific knowledge as a base for high performance programs, and a concentration on problems taken from real world settings. Both of these mean an emphasis on the accumulation and management of large collections of knowledge. In many systems embodying these trends much time has been spent on building and maintaining such knowledge bases. Yet there has been little discussion or analysis of the concomitant problems.

This section of the book attempts to define some of the issues involved, and explores steps taken toward solving a number of the problems encountered. It describes the organization, implementation, and operation of a program called TEIRESIAS, designed to make possible the interactive transfer of expertise from a human expert to the knowledge base of a high performance program, in a dialog conducted in a restricted subset of natural language.

The two major goals set were (i) to make it possible for an expert in the domain of application to "educate" the performance program directly, and (ii) to ease the task of assembling and maintaining large amounts of knowledge.

The central theme of this work is the exploration and use of what we have labelled meta level knowledge. This takes several different forms as its use is explored, but can be summed up generally as "knowing what you know". It makes possible a system which has both the capacity to use its knowledge directly, and the ability to examine it, abstract it, and direct its application.

We report here on the full extent of the capabilities it makes possible, and document cases where its lack has resulted in significant difficulties. We describe efforts to enable a program to explain its actions, by giving it a model of its control structure and an understanding of its representations. We document the use of abstracted models of knowledge (rule models) as a guide to acquisition and demonstrate the utility of describing to a program the structure of its representations. Finally, we describe the use of strategies in the form of meta rules, which contain knowledge about the use of knowledge.

Chapter 1

Introduction

I will tell you the whole truth.

Sophocles
Oedipus the King, line 800

1–1 CONTEXT

The creation and management of large knowledge bases has become a central problem of artificial intelligence (AI) research. This is a result of two recent trends: an emphasis on the use of large stores of domain-specific knowledge as a base for high-performance programs, and a focus on problems taken from real world settings. These trends are motivated by the belief that artificial problems may, in the long run, prove more of a diversion than a base for development and by the belief that the field of AI has progressed far enough to provide high performance systems capable of solving real problems. Both of these mean an emphasis on the accumulation and management of large collections of knowledge; and in many systems embodying these trends (*e.g.*, [MACSYMA74], [Buchanan71], [Finkel74], [Hart75]), much time has been spent building and maintaining such knowledge bases. Yet there has been little discussion or analysis of the concomitant problems. We attempt to define here some of the issues involved and explore the steps taken toward solving a number of these problems. We describe a computer program called TEIRESIAS[1] that has been designed and implemented to deal with some of the important issues.

1–2   TASK

The fundamental problem discussed in the following chapters is the creation of a set of tools for the construction, maintenance, and use of large, domain-specific knowledge bases.

Two major goals were used as guidelines in creating those tools. First, it should be possible for an expert in the domain of application to "educate" the performance program interactively, commenting on and correcting its behavior.[2] Second, it should be possible for the expert to assemble and maintain a large body of knowledge.

Concerning the first goal, consider the two alternative approaches shown in Figure 1–1. In the traditional approach, the behavior of the program is interpreted by an assistant for the benefit of an expert who knows little or no programming. The expert's comments on and corrections to program behavior are in turn interpreted by the assistant who then makes the appropriate changes to the program.

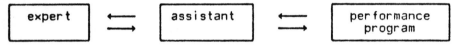

The traditional approach to building high performance programs

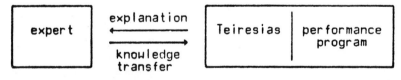

The alternative discussed here

Figure 1–1   Building high-performance programs.

The alternative approach puts the expert in more direct communication with the program, so that he can discover what the program is doing and why, and can modify it himself to produce the desired behavior. It is this alternative toward which we have been working.

---

[1] The program is named for the blind seer in. *Oedipus the King* [Sophocles27], and selected quotes from the play are scattered. through the text. As will become clear, the program, like the prophet, has a "higher order" of knowledge. However, this rather thin analogy should not be pursued too vigorously. Most of the virtue in having a name for the program lies in the convenience it offers for reference to a large body of code.

[2] "Expert" is used to mean someone expert in an applications domain but assumed to be inexperienced in programming.

In this situation, the interaction between the expert and the program resembles that of a teacher who continually challenges a student with new problems to solve and carefully observes the student's performance. The teacher may interrupt the student to request a justification of some particular step taken in attacking the problem or he may challenge the final result (both of these are information transfer from right to left, which we label "explanation"). This process may uncover a fault in the student's knowledge of the subject and result in the transfer of information to correct it (information flow from left to right, "knowledge transfer").

The second goal was to make it possible for the expert to assemble and maintain a large body of knowledge. It is rarely possible to put together a large knowledge base in one or even a few passes. The process is, instead, one of constant trial and reevaluation, an incremental approach to competence. When knowledge is accumulated over a long period of time, the knowledge base undergoes numerous changes. If it is to grow very large, making those changes must be a reasonable task. From this simple observation comes one major theme of this work: the search for knowledge representations and system designs that offer a high degree of flexibility in the face of changes. One way to achieve flexibility is to build a separate acquisition program specifically tailored to the structure of the knowledge base. A more fundamental solution would involve designing a knowledge base that is inherently flexible, one that would easily accommodate changes. Elements of both these approaches will be found in the chapters that follow.

Not surprisingly, both goals—forging a direct link between expert and program, and assembling large amounts of knowledge—have significant impacts on the design of the performance program. In particular, attempting to achieve both of them simultaneously is predicated on an important assumption: that it is possible to distinguish between basic *formalism* and *degree of expertise* or, equivalently, that the control structure and representation can be considered separately from the knowledge base. [3] The basic control structure(s) and representations employed in the performance program are assumed to be established and debugged, and the fundamental approach to the problem is assumed acceptable. The task of the expert, then, is to enlarge the knowledge base by adding new knowledge to be used in one of the established ways. In other words, we are assuming that *how* the knowledge is to be used can be settled by the selection of one or more of the available representations and control structures. The expert's task is thus to enlarge *what* it is the program knows.

There is a corollary assumption in the belief that the control structures and representations are comprehensible to the expert (at the conceptual level), so that he can express his knowledge with them. This is required to insure that the expert understands system performance well enough to know what to correct and

---

[3] Note that this distinction is not specific to any particular system or knowledge representation. As long as it is possible to make this distinction, the general approach used here will remain valid.

to assure that he knows how to express the required knowledge. What the expert sees and wants to change is the external behavior of the system. Mapping from the desired (external) behavior to the necessary internal modification is often quite subtle and requires an intimate understanding of the system structure. Part of the "art of debugging" is an understanding of this mapping. We are thus assuming that the representation of knowledge and the manner in which knowledge is used will be sufficiently comprehensible to the expert that he can understand program behavior.[4] It follows, from these two assumptions, that the performance programs should have the architecture suggested in Figure 1–2. The *knowledge base* is the program's store of task-specific knowledge that makes possible high performance. The *inference engine* is an interpreter that uses the knowledge base to solve the problem at hand.

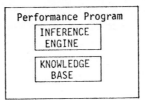

Figure 1–2   The architecture of the performance program.

The main point here is the explicit division between these two parts of the program. This design is in keeping with the assumption noted above that the expert's task would be to augment the knowledge base of a program whose control structure (inference engine) is assumed both appropriate and debugged. If all of the control structure information is kept in the inference engine, then we can engage the domain expert in a discussion of the knowledge base and be assured that the discussion will deal only with issues of domain-specific expertise (rather than with questions of programming and control structures). If all of the domain-specific knowledge is kept in the knowledge base then the program should have a degree of domain independence, that is, it should be possible to "unplug" one knowledge base and "plug in" another.

This division is also in keeping with the aim of accumulating large amounts of knowledge. Experience in constructing large, task-oriented systems [Feigenbaum 71] suggests that this separation makes augmentation of program performance a far easier task than would be the case if the distinction were not maintained.

---

[4] In terms of a performance program that uses a rule-based representation of knowledge, for instance, this means, more specifically, that we assume the expert is familiar with the fundamental structure, organization, and use of production rules. He need only understand them at the conceptual level, since part of establishing the link between expert and program involves insulating him from details of implementation. The central issue is that they share a common language of knowledge expression and use.

Given this general architecture, we can picture the situation in Figure 1–1 in more detail, viewing TEIRESIAS as a means of establishing a link between the domain expert and the performance program, Figure 1–3.

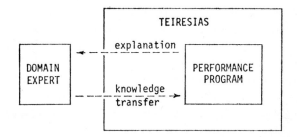

Figure 1–3   The expert, TEIRESIAS, and the performance program.

Given the range of detailed tasks associated with knowledge base construction, it is not always easy to put the expert in direct contact with the program and keep the dialog comprehensible. In response, we have devoted extensive efforts to making the interaction as "high level" as possible. To the extent that it is feasible, for instance, questions from the system are phrased in terms of the manipulation of objects in the domain and not as manipulations of program structures. This helps "insulate" the expert from implementation-level details (see especially chapters 6 and 7).

Our success with this problem has been varied. Viewed in terms of who might be able to use TEIRESIAS, there are operations that could be performed by someone who had only the briefest introduction to the system; others require more extensive experience; still others presume some programming experience; and some require interactions comprehensible only to the program's author. There are far more of the first sort and reassuringly few of the last. Those that remain low level are invariably tasks that are both conceptually difficult and unfamiliar to nonprogrammers (*e.g.*, designing a data structure for a new representation).

1–3 SCOPE OF THE PROBLEM

Chapters 3 through 7 deal with four problems encountered in attempting to reach the pair of goals outlined above. Each of these problems supplied a major topic of investigation and was considered individually in broadly applicable terms. Each is characterized below by a description of the problem and an indication of an acceptable solution. The chapters that follow describe the attempts to solve these problems and explore the extent to which an acceptable level of performance has been achieved.

Chapter 3 discusses efforts to enable the performance program to explain its actions. The fundamental goal was to design a facility that would allow the program to explain itself to a wide-ranging audience that might include: an expert who wanted to debug its knowledge base, a user who requested its services, and a student with minimal experience in the field who wanted to learn from it.

Chapter 4 provides a brief overview of our perspective on knowledge acquisition, while chapter 5 describes techniques that make it possible for the expert to supply new inference rules, using a restricted subset of the language and vocabulary natural to the domain. It illustrates the utility of setting knowledge acquisition in the context of shortcomings in the knowledge base and describes how the program forms expectations during its interaction with the expert. The basic goal here was to make the knowledge transfer process both easy enough and "intelligent" enough so that the expert alone could make significant additions to the knowledge base.

Chapter 6 discusses the acquisition of new conceptual primitives. This chapter views the process in terms of a knowledge base and data structure management task and describes the techniques developed for effective performance when data structures and representations are uncomplicated. More generally, it explores the use of meta-level knowledge as a tool for knowledge base management. The goal here was to make it possible for the expert to build an entire knowledge base from scratch.

Finally, chapter 7 examines the problem of representation and use of strategies that enable a program to make more efficient use of its knowledge base. It also explores the larger question of meta-level knowledge as a framework for the organization and expression of strategies and examines issues of implementation and efficiency.

1–4 METHOD

The central theme of this work is the exploration and use of what we have labeled *meta-level knowledge*. This concept takes several different forms as its use is explored, but can be summed up as "knowing what you know." It makes possible a system with both the capacity to use its knowledge directly and the ability to examine it, abstract it, and direct its application.

To see how this might be done, recall that one of the principal problems of AI is the question of representation and use of knowledge about the world. Much progress has been made and numerous techniques have been developed. One way to view what we have done is to imagine turning this idea of knowledge representation in on itself, using some of these same techniques to describe parts of the program itself. Thus we have a program containing both object-level representations describing the external world and meta-level representations describing the internal world of representations.

In the general context of building a large knowledge base, meta-level knowledge has been used as a tool for the management of object-level knowledge. We report on the capabilities made possible by this approach and document cases where its absence has resulted in significant difficulties. Chapter 3 describes the explanation system, which involves giving the performance program a model of its control structures and an "understanding" of its representations; chapter 5 documents the use of abstracted models of knowledge as a guide to acquisition; chapter 6 demonstrates the utility of describing to the system the structure of its knowledge base; and chapter 7 describes the use of strategies that contain knowledge about the use of knowledge.

Keep in mind that meta-level knowledge does not refer to a single entity but is used as a generic term for several different kinds of information. Each of these chapters explores one or more manifestations of it.

1–5   RANGE OF APPLICATION

We noted above that it is the expert's task to enlarge what it is the program knows, working within the existing set of representations and control structures to correct shortcomings he finds in the knowledge base. Within this framework we can imagine a range of different shortcomings that he might uncover:

Ignorance   Some piece of knowledge is missing.

Stupidity   Some piece of knowledge is incorrect.

Incompetence   The current set of conceptual primitives is incapable of expressing a needed piece of knowledge.

Formalism bug   The control structure has a bug, or the set of available representations is inadequate.

From these we can get a feeling for the range of application of the techniques described in subsequent chapters. We will be concerned here with the first three (although there is an important class of incompetence-type errors that cannot be handled; see chapter 6) and will make no attempt to deal with the last. This means that the tools provided are capable of making extensive changes to the knowledge base but none at all to the basic control structures.

Since the expert is constrained to work with the available set of representations and control structures, our approach is also limited to dealing with knowledge in the application domain that can be formalized and expressed within the range of available techniques. This is a substantial assumption, since knowledge in some domains is ill-specified and it is unclear what even the basic conceptual primitives should be. In other domains, processes may be so well understood that definitive algorithms can be specified, eliminating the need to accumulate large amounts of informal knowledge.

Our approach to knowledge acquisition is geared to domains whose level of formalization falls somewhere between these two extremes. The "vocabulary" of conceptual primitives should be established, but knowledge should still be incomplete enough that problem solving is a heuristic process. The knowledge should also be decomposable into small, modular "chunks" that can be expressed with a simple syntax. The latter implies that both the number of interacting factors and the complexity of their interaction are limited. For a range of tasks, knowledge expressed in production rules meets both constraints.

1–6   A WORD ABOUT NATURAL LANGUAGE

Natural language has not been a major focus of this work; for the most part, we have used the simplest techniques that would support the level of performance required. All questions and responses from TEIRESIAS are either pre-formed or based on a simple template completion mechanism (as evidenced by the appearance of phrases like "a area"). Responses from the user are of three general types: single-token answers to multiple choice questions, strings belonging to a synthetic language with a formal grammar, and heavily stylized natural language sentences using a restricted vocabulary (examples of all of these are seen in subsequent chapters). The first is handled in the obvious way, the second relies on a simple parser that matches user input against a BNF specification of valid responses, and the last relies on straightforward keyword analysis.

   This approach has served thus far to keep the interaction acceptably "natural," without unreasonable processing overhead. It appears to be viable where unrestricted dialog is not the goal and for domains where there is available a semiformal technical language with a low degree of ambiguity. Since, in our experience, technical interchange in such domains is often ungrammatical (relying instead on technical terms to convey meaning), a heavily grammar-based approach might not have fared well in any case.

1–7   THEMES

There are at least two different, completely orthogonal organizations of the ideas presented here. The first is suggested by the table of contents, which indicates chapters dealing with four basic tasks:

1   Explanation.
2   Acquisition of new inference rules.
3   Acquisition of new conceptual primitives.
4   Encoding, organization, and use of strategies.

All of these employ techniques based on different varieties of meta-level knowledge.

   The second organization of the material is suggested by the collection of catch-phrases below. These represent themes that recur throughout the remainder of this work. It will be useful to keep these in mind as an alternative set of issues addressed by the work. They will be revisited in the final chapter to see how close TEIRESIAS has come to some of the ideals they imply. They are purposely oversimplified here for the sake of clarity and are intended only to be suggestive, conveying by keywords and phrases some of the character of the work that follows.

1   Task-specific high-level languages make code easier to read.

2   Knowledge in programs should be explicit and accessible.

3   Programs can be self-understanding.

4   Programs can have access to and an understanding of their own representations.

5   Programs can have some grasp of their own complexity.

6   Programs can be self-adjusting.

7   Representations can usefully be more than a densely encoded string of bits.

Chapter 2

Background

It vexes me what ails him.

Sophocles
Oedipus the King, line 74

2–1 INTRODUCTION

The first part of this chapter provides a brief overview of TEIRESIAS and the sort of performance programs it is designed to help build. We describe the knowledge representations used, review the control structure, and introduce several concepts and terms that will be useful vocabulary in subsequent chapters.

Section 2–4 explores some general ideas about production rules, showing how they have been used to develop what amounts to a high-level language and indicating how this language forms the basis for many of the capabilities discussed later.

Section 2–5 considers briefly the problem of high performance *vs.* generality and examines the work we have done in that light, considering in particular the benefits of a hierarchical layering of types of knowledge.

2–2 ᵒ COMPUTER CONSULTANTS

The recent growth of interest in the class of programs known as computer consultants can be seen as a logical consequence of the two trends noted in chapter 1—an emphasis on large stores of domain-specific knowledge and the concentration on problems taken from real world settings. These programs are intended to provide expert-level advice on a difficult cognitive problem, perhaps one for which human expertise is in short supply.[1]

Several programs of this type are currently under development. A program for diagnosis of glaucoma is described in [Kulikowski73]; internal medicine is the domain for another effort described by [Pople75]; and work on a consultation program for electro-mechanical repair tasks is reported in [Hart75]. These programs all rely on large stores of domain-specific knowledge for their performance, and thus could be considered candidates for the kind of performance program TEIRESIAS has been designed to help construct.

2–2.1   Mycin

One such program, the MYCIN system ([Shortliffe76], [Davis77b]), provided the context in which TEIRESIAS was developed and played the role of the performance program in Figure 1–3. MYCIN was designed to provide consultative advice on diagnosis and therapy for infectious diseases. Such advice is often required in the hospital because the attending physician may not be an expert on infectious disease—as, for example, when a cardiology patient develops an infection after heart surgery. Time considerations compound the problem. A specimen (blood, urine, etc.) from a patient can show some early evidence of bacterial growth within 12 hours, but 24 to 48 hours (or more) are usually required for positive identification. The physician must therefore often decide in the absence of complete information whether or not to start treatment and what drugs to use if treatment is required. Both of these may be difficult questions.

Figures 2–1 and 2–2 show the initial and final parts of a sample interaction between a physician and the program (italicized comments at the right provide additional commentary but are not part of the actual dialog). MYCIN in effect "interviews" the doctor about his patient, collecting information that will allow it to infer the diagnosis and select an appropriate therapy.

2–3   TEIRESIAS: SYSTEM ORGANIZATION

As we have noted, TEIRESIAS provides a number of tools designed to aid in the

---

[1] The concept is defined here in terms that assume the existence of human experts to insure that knowledge in the domain is sufficiently advanced that it can reliably support high performance. Human experts also supply one of the best sources for this knowledge (learning from textbooks has also been considered) and offer a standard by which to gauge program performance. The definition includes only cognitive tasks, to minimize complicating factors that result from the reliance of human performance on highly specialized processors (as appears to be true for vision and manipulation).

```
- - - - - - - - PATIENT-1 - - - - - - - -
(1) Patient's name: (first-last)
**FRED SMITH
```
                                                    {background data}
```
(2) Sex:
**MALE
(3) Age:
**55
(4) Have you been able to obtain positive cultures from a site at which Fred Smith
    has an infection?
**YES
    - - - - - - - - INFECTION-1 - - - - - - - -
    (5) What is the infection?
    **PRIMARY-BACTEREMIA
    (6) Please give the date and approximate time when signs or symptoms of the
        primary-bacteremia (INFECTION-1) first appeared. (mo/da/yr)
    **MAY 5, 1975
The most recent positive culture associated with the primary-bacteremia
(INFECTION-1) will be referred to as:
    - - - - - - - - - CULTURE-1 - - - - - - - -
    (7) From what site was the specimen for CULTURE-1 taken?
    **BLOOD
    (8) Please give the date and time when this blood culture (CULTURE-1)
        was obtained. (mo/da/yr)
    **MAY 9, 1975
The first significant organism from this blood culture (CULTURE-1)
will be referred to as:
    - - - - - - - - ORGANISM-1 - - - - - - - -
    (9) Enter the identity of ORGANISM-1:
    **UNKNOWN
```
                        {typically the identity is not known and must be inferred}
```
    (10) Is ORGANISM-1 a rod or coccus (etc.):
    **ROD
    (11) The gram stain of ORGANISM-1:
    **GRAMNEG
    (12) Have there been POSITIVE cultures from sites which are NOT
         associated with infections about which you are seeking advice?
    **NO
    (13) Did ORGANISM-1 grow aerobically?
    **YES (8)
    (14) Did ORGANISM-1 grow anaerobically?
    **YES
    (15) What is the suspected portal of entry of ORGANISM-1
         into this sterile site?
    **GI (6)
        . . .
```

{more questions follow, to gather sufficient information to infer possible identities of the infecting organisms}

FIG. 1. Initial segment of a session with the consultation system. User responses are in **boldface** and follow the double asterisks. Italicized comments at the right are not part of the actual dialog.

Figure 2–1   The initial part of a consultation.

My therapy recommendation will be based on the following probable infection(s)
and potential causative organism(s):

INFECTION–1 is PRIMARY–BACTEREMIA

{possible identities}

⟨Item 1⟩ The identity of ORGANISM-1 may be PSEUDOMONAS-AERUGINOSA
⟨Item 2⟩ The identity of ORGANISM-1 may be KLEBSIELLA-PNEUMONIAE
⟨Item 3⟩ The identity of ORGANISM-1 may be E. COLI
⟨Item 4⟩ The identity of ORGANISM-1 may be BACTEROIDES-FRAGILIS
⟨Item 5⟩ The identity of ORGANISM-1 may be ENTEROBACTER
⟨Item 6⟩ The identity of ORGANISM-1 may be PROTEUS-NON-MIRABILIS

   (46) On a scale of 0 to 4, where higher numbers indicate increasing severity
        how would you rate Fred Smith's degree of sickness?
   **3
   (47) Does Fred Smith have a clinically significant allergic reaction to any
        antimicrobial agent?
   **NO
   (48) Fred Smith's weight in kilograms (or ⟨number⟩ POUNDS):
   **70

{note that 2 drugs cover for 6 potential organisms}

[Rec 1] My preferred therapy recommendation is as follows:
   In order to cover for Items ⟨1 2 3 5 6⟩:
      Give: GENTAMICIN
      Dose: 119 mg (1.7 mg/kg) q8h IV [or IM] for 10 days
      Comments: Modify dose in renal failure
   In order to cover for Item ⟨4⟩:
      Give: CLINDAMYCIN
      Dose: 595 mg (8.5 mg/kg) q6h IV [or IM] for 14 days
      Comments: If diarrhea or other GI symptoms develop, patient
         should be evaluated for possible pseudomembranous colitis.

Do you wish to see the next choice therapy?

{alternative choices are available}

**Y
Which, if any, of the above drugs do you wish eliminated from consideration?
**CLINDAMYCIN

[Rec 2] Next best therapy recommendation:
   In order to cover for Items ⟨2 3 4 5 6⟩:
      Give: CHLORAMPHENICOL
      Dose: 1 gm (15 mg/kg) q6h IV for 14 days
      Comments: Monitor patient's white count
   In order to cover for Item ⟨1⟩:
      Give: GENTAMICIN
      Dose: 119 mg (1.7 mg/kg) q8h IV [or IM] for 10 days
      Comments: Modify dose in renal failure

Figure 2–2   The final part of a consultation.

construction, maintenance, and use of the knowledge base in the performance program. The overall structure of the system is shown in Figure 2–3, a more detailed version of Figure 1–3. In order to focus on the issues of knowledge acquisition, explanation, etc., covered in later chapters, we will henceforth adopt the perspective suggested in Figure 2–3 and consider the performance program as the simple entity indicated there. MYCIN is of course more complex, but this abstraction contains all the detail necessary for our purposes.

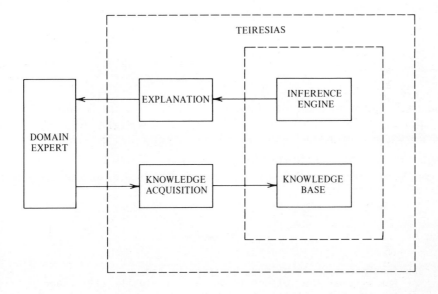

Figure 2–3   TEIRESIAS: System organization.

TEIRESIAS's *explanation* facility (see chapter 3) uses both the information in the knowledge base and an understanding of the design of the inference engine to provide the expert with explanations of the performance program's behavior. The *knowledge acquisition* facility (chapters 4-6) allows the expert to transfer his knowledge of the field into the knowledge base, in order to increase the performance program's competence. Finally, the base of *strategy knowledge* (chapter 7) provides a mechanism for expressing strategies concerning the use of information in the knowledge base. [2]

TEIRESIAS is written in INTERLISP, an advanced dialect of the LISP language,

---

[2] Ideally, it should be possible for the expert to add strategy knowledge to the system using the knowledge acquisition facility, but this has not as yet been implemented. See chapter 7 for details.

and runs on a DEC PDP-10 under Tenex. The knowledge acquisition program occupies approximately 40,000 (36-bit) words; the explanation program, 10,000; and the strategy knowledge base, 5,000.

2–3.1   Performance Program: Knowledge Base Organization

In time you will know all with certainty.

Sophocles
Oedipus the King, line 613

TEIRESIAS is designed to deal with knowledge encoded in the form of inference rules of the sort shown in Figure 2–4. The rules are stored internally in the INTERLISP form shown, from which the English version is generated. Each rule is a single "chunk" of domain-specific information indicating an *action* (in this case a conclusion) that is justified if the conditions specified in the *premise* are fulfilled.

<u>RULE050</u>

```
If      1) the infection is primary-bacteremia, and
        2) the site of the culture is one of the sterile sites, and
        3) the suspected portal of entry of the organism is the gastro-
           intestinal tract,
Then there is suggestive evidence (.7) that the identity of the organism is
    bacteroides.
```

```
PREMISE         ($AND (SAME CNTXT INFECT PRIMARY-BACTEREMIA)
                      (MEMBF CNTXT SITE STERILESITES)
                      (SAME CNTXT PORTAL GI))
ACTION          (CONCLUDE CNTXT IDENT BACTEROIDES TALLY .7)
```

Figure 2–4   An inference rule.

Note that the rules are judgmental, that is, they make inexact inferences. In the case of the rule in Figure 2–4, for instance, the evidence cited in the premise is enough to assert the conclusion shown with a mild degree of confidence: .7 out of 1.0. This number is called a "certainty factor," or CF, and embodies a model of confirmation described in [Shortliffe75b]. The details of this model need not concern us here; we need only note that rules in this case are typically inexact inferences, rather than statements made with certainty. [3]

The premise of each rule is a Boolean combination of one or more *clauses*, each of which is constructed from a *predicate function* with an *associative triple* (*attribute, object, value*) as its argument. Thus each clause of a premise has the following four components:

<predicate function>   <object>   <attribute>   <value>

For the third clause in the premise of Figure 2–4, for example, the predicate function is SAME, and the triple is "*portal-of-entry* of *organism* is *GI-tract.*" (CNTXT is a free variable which is bound to the specific object [also called a "context"] for which the rule is invoked.) There is a standardized set of some 24 domain-independent predicate functions (*e.g.*, SAME, KNOWN, DEFINITE) and a range of domain-specific attributes (*e.g.*, IDENTITY, SITE), objects (*e.g.*, ORGANISM, CULTURE), and associated values (*e.g.*, E.COLI, BLOOD). These form a "vocabulary" of conceptual primitives available for use in constructing rules.

A rule premise is always a conjunction of clauses, but it may contain arbitrarily complex conjunctions or disjunctions nested within each clause. (Instead of writing rules whose premise would be a disjunction of clauses, a separate rule is written for each clause.) The action part indicates one or more conclusions that can be drawn if the premises are satisfied, making the rules purely inferential.

Each rule is intended to embody a single, independent chunk of knowledge and states all necessary information explicitly in the premise. Since the rule uses a vocabulary of concepts common to the domain, it forms, by itself, a comprehensible statement of some piece of domain knowledge. As will become clear, this characteristic is useful in many ways.

Each rule is highly stylized, with the if/then format and the specified set of available primitives. While the LISP form of each is executable code (the premise, in fact, is simply EVALuated by LISP to test its truth; and the action EVALuated to make its conclusions), this tightly structured form makes it possible to examine the rules as well as execute them. This, in turn, leads to some important capabilities, described below. As one example, the internal form (*i.e.*, LISP) can be translated into the English form shown in Figure 2–4.

Facts about the world (Figure 2–5) are represented as 4-tuples made up of an associative triple and its current CF. Positive CFs indicate a predominance of evidence confirming a hypothesis; negative CFs indicate predominance of disconfirming evidence.

---

[3] $AND (the multivalued analogue of the Boolean AND) performs a minimization operation; $OR (similar) does a maximization. Note that, unlike standard probability theory, $AND does not involve any multiplication over its arguments. Since CFs are not probabilities, there is no *a priori* reason why a product should be a reasonable number. There is, moreover, a long-standing convention in work with multivalued logics which interprets AND as *min* and OR as *max* [Lukasciewicz70]. It is based primarily on intuitive grounds: If a conclusion requires all of its antecedents to be true, then it is a relatively safe and conservative strategy to use the smallest of the antecedent values as the value of the premise. Similarly, if any one of the antecedent clauses justifies the conclusion, it is safe to take the maximum value.

```
(SITE CULTURE-1 BLOOD 1.0)
(IDENT ORGANISM-2 KLEBSIELLA .25)
(IDENT ORGANISM-2 E.COLI .73)
(SENSITIVS ORGANISM-1 PENICILLIN -1.0)
```

Figure 2-5   Examples of representation of facts.

Note that the model of inexact logic permits the coexistence of several plausible values for a single attribute, if suggested by the evidence. Thus, for example, after attempting to deduce the identity (IDENT) of an organism, MYCIN may have concluded (correctly) that there is evidence both for E.coli and for Klebsiella.

There are thus two major forms of knowledge representation in use in the performance program: (*i*) the attributes, objects, and values—which form a vocabulary of domain-specific conceptual primitives, and (*ii*) the inference rules expressed in terms of these primitives. There are, correspondingly, two forms of knowledge acquisition: (*i*) the acquisition of new primitives—to expand the performance program's vocabulary of concepts, and (*ii*) the acquisition of new rules expressed in terms of existing primitives. TEIRESIAS makes possible both of these; chapter 6 deals with the first, and chapter 5 describes the second.

2-3.2   Performance Program: The Inference Engine

Know that I have gone many ways wandering in thought.

Sophocles
Oedipus the King, lines 66-67

The rules are invoked in a simple backward-chaining fashion that produces an exhaustive depth-first search of an and/or goal tree. Assume that the program is attempting to determine the identity of an infecting organism. It retrieves all the rules that make a conclusion about that topic (*i.e.*, they mention IDENT in their action) and invokes each one in turn, evaluating each premise to see if the conditions specified have been met. For the rule in Figure 2-4, this process would begin with determining the type of the infection. This, in turn, is set up as a subgoal and the process recurs.

The search is thus depth-first (because each premise condition is thoroughly explored in turn); the tree that is sprouted is an and/or goal tree (because rules may have OR conditions in their premise); and the search is exhaustive (because the rules are inexact; so that even if one succeeds, it was deemed to be a wisely conservative strategy to continue to collect all evidence about the subgoal.)

Note that the subgoal that is set up is a generalized form of the original goal. Thus, for the first clause in Figure 2-4 ("the infection is primary-bacteremia"), the subgoal set up is "determine the type of infection." The subgoal is therefore always of the form "determine the value of <attribute>" rather than "determine whether the <attribute> is equal to <value>." By setting up the generalized goal of collecting all evidence about an attribute, the performance program effectively exhausts each subject as it is encountered, and thus tends to group together all questions about a given topic. This results in a system that displays a much more focused, methodical approach to the task, which is a distinct advantage where human engineering considerations are important. The cost is the effort of deducing or collecting information that is not strictly necessary. However, since this occurs rarely—only when the <attribute> can be deduced with certainty to be the <value> named in the original goal—it has not proven to be a problem in practice.

If after trying all relevant rules (referred to as "tracing" the subgoal), the total weight of the evidence about a hypothesis falls between —.2 and .2 (an empirical threshold), the answer is regarded as still unknown. This may happen if no rules are applicable, if the applicable rules are too weak, if the effects of several rules offset each other, or if there are no rules for this subgoal at all. In any of these cases, when the system is unable to deduce the answer, it asks the user for the value of the subgoal (using a phrase that is stored along with the attribute itself).

The strategy of always attempting to deduce the value of a subgoal and asking the user only when deduction fails, insures a minimum number of questions. It would also mean, however, that work might be expended searching for a subgoal, arriving perhaps at a less than definite answer, when the user might already know the answer with certainty. To prevent this inefficiency, some of the attributes have been labeled "laboratory data," to indicate that they represent information available to the physician as results of quantitative tests. In these cases the deduce-then-ask procedure is reversed and the system will attempt to deduce the answer only if the user cannot supply it. Given the desire to minimize both tree search and the number of questions asked, there is no guaranteed optimal solution to the problem of deciding when to ask for information and when to try to deduce it. But the distinction described has performed quite well and seems to embody a very appropriate criterion.

Two other additions to straightforward tree search increase the inference engine's efficiency. First, before the entire list of rules for a subgoal is retrieved, the program attempts to find a sequence of rules that would establish the goal with certainty, based only on what is currently known. Since this is a search for a sequence of rules with $CF=1$, the result is termed a *unity path*. Besides efficiency considerations, this process offers the advantage of allowing the program to make "common sense" deductions with a minimum of effort (rules with $CF=1$ are largely definitional). Because there are few such rules in the system, the search is typically very brief.

Second, the inference engine performs a partial evaluation of rule premises. Since many attributes are found in several rules, the value of one clause (perhaps the last) in a premise may already have been established while the rest are still unknown. If this clause alone would make the premise false, there is clearly no reason to do all the search necessary to establish the others. Each premise is thus "previewed" by evaluating it on the basis of currently available information. This produces a Boolean combination of TRUEs, FALSEs, and UNKNOWNs; straightforward simplification (*e.g.*, $F \wedge U \equiv F$) indicates whether the rule is guaranteed to fail. This procedure is examined in more detail in Section 2–4.4.

The final aspect of the control structure is the tree of objects (or contexts) that is constructed dynamically from a fixed hierarchy as the consultation proceeds (Figure 2–6). This tree serves several purposes. First, bindings of free variables in a rule are established by the context in which the rule is invoked, with the standard access to contexts that are its ancestors. Second, since this tree is used to represent the relationships of objects in the domain, it helps structure the consultation in ways already familiar to the user. For example, in the medical domain, a patient has one or more infections, each of which may have one or more associated cultures, each of which in turn may have one or more organisms growing in it, and so on.

2–3.3   Domain Independence and Range of Application

The fundamental design and implementation of the system in Figure 2–3 does not restrict its use to medical domains. This is due primarily to the modularization suggested in that figure and to the fact that TEIRESIAS is oriented solely around the concepts of rules, attribute-object-value triples, etc.

The clear distinction between the inference engine and the knowledge base, for instance, makes it possible to remove one knowledge base from the performance program and replace it with another. It has proven possible, for instance, to build separate knowledge bases for such disparate areas as auto mechanics and chemotherapy for psychiatry. In the first such effort ([vanMelle74]), a small part of an auto repair manual was rewritten as production rules and inserted in place of the bacteremia knowledge base. What resulted was a very simple but fully functional consultant capable of diagnosing and suggesting remedies for problems in parts of an auto electrical system. More recently, a pilot system for psychiatric diagnosis and chemotherapy was assembled. While this program had only 50 rules, it too was fully functional and displayed primitive but encouraging performance. In both systems, all of the established explanation facilities worked as designed, without modification.

There are, naturally, some domains that might be less profitable to explore. One of the interesting lessons of the auto repair system was that domains with little inexactness in the reasoning process—those for which algorithmic diagnostic routines can be written—are not particularly appropriate for this methodology. The precision in these domains means that little use is made of the certainty factor mechanism, and many of the more complicated (and computationally expensive) features go unused. The effect would be akin to swatting a fly with a large doctoral thesis—all that work and weight are unnecessary when something far simpler would do.

Nor is it reasonable to expect to be able to write inference rules built from attribute-object-value triples for an arbitrary domain. As knowledge in an area

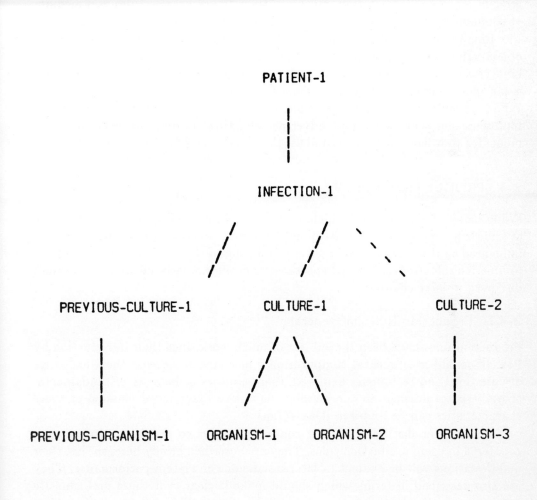

Figure 2-6   A sample tree of objects

accumulates, it becomes progressively more formalized. There is a certain stage in this formalization process when it is appropriate to use rules of the sort shown above. Earlier than this the knowledge is too unstructured; later on it may (like the auto repair system) be more effective to write straightforward algorithms.

It is also possible that the knowledge in some domains is inherently unsuited to a rule-like representation, since rules become increasingly awkward as the number of premise clauses increases. Dealing with a number of interacting factors may be difficult for any representation, but given the reliance here on rules as a medium of communication of knowledge, the problem becomes especially significant.

Finally, the current performance program makes extensive use of the attribute-object-value associative triple. This is perhaps the most limiting factor, since this kind of representation is effective only in simpler domains. It is also, however, a far more implementation-dependent factor than the other two mentioned. While it would be difficult, the triples could be replaced by a more powerful representation scheme without adversely affecting the feasibility of the techniques for knowledge acquisition and use that are described in subsequent chapters.

2–4   PRODUCTION RULES

While many of the ideas on which TEIRESIAS is based are applicable to a range of knowledge representations, its design and implementation have been strongly influenced by the use of a rule-based encoding of knowledge. This section explores production rules from several perspectives, to provide a basis for some of the issues discussed in later chapters.

2–4.1   Production Rules in General

Production rules have been the subject of much work since their introduction by Post ([Post43]) as a general computational mechanism. Across the wide range of variations and techniques explored, there appears to be a set of fundamental characteristics intrinsic to the methodology. (An extended discussion of these characteristics can be found in [Davis77a].)

The present discussion will be concerned with two problems typically encountered in using production rules. They are described briefly here, so that their manifestations will be evident in later discussions of system performance. They are also described in terms which should make it clear that these problems are inherent in the production system methodology itself. This will enable the reader to distinguish them from shortcomings that may have arisen from our approach to various uses of meta-level knowledge. Thus, while TEIRESIAS displays certain limitations, some of these are a result of the approach, while others are a legacy of the particular representation of knowledge chosen early in the development of the performance program.

One problem is the limit on the amount of knowledge that can be expressed conveniently in a single rule. Actions that are "larger" than this limit are often achieved by the combined effects of several rules. For many reasons (see

[Davis77a], section 5), this is difficult to do and often produces opaque results. We will see that this is a significant consideration when judging the utility of production rules as a knowledge representation.

Second, there is what has been labeled the implicit context problem. Perhaps the simplest example can be found in a production-rule-based system that uses a sequential left-hand side (LHS) scan—that is, it starts out at the beginning of the rule set and searches sequentially through it, examining the LHS of each rule until one is found that meets the desired criteria. Suppose the LHS of the first three rules are:

$$
\begin{array}{rl}
\text{R1:} & A \wedge B \wedge C \implies \ldots \\
\text{R2:} & D \implies \ldots \\
\text{R3:} & E \wedge F \implies \ldots
\end{array}
$$

Figure 2–7

R3 won't be tested unless D is false and either A, B, or C is false. The rule thus, effectively, has two extra, implicit clauses of the form $(notD)$ and $((notA) \vee (notB) \vee (notC))$, simply because of its location in the rule set. Note that the location is not *necessarily* critical—the entire thrust of the rule could possibly be summed up in the presence of just E and F. But often the location *is* an important element and the implicit clauses are significant. [4]

It is tempting to make use of implicit context to take advantage of the resulting conciseness—consider how short R3 is and how long an explicit statement of the 99th rule might be if it depended on the failure of the first 98. While the point has been illustrated via an ordered rule set, the same problem can arise from other causes. MYCIN's rules are not ordered, but they are classified according to the object to which they apply and similar problems arise from this.

The essential point here is twofold: First, *any* piece of structuring in the system carries information. Second, this information can be implicitly passed on to the rules in subtle ways. We will see examples of this in discussing the organization of meta-rules in chapter 7.

2–4.2   Production Rules as a Knowledge Representation

TEIRESIAS's first goal—putting a domain expert in direct communication with a high performance program—requires a common language of communication. This is especially important for the specification of knowledge that the expert wants to add to the system. He must be able to express it in a form that is the same as (or transformable into) the one used internally by the program. Thus, the ease of establishing the link between expert and program is strongly affected by the knowledge representation chosen.

While we cannot offer formal arguments, there are several reasons why production rules of the sort shown in Figure 2–4 are a useful representation. First,

---

[4] Indeed, [Waterman70] uses this idea to great advantage.

the general task of deduction is one that fits quite well into the situation/action character of production rules. There is therefore less transformation necessary between the knowledge as expressed by the expert and its final encoding inside the system.

Next, the rules are, by themselves, comprehensible chunks of knowledge, since they carry in their premise a full specification of their applicability. Their independence also facilitates the incremental growth of the knowledge base: Rules can be added one by one, and performance improves with each addition.

Rules are also retrieved and invoked on the basis of the content of their right-hand side (rather than on the basis of their name) and never reference one another. As a result, adding (or changing) a rule is a far easier task than would be the case if there were extensive references to the rule's name in many places. Consider the difficulty, by contrast, of editing a procedure in an ALGOL-like language and then having to go back and find all the places it is called to see if those calls are still appropriate.

The rules also seem to capture a "chunk" of knowledge of the appropriate size. A significant amount of knowledge of bacteremia diagnosis and therapy has been encoded in rules that have between two and five premise clauses and one or two actions. While all domains may not offer such convenient "bite-size" chunks, the success of the systems in the other two domains that have been explored is encouraging.

The control structure—backward chaining—also appears to be reasonably intuitive. While such *modus ponens* reasoning is not often recognized explicitly, it is common cognitive behavior and should therefore not be alien to the expert.

Finally, the rules are, for the most part, what may be labeled a "single level" mechanism. They are composed of elements that are conceptual primitives and require no further decomposition to be understood. It is clear to the user, for instance, what is meant by "the site is X," or "conclude that the identity is Y." Compare this with the difficulty that would arise if the action of a rule were the invocation of a deep and complex calculation.

As a result of all of these factors, production rules of the sort shown above have proven to be an effective and useful representation.

2–4.3 Impact on Knowledge Organization

Production rules also contribute their own perspective on the fundamental organization of knowledge in a program, a perspective quite different from that associated with procedure-oriented representations. Production rules tend to deemphasize the hierarchical control structure natural to procedural languages and substitute a single, uniform collection of knowledge "chunks" (the rules). Since each rule is retrieved on the basis of its contents (as the rule in Figure 2–4 is retrieved on the basis of its conclusion), no rule is ever called directly, in the style of procedures. Thus, the addition (or deletion) of a rule does not require the modification of any other rule to provide for (or delete) a call to it. The result is a program whose knowledge base is easily modified and whose behavior is relatively stable in the face of those changes.

This stability might be demonstrated by repeatedly removing rules from a production-rule-based program. Many such systems will continue to display some sort of "reasonable" behavior, up to a point. By contrast, adding a procedure to an ALGOL-like program requires modification of other parts of the code to insure that it is invoked, while removing an arbitrary procedure from such a program generally cripples it.

Note that the issue here is more than simply the "undefined function" error message that would result from a missing procedure. The problem persists even if the compiler or interpreter is altered to treat undefined functions as no-ops. The issue is a much more fundamental one concerning organization of knowledge: Programs written in procedure-oriented languages stress the kind of explicit passing of control from one section of code to another that is characterized by the calling of procedures. This is typically done at a selected time and in a particular context—both carefully chosen by the programmer. If a no-op is substituted for a missing procedure, the environment upon return will not be what the programmer expected, and subsequent procedure calls will be executed in increasingly incorrect environments. Similarly, procedures that have been added must be called from *somewhere* in the program, but the location of the call must be chosen carefully if the effect is to be meaningful.

Production systems, on the other hand, emphasize the decoupling of control flow from the writing of rules. Each rule is designed to be a modular chunk of knowledge with its own statement of relevance. Thus, where the ALGOL programmer carefully chooses the order of procedure calls to create a selected sequence of environments, in a production system it is the environment which chooses the next rule for execution. And since a rule can only be chosen if its criteria of relevance have been met, the choice will continue to be a plausible one, and system behavior will remain "reasonable," even as rules are successively deleted.

2–4.4   Production Rules as a High-Level Language

As noted, the inference rules are composed of clauses made up of predicate functions and attribute-object-value triples. The entire collection of these elements forms a set of conceptual primitives for any given domain. Thus in dealing with infectious disease, for example, there are cultures with sites like blood.

If we consider pushing this back one level, it becomes plausible to consider the concepts *predicate function, attribute, object,* and *value* as conceptual primitives in the more general domain of knowledge representation. We consider each of them an indication of a whole class of objects, with individual instances supplied by the domain of application. This suggests treating them as extended data types, which is a useful analogy to keep in mind. There are 13 such "data types," used as a set of conceptual primitives for expressing knowledge in rule form. They are the data types of what is, in effect, a high-level programming language—one whose syntax is very restricted and whose sole statement type is a rule. Since we refer to them often in what follows, they are listed and described below, for reference:

This concept, of a high-level language with a restricted syntax and a small number of data types, forms an important base underlying many of the the capabilities of TEIRESIAS. Perhaps the most fundamental of these is the ability to make multiple uses of a single body of knowledge. Because TEIRESIAS can both assemble and dissect rules, we have a system that can not only use its knowledge of a domain directly, but can also examine it, alter it, abstract it, and draw conclusions about it. The rules are thus, at different times, both code and data and are used in both capacities almost equally. A large number of interesting and useful features follow from this; they are explored in subsequent chapters. To clarify this point, however, we offer a simple but illustrative example.

As indicated earlier in our discussion of the control structure, before invoking a rule the system performs a partial evaluation of its premise to make sure that the rule is not already guaranteed to fail. But performing this evaluation is nontrivial. The system requires a way to tell if any clause in the premise is known to be false. It cannot simply EVALuate each clause individually, since a subgoal that had never been traced before would send the system off on its recursive search.

However, if the system can establish which attribute is used in the clause, it is possible to determine whether this attribute has been traced previously (by reference to internal flags). If so, the clause can be EVALuated to obtain the value.

This process is made possible by a TEMPLATE associated with each predicate function. It describes the format of any call of that predicate function, by giving the generic type and order of the arguments to the function. It thus resembles a simplified procedure declaration.

Function	Template	Sample function call
SAME	(SAME CNTXT PARM VALUE)	(SAME CNTXT SITE BLOOD)

Figure 2–8   Example of a function template.

The template is not itself a piece of code but is simply a list structure of the sort shown above, indicating the appearance of an interpreted call to the predicate function. Since rules are kept in interpreted form, as shown in Figure 2–4, the template can be used as a guide to dissect a rule. For each clause in a rule, TEIRESIAS retrieves the template associated with the predicate function found in that clause (*i.e.*, the template associated with the CAR of the clause) and uses it to guide the examination of the clause. In the case of the function SAME, for instance, the template indicates that the attribute (ATTRIB) is the third element of the list structure that comprises the function call. The previewing mechanism uses the templates to extract the attribute from the clause in question and can then determine whether or not it has been traced.

There are two points of interest here:

1   Part of the system is examining the code (the rules) being executed by another part.

2   This examination is guided by the information carried in components of the rules themselves.

The ability to examine the code could have been accomplished by requiring all predicate functions to use the same format, but this is obviously awkward. Allowing each function to describe the format of its own calls permits code to be stylized without being constrained to a single form, and hence is flexible and much easier to use. This approach requires only that each form be expressible in a template built from the current set of conceptual primitives. It also insures that the capability will persist in the face of future additions to the system. The result is one example of the general idea of giving the system access to, and an "understanding" of, its own representations. Additional examples of this concept are spread throughout the remainder of this work.

2–5   LEVELS OF KNOWLEDGE

The concept of meta-level knowledge introduced in chapter 1 can be defined more generally as multiple levels of knowledge. [5] This idea has several important applications in the work reported here. In chapter 7, strategies are defined in terms of a knowledge hierarchy with an arbitrary number of levels. A different sort of hierarchy is responsible for much of the performance and generality of TEIRESIAS's knowledge acquisition routines. In this hierarchy, knowledge is stratified into three distinct levels. A brief description of it here will help to clarify many of the ideas involved and illustrate their power.

The first level of the hierarchy contains the object-level knowledge—medical knowledge of cultures, organisms, drugs, etc. High performance on the task of diagnosis and therapy selection is supported by an extensive collection of knowledge about objects in the medical domain. This first level is naturally limited to this single domain.

The next level is concerned with the conceptual building blocks of the knowledge representation—the predicate functions, attributes, values, rules, and so on. Performance on the task of knowledge acquisition is dependent upon an extensive body of knowledge about these building blocks. That is, there is assembled at this level a large amount of knowledge about the representational primitives. As will become clear in chapters 5 and 6, the system has an "understanding" of what an attribute is, what roles it plays, etc. Since no reference is made at this level to any specific instance of any of the primitives, this level of knowledge has a degree of domain independence. Over the range of domains in which knowledge can be represented in terms of these primitives, the knowledge acquisition routines are similarly domain independent.

Knowledge at the third level is concerned with the conceptual primitives behind representations in general. To make this clearer, consider the recursion of ideas: To aid the construction of a high-performance (object-level) program, we build a (meta-level) system that can acquire object-level knowledge. Its performance at this task is based on an extensive store of knowledge about specific representations. *But it in turn is "just" another knowledge-based system.* By supplying the proper set of representation-independent primitives (and a store of knowledge about them), we can use precisely the same formalism (indeed, the same code) to provide a system for acquiring knowledge about individual representations. [6]

In this way, the second-order system can be used to acquire knowledge about a representation. This, in turn, becomes the knowledge base for the meta-level system, which then facilitates the construction of the knowledge base for the object-level performance program. The two stages of this process are shown below.

Note, however, that while this indicates the process as it appears conceptually, a more accurate system view is shown below. Here we have only two systems,

---

[5] There have been other uses of the term "levels of knowledge," most notably to describe the hierarchy of domain knowledge in the HEARSAY II system [Lesser74] (*e.g.*, phoneme, word, syntax, semantics, etc.). We use the term here in a different sense, that of a hierarchy of *types* of knowledge, and intend that meaning throughout.

[6] The details and examples of this bootstrapping process are given in chapter 6.

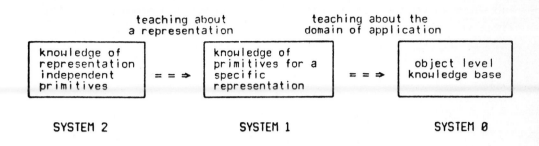

Figure 2–9   The conceptual process.

because there is in fact only a single higher level system. This is possible because the process of teaching about a *representation* can be made computationally identical to the process of teaching about specific *instances* of that representation. The two are therefore accomplished with precisely the same mechanism.

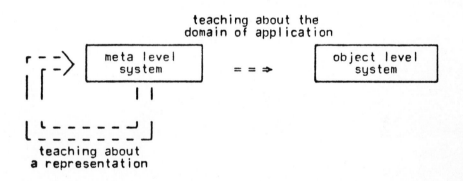

Figure 2–10   The computational process.

In TEIRESIAS, the recursive application of the knowledge acquisition system offers a certain degree of representation independence; its extent and limitations are examined in chapter 6.

We began this report by noting that the original search for generality—set in the domain of problem-solving methods—has proved unsuccessful thus far. Knowledge-based methods have been suggested as an alternative, but each has a sharply limited range of application, and the lure of generality remains. Is there another way to salvage it?

One of the underlying themes of this work is the attempt to capture a different form of generality, one that has its source in knowledge acquisition rather than in problem-solving methods. That is, if programs require large stores of knowledge for performance, then can we not take a step back and discover powerful, broadly applicable techniques for accomplishing the transfer of knowledge from expert to program? The resulting man-machine combination would be a semi-automatic system, whose generality arose from access to the appropriate human experts and whose power was based on the store of knowledge it acquired from them. The next five chapters discuss several steps toward the realization of this aim.

Chapter 3

Explanation

*What do you mean? What you have said so far leaves me uncertain whether to trust
or fear.*

Sophocles
Oedipus the King, lines 88–90

*"No, no! The adventures first," said the Gryphon in an impatient tone: "explanations
take such a dreadfully long time!"*

Lewis Carroll
Alice's Adventures in Wonderland

3–1 INTRODUCTION

The fundamental goal of an explanation facility is to enable a program to display
a comprehensible account of the motivation for all of its actions. This chapter
explores steps taken toward this goal, examining the extent to which "all" actions
of a program can be explained. It considers what is required for a "comprehensible"
account and offers a framework in which to understand "motivations" for one
particular system.

The utility of an explanation facility should be clear. Even for an experienced programmer, the attempt to account for program behavior by hand simulation is difficult for any sizable program. It is often difficult enough to discover how a program got to where it is. Trying to account for past behavior (*e.g.*, function calls that have long since exited) is often impossible because critical variables have been overwritten.

For consultation programs, in particular, the problem of explanation is worse because they deal with an audience assumed to know nothing about programming. This requires a different standard of comprehensibility, one defined in terms of the application domain rather than in the language of computation. A naive user (*e.g.*, a student) should find the explanations educational; a more experienced user should find them reassuring, employing them to satisfy himself that the conclusions the system has reached are based on acceptable reasoning; while an expert should find them useful in discovering gaps or errors in the knowledge base. We describe below how each of these objectives is accomplished.

This chapter begins by outlining and discussing the plausibility of the fundamental assumptions behind the techniques used in TEIRESIAS. This is followed by several examples of the capabilities that have been developed and a description of how they are achieved. Finally, as a prelude to knowledge acquisition, we end by exploring how TEIRESIAS may be used to discover the source of problems in the knowledge base.

3-2   BASIC ASSUMPTIONS

The techniques used in TEIRESIAS for generating explanations are based on a number of assumptions about the system being explained. These assumptions are reviewed here to help motivate what follows and to characterize their range of applicability.

3-2.1   Generalities: Two Assumptions

We assume, first, that a recap of program actions can be an effective explanation as long as the correct level of detail is chosen. This assumption simplifies the task considerably, since it means that the solution requires only the ability to record and play back a history of events. In particular, it rules out any need to simplify those events.

But this assumption is perhaps the source of greatest limitation as well. It is not obvious, for instance, that an appropriate level of detail can always be found. A large program with cooperating parallel processes might prove sufficiently complex that it required a sophisticated interpretation and simplification to be comprehensible. Nor is it obvious how this approach can be applied to programs that are primarily numeric. With a program that does symbolic reasoning, recapping offers an easily understood explanation. But simply recapping the arithmetic involved in determining parameters of a complex electrical network, for example, would explain little of the reasoning involved and would teach little physics. Understanding it requires a much higher level of sophistication:

It assumes that the viewer can interpret each numeric step in symbolic terms. The lack of any mechanism for either simplifying or reinterpreting computations means our approach is basically a first order solution to the general problem of explaining program behavior.

If a simple recap is going to be effective, there must be several constraints on the level of detail chosen. It must be *detailed enough* that the operations it cites are comprehensible. For example, if a chess program were to explain a move with the justification that it "picked the best choice," the explanation would explain very little because it wouldn't reveal what was involved in the operation of choosing. Some explanation in terms of alpha/beta search and evaluation functions might provide the relevant information.

The level must also be *high enough* that the operations are meaningful to the observer and that unnecessary detail is suppressed. Describing the chess program in terms of register-transfer operations, for instance, would lose any sense of task specificity and introduce pointless detail.

Finally, the explanation must be *complete enough* that the operations cited are sufficient to account for all behavior. Completeness is easiest to achieve if the operations are free of side effects and the system design is reasonably "clean." If the alpha/beta search used in the chess program had numerous subtle side effects, it would be difficult to find a level of detail that could account for the side effects without introducing other irrelevant information.

The second major assumption is that there exists some framework for viewing the program's actions that will allow them to be comprehensible to the observer. The likely validity of this assumption depends on both the program's fundamental mechanisms and the level at which these are examined. Consider a program that does medical diagnosis using a statistical approach based on Bayes' Theorem. It is difficult to imagine what explanation of its actions the program could give if it were queried while computing probabilities. No matter what level of detail is chosen, the approach is not (nor is it intended to be) an accurate model of the reasoning process typically employed by physicians (see [Tversky74] for some experimental verification). As effective as these actions may be, there is no easy way to interpret them in terms that will make them comprehensible to a physician unacquainted with the program.

With the current state of the art, then, the desire to have a program capable of explaining its actions strongly constrains the methodology chosen and the control structure that can be used. There do not yet appear to be general principles for generating explanations of arbitrary control structures in the way, for example, that an experienced programmer can read unfamiliar code and then explain it to someone else. As a result, the capability cannot now be tacked on to an existing system. To make the problem tractable, the desired capabilities must be taken into account early in the system-design process.

3–2.2   Specifics: How the Assumptions Were Applied

The fundamental organization of the performance program described earlier provides an environment in which both of these assumptions can be satisfied. The simple and/or goal-tree control structure and the domain-specific rules invoked in a *modus ponens* mode offer a basis for explanations that typically need little additional clarification. The invocation of a rule is taken as the fundamental action of the system. This, along with the goal tree as a framework, accounts for enough of the system's operation to make a recap of such actions an acceptable explanation. In terms of the constraints noted earlier, it is sufficiently detailed— the actions performed by a rule in making a "conclusion," for instance, correspond closely enough to the normal connotation of this word that no greater detail is necessary. It is still at an abstract enough level that the operations are meaningful. Finally, it is generally complete enough—there are typically no other mechanisms or sources of information that the observer needs to know in order to understand how the program reaches its conclusions. [1]

The success of this technique relies to some extent on the claim that the performance program's approach to its domain is sufficiently intuitive that a summary of those actions is a reasonable basis for explanation. While we have not yet attempted to prove the claim in any formal sense, there are several factors that suggest its plausibility.

First, the performance program is dealing with a domain in which deduction, and deduction in the face of uncertainty, is a primary task. The use of production rules seems therefore to be a natural way of expressing things about the domain and the display of such rules should be comprehensible. Second, the use of such rules in a backward-chaining mode seems to be a reasonably intuitive scheme. *Modus ponens* is a well-understood and widely (if not explicitly) used mode of inference. Thus, the general form of the representation and the way it is employed should not be unfamiliar to the average user. More specifically, however, consider the source of the rules. They are supplied by human experts who were attempting to formalize their own knowledge of the domain. As such, the rules embody accepted patterns of human reasoning, implying that they should be relatively easy to understand, especially for those familiar with the domain. As such, they also attack the problem at what has been judged an appropriate level of detail. That is, they embody the right size "chunks" of the problem to be comprehensible.

Many of the capabilities of the current explanation system also depend on the presence of a high-level language of the sort described in chapter 2. Extensive use is made of the stylized code and the small number of classes of primitives found in this language. This makes possible, in particular, dissection and interpretation of the rules, techniques which form the basis for many of TEIRESIAS's capabilities.

We have referred several times to explanations that are "comprehensible" and "complete," which raises the questions Comprehensible to whom? and Complete enough for whom? As indicated, our efforts have been directed at users from the

---

[1] The hedging here arises because, on those occasions when explanations produced by TEIRESIAS are cryptic, it is often a result of incompleteness of this sort. There are, for instance, rules in the performance program whose format and content have been influenced by the attempt to take advantage of subtle aspects of the control structure (*e.g.*, ordering the clauses of a premise so that certain attributes are traced first). Since there is in the system no indication of which rules have been so modified, the simple goal-tree model is incomplete is this respect.

application domain. It is with respect to this audience that "comprehensible" and "complete" are used, and it is with respect to their conceptual level that appropriate explanations must be produced. While a different level would have to be chosen for a different audience (*e.g.*, experienced programmers), the criteria above remain valid if the explanations are to be based on a recap of program actions.

3-3   DESIGN CRITERIA

There were three criteria central to the design of the explanation facilities.

1   *Accuracy.* Above all else, the explanations generated had to provide an accurate picture of what was going on in the performance program. This meant overcoming several temptations; in particular, the desire to "dress things up just a bit," to cover over some of the less impressive (or less transparent) aspects of MYCIN's behavior. If the facilities were to be an effective debugging tool, they had to be accurate.

2   *Comprehensibility.* Since computer consultants are intended for use by a nonprogramming audience, the explanations generated by TEIRESIAS had to be tailored accordingly. This meant restrictions on content and vocabulary and an emphasis on brevity. This criterion was the main source of the temptation to gloss over parts of MYCIN's behavior, to avoid having to justify in layman's terms the decisions that were based on computational considerations.

3   *Human engineering.* Consideration was also given to a collection of user-oriented factors like ease of use, power, and speed.

As might be expected, (1) and (2) occasionally conflict, in part because the facilities are powerful enough to allow the user to examine aspects of the performance program not normally intended for display. As one example, the first eight or nine questions of a consultation are generated as part of the initialization phase of the program and hence use a few nonstandard mechanisms. Their external appearance is the same as those generated by the standard method of backward chaining of rules, but the user can (perhaps unwittingly) uncover some perplexing operations if he explores this part of the process with the explanation facilities. There are good reasons for all of these operations, but it would take some extended discussion to make them clear to a nonprogrammer.

Wherever conflicts did arise, they were resolved using the design goals in the order listed. The facilities present an accurate picture of system performance; they do so as comprehensibly as possible and attempt to be fast and easy to use.

3-4   BASIC IDEAS

The basic ideas behind the design of the explanation facilities can be viewed in terms of the four steps discussed below.

1 *Determine the program operation that is to be viewed as primitive.* This gives the smallest unit of program behavior that can be explained. Examples further on will demonstrate that it is possible to generate different degrees of abstraction, but the level chosen in this step determines the level of maximum detail. In our case, the invocation of an individual rule was selected as the primitive operation.

2 *Augment the performance program code to leave behind a record of behavior at this level of detail.* The result is a complete trace of program behavior, a history of performance. The relevant sections of the performance program's control structure (*i.e.*, the inference engine) were augmented in this way to write a history of rule invocation attempts.

3 *Select a global framework in which that trace can be understood.* This framework is important especially where computationally naive users are concerned. The trace provides a record of behavior, but the framework supplies a way of understanding that behavior. Its selection is thus a central task in the construction of the facilities.

The framework was readily supplied by the performance program's control structure—the and/or goal tree offered a natural perspective in which to view program behavior and its explanation. The tracing task is structured in terms of tree traversal, and the user is offered a set of commands designed around it. The goal-tree view is of course specific to this particular control structure, but analogous frameworks are possible for other system designs.

4 *Design a program that can provide the user with an interpretation of the trace.* The program should be capable of systematic examination of the trace and should use the framework chosen to provide an interpretation of events recorded there. A body of code to do this forms the explanation program in TEIRESIAS and enables the user to examine the behavior of the performance program. It interprets the trace in terms of the and/or goal-tree framework and provides a set of commands that allows the user to examine previous, current, or future (potential) behavior.

These ideas form the foundation for the basic set of explanation capabilities. They are illustrated below with a number of annotated examples.

3–5 TRACE OF SYSTEM PERFORMANCE: EXPLANATIONS FOR PERFORMANCE VALIDATION

Modern-day computers are amazing pieces of equipment, but most amazing of all are the uncertain grounds on account of which we attach any validity to their output.

E. Dijkstra, *et al.*
Structured Programming

During a consultation, the performance program takes the initiative, asking questions of the user. If one of those questions seems inappropriate, the user can interrupt and use TEIRESIAS's explanation facilities to find out what's going on. By examining the chain of reasoning that prompted the question, he can find out if the reasoning was motivated by plausible considerations.

Since explanation is viewed in terms of traversal of the and/or goal tree, the command set is designed accordingly. The two basic commands are "why" and "how," corresponding to ascent and descent of the tree. It is the performance program's invocation of rules in a goal-directed fashion that makes tree traversal operations plausible interpretations of the commands.

Several annotated examples are given below, in this and subsequent sections. In each case, a single question from the consultation has been extracted and the explanation facilities have been used to examine the reasoning behind it. Figure 3–1 shows the part of the reasoning tree being examined in the first example.

In the trace below, computer output is in mixed upper and lower case in this font, user responses are in BOLDFACE CAPITALS, while annotations are indented in {*italics inside braces*}.


```
In light of the site from which the culture was obtained and
the method of collection, do you feel that a significant
number of ORGANISM-1 were obtained?
** WHY
[i.e., Why is it important to determine whether a ORGANISM-1
 was observed in significant numbers?]
[1.0] This will aid in determining whether there is
         therapeutically significant disease associated with
         this occurrence of ORGANISM-1.
      It has already been established that
[1.1] the method of collection is sterile,
         therefore, if:
[1.2] the organism was observed in significant numbers, and
[1.3] the site of the culture is not one of those which are
         normally sterile,
      then
there is strongly suggestive evidence (.9) that there is
therapeutically significant disease associated with this
occurrence of the organism.
[Also: there is strongly suggestive evidence (.8) that the
 organism is not a contaminant.]
[RULE054]
```

{*As Figure 3–1 shows, the issue of "a significant number of organisms" is one subgoal, "therapeutically significant disease" is another at the next level up, and rule 54 links them. The "reason" for asking the original question, then, is to invoke rule 54 to determine the higher subgoal, and the answer to "why" is simply a display of the goals and the rule linking them.*

Considerable attention has been paid to making this as lucid a display as possible. First, since "why" has several other interpretations and no more extensive natural language capabilities are available, the question is expanded by TEIRESIAS *to indicate the sense in which it will be answered. The higher level goal is then presented, followed by the rule. The premises of the rule are divided into those already established and those yet to be determined, using the template mechanism described in chapter 2. Finally, since rules may have multiple conclusions about different attributes, the relevant conclusion is presented first and all others follow.}*

** WHY

{Further sections of the reasoning chain can be examined by repeating the command.}

```
[i.e., Why is it important to find out whether there is
therapeutically significant disease associated with this
occurrence of ORGANISM-1?]
[2.0]... in order to find out a locus of infection in
      PATIENT-1.  It has already been established that:
  [2.1] the number of days since the specimen for the culture
        was obtained is less than 7,
        therefore, if:
  [2.2] there is therapeutically significant disease
        associated with this occurrence of the organism
        then
it is definite (1.0) that the site of the culture is a
locus of infection in the patient.
[RULE021]
```
** WHY
```
[i.e., Why is it important to determine a locus of infection
in PATIENT-1?]
[3.0]...in order to find out about an organism or class of
      organisms for which therapy should cover.
      It has already been established that:
  [3.1] the site of the culture is blood, and
  [3.2] the stain of the organism is grampos, and
  [3.3] the portal of entry of the organism is GI,
        therefore, if:
  [3.4] [A - abdomen is a locus of infection in the patient,
        or,
            B - pelvis is a locus of infection in the patient]
        then
there is strongly suggestive evidence (.9) that
enterobacteriaceae is a class of organisms for which
therapy should cover.
[RULE095]
```
** HOW [3.0]

{*HOW can be used to climb "down" the reasoning chain and gives a picture of all the ways any subgoal may be achieved. In the examples demonstrating its use, numbers following the command refer to the corresponding items above (e.g., the* [3.0] *above).*}

[i.e., How were you determining an organism or class of
organisms for which therapy should cover?]
[4.0] At that point RULE095 was being used. In addition,
 [4.1] RULE162 was used to conclude that bacteroides is an
        organism for which therapy should cover, and
 [4.2] RULE115 will be tried later, as well.

{*Once again the question is underspecified and is expanded by* TEIRESIAS. *Note that the system can indicate reasoning chains previously followed, those currently being examined, and those yet to be tried. Each can be further explored.*}

** HOW [4.1]
[i.e., How was RULE162 used?]
[5.0]   It has already been established that:
 [5.1] the site of the culture is blood, and
 [5.2] the portal of entry of the organism is GI, and
 [5.3] the patient is a compromised host.
        Therefore,
it is definite (1.0) that bacteroides is an organism for
which therapy should cover.
 [RULE162]
** HOW [4.2]
[i.e. How will RULE115 be used?]
 If [6.0] brain-abscess is an infectious disease diagnosis
        for the patient,
 then   there is weakly suggestive evidence (.2) that
          streptococcus-anaerobic is an organism for which
          therapy should cover.
          [RULE115]

3-6   THE NEED FOR AN INFORMATION METRIC

[In an explanation] we must not carry reasoning too far back, or the length of our argument will cause obscurity; neither must we put in all the steps that lead to our conclusion, or we shall waste words in saying what is manifest.

Aristotle

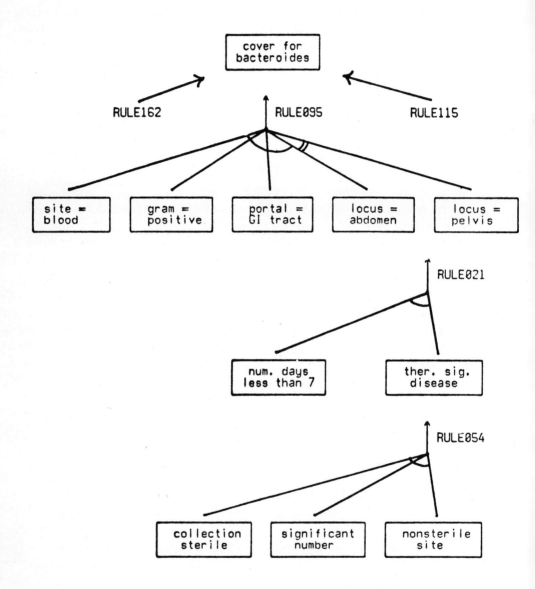

Figure 3-1   Reasoning tree for the first set of explanation examples.

One problem anticipated in the use of the WHY command, and one that is common to explanations in general, is the issue of an appropriate level of sophistication and detail. It is generally of little use to discover that

```
If:   1) The gram stain of the organism is grampos, and

      2) The morphology of the organism is rod

Then:  It is definite (1.0) that the category of the

       organism is grampos-rods.
```

Figure 3–2   RULE140.

Depending on the individual user, it might be best to display all steps in a reasoning chain, to omit those that are definitional or trivial, or, for the most sophisticated user, to display only the highlights. This presumes that we have some idea of what constitutes "the details." In terms of the goal tree, it means knowing how "far" it is conceptually from one node to another, which is difficult since this depends very much on the (constantly changing) state of the user's knowledge. It is also very important since the best explanations are those based on a clear understanding of the extent of the user's comprehension.

In a very rough analogy to information theory, we use -(log CF) to provide this measure. Definitional rules (with CF = 1.0) thus have no information, while those with smaller CFs have progressively more. This is clearly imperfect. It does not take into account the state of the user's knowledge, and since CFs are not probabilities there is no formal justification that -(log CF) is a meaningful number. It's primary utility, however, is as a "dial" with which the user can adjust the level of detail in the explanations. Absolute settings are less important than the ability to make relative adjustments.

The adjustment is made via an optional argument to the WHY command. The entire "distance" from the current node to the top of the goal tree is normalized to 10, and the argument following the WHY is taken as some fraction of that distance. Thus, rather than the multiple WHYs seen above, the user might have asked "WHY 4":

```
We are trying to find out whether the organism has been observed in
significant numbers, in order to determine an organism or class of
organisms for which therapy should cover.
```

Figure 3-3   A "high-level" explanation.

Since the three steps in the chain shown in Figure 3–1 constitute roughly two-fifths of the "distance" to the top, they are compressed into a single answer. This command may be repeated as often as necessary, allowing the user to follow the reasoning chain in step sizes of his own choosing.

The user may occasionally choose a step size that is too big, compressing too many steps into a single answer, leaving him with an incomprehensible explanation. In this case he can invoke the EXPLAIN command, which will cover the same starting and ending points in the reasoning, but in more detail. Thus, if the explanation in Figure 3–3 above proved to be too obscure, the user might say EXPLAIN and have it expanded out in complete detail. He might also say EXPLAIN 2, to have it expanded out in steps roughly half as big as in Figure 3–3 (the argument has the same meaning for both the WHY and EXPLAIN commands).

3–7   MORE SOPHISTICATED HOWS

Previous examples have demonstrated that HOW questions can have a range of possible meanings, depending on the referent of the question. Examples above showed its use in determining how the value of an attribute was reached and how different rules had been (or might be) used. A more complex situation arises if the question refers to a clause from a premise of a rule, as in:

```
Is the patient's illness with ORGANISM-1 a hospital-acquired
infection?
**  WHY
[i.e., WHY is it important to determine whether or not the
 infection with ORGANISM-1 was acquired while the patient
 was hospitalized?]
[2.0] This will aid in determining the category of
       ORGANISM-1.  It has already been established that
  [2.1] the gram stain of ORGANISM-1 is gramneg, and
  [2.2] the morphology of ORGANISM-1 is rod, and
  [2.3] the aerobicity of ORGANISM-1 is facultative
```

```
          Therefore, if
[2.4] the infection with ORGANISM-1 was not acquired while
      the patient was hospitalized
      then
there is strongly suggestive evidence (.8) that the
category of ORGANISM-1 is enterobacteriaceae
[ALSO: there is weakly suggestive evidence (.1) that the
  identity of ORGANISM-1 is pseudomonas-aeruginosa]
[RULE037]
```
** HOW [2.3]
```
[i.e., HOW was it established that the aerobicity of
ORGANISM-1 is facultative?]
The following were used:
[3.1] RULE027 indicated there is strongly suggestive
      evidence (.8) that the aerobicity of ORGANISM-1 is
      facultative
[3.2] RULE033 indicated there is weakly suggestive evidence
      (.2) that the aerobicity of ORGANISM-1 is not
      facultative.
Since this gave a cumulative CF of (.6) for facultative, the
evidence indicates that the aerobicity of ORGANISM-1 is
facultative.
```
Figure 3–4

To answer the question about aerobicity accurately, we must determine from the execution trace the subset of rules that actually contributed to the conclusion mentioned in clause [2.3]. In this case it is straightforward, since the set of all rules invoked about aerobicity is available from the execution trace and the appropriate subset (those that concluded that aerobicity was facultative) can be determined using the template mechanism to examine the conclusion of each of them.

A second example, from a different consultation, shows a more complex response.

```
Is PATIENT-1 immunosuppressed or immunodeficient?
```
** WHY
```
[i.e., Why is it important to determine if the patient is
  immunosuppressed or immunodeficient?]
[5.0] This will aid in determining the category of
      ORGANISM-1.  It has already been established that
[5.1] the site of CULTURE-1 is blood, and
[5.2] the gram stain of ORGANISM-1 is gramneg, and
[5.3] the morphology of ORGANISM-1 is rod,
      Therefore, if
[5.4] the patient is immunosuppressed or immunodeficient,
      then
```

there is weakly suggestive evidence (.3) that the category
of ORGANISM-1 is enterobacteriaceae
[RULE085]
**WHY
[i.e., Why is it important to determine the category of
ORGANISM-1?]
[6.0] This will aid in determining the identity of
       ORGANISM-1. It has already been established that
  [6.1] the site of CULTURE-1 is blood, and
  [6.2] the gram stain of ORGANISM-1 is gramneg, and
  [6.3] the morphology of ORGANISM-1 is rod,
       Therefore, if
  [6.4] the category of ORGANISM-1 is not known with certainty,
       then
there is weakly suggestive evidence (.3) that the identity
of ORGANISM-1 is proteus.
[RULE093]
** HOW [6.4]
[i.e., How will it be established that the category of
ORGANISM-1 is known, but not with certainty?]
[7.0] Currently RULE085 is being used.
       In addition, the following was also used:
  [7.1] RULE084 indicated that there is strongly suggestive
       evidence (.8) that the category of the organism is
       enterobacteriaceae.
       Based on current patient data, the following may also
       prove useful later in the consultation:
  [7.2] RULE176
  [7.3] RULE021
If, after trying these rules, the cumulative CF of any value
of the category of ORGANISM-1 is equal to or greater than .2
and less than 1.0, it will be established that the category
of ORGANISM-1 is known, but not with certainty.

Figure 3–5

In this case the performance program has not yet finished determining the
organism's identity, and the user has asked how the process will establish the
answer with the indicated range of certainty. Several sources of information are
required to provide an accurate and informative response. First, TEIRESIAS needs
some indication of the "meaning" of the predicate function "known, but not with
certainty."

There is a simple framework in which all of the predicate functions can be
viewed, and which provides the basis for our representation of this information.
Each function can be seen as some segment of the number line $[-1.0, 1.0]$ that
defines the range of certainty factors (several examples are indicated in Figure

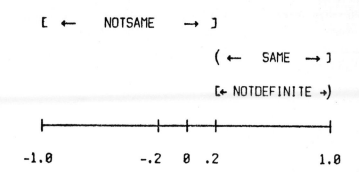

-1.0   -.2 0 .2   1.0

[- closed interval

(- open interval

Figure 3-6   Predicate functions: Segments of the number line.

3–9 below, see [Shortliffe76] for the entire list). Associated with each predicate
function is a numerical definition in these terms.

For NOTDEFINITE (the predicate function used in clause [6.4]), the definition
is

$$(AND \ (GTE \ CF \ .2) \ (LT \ CF \ 1.0))$$

Since experience has shown that the "canned" English phrases associated with
the predicate functions are often unclear, TEIRESIAS prints the interval definition
at the end of the explanation. This makes clear to the user the criterion used
to judge the truth or falsity of a clause. In the current case, for example, it
is judged to be true that "the category of ORGANISM-1 is not known
with certainty" if some value has been established for it with a CF greater
than or equal to .2 and less than 1.0.

The set of answers obtained by the user during the consultation is the second
major source of information. This set makes possible a well-constrained list of
rules that "may prove useful later in the consultation" (as in [7.2]
and [7.3] above). The entire list of rules about identity is available internally; the
subset of them yet to be invoked can be determined by reference to the execution
trace. The premise of each of these is checked (using the partial evaluation
technique discussed in chapter 2), disqualifying those that are known to be false
based on currently available information. This helps TEIRESIAS keep the answer
brief and avoid leading the user down a path in the reasoning tree known to be
a dead end.

The major contribution of these various sources of information is to allow
TEIRESIAS to construct explanations that are as sharply focused, precise, and in-

formative as possible. The system's ability to constrain the set of rules considered means that the user will not be inundated by large numbers of possible paths, even when there are quite a few rules in the knowledge base. The system's ability to present some indication of the definition of the predicate functions means that it can be terse in its normal translation of a rule and still give the user some idea of the less obvious aspects of the model of confirmation.

3–8   SPECIAL PURPOSE RESPONSES

The goal-tree framework accounts for a very large part of MYCIN's performance, but not all of it. In order to meet the primary design goal of accuracy, it was necessary to implement a small number of special purpose responses in TEIRESIAS's explanation program.

The description of the control structure in chapter 2 noted that each object (a patient, culture, organism, etc.) has a number of its associated attributes marked as "primary" and that these attributes are automatically traced when the object is instantiated.[2] Since this process is not part of the standard goal-tree search, a separate mechanism is required to provide a response to a WHY inquiry at this point. An example is shown below: It is a brief statement of fact, augmented by a very simple form of generalization.

```
From what site was the specimen for CULTURE-1 taken?
** WHY

[i.e. Why is it important to determine the site of CULTURE-1?]
[8.0]    There are 2 standard clinical parameters that are important to
   determine in discussing a culture, and the site of the culture is
   one of them.
      The site of CULTURE-1 may be useful later in the consultation.   For
   example, it is very important in determining the identity of an
   organism, and is significant in determining whether or not an
   organism is a contaminant.
```

Figure 3–7

This response takes account of the motivation for automatically tracing the primary attributes: They are often the most informative pieces of information about the problem. In response, the explanation routines examine the knowledge base to see how the answer may be used and select the most common uses. The piece of information originally requested is then classified as being "very important," "significant," or "relevant" to each of those uses, according to the number of rules found. In the example above, of all the rules which mention culture site in their premise, there are a large number that conclude about organism identity and a smaller number that conclude about possible contaminants.

A second special purpose mechanism is employed to make sure that implicit deductions do not confuse the user. Consider a consultation in which the user indicates that the culture site is blood. In printing out a rule later on, the system might make reference to the fact that *the site of the culture is one of those sites that are normally sterile.* If the user asks how this fact was established, the program responds:

---

[2] This is in response to the stylized presentation of information that is common in the domain: A clinician is accustomed to offering certain standard pieces of information about each topic. Tracing the primary attributes of each object as soon as the object is created means that the consultation presents a familiar format.

```
[i.e. How was it established that the site of CULTURE-1 is one of those sites
      that are normally sterile?]

You said so [question 4].
[Those sites that are normally sterile are: UPPER-GU, BLOOD, BONE, BRAIN, CSF,
LIVER, LOWER-RESP, PERICARDIUM, PLEURAL-SPACE, SINUS.]
```

Figure 3–8

Since the user only said that the site was blood, and may not be aware of exactly which sites are sterile, this additional information is made clear to him.

3–9   LIMITATIONS

There are several sources of limitations in the approach we have taken.

3–9.1   Restriction to a Single Framework

First, the choice of a single primitive operation (rule invocation) and a single framework (the goal tree) restricts the class of events that can be explained. We have seen that behavior caused by mechanisms outside this framework must either be explained with special purpose routines or left unaccounted for. In terms of the current performance program (MYCIN), the most serious example of the latter is drug selection. While some part of that process is expressed in rules, much of the optimization phase (minimizing the number of drugs and side effects and maximizing coverage) is in complex LISP code and hence inaccessible to the methods used in TEIRESIAS.

Two possible approaches to solving this are (i) put everything in rules, or (ii) provide multiple frameworks. Some preliminary steps toward the former are discussed in chapter 7, which describes the use of meta-rules to express many types of knowledge. This appears to be only a partial solution, however. While production rules are a general computational mechanism, their utility as a representation for some tasks is questionable (see [Davis77a] for a discussion of this issue). Developing multiple frameworks appears to be a more general solution, but has not yet been explored.

3–9.2   Lack of a General Model of Explanation

A more fundamental conceptual limitation arises out of the priorities of our design criteria. TEIRESIAS's explanation facilities do indeed supply an effective tool for discovering the basis for the performance program's behavior and for examining its knowledge base. They do not, however, contain a particularly sophisticated model of explanation. This becomes evident in several ways. It was noted earlier, for instance, that "why" and "how" are underspecified and must necessarily be expanded by TEIRESIAS to avoid misinterpretation by the user (*e.g.*, "Why" might mean "Why did you ask about that instead of...," or "Why did you ask about that now," etc.). These other interpretations are valid questions about the system, yet there is no way in the current framework to answer them.

As another example, there are certain types of information that are missing from the system entirely, which are judged necessary if we are to supply a truly comprehensive explanation capability. Consider the following example.

```
Was the infection with ORGANISM-1 acquired while the patient was
hospitalized?
** WHY
[i.e. Why is it important to determine if the infection with ORGANISM-1 was
acquired while the patient was hospitalized?]


[1.0] This will help to determine the identity of ORGANISM-1.
      It has already been established that
          [1.1] the gramstain of ORGANISM-1 is gramneg, and
          [1.2] the morphology of ORGANISM-1 is rod, and
          [1.3] the aerobicity of ORGANISM-1 is facultative,
      Therefore, if
          [1.4] the infection with ORGANISM-1 was acquired while the patient
                was hospitalized,
      Then
          there is weakly suggestive evidence (.2) that the identity of the
          organism is pseudomonas.
      [RULE050]
```

Figure 3–9

A naive user might now be tempted to ask a different sort of "why": *Why is it true that a gram negative facultative rod in a hospital setting is likely to be a pseudomonas?* The answer is that certain sorts of bacteria are very common in the hospital environment, but there is currently no representation of this in the system. Since the sequence of "why" questions of this sort can be continued indefinitely (*Why are some bacteria more common in the hospital?*, etc.), it is not unreasonable to cut off at some point. But currently the question cannot be answered even once, and in a more general explanation model, this should be possible.

The lack of a user model in the information metric has been mentioned, and this too is an important element. In our current model, two rules with the same certainty factor have the same information content, yet a user who is familiar with only the first of them will find much more information in the second.

Next, while our approach generates high-level explanations by leaving out detail, there is another sort of abstraction that would be very useful. The system should be.able to describe its actions at different conceptual levels, perhaps at levels ranging from rule invocation to LISP interpretation, to function calls, etc. A limited form of this kind of ability is described in [Sacerdoti77], but there it arises from code that has been intentionally structured in this multilevel form. More interesting would be an ability to generate such explanations from an understanding of the process at each level. Some of the work on models of disease processes described in [Kulikowski73] may be relevant here.

Finally, there is the possibility of decoupling explanation from control flow. Section 3-2 pointed out a fundamental assumption of our approach: that a recap of program actions can be a plausible explanation. This assumption need not be made and explanations could be considered separately, distinct from execution (as in [Brown75]). This is common human behavior—the account someone gives of how he solved a complex problem may be quite different from a simple review of his actions. The difference is often more than just leaving out the dead ends or omitting the details of the solution. Solving the problem often produces new insights and shows results in a totally different view, one which often admits a much more compact explanation. There is greater flexibility from an approach of this kind since it can be used to supply a wider variety of explanations; but it also requires a new and separate basis for generating explanations and, hence, is more difficult.

All of these examples point the way to useful extensions to TEIRESIAS that would give it a far more general and powerful explanation capability.

3–9.3   Lack of Ability to Represent Control Structures

The third, and most relevant, limitation is the lack of a substantive ability to represent control structures. In the current system, the closest approximation comes from the use of the goal-tree framework as a model of the control structure. But this "model" exists only implicitly, expressed by the organization of code in the explanation facility rather than as a separate entity. Shortcomings are evidenced by the fact that almost any alteration of the control structure of the performance program requires an analogous recoding of TEIRESIAS's explanation routines. If there were instead some representation of the control structure that the explanation routines could examine, the system would be much more flexible. The general scheme would be as pictured below:

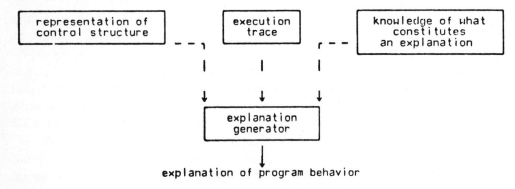

Figure 3-10   A more sophisticated explanation-generation scheme.

Given some representation of the control structure and a body of knowledge about what an explanation is, TEIRESIAS would generate a comprehensible account of performance program behavior. Supplying either of these seems to be a formidable but interesting prospect.

The fact that a programmer can scan a strange piece of code and then explain the behavior of a program executing it, suggests that the task is at least plausible. Formalizing the knowledge of what it means to "explain" does not seem to have received extensive attention. Some of the work on affects and intensions by [Faught74] may be relevant, as may be the conceptual dependency work in [Reiger74] and the work on computer-aided instruction in [Brown75].

Some small steps toward representing the control structure in an accessible form are described in chapter 7. There we explore the use of meta-rules to express certain aspects of the performance program's control structure, and hence render them accessible to the current explanation mechanism.

A more sophisticated form of representation is needed, however. The source code of a program is not a particularly good choice for two reasons. First, it carries too much implementation detail. It may be useful to know only that a piece of code is, for instance, an iterative loop, and the detail of how it is implemented often only confuses the issue. Second, it carries too little intentional information. LISP's CAR operation, for example, can usually be read as *first element* of a list; but inside a loop, it might be more appropriately viewed as *next element*.

The task requires some way of suppressing implementation detail and emphasizing intentions. There is a common style of programming that accomplishes some of this. It emphasizes the use of extended data types (*e.g.*, record structures) and macros (or functions) designed for the task at hand. It may include two functions called FIRST and NEXT, for instance, even though both perform the same CAR operation. Something along this line has been suggested in [Hewitt71], but the emphasis there is on program correctness and automatic programming. The point here is simply to give the programmer a way of expressing his (perhaps informal) intentions for each section of code so that the program can later be explained. Note that these intentions might include not only descriptions of control structure but might go on to specify many other things about the code: design considerations, algorithm choices, and perhaps other kinds of information of the sort found in well-written documentation. Thus, where the efforts in program correctness have concentrated on describing precisely "what" a program should do, intentional information might include descriptions of the "how" of program design. The work in [Goldstein74] suggests the multiple uses that might be made of such annotations: That system based its debugging of simple programs on an understanding of common error types plus remarks in the code that indicated the programmer's "plan" for solving the problem.

Flowcharts are a second possibility; some text-oriented representation of them might prove useful. In an analogy to some of the work on program correctness, they might be annotated with "motivation conditions," providing, thereby, both a representation of the control structure and the information necessary to explain it. Both of these are clearly very speculative; there is much room for additional work.

3–9.4   Other Communication Media

We have not yet explored any graphics-oriented explanations, but Figure 3–1 illustrates that they might be very useful. The tree shown there makes clear what otherwise takes many lines of text. Considering the natural interpretation of the performance program's control structure in graphic form and the desire to be as brief as possible, it appears to be an excellent medium.

3–10   TRACE OF SYSTEM PERFORMANCE: EXPLANATIONS FOR SYSTEM DEBUGGING

And you are wrong if you believe that one.

Sophocles
Oedipus the King, line 554

Work on giving a program the ability to explain its actions ([Shortliffe75a]) was originally motivated by concerns about comprehensibility: Consultation programs are unlikely to be accepted by users if they function as "black boxes" that simply print their final answers. Much of the work described earlier in this chapter is in the same vein.

But there is another, different, and very useful application of explanation: program debugging, in particular as a means of setting an appropriate context for knowledge acquisition. As an introduction to the knowledge acquisition sections that follow, an example below demonstrates how the explanation routines in TEI- RESIAS have been designed to allow the domain expert to track down the source of an error in the knowledge base.

One of the options available to the expert is having the system stop after it has presented its diagnosis, to give him a chance to comment on it. This pause provides a natural starting place for evaluation and debugging. Once the bug is found, the acquisition session, described in later chapters, then goes on to repair the problem by teaching the system the new rule.

The example presented here will be carried on through the knowledge ac- quisition chapters and developed in detail. In order to present a single example that would include all the features to be displayed, it was necessary to create a bug by removing a rule from the performance program's knowledge base and eliminating all references to it. The example is special in no other sense, however, and with the obvious exceptions of font changes, annotations, and slight refor- matting, the interaction appears just as it does here. For completeness, the entire consultation is presented below.

```
MYCIN   24-NOV-76 ...
Special options (type ? for help):
** RD SAVE
Hello, Dr. Davis
```

{The expert identifies himself to the system and indicates that he wants a record of this consultation kept in the case library. }

This will be patient 281.
If you would care to enter a brief clinical summary of your patient's case, to be used for easy future reference to this file, please do so now (type as many lines as required, terminate with a blank line):
**CLASSIC CASE OF GRAM NEGATIVE ROD INFECTION FOR A
**PATIENT WITH A NON-NOSOCOMIAL DISEASE
**
--------PATIENT-281--------
1) Patient's name: (first-last)
** ALBERT HALL
2) Sex:
** MALE
3) Age:
** 34
4) Have you been able to obtain positive microbiological information about a possible infection of Albert Hall?
** YES
--------INFECTION-1--------
5) What is the infection?
** PRIMARY-BACTEREMIA
6) Please give the date and time when signs or symptoms of the primary-bacteremia (INFECTION-1) first appeared.
** 15 DECEMBER 77 12:00
The most recent culture yielding positive microbiological information about the primary-bacteremia (INFECTION-1) will be referred to as:
--------CULTURE-1--------
7) From what site was the specimen for CULTURE-1 taken?
** BLOOD
8) Please give the date and time when this blood culture (CULTURE-1) was obtained. (mo/da/yr time)
** 16 DECEMBER 77 12:00
The first significant organism from this blood culture (CULTURE-1) will be referred to as:
--------ORGANISM-1--------
9) Enter the identity of ORGANISM-1:
** UNKNOWN
10) Is ORGANISM-1 a rod or coccus (etc.):
** ROD
11) The gram stain of ORGANISM-1:

** GRAMNEG

12) Did ORGANISM-1 grow in the aerobic bottle?

** YES

13) Did ORGANISM-1 grow in the anaerobic bottle?

** YES

14) Is the patient's illness with ORGANISM-1 a hospital-
     acquired infection?

** NO

15) Have there been POSITIVE cultures yielding organisms
     about which you will NOT be seeking advice?

** NO

16) Is Albert Hall a burn patient?

** NO

17) Do you consider Albert Hall to be a compromised host
     (alcoholic, immunosuppressed, etc.)?

** NO

18) What is the suspected portal of entry of ORGANISM-1
     into this sterile site?

** GI

19) Has Albert Hall had any G-U surgery or manipulation of
     the urinary tract (eg. catheter, cystoscopy, etc.)?

** NO

20) Including this blood culture (CULTURE-1), how many times
     during this series of cultures was this site cultured?

** 3

21) In this series, how many of the cultures from this
     site were positive for ORGANISM-1?

** 3

22) Any other significant organisms isolated from this blood
     culture (CULTURE-1)?

** NO

23) Did any additional cultures yield positive microbiologi-
     cal information which you believe is associated with the
     primary-bacteremia (INFECTION-1)?

** NO

24) Does Albert Hall have any other infection about which you
     have obtained positive microbiological information?

** NO

25) Do you suspect an infection at a site which you have been
     unable to culture, or from which all cultures were
     negative?

** NO

26) Is Albert Hall currently receiving therapy with any
     antimicrobial agent?

** NO

27) During the present illness, has Albert Hall been treated
    with an antimicrobial agent which is no longer being
    administered?
** NO

My therapy recommendation will be based on the following
probable infection(s) and potential causative organism(s):
INFECTION-1 is PRIMARY-BACTEREMIA
        <Item 1> E.COLI [ORGANISM-1]
        <Item 2> PSEUDOMONAS-AERUGINOSA [ORGANISM-1]
Are all these identities correct?
++** N

{*At this point* TEIRESIAS *steps in, asks for the expert's opinion, and is told that something is wrong. From here on, the interaction is between the expert and* TEIRESIAS, *with the performance program in the background being manipulated by* TEIRESIAS. }

Are there any identities missing?
++** Y
Which one(s)?
++** KLEBSIELLA-PNEUMONIAE PROTEUS-NON-MIRABILIS
Are there any identities that shouldn't have appeared?
++** Y
Which one(s)?
++** PSEUDOMONAS-AERUGINOSA
We'll start with the PSEUDOMONAS-AERUGINOSA first.

{*Heuristics derived from our experience in debugging are built into the system. They suggest that the best approach is (a) to track down one problem at a time, and (b) to start with an answer that shouldn't have appeared, if there is one. Experience has suggested that values which appear inappropriately are often the result of a bug causing several problems; so curing one often removes a number of problems at once.* }

Do you want to
        1] track down the problem yourself, or
        2] allow me to guide the debugging, or
        3] ignore it for now and fix it another time?
Type 1, 2 or 3
++** 1

{*The first option allows the expert to use all the standard explanation facilities and will be demonstrated here. The second is based on an analysis of the control structure that drives the consultation and is explored in the next chapter. The final option is for human engineering purposes and allows the expert to sidestep the whole process if he should decide to do so. }*

```
The following rules were used in deducing that the identity of
          ORGANISM-1 is pseudomonas-aeruginosa
RULE184
-------

Since [1.1] the category of ORGANISM-1 is not known
      [1.2] the gram stain of ORGANISM-1 is gramneg
      [1.3] the morphology of ORGANISM-1 is rod
      [1.4] the aerobicity of ORGANISM-1 is facultative
  There is weakly suggestive evidence (.3) that the identity of
          ORGANISM-1 is pseudomonas-aeruginosa
Now use the standard explanation commands (WHY HOW, etc.) to
find the bug.  When you've discovered what you think the
problem is, type ''OK'', and we can try to fix it
```
     ** HOW [1.1]
```
[i.e. HOW was it established that the category of ORGANISM-1
 is not known?]
There were no rules successfully invoked to deduce the category
of ORGANISM-1.  The following rules failed:
      [2.1] RULE050
      [2.2] RULE116
```

{ When the expert is tracking down a bug, the answer to a "how" question includes an indication of rules that might have been executed but which failed. This is not normally useful to the average observer and so is omitted in other circumstances. }

     ** HOW [2.1]
```
It was established that
      [3.1] the gram stain of ORGANISM-1 is gramneg, and
      [3.2] the morphology of ORGANISM-1 is rod, and
      [3.3] the aerobicity of ORGANISM-1 is facultative
But it was never established that
      [3.4] the infection with ORGANISM-1 was acquired while
            the patient was hospitalized
[And the conclusion could not be made that
 there is strongly suggestive evidence (.7) that the category
 of ORGANISM-1 is enterobacteriaceae]
[RULE050]
```
     ** HOW [2.2]
```
It was established that
      [4.1] the identity of the organism is not known,
But it was never established that
```

```
    [4.2] the gram stain of the organism is not known,
    [4.3] the morphology of the organism is not known, and
    [4.4] the site of the culture is csf, and
    [4.5] the infection is meningitis, and
    [4.6] the age (in years) of the patient is less than or
          equal to .17
[And the conclusion could not be made that
 there is weakly suggestive evidence (.3) that the category
 of ORGANISM-1 is enterobacteriaceae]
[RULE116]
    ** OK
Good, now do you want to:
    1] give me a new rule
    2] modify an existing rule
++** 1
The new rule will be called RULE383
  If:    1 -
```

The expert has tracked down one problem: The performance program should have been able to deduce the probable category of the organism. TEIRESIAS is now ready to accept a new rule to fix the problem. We're going to stop at this point and start again in chapter 5 in order to see how the acquisition process proceeds.

3–11   SUMMARY

Three different means of generating explanations have been explored in this chapter. The first technique, which explores branches of the tree not yet traversed by the consultation program, is used in producing answers to "how" questions (*e.g., How will you determine the identity of ORGANISM-1?*). These are produced by having the explanation program simulate the operation of the consultation program via special-purpose software. It is thus a hand-crafted solution.

More general is the use of the goal-tree concept as a basis for explanation. Since the notion of a goal tree models a large part of the control structure, it provides a single, uncomplicated model for much of the performance program's behavior. As a result, a simple formalism that equates "why" and "how" with tree traversal offers a reasonably powerful and comprehensive explanation capability.

The most general technique involves having TEIRESIAS directly examine the rules in the knowledge base, as in the use of the templates to determine whether a premise clause has already been established or is still untested. In doing this, TEIRESIAS's explanation facility examines and interprets the same piece of code that the performance program is about to execute. The resulting explanation is thus constructed with reference to the content of the rule, and this referral is guided by information (the templates) contained in the rule components themselves.

We have also seen two distinct uses for the explanations that TEIRESIAS can generate. They can help make a performance program more comprehensible by displaying the reasoning it employed and can aid in uncovering shortcomings in the knowledge base. The next three chapters follow up on this second theme and show how to rectify the errors discovered.

Chapter 4

Knowledge Acquisition: Overview

The essence of knowledge is, having it, to apply it; not having it, to confess your ignorance.

Confucius

4–1   INTRODUCTION

Before describing the range of knowledge acquisition capabilities in TEIRESIAS, there are a few introductory comments that will help to establish a global perspective on what follows. First, since the term "knowledge acquisition" has been used previously to describe a range of tasks, we characterize our view of it.

4–2   PERSPECTIVE ON KNOWLEDGE ACQUISITION

We view the interaction between the domain expert and the performance program as *interactive transfer of expertise.* We see it in terms of a teacher who continually challenges a student with new problems to solve and carefully observes the student's performance. The teacher may interrupt to request a justification of some particular step the student has taken in solving the problem or may challenge the final result. This process may uncover a fault in the student's knowledge of the subject (the debugging phase) and result in the transfer of information to correct it (the knowledge acquisition phase).

Other approaches to knowledge acquisition can be compared to this by considering their relative positions along two dimensions: (i) the sophistication of their debugging facilities and (ii) the independence of their knowledge acquisition mechanism.

The simplest sort of debugging tool is characterized by a program like DDT, which is totally passive (in the sense that it operates only in response to user commands), is low level (since it operates at the level of machine or assembly language), and knows nothing about the application domain of the program.

Debuggers like BAIL [Resier75] and INTERLISP's break package [Teitelman75] are a step up from this since they function at the level of programming languages like SAIL and INTERLISP.

The simple "how" and "why" commands in TEIRESIAS represent another step, since they function at the level of the control structure of the application program. The guided debugging which TEIRESIAS can also provide (see chapter 5) represents yet another step, since here the debugger is taking the initiative and has enough built-in knowledge about the control structure that it can track down the error. It does this by requesting from the expert an opinion on the validity of a few selected rules from among the many that were invoked.

Finally, at the most sophisticated level are knowledge-rich debuggers like the one found in [Brown78]. Here the program is active, high-level, and informed about the application domain, and is capable of independently localizing and characterizing bugs.

By independence of the knowledge acquisition mechanism, we mean the degree of human cooperation necessary. Much work on knowledge acquisition has emphasized a highly autonomous mode of operation. There is, for example, a large body of work aimed at inducing the appropriate generalizations from a set of test data (see, *e.g.*, [Buchanan78] and [Hayes-Roth77]). In these efforts user interaction is limited to presenting the program with the data and perhaps providing a brief description of the domain in the form of values for a few key parameters; the program then functions independently.

Winston's work on concept formation [Winston70] relied somewhat more heavily on user interaction. There the teacher was responsible for providing an appropriate sequence of examples (and non-examples) of a concept.

In describing our work, we have used the phrase "interactive transfer of expertise" to indicate that we view knowledge acquisition as information transfer from an expert to a program. TEIRESIAS does not attempt to derive new knowledge on its own, but instead tries to "listen" as attentively as possible and comment appropriately, to help the expert augment the knowledge base. It thus requires the strongest degree of cooperation from the expert.

4–3 KNOWLEDGE ACQUISITION IN CONTEXT

TEIRESIAS is designed to work with performance programs that accommodate inexact knowledge. Such programs find their greatest utility in domains where knowledge has not been extensively formalized. In such domains there are typically no unifying laws on which to base algorithmic methods; instead there is a collection of informal knowledge based on accumulated experience. As a result, an expert specifying a new rule in this domain may be codifying a piece of knowledge that has never previously been isolated and expressed as such. This process of explicating previously informal knowledge is difficult, and anything which can be done to ease the task will prove very useful.

In response, we have emphasized knowledge acquisition in the context of shortcomings in the knowledge base. To illustrate the utility of this approach, consider the difference between asking the expert

<blockquote>What should I know about bacteremia?</blockquote>

and saying to him

> Here is a case history for which you claim the performance program incorrectly deduced the presence of pseudomonas. Here is how it reached its conclusions, and here are all the facts of the case. Now, *what is it that you know that the performance program doesn't,* which allows you to avoid making that mistake?

Consider how much more focused the second question is and how much easier it would be to explicate the relevant knowledge.

The focusing provided by the context is also an important aid to TEIRESIAS. In particular, it permits the system to build up a set of *expectations* concerning the knowledge to be expressed, facilitating knowledge transfer and making possible several useful features illustrated in the next chapter.

This approach should be distinguished from the one commonly described by the phrase *knowledge as debugging,* illustrated by the work of [Sussman75] and [Goldstein74]. That technique suggests that an important part of problem solving is knowing how to correct "nearly right" solutions. The emphasis there is on developing a taxonomy of problem-solving errors and assembling a store of knowledge about corresponding repairs. There is some knowledge of this sort in TEIRESIAS's knowledge acquisition routines, but it is largely hand-tailored and designed to deal with details of the performance program's operation. More of it, and a more general foundation for it, would add useful capabilities. They would be distinct, however, from the advantages illustrated here, which accrue from the explication of knowledge in the context of an error.

4–4 KNOWLEDGE BASE MANAGEMENT

A third aspect of the approach in TEIRESIAS lies in viewing some elements of knowledge base management in terms of database management. That is, part of the task looks like the sort of data-structure manipulation that has been the focus of previous work on databases (*e.g.,* [Sandewall75], [McLeod76], [Johnson75]). But our work differs in several respects. For one thing, it involves constructing an integral part of the high-performance program, rather than simply a database from which information is retrieved. In most standard database tasks, the retrieval or storage of information is the ultimate aim. In TEIRESIAS, we are assembling large amounts of information that will be used by the performance program and that will enable it to reason about the domain. Where database work concentrates solely on the management of facts, our system is also concerned with the management of a set of inference rules.

Another basic difference is the reliance on meta-level knowledge. Examples in later chapters will illustrate that management of the knowledge base can be founded on both the system's access to and "understanding" of its own representations.

Finally, our system focuses primarily on making additions to the knowledge base. [1] Concentrating on this single operation will focus the discussion yet still cover most of the interesting problems.

4–5 SYSTEM DIAGRAM

Figure 2–3 offered one view of TEIRESIAS and its relation to the performance program. "Zooming in" on the knowledge acquisition box shown in that figure produces the view presented in Figure 4–1, which is a complete overview of the capabilities described in chapters 5 and 6. The figure shows both the processes (standard boxes) and different repositories of knowledge (double-walled boxes) divided up according to their conceptual appearance (rather than their physical structure). Both the "new schema acquisition" and "new instance acquisition" are accomplished with the same body of code (described in chapter 6). Other paths of information flow have been omitted from this diagram for the sake of clarity. They will all be described in the next two chapters. Chapter 5 deals with acquisition of new inference rules expressed in terms of known conceptual primitives (*e.g.*, known attributes, objects, and values), while acquisition of new conceptual primitives is described in chapter 6. As we will see, these two are related but distinct problems, each requiring substantial effort for solution.

The final introductory point to be made is the mixed-initiative nature of the TEIRESIAS-expert interaction. In general, the user indicates what he wants to do. TEIRESIAS then takes over and structures the task, requesting information from the user and getting his approval before taking any important steps. Numerous examples of this will be encountered in the next two chapters.

---

[1] Since deletion of structures can often be viewed as the inverse of addition, and modification viewed as deletion followed by addition, little generality is lost.

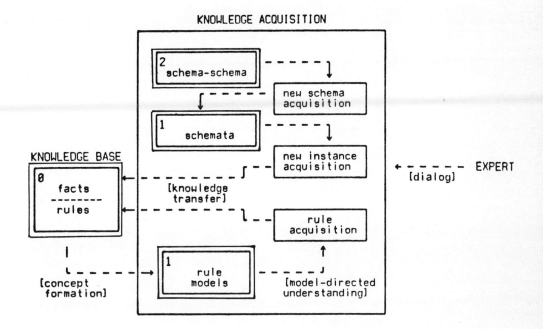

Figure 4-1   Close-up view of knowledge acquisition. Double-walled boxes with numbers in the upper left-hand corner contain various sorts of knowledge; the number indicates the level of knowledge they contain. The original performance program knowledge base is at the left with a "O," indicating object-level knowledge. Standard boxes without numbers indicate the three knowledge acquisition processes available for educating the system. Dashed arrows indicate information flow and are labeled (in brackets) when that information flow has a familiar name.

Chapter 5

Knowledge Acquisition I

Knowledge is that small part of ignorance that we arrange and classify.

Ambrose Bierce

5–1 INTRODUCTION

When last we left him in chapter 3, the expert had noticed something wrong with the identities deduced and had tracked down the problem himself, using the explanation facilities in TEIRESIAS. In this chapter, the same example is explored to show how the system can direct the debugging process. Then, in order to present the entire interaction at once, the example continues through the acquisition of a new rule that fixes the problem. The remainder of the chapter presents a global overview of the ideas used that make possible the system's performance and reviews the trace in detail to explain the basis for some of the capabilities displayed.

5–2 TRACE OF SYSTEM PERFORMANCE: DEBUGGING EXAMPLE CONTINUED

It should be emphasized that this example has been chosen because it displays, in

a single pass, a large number of the features of the system. In particular, it shows
initial failure of the primary natural language handling routines and allows the
demonstration of many of the secondary features. The interaction shown below
is thus longer than most. As before, annotations are in italics, and user responses
in boldface capitals.

```
My therapy recommendation will be based on the following
probable infection(s) and potential causative organism(s):
INFECTION-1 is PRIMARY-BACTEREMIA
     <Item 1>   E.COLI [ORGANISM-1]
     <Item 2>   PSEUDOMONAS-AERUGINOSA [ORGANISM-1]
Are all these identities correct?
++** N
```

{ *As before, the expert disagrees with the results and indicates to* TEIRESIAS
the identities that he thinks should have resulted. }

```
Are there any identities missing?
++** Y
Which one(s)?
++** KLEBSIELLA-PNEUMONIAE   PROTEUS-NON-MIRABILIS
Are there any identities that shouldn't have appeared?
++** Y
Which one(s)?
++** PSEUDOMONAS-AERUGINOSA
Do you want to
     1] track down the problem yourself, or
     2] allow me to guide the debugging, or
     3] ignore it for now and fix it another time?
Type 1, 2 or 3
++** 2
```

{ *Recall that in chapter 3 the expert followed option #1.* }

```
We'll start with the PSEUDOMONAS-AERUGINOSA first.
```

{ *This time,* TEIRESIAS *will guide the process. Again it applies the heuristic
of starting with an identity that appeared incorrectly.* }

```
The following rules were used in deducing that the identity of
ORGANISM-1 is pseudomonas-aeruginosa
RULE184
--------

Since [1.1] the category of ORGANISM-1 is not known
      [1.2] the gram stain of ORGANISM-1 is gramneg
```

[1.3] the morphology of ORGANISM-1 is rod
[1.4] the aerobicity of ORGANISM-1 is facultative
There is weakly suggestive evidence (.3) that the identity of
ORGANISM-1 is pseudomonas-aeruginosa
Is this rule correct?
++** Y
Should its premise have failed for this case?
++** Y
Which clause of the premise should have been false? [give #]
++** 1
No conclusions were reached concerning the category of
ORGANISM-1.
Should it have been possible to conclude a category?
++** Y
Which one?
++** ENTEROBACTERIACEAE
There were no rules successfully invoked in the attempt to
deduce that the category of ORGANISM-1 is enterobacteriaceae.
The following (potentially applicable) rules were NOT executed
because the starred [**] clause failed:
RULE116

If   1) the identity of ORGANISM-1 is not known
  ** 2) the gram stain of ORGANISM-1 is not known **
      3) the morphology of ORGANISM-1 is not known
      4) the site of CULTURE-1 is csf
      5) the infection is meningitis
      6) the age (in years) of Albert Hall is less than or
         equal to .17
then   There is weakly suggestive evidence (.33) that the
       category of ORGANISM-1 is enterobacteriaceae
RULE050

If   1) the morphology of ORGANISM-1 is rod
      2) the gram stain of ORGANISM-1 is gramneg
      3) the aerobicity of ORGANISM-1 is facultative
   ** 4) the infection with ORGANISM-1 was acquired while the
         patient was hospitalized **
then   There is suggestive evidence (.7) that the category of
       ORGANISM-1 is enterobacteriaceae
Are all these rules correct?
++**Y
Should any of them have been successfully invoked?
++** N

{ This would be the case if one of the starred premise clauses was false because it had been "stepped on" by yet another rule further back in the chain. }

```
Is there a rule missing?
++**Y
Ok, then I need a rule that would allow me to deduce that the
category of ORGANISM-1 is enterobacteriaceae.
Would you like to give me such a rule now?
++**Y
Good...
```

{ To review briefly: The expert is tracking down the reason why MYCIN incorrectly concluded that the identity was pseudomonas-aeruginosa. Shown below is the sequence of rules which were involved:

```
IDENITY
GRAMST.
MORPH.
SITE      -- RULE116 -->⎤
INFECT.              ⎟
AGE                 ⎬   CATEG.
                    ⎟   GRAMST. -- RULE184 --> IDENT = PSEUD-AERUG.
MORPH.    -- RULE050 -->⎦  AEROB.
GRAMST.             MORPH.
AEROB.
HOSP.
```

Pseudomonas-aeruginosa appeared because RULE184 executed successfully. This occurred in part because category was unknown. Category was unknown because all rules to conclude it (50 and 116) failed. Since the expert believes all existing rules are correct, the knowledge base must be missing a rule that will conclude about category; in particular, that the category is enterobacteriaceae. This will cause category to be known, inhibiting rule 184, fixing at least this first problem, the incorrect conclusion about pseudomonas-aeruginosa.

Note how sharply focused the issue has become, for both the expert and TEIRESIAS, *as a result of the large amount of contextual information available. The doctor is not being asked to "discuss bacteremia"; instead, the system can at this point say*

```
I need a rule that would allow me to deduce that the ca-
tegory of ORGANISM-1 is enterobacteriaceae.
```

and it must be a rule which is invocable in the context of this patient. This focus makes it easier for the expert to specify a rule that may never have been explicitly stated or recognized as such. This can be an important advantage in any domain where the knowledge is not yet fully formalized.

The contextual information is useful for TEIRESIAS *as well. It provides a number of expectations about the content of the rule that are useful both in understanding what the expert types in and in checking the new rule to make sure that it does indeed solve the problem at hand. Details of this process are explained below.*

The trace continues with the expert typing in the rule...}

```
The new rule will be called RULE383
   If:     1 -     THE PATIENT'S INFECTION IS PRIMARY-
                   BACTEREMIA
   and     2 -     THE SITE IS ONE OF THE STERILE SITES
   and     3 -
   Then:   1 -     THERE IS EVIDENCE (.8) THAT THE CATEGORY IS
                   ENTEROBACTERIACEAE
   and     2 -
This may take a few moments...
```

{Generally, it takes on the order of 10 to 30 seconds of cpu time. }

```
This is my understanding of your rule:
RULE383
--------

   If:    1) Primary-bacteremia is an associated infection for
             which therapy should cover, and
          2) The infection with the organism was acquired while
             the patient was hospitalized, and
          3) The culture was taken from a sterile source, and
          4) The organism is not normally found at this site
   Then:     There is strongly suggestive evidence (.8) that the
             category of the organism is enterobacteriaceae
```

*{*TEIRESIAS*'s initial interpretation of the natural language is incorrect (recall that the example was chosen in part for this reason). In the system's first attempt to understand the rule, each line of the original text has been interpreted as two clauses. This results primarily from the word-by-word approach to meaning. For instance, despite the obvious grammatical simplicity of the first line of text, the system used the word "primary-bacteremia" as the basis for generating the first clause, and it used the word "infection" to generate the second. In the second line of text the word "sterile" was responsible for clause #3, and the word "sites" used as the basis for clause #4. The details of this process are explained below, where it will become clear that while the translation is wrong, it is not unreasonable given the simple natural language facilities.*

Nor is it unreasonable that TEIRESIAS *has turned each line of English into more than one premise clause. The expert is not restricted to typing the*

English equivalent of a single premise clause on each line. If he were, rather than typing "the organism is a gram negative aerobic rod," he would have to type three lines, "the organism is gram negative," "it is aerobic," "it is a rod." The cost of this capability, however, is shown here: It may result in spurious clauses.

We will see later that while TEIRESIAS's interpretations are incorrect, they are all "reasonable" and "consistent," in light of the system's somewhat primitive approach to natural language. The rest of the example shows that even when the initial guesses are incorrect, straightening things out may conceivably be very easy. }

```
Okay? (Yes or No)
++**N
```

{ The expert indicates that there is a problem with the interpretation and uses the system's rule editor to specify the changes needed. }

```
Change premise?
++**Y
What clause should be changed in premise?
(type HELP for list of commands)
++**CHANGE 1
Suppose (1) were changed to read—
        1 - The infection is primary—bacteremia
Would that be ok?
++**Y
```

{ Several simple heuristics are invoked to select the next most likely interpretation, based on the English source of this clause and the set of interpretations already rejected. In this case, the second choice is correct. }

```
Then you'll probably want to delete:
        2) The infection with the organism was acquired while
           the patient was hospitalized
Correct?
++** Y
```

{ TEIRESIAS enforces consistency constraints on its interpretation of the English text. One of these constraints indicates that if the new interpretation of clause #1 is correct, then clause #2 must have arisen spuriously. That is, the system realizes it cannot get both the new version of clause #1 and the old clause #2 from the same line of text, and indicates this to the expert. }

```
Anything else?
++**D 3
```

```
clause(s) 3 deleted.
```

{*Realizing that there was another spurious clause, the expert deletes clause #3, but then has second thoughts about the one he chose, so he checks, using the "?" command.* }

```
Anything else?
++**?
      1 - the infection is primary-bacteremia
 and 2 -    <deleted>
 and 3 -    <deleted>
 and 4 - the organism is not normally found at this site
```

{*He then discovers that he has typed the wrong number, undoes the damage, and deletes the one initially intended.* }

```
Anything else?
++**U 3
clause(s) 3 undeleted.
Anything else?
++**D 4
clause(s) 4 deleted.
```

{*There is one last correction to be made (all commands can be abbreviated to a single letter)...* }

```
Anything else?
++**C 3
Suppose (3) were changed to read-
        3 - The site of the culture is one of: those sites that
            are normally sterile
Would that be ok?
++**Y
Anything else?
++**?
      1 - the infection is primary-bacteremia
 and 2 -    <deleted>
 and 3 - the site of the culture is one of: those sites that
            are normally sterile
 and 4 -    <deleted>
++**OK
```

{*...and at last he's happy with the rule.* }

```
Change action?
```

++**N

This is my understanding of your rule:
RULE383

  If: 1) The infection is primary—bacteremia, and
        2) The site of the culture is one of: those sites that
           are normally sterile
Then: There is strongly suggestive evidence (.8) that the
      category of the organism is enterobacteriaceae
Okay? (Yes or No)
++**Y

{ *This is the classic test of comprehension: The original English text has been turned into a rule coded in* LISP; *the* LISP *is then translated back into English for approval. Compare the results with the expert's original input. Now that the expert is satisfied that the system understands the rule as he has entered it,* TEIRESIAS *checks several things about the rule to see if "it is satisfied. }*

I hate to criticize, Dr. Davis, but did you know that most
rules about what the category of a organism might be, that
mention—
          the site of a culture
          the infection
ALSO mention—
    [A] — the portal of entry of a organism
Shall I try to write a clause to account for [A] ?
++**Y

{ *The mechanism that makes possible this sort of "second guessing" by* TEI-RESIAS *is explained in detail below. Briefly, the system maintains a model of the knowledge base. In checking to see how this new piece of information "fits in" to that model, it discovers that its expectations have been only partially met. It indicates to the expert what expectations were left unfulfilled and asks if it should attempt to fill in the missing parts. }*

How about—
    [A] The portal of entry of the organism is gi
Ok?
++**Y

{ *The expert agreed to the inclusion of a clause about the portal of entry, this determines which attribute to use.* TEIRESIAS *examines its model of the knowledge base to see which predicate function is likely to be the right one; the model evidently suggested the function* SAME. *Finally, in order to fix the original bug, it must be possible to invoke the new rule for this patient.*

Since, in answer to question 18 of the original consultation (see Figure 3–10), the expert responded that the portal of entry was GI, this is a plausible guess at the value to use. This demonstrates another benefit of the "knowledge acquisition in context" methodology described in chapter 4. }

```
Also, most rules about what the category of a organism may be
ALSO conclude about—
     [A] — the identity of a organism
Shall I try to write a clause to account for [A] ?
++**N
```

{ The system noticed another unfulfilled expectation concerning the action part of the rule, but the expert always has the option of overriding the system's suggestions, and does so. }

```
The rule now reads:
RULE383
———————

  If:  1) The infection is primary—bacteremia, and
       2) The site of the culture is one of: those sites that
          are normally sterile, and
       3) The portal of entry of the organism is gi
  Then:   There is strongly suggestive evidence (.8) that the
          category of the organism is enterobacteriaceae
```

{ Now that both the expert and TEIRESIAS are satisfied with the rule, there is a bit of bookkeeping to do. First, the new rule is checked by the system (behind the scenes) to be sure that there is nothing obviously wrong with it—for instance, one of the tests insures that none of the premise clauses is currently known to be false. This might have happened if the expert had mistakenly typed the site is not one of the sterile sites. *Had this been the case, the system would have noticed at this point that that clause was guaranteed to fail for the current patient, and the expert would have been given the option of returning to the rule editor to fix the problem. There are several other things the system checks at this point, but this rule passes all the tests, and hence there is no indication of any problem.*
}

```
Please describe briefly why you added (or changed) this rule.
Type an empty line when done.
++**THE SYSTEM FAILED TO REALIZE IT COULD CONCLUDE
++**CATEGORY, AND THIS ALLOWED RULE184 TO INCORRECTLY
++**CONCLUDE IDENTITY
++**
```

{ Over the years of MYCIN *development, the experts associated with the project have occasionally looked in astonishment at a rule which, though it had been around for some time, seemed, superficially at least, to make very little sense. The question then arises as to why that rule was added to the knowledge base. To avoid this problem, the expert is required to explain why he wrote (or changed) the rule.*

There are also a number of other bookkeeping-type chores that are being attended to here (again, behind the scenes). TEIRESIAS *takes care of tagging the rule with information that will simplify keeping track of the large, and constantly changing, body of rules. We will see in a moment how that information is accessed. }*

```
RULE383 has now been added to the knowledge base.
 I will now re-run the consultation to check the effectiveness
of your new rule. Get comfortable, since this may take a bit.
    Also, new questions may be asked as a result of this new
rule. If a question is printed, please answer it with refe-
rence to this current patient.
```

{ TEIRESIAS *now invokes the performance program as a subprocess to make sure the bug is fixed, and to test for any other side effects. Since* MYCIN *has saved all the answers from the initial consultation, the process is fairly inexpensive. The expert is warned about new questions because his new rule may mention an attribute that was not previously traced, or it may indirectly cause the tracing of one.*

While there are some cases in which it is possible to compute the incremental effect on a given consultation of adding a single new rule to the knowledge base, these are rare enough that in the long run it is computationally cheaper to simply rerun the consultation. }

```
18-DEC-75 16:30:46
    --------PATIENT-281--------
      --------INFECTION-1--------
        --------CULTURE-1--------
          --------ORGANISM-1--------
```

{ The answers to all questions were available internally, so the performance program asks nothing new. (The headings are printed to let the expert follow the progress of the consultation.) }

```
My therapy recommendation will be based on the following
probable infection(s) and potential causative organism(s):
INFECTION-1 is PRIMARY-BACTEREMIA
    <Item 1>  E.COLI [ORGANISM-1]
    <Item 2>  KLEBSIELLA-PNEUMONIAE [ORGANISM-1]
```

    <Item 3> PROTEUS—NON—MIRABILIS [ORGANISM-1]
Well, it appears that things are straightened out.

> *{ The new conclusions are the ones the expert indicated earlier as the correct answers. This does not go unnoticed by* TEIRESIAS, *which, as before, interrupts the consultation at this point to check the validity of the answers produced.*
> *}*

Are all these values correct now?
++**Y

> *{ As always,* TEIRESIAS *gives the expert the last word and waits for approval before proceeding. }*

Good, then the problem's been fixed.
    ...continuing with therapy selection now.

> *{ At this point* TEIRESIAS *allows the performance program subprocess to continue with the normal therapy-selection phase. This has been omitted here for brevity.*
> *The reader may be wondering why three errors disappeared with the addition of one rule. This is explained schematically below:*

```
** RULE116 **
** RULE050 **
   RULE383     -- CATEG. -->  ** RULE184 **  --> IDENT = PSEUD-AER.

                                 RULE084      --> IDENT = KLEB-PNEU
                                                           PROTEUS-NON-M.
```

> *As before, 116 and 50 have failed (hence the **s), but now the new rule, 383, has succeeded, supplying a value for category. In turn, 184 now fails, as hoped, and thus no conclusion is made about pseudomonas-aeruginosa.*
> *However, rule 84, which requires a value of category and failed last time because the system was unable to deduce one, can now fire and yields the desired, missing identities. }*

                    ****

> *{ All of the bookkeeping that was done is accessible via the INFOrmation command added to the question-answering facility of the performance program. This gives the expert the background for any rule in the system.*
> *}*

** INFO 383
RULE383

----

        was written by Dr. Davis
        on December 18, 1975
        for the following reason:
                THE SYSTEM FAILED TO REALIZE IT COULD CONCLUDE
                CATEGORY, AND THIS ALLOWED RULE184 TO INCORRECTLY
                CONCLUDE IDENTITY.
        for patient 281
            [who was described as follows:
                CLASSIC CASE OF GRAM NEGATIVE ROD INFECTION FOR A
                PATIENT WITH A NON—NOSOCOMIAL DISEASE]

5–3   RULE MODEL OVERVIEW

The utility of knowledge acquisition in context should now be clear. In this
example we have seen how the availability of the contextual information has
made it much easier for the expert to specify the knowledge required and how it
has supported, as well, many of the "intelligent" actions taken by the program.

One of the uses of this contextual information is as a source of expectations
about the content of the expert's new rule. The concept of an "expectation"
is precisely defined in TEIRESIAS, and in order to provide some perspective on
its intellectual origins and development, we consider the concept of *models* [1]
and *model-based understanding*.

The use of models in computer programs as a guide to understanding dates
back to early efforts in AI. The author's first encounter with it was in work on
computer vision, and since this offers a particularly clear introduction to the
ideas involved, we digress for a moment to introduce some useful concepts from
that field. (The treatment here is necessarily superficial. For a broader review of
current work, see [Barrow75]; for an interesting introduction to the capabilities
of the human visual system, see [Gregory66].)

5–3.1   Perspective: Model-Based Computer Vision

Computer interpretation of a scene typically starts with digitization, in which
the picture is turned into a large array of numbers indicating the light intensity
at each point. The task is then to determine which physical objects in the scene
produced each of the different regions of intensity values in the array. Among the
tools used are various types of edge detectors. These are mathematical operators
that are sensitive to certain sorts of changes in the intensity level values, usually

---

[1] The concept of a model has been an integral part of science and philosophy for quite
some time. The work described here can be seen in terms of the standard definitions that
have evolved, and it fits quite easily into the frameworks that have been developed. Since the
literature on the subject is extensive, we will not deal with it here. For a useful introduction,
see [Harre70], especially chapter 2.

sharp gradients or step functions, which suggest the end of one region and the beginning of another.

One of the first significant stumbling blocks encountered in scene under-standing was the presence of shadows and noise. [2] Real scenes rarely contain all the detail seen (or interpreted) by the human eye/brain processor. Many of the edges of objects, for instance, are lost in shadows; these same shadows often suggest false edges as well. As a result, the uniform application of an edge detector results in a large collection of "edges," only some of which are real. It is in part because human vision is an eye *and* brain process that we are not similarly confused—we are able to classify objects being viewed and, based on this classification, can ignore false edges and supply missing ones.

Some of the first vision work to take these problems into account was done by Falk [Falk70], building on the work of Roberts [Roberts63] and Guzman [Guzman68]. The key elements of this work that are of interest here are (i) a set of *prototypes* (or models) that *embody knowledge* about the objects being viewed and (ii) the use of these prototypes as a way of *guiding the process of understanding*.

Falk's system (like many others) viewed scenes containing a number of children's blocks selected from a known set of possible objects. His prototypes were similar to wire frame models of each of the blocks and thus embodied a "high-level" description that indicated the structure of each object. This compact, high-level description was then used to guide the lower level processing of the intensity values. After detecting a number of edges in the scene, his system attempted to fit a model to each collection of edges and then used this model as a guide to further processing. If, for instance, the model accounted for all but one of the lines in a region, this would suggest that the extra line might be spurious. If the model fit well except for some line missing from the scene, this was a good hint that a line had been overlooked and also an indication of where to go looking for it.

One other idea necessary to complete a general perspective on the use of models to guide understanding is described quite well by a distinction drawn in [Baumgart74]. As he points out (also in the context of scene understanding, but it generalizes easily), three different approaches can be identified:

1   *Verification.* "Top down" or completely model-driven processing con-centrates on verifying the details in a scene about which much is already known.

2   *Description.* "Bottom up" or data-driven processing involves searching an unfamiliar scene for any suggestive features that might indicate what is present.

3   *Recognition.* "Bottom up into a prejudiced top" is processing where there is available some idea of what to expect, and where perhaps a small set of possibilities can be specified, but none definitely. The data is allowed to suggest interpretations, but the set of items to be considered is constrained to those expected.

---

[2] Noise can be electronic, can be due to digitization effects, or can simply be the result of smudges or dirt on the objects in the scene.

The first approach is useful when the contents of the scene are known and when the task concerns only settling details of orientation or precise location. The second can be used as the initial approach to an unfamiliar scene, and the third is relevant if there is some idea of what is present, but nothing definite. (Of course, all three might well be used on the same scene at different points in the processing.)

Finally, note that one of the long recognized potential weaknesses of a model-based approach is the dependence on a fixed set of models. Since the scope of the program's "understanding" of the world may be constrained by the number of models it has, "...it would be desirable [for a program] to be able to 'learn' new structural descriptions of models" [Falk70].

5–3.2   Rule Models: Overview

For rule acquisition the primary problem to be solved is the interpretation of the new rule. Note that this problem can be viewed as analogous to a problem in perception: (a) There is a signal to be processed (text); (b) the signal is noisy ("noise" words that convey no information); and (c) there is a large amount of context available (from tracking down the error) on which to base expectations about the signal content. It would prove useful, then, to have something analogous to Falk's prototypes, something to capture the "structure" of the physician's reasoning, that would offer a way of expressing expectations and guiding the interpretation of his statement of the rule. In short, we are asking for the cognitive analogue of the polyhedra prototypes.

But is it reasonable to expect that such structures exist? There are several reasons why the idea seems plausible. Concepts in human memory, for instance, are structured in an implicit, but highly complex fashion. They rarely exist independently, but rather have a number of cross references and interrelationships. New knowledge is typically "filed away," rather than just deposited, and it is clear when some new item "doesn't fit" into the established structure (see, *e.g.*, [Norman75]).

There are also suggestive regularities in the set of rules in the MYCIN system. They were first noticed in a naive survey of the knowledge base when the author began working with the system and were later verified by a simple experiment which demonstrated that three of the clinicians associated with the project each, independently, detected the same regularities. [3]

The cognitive models will thus be based on uniformities in subsets of rules and will look like abstract descriptions of those subsets, based on a set of empirical generalizations about them. They are referred to as *rule models*. As will become

---

[3] Each of the clinicians was given a complete set of rules and asked to sort them into "similarity classes," subsets of rules that seemed to belong together. The criteria for similarity were purposefully left up to each clinician, who was asked to label each subset to explain what kind of rules it contained. The results strongly confirmed initial impressions—all the clinicians chose the same set of similarity classes (except that some classes had occasionally been further subdivided), and of 300 rules, there were substantial disagreements on the classification of only six.

clear, they represent a simple form of concept formation—the concept of a "typical" rule in that subset. They will be used to express expectations about the expert's new rule and to guide processing of the English text.

Rule models are composed of four parts (Figure 5–1).

```
EXAMPLES          the subset of rules which this model describes

DESCRIPTION       characterization of a ''typical'' member
                       of this subset
                         characterization of the premise
                         characterization of the action
                               which attributes ''typically'' appear
                               correlations of attributes


MORE GENERAL      pointers to models describing more general
MORE SPECIFIC     and more specific subsets of rules
```

Figure 5–1   Rule model structure.

They contain, first, a list of EXAMPLES, the subset of rules from which this model was constructed. Next, a DESCRIPTION characterizes a typical member of the subset. Since we are dealing in this case with rules composed of premise-action pairs, the DESCRIPTION currently implemented contains individual characterizations of a typical premise and a typical action. Then, since the current representation scheme used in those rules is based on associative triples, we have implemented those characterizations by indicating (a) the attributes that typically appear in the premise (action) of a rule in this subset, and (b) the correlations of attributes appearing in the premise (action).

Note that the central idea is the concept of *characterizing a typical member of the subset.* Naturally, that characterization would look different for subsets of rules, procedures, theorems, etc. But the main idea of characterization is widely applicable and not restricted to any particular representational formalism.

The two other parts of the rule model are pointers to other models describing more general and more specific subsets of rules. The set of models is organized into a number of tree structures, Figure 5–2. At the root of each tree is the model made from all the rules that conclude about a given attribute (*e.g.*, the CATEGORY model); below this are two models dealing with all affirmative and all negative rules (*e.g.*, the CATEGORY–IS model); and below this are models dealing with rules that affirm or deny specific values of the attribute.

For any given attribute, some of the branches may not exist since we require (empirically) that there must be at least two relevant rules before the corresponding model is created (which was why there was no CATEGORY–IS–ENTEROBACTERIACEAE model in the current system).

The fact that the models are organized around the contents of the action part assumes that rules which conclude about the same thing have useful similarities in their premises. This assumption was made plausible by several considerations.

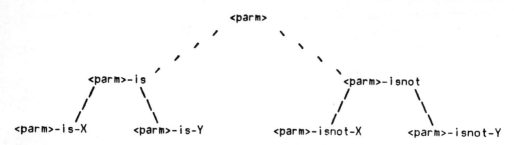

Figure 5–2   Organization of rule models.

To begin with, this organization paralleled the one used by the clinicians when they were asked to sort the rules. It was also hoped that the models would be more than just a description of a subset of rules, that they might also suggest things about the reasoning process itself. It is possible, for instance, that simple correlations among terms in rules might actually reflect a valid generalization about the way an expert reasons in this domain. In the current implementation, therefore, the models are organized around the action part of the rule; but, as discussed below, other organizations are possible.

Rather than being hand-tooled, the models are assembled by TEIRESIAS on the basis of the current contents of the knowledge base, in what amounts to a very simple (*i.e.*, statistical) form of concept formation. Thus, the combination of TEIRESIAS and the performance program presents a system that has a model of its own knowledge, a model it forms by itself.

5–3.3   Rule Models: Example

Shown below is an example of a rule model from the current system. This particular model describes the subset of rules that conclude affirmatively about the category of an organism and is the one that was used by the system in the trace shown earlier. Each of the pieces of the model will be described in some detail, to give the reader a feeling for the concepts involved. The usual warnings apply, however: It is the global concepts that are important here, rather than the precise format or location of every parenthesis. The models are also fairly compact, in the sense that they contain a great deal of information. We will see that all of it is used eventually.

This model was formed from the six rules listed in the EXAMPLES part of Figure 5–3. (The numbers between zero and one associated with the rules are the relevant certainty factors from the conclusions; these are used when updating the models in response to changes in the knowledge base.)

The DESCRIPTIONs of the premise and action indicate regularities found in the subset of rules listed in EXAMPLES. The two types of description noted above are each encoded in their own format: There are "singlets" indicating which attributes typically appear and "ntuples" indicating (empirical) correlations of attributes. For instance, the first singlet in the premise description above

(GRAM SAME NOTSAME 3.83)

CATEGORY-IS

```
EXAMPLES    ((RULE116 .33)
             (RULE050 .70)
             (RULE037 .80)
             (RULE095 .90)
             (RULE152 1.0)
             (RULE140 1.0))


P-ADVICE    ((GRAM SAME NOTSAME 3.83)
             (MORPH SAME NOTSAME 3.83)
             ((GRAM SAME) (MORPH SAME) 3.83)
             ((MORPH SAME) (GRAM SAME) 3.83)
             ((AIR SAME) (NOSOCOMIAL NOTSAME SAME) (MORPH SAME) (GRAM SAME) 1.50)
             ((NOSOCOMIAL NOTSAME SAME) (AIR SAME) (MORPH SAME) (GRAM SAME) 1.50)
             ((INFECTION SAME) (SITE MEMBF SAME) 1.23)
             ((SITE MEMBF SAME) (INFECTION SAME) (PORTAL SAME) 1.23))


A-ADVICE    ((CATEGORY CONCLUDE 4.73)
             (IDENT CONCLUDE 4.05)
             ((CATEGORY CONCLUDE) (IDENT CONCLUDE) 4.73))


MORE-GENL·  (CATEGORY-MOD)


MORE-SPEC   NIL
```

Figure 5-3   Rule model for rules concluding affirmatively about category.

indicates that gramstain (GRAM) typically appears and is often associated with the functions SAME and NOTSAME. (The 3.83 is explained below.)

The third item in the premise description of Figure 5-3 is an example of an ntuple:

$$((\text{GRAM SAME}) (\text{MORPH SAME}) \ 3.83) \ .$$

It indicates that whenever gramstain appears in a rule premise, morphology (MORPH) is typically found as well.

A collection of this sort of information can provide a fairly detailed picture of the "typical" appearance of a rule from this subset. In this case, rules that conclude affirmatively about category "typically" mention gramstain and morphology; when one of these appears, the other tends to appear also, and so on.

Finally, the MORE-SPEC and MORE-GENL pointers indicate that there is no rule model more specific than this one in the current system and that the CATEGORY model is more general.

5-3.3.1   Details of the DESCRIPTION Implementation

Each singlet is of the form

$$(\ \text{<attrib>} \ \text{<predicate-function>}^{+} \ \text{<cf-sum>} \ )$$

where the superscript "+" indicates one or more of instantiations of the item. A singlet of this sort will be constructed for any attribute that appears in the premises of at least 30% of the rules in the subset.[4] Enough predicate functions are then supplied to account for at least 75% of the appearances of the attribute. Thus the example cited above means that (a) gramstain occurs in a premise clause of at least 30% of the rules listed in EXAMPLES, and (b) 75% of those clauses containing gramstain use either SAME or NOTSAME as the predicate function.

The 3.83 at the end is the sum of the certainty factors of the rules that had premise clauses mentioning gramstain. As will become clear, the DESCRIPTIONs contained in the rule models provide TEIRESIAS with "advice" about what to expect to find in a newly acquired rule; in these terms, the numbers become an indication of the "strength" of this advice. While its origin is purely empirical, there are reasons why it appears to be plausible. First, by summing up CFs, the strongest advice will arise from the factors that appear the most often. Since the model is supposed to characterize the typical content of a rule, a dependency of strength on frequency of appearance seems reasonable. Second, rules with high CFs tend to be those that are the soundest and perhaps the closest to being based on an understanding of underlying processes rather than simply on experience. Thus, given equal frequency of appearance, advice arising from more definite rules will be stronger. Finally, it appears to give a satisfying range of strengths; in the current system, the largest such value is close to 21, the smallest is 0.7.

To review, the first singlet in the rule model of Figure 5–3 means that at least 30% of the rules in EXAMPLES had a premise clause containing gram stain, that at least 75% of those clauses used either SAME or NOTSAME and, finally, that the sum of the CFs of those rules was 3.83.

The general form of the ntuples is

$$(\ (\texttt{<attrib>} \ \texttt{<predicate-function>}^+)^+ \ \texttt{<cf-sum>} \ )$$

and the first example in this model is

$$\texttt{((GRAM SAME) (MORPH SAME) 3.83)} .$$

This ntuple means that whenever gram stain appeared in a rule premise, morphology (MORPH) also appeared at least 80% of the time. The implication is unidirectional—if it is also true that whenever morphology appears, gram stain also appears (at least 80% of the time), then there would be another ntuple expressing this fact (as there is in this case).[5] All this generalizes to more than two attributes so that, for example, the fifth element of the DESCRIPTION indicates that the presence of aerobicity (AIR) indicates the likely presence of several other attributes.

---

[4] This and all other thresholds cited are purely empirical. They were chosen solely on the basis of producing results that were similar to those suggested by the rule sorting experiment performed with the clinicians.

[5] The interpretation of the <predicate-function> and <cf-sum> is the same, except that the <predicate-function>s are taken only from those instances in which the <attrib>s actually did appear together. This accounts for the fact that NOTSAME does not appear. Evidently, when gram and morph appear together, they tend to use just SAME.

5–3.4 Rule Models as Concept Formation

As noted, the rule models are constructed by TEIRESIAS from the rules in the performance program's knowledge base—the description of the rule-model components given in the previous section is an informal specification of the algorithm used.

Despite this automated construction, however, there are several reasons why the rule models are only a weak form of concept formation. First, and perhaps most important, the concepts are expressed in terms of a predefined set of patterns: the singlets and ntuples, both used to describe the fixed subsets of rules described in the previous section. While it would not be difficult to add the ability to detect other types of patterns in subsets organized along different criteria, this would not confront the more fundamental problem of concept formation: the judicious selection of the "proper" organization of the examples to detect "important" regularities and the ability to discover unpredicted patterns.

In addition, the current implementation commits what Winston calls the "fallacy that frequent appearance means importance" [Winston70]. While the strength of each piece of advice in the models does provide some measure of differential importance (similar to the "must-have" link in [Winston70]), that measure is acquired purely on the basis of frequency. This strongly limits the range of concepts that can be defined: There is no way, for instance, to infer a link equivalent to a "must-not-have" link. Nor is there any notion of *why* a particular collection of attributes tend to appear together. The current approach can not distinguish between statistical accidents and a meaningful correlation. In the absence of a carefully constructed set of teaching examples (in particular, there are none of the "near misses" Winston uses to great advantage), the system uses the only information it has and assumes that all rules in the knowledge base are equally good instances.

Finally, the pattern detection routines all use an exhaustive search of the knowledge base. This is not particularly sophisticated, and a more powerful approach to concept formation should be more efficient.[6]

Despite the simplicity of the techniques used, the rule models present an adequate picture of the concept of a "typical" rule. There are several reasons why this is so. First, the concept is ill-defined to begin with and is being formed from a very limited set of data. This implies that it might not be wise to devote extensive amounts of computation to sophisticated concept-formation routines. Second, the fundamental task here is comprehension rather than concept formation, and the models are not the end product of the program. The models are instead used later in a support role to provide more sophisticated comprehension. Finally, exhaustive search for patterns does not present significant problems because the knowledge base is built incrementally, hence rule model computation can proceed in parallel. (As long as intermediate results are kept for reference, the incremental

---

[6] A recent report [Hayes-Roth76] discusses more formal and efficient methods for a similar sort of concept formation task.

computation is not time consuming.) Improvements could still be made in all of these areas, but the point here is simply that very sophisticated techniques are not required for adequate performance.

5–3.5   Implications

A number of implications follow from the design and automated construction of the models. First, the use of the singlets and ntuples is really only one instance of a more general idea. In fact, any kind of pattern involving any of the components of a rule could be used. While they were not included (for the sake of simplicity), patterns in the values of the attributes or certainty factors might also have been considered. Straightforward extensions to the current implementation would make it possible to look for any specified pattern involving any of the components and to use this in much the same way as a picture of what to expect in a rule of this subset.

As noted, the rule models are assembled by the system from the rules in the knowledge base. This automatic generation and updating has a number of advantages.

In our discussion of Falk's original concept of models, for instance, we noted both the potential disadvantage of a fixed set of models and the utility of being able to add new models easily. The system described here has avoided the disadvantage of a fixed set and has the ability to add new models without difficulty. In addition:

1   The expert need never concern himself with adding models, since TEIRESIAS takes care of all the work involved. Indeed, the expert may never know of the models' existence.

2   TEIRESIAS builds and updates the models on the basis of *experience*, a capability that is intuitively appealing. Every time a new rule is added to the knowledge base or an existing rule is modified, the appropriate model(s) is recomputed.

There are other implications as well. It was noted above that the model might be used to characterize many kinds of features displayed by the rules. The correlation detection operators used to form the ntuples can be viewed as demons, lying dormant until enough examples have accumulated to trigger them, at which time they add their newfound correlation to the appropriate model.

It was also mentioned above that the trees around which the models are organized are quite often incomplete, since there may be too few rules about a particular attribute. It should now be clear that this tree is constantly growing (and shrinking), exactly paralleling the changes in the knowledge base. The entire model set is thus kept current with the growing knowledge base, evolving along with it, and reflecting the shifting patterns it contains.

The models are also one of the primary examples of a central theme of this work: higher level knowledge. While the rules are a representation of (medical) knowledge, the models are a representation of rules and, hence, are a representation of a representation. As generalizations of a set of rules, they may suggest some of the regularities in the structure of the reasoning embodied in the rules in the knowledge base.

The models are also "fuzzy." Just knowing that a rule concludes about a particular attribute is insufficient information to completely specify its premise, but it is enough to permit a number of plausible suggestions. The representation thus requires a form of inexactness that allows the specification of a range of possibilities, along with the likelihood of each. The DESCRIPTIONs of premise and action offer this fuzziness.

There is also a certain "critical mass" effect. Early in the construction of a knowledge base, there will be few models and their advice will be somewhat unreliable, since the system is, in effect, generalizing from too small a sample. As the knowledge base grows, the system's own picture of its knowledge gets progressively better, trends become more evident, and the models will make more effective contributions.

The way in which the models are used implies that the system will tend to "hear what it expects to hear," and "hear what it has heard before." This will be explored in detail below, but note that it is not unlike the typical human response in the same situation.

Perhaps most interesting, the presence of the models means that the system has a model of its own knowledge. As will become clear further on, in a primitive sense it "knows what it knows, and knows where it is ignorant" and, in a rudimentary way, can discuss both of these.

5–3.6   CHARACTER AND USE OF THE MODELS

Two further points remain to be made before reviewing the details of the trace of system performance. First, recall that the design and use of models was described in terms of three important facets: They were to be a high-level description, they could be used to express expectations about the world, and they could be used to guide interpretation and "understanding." The role of rule models as high-level descriptions should be clear from the previous discussion. The reader may by now have recognized their use in expressing expectations: In the trace, after narrowing down the source of the problem, TEIRESIAS indicates that

```
I need a rule to deduce that the category of ORGANISM-1 is
enterobacteriaceae.
```

This is both a set of instructions to the user about how to fix the problem and an indication of the sort of rule the system will expect—it indicates the rule model that will be employed.

The use of the models as a guide to understanding is the final point. With the expectations that arise from doing acquisition in the context of a shortcoming in the knowledge base, the system is not entering the rule interpretation process blindly. In terms of the three methodologies mentioned earlier, then, the *descriptive* approach is inappropriate. But the program should not be restricted to understanding only rules that look like previous rules in the model, since the new ones may be different from all previous examples. It would thus be too inflexible to use a *verification*-oriented approach, and the *recognition* technique appears to be just right. There are expectations, but it is not certain that they will be fulfilled. Hence the rule text is processed "bottom up," but with a strong set of biases about where that processing should eventually lead. In addition, the rule models, like the polyhedra models, will be used to direct the processing of the text and to help identify both noise and gaps in the signal.

5–4 HOW IT ALL WORKS

At this point we begin the trace again, reviewing it piece by piece, as a background for discussing some of the more interesting ideas in TEIRESIAS and as a way of exploring features not yet illustrated. To avoid the necessity of flipping pages, the relevant sections of the trace have been reproduced below, set off by horizontal lines.

It is both difficult and not particularly informative to attempt to review all the options in the system, so only the more interesting examples will be explored. In general, however, the proper facilities exist for handling all cases, and short of purposeful attempts to supply inconsistent answers, TEIRESIAS takes the appropriate action.

For the sake of consistency, we will work with the single example shown in the original trace. It is occasionally necessary, however, to illustrate additional points by examining the system's action on hypothetical responses from the user. These will be clearly indicated.

There are seven general phases to the rule acquisition process:

(a)   Tracking down the bug.
(b)   Deciphering the English text of the new rule.
(c)   Checking preliminary results.
(d)   "Second guessing."
(e)   Final checkout.
(f)   Bookkeeping.
(g)   Rerunning the consultation.

Each is reviewed in turn.

5–4.1 Tracking Down the Bug

I will not be persuaded to leave off the chance of finding out the whole thing clearly.

Sophocles
Oedipus the King, lines 1065–1066

The performance program's diagnosis is used as an entry point to the debugging routine. This is a logical evaluation point since most of the consultation is aimed toward determining it. It is possible that the diagnosis may be correct due to offsetting errors in the course of the consultation. However, since the expert can interrupt the consultation at anytime during the processing to use the explanation and acquisition routines, we make the plausible (but imperfect) assumption that if he got this far and the diagnosis is correct, then everything else is correct also.

```
My therapy recommendation will be based on the following
probable infection(s) and potential causative organism(s):
INFECTION-1 is PRIMARY-BACTEREMIA
     <Item 1>   E.COLI [ORGANISM-1]
     <Item 2>   PSEUDOMONAS-AERUGINOSA [ORGANISM-1]
Are all these identities correct?
++**N
Are there any identities missing?
++** Y
Which one(s)?
++** KLEBSIELLA-PNEUMONIAE   PROTEUS-NON-MIRABILIS
Are there any identities that shouldn't have appeared?
++** Y
Which one(s)?
++** PSEUDOMONAS-AERUGINOSA
```

The focusing process begins immediately, as the expert is required to specify exactly why he doesn't like the diagnosis shown. There must either be an inappropriate answer present; one that is missing; or, as in the current example, both.

```
Do you want to
     1] track down the problem yourself, or
     2] allow me to guide the debugging, or
     3] ignore it for now and fix it another time?
Type 1, 2 or 3
++** 2
```

Alternative #1 was explored in chapter 3, and #2 is reviewed here. Alternative #3 is part of the emphasis on human engineering. Since the process of tracking down and fixing the bug is a substantive task, the expert is given a chance to avoid it. If he takes this option, the system reminds him to "try to remember to fix it some time" and (quietly) composes and sends a note to a bug-reporting file, giving the case number and the list of incorrect or missing answers indicated by the user. This file is routinely examined by system programmers, who can either fix the problem or simply make sure that it gets attention later.

```
We'll start with the PSEUDOMONAS-AERUGINOSA first.
```

```
The following rules were used in deducing that the identity of
ORGANISM-1 is pseudomonas-aeruginosa
RULE184
-------
Since [1.1] the category of ORGANISM-1 is not known
      [1.2] the gram stain of ORGANISM-1 is gramneg
      [1.3] the morphology of ORGANISM-1 is rod
      [1.4] the aerobicity of ORGANISM-1 is facultative
 There is weakly suggestive evidence (.3) that the identity of
 ORGANISM-1 is pseudomonas-aeruginosa
Is this rule correct?
++** Y
Should its premise have failed for this case?
++** Y
Which clause of the premise should have been false? [give #]
++** 1
```

The last three questions directed to the user demonstrate the methodical unwinding process that forces criticism to be very specific. At each point, the expert must either approve of the rules invoked and the values obtained or indicate which one was in error and supply the correction. An analysis of the performance program's control structure indicates that if the value of an attribute A is incorrect, then (if S is the set of rules in the knowledge base that conclude about A) either:

(a) Some rule in S which was executed had an error in its conclusion.

(b) Some rule in S was not executed and should have been (either because of an error in its premise or because a clause of the premise incorrectly evaluated to "false").

(c) Some rule in S was executed and should not have been (either because of an error in its premise or because a clause of the premise incorrectly evaluated to "true").

(d) The set S is incomplete, and one or more rules is missing.

The routines in TEIRESIAS reflect this analysis and can account for all error sources within the current control structure. Thus, had the expert indicated that rule 184 was incorrect, he would have been invited to use the rule editor to fix it. Had he indicated that it was correct and that it was not inappropriately invoked, the assumption would have been that there was a rule missing that concluded negatively about the presence of pseudomonas-aeruginosa (the missing rule would offset the action of 184 and, hence, remove the inappropriate identity).

The possibility remains, however, that the framework itself may break down some day. That is, the expert may claim that all the rules are individually correct, that they were all executed correctly, that no rule is missing, and yet the final answer is still incorrect. This is most likely to come about as a result of the possible inapplicability in a new domain of the performance program's control structure or certainty factor mechanism. If the expert does indicate that none of the established classifications of the problem is correct, TEIRESIAS will indicate its inability to help further and use the bug reporting mechanism noted above to make a note of the problem.

In this case, however, the expert has indicated that the first clause of rule 184 ("the category of the organism is not known") incorrectly evaluated to "true." The process continues from there.

```
No conclusions were reached concerning the category of
ORGANISM-1.
Should it have been possible to conclude a category?
++** Y
Which one?
++** ENTEROBACTERIACEAE
There were no rules successfully invoked in the attempt to
deduce that the category of ORGANISM-1 is enterobacteriaceae.
The following (potentially applicable) rules were NOT executed
because the starred [**] clause failed:
RULE116
-------

If     1) the identity of ORGANISM-1 is not known
   ** 2) the gram stain of ORGANISM-1 is not known **
       3) the morphology of ORGANISM-1 is not known
       4) the site of CULTURE-1 is csf
       5) the infection is meningitis
       6) the age (in years) of Albert Hall is less than or
          equal to .17
then   There is weakly suggestive evidence (.33) that the
       category of ORGANISM-1 is enterobacteriaceae
RULE050
-------

If     1) the morphology of ORGANISM-1 is rod
       2) the gram stain of ORGANISM-1 is gramneg
       3) the aerobicity of ORGANISM-1 is facultative
   ** 4) the infection with ORGANISM-1 was acquired while the
          patient was hospitalized **
then   There is suggestive evidence (.7) that the category of
       ORGANISM-1 is enterobacteriaceae
```

Since the need to deal with large numbers of rules was anticipated, the rule unwinding process is kept as constrained as possible. Before displaying all the rules that might have concluded any value of category, the expert is asked which category it should have been. Then, only rules that are appropriate to his answer need be considered.

```
Are all these rules correct?
++**Y
Should any of them have been successfully invoked?
++** N
Is there a rule missing?
++**Y
Ok, then I need a rule that would allow me to deduce that the
category of ORGANISM-1 is enterobacteriaceae.
Would you like to give me such a rule now?
++**Y
Good...
The new rule will be called RULE383
```

   If: 1 –   THE PATIENT'S INFECTION IS PRIMARY-
                       BACTEREMIA
  and   2 –   THE SITE IS ONE OF THE STERILE SITES
  and   3 –
Then: 1 –   THERE IS EVIDENCE (.8) THAT THE CATEGORY IS
                       ENTEROBACTERIACEAE
  and   2 –

```
This may take a few moments...
```

The problem has finally been tracked down and characterized with an indication of exactly what sort of rule is needed. As noted earlier, this characterization also serves the purpose of setting up TEIRESIAS's expectations about the sort of rule it is about to receive. Since there is not necessarily a rule model for every characterization, the system chooses the model that matches most closely. This is done by starting at the top of the tree of models and descending until either reaching a model of the desired type or encountering a leaf of the tree. In this case, the process descends to the second level (the CATEGORY-IS model), notices that there is no CATEGORY-IS-ENTEROBACTERIACEAE model at the next level, and settles for the former. This technique is used in several places throughout the knowledge transfer process and, in general, supplies the model that best matches the current requirements. Note that it can deal with varying levels of specificity in the stated expectations. If, for instance, the system had known only that it expected a rule that concluded affirmatively about category, it would have descended just that far in the model tree and looked no further.

5–4.2   Deciphering the English Text

It was suggested earlier that interpreting the natural language text of the rule can be viewed as a "recognition" process in which the data are allowed to suggest interpretations, but the system maintains certain biases about which interpretation is likely to be correct. TEIRESIAS does this, generating all consistent interpretations of each line of English text and then evaluating each interpretation in the light of the biases expressed by the choice of a specific rule model. The interpretations suggested by the text (data-driven, "bottom up" mode) are thus intersected with the expectations (hypothesis-driven, "top down" mode) provided by the debugging process.

The interpretation process works in a strictly line-by-line fashion, processing each line of text independently. This method is a source of some deficiencies, some of which are trivially fixed, while others are superficial manifestations of interesting and complex problems. Each of them is discussed in subsequent sections below.

Deciphering the text occurs in four stages:

(a) Preprocessing the text.
(b) Checking the rule model.
(c) Generating the set of plausible LISP interpretations.
(d) Scoring the interpretations by reference to the rule model.

As will become clear, our approach to natural language is very simple, yet powerful enough to support the performance required. The problem is made easier, of course, by the fact that we are dealing with a small amount of text written in a semi-formal technical language, rather than with large amounts of text in unrestricted dialog. Even so, the problem of interpretation is substantial. The source of TEIRESIAS's power and performance lies in its use of a multiplicity of knowledge sources. These are listed and described briefly below; their use is explored in more detail in the sections that follow. Since much of the interpretation process can be viewed in terms of forming hypotheses (interpretations) from a set of data (the text), each knowledge source is also labeled in these terms.

Data-driven knowledge sources:

1 *Connotations of individual words* (data interpretation). As explained in more detail below, each English word may have associated with it a number of connotations of varying strength. These indicate attributes, objects, values, or predicate functions to which the word may plausibly be referring.

2 *Degree of ambiguity of individual words* (ambiguity of the data). This is used to constrain the search for an interpretation of the text.

3 *Function template* (structure of the hypothesis). As noted in chapter 2, there is associated with each predicate function a template indicating the order and generic type of its arguments. Generating code is essentially a process of filling in this template; it thus provides a primary source of direction for the interpretation process.

4 *Degree of success of the template completion process* (degree of success of hypothesis construction). The expert may be terse enough in his rule statement that the contents of certain slots in the template must be inferred rather than sought in the text. Such inferences are made with different degrees of confidence.

5 *Consistency of meaning assignment* (consistency of data interpretation). Where ambiguity exists, several plausible interpretations of a clause may arise;

the appropriate bookkeeping is done to assure that each word is understood in only one way for any given interpretation.

6   *Accounting for all words in the text* (accounting for all the data). Preference is given to those interpretations that leave fewer words unaccounted for in a line of text.

7   *Consistency of attribute, object, and value interrelationships* (internal consistency of hypothesis structure). This is used in several ways. For instance, in assembling an interpretation, ambiguity can sometimes be resolved simply by restricting interpretation to syntactically valid triples (*e.g.*, there may be several attributes and values suggested by the text, but perhaps only one of the possible pairings is syntactically valid). Also, knowing one of the three may help guide the search for another (*e.g.*, if the attribute is known [or postulated], then TEIRESIAS can refer to it to determine the appropriate kinds of values to seek).

Expectation-driven knowledge sources:

The rule model. As noted above, the model chosen during debugging is used as a source of advice (or hints) about the possible content of the new rule.

5–4.2.1   Terminology and Dictionary Structure

The English version of a rule will be referred to as "text," while each of the components of the LISP version will be referred to as a "LISP clause." Thus *the infection is primary-bacteremia* is text, and the corresponding LISP clause is (SAME CNTXT INFECTION PRIMARY–BACTEREMIA). The terms "parse" or "interpretation" are used to mean the creation of a single LISP premise or action clause.

The natural-language-understanding capabilities are purely keyword based. The connotation of a single word is determined by a number of pointers associated with it.[7] These are, in general, inverse pointers derived from the English phrases ("translations") associated with many of the data structures in the system. For instance, a list like STERILESITES has a translation of *those sites which are normally sterile*. As a result, associated with the word *sterile* is a pointer to the name STERILESITES. The creation and updating of these pointers are handled semi-automatically by routines that help to minimize the bookkeeping task.

For ease of reference later on, the names of those pointers are listed below, along with an indication of what they supply.

```
<WORD1>
pointer           value
INATTRIB    <word1> appears in the translation of these attributes
INOBJECT    <word1> appears in the translation of these object types
INFUNCS     <word1> appears in the translations of these predicate functions
VALUEOF     <word1> is a legal value of these attributes
```

---

[7] The current structure of the dictionary is the result of work by a succession of people associated with the project, in addition to the author.

INLTRANS   <word1> appears in the translation of these list names

Figure 5–4   Dictionary structure.

They are referred to collectively as "connotation pointers." (There are additional pointers to handle synonyms, but they are not relevant here.) The important point is that the appearance of any given word can be taken as evidence that the expert was talking about one of the attributes, objects, predicate functions, values, or list names indicated by the pointers for that word.

5–4.2.2   Pre-processing the Text

The first step in processing the new rule is to take a single line of text and replace each word with its root word equivalent. (Root words provide a canonical form for plurals and other simple variations.) Common words like *a, and, the,* are explicitly marked in the dictionary as content free, and are ignored.

All the connotations of each word are then obtained by referring to the appropriate pointers. Figure 5–5 below shows the result of this process.

As should be clear, this technique is strictly word by word. A more sophisticated approach would have some grasp of grammar and would attempt to assign meanings to entire phrases. We have been fairly successful in spite of the primitive approach, primarily because of the semi-formal nature of the technical language used: It tends to be terse, relatively unambiguous, and has a high information content. TEIRESIAS is thus not often led astray by ambiguities or "noise" words in the text. The common lack of correct grammar in the expert's responses also suggests that any extensive or computationally expensive use of a grammar-based approach might not pay off very well.

```
TEXT              ROOT WORDS      CONNOTATIONS

the               the             NIL
patient's         patient         [NIL (INFECTION) (CURINF) NIL NIL]
infection         infection       [NIL (INFECTION TREATALSO CYTOTOXIC
                                       NOSOCOMIAL WHENINFECT)
                                       (CURINF SUSPINF SUSPORG) NIL
                                       (ALLINFECTIONS)]

is                be              [(SAME) NIL NIL NIL NIL]
primary-          primary-        [NIL NIL NIL (PRIMARY-BACTEREMIA) NIL]
bacteremia        bacteremia
```

Figure 5–5   Original text, root words, and connotations. The connotations are listed in the order: predicate function, attribute, object, value, list name. Thus, *patient* can be interpreted as an indication of either an attribute or an object, while *infection* has numerous connotations.

5–4.2.3   Checking the Rule Model

TEIRESIAS's next step is to verify the applicability of the rule model that was suggested by the debugging process (or supply a model, if it "came in cold"). This is achieved by scanning each of the words in the action part of the rule and checking their connotation pointers to see which attributes or values are implicated.

If the debugging process has indicated which rule model to use, TEIRESIAS attempts to reconcile that model with the indications from the scan of the action text. If there is agreement, nothing unusual happens. If, however, it cannot reconcile any of the indications from the action text with the given model, the system indicates this problem and asks the expert for help. A trace of this process is shown below. Assume the system entered as before, expecting a rule about category, but the expert suddenly thinks of another rule he has been meaning to enter:

```
The new rule will be called RULE384
  If     1 -    THE ORGANISM IS A GRAMNEGATIVE ROD
    and  2 -    IT IS ANAEROBIC
    and  3 -
  Then:  1 -    THE ORGANISM MIGHT BE A BACTEROIDES (.6)
    and  2 -
Hmm... it seemed that this was going to be a rule to
deduce the category of a organism.  But it doesn't appear to
be...

To aid in analyzing this rule, please answer yes or no (Y or
N) to each of the following.

Is this a rule to deduce:
    an organism or class of organisms for which therapy
    should cover
**  N
    a likely identity of an organism causing a infection
**  N
    the identity of a organism
**  Y
Thank you...
```

The important thing here is a fast and very simple checking process. The first two incorrect guesses are the result of other connotations of the word *organism*. There are rarely more than four or five connotations in any case, so even at worst, the expert only sees a few bad guesses.

If the system had "come in cold," the process would start at the point where it says "To aid in analyzing..." Even without the debugging process, then, all the benefits of the recognition-oriented approach are still available.[8]

Once a model is selected, the interpretation process begins. As indicated, it proceeds line by line and is oriented primarily toward doing the best job possible with the limited natural language techniques available. There are two important points to note. First, the system does what might be called "template-directed code generation," analogous to the way English is often generated by "filling in the blanks" of a template. [9] Second, the system maintains several types of consistency in the parses that it generates.

5–4.2.4   Generating a LISP Clause

The next step is to generate the tree of possible parses. One example of the generation process will serve to illustrate the important ideas and explain what is meant by a tree of parses.

The process begins by determining which predicate function the expert might have had in mind, scanning the list of connotations, and choosing the predicate function that turns up most often. The template for this function is retrieved, and the rest of the process of creating a clause is guided by the attempt to fill in the template. [10] For example, suppose the function is SAME and the template is

(SAME CNTXT ATTRIB VALUE)

Associated with each of the primitives in the high-level "language" is a routine that embodies much of the semantics of each primitive. The template is filled in by calling each routine as needed and allowing it to examine the list of connotations to find the kind of object it requires. Consider the text from the first line in the trace, *the patient's infection is primary-bacteremia*. The routine for VALUE would discover that the only object of type VALUE suggested by the text was PRIMARY–BACTEREMIA. The routine for ATTRIB would find several objects of type ATTRIBUTE, since the word *infection* has a large number of connotations. However, since the VALUE routine has already filled in PRIMARY–BACTEREMIA as a VALUE, this narrows the choice to those attributes for which PRIMARY–BACTEREMIA is a legal value, and the routine takes the first of them (INFECTION) initially. The routine for CNTXT notices that *patient* can be interpreted as an

---

[8] While modeling human performance was not one of our motivations, it is interesting to note that both of these reactions are similar to human behavior. Sudden changes in the topic of a conversation can violate expectations about what is to follow, resulting in an expression of surprise. Similarly, arriving in the middle of an ongoing conversation often requires a moment to become oriented and prompts a request for information. Elements of both of these are seen above.

[9] The basic concept of filling in a template to generate code is taken from the original design in [Shortliffe76]. All the rest of the process that guides the template completion was designed by the author, including the view of attributes, values, etc., as extended data types.

[10] Note that this is the same template described in chapter 2 as the basis for the system's ability to dissect a rule.

It has recently been pointed out to me that the techniques used to fill in the template are similar to some of the work on natural language parsing using case grammars (see, *e.g.*, [Rumelhart73]).

object,[11] one that is a valid object for the attribute INFECTION, and hence marks it as such. It returns the literal atom CNTXT, reflecting the fact that CNTXT plays the role of a free variable that is bound when the rule is invoked.

This produces the clause [12]

(SAME CNTXT INFECTION PRIMARY—BACTEREMIA)

All the nontrivial words in the text have been assigned a meaning, so no more clauses can be derived from it. There are, however, alternate interpretations for two of the words (*patient* and *infection*). The system uses a standard depth-first search with backtracking and, at this point, undoes its current set of meaning assignments and tries all the alternatives. Other clauses are generated as alternate interpretations.

It will be instructive to examine one type of failure that can occur as clauses are generated. This will illustrate the point made in chapter 2, that knowledge acquisition is based in part on giving the system access to and an "understanding" of its own representations. To see this, consider the system's response to a line like *the site of the culture is blood.* The system will generate several clauses, including the correct one (which uses SAME as the predicate function and interprets *culture* as the object, *site* as the attribute, and *blood* as the value). In one of its later attempts to construct other clauses, it will discover it has used all the VALUEs it can find, and the VALUE routine thus fails. The routine for ATTRIB then finds it has not yet tried to interpret *culture* as an indication of the attribute "the number of cultures in this series" (NUMCULS) and makes this assignment. It then invokes the VALUE routine with instructions to look for a value for NUMCULS. [13] That routine, in turn, uses its knowledge of the structure of an attribute to examine NUMCULS, discovers that it takes an integer between 1 and 15 as a value, and finds none in the text. The attempt to interpret *culture* as an indication of NUMCULS thus fails, the assignment is undone, and the next alternative is tried. Maintaining the internal consistency of the clauses generated is thus based in part on giving the system the ability to examine its own representations; in this case, an attribute is examined to find out what kind of values are associated with it.

As may be clear, the template parts are not necessarily filled in the order in which they appear in the template. The VALUE part (if there is one) is always tried first, for instance, since words indicating values in this domain are often

---

[11] Recall that objects are also referred to as "contexts," for historical reasons.

[12] Since the clauses are later scored for likely validity, the first clause generated is not necessarily the system's first guess.

[13] The VALUE routine can be re-invoked, despite its previous failure, because there are a number of cases in which the word-by-word approach fails. It is then profitable to go back and take another look as long as there is some idea of what to look for. For attributes which are either true or false, for instance, an indication of the VALUE rarely appears explicitly in the text (*e.g.,* the text might be *the patient is a compromised host* rather than *it is true that the patient is a compromised host*).

totally unambiguous.[14] This simple "first pass" strategy is built into the driver routines, but, since one routine may invoke another, the order may soon become more complex.

The entire tree of parses is generated using the depth-first search with the backup noted earlier. The result is a tree of clauses of the sort shown below (part of the tree generated from the first line of text is shown). At each node of the tree is a potential premise clause, and any single path through the tree from the root to a leaf is a set of consistent interpretations.

(SAME CNTXT INFECTION PRIMARY-BACTEREMIA)   (SAME CNTXT TREATALSO PRIMARY-BACTEREMIA)

(SAME CNTXT CYTOTOXIC)   (SAME CNTXT NOSOCOMIAL)

Figure 5-6

Generation of the tree with alternative word meanings in different branches provides the notion of consistency between interpretations. Consistency is required in order to permit TEIRESIAS to get more than one LISP premise clause from a single line of text without making conflicting assumptions about that text. The current implementation takes care of the most obvious sources of such conflicts by insuring that only one meaning is chosen for each word.

There are a number of factors that prevent the tree of parses from becoming unreasonably large. To explain the first factor, it is necessary to refine the statement above which claimed that, in choosing a predicate function, the first one chosen is "the one that turns up most often." More precisely, when choosing a predicate function (or any item to fill in one of the blanks), the first one chosen is "the one that turns up most often, *and* was suggested by unambiguous words." This means that the tree is generated far more efficiently, with less backup. An example is shown below, in two versions of a fragment of a parse tree that would result from the text *the organism is an aerobic rod*. *Aerobic* is ambiguous (it can be either an aerobicity value or an organism subtype), while *rod* is unambiguously a morphology value.

---

[14] They are also sufficiently strong clues as to text content that the ATTRIB routines will supply the attribute which belongs with a given VALUE, even if no other indication of that attribute can be found. This is what allows the system to parse something like *the organism is a gramnegative rod*, even though there are no other indicators of gram stain (other than the value *gramnegative*) or morphology (other than the value *rod*).

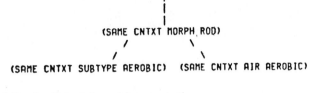

```
                              |
                              |
                              |
                   (SAME CNTXT MORPH ROD)
                      /              \
                    /                  \
     (SAME CNTXT SUBTYPE AEROBIC)   (SAME CNTXT AIR AEROBIC)
```

Figure 5-7   Inefficient tree of interpretations.

```
                      /   \
                    /       \
                  /           \
     (SAME CNTXT SUBTYPE AEROBIC)   (SAME CNTXT AIR AEROBIC)
                  |                          |
                  |                          |
     (SAME CNTXT MORPH ROD)         (SAME CNTXT MORPH ROD)
```

Figure 5-8   More efficient tree of interpretations.

Second, the insistence on consistency within a parse is simple but very effective. It is more efficient to avoid producing invalid parses than to generate them and prune them out later.

Finally, and perhaps most important, there is a very small amount of text and most of it is relatively unambiguous. While the expert is permitted to type an arbitrary amount in each text line, there are typically no more than 15 or so words.

At this point the system has generated a tree of interpretations for a single line of text. Any path in that tree from root to leaf represents a consistent and plausible set of LISP clauses that contain all of the meaning that could be found in the text.

As each clause is completed, it is given a preliminary score that reflects how it was assembled. For instance, those clauses for which independent evidence was found for both VALUE and ATTRIB are given the highest score. If the ATTRIB must be implied by the presence of a value, the score is somewhat lower. There are a number of other criteria that are also used in composing the score. The main idea is simply to provide some measure of how strongly the data (the text) suggested the interpretations (the LISP clauses) that were made.

5-4.2.5   Scoring the Parses

The next step is to select a single interpretation for the text by choosing a path through the tree of clauses. This is done with reference to the rule model chosen during the debugging phase. Each path is scored according to how well it fulfills the expectations expressed by the model. The singlets in the model predict the appearance of clauses containing specific attributes and predicate functions, while the ntuples predict the appearance of associations of clauses containing certain attributes. The score for each path is the sum of the strengths of the predictions that it fulfills.

There are thus two scores. The individual score for a given LISP clause indicates how strongly the clause was suggested by the English text. The score for an entire path indicates how well the set of clauses meets expectations. These two are combined in a way that emphasizes the expectations (the recognition-oriented approach), and candidates are ranked according to the outcome. The system will thus "hear what it expects to hear" if that is at all possible; otherwise, it will choose the best alternative interpretation.

5–4.3 Checking Results

May I say what I think second best? If there's a third best, too, spare not to tell it.

Sophocles
Oedipus the King, lines 282–283

Having chosen a likely interpretation for each line of text typed by the expert, the system displays the entire rule and asks for approval.

```
This is my understanding of your rule:
RULE383
--------

  If:   1) Primary-bacteremia is an associated infection for
           which therapy should cover, and
        2) The infection with the organism was acquired while
           the patient was hospitalized, and
        3) The culture was taken from a sterile source, and
        4) The organism is not normally found at this site
  Then:   There is strongly suggestive evidence (.8) that the
          category of the organism is enterobacteriaceae
Okay? (Yes or No)
--** N
```

When the expert indicates a problem, the system invokes a rule editor that allows him to make changes. He can add a clause (the system prompts for a new line of text), delete one, undo a deletion ("undeleting"), or ask to change a clause.

```
Change premise?
--** Y
What should be changed in premise? (type HELP for list of
commands)
++** CHANGE 1
Suppose (1) were changed to read-
        1 - The infection is primary-bacteremia
Would that be ok?
++** Y
Then you'll probably want to delete:
        2) The infection with the organism was acquired while
           the patient was hospitalized.
Correct?
```

```
++**  Y
```

The "change" command makes use of the fact that all the alternative interpretations of each text line have been saved. Given a clause to be changed, the system invokes several heuristics to find the next most likely interpretation. The primary heuristic is to examine the clause for a component (a predicate function, attribute, value, etc.) that was suggested by an ambiguous word in the text, to see if there is an alternative clause that uses one of the other connotations of that word. The system thus tries to reinterpret by making the smallest change it can, acting on the assumption that the original clause is probably close to correct. If this fails, the clause with the next highest overall score is chosen.

The alternatives are presented one by one for approval. If none of them is acceptable, the system prompts for a new line of text. There are two reasons for showing all the current alternatives before asking for new text. First, the selection of an alternative is very fast, because all necessary data structures are already present. Reprocessing a new line of text would take much longer. More important, however, the expert gets a good idea of what he might have said that triggered the system's incorrect interpretations and can then rephrase his statement appropriately. This can become important if there are only subtle differences in the translations of several functions, attributes, etc.

This segment also demonstrates the utility of even the very limited form of consistency checking that is available. TEIRESIAS maintains a record of the tree of parses, and whenever a clause is changed by selecting an alternative, it checks to make sure that the new alternative is consistent with all the other clauses derived from the same line of text. Once again, the process is very fast, since all the data structures already exist.

```
Anything else?
++**  D 3
clause(s) 3 deleted.
Anything else?
++**  ?
     1 - the infection is primary-bacteremia
 and 2 -    <deleted>
 and 3 -    <deleted>
 and 4 - the organism is not normally found at this site
Anything else?
++**  U 3
clause(s) 3 undeleted.
```

No deletions are actually done until exiting from the editor, making it possible to undo mistaken deletions.

```
Anything else?
++**  D 4
```

```
clause(s) 4 deleted.
Anything else?
++** C 3
Suppose (3) were changed to read-
        3 - The site of the culture is one of: those sites
              that are normally sterile
Would that be ok?
++** Y
Anything else?
++** ?
     1 - the infection is primary-bacteremia
 and 2 -    <deleted>
 and 3 - the site of the culture is one of: those sites that
           are normally sterile
 and 4 -    <deleted>
++** OK
Change action?
--** N
This is my understanding of your rule:
RULE383
-------
   If:  1) The infection is primary-bacteremia, and
        2) The site of the culture is one of: those sites
             that are normally sterile
   Then:  There is strongly suggestive evidence (.8) that the
            category of the organism is enterobacteriaceae
Okay? (Yes or No)
++** Y
```

After making all the changes that the expert wanted, the system again displays the rule and asks for approval. This time the expert is satisfied with the interpretation.

This segment of the trace also displays one weakness of the current implementation: Efficient use of the rule editor requires a familiarity with the nature of the mistakes produced by the natural language routines. Since all four lines of the system's original interpretation are incorrect, the command "CHANGE 1 2 3 4" seems plausible. It takes a certain level of familiarity with TEIRESIAS to realize that clauses 1 and 3 are close but incorrect, while 2 and 4 are purely spurious. While the expert need not understand how the natural language routines work, and might acquire the necessary sophistication through experience, the nontransparency of this part of the system still presents a problem, and is a likely topic for future work.

5–4.4   Second Guessing

*Do you know what you are doing? Will you listen to words to answer yours, and then
pass judgment?*

Sophocles
Oedipus the King, lines 543–544

So clear in this case were the oracles; so clear and yet false.

Sophocles
Oedipus the King, lines 722–723

Now that the expert has indicated that the interpretation of his text is
correct, TEIRESIAS double-checks the rule. The basic idea is to use the rule model
to see how well this new rule "fits in" to the system's model of its knowledge,
that is, does it "look like" a typical rule of the sort expected?

The point here is to take advantage of several unique characteristics of
the "student" being tutored: TEIRESIAS has "total recall" of every rule in the
knowledge base and has a great capacity for dealing with large amounts of detail.
Both of these characteristics are put to use in constructing the rule models. Since
the expert may be expressing rules that have never previously been formalized,
any help that the system can offer will prove very useful. The models help by
providing a basis for suggesting details that may have been overlooked. In doing
so, they also give the expert a hint of the "world view" implicit in the rules
already in the knowledge base.

The presence of a partial match between the new rule and the generalizations
in the rule model trigger a response from the system. Recall the last ntuple of
the premise description in the rule model of Figure 5–3:

```
((SITE MEMBF SAME) (INFECTION SAME) (PORTAL SAME) 1.23))
```

This means that when culture SITE appears in the rule, INFECTION type and
organism PORTAL often appear as well. The new rule has the first two but lacks
the last, and the system points this out:

```
I hate to criticize, Dr. Davis, but did you know that most rules
about what the
category of a organism might be, that mention-
              the site of a culture
              the infection
ALSO mention-
     [A] - the portal of entry of a organism
Shall I try to write a clause to account for [A] ?
++** Y
How about-
```

```
     [A] The portal of entry of the organism is gi
Ok?
++** Y
```

Since the expert has agreed to a clause about portal of entry, the system constructs it. The predicate function (SAME) is supplied by the ntuple. The template for SAME is then completed in the usual way, except that the system first checks in the record of the consultation. In this case, it needs a VALUE for PORTAL, which is available as the answer to question 18, asked during the consultation (Section 3–10). Nothing further is needed, so the system requests no assistance. (Had the desired information not been available—as would be the case if it had "come in cold" rather than from the consultation—the expert would have been asked to supply whatever was needed.) The result is a plausible guess, since it insures that the rule will in fact work for the current case (note the further use of the "knowledge acquisition in context" idea). It is not necessarily correct, of course, since the desired clause may be more general, but it is at least a plausible attempt.

```
Also, most rules about what the category of a organism might be
ALSO conclude about-
     [A] - the identity of a organism
Shall I try to write a clause to account for [A] ?
++** N
```

There are also ntuples (in the description of the action) that indicate patterns in the action of the rule, and one of these is applicable to the new rule. As always, the expert can override the system's suggestions, and does so in this case.

It should be noted that there is nothing in this concept of "second guessing" that is specific to the rule models as they are currently designed, or indeed to the rules as a knowledge representation. The most general and fundamental point is that mentioned above, of testing to see how something "fits in" to the system's model of its knowledge. At this point, the system might perform any kind of check, for violations of any established prejudices about what the new chunk of knowledge should look like. For rules, these checks might concern the size of its certainty factor, the number of clauses in the premise, etc., in addition to the current checks. Checks used with, say, a procedural encoding might involve the number and type of arguments passed to the procedure, the use of global variables, the presence of side effects, etc. In that case, for example, we can imagine adding a new procedure to a system that then responds by remarking "...*most procedures that do hash-table insertion also have the side effect of incrementing the variable* NUMBERELEMENTS. *Shall I add the code to do this?*" In general, this "second guessing" process can involve any characteristic that the system may have "noticed" about the particular knowledge representation in use.

5–4.5   Final Checkout

Now that both the expert and TEIRESIAS are satisfied, there is one final sequence of tests to be performed, reflecting once again the benefit of knowledge acquisition in context.

At this point, TEIRESIAS examines several things about the rule, attempting to make sure that the rule will, in fact, fix the problem uncovered. In this case, for instance, the action of the new rule should be a conclusion about category; the category mentioned should be enterobacteriaceae, and the conclusion should be affirmative. The premise should not contain any clauses that are sure to fail in the context in which the rule will be invoked. (Note that these tests require the ability to dissect and partially evaluate the rule, and they rely heavily on the use of the function templates to guide that dissection.) All of these are potential sources of error that would make obvious the fact that the rule will not fix the bug.

The new rule in the current example passes all these tests, but note what would have happened if the user had (accidentally) typed initially *the site is* not *one of the sterile sites.* Everything would have been the same up until this point, when the following exchange would have occurred.

```
The rule now reads:
RULE383
--------
   If:   1) The infection is primary-bacteremia, and
         2) The site of the culture is not one of: those sites
      that are normally sterile, and
         3) The portal of entry of the organism is gi
      Then:   There is strongly suggestive evidence (.8) that the
      category of the organism is enterobacteriaceae
Sorry, but this rule won't work.   In the context of
ORGANISM-1, clause 2 ("the site of the culture is not one of:
those sites that are normally sterile") is sure to fail.
Would you like to change the rule?
++**
```

The expert then has the option of either editing the current rule or writing an entirely new one (since the current rule may be correct, only inapplicable to the current problem). If he edits it, the tests are run again, until the system is satisfied that there is nothing obviously wrong with the rule.

5–4.6   Bookkeeping

There are a number of straightforward bookkeeping tasks to be performed. Some of them involve hooking the new rule into the knowledge base so that it is retrieved and invoked appropriately. TEIRESIAS does this by scanning the clauses of the action part and adding the rule number to the proper internal lists (*e.g.*, in this case, it adds the rule number to the list of rules that conclude about CATEGORY.) This task is not difficult because meta-rules can be used to express all necessary ordering of rule invocation (see chapter 7). As a result, the lists can be stored unordered, so adding a new rule to them is easy. All of this is taken care of without assistance from the user.

Another of the bookkeeping tasks involves tagging the rule with information which facilitates maintaining the large and constantly changing body of rules. Each rule is tagged with the name of the author, the date of creation, the case number that prompted its creation (if there is one), and the user's own comments on why he added (or changed) the rule. This last item gives the expert a way of recording the reasons for any rules or parts of rules that are not obvious. Since the rule in this example is fairly straightforward, so are the user's comments.

```
Please describe briefly why you added (or changed) this rule.
[Type an empty line when done.]
** THE SYSTEM FAILED TO REALIZE IT COULD CONCLUDE CATEGORY,
** AND THIS ALLOWED RULE184 TO INCORRECTLY CONCLUDE
** IDENTITY.
**
RULE383 has now been added to the knowledge base.
```

It should be noted that rule 383 gets added only to the current "working" knowledge base. All changes made by any individual are stored away at the end of the session, filed under the individual's name. When the expert signs on again, the system automatically searches for a file of the proper name and asks if the changes should be reinstated. This allows each expert to build up a knowledge base that includes his own personal preferences and yet does not cause problems with maintaining a standard, functioning system for other users. Permanent changes to the performance program knowledge base are made after agreement from the experts.

At this point, the system also performs any necessary recomputation of rule models.[15] The operation is very fast, since it is clear from the action part of the rule which models may need to be recomputed, and the EXAMPLES part supplies the names of the other relevant rules. Note that this means that TEIRESIAS's model of the knowledge base is kept constantly up-to-date, immediately reflecting any changes. As a result, performance on the acquisition of subsequent rules may conceivably be better. Since the updated rule models are filed away with the other changes, this also means that the system will again reflect the "structure" of this expert's reasoning the next time he logs in.

5-4.7 Rerunning the Consultation

TEIRESIAS then invokes the performance program as a subprocess, rerunning the

---

[15] The models are recomputed when any change is made to the knowledge base, including rule deletion or modification, as well as addition.

consultation to insure that additional effects of the new rule are discovered. To do this, TEIRESIAS first erases everything from the database except the expert's responses to questions asked during the original consultation. When the consultation is rerun, the information-requesting routines look in the database for answers before asking the expert.

In this case, the single new rule has repaired all the problems.

5–5   OTHER USES FOR THE RULE MODELS

There are other applications of the rule models that help to characterize their role in allowing the system to "know what it knows," and which make plausible the claim that they indicate useful regularities in the knowledge base.

5–5.1   "Knowing What You Know": Rule Models as Abstract Descriptions of Knowledge

The rule models have also been integrated into the question-answering program that is part of MYCIN. Previously, MYCIN would respond to a question like *How do you determine the identity of an organism?* by typing out the names of all the relevant rules and asking which the user wanted to see. But a rule model, as a generalization of an entire class of rules, answers the question too.

```
**  HOW DO YOU DECIDE THAT AN ORGANISM IS`   PSEUDOMONAS
AERUGINOSA?
Rules which conclude that the identity of the organism is
pseudomonas-aeruginosa generally use one or more of the
following pieces of information:
     the site of the culture
     the gram stain of the organism
     the morphology of the organism
Furthermore, the following relationships hold:
     The gram stain of the organism and the morphology of the
     organism tend to appear together in these rules.
RULE184, RULE116, RULE047, RULE085, and RULE040 conclude that
     the identity of the organism is pseudomonas-aeruginosa.
Which of these do you wish to see?
**
```

By simply "reading" the rule model to the user, the system first supplies an overview of the knowledge in the relevant rules and then allows the user to examine any of those rules for specific details. This overview suggests the structure of global trends in the knowledge of the experts who assembled the knowledge base and thus helps to define the overall approach to any given topic.

5–5.2 "Knowing What You Don't Know"

There are models in the current system made from between 2 (the defined minimum) and 35 rules. We have defined a metric to measure the "strength" of a model and have based it on both the total number of rules from which the model was constructed and the size of the CF for each of those rules. [16] The entire model set is kept ordered from weakest to strongest, giving the system some indication of its likely competence on a range of subjects. In a very primitive way, it thus gains a knowledge of where it is ignorant.

This feature makes possible a new option for the expert. Instead of adding a rule to fix a bug, he can ask the system what it would like to learn. (There is currently no real language processing done on the question below; the system checks for precisely the sequence of words shown.)

```
--** WHAT WOULD YOU LIKE TO KNOW?
There are only 2 rules for concluding that the identity of a
organism might be enterococcus. Would you like to give me a
rule for that?
++** N
There are only 2 rules for concluding that a infection might be
infective-endocarditis.  Would you like to offer a rule for
that?
++** Y
The new rule will be called RULE384
 If       1-
```

The system cycles through the rule models in order, indicating the weakest topics first. The current implementation ignores topics for which no rule models exist. It also makes the (imperfect) assumption that subjects for which there are no rules at all are the sorts of things that would not ordinarily be deduced.

This is a first order solution to the problem of giving the system an indication of its weaknesses. A better solution would supply an indication of how much it knows about a subject, as compared with how much there is to know. There surely are subjects for which three or four rules exhaust the available knowledge, while for others a hundred or more rules may not suffice. The issue is related to work described in [Carbonell73], on closed vs. open sets. That paper offers some interesting strategies for allowing a program to decide when it is ignorant and how it might reason in the face of the inability to store every fact about a given topic.

There appear to be no easy ways to deduce the incompleteness of the knowledge base using only the information stored in it. It is not valid to say, for

---

[16] In more detail: Model M1 is "stronger" than model M2 (a) if M1 was constructed from more rules than M2, or (b) when the number of rules in both is the same, if the sum of the certainty factors of the rules from which M1 was made is larger than the corresponding sum for M2.

instance, that there ought to be even a single rule for every attribute (how could a patient's name be deduced?). Nor is there a well-defined set of attributes for which no rules are likely to exist. Nor is it clear what sort of information would allow the incompleteness to be deduced.

The issue is a significant one, since a good solution to the problem would not only give TEIRESIAS a better grasp of where the performance program was weak but would also provide several important capabilities to the performance program itself. It would, for example, permit the use of the "if it were true I would know" heuristic in [Carbonell73]. Roughly restated, this says that "if I know a great deal about subject S, and fact F concerns an important aspect of S, then if I don't already know that F is true, it's probably false." Thus, in certain circumstances a lack of knowledge about the truth of a statement can plausibly be used as evidence suggesting that the statement is false. [17]

5–6 PERSONALIZED WORLD VIEWS

One of the likely problems of collecting knowledge from several experts is that of conflicting world views. Since, currently, individual modifications to the rule base are stored away separately for each individual user, the established knowledge base is kept distinct from local modifications. At some time, however, it might prove useful to be able to deal with contributions from several experts and keep them in the knowledge base all at once. Some very limited capabilities in this direction are made possible by tagging each rule with the name of its author (as illustrated earlier) and by building a set of rule models for each individual's personal knowledge base.

Individualized rule models make it possible, for instance, to ask the system *How would Dr. Jones deduce the identity of an organism?* and to compare this with the reasoning indicated by a rule model for a different expert. The tags on rules make it possible to focus conveniently on the effects of the contributions of different experts. We can imagine, for instance, a meta-rule of the form *When trying to deduce the identity of an organism, only use rules written by Dr. Jones or Dr. Smith, or ...only those written by the expert currently running the program.* (There might even be a preference ordering on the rules, based on length of experience of the rule author. See chapter 7 for the details of meta-rule operation.) Using both of these capabilities, it is possible to see both how a given expert reasons about a subject and how he might handle a single, given aspect of a case.

While this provides a handle on manipulating different world views, it clearly does not confront the deeper problem of resolving any conflicts between them. More work on this subject is required.

---

[17] Note that this is another, very useful, form of meta-level knowledge.

5–7 MORE ON MODELS AND CONCEPT FORMATION

Now that the organization, structure, and function of rule models in the system
is clear, let's take another look at the general idea of models, concept formation,
and model-based understanding.

5–7.1 Model-Based Understanding

Many AI programs have incorporated explicit models and used them as a guide
to understanding. The work of Falk and Roberts in vision has been mentioned;
the idea has been extended to a range of other sensory modalities as well. Viewed
in the broadest terms, the process may be considered one of signal interpretation,
as suggested by the figure below.

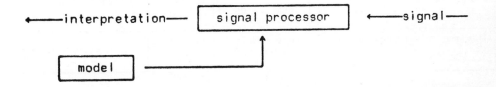

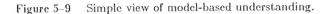

Figure 5–9   Simple view of model-based understanding.

Some signal-processing operation is performed on the incoming signal, with
guidance and/or advice from a model. The result is an interpretation of the
signal (or some action based on it), which gives evidence that it was understood.
The table below lists six different systems that can be viewed in these terms
(including ours) and compares them along several dimensions.

The examples illustrate the two sorts of models in use. "World model" is
used in the usual sense and refers to a collection of information that characterizes
the domain of interest. The system described in [Reddy73], for example, had a
model of the world of chess that included information about plausible moves and
appropriate vocabulary. The vision system in [Waltz72] contained a complete
classification of the types of vertices that could be a part of a convex planar-faced
polyhedron and used this as its model of the blocks world.

An "object model," on the other hand, is used to characterize the expected
content of the signal to be processed. Falk's system, for example, had models of the
individual polyhedra from which scenes would be constructed. Understanding a
scene was then viewed in terms of choosing specific models and assigning locations
and orientations to each.

The two sorts of models tend to be used somewhat differently. In very general
terms, we can say that since object models provide characterizations of signal
content, "understanding" can be approached as a comparison between the model
and the signal. World models provide a source of knowledge that is typically
used to check the plausibility of potential interpretations of the signal. Object
models are thus typically used in some manner of matching process, while world
models are used inferentially.

Model-based systems

reference	signal	model	model type	evidence of understanding
[Falk70]	light	polyhedra	object	synthesized reconstruction of picture
[Winograd72]	English text	blocks world	world	block manipulation, coherent dialogue
[Waltz72]	line drawings	vertex classification	world	analysis of picture
[Reddy73]	sound	chess game	world	typed version of spoken sentence
[Goldstein74]	annotated program	verbal description of picture	world	debugged program
Davis	English text	rule models, medical knowledge base	object world	re-translated rule

Table 5-1   Model-based systems.

The two models are really at either extreme of the continuum shown below, which emphasizes the distinction by considering two vision programs that performed similar tasks.[18] Where Falk's program had models of individual polyhedra (models characterizing the signal content), Waltz's program used knowledge about the "world" of polyhedra in general, without reference to any specific instance.

MODEL	PROCESS	EXAMPLE
World model	Inferential	[Waltz72]
Object model	Matching	[Falk70]

Figure 5-10   Object models and world models: Comparison.

The rule models used in TEIRESIAS fall somewhere in between. They are a type of object model, since they represent the content expected in the signal. But they are not themselves rules and cannot therefore simply be matched against the signal. The information they carry, however, can be used to help direct the interpretation process. In addition, the knowledge base provides the system with a world model. As will become clear in the next chapter, the knowledge base contains many data structures that indicate such things as which values belong with which attributes. The system relies on this information to maintain

---

[18] Remember that selected aspects of each program have been singled out here for the sake of discussion. All of the programs here and in Table 5-1 were more complex than the simple characterizations given.

the internal consistency of the clauses it assembles and will, as a result, never produce a clause of the form "The site of the culture is e.coli."

5-7.2 Concept Formation

There has also been much work done in AI on concept formation; a recent example noted earlier is [Winston70]. A much simplified view of the information flow in the task is shown below, where a set of examples is used as the basis for inferring a concept.

Figure 5-11   Simplified view of concept formation.

5-7.3 A Synthesis

Now consider the process of model-directed understanding combined with concept formation, producing the figure below. In terms of our system, the "signal" is the new rule text, "signal processing" is done by the rule acquisition routines, the interpretation is the new rule in LISP terms, and the "model" is provided by the set of rule models. For concept formation, the rule base supplies the examples from which the concepts—the rule models—are constructed.

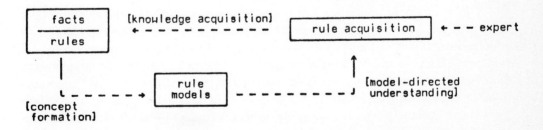

Figure 5-12   Synthesis of concept formation and model-based understanding.

The result is an interesting form of closed-loop behavior. The existing rule models are used to guide the process of acquisition, the new rule is added to the knowledge base and the relevant rule models are recomputed. The system is thus constructing its models (its picture of its own knowledge) on the basis of experience, keeping those models up-to-date with the current knowledge base and using them to help acquire new knowledge.

This loop has a number of interesting implications. First, performance on the acquisition of the next rule may be better because the system's "picture" of its knowledge base has improved—the rule models are now computed from a larger set of instances and their generalizations are more likely to be valid.

Second, since the relevant rule models are recomputed each time a change is made to the knowledge base, the picture they supply is kept constantly up-to-date; thus, they are at all times an accurate reflection of the shifting patterns in the knowledge base.

Finally, and perhaps most interesting, the models are not hand-tooled by the system architect or specified by the expert. They are instead formed by the system itself and formed as a result of its experience in acquiring rules from the expert. Thus, despite its reliance on a set of models as a basis for understanding, TEIRESIAS's abilities are not restricted by the existing set of models. As its store of knowledge grows, old models become more accurate, new models are formed, and the system's stock of knowledge about its knowledge continues to expand. This appears to be a novel capability for a model-based system.

5–8   ASSUMPTIONS AND LIMITATIONS

As noted, our approach involves knowledge transfer that is interactive, that is set in the context of a shortcoming in the knowledge base, and that transfers a single rule at a time. Each of these has implications about TEIRESIAS's range of applicability.

Interactive knowledge transfer seems best suited to task domains involving problem solving that is entirely or primarily a high level cognitive task, with a number of distinct, specifiable principles. Consultations in medicine or investments seem to be appropriate domains, but the approach would not seem well suited to those parts of, say, speech understanding or scene recognition in which low level processes play a significant role.

The transfer of expertise approach presents a useful technique for task domains that do not permit the use of programs (like those noted in chapter 4) which autonomously induce new knowledge from test data. This may occur most commonly because the data for a domain simply don't exist yet. In quantitative domains (like mass spectrum analysis [Mitchell78]) or synthesized ("toy") domains (like the line drawings in [Waltz75]), a large body of data points is easily assembled. This is not currently true for many domains, consequently induction techniques cannot be used. In such cases interactive transfer of expertise offers a useful alternative.

Knowledge acquisition in context appears to offer useful guidance wherever knowledge of the domain is as yet ill-specified, but the context need not be a shortcoming in the knowledge base uncovered during a consultation, as is done here. Our recent experience suggests that an effective context is also provided by examining certain subsets of rules in the knowledge base and using them as a framework for specifying additional rules. The overall concept is limited, however, to systems that already have at least some minimal amount of information in their knowledge base. Earlier than this, there may be insufficient information to provide any context for the acquisition process.

Finally, the rule-at-a-time approach is a limiting factor. The example given earlier works well, of course, because the bug was manufactured by removing a single rule. In general, acquiring a single rule at a time seems well suited to the later stages of knowledge base construction, in which bugs may indeed be caused by the absence of one or a few rules. We need not be as lucky as the present example, in which one rule repairs three bugs; the approach will also work if three independent bugs arise in a consultation. But early in knowledge base construction, where large sub-areas of a domain are not yet specified, it appears more useful to deal with groups of rules, or, more generally, with larger segments of the basic task (as in [Waterman78]).

In general then, the interative transfer of expertise approach seems well suited to the later stages of knowledge base construction for systems performing high-level tasks, and offers a useful technique for domains where extensive sets of data points are not available.

5-9   UNSOLVED PROBLEMS AND FUTURE WORK

There are a number of problems left unsolved by the current implementation that suggest several directions for future work. They are of two forms: minor problems whose solution involves extensions and refinements to existing methods, and major problems requiring new solutions.

5-9.1   Minor Problems

As with all first-generation systems, TEIRESIAS has many rough spots and inconveniences. These will have to be smoothed out before the acquisition routines can become a powerful user-oriented system. For instance, the system's guidance of the debugging process could be improved. It currently derives much power from its methodical approach, forcing the expert's criticism to be sharply focused. But it is also somewhat inflexible and unforgiving: In most cases there is no way to change a response once a question is answered, for instance.

There are other tasks suggested by the larger context in which acquisition occurs. It would be useful, for example, to provide several sorts of feedback on the consultation system's performance. A recent addition to MYCIN keeps extensive statistics on the use of each rule in the knowledge base. These should be routinely scanned by the acquisition system to detect potential bugs (*e.g.*, a rule that is never invoked successfully is likely to have an error in its premise). A more sophisticated solution might even be capable of suggesting plausible corrections, based on an examination of the situations under which failure occurred. It should also be possible to provide some feedback after the complete information on a case is available. Original diagnoses, for instance, could be evaluated in light of the final results from the laboratory, possibly suggesting modifications to the knowledge base.

The rule editor could also be improved in several respects. It should be possible, for instance, to make a number of routine changes to a rule with less machinery than is currently used. The rule editor can currently be invoked separately to accomplish some of these, but it would require a larger command set to be adequately powerful. A more substantive improvement concerns the problem noted earlier, of knowing exactly what to change and what to delete in a rule that has been misunderstood: While the primitive approach to natural language is the fundamental source of the problem (see below), there are several things that could be done to ease the difficulties. It would be a great help simply to make clear which interpretations came from which lines of the original input text. This might be done as easily as grouping the appropriate lines together as they are printed, making the nature of the system's misunderstandings more obvious.

Since the process of tracking down the original problem in the knowledge base is easily viewed as diagnosis and therapy, there is the interesting possibility of expressing it too in rules. Such a body of rules would allow running a "mini-consultation" to uncover the problem and initiate corrective action. It would have the substantive advantage of allowing all the explanation (and conceivably, acquisition) routines to be used during the debugging process. Rules to do this have been drafted but have not yet been implemented.

5–9.2   Major Problems

5–9.2.1   Better Techniques for Rule Model Generation

The shortcomings of the present approach to rule model generation were outlined earlier. The primary problem is the use of a purely statistical approach to concept formation. This approach was motivated, in part, by the desire to make the models transparent to the expert. More sophisticated sorts of concept formation would be possible if the model construction process were made interactive. With this approach, each time a change had been made to the knowledge base, TEIRESIAS would indicate to the expert any new patterns that had become evident and would ask him for an evaluation of each. With this sort of advice, it would become possible to distinguish accidental correlations from valid interrelations. It would also be possible to construct models with a much finer degree of control. The utility and sophistication of TEIRESIAS's second guessing would increase proportionally.

5–9.2.2   Natural Language

Of the major problems, the weakness of the natural language understanding techniques presents the largest barrier to better performance. Even without introducing more sophisticated grammar-oriented techniques, however, there are several steps that might be taken to strengthen the system. Processing each line of the text independently is one source of weakness. The rule models are currently used to score the interpretation of each line independently, but the ntuples might easily be used to score an entire premise at once.

Also, as shown, there is substantive advantage in being careful about the consistency of the parses generated for a single line of text. A similar technique should be developed to consider consistency between lines. This is a much harder problem, however, since it requires a considerably large store of world knowledge. For instance, it makes sense to have a rule say *if the identity of an organism is likely to be X and likely to be Y* (*i.e.*, there's evidence for both X and Y). But it does not make sense to say *if the site of the culture is likely to be X and likely to be Y*, because the site from which a culture is obtained is rarely in doubt. This requires more knowledge about things like identities and sites than currently exists in the system, or than is easily added.

Another manifestation of the weakness of the line-by-line treatment of natural language appears in the way the English versions of the rules are printed. Some rules are quite awkward when translated line by line, yet often they have very simple restatements in other terms. More sophisticated translation routines should be developed to handle an entire rule at once.

There are obvious weaknesses, too, in the word-by-word approach to meaning. As the knowledge base grows larger, significant numbers of attributes are beginning to use similar terms. The appearance of that term in text then yields numerous connotations and an awkwardly large number of clauses are generated.

The rule models should also be integrated deeper into the natural language interpretation process. Rather than generating all the parses, the models should be used to help choose which branch of the parse tree to explore. The tree would be generated a path at a time, under the guidance of the rule model, which might be far more efficient and have a better chance of arriving at the right answer sooner.

5–9.2.3 Impact on the Knowledge Base

There is a rather vast problem, which we have examined only very briefly, concerning the impact of any new or changed rule on the rest of the knowledge base. [19] There are two general classes of interactions, corresponding to syntactic and semantic conflicts. The difficulty in syntactic problems arises out of the use of certainty factors. Except in very simple cases (*e.g.*, two rules identical except for their CFs), there is some question of what constitutes contradiction and subsumption for this form of reasoning rule.

The lack of a precise definition of inconsistency makes detecting indirect contradictions (which result from chaining several rules together) especially difficult. As an example, consider the rules below. They are valid under the current CF model but would be a contradiction in ordinary binary-valued logic. (A well-specified set of organisms belong to a given category, so just knowing the category of an organism gives a hint about its identity. But the rule set below is plausibly correct if all the members of the category except one [identity A] have the same aerobicity.)

Thus, there are two patterns of the form

$$CATEGORY\ =\ .4 \Rightarrow IDENTITY\ =\ -1.0 \Rightarrow AEROBICITY$$

[19] See [Shortliffe76] for additional thoughts on this topic.

R1:   CATEGORY is X ═══ .4 ═══▶ IDENTITY is A
                          [knowing category is X gives some hint of identity]

R2:   IDENTITY is A ═══ -1 ═══▶ AEROBICITY is B
                          [knowing identity is A can be used definitely to rule out the
                          aerobicity value which is different than the aerobicity of A]

R3:   CATEGORY is X ═══ .2 ═══▶ AEROBICITY is B
                          [but the category is evidence about aerobicity also, and might
                          indicate that it's B, if all the other members of the category
                          have aerobicity B]

Figure 5–13

and

$$\text{CATEGORY} = .2 \Rightarrow \text{AEROBICITY}$$

In this way, CATEGORY can be both evidence in favor of and against AEROBICITY, depending on the reasoning chain used.[20] Now consider what happens if the CFs for R1 and R3 above are changed slowly and allowed to approach 1.0. Since the CF model becomes Boolean logic when all CFs are either 1.0 or —1.0, at some point the rule set above will become inconsistent; but the question is when.

Boolean logic has the constraint that P(HfiE) + P(not-HfiE) = 1.0, an equality from which the value of either probability can be computed when given the other. For CFs there may conceivably be an inequality from which to compute the legal range of a certainty factor for one rule in a particular set of rules, but it has not been derived as yet. The first step in detecting inconsistencies is thus to define the concept more precisely.

Even with a rigorous definition, however, the problem of inconsistency detection would remain difficult. One possible approach would be to view the rule base as a directed graph, where nodes correspond to attributes, and links correspond to rules, with weights on the links equal to the certainty factors of the rules. In these terms, the example above would look like two different paths from category to aerobicity. We might then attempt to develop a taxonomy of topologic forms that were "suspicious" and take the proper action (or just warn the expert) if a new rule ever resulted in such a form. (Note that the problem is a good deal easier with this incremental approach. By guaranteeing the integrity of the current knowledge base, there is far less work to do when a new rule is added.)

---

[20] This is not unreasonable. Conditional probabilities in standard Boolean logic present an analogous situation. Given an hypothesis H and a piece of evidence E, E can be both evidence in favor of H (P[HfiE] = .8) and evidence in favor of not-H (P[not-HfiE] = .2).

"Semantic" conflicts are more difficult to handle. How, for instance, can the system know that it is a contradiction to have two rules conclude that *it is definite that the site of the culture is one of the sterile sites* and that *it is definite that the site is one of the nonsterile sites.* The important point is that these two classes are mutually exclusive. There might be a rule of the form *if a site is sterile then it is not nonsterile*, but attempting to account for such problems on a case-by-case basis is difficult to do for any large knowledge base. Consider, for instance, the difficulty that would be encountered when it became clear that the two classes are not exhaustive and that there is a third class of sites that are "questionably" sterile. A more fundamental solution to the problem requires, once again, an extensive body of world knowledge not currently a part of the system. We have not yet investigated the question of dealing with this sort of conflict.

5–9.2.4 Limits of the Interactive Transfer of Expertise Approach

While TEIRESIAS has not as yet been tested by having experts use it, our experience with manual knowledge acquisition provides a perspective on its likely area of greatest utility. As noted, our approach involves knowledge transfer that is interactive, that is set in the context of a shortcoming in the knowledge base, and that transfers a few rules at a time. Each of these implies certain constraints on the range of applicability of this system.

Interactive knowledge transfer seems best suited to task domains involving problem solving that is entirely or primarily a high-level cognitive task, with a number of distinct, specifiable principles. Medical diagnosis seems an appropriate domain, but the technique would not seem well suited to those parts of, say, speech understanding or scene recognition in which low-level processes appear to play a significant role.

Knowledge acquisition in context appears to offer a useful guide wherever knowledge of the domain is as yet ill-specified, but the context need not be a single consultation, as used here. Our recent experience suggests that an effective context is also provided by examining certain subsets of rules in the knowledge base, using them as a framework for specifying new rules.

Finally, the rule-at-a-time approach is perhaps the most limiting factor. The example given earlier works well, of course, because the bug was manufactured by removing a single rule. In general, the approach seems well suited to the later stages of knowledge base construction, in which bugs may indeed be caused by the absence of one or a few rules. We need not be as lucky as the present example, in which one rule repairs three bugs; the approach will also work if three independent bugs arise in a given consultation. But early in knowledge base construction, where large sub-areas of a domain are not yet specified, it appears more useful to deal with groups of rules or, more generally, to deal with larger segments of the basic task, as for example in [Waterman77].

In general, then, this approach seems well suited to the later stages of knowledge base construction for systems performing high-level tasks.

5–10   SUMMARY

This chapter has explored and illustrated a number of issues. First, by doing knowledge acquisition in the context of a shortcoming in the knowledge base, TEIRESIAS's acquisition system can build up a set of expectations about the class of rule it is going to get.

Second, in the set of rule models TEIRESIAS has a model of the information in the knowledge base, and it is by selecting one part of that model (a specific rule model) that it expresses its expectations.

Third, because it has a model of the knowledge base, TEIRESIAS can tell whether some new piece of information "fits in" to what is already known. It is the occurrence of a partial match between the expectations in the rule model and the new rule that prompts the system to make suggestions to the expert.

Fourth, the rule models are computed directly from the set of rules in the knowledge base and are updated whenever a new rule is added. This means that the system's model of its knowledge is both derived from its "experience" and constantly evolving along with the knowledge base itself.

Chapter 6

Knowledge Acquisition II

Yes, but I see that even your own words miss the mark...

Sophocles
Oedipus the King, line 324

6–1 INTRODUCTION

The techniques described in the previous chapter make it possible for the expert to teach the system new rules, expressed in terms of known concepts. But this capability alone would be insufficient for any substantial education of the system since gaps in the knowledge base might require rules dealing with concepts not yet known to the system. This chapter describes how the expert can teach the system new conceptual primitives and new types of conceptual primitives. [1]

This capability requires dealing with a new set of problems, in addition to those faced earlier. There will, in particular, be a greater emphasis on the manipulation of data structures in the knowledge base. Acquisition of new rules dealt with a single type of structure, one which was understood in terms of a

---

[1] A "new conceptual primitive" means a new instance of one of the 13 primitives listed in Section 2–4.4. A "new type of conceptual primitive" refers to teaching the system about a new kind of primitive in addition to the existing 13.

combination of available primitives. There was thus a single, uniform process for acquisition and integration, with an emphasis on understanding and interpreting the English text. Here, in the acquisition of new conceptual primitives, it is necessary to deal with a wide range of data structures, each of which may have its own requirements for integration into the knowledge base. The problem thus has two major aspects to it: (i) knowledge acquisition and (ii) knowledge base management. In response, the techniques used address both the difficulties presented by the knowledge transfer process and the general issues of constructing and maintaining a large collection of data structures.

This chapter is divided into three main parts. The first part introduces the idea of a *data structure schema*, a device for describing representations, and contains the bulk of the discussion about it. It begins with a general overview of the fundamental problems attacked and the basic ideas used. It then continues with traces that show how TEIRESIAS directs the acquisition of a new value for an attribute, demonstrating a simple example of "filling out" an existing schema to produce a new instance. Section 6–8 and Section 6–9 then discuss the organization and use of the knowledge carried in the schemata.

Section 6–10 starts the second part with an example and an explanation of the acquisition of a new attribute. This part demonstrates the use of the schemata on more complex data structures and indicates how a new schema can be acquired using the same techniques employed for acquiring new instances.

The last part begins with Section 6–12, which describes how to start the knowledge acquisition process when building an entirely new knowledge base. It shows an example of TEIRESIAS's performance on this task.

6–2 KEY IDEAS: OVERVIEW

The discussion below requires including a certain amount of detail concerning both the schemata and internal data structure implementation. It also ranges over a large number of topics and examines steps toward solving many of the problems. To insure that the more important ideas are not lost in the mass of detail, they are summarized below and labelled with the section in which they first appear.

The most basic observation we make is that

1   By supplying a system with a store of knowledge about its own representations, both knowledge acquisition and knowledge base management can be carried out in a high-level dialog that transfers information relatively easily. (Section 6–5.)

Further observations dealing with the store of knowledge about representations include:

2   Each of the conceptual primitives (knowledge representations) from which rules (and other structures) are built will be viewed as an extended data type.

Each such extended data type is described by a *data structure schema*, a record-like structure augmented with additional information (such as data structure interrelations). (Section 6–5.)

3   The schemata provide a language and mechanism for describing representations and hence offer a way of expressing a body of knowledge about them. (Section 6–6.2.)

4   The body of knowledge is organized around the representational primitives in use (such as, in this case, the notion of *attribute*, *object*, *value*, etc.). (Section 6-8.2.)

5   Knowledge is represented as a collection of prototypes (the schemata). (Section 6–8.)

6   Knowledge can be viewed in terms of different levels of generality: (*i*) schema instances, (*ii*) schemata, and (*iii*) "schema-schema." (Section 6–13.)

7   The techniques we use gain a certain degree of generality by keeping the knowledge carefully stratified according to those levels. (Section 6–13.)

8   The set of schemata can itself be organized into a generalization hierarchy. (Section 6–8.1.)

Observations dealing with knowledge base management include:

9   It is useful to consider the terms *data structure*, *extended data type*, and *knowledge representation* as interchangeable. (Section 6–6.1.)

10   The system is "totally typed" in the sense that ideas (4) and (5) above are applied exhaustively to all representations and data structures in the system. (Section 6–6.3.)

11   Unlike ordinary record structures or declarations, the schemata are a part of the system itself and are available to the system for examination. (Section 6–6.3.)

Ideas relevant to knowledge acquisition include the suggestions that:

12   Knowledge acquisition can proceed by interpreting the information in the schemata as a set of instructions for the construction and maintenance of the relevant knowledge representations. Hence it is the process of schema instantiation that drives knowledge acquisition. (Section 6–9.)

13   Doing knowledge acquisition via the schemata offers a certain level of knowledge base integrity. (Section 6–6.4.)

14   Acquisition of a new *instance* of an existing conceptual primitive is structured as a process of descent through the schema hierarchy noted above. (Section 6–8.1.)

15   Acquisition of a new *kind* of conceptual primitive is structured as a process of adding new branches to the schema hierarchy. (Section 6–10.)

6–3   THE FUNDAMENTAL PROBLEM

Viewed from the perspective of knowledge representation and knowledge base management, the problem of acquiring a new conceptual primitive can be seen in terms of adding a new instance of an extended data type to a large program. Using the standard approach, a programmer attempting this task would have to gather a wide range of information, including the structure of the data type and its interrelations with other data types in the program. Such information is typically recorded informally (if at all) and is often scattered through a range of sources; it might be found in comments in program code, in documents and manuals maintained separately, and in the mind of the program architect. Just finding all of this information can be a major task, especially for someone unfamiliar with the program.

In this situation, two sorts of errors are common: The new instance may be given the wrong structure or it may be improperly integrated into the rest of the program. Since an extended data type may be built from a complex collection of components and pointers, it is not uncommon that a new instance receives an incorrect internal organization, that extraneous structures are included, or that necessary elements are inadvertently omitted. Since data structures in a program are not typically independent, the addition of a new instance often requires significant effort to maintain the existing interdependencies. Errors can result from doing this incorrectly, by violating the interrelationships of existing structures or (as is more common) by omitting a necessary bookkeeping step.

6–4   SOURCES OF DIFFICULTY

A basic source of difficulty in solving the problem of acquiring a new conceptual primitive arises from our desire to deal with the issues noted above (insuring correct structure for a newly added primitive and maintaining existing inter-relationships) in the context of the global goals set out at the beginning. That is, a nonprogrammer should be able to build the knowledge base and be able to assemble large amounts of knowledge. The first of these goals means that the user cannot (nor should he be expected to) deal with the system at the level of data structures; he needs a dialog at a higher level. This is accomplished by having TEIRESIAS take care of the "details" and having the user supply only domain-specific information.

The second global goal—building a large knowledge base—brings with it the problem of complexity. There is a well-known phenomenon in all programs (but most obvious in large systems) referred to as the "1 + epsilon bug" phenomenon: A change introduced to fix a known bug may result, on the average, in the creation of *more than* one new bug. The system may thus be inherently unstable, since any attempt to repair a problem may introduce more problems than it repairs.

Complexity arises in our case primarily because of size: the size of the performance program's knowledge base and the wealth of detail involved in fully describing its knowledge representations. There is, for example, a large number of different data types, each with its own structural organization, its own set of interrelations with other data types, and its own set of requirements for integration into the program. There is also a large number of instances of each data type. Since modifications to a data type design have to be carried out on all of its instances, the efficient retrieval and processing of this set is another problem that involves the management of large numbers of structures.

In order to make the acquisition of new conceptual primitives possible in the context of our original goals, then, we have to provide the user with a system that carries on a high-level dialog and that keeps track of the numerous details of data structure implementation. The first of these design requirements will insure that the system is comprehensible to the user; the second will insure that new bugs are not inadvertently created while fixing old ones.

Note that this emphasis on the necessity of avoiding bugs during the process of acquiring new primitives is really no different from the view presented earlier in discussing explanation and rule acquisition. When dealing with rules, we noted that the large amount of knowledge required for high performance makes shortcomings in the knowledge base inevitable, and we emphasized the benefits of using these shortcomings to provide the context and focus for knowledge acquisition. We will similarly use shortcomings in the knowledge base to provide the context for the acquisition of new conceptual primitives.

In both cases, we must avoid introducing errors during the process of knowledge acquisition. This is of greater concern during acquisition of new conceptual primitives for reasons arising out of the nature of the errors encountered and the objects involved.

As noted earlier, conceptual primitives are each individually far more complex in their structure than rules. In addition, there is only a single rule format, while there are many different conceptual primitive structures. There is, thus, far greater opportunity for error.

In addition, where the rules are designed to be fundamentally independent, data structures used to represent the conceptual primitives are often interrelated in subtle ways and the character of the errors produced is very different. The independence of rules means that their interaction during a consultation can be understood by a simple model in which the contribution of each rule is considered individually. This is manifestly untrue of complex data structures, where errors in format can result in subtle interactions.

Finally, there is the issue of the conceptual level of the objects being manipulated, that is, their likely familiarity to the expert. It seems reasonable to assume that domain-specific rules will deal with knowledge sufficiently familiar to the expert that he will be able to understand the program in these terms. We do not assume that he is familiar enough with data structures and representations to be able to manipulate or debug them.

In summary, recall the distinction drawn in chapter 1 between expertise and formalism. Because rules are designed to have a sharply constrained degree of interaction and to be comprehensible to the expert, errors in the knowledge base may properly be considered shortcomings of expertise. The complex interrelations of data structures used to represent conceptual primitives and the subtle nature of the bugs they produce puts them in the domain of errors of formalism. In dealing with the creation of new conceptual primitives, therefore, strong emphasis is placed on techniques that assure a high degree of integrity.

6–5   THE SOLUTION

In the simplest terms, the solution we suggest is to give the system a store of knowledge about its representations and the capability to use this knowledge as a basis for the construction and management of them.

In more detail: We view every knowledge representation in the system as an extended data type. Explicit descriptions of each data type are written, descriptions that include all the information about structure and interrelations that was noted earlier as often being widely scattered. Next, we devise a language in which all of this information can be put in machine-comprehensible terms and write the descriptions in those terms, making this store of information available to the system. Finally, we design an interpreter for the language so that the system can use its new knowledge to keep track of the details of data structure construction and maintenance. This is, of course, easy to say but somewhat harder to do. Some difficult questions arise:

> What knowledge about its representations does a system require in order to allow it to do a range of nontrivial management tasks? How should this knowledge be organized? How should it be represented? How can it be used?

All these issues are dealt with below. We demonstrate, for instance, that the relevant knowledge includes information about the structure and interrelations of representations and show that it can be used as the basis for the interactive transfer of domain-specific expertise.

The main task here, then, is the description and use of knowledge about representations. To accomplish this, we use a *data structure schema*, a device that provides a framework and language in which representations can be specified. The framework, like most, carries its own perspective on its domain. One point it emphasizes strongly is the detailed specification of many kinds of information about representations. It attempts to make this specification task easier by providing an organization for the information and a relatively high-level vocabulary for its expression.

Note that the schemata form the second major example of meta-level knowledge. While a particular data structure may be used to represent an object in the domain, the schemata (as descriptions of representations) are meta-level objects.

6–6   KEY IDEAS: COMMENTS

To provide some background for understanding the examples of system performance that follow, we present below some brief comments on several of the ideas listed in Section 6–2.

6–6.1 Vocabulary

In the discussion that follows, the terms *data structure, extended data type,* and *representation* will be used interchangeably. Equating the first two implies extending the idea of data types to cover every data structure in a system. The utility of this view appears to be widely accepted and, in the case at hand, will influence our approach to determining what information about data structures is relevant and how that information should be organized.

The equivalence of the last two suggests our perspective on the design and implementation of knowledge representations. These two tasks—design and implementation—are typically decoupled, and, indeed, the desirability of transparency of implementation has been stressed from many quarters (*e.g.,* [Bachman75], [Balzer67], [Liskov74]). But what might we learn by considering them simultaneously? That is, what can we learn about representation design by considering issues that arise at the level of implementation and technical detail? Conversely, what can we learn about the organization or design of data types by viewing them as knowledge representations? We examine these questions below.

6–6.2 Schemata as Knowledge Representation Descriptions

As noted, the schemata are the primary vehicle for describing representations. They were developed as a generalization of the concept of record structures and strongly resemble them in both organization and use. Many of the operations with the schemata can be seen in terms of variations on the task of creating a new instance of a record-like structure. We will see that these operations proceed in a mixed-initiative mode: The need to add a new data structure is made evident by an action on the part of the user; TEIRESIAS then takes over, retrieving the appropriate schema and using it to guide the rest of the interaction.

The schemata take from records the concept of structure description, the separation of representation from implementation, and the fundamental record creation operation. Records provide a simple language for describing data structures, and this was used as the basis for the structure syntax in the schemata. Records also isolate conceptual structures from details of implementation. Thus, code may uniformly refer to field F of record R despite changes in the way the record is actually stored. Finally, the operation of creating a new instance of a record was used as the fundamental paradigm for this part of the knowledge acquisition task. At the global level, much that happens in this chapter can be viewed in terms of creating instances from one or more kinds of records.

6–6.2.1 Extensions—Data Structure Syntax

The basic idea of a record-like descriptor was then extended to make possible the capabilities we require. The structure syntax was extended by adopting some of the conventions of BNF, so that a certain variability could be described. For instance, a schema can indicate that a structure has a *minimum of 1, a maximum of 4, and typically 2* components of a given form.[2]

6-6.6.2   Extensions—Data Structure Interrelationships

In addition, we introduced a syntax of data structure interrelations. As noted above, data structures in a program are not typically independent and the addition of a new instance of some data type to the system often requires extensive bookkeeping to maintain the existing interdependencies.

This problem has been considered previously, primarily with techniques oriented around demon-like mechanisms (*e.g.*, the demons in QA4 [Rulifson72]). The approach taken here differs in several respects. While, as in previous approaches, demon-like mechanisms were employed to help model the domain, they will also be used extensively at the level of data structures, as a tool to aid in management of the knowledge base. They become an important component of our representation methodology and will be seen to have an influence on the organization of knowledge in the system.

Previous uses of demons have also involved the full power of the parent programming language, as in QA4 or PLANNER, where the body of a demon can be an arbitrary computation. For reasons which will become clear later, significant effort was put into avoiding this approach. We have instead developed a small syntax of interrelationships that expresses the relevant facts in a straightforward form.

The fundamental point here is simple enough: Whatever the interrelationships, they should be made explicit. All too often, the interdependencies of internal data structures are left either as folklore or, at best, mentioned briefly in documentation. In line with the major themes of this work, we want to make this knowledge explicit and accessible to the system itself. The interrelationship syntax was the tool employed to do this.

6-6.3   A "Totally Typed" Language

The basic approach, then, was to view the representation primitives as extended data types in a high-level language, use an augmented record-like structure to describe each of them, and then make those structures available for reference by the system itself. The next step was to apply this exhaustively and uniformly to every object in the system. That is, the "language" should be "totally typed," and every object in the system should be an instance of some schema. One reason for this is data base integrity. A totally typed language makes possible exhaustive type checking and one level of knowledge base integrity. In addition, since many of the extended data types correspond to domain-specific objects, the knowledge acquisition dialog can be made to appear to the expert to be phrased in terms of objects in the domain, while to the system it is a straightforward manipulation of data structures. It thus helps bridge the gap in perspectives. Finally, since we were concerned with the large amount of knowledge about representations

---

[2] This variability is what led to calling them *schemata*, rather than declarations or records, since the latter typically describe structures with fixed formats.

that is typically left implicit, applying the schema idea to every object in the system offered some level of assurance that we had made explicit some significant fraction of this information.

Exhaustive application of the schema idea presents several implications. First, it means that even the components from which a schema is built should also be instances of some (other) schema, and we will see that this is true. Second, since we claim both that the schemata should be a part of the system and that every object in the system should be an instance of some schema, then the schemata themselves should be an instance of something. In more familiar terms, *if the structure declarations are to be objects in the program, and if everything is to be a data type of some sort, then the declarations themselves must be a data type.* This was done. There is a "schema-schema," which specifies the structure of a schema, and all schemata are instances of it.

Since the schema-schema indicates the structure of a schema, it can be used to guide the creation of new data types. This offers the same benefits as before, of a certain level of integrity and a relatively "high- level" dialog. Note that it deals, however, with the fairly sophisticated task of specifying a new data structure.

While the recursive application of the schema idea was motivated initially by purely utilitarian considerations, it led to a useful uniformity in TEIRESIAS: There is a single process by which both the schema-schema can be instantiated to create a new schema (a new knowledge representation) and by which a schema can be instantiated to create a new instance of an existing knowledge representation. This not only made possible bootstrapping the system (described later in this chapter) but also supplied much of the generality of the approach. Part of Figure 4–1 has been reproduced below to illustrate this multi-level organization.

6–6.4 Knowledge Base Integrity

Avoiding bugs when manipulating data structures is also known as "assuring the integrity of the data base" and has been investigated within the framework of several organizational paradigms (see, *e.g.*, [McLeod76] and [Eswarn75]). Previous efforts have emphasized the utility of extensive type checking for extended data types and have studied aspects of integrity specific to a particular paradigm. We use many of these same techniques here, but focus on the problem of interrelationships between data structures in general and concentrate on dealing with the effects of additions on the integrity of the knowledge base.

While it has not been possible to devise ways of assuring the total integrity of the knowledge base, the capabilities of our system can be broadly classified by considering three error sources. First, the system can assure a form of completeness, by making sure both that the expert is reminded to supply every necessary component of a structure and that all other appropriate structures are informed of the newly added item ("informed" is elaborated below). Second, it can assure "syntactic" integrity. There is complete type checking, and no interaction with the expert will result in incorrect data types in the knowledge base.

Finally, it can assure a certain level of "semantic" integrity. The semantics of any individual data structure will be properly maintained, so that, for instance, a

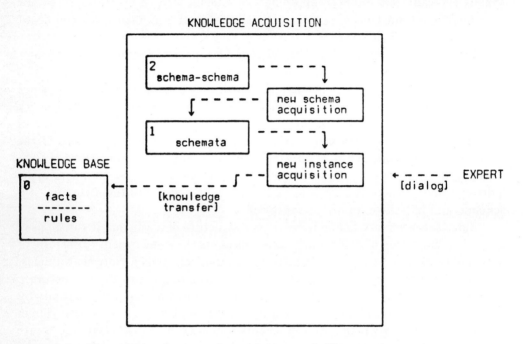

Figure 6-1   The multi-level process of acquiring new primitives.

new attribute will be given all the descriptors appropriate to it, in the correct form. It can also assure some semantic consistency in two or more related structures, but this is as yet incomplete, since some inconsistencies can arise that require more knowledge about the domain than is currently available. For instance, in the medical domain, while describing a new organism a user might indicate that it is an "acid-fast coccus" ("acid-fast" describes a response to a kind of stain) when, in fact, the combination is biologically meaningless. Each individual answer is correct but the combination is inconsistent for reasons that are not easily represented.

6–6.5   Summary

The schemata and their associated structures provide a language and framework in which representations can be specified. It should be emphasized that all of the work reported here was at the level of the design and the implementation of this language and framework in TEIRESIAS. Some of the representations that the language can describe are those used in the current performance program (MYCIN); later sections of this chapter examine the limits of its expressive power. Within those limits, the system deals with the general issue of the design and specification of representations. Nothing here is specific to medicine or to the attribute-object-value representations that we will see employed. Within the range of representations that our framework permits, the system is domain independent and has a degree of representation independence as well. This generality results from the isolation and stratification of the three different levels of knowledge in the system, discussed in detail in Section 6–13.

6–7 TRACE OF SYSTEM PERFORMANCE: ACQUIRING NEW VALUES

Two examples—the acquisition of new values for organism identity and for culture site—will provide an overview of TEIRESIAS's capabilities. This demonstration uses a version of the performance program with a very simple knowledge base, as it might appear in an early stage of development when it contains only a few attributes and a few values for each.

Some preliminary comments should be made about these examples. First, since we will be dealing with some complex data structures from a specific performance program, much of what happens in the trace derives from implementation conventions that are part of that program. Since TEIRESIAS's acquisition process has to be thorough, it takes care of all of them. The important point to note is not what these conventions are but that TEIRESIAS can deal with them.

Second, the dialogs are at times deceptively simple. This is in part some measure of success, since we have managed to delegate much of the detail to TEIRESIAS, which takes care of it quietly in the background. To see this point most clearly, consider after reviewing the traces the amount of work that would be needed to do the same tasks by hand: There are a number of details of system construction that would have to be memorized and a significant amount of effort expended to create and edit the structures by hand. Much more work would be involved if it were necessary to teach the expert (who may never have programmed before) how to do the same things. TEIRESIAS attends to the details, does most of the work, and maintains a relatively high-level dialog.

6–7.1 Acquisition of a New Organism Identity

The first example shows how TEIRESIAS guides the process of describing a new kind of organism. It demonstrates primarily the ability of the schemata to keep track of all the structural details in a data structure. It also illustrates some of the human engineering features of the system.

> { *The expert is in the middle of a normal rule acquisition sequence when he mentions an organism name that the system has never encountered before.* }

```
The new rule will be called RULE384
    If 1 - THE SITE OF THE CULTURE IS BLOOD
       2 - THE PORTAL OF ENTRY OF THE ORGANISM IS THE
URINARY TRACT
       3 - THE PATIENT HAS NOT HAD A GENITO-URINARY
MANIPULATIVE PROCEDURE
       4 - CYSTITIS IS NOT A PROBLEM FOR WHICH THE
```

PATIENT HAS BEEN TREATED
         5 –
Then
         1 – THE ORGANISM IS LIKELY (.4) TO BE AN E.COLI
Sorry, but I don't understand
      THE ORGANISM IS LIKELY (.4) TO BE AN E.COLI
because these words are unknown: E.COLI

{TEIRESIAS *finds it cannot generate any interpretations of the text, so it reprints the original line and specifies where the trouble is. This makes it possible for the expert to figure out what it is that is new to the system.* }

Would you care to try rephrasing that?
++* Y
(Please use *'s to mark what you think might be a new attribute
  or a new value of a attribute.)
         1 –   THE ORGANISM IS LIKELY (.4) TO BE AN * E.COLI *

{*While the language in this example is very simple, there are more complex cases where it would be quite hard to decide from the context what sort of new item the expert had in mind. To avoid the necessity for more sophisticated natural language handling, he is asked to mark off the new word or phrase with asterisks...* }

It looks as though
         E.COLI
refers to a new value of an attribute, correct?
++* Y
  ... is it a new value of the identity of a organism?
++* Y

{*and with the new item clearly marked, the system can then do some very simple pattern matching to decide what's going on.* }

Now please tell me a few things about it...

{TEIRESIAS *retrieves the schema for an organism identity and "reads" it to find out what it needs to know about any organism.* }

Please give the full, formal name for ''E.COLI''
++* ESCHERICEA COLI
= ESCHERICEA-COLI

{Many long medical terms have abbreviations, so the system requests the formal name first. (Hyphens are inserted to make a single identifier out of it.) }

Now please give all synonyms or abbreviations for ESCHERICEA-
COLI which you would like the system to accept:
[type an empty line when done]
++* E.COLI
++**

{The system requests synonyms and abbreviations so that they can be used in the future. The first of them is then used through the rest of the dialogue. }

Please give a short description of E.COLI as a identity of a
organism.
++* ?
[e.g., for PSEUDOMONAS, the description is ''AN ORGANISM
 COMMONLY FOUND IN THE HOSPITAL, QUITE OFTEN A SOURCE OF
 SECONDARY INFECTIONS IN PATIENTS WHOSE IMMUNE RESPONSE IS
 WEAKENED'']
[type an empty line when done]
++* NORMAL FLORA IN THE LOWER INTESTINE, BUT A
++* CAUSE OF SEPTICEMIA WHEN TRANSMITTED TO THE
++* BLOOD STREAM
++**

{Two useful capabilities are displayed here. First, the expert is asked to describe every structure he creates, providing a form of on-line documentation for all data structures. Since the documentation is acquired incrementally along with the rest of the knowledge base, the task is much easier than attempting to document an entire system at once.

Second, TEIRESIAS can generate sample answers for any of its questions. In some previous session, the expert had evidently taught the system about pseudomonas. Since each schema has an indication of all of the instances that were created from it, the system picks one of those instances and displays the answer to this question for that instance. }

What is the aerobicity of a E.COLI?
The answer should be in the form of 1 or more of the
following—
          <aerobicity> <certainty factor>
[Type 1 set to a line, then an empty line when done.]
++* FACULTATIVE .8
++* AEROBIC .2

++**

{*Each of the questions from the system is prompted by the attempt to fill in some component of the data structure being built, according to the representation conventions indicated by the schema. One of those conventions indicates that aerobicity, gramstain, and morphology are stored as part of an organism. The schema also indicates the format for each piece of substructure, and this is displayed as instructions to the user.* }

```
What is the gramstain of a E.COLI?
The answer should be in the form of a
        <gramstain>
[Type 1 set to a line, then an empty line when done.]
++* ROD
   Sorry, but the following are invalid -
      ROD is not a recognized <gramstain>
   Please answer again [use the same answer if you really
   meant it.]
++* GRAMNEG
++**
```

{*The formatting information also allows a check on the validity of each answer, to insure that all information added to the knowledge base is properly structured. This time the expert made a mistake. It can happen, however, that the answer is correct but the performance program simply hasn't heard of it yet. Early in its "education," the knowledge base may, for instance, not yet have information about all the gramstain values, and this might become evident in the course of teaching it about a new organism. Examples of this are found in additional traces later in this chapter, which demonstrate that* TEIRESIAS *sets up new subtopics as required.* }

```
What is the morphology of a E.COLI?
The answer should be in the form a
        <morphology>
[Type 1 set to a line, then an empty line when done.]
++* ROD
++**
[Adding E.COLI to ORGANISMS]
```

{*In addition to creating the new structure, it's necessary to add it to an internal list called* ORGANISMS. *The message is printed simply to indicate that the proper step has been taken.* }

```
Ok, done with E.COLI now...
Back to the rule.
```

This may take a few moments.

{*Acquiring the rule then can continue as before.*}

6–7.2   Acquisition of a New Culture Site

Having taught the performance program about e.coli, the expert might later start adding rules about the urinary tract and for the first time mention urine as a culture site. The next example shows how this would proceed and demonstrates TEIRESIAS's handling of a fairly complex set of data structure interrelationships.

```
The new rule will be called RULE384
    If 1 - THERE IS NO HISTORY OF PYELONEPHRITIS
       2 - THE ORGANISM WAS CULTURED FROM THE URINE
       3 - THERE IS NO HISTORY OF RECURRENT UTI'S
       4 -
    Then
       1 - THE ORGANISM IS LIKELY (.3) TO BE E.COLI
Sorry, but I don't understand
    THE ORGANISM WAS CULTURED FROM THE URINE
because these words are unknown:   URINE
Would you care to try rephrasing that?
++* Y
    (Please use *'s to mark what you think might be a new
     attribute or a new value of an attribute)
          3 - THE SITE OF THE CULTURE IS * URINE *
It looks as though
       URINE
refers to a new value of an attribute, correct?
++* Y
... is it a new value of the site of a culture?
++* Y
    Now tell me a few things about it...
    Please give the full, formal name for ''URINE''
    ++* URINE
    Now please give all synonyms or abbreviations for URINE
    which you would like the system to accept:
    [type an empty line when done]
    ++**
    Please give a short description of URINE as a culture site.
    [type an empty line when done]
    ++* THERE ARE SEVERAL METHODS OF OBTAINING URINE
    ++* SPECIMENS, SOME MORE LIKELY TO PRODUCE STERILE
    ++* RESULTS. BECAUSE OF THE LARGE POSSIBILITY OF
```

++* CONTAMINATION, CULTURES ARE NOT CONSIDERED
++* SIGNIFICANT UNLESS COLONY COUNT IS 100,000 OR
++* MORE.
++**
Should this new item be added to—
    1 - those sites that are normally sterile, or
    2 - those sites that are normally nonsterile, or
    3 - those sites from which the sterility of cultures
  depends upon the method of collection
Select one of the above
++* 3
[Adding URINE to OTHERSITES]

> {Here we begin to encounter the interactions with other data structures. The first problem is to find out whether the site is to be considered sterile, nonsterile, or indeterminant, so that it can then be added to the proper internal collection of sites. }

[Adding URINE to ALLSITES]

> {The schema also indicates that there is an internal list (called ALLSITES) that contains all the sites. The system adds the new site to it without having to ask. }

Please indicate the infections which can occur at the
site: URINE. The answer should be in the form of 0 or
more of the following—
        <an infection name>
[Type 1 set to a line, then an empty line when done.]
++* ACUTE-PYELONEPHRITIS
++* PYELITIS
++* URETHRITIS
++* CYSTITIS
++**

> {A third data structure keeps track of which infections occur at which sites. }

Should this new item be added to —
      — those sites for which a positive culture implies a
  specific infection .
++* N

> {A fourth contains the list of all sites for which a positive culture implies a specific infection. }

Please indicate the methods of collection generally
associated with a culture taken from the URINE, and the
likelihood that the culture will be sterile.
The answer should be in the form of 0 or more of the
following—
     <the method of collection of a culture> <certainty factor>
[Type 1 set to a line, then an empty line when done.]
++* VOIDED .7
++* FOLEY-CATH-ASPIRATION 1.0
++* FOLEY-BAG-DRAINAGE .9
++* URETERAL 1.0
++**

{ *The fifth keeps track of the various ways samples can be collected at different
sites and notes their likely sterility.* }

What are the likely pathogens to be found at the site: URINE?
The answer should be in the form of 0 or more of the
following—
     <identity of an organism> <certainty factor>
[Type 1 set to a line, then an empty line when done.]
++* E.COLI .3
++* PSEUDOMONAS .2
++* ENTEROCOCCUS .2
++* PROTEUS .2
++* KLEBSIELLA .1
++**

{ *And the last keeps track of which organisms are typically found at specific
sites. Note that all of this information is required for every new site that is
added to the system.* }

Ok, done with URINE now...
Back to the rule.

{ *Having finished with the new site,* TEIRESIAS *returns to parsing the new
rule.* }

This may take a few moments.

6–8 KNOWLEDGE ABOUT REPRESENTATIONS: ORGANIZATION

We have emphasized earlier that performance of the acquisition system (TEIRE-
SIAS) depends on an extensive store of knowledge about the representations used

by the performance program (MYCIN). There are several kinds of information involved (Figure 6–2 below). First, a generalization hierarchy links the schemata together, indicating what categories of data structures exist in the system and the relationships between them. Second, there are the individual schemata, each indicating the structure and interrelationships of a single type of data structure. Finally, there are the "slotnames" (and associated structures) from which the schemata are built; these offer knowledge about specific conventions at the programming-language level. Each of these supplies a different sort of information; together they compose an extensive body of knowledge about the structure and organization of the representations.

```
schema hierarchy     — indicates categories of representations and
                         interrelations
individual schema  — describes structure of a single representation
slotnames            — the schema building blocks, describe implementation
                         conventions
```

Figure 6–2   Types of knowledge about representations.

6–8.1   The Schema Hierarchy

The schemata are organized into a generalization hierarchy that has several useful properties. Part of the hierarchy for the current performance program is shown in the figure below.[3]

KSTRUCT–SCHEMA (knowledge structure) simply provides a root for the network; its schema is empty. Below it are the schemata for value and attribute, and each of these is further subdivided into more specific schemata. The right branch of the network illustrates the fact that a schema can have more than one parent.

The major contribution of the hierarchy is as an organizing mechanism that offers a convenient overview of all the representations in the system. It also indicates their global organization. The right branch above, for instance, indicates that there are two different breakdowns of the set of attributes: one containing four categories,[4] the other containing three categories.[5] As will be illustrated further on, acquisition of a new instance of a conceptual primitive is, in part, a

---

[3] The schemata for *blank, advice, slotname,* and the remainder of the primitives in Section 2–4.4 each form a branch of the network one level below KSTRUCT–SCHEMA. They are omitted here for simplicity.

[4] The attributes can be classified according to which object they are an attribute of (*e.g.*, patient, infection, culture, organism).

[5] They can also be broken down into "single-valued," "multiple-valued," and "true/false" types. Single-valued attributes can have only one value known with certainty (*e.g.*, an organism can have only a single identity that has a CF of 1.0), while multiple-valued attributes can have more than one (*e.g.*, there may be more than one drug to which the patient is definitely allergic). The final category contains attributes that ask questions answered by "yes" or "no" (*e.g.*, "Did the organism grow in the aerobic bottle?").

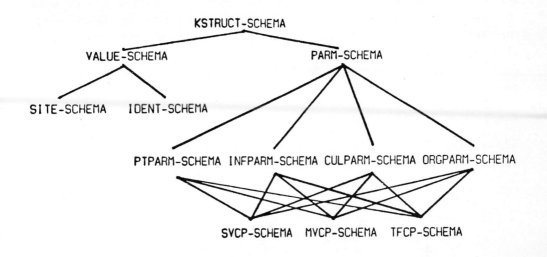

Figure 6-3   Part of the schema hierarchy.

process of descent through this hierarchy, so it provides a useful structuring of the acquisition dialog.

Since the acquisition of new types of conceptual primitives is viewed as a process of adding new branches to this network, it is important that network growth be reasonably smooth and convenient. Later sections will demonstrate that it does, in fact, arise as a natural part of enlarging the knowledge base and that this new growth is automatically reflected afterward in future dialogs.

In the network, extensive use is made of the concept of inheritance of properties. The left branch above, for instance, indicates that culture site and organism identity are more specific categories of the data type VALUE. All of the characteristics that site and identity have in common as VALUEs are stored in the VALUE—SCHEMA. Thus the structure description part of the VALUE—SCHEMA (shown in the next section) describes the structural components that are common to all VALUEs. The network then branches at this point because an organism identity is a different type of data structure than a culture site, and differs in some details of structure. As the next section illustrates, this inheritance of properties is used for all the different types of information stored in the schema.

This hierarchical distribution of information also offers some handle on the issue of the level of abstraction at which data types are described, since the hierarchy stores at each level only those details relevant to that particular level.[6]

While it is not evident from the segment of the schema network shown above, functions constitute a branch of the network. Included there, for instance, are the predicate functions used in rules. We are thus viewing functions as another

_____

6 The schema hierarchy can also be seen as a data structure version of the sort of hierarchy often represented with the *class* construct in SIMULA [Dahl70].

type of data structure. Restated in LISP terms, a function is "just" another data structure that happens to have an item on its property list called EXPR (where the definition is stored). As will become clear, it is at times useful to take this view, but it is not in any sense exclusive. Functions will be viewed as both data structures and procedures, depending on which is the most relevant at the moment.

6–8.2　Schema Organization

The schemata are the second of the three kinds of knowledge about representations noted in Figure 6–2. Each contains several different types of information:

(a)　The structure of its instances,
(b)　interrelationships with other data structures,
(c)　a pointer to all current instances,
(d)　inter-schema organizational information, and
(e)　bookkeeping information.

Figure 6–4 shows the schema for the value of an attribute and the schema for the identity of an organism. In both, information corresponding to each of the categories listed above is grouped together (the numbers at the right are for reference only).

Note that, since the VALUE–SCHEMA is the parent of the IDENT–SCHEMA in the hierarchy, information in the former need not be reproduced in the latter. Hence the complete specification for an organism identity is given by considering information in both schemata.

Note also that the schema use what is known as an "item-centered" factorization and indexing of knowledge. That is, the items dealt with (IDENTities, VALUEs, etc.) are used as the main indexing points for the body of knowledge about representations, and all information about a particular item is associated directly with that item. The advantage of this approach lies in making possible a strongly modular system in which it is relatively easy to organize and represent a large body of knowledge. The twenty-five or so schemata that make up that body of knowledge encode a significant amount of information about the representation conventions of a large and complex program. They were reasonably easy to construct because the individual representations are "mostly independent" (*i.e.*, they have only a few, well-specified kinds of interactions) and because the item-centered organization encourages taking advantage of that modularity.

6–8.2.1　Instance Structure

The part of the schema that describes the structure of its instances (lines 1–7, 15–20) is the element that corresponds most closely to an ordinary record descriptor. The current implementation takes a very simple view of LISP data structures. It assumes that they are composed of a print name, a value, and a property list, with the usual conventions for each: The print name is a single identifier by which the object is named, the value is an atom or list structure, and the property list is composed of property-value pairs. The first three items in the first schema above deal with each of these in turn.

Each item is expressed as a triple of the form:

<slotname> <blank> <advice>

(We use the term "slot" from the work on frames [Minsky74] since the concept is similar, but the schemata grew out of, and are fundamentally an extension of, the idea of a record structure.) For the print name of any value of an attribute, then, the *slotname* is PNTNAME, the *blank* is ATOM, and the *advice* is ASKIT.[7]

The *slotname* labels the "kind" of thing that fills the *blank* and provides access to other information that aids in the knowledge transfer process. Slotnames are the conceptual primitives around which representation-specific and representation-independent knowledge in the system is organized. All of the semantics of a print name, for instance, are contained in the PNTNAME slot and the structures associated with it (described in Section 6–8.3).

The *blank* specifies the exact format of the information required. A translated form of it is printed out when requesting information from the expert and is then used to parse his response and insure its syntactic validity. The blank has a simple syntax but can express a range of structures. The term KLEENE, for instance, is taken from the Kleene star and implies a repetition of the form within the angle brackets. The parenthesized numbers that follow it indicate the typical, minimum, and maximum number of occurrences of the form. The appearance of a term of the form <datatype>-INST indicates some instance of the <datatype>-SCHEMA. Thus,

(KLEENE (1 1 2) <(AIR-INST CF-INST)>)

from the identity schema above indicates that the aerobicity of an organism is described by 1 or 2 lists of the form (<aerobicity> <certainty-factor>).

The *advice* suggests how to find the information. Various sorts of information are employed in the course of acquiring a new concept from the expert. Some of it is domain specific (*e.g.*, the gramstain of a new organism) and clearly must be supplied by the expert. Other parts of it are purely representation specific. These should be supplied by the system itself, not only because they deal with information that the system already has (and therefore should not have to ask), but because the expert is assumed to know nothing about programming. Even a trivial question concerning internal data structure management would thus appear incomprehensible to him. The *advice* provides a way of expressing instructions to the system on where to find the information it needs. There are five such instructions that can be given.

---

[7] All symbols in the schemata are purely tokens. They were chosen to be mnemonic, but no significance is attached to any particular name, and nothing depends on the use of the particular set of names chosen.

```
VALUE-SCHEMA
    PNTNAME      (ATOM       ASKIT)                                              [1
    VAL          (PNTNAME    INSLOT)                                             [2
    PLIST        [(INSTOF  (VALUE-SCHEMA                     GIVENIT)            [3
                  DESCR    (STRING                           ASKIT)             [4
                  AUTHOR   (ATOM                             FINDIT)            [5
                  DATE     (INTEGER                          CREATEIT))         [6
                 CREATEIT]                                                       [7


    STRAN        the value of a clinical parameter                              [8
    FATHER       (KSTRUCT-SCHEMA)                                               [9
    OFFSPRING    (IDENT-SCHEMA  SITE-SCHEMA)                                     [10


    DESCR        the VALUE-SCHEMA describes the format for a value of a clinical parameter   [11
    AUTHOR       DAVIS                                                          [12
    DATE         1115'                                                          [13
    INSTOF       (SCHEMA-SCHEMA)                                                [14




IDENT-SCHEMA
    PLIST        [(INSTOF  (IDENT-SCHEMA                     GIVENIT)           [15
                  SYNONYM  ((KLEENE (1 0) < ATOM >)          ASKIT)             [16
                  AIR      ((KLEENE (1 1 2) <(AIR-INST CF-INST)> ) ASKIT)      [17
                  GRAM     (GRAM-INST                        ASKIT)             [18
                  MORPH    (MORPH-INST                       ASKIT)             [19
                 CREATEIT]                                                      [20


    UPDATES      ((ADDTO (AND* ORGANISMS)))                                     [21


    INSTANCES    (ACINETOBACTER ACTINOMYCETES AEROMONAS  ...  XANTHOMONAS YERSINA)   [22


    STRAN        the identity of an organism                                    [23
    FATHER       (VALUE-SCHEMA)                                                 [24
    OFFSPRING    NIL                                                            [25


    DESCR        the IDENT-SCHEMA describes the format for an organism           [26
    AUTHOR       DAVIS                                                          [27
    DATE         1115                                                          [28
    INSTOF       (SCHEMA-SCHEMA)                                                [29
```

Figure 6–4   Two schemata.

ASKIT	ask the expert
CREATEIT	manufacture the answer
FINDIT	the answer is available internally, retrieve it
GIVENIT	use the contents of the blank as is (like QUOTE in LISP)
INSLOT	use the contents of the slot indicated

The first triple in Figure 6–4 (line 1) indicates then that the print name is an atom and that it should be requested from the expert. The second (line 2) indicates that the organism name should evaluate to its print name, and the third (lines 3 - 7) indicates the form of the property list. Note that the *blank* for the last of these consists of, in turn, a set of *slotname-blank-advice* triples describing the property list.

6–8.2.2 Interrelationships

A second main function of the schema is to provide a record of the interrelationships (line 21) of data structures. The RELATIONS slot contains this information, expressed in a simple language for describing data structure relationships. In BNF terms, it looks like:

```
<update>     =  ( <command> ( <switch> <structure>+)+)
<command>    =  ADDTO | EDITFN
<switch>     =  AND* | OR*  | XOR* | (<switch> <structure>+)
<structure> =  <any data structure or function name>
```

(The superscript "+" means "one or more.") ADDTO indicates that some other structure in the system should be told about the new instance, while EDITFN indicates that some function may need to be edited as a result of creating the new instance. The three switches indicate that the action specified by <command> should be taken on all (AND*), 1 or more (OR*), or exactly 1 (XOR*) of the structures that follow. In the case of a new organism, the update is a simple one, and its name is added to the structure called ORGANISMS.

The recursive definition allows construction of conditional expressions, as in the RELATIONS information in the schema for a culture site:

```
((ADDTO (XOR* STERILESITES NONSTERILESITES OTHERSITES))
 (ADDTO (AND* ALLSITES SITE-INFECT))
 (ADDTO (OR*  PATHOGNOMONIC-SITES))
 (ADDTO ((OR* NONSTERILESITES OTHERSITES) PATH-FLORA))
 (ADDTO ((AND* OTHERSITES) METHOD))))
```

Here, the first three tasks are straightforward, but the fourth line indicates that if the site is either nonsterile or indeterminant then it should be added to the structure called PATH—FLORA. The last line indicates that all indeterminant sites should be added to the structure called METHOD.

The key point here is to provide the system architect with a way of making explicit all of the data structure interrelationships upon which his design depends. The approach we use differs slightly from the one more typically taken, which relies on a demon-like mechanism that uses the full power of the underlying programming language. We have avoided the use of an arbitrary body of code and emphasized instead the use of a task-specific high-level language.

This formalization of knowledge about data structure interrelationships has several useful applications. First, since the domain expert cannot, in general, be expected to know about such representation conventions, expressing them in machine-accessible form makes it possible for TEIRESIAS to take over the task of maintaining them. Second, having TEIRESIAS attend to them insures a level of knowledge base integrity without making unreasonable demands on the expert. Finally, it keeps knowledge in the system accessible since the RELATIONS make explicit the sort of knowledge that is often left implicit, or which is embedded in code and hence is inaccessible. There are several advantages to this accessibility of knowledge. For example, by adding to TEIRESIAS a simple analyzer that could "read" the RELATIONS, a programmer could ask questions like *What else in the system will be affected if I add a new instance of this data structure?* or *What are all the other structures that are related to this one?* This would be a useful form of on-line documentation.[8]

There are additional advantages that will become apparent in Section 6–9.1.2, which describes how the updating is actually performed.

6–8.2.3 Current Instances

Each schema keeps track of all of its current instances (line 22), primarily for use in knowledge base maintenance. If it becomes necessary to make changes to the design of a particular representation, for instance, we want to be sure that all instances of it are modified appropriately. Keeping a list of all such instances is an obvious but very useful solution.

6–8.2.4 Organizational Information

FATHER indicates the (more general) ancestors of this schema in the hierarchy and OFFSPRING indicates its more specific offspring (lines 9-10). STRAN (line 8) is an English phrase indicating what sort of thing the schema describes and is used in communicating with the expert.

6–8.2.5 Bookkeeping Information

Much the same sort of bookkeeping information (lines 11-14) is maintained for each data structure as is kept for rules; DESCRiption, AUTHOR, and DATE are

---

[8] This is the data structure analogue for the facility of INTERLISP called MASTERSCOPE, which can analyze a set of function definitions and answer questions like *Who calls function F?*, *Which function binds X?*, etc.

the analogous items. INSTOF is the inverse of INSTANCES and indicates which schema was used to create this data structure.

Note that in the current example it is the organism schema itself that is being described by all of this bookkeeping information, and, as shown, it is an instance of the SCHEMA–SCHEMA (described in Section 6–11).

6–8.3   Slotnames and Slotexperts

The most detailed knowledge about representations is found in the slotnames and the structures associated with them. They deal with aspects of the representation that are at the level of programming-language constructs and conventions. The overall structure of a slotname is shown below.

```
<slotname>
----------
PROMPT   an English phrase used to request the information to fill the slot
TRANS    an English phrase used when displaying the information
         found in the slot
EXPERT   the name of the slotexpert
```

Figure 6–5   Information associated with a slotname.

The PROMPT and TRANS are part of the simple mechanism that makes the creation of a new data structure an interactive operation. The former is used to request information, the latter is used when it is necessary to display information that has previously been deposited in a slot. [9]

Associated with each slotname is a procedure called a *slotexpert* (or simply, *expert*). It serves primarily as a repository for useful pieces of knowledge concerning the implementation of the representations. For example, names of data structures have to be unique to avoid confusion or inadvertent mangling. Yet, in knowledge acquisition, new data structures are constantly being created and many of their names are chosen by the user. Part of the task carried out by the *expert* associated with the PNTNAME slot is to assure this uniqueness.

The slotexperts are organized around the different sorts of advice that can be used in a slot. Their general format is shown below. Since not all pieces of advice are meaningful for all slotexperts, in general not every slotexpert has an entry for every piece of advice.

```
(<slotexpert> [LAMBDA (BLANK ADVICE)
      (SELECTQ ADVICE
            (ASKIT      ...)
            (CREATEIT   ...)
            (FINDIT     ...)
            (INSLOT     ...)
```

---

[9] The idea of a PROMPT and TRANS were adapted from work in [Shortliffe76].

```
(GIVENIT   ...)      etc.])
```

Figure 6-6   The structure of a slotexpert, SELECTQ can be thought of as a *case* statement for symbolic computation. Thus the code above is equivalent to *if ADVICE = ASKIT then ...else if ADVICE = CREATEIT then ... etc.*

The individual chunks of code that make up the parts of the *experts* are the smallest units of knowledge organization in our framework. They embody knowledge about things like where to find or how to create the items needed to fill the *blank* for a particular slot. For instance, we noted that the *expert* associated with the PNTNAME slot insures the uniqueness of names that are supplied by the user. This routine would be found in the ASKIT section of the *expert*. Code in the CREATEIT section uses a number of heuristics that help to generate print names that are between 4 and 10 characters long and that are reasonably mnemonic. This is used when the system itself creates a name for a new internal data structure. [10]

Recall that we set out to describe representations in order to make possible the interactive acquisition of new conceptual primitives. The slotname and associated expert organize the knowledge needed and provide the English to make the operation interactive. The blank provides an indication of the format of the answers to questions and a check on their syntax. The advice allows the embedding of an additional sort of knowledge that makes the process function efficiently and "intelligently."

6-8.3.1   Slotnames as Data Structures, "Circularity" of the Formalism

While discussing the use of a typed language, it was noted that everything in the system should be an instance of some schema. One implication of this was that both the schemata and their components were themselves considered extended data types. Evidence of this can be seen in the slotnames. There is a SLOTNAME–SCHEMA that describes the structure of a slotname and makes it possible to acquire new slotnames interactively.

One of the consequences of this approach is a circularity in the definitions of the data types. For instance, DESCRiption is a slotname and, hence, an instance of the SLOTNAME–SCHEMA. But part of the structure of every slotname is a DESCRiption specifying what that slotname represents. Hence, there is a DESCRiption of DESCRiption. Similarly, in acquiring a new slotname, the system requests a prompt for it, using the prompt for PROMPT: *Please give me a short phrase which can be used to ask for the contents of this slot.* This circularity is a result of the systematic application of the use of the extended data types

---

[10] While the slotnames are currently globally unique (the SYNONYM slot in Figure 6-4, for instance, is presumed to mean the same thing for all types of data structures), this is not critical to the formalism. Slotnames could easily be made local to a given schema, and the schema name would become another index in the knowledge organization framework. Thus, instead of indexing the knowledge in the slotexperts by slotname and advice, we would index by schema name, slotname, and advice. The power and limitations of the framework would remain unchanged.

and makes possible the sort of bootstrapping behavior demonstrated later in this chapter.

6–9   KNOWLEDGE ABOUT REPRESENTATIONS: USE

Section 6–8 described the organization and content of the knowledge about representations embodied in the schemata and associated structures. This section describes how that information is used; in particular, the way it enables the expert to teach the system about new conceptual primitives. Other uses (*e.g.*, for information storage and retrieval) are also described.

6–9.1   Schema Function: Acquisition of New Instances

We begin at the point where some schema in the network has been selected as a starting point (Section 6–9.2 discusses how this decision is made). Since information is distributed through the schema network, the first step is to get to the root, keeping track of the path while ascending. TEIRESIAS "climbs" up the FATHER links, marking each schema along the way. [11] The system eventually arrives at the root, with all or some part of the path marked back down to a terminal schema. (Parts may be unmarked either because it jumped over non-unique parents or because the starting point chosen was not a terminal of the network. The latter case would arise if, for instance, TEIRESIAS knew only that the expert wanted to create a new kind of value but was not able to discover which type.)

The next step is to descend back down the network along the marked path, using each schema along the way as a further set of instructions for acquiring the new instance. If the process encounters a part of the path that is not marked, the expert's help is requested. This is done by displaying the English phrase (the STRAN) associated with each of the OFFSPRING of the current schema and asking the expert to choose the one which best describes the item being constructed.

At each node in the network the acquisition process is directed by a simple "schema interpreter" whose control structure consists of three basic operations:

(a)   Use the structure description part of the schema to guide the addition of new components to the instance,

(b)   attend to any updating according to the information specified in the RELATIONS, and

---

[11] If it encounters a schema that has multiple parents, it jumps directly to the network root. This is a sub-optimal solution; a better approach would have a more sophisticated treatment of the network. It might, for instance, be able to recognize the situation in which all the parents had a common "grandparent" and thus jump only two levels (over the ambiguous section), rather than straight to the root.

(c)   add the new item to the schema's list of instances. [12]

6–9.1.1   Adding to the Structure of the New Concept

The process of adding new components to the new instance involves filling in slots, as guided by the information provided in the *blank*. Computationally, the process involves sending the *blank* and *advice* as arguments to the appropriate slot expert: [13]

     (APPLY* (GETEXPERT <slotname>) <blank> <advice>)

The segment of code in the SLOTEXPERT associated with the *advice* then determines how to go about filling in the blank. For example, when that *advice* is ASKIT, the expert is consulted. As we have seen, this appears to the expert as a process of supplying information in a form specified by the system: TEIRESIAS first prints a "translated" version of the *blank* to guide the expert, then uses the same *blank* to parse his response.

     This approach makes possible a particularly simple form of "schema interpreter." For instance, the part of the interpreter that handles this addition of new substructure is just the single line of code shown above. The task of filling in the blank is thus handed off to the appropriate *expert*. The *expert*, in turn, hands it to the segment of code associated with the indicated piece of *advice*. That code may, in turn, request each part of the *blank* to supply a "translation" of itself for display to the user. Thus, rather than trying to write a clever interpreter that had a lot of information about each representation, we have instead written a simple interpreter and allow the representations themselves to supply the information.

     There are also several human engineering features available when the advice indicates that the information to fill the slot should be requested from the expert. We have seen the use of the *blank* in guiding the expert and in parsing his answer. There is also the ability to display a sample answer (in response to a "?") or all legal answers (in response to a "??"). All of these help to make the interaction relatively painless.

6–9.1.2   Attending to Data Structure Interrelations

The next step—dealing with necessary updates to other structures—relies on the information specified in the RELATIONS slot. The basic idea is to consider this information as a list of potential updating tasks to be performed whenever a new instance of the schema is acquired.

     Maintaining existing interdependencies of data structures in the face of additions to the system requires three kinds of information:

---

[12] For the sake of efficiency, only schemata at the leaves of the network keep track of instances. Each new item carries a record of its path through the network (in its INSTOF property); this allows disambiguation when a schema has more than one parent in the network.

[13] APPLY* applies its first argument to its remaining arguments. Thus, (APPLY* (QUOTE CONS) (QUOTE A) NIL) = (A) .

1   What other structures might need to be updated in response to the new addition?

2   If those other structures are not all independent, what interrelationships exist between them?

3   What effect should the new addition have on each structure?

As an example, consider the acquisition of the new culture site shown earlier. The first updating task encountered is the decision whether to add the new site to the collection of sterile, nonsterile, or indeterminant sites. We describe this by saying that the data type SITE is the "trigger" for an action that may need to be performed on one or more "targets." In these terms, the targets are the answers to question 1 above (other structures that may need to be updated), and the fact that the categories are mutually exclusive is the answer to question 2 (the constraints on the effects). Information needed to answer question 3 (the effect on each target) may come from two sources. First, the data type and organization of the target is always relevant. A partially ordered list, for example, will be updated one way, while a set will be updated in another. Second, the trigger may or may not carry relevant information. In the example above, it does not. Adding a new site to any one of the three categories requires no information about the site itself; the system need only know to which target it should be added. The approach used here is particularly well suited to this situation (in which the trigger does not determine the effect on the target) and takes advantage of it by minimizing the distribution of the required knowledge (this point will be clarified below).

The "language" of the RELATIONS is a syntax of data structure interrelationships and provides a way of expressing the answers to questions 1 and 2. For the current example, part of the RELATIONS of the SITE–SCHEMA is

(XOR* STERILESITES NONSTERILESITES OTHERSITES)

which indicates which structures are potentially affected and the constraint of mutual exclusion. The information for question 3 is supplied by updating functions (described below), which are included in some of the schemata.

One example of how the updating process works will make all of this clearer and illustrate the advantages it presents. The first step is to determine which structures should actually be updated. If the <switch> is OR* or XOR*, the expert's help is requested;[14] otherwise (AND*, or a recursive definition), the system itself can make the decision. In this case the system displays the three choices (sterile, nonsterile, and indeterminant) and asks the expert to select one.

The rest of the process can best be viewed by adopting the perspective of much of the work on "actors" [Hewitt75] and the SMALLTALK language [Learning76], in which data structures are considered active elements that exchange messages. In

---

[14] Recall that all data structures in the knowledge base have associated with them a descriptive English phrase (the DESCR part) supplied during the acquisition process. It is this description that allows TEIRESIAS to "talk" about various data structures.

these terms, the next step is to "send" the new culture site to the target selected (OTHERSITES), along with the command to the target to "Add this to yourself." The target "knows" that knowledge about its structure is stored with the schema of which it is an instance, so it finds a way to pass the buck: It examines itself to find out which schema it is an instance of (*i.e.*, it examines the contents of its INSTOF slot). Determining that it is an instance of the schema for alphabetically ordered linear lists (the AOLL—SCHEMA), it sends a request to this schema, asking the schema to take care of the "add this" message.

Recall that the schema is a device for organizing a wide range of information about representations. Part of that information indicates how to augment existing data structures. The AOLL—SCHEMA (like others) has an "updating function" capable of adding new elements to its instances (alphabetically ordered linear lists) without violating their established order. Thus, in response to the request from OTHERSITES, the AOLL—SCHEMA invokes its updating function on the new culture site and the list OTHERSITES, adding the new element to the list in the proper place.

To review:

- SITE—SCHEMA asks the expert if the new site is *sterile, nonsterile,* or *indeterminant.*
- The expert indicates *indeterminant.*
- SITE—SCHEMA sends the new site to OTHERSITES, with the message "Add this to yourself."
- OTHERSITES examines itself, finds it is an instance of AOLL—SCHEMA, and sends a message to AOLL—SCHEMA saying "Add this new site to me."
- The updating function associated with AOLL—SCHEMA adds the new site to OTHERSITES.

There are several advantages to the distribution of knowledge this technique employs. To make them clear, consider the generalized view of the process shown in Figure 6–7. Shown there is one trigger (SITE), three targets, and a structure called a "traffic director" (which is a generalized version of the RELATIONS). In this view, each schema would have its own traffic director that tells it what to do with new instances. The basic issue is organization of knowledge and, in particular, how that knowledge should be distributed between the updating functions and the traffic director.

In the current example, a new culture site is "sent" to the traffic director for instructions. It might receive three kinds of directions, depending on how much information is stored there. The traffic director might know:

DESIGN A: the names of the targets.
DESIGN B: the names of the targets and the constraints among them.
DESIGN C: the names of the targets, the constraints among them, and the structure of each target.

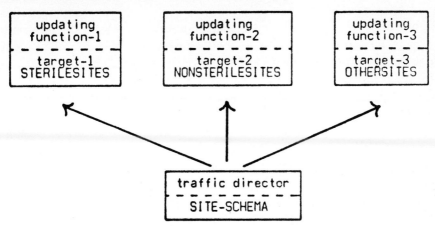

Figure 6–7   Generalized view of attending to data structure interrelations.

Design C organizes the updating process around each trigger, corresponding closely to the standard demon-like approach. In this case the traffic director can "tell" the new site exactly which target(s) to go to and how to "add itself" to each. This would mean most of the knowledge is stored in the traffic director, which has to know both the organization and the structure of all current targets.

Design A organizes the process around the target. Here the traffic director can only say "Here's all the places you might (or might not) belong, try them all and ask when you get there." In this case the bulk of the knowledge is stored with the updating functions: They will be responsible for adding the new site to the target and for maintaining the necessary interrelations between the targets.

Design B is how the RELATIONS are designed. In this case the traffic director can decide exactly which target(s) the new site should be added to, but it does not know how to add it there. This time it would say, "Here's where you belong, ask about how to be added when you get there."

Now consider the advantages and difficulties associated with each alternative. Design A requires that the targets (or the expert) must be sure to maintain the necessary constraints. In terms of the current example, this would mean either including in the updating function for each category of site a test to insure mutual exclusion with the other two categories (which would be slow and redundant) or, when asking the expert about each category of site individually, relying on him to maintain the requirement of mutual exclusion (which would be slow, redundant, and less reliable). The traffic director in design B has enough information to present the expert with a single coherent picture of the choice to be made (e.g., asking him to choose just one of the three alternatives), rather than requiring him to reconstruct it from a sequence of questions.

Design C has the disadvantage that adding a new representation to the system would be rather involved, since describing its traffic director would require keeping in mind the structure of each target. In addition, any changes in the structure of the targets would be harder to accommodate since knowledge about that structure might be widely distributed among several traffic directors. With alternative B, all the necessary changes can be made by editing a single schema.

Design B has the advantage that all of the information relevant to a representation is associated directly with it. This offers a convenient framework for its initial acquisition and can mean modifications are easier to make. In terms of these alternatives, it can be seen as a compromise between having the information associated primarily with the trigger (*i.e.*, stored in the traffic director, as in alternative C) and having it associated primarily with the targets (*i.e.*, stored in the updating functions, as in alternative A). In the most general terms, Design B succeeds because *it keeps the distribution of information about data structures constrained to the fewest number of locations.*

Note that this updating technique is applicable to a wide range of data structures. SITE–INFECT, for instance, is a table with a culture site labeling each row and an organism identity labeling each column. The entry in that row and column is the CF that an infection at site <rowname> is caused by the organism <columnname>. A newly acquired site will eventually be sent to SITE–INFECT as part of the response to the updating command:

$$\text{(ADDTO (AND* ALLSITES SITE–INFECT))}$$

In this case, SITE–INFECT sends a request to the schema of which it is an instance; this schema then invokes its updating function, which results in the interaction seen earlier in the trace ("What are the likely pathogens to be found at the site: URINE?"). The answer is used to create a new row in the SITE–INFECT table.

The caveat mentioned above should be reemphasized. The current design scheme takes advantage of a degree of modularity in the data structures. It is applicable only where target updating is not dependent on extensive information from the trigger. That is, the updating functions of each target in Figure 6–7 must be able to add new elements to their targets without knowing which traffic director sent them the new element. Since this modularity is not present in all data structure designs, it forms a limiting factor in the approach.

6–9.1.3   Noting the New Instance

The final step in "interpreting" a schema is to add the newly created structure to the list of INSTANCES of the schema. This is done primarily for bookkeeping purposes, but it also has other useful applications which will be demonstrated later.

6–9.2   Where to Start in the Network

The description of the use of schemata to guide acquisition assumed that the question of where to start in the schema hierarchy had already been settled. While the mechanisms used to make this decision are not complex, they illustrate an interesting issue.

One mechanism provides a default starting place for the case in which the user indicates, outside of the context of any consultation, that he wants to teach the system about some new instance. (While we have seen the acquisition of a new value illustrated in the context of rule acquisition, it is also possible to acquire new instances of any data type as a separate operation.) Since there is no context to rely on, the default is to start at the root of the schema network and ask the expert to choose the path at every branch point. This presents a reasonable dialog since it requests from the expert a progressively more detailed specification of the concept he has in mind. Each individual inquiry will appear sensible since, without contextual information, there is no way the system could have deduced the answer. (In the excerpt below, only the sequence of questions is shown; everything else has been edited out.)

```
++* ?
Commands are
 NR - enter a new rule
 ER - edit an existing rule
 DR - delete rule
 NP - enter a new primitive (attribute, value etc.)
++* NP
Which of the following best describes the new primitive?
[Choose the last if no other is appropriate]
      1 - an attribute, or
      2 - a value of an attribute, or
      3 - None of the above
Choose one
++** 1
```

> {*At this point, acquisition of the new item would begin; it is omitted here.*
> }

```
Which of the following best describes the new attribute?
[Choose the last if no other is appropriate]
      1 - an attribute of a patient
      2 - an attribute of a infection
      3 - an attribute of a culture
      4 - an attribute of a organism
      5 - None of the above
Choose one
++** 3
```

> {*Here we would see additional acquisition of information about the item;
> again, omitted.* }

```
Which of the following best describes the new attribute?
[Choose the last if no other is appropriate]
      1 - a single-valued attribute, or
      2 - a multi-valued attribute, or
```

```
    3 - an attribute whose value is ''true'' or ''false'', or
    4 - None of the above
Choose one
++** 3
```

When a new concept is mentioned during a rule acquisition, however, there is an extensive amount of context available. The same sort of default approach would look "dumb" in this case, since there are numerous clues indicating which kind of data type is being mentioned. In the example in Section 6–7.1, for instance, it was not difficult to discover that the concept was a new identity of an organism. As was indicated, this is accomplished by some simple pattern matching. Each schema in the network has one or more patterns associated with it. For example, the pattern

```
         the <attribute> of <object> is---
```

is associated with the VALUE–SCHEMA. Each of these is tested against the line of text that prompted acquisition of the new item, and the outcome supplies a starting place in the network. (If all matches fail, the system starts as before with the root of the network.)

The patterns thus make it possible to use contextual information from the rule acquisition dialog in order to select a starting place in the schema network. Note that this link between the natural language dialog and the data type hierarchy represents part of the semantics of each data type. Since the schemata were designed initially to represent only the syntax of the data types, at present they contain only the very limited and somewhat ad hoc semantic information in the patterns. Such information is clearly needed, however, and would represent a useful and natural extension to the current implementation. It would mean that, along with the syntax of each data type, some of its semantics would be described, perhaps in the form of a more systematic set of patterns than those currently in use, or other more sophisticated devices. The system would then always start at the root of the network and could use the semantic information stored with each schema to take advantage of context from the dialog, guiding its own descent through the network.

6–9.3   Schema Function: Access and Storage

The schema concept was introduced by describing it as an extension of the notion of a record structure, and we have seen how it guides the acquisition of a new instance. A second important use of record structures is for access and storage, and the schemata have the parallel capability. If slotnames are viewed as analogous to the fields of a record, then the mechanism used in TEIRESIAS looks quite similar to the standard record *fetch* and *store* operations.

Our approach is based on generalizing the use of the *advice* construct by using four additional types of advice (shown below). To carry out a storage or access operation, the relevant slotexpert is sent the the name of the data structure and one of these pieces of advice.

GETONE   retrieve one instance of whatever fills this slot in the indicated data structure

GETALL   retrieve all instances of whatever fills this slot in the indicated data structure

GETNEXT   retrieve one new instance at each request

STOREIT   store an item in the slot of the indicated data structure

Figure 6–8   Four pieces of advice used for access and storage.

For instance

(APPLY* (GETEXPERT AIR) 'E.COLI 'GETONE)

will retrieve one of the aerobicity values of E.COLI, while

(APPLY* (GETEXPERT AIR) 'E.COLI 'GETNEXT)

functions as a generator and will retrieve them all one by one. Since the slotexperts are organized around the pieces of advice, the relevant code for storage or retrieval is similarly organized in each slotexpert.

This feature, too, has been influenced by the work on actors and SMALLTALK noted earlier. However, where that work concentrates on issues of programming and program correctness, we intend here nothing quite so formidable. We use it because it was a natural extension to our approach, with much the same perspective on organization of knowledge.

Our implementation offers, for instance, the well-known benefits supplied by any record-like structure that provides a level of "insulation" between representation and implementation. The use of slotexperts and advice turns accessing a structure into a process of sending a request to the data structure itself, which then "answers" by providing (or storing) the desired item. All access and storage is thus funneled through the individual structures (via the slotexperts), and explicit reference is made to the configuration of the structure in only one place in the system. As with standard record structures, this technique makes it possible to access a data structure without reference to the details of how it is actually stored and without the need to change the code if the storage implementation is modified. In addition, the slotexperts make it easy to use an arbitrary function for storage and retrieval. Dates, for example, are stored in the system as integers (for efficiency), and the DATE–EXPERT takes care of decoding and encoding them on access and storage.

6–10   TRACE OF SYSTEM PERFORMANCE: ACQUIRING A NEW ATTRIBUTE

A more sophisticated example—the acquisition of a new attribute—will illustrate several other aspects of our approach to handling data structures. It will demonstrate, for instance, the utility of the schema network as a device for structuring the acquisition process. The network is used to organize the dialog and to insure that the expert is presented with a comprehensible sequence of questions. It also offers a foundation for adding new data structures to the system, making the task reasonably simple both conceptually and computationally.

Since an attribute is a more complex structure than those encountered in previous examples, the acquisition process is correspondingly more complex. In particular, the presence of several different data types in the substructure of the attribute guides the dialog through a parallel sequence of several different topics.

The example presents a borderline case for the distinction drawn earlier between formalism and degree of expertise. To describe a new attribute it is necessary to describe the values associated with it. It may happen that these values require a data type as yet unknown to the system, and creating that data type becomes, in turn, a new subproblem. But describing a new kind of data type is a complex operation that typically has an impact on the underlying formalism of the performance program. The current example is a borderline case because that impact can be avoided, but it will demonstrate how the problem arises.

The dialog below is presented in two parts. After the first half there is a brief review of what has happened so far and an indication of what is yet to occur. Recall that the knowledge base appears as it would during the early stages of construction.

```
The new rule will be called RULE383
  If:     1 - THE ORGANISM IS A GRAM NEGATIVE ROD
     and  2 - PATIENT IS A COMPROMISED HOST
     and  3 - THE NUTRIENT OF THE CULTURE MEDIUM IS
     BLOOD-AGAR
     and  4 -
  Then:   1 - THERE IS EVIDENCE (.8) THAT THE CATEGORY IS
     ENTEROBACTERIACEAE
     and  2 -
This may take a few moments...
I don't understand
          THE NUTRIENT OF THE CULTURE MEDIUM IS BLOOD-AGAR
because these words are unknown: NUTRIENT MEDIUM BLOOD-AGAR
```

{ *The expert is typing in a new rule and uses several words* TEIRESIAS *doesn't recognize. As before, the system indicates its inability to parse one of his lines and displays the unfamiliar words.* }

```
Would you care to try rephrasing that?
++* Y
   (Please use *'s to mark what you think might be a new
    attribute or a new value of an attribute)
        3 - * THE NUTRIENT * OF THE CULTURE MEDIUM IS
```

```
        BLOOD-AGAR
It looks as though
        THE NUTRIENT
refers to a new attribute, correct?
++** Y
 ... is it a new attribute of the culture?
++** Y
```

{ *Once again, the language is sufficiently simple that with the relevant phrase marked off, straightforward pattern matching succeeds in determining what the new item is. The system then retrieves the schema for attributes and begins to fill it out.* }

```
Now tell me a few things about this new attribute ...
If there is one word which neatly sums up ''THE NUTRIENT'',
please give
it (else press RETURN)
++** NUTRIENT
```

{ *The new data structure needs a name, so the system asks the expert to supply one. If he declines, it will create one, using the phrase delimited by the asterisks and a few simple heuristics for creating mnemonic variable names.* }

```
If someone said WHAT DO YOU MEAN BY NUTRIENT, what would you
say?
[type an empty line when done]
++** CULTURE MEDIA COME WITH A WHOLE RANGE OF
++** NUTRIENTS, AND SOME BACTERIA ARE VERY PARTIAL
++** TO ONE NUTRIENT OR ANOTHER
++**
```

{ *As before, the author of a new concept is responsible for describing it.* }

```
Please give a phrase with which I can talk about the value
of NUTRIENT
++** THE NUTRIENT OF THE MEDIUM OF *
```

{ *All attributes have a phrase associated with them that can be used to talk about their value. It is used in many places throughout the system (e.g., to produce the natural language version of the rules). The asterisk is filled in with the name of the relevant object, to produce, for instance, "the nutrient of the medium of CULTURE-1."* }

```
Now we want to select some keywords which might be good
```

indicators that a speaker was referring to this new
attribute. There are two classes of keywords (strong and
weak) that are used to classify each of the non-trivial
words in the phrase you just typed.
Should NUTRIENT be a keyword?
++** Y
Strong?
++** Y
Should MEDIUM be a keyword?
++** Y
Strong?
++** Y
If you want to add any additional keywords,type them now.
[type an empty line when done]
++** ENERGY-SOURCE
Strong?
++** N
++**

{ As described in chapter 5, natural language capabilities are based on keywords selected from the English phrases associated with some of the data types. Here the dictionary is updated to include the keywords from the new attribute.
}

Is this attribute the result of a quantitative laboratory
procedure?
++** Y

{ The answer will be important during consultations: Recall that for this type of attribute, the consultation system asks for the value before attempting to deduce it. }

Which of the following best describes concepts like NUTRIENT
[Choose the last if no other is appropriate]
        1 - a single-valued attribute, or
        2 - a multi-valued attribute, or
        3 - an attribute whose valued is ''true'' or ''false'', or
        4 - None of the above
Choose one
++** 1

{ The expert has supplied all the information required by the CULATTRIB-SCHEMA, and TEIRESIAS *now attempts to descend further down the schema network. As Figure 6-3 illustrated, however, there is a three-way branch*

here. Since the system has no way of knowing which way to go, it asks the expert, who responds by further specifying the concept he has in mind. }

```
Please give all the legal values for NUTRIENT
The answer should be in the form of 1 or more of the
following-   <a value of an attribute>
++** BLOOD-AGAR
++** THAYER-MARTIN
++**
```

{ *One of the components of an attribute is a list of the values associated with it. This is indicated in the relevant schema with the slotname-blank-advice triple.*

$$\text{LEGALVALUES (KLEENE (1) <VALUE-INST >) ASKIT}$$

which says that an attribute has one or more objects associated with it that are of type VALUE *and that they should be obtained from the expert.* }

```
Now I need to know a few things about each of these values...
First BLOOD-AGAR
```

{ *Since they are new to the system, the expert is asked to describe each of them. Since the triple shown above indicates that each is an instance of the* VALUE *schema, the system starts by retrieving that schema and filling it in.* }

```
Please give the full, formal name for ''BLOOD-AGAR''
++** BLOOD-AGAR .
Now please give all synonyms or abbreviations for
BLOOD-AGAR which you would like the system to accept:
++**
Which of the following best describes concepts like BLOOD-AGAR
[Choose the last if no other is appropriate]
     1 - identity of an organism, or
     2 - the site of a culture, or
     3 - None of the above
Choose one
++** 3
```

{ *After finishing with the* VALUE–SCHEMA, *the system is again faced with a choice of paths (see Figure 6–3) and must ask for advice. Since two different attributes can have values in common, there is no guarantee that the values of this new attribute are unique. Also, since the phrases like "the site of a culture" are simply strings associated with each schema, the system has no*

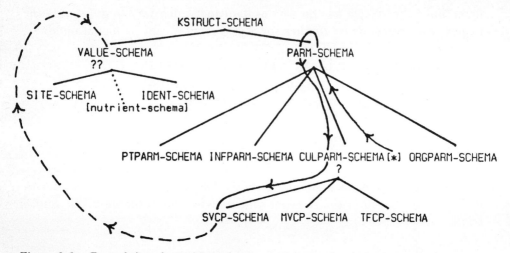

Figure 6–9   Part of the schema hierarchy.

way of knowing what each choice represents. The expert indicates that the
concept he is talking about is new by choosing the third item. }

Ok, then you'll have to tell me a few things about it...
****

Let's take a moment out to review what's happened so far and to see where
we are going from here. (A revised version of Figure 6–3 is reproduced below for
reference. It includes an indication of the path this example takes through the
network and omits several other network branches for clarity.)

The system was able to use its pattern-matching routines to guess from
the dialog that the new object being discussed was an attribute of a culture.
The expert verified this guess and the system used as its starting point the
CULATTRIB–SCHEMA, since it was the schema associated with the pattern that
matched. From there (indicated in Figure 6–9 by the asterisk), the system
"climbed" up one level in the network[15] and started back down. The first schema
to be filled out is the ATTRIB–SCHEMA; this supplied the direction for the initial
part of the dialog. Then, since the path had been marked (during the ascent), it
descended to the CULATTRIB–SCHEMA and used that to continue the dialog.

At that point, the system encountered a branch in the network for which it
had no directional information (indicated by the single question mark) and hence
had to ask "Which of the following best describes concepts like
NUTRIENT?" The process continued after the expert indicated the correct choice.

In filling out this schema, however, the system encountered a link to another
type of data structure. Since each attribute carries with it a list of its associated
values, constructing a new attribute leads to the acquisition of new values. As

---

[15] Since the KSTRUCT–SCHEMA is empty, there is no need to go all the way to the root.

```
new rule acquisition requires a
    new clinical parameter which has its associated
        new values But these are a
            new data type which means adding a new schema to the network.
        new values then Instantiate the new schema, and finally the
    new clinical parameter is finished up, so the system returns to the
new rule
```

Figure 6–10

shown in the trace, this is triggered by encountering

LEGALVALUES (KLEENE (1) <VALUE–INST >) ASKIT

in the SVA–SCHEMA. After listing all of the associated values, the expert was asked to describe each. The description task is set up as a subproblem (indicated by the dashed line) with the starting point in the network given by the schema named in the triple.

Consider the description of the first value. The system started with the VALUE–SCHEMA, but then reached a branch point for which it had no information (the double question mark) and again had to ask the expert "Which of the following best describes things like BLOOD–AGAR?" This time, however, the expert indicated that the object being acquired was of a type not yet known to the system. The acquisition of a new schema to describe the new data type is then set up as a sub-subproblem.

The next step in the dialog, then, will be the description of the new "data type" NUTRIENT, accomplished by filling out the SCHEMA–SCHEMA to produce the NUTRIENT–SCHEMA. This will become a part of the network as a new branch below the VALUE–SCHEMA. Note that the network thus "evolves," growing larger in a relatively smooth and natural way as the number of data types increases. In this particular case, almost all of this operation can be carried out by the system itself, and it is thus almost totally transparent to the expert.

The process then returns to the subproblem of describing the values and continues with BLOOD–AGAR where it left off. That is, after describing the new data type (sprouting the new branch of the network), the process will continue down into that branch and will request a description of the first instance of the new data type, using the new schema as a guide.

After all the values have been described, the dialog goes back to finish up acquisition of the new attribute. The entire sequence of topics is shown in Figure 6–10.

Let's continue with the trace, picking it up at the point where the system requested help in choosing the path to follow below the VALUE–SCHEMA.

Which of the following best describes things like BLOOD–AGAR
[Choose the last if no other is appropriate]

```
    1 - identity of an organism, or
    2 - the site of a culture, or
    3 - None of the above
Choose one
++* 3
Ok, then you'll have to tell me a few things about it...
```

{ TEIRESIAS retrieves the SCHEMA—SCHEMA to direct the acquisition of the new data type. }

```
Please give a phrase (like the ones above) to describe this
new type of value.
++* THE NUTRIENT OF A CULTURE MEDIUM
Ok, finished describing the new type of value; now back to
BLOOD-AGAR
```

{ In this case, most of the task of constructing the new schema can be handled by the system itself, so the dialog returns to the problem of describing the new instances of the (new) data type. }

```
Finished with BLOOD-AGAR; now THAYER-MARTIN
```

{ And there's nothing else to do in describing the first value, so the system continues with the second. }

```
Please give the full, formal name for ''THAYER-MARTIN''
++* THAYER-MARTIN
Now please give all synonyms or abbreviations for
THAYER-MARTIN which you would like the system to accept:
++* CHOCOLATE-AGAR
++* TM
++**
Finished with THAYER-MARTIN
OK done with the values for NUTRIENT now...
```

{ The second instance is likewise described in short order, and the dialog returns to the original problem—describing the new attribute. There is just one more part to be acquired. }

```
Please give a phrase which can be used to ask about the
value of NUTRIENT
[Type as many answers as are appropriate, then an empty
  line.]
++* WHAT IS THE NUTRIENT OF THE MEDIUM FOR *
++**
```

```
Ok, finished with describing the new attribute now.
Returning to parsing the new rule.
This may take a few moments...
This is my understanding of your rule:
RULE383
-------
```

```
  If:  1) The gramstain of the organism is gramnegative, and
       2) The morphology of the organism is rod, and
       3) The patient is a compromised host, and
       4) The nutrient of the medium of the culture is
    blood-agar
  Then:  There is strongly suggestive evidence (.8) that the
  category of the organism is enterobacteriaceae
Okay? (Yes or No)
++* Y
```

{Finally, we have the new rule, with its new attribute and value. }

6–10.1 Comments on the Trace

The creation of the new attribute is an extensive operation involving several different data types. By structuring it properly, however, the task becomes comprehensible. There are several sources of this structuring information. First, the schemata take advantage of the decomposability of individual data types to present a series of straightforward, independent questions. Next, the schema network relies on the fundamentally simple organization of the data types to provide a comprehensible sequence of topics. The slots and slotexperts, in turn, make it possible to represent many conventions of the data types in ways that permit the system to perform many of the routine tasks, considerably simplifying the entire operation. Finally, the correspondence between data types and objects in the domain makes it possible to present a dialog that appears comprehensible to the expert, yet which deals effectively with questions of data structure manipulation. The result of all this is the construction of some complex data structures with numerous internal conventions and interrelationships, in a fashion that makes it a reasonable task for the expert.

The growth of the schema network to encompass a new data type demonstrates the degree of flexibility in the system. The flexibility arises from the use of the schemata as a language and framework for the specification of representations. Knowledge about any specific representation is contained entirely in the "statements" of that language, rather than in special purpose code. This provides a greater range of applicability and flexibility than would be possible if separate, hand-tailored acquisition routines were written for each different data type.

Additional flexibility arises from the inherently extensible nature of the schema network. As with all generalization hierarchies, it is a relatively simple operation to add new branches at any level in the network. Since the representation language interpreter "reads" the network to structure the dialog, the addition will be reflected in future acquisition sessions. That is, the next time TEIRESIAS reaches the VALUE–SCHEMA node and requests advice about which way to go, it will present the expert with four options: the three shown in the previous trace plus the new one of culture medium nutrient.

The trace also demonstrates that the description of the structure of one data type may mention another (as the description of an *attribute* mentions *values*). In the acquisition process this gets translated into a new direction for the dialog, as one topic (describing the new attribute) leads naturally into another (describing its associated values). These "new directions" are currently followed as they arise (*i.e.*, the search is depth-first). This can prove to be a distraction at times, since the dialog goes off on a subtopic and later returns to the main topic to finish up. This could easily be changed to a modified breadth-first search, which would result in a dialog that exhausted each topic (each data structure) in turn before beginning another.

One final comment concerns the simplicity of acquiring the new schema that describes the values of the new attribute. There are several reasons why the operation is in this case almost totally transparent to the expert when in general it is a much more complex operation. It is in part a fortuitous side effect of the conventions used in the current set of representations. Most of the important conventions concerning the representation of a value are common to all values and hence are expressed in the network at the level of the VALUE–SCHEMA. There is thus relatively little more that the schemata at lower levels have to add.

This transparency also results from the assumption that the expert will not be expected to make changes in the basic formalism of the performance program. In line with this assumption, when dealing with the expert, the schema interpreter does not request two types of information that would normally be part of the description of a new data type: substructure and interrelationships. Wherever a new schema is added to the network, there is the possibility that the data structure it describes has additional substructure and interrelationships beyond those described by its ancestors in the network. To be complete, the system should naturally ask about them. But notice that the answer to either the question of substructure or interrelationship requires a knowledge of, and implies potential alterations to, the underlying formalism of the performance program. Any substructure in a new data type would have to be referenced somewhere in the performance program if it is to be of use, implying that the performance program code would have to be changed. The ability to specify new interrelationships between data types implies an understanding of the data types that already exist. Since both of these clearly require an understanding of elements of the system that would be alien to the expert, they are omitted. (We will see later that they are asked under other circumstances.)

This approach allows the expert to teach the system about new attributes and values without getting involved in programming details. The price is a small possibility that he may compromise the integrity of the data base, if the new data type in fact should be related to some existing structure.

There is really a more fundamental problem here: The current design of MYCIN's representations makes each kind of VALUE its own data type. This is what makes it necessary to acquire a new schema and pushes the task into the realm of changes to the performance program. With some redesign of the data structures involved, it would be possible to have just a single kind of VALUE data type, and avoid all this. But as indicated, it was necessary to work within the existing representations in MYCIN and still make it possible for the expert to educate the system.

6–11 KNOWLEDGE ABOUT KNOWLEDGE ABOUT REPRESENTATIONS

TEIRESIAS was designed to make possible interactive transfer of expertise. As we have seen, one kind of expertise it can transfer is domain-specific information, the kind supplied by an expert to improve the operation of a performance program. But recall that high performance on the transfer of expertise task required a store of knowledge about representations. If TEIRESIAS is designed to make possible interactive transfer of expertise independent of domain, why not apply it to the task of acquiring and maintaining the requisite base of knowledge about representations? That is, why not push this back a level and consider the knowledge about representations as a candidate for interactive transfer of expertise? This has been done and involves using TEIRESIAS in two phases (Figure 6–11).

As we have seen, the domain expert uses TEIRESIAS to teach the performance program about the domain of application. High performance on this task is made possible by the base of knowledge about representations provided by the schemata. But the system architect can also use TEIRESIAS to teach about a particular set of representations. High performance on this task is made possible by the *schema-schema*, a base of "knowledge about knowledge about representations," which is used to guide the process of describing a new representation. It is, in effect, a set of instructions describing how to specify a representation. Since the instructions are in the same format as those in an ordinary schema, the process of following them is identical. As a result, we need only a single "schema interpretation" process. Teaching about a representation (acquiring a new schema) is thus computationally identical to teaching about the domain (acquiring a new instance of a schema); indeed, both teaching tasks shown in Figure 6–11 are done with a single body of code.

Earlier sections of this chapter displayed three examples from the process of teaching about the domain and demonstrated how each could be understood in terms of filling out one or more schemata. This section explores an example of the first process—teaching about a representation—and views it in terms of *augmenting the schema network*.

This view is useful both computationally and conceptually. The computational task is simplified because much is accomplished by adding a single branch

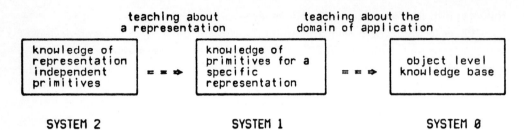

Figure 6–11   The two applications of schema instantiation.

to the schema network, which is an information-rich structure. The new schema will inherit all of the information represented in its ancestors in the network and hence need not replicate it. The task becomes easier conceptually since the network offers a useful framework for organizing and understanding all the different representations in a program.

This approach assumes, of course, that the different data types in a program can, in fact, be organized into a generalization hierarchy. If this is true, the hierarchy can be used to provide another tool for dealing with complexity, providing a useful organizational overview when there are a number of related data types.

Building the schema network also provides one useful test of the generality of this part of the system. If the techniques used are sufficiently general, it should be possible to grow the entire network from a foundation that is not specific to any particular representation. This was made one of the design criteria for the system, and has provided useful guidance.

We will see that the schemata have been applied to a variety of data structures. This will help make plausible the claim that they form a useful tool for attacking one central problem faced in building knowledge bases: the construction and maintenance of large collections of varied data structures.

Since this stage of knowledge base construction deals with the process of describing representations, we do not expect that it would be accomplished by the expert from the application domain. The task requires a knowledge of programming and may require changes to the basic formalism of the performance program. In this use, then, the schemata are more properly viewed as a "programmer's assistant" tool, to be used by someone with the appropriate background. The language of the next dialog will reflect this new orientation, since it assumes a familiarity with both general programming issues and the language of the schemata.

6–11.1   The SCHEMA-SCHEMA

As noted earlier, in our framework the process of describing a new representation can be made computationally identical to that of describing new instances of a representation. This uniformity is made possible by the schema-schema, shown below.

The schema-schema, along with some associated structures, provides a foundation of representation-independent knowledge that can be used for constructing an entire knowledge base. The nature and extent of this knowledge is outlined below, to characterize the assumptions behind the use of the schema-schema and, hence, the range of representations for which it is applicable.

Knowledge embedded in the schema-schema assumes that:

1   Data structures have a well-specified syntax. That is, they have a certain static quality and maintain the same structure and organization over a lifetime that includes a number of access, storage, and creation operations. One obvious set of candidates are those structures that do not change while the program is executing. Conversely, applying this to temporary structures which are quickly modified would be less successful.

2   Data structures can be specified in terms of distinct sub-units, each of which has a straightforward syntax and is for the most part independent of the others.

3   Data structures may be interdependent. Thus, part of the task of specifying a new representation is to describe any interrelationships it may have with other structures.

4   There is more than one instance of each data type. The utility of the schema as a tool for dealing with program complexity is dependent on a useful instance-to-schema ratio. If every data structure in a program were distinct (a 1:1 ratio), the schemata would offer little advantage in knowledge base maintenance.

Since the schemata were devised as an extension to the notion of a record structure, it is not surprising to find that several of these assumptions are common to the use of record structures as well.

6–12   TRACE OF SYSTEM PERFORMANCE: BUILDING THE SCHEMA NETWORK

This example demonstrates the process of adding a new schema to the network in the very early stages of knowledge base construction. At this point the system does not yet know anything about the concept of organism identity.

```
Schema network editor
Command?
++* DOWN
    Level 1:
 1) attribute
 2) value of an attribute
```

{ *There is a simple editor that allows the user to examine the network and perform various operations on it. Here he descends from the root...* }

```
++* SHOW 2
VALUE-SCHEMA
```

SCHEMA-SCHEMA


```
PNTNAME        (ATOM      CREATEIT)
STRUCT         (PNTNAME   INSLOT)
PLIST
        [ (PNTNAME    ((BLANK-INST ADVICE-INST) ASKIT)
          STRUCT    ((PNTNAME INSLOT)        GIVENIT)
          PLIST
                  [ (INSTOF       (( (PNTNAME INSLOT) GIVENIT )              CREATEIT)
                    DESCR       ((STRING   ASKIT)                    GIVENIT)
                    AUTHOR      ((ATOM     ASKIT)                    GIVENIT)
                    DATE        ((INTEGER CREATEIT)                  GIVENIT)
                    KLEENE      ((SLOTNAME-INST (BLANK-INST ADVICE-INST)) ASKIT))
                CREATEIT]
          FATHERMOD ( SCHEMA-INST         FINDIT)
          INSTANCES ( LIST               ASKIT)
          STRAN     ( STRING             FINDIT)
          INSTOF    ( SCHEMA-SCHEMA      GIVENIT)
          DESCR     ( STRING            CREATEIT)
          AUTHOR    ( ATOM              ASKIT)
          DATE      ( INTEGER           CREATEIT)
          OFFSPRING ( (KLEENE (0) < SCHEMA-INST >)  ASKIT)
          UPDATES    ((KLEENE (0) <(UPDATECOM-INST KLEENE (1)
                                <(SWITCHCOM-INST KLEENE (1) <KSTRUCT-INST>)>)>)
                          ASKIT))
        CREATEIT]
  FATHERMOD  (SCHEMA-SCHEMA)
  INSTANCES  ((ALLSCHEMA))
  STRAN      "knowledge structure"
  INSTOF     (SCHEMA-SCHEMA)
  DESCR      "the schema-schema describes the format for all other schemata"
  AUTHOR     DAVIS
  DATE       876
  OFFSPRING  NIL
  UPDATES    ((ADDTO (AND* ALLSCHEMA)))
```


Figure 6–12   The schema-schema.

```
PNTNAME        (ATOM        ASKIT)
VAL            (PNTNAME     INSLOT)
PLIST          [(INSTOF  (VALUE-SCHEMA      GIVENIT)
                DESCR    (STRING            ASKIT)
                AUTHOR   (ATOM              FINDIT)
                DATE     (INTEGER     CREATEIT))
CREATEIT]
STRAN          the value of a attribute
FATHER         (KSTRUCT-SCHEMA)
OFFSPRING      (SITE-SCHEMA)
DESCR          the VALUE-SCHEMA describes the format for a
               value of any attribute
AUTHOR         DAVIS
DATE           1115
INSTOF         (SCHEMA-SCHEMA)
```

{examining schemata along the way...}

++* DOWN 2
```
    Level 2:
    2.1) site of a culture
```
++* ADD 2.2

{until he has found the right spot and then indicates that he wants to add a new schema. The system retrieves the SCHEMA-SCHEMA and uses it to guide the process of describing the new data type.}

```
Please give a phrase to describe this new type of value of an
attribute.
```
++* IDENTITY OF AN ORGANISM
```
    If there is one word which neatly sums up ''identity of an
    organism'', please give it (else press RETURN)
```
++* IDENT

{The system needs a name for the new schema and asks the user first. If he declines to supply one, the system will manufacture one out of the phrase "identity of an organism."}

```
Please describe any additional properties of a identity of
an organism. The answer should be in the form of one or
more of the following-
     <slot name> <blank specifier> <slot advice>
[Type 1 set to a line, then an empty line when done.]
```
++* AIR   (KLEENE (1 1 2) <(AIR-INST CF-INST)>) ASKIT

```
++* GRAM      GRAM-INST     ASKIT
++* MORPH     MORPH-INST    ASKIT
++* SYNONYM   (KLEENE (1 0) < ATOM >)   ASKIT
++**
```

{ *The user indicates several structural components that are part of the new data type, describing them in the standard slotname-blank-advice format. These are in addition to the structural conventions it inherits by virtue of being a type of* VALUE. }

```
Sorry, but the following are invalid —
     SYNONYM is not a known <slot name>
Please answer again [use the same answer if you really
meant it.]
++* SYNONYM (KLEENE (1 0) < ATOM >) ASKIT
```

{ *The concept of a synonym is as yet unknown to the system; so it too has to be described. This is set up as a subproblem, and the* SLOTNAME–SCHEMA *is used to guide the description.* }

```
Please tell me a few things about the concept of SYNONYM
as a <slot name>.
   Please give a short phrase which can be used to ask for
   the contents of this slot.
   [type an empty line when done]
   ++* PLEASE GIVE ALL SYNONYMS OR ABBREVIATIONS
++* FOR * WHICH YOU WOULD LIKE THE SYSTEM TO
++* ACCEPT.
++**
```

{ *Recall that the asterisk is used to indicate a gap to be filled in the template. In this case it will be filled in with the name of the new identity being acquired.* }

```
   Please give a short phrase which can be used to display
   the contents of this slot.
   [type an empty line when done]
   ++* THE SYNONYMS OF * ARE
++**
   Please give a description of SYNONYM.
   [type an empty line when done]
   ++* SINCE MANY ORGANISM NAMES ARE LONG AND
   ++* UNWIELDY, SHORTER SYNONYMS ARE OFTEN
   ++* USED. THOSE SYNONYMS ARE PART OF THE
   ++* DATA STRUCTURE WHICH REPRESENTS AN
```

++* ORGANISM IDENTITY.

++**

Please edit and complete this skeleton function
definition for the SYNONYM-EXPERT:

```
[NLAMBDA (BLANKS ADVICE)
  (SELECTQ ADVICE
    (ASKIT (ASK-XPERT BLANKS (QUOTE SYNONYM)))
    (GIVENIT BLANKS)
    (FINDIT )
    (CREATEIT )
    (INSLOT (APPLY* (GETEXPERT BLANKS) SCHEMA
      (QUOTE GETALL)))
    [GETONE (CAR (GETP KSNAME (QUOTE SYNONYM]
    (GETALL (GETP KSNAME (QUOTE SYNONYM)))
    (GETNEXT (NEXTONE SCHEMA (QUOTE SYNONYM))
    (NOADVICE BLANKS (QUOTE SYNONYM-EXPERT]
        tty:
```

*

{Since there is a slotexpert associated with every slotname, the acquisition
of the slotexpert becomes a new sub-task. Recall that even though it is a
function, the slotexpert is viewed for the moment as simply another data
type, one of whose components is a function definition. All of the other
components are sufficiently stylized that they can be manufactured by the
system itself, and this occurs without aid from the user.

The function definition is complex enough to be an exception to this,
but even here there is enough stylization that the system can prepare a
useful skeleton to be completed by the user. The standard INTERLISP editor
is invoked (announcing itself with the "tty:" prompt), to allow the user to
make any necessary changes. Since not every piece of advice makes sense
for every slotexpert, the user may delete some of the entries. Other entries
may be expanded to account for additional representation conventions, or
edited because the original skeleton is at best a rough guess. The point in
having the system produce the skeleton is not to automate the creation of
code, but rather to make it as easy as possible for the user to supply all the
information that the system will eventually need. }

.
.
.

OK

{The user finishes the editing (which has been omitted here). }

Done with the concept of SYNONYM as a <slot name> now.

{Having finally finished with the new slotname, the dialog returns to the last item needed for the new schema... }

```
Please specify all updating to other data structures which
will be necessary when a new instance of a identity of an
organism is acquired.  The answer should be in the form of
one or more of the following—
<update command> [1 or more: <selection command>
     [1 or more: <data structure>]]
[Type 1 set to a line, then an empty line when done.]
```
++∗ ADDTO (AND∗ ORGANISMS)
```
++∗∗
Ok, finished defining IDENT-SCHEMA.
  Level 2:
    2.1) site of a culture
    2.2) identity of an organism
Command?
++∗∗
```

{...and then is done. }

6–12.1 Comments on the Trace

The system requires only a very small core of knowledge as the basis for the schema network construction shown in this trace. In addition to the network editor and the schema interpreter, it requires only five schemata and a small number of instances.[16] From this core of knowledge everything else can be built. As a demonstration, the network shown above in Figure 6–3 was constructed in this fashion. The single process of schema interpretation was used to guide the construction of the base of representation-specific knowledge and then used to instantiate it in order to build a small object-level knowledge base. The system was thus bootstrapped from the schema-schema and a few associated structures.

In practice, the content of the knowledge base would not already be determined, so the process would proceed slightly differently. A basic skeleton of the schema network should be constructed first, using the network editor. After a few major branches have been supplied, it is then convenient to go back to typing in new rules and to allow the system to guide the necessary network growth. As in the example of acquiring a new attribute, this means that a new rule might

---

[16] Since the schema-schema needs to refer to the concepts of slotnames, slotexperts, advice, and blanks, the schemata for these must be supplied and cannot be bootstrapped. The instantiations required are the slotname and slotexperts for each of the slotnames found in a schema, and instantiations of the advice schema for the nine pieces of advice.

trigger the addition of a new branch to the network (the new data type) and then trigger several instantiations of it (the nutrients).

While rules can be entered from the very beginning of knowledge base construction, this tends initially to produce dialogs that are difficult for the user to follow. With an empty schema network, the first line of the first rule will trigger a long and deeply recursive dialog. In general, early in knowledge base construction, the smallest addition tends to trigger many other additions. It is easiest to start by building a basic network a piece at a time with the editor.

Since the network can conceivably grow quite complex, some simple heuristics have been embedded in the editor. To help deal with the problem of potential interconnections of a new schema, the editor can propose candidates. If a new schema were added in the third level of the network of Figure 6–3, the editor would suggest:

```
Listed below are 1 or more possible sub-classifications of
this new concept. Please indicate [Y or N] each one that
applies.
  1 - an attribute whose value is ''true'' or ''false''
  ++* YES
  2 - a multi-valued attribute
  ++* YES
  3 - a single-valued attribute
  ++* YES
```

Figure 6–13   Proposing potential connections.

The editor examines the siblings of the new schema and notes to which other schemata they are connected. If a sufficient percentage of the siblings share a common offspring, that offspring becomes a potential connection in the schema network. In this case the editor (correctly) proposes the three schemata to which all the other five siblings are attached.

An analogous sort of aid is available when specifying the structure of a new data type. The network editor examines the three structure-defining slots (the print name, value, and property list) of the new schema's siblings and detects regularities in a manner similar to the way rule models are created. These are then displayed to the user and, like the rule models, can be useful reminders of overlooked details.

6–13   LEVELS OF KNOWLEDGE

The mechanisms reviewed above provide an extensive amount of machinery for encoding knowledge about representations. But it is not enough simply to provide the machinery—if the result is to be something more than "yet another knowledge representation formalism," there must be some sense of organization and methodology that suggests how all this ought to be used.

Organization is provided by a common theme that serves to unify all of the proposed mechanisms: the notion of *levels of knowledge*. There are several different (and independent) stratifications of knowledge implicit in the formalism developed above. Two of the most important involve:

(a) describing knowledge in the system at different levels of detail, and
(b) classifying it according to its level of generality.

In both cases, the important contribution is a framework for organizing the relevant knowledge about representations. The idea of different levels of detail indicates that representations (*e.g., value* or *attribute*) can be described at the level of global:

- organization (as in the schema hierarchy),
- of logical structure (as in the schemata), and
- of implementation (as in information associated with the slotnames).

These levels provide an organizational scheme that makes it easier to specify and to keep track of the large store of information about representations required by the acquisition task. The different levels of generality for classifying knowledge include:

- domain specific,
- representation specific, and
- representation independent.

As explained below, the idea of maintaining clear distinctions between these different kinds of knowledge is an important contributor to much of TEIRESIAS's current range of application.

6–13.1   Level of Detail

As noted in Section 6–8, the schema hierarchy, individual schemata, and slotnames each encode their own form of knowledge about representations. The hierarchy indicates the global organization of representations in the system and provides a foundation for both the acquisition of new instances of existing primitives (a process of descent through the hierarchy and instantiation of the schemata encountered) and the acquisition of new kinds of primitives (a process of adding new branches to the hierarchy). [17] The schemata describe the logical structure and logical interrelationships of individual representations and, as prototypes, provide a focus for the organization of knowledge about a representation. The slotnames have associated with them information concerning the implementation

---

[17] Note that the entire schema hierarchy is viewed here as dealing with information at a single level of detail (viz., global organization of representations). Viewed by itself, it is of course yet another (independent) structuring of knowledge in the system into various levels.

(0)   The knowledge base of the performance program contains:
      object–level knowledge that is
      domain specific and is formed by
      instantiating the appropriate schema to form a *new instance of
          an existing conceptual primitive.*

(1)   The knowledge about representions (the schemata) contains:
      meta–level knowledge that is
      representation specific and is formed by
      instantiating the schema–schema to form a *new type of
          conceptual primitive.*

(2)   The schema–schema contains:
      second order meta–level knowledge that is

      representation independent and is formed by
      hand.

Figure 6–14   Levels of generality of knowledge about representations.

of a specific representation, information at the level of programming-language constructs and conventions (*e.g.*, variable name uniqueness, etc.).

6–13.2   Level of Generality

Much of the range of applicability of TEIRESIAS results from the isolation and stratification of the three kinds of knowledge shown below. The base of *domain-specific* knowledge at level 0 consists of the collection of all instances of each representation.

The base of *representation-specific* knowledge at level 1 consists of the schemata, which are, in effect, the declarations of the extended data types. These have a degree of domain independence since they describe what an attribute is, what a value is, etc., without requiring *a priori* knowledge of the domain in which those descriptions will be instantiated.

The base of *representation-independent* knowledge at level 2—the schema-schema—describes what a declaration looks like. At this level resides knowledge about representations in general and about the process of specifying them via declarations.

While level 2 is formed by hand, it is the only body of knowledge in the system for which this is true, and it forms a small core of knowledge from which everything else can be built. For example, the schema hierarchy shown in Figure 6–3 (and all associated structures) was constructed by bootstrapping from the schema-schema and the core of structures noted in Section 6–12.1. The single process of schema interpretation was used to guide the construction of the base of representation-specific knowledge (the hierarchy and schemata) and then used to instantiate it to build a small object-level knowledge base.

One reason that this is a practical approach is the great leverage in the notion of a schema as a prototype. The current performance program, for instance, contains knowledge about some 125 organisms, but a single schema serves to characterize every one of them. There are some 25 different representations in the program, requiring 25 schemata; yet a single schema-schema serves to characterize all of them.

It was, in fact, precisely such utilitarian considerations that motivated the initial creation of the schema-schema. Recall that the schemata were developed because there were many details involved in creating a new object and adding it to the system. But there turned out to be a large number of details involved in creating all the necessary schemata, too. The schema-schema was thus the result of the straightforward recursive application of the basic idea, for precisely the same reason.

6–13.3 Impact

The direct advantages of this stratification arise from the capabilities it supports. The compartmentalization of knowledge suggested by the levels of generality, for instance, provides an increased range of applicability of the system. The single schema-instantiation process can be used with the core of representation-specific knowledge in a range of different domains, or it can be used with the representation-independent knowledge over a range of representations. Describing representations at different levels of detail, on the other hand, offers a framework for organizing and keeping track of the required information. It also provides a useful degree of flexibility in the system, because the multiple levels of description insulate changes at one level from the other levels. Thus, in the same way that modifications to information associated with the slotnames can change the implementation of a representation without impacting its logical structure (exactly in the manner of record structures [Balzer67]), so changes can be made to logical structure (the schemata) without impacting the global organization of representations (the hierarchy).[18]

In a more general sense, both stratifications provide guidance in using the representational machinery proposed above. In both cases we have a set of general guidelines that suggests the appropriate mechanism to use for each of the forms of knowledge necessary for the acquisition task. These guidelines (Figure 6–2 and Figure 6–14) deal with dimensions of knowledge organization that are broadly applicable and hence are not limited to a single domain of application nor to a single representational formalism. They thus help to "make sense" of the representation scheme outlined here.

6–14 LIMITATIONS

One of the primary shortcomings of the current implementation is the simplicity

---

[18] Changes at one level may quite possibly require additional changes at that same level in order to maintain consistency of data structure specifications or to assure the continued operation of the program. But by organizing the information in the levels described, the effects of changes will not propagate to the other levels of description.

of the structure syntax. While the *slotname-blank-advice* triples can be combined in various ways and the *blank* is capable of describing a range of structures, the result is still somewhat rudimentary. The schemata need a more powerful language for describing the "shape" of data structures before they can be widely applicable.

More fundamental limitations arise out of the organization of the slotexperts. They rely, for instance, on the assumption that knowledge about the representations being described can be broken down into basically independent chunks indexed by the slotname and advice. This requires a certain modularity in the design of a representation that is not always possible to supply.

Independence of slotnames implies that a representation can be decomposed into a collection of independent subparts, and this is not always true. While the current implementation is able to deal with a limited amount of interdependence between slots, more complex interdependencies do not appear to be accommodated easily. The current implementation can, for example, make it possible for one slot to use the contents of another but cannot deal with the situation in which the contents of one slot restrict the set of admissible contents of another.

This inability to deal with more complex interrelationships of representations is currently the system's primary shortcoming. Related attempts to formalize such information have come from many directions (*e.g.*, [Spitzen75], [Stonebreaker75], [Suzuki76]) and have encountered similar difficulties. Specifying complex integrity constraints is fundamentally a problem of knowledge representation and confronts many of the same difficult issues.

Another limitation arises from the assumption in the design of the *advice* concept that the question of where to get the information to fill a slot can be broken down into a collection of cases that are (*i*) broadly applicable and (*ii*) independent. The issue is not so much precisely which cases are chosen, but that some set of them can be assembled that will provide a "language" for designating the sources of knowledge used in creating a data structure. The range of application of the set determines the ease with which the whole approach can be used. If, for instance, there are important differences in the implications of CREATEIT for two different slotexperts, then whoever constructs a schema has to know this fact. But then little is gained by the whole approach. It becomes far less transparent, and the slotname/advice indexing scheme becomes an obscure way of invoking particular pieces of code. More serious problems would arise if the question of where to get the information to fill the slots could not even be decomposed into any set of distinct, independent cases.

Several of the traces demonstrated that the acquisition of one kind of data structure can lead to acquisition of another, as in the case of an attribute leading to its associated values. This is a useful feature, since it means that the system tends to request coherent blocks of information from the expert. It depends, however, on explicit structural interconnections between data types—the attribute leads to acquiring values because those values are part of its structure. Had this not been the case, the link would not have been made and the system would have acquired each new value as it was mentioned. This means that the design of the representations used can have an important impact on the coherence of the acquisition dialogs.

Requesting the expert's help in descending the schema network assumes that the display of the alternative paths will be comprehensible to him. This presumes a correspondence between the representations in the program and objects in the application domain. While it does seem likely that such a correspondence will exist, its absence would present a significant problem for our system.

While the schemata make possible a number of useful features, they are not without associated costs. Most of this cost tends to be borne by the system designer, to the benefit of the expert who wants to augment the knowledge base. This is because the schemata impose a certain discipline on the system designer, requiring, in particular, that he view the representations in the system in fairly general terms and fit them into the framework provided. While there are advantages to doing this, it may not be an easy task. Especially during the early stages of system design, when numerous changes are made, the cost may outweigh its advantages. In their present state of development, then, the tools described in this chapter are more appropriate to ongoing knowledge base maintenance than to the initial phases of knowledge base construction.

Perhaps the most general limitation of the techniques outlined here concerns the conceptual level of the system's task. It is no accident that we have emphasized at many points the use of a high-level language and the manipulation of extended data structures that correspond to objects in the world being modeled. There clearly are tasks and system designs for which this correspondence cannot be maintained. However, to the extent that a system can be viewed successfully in these high-level terms, the methodology can be very useful. In general, the higher the level of the language and programming, the more applicable the techniques will be.

Finally, the current system cannot yet acquire new objects (i.e., "objects" as in the second part of an attribute-object-value triple) or new predicate functions. Of these, the latter is more difficult, since it is basically a problem in automatic programming and no attempt has been made to solve it. Objects present a different challenge, since they are represented by some highly convoluted data structures (they are designed currently for maximum efficiency, at the price of comprehensibility). Schema syntax will have to be extended before it is capable of describing them, but it is not clear whether this arises solely from a shortcoming in the expressive power of the schemata or whether the convoluted design of objects contributes to the problem as well. It is not reasonable, of course, to design a language and then claim that anything it cannot express should not be said. But every language carries its own perspective, and the schemata stress the simplicity of design that arises from decomposability. (As discussed above, they currently rely *too* heavily on this.) One of the potential long-term benefits of a representation language, however, is as a vehicle for developing and formalizing principles of good design. Given a language based on such principles, it might then be said with some justification that what could not easily be stated might profit from reconsideration. The schemata are, naturally, only a single step in this direction and much more work is needed.

6-15   FUTURE WORK

6-15.1   Minor Extensions

As is apparent from a number of the traces, the system's "depth-first" approach to acquisition can be difficult to follow. Despite the messages printed by the system and the indication of level given by the indentation of the dialog, it is not always easy to remember which problem the system is returning to after it finishes up with a subproblem. As noted, this could be solved by using a modified breadth-first search, in which the system finished acquiring all the necessary components at its current level before taking up any subproblems. In acquiring a new attribute, for example, this would mean that acquisition of the new attribute would be finished before starting to deal with its associated values.

It should also be possible to suspend the acquisition task temporarily. The expert can at times find himself involved in a protracted dialog that is not immediately relevant to the bug he started to correct. All the information requested will prove necessary eventually, but it may prove to be an unreasonable distraction to have to deal with every detail before getting back to the original problem.

The system is currently an effective listener for anyone who knows just what he wants to say, but it is not at all forgiving. It enforces a one-pass, "get-it-all-right-the-first-time" approach, and this is clearly an unrealistic view of knowledge base development. For example, the schema network may require reorganization as a result of several causes. This may become necessary because of mistakes in describing the schemata originally, because further development of the performance program dictates redesign of some representations, or because the addition of a new schema to the network requires it in order to maintain the proper inheritance of properties. This makes the network editor a good candidate for additional work. As currently implemented, it does not offer any mechanism for reorganizing existing schemata; to be a truly useful maintenance tool, it should be extended to provide a wider range of such capabilities. (See [Sandewall75] for some suggestions on similar data base reorganization problems.)

Once it becomes possible to modify existing representations, there is an auxiliary capability that would prove extremely useful. After the user has finished modifying any schema, the editor should be prepared to execute those same modifications on all current instances of the schema. That is, the system should "look over the user's shoulder" and then make the same changes to all instances of the schema. Simple deletions or reorganizations could be performed unaided; where new components had been added, the system would prompt for the appropriate entry for each instance. This would allow extensive changes in representation design with relatively little effort and a reduced probability of introducing errors.

6–15.2   Major Extensions

Perhaps the most interesting major extension to the system would be the addition of semantic information to the schemata. They were designed originally to convey the syntax of data structures, but as Section 6–9.2 illustrated, inclusion of semantic information would prove very useful—it would make the system appear "smarter" by allowing it to take advantage of context from the debugging dialog to guide its own descent through the schema network. Representation of the semantics might be based initially on more extensive use of patterns like those described above, but more sophisticated mechanisms should eventually be devised.

6–16   SUMMARY

6–16.1   Review of Major Concepts

At the beginning of this chapter we suggested that it would be instructive to consider the terms *knowledge representation*, *extended data type*, and *data structure* as equivalent, to see what might be learned by viewing each of them in the perspective normally reserved for one of the others. A number of the key ideas involved in the design and use of the schemata were inspired by this mixing of perspectives.

The fundamental idea of a *base of knowledge about representations*, for instance, was suggested by the view of representations as extended data types and motivated by the desire to organize and represent knowledge about those data types. This led to the idea of the *schemata as a language and mechanism for describing representations*, and it strongly influenced schema design by indicating what sort of information they ought to contain (*e.g.*, structure and interrelationships). This view also suggested the organization of that information and led to *organizing it around representational primitives* (*e.g.*, attribute, object, value, etc.), which were, in turn, *represented as prototypes* (the schemata) and *instantiated to drive the interactive transfer of expertise process*.

Viewing extended data types from the perspective of knowledge representations led to incorporating the *advice* mechanism in those data types. This provided an additional source of knowledge about those structures and allowed a "high-level" dialog that was coherent to the domain expert.

Blurring the distinction between data type and knowledge representation offered an interesting consideration for knowledge base design. To see how this consideration arose, note that a subtle factor that added to the coherence of the acquisition dialogs earlier was the somewhat fortuitous correspondence between data structures and domain-specific objects (*e.g.*, organisms). This meant that the acquisition dialog appeared to the expert to be phrased in terms of objects in the domain, while to the system it was a straightforward manipulation of data structures. Such a correspondence helps to bridge the gap in perspectives, and the purposeful attempt to insure its presence in a system can be a very simple, but useful consideration in the initial design of a knowledge base.

A second set of major ideas involved in the schemata arose from the notion of *levels of knowledge* described above. As noted, this stratification of knowledge provided an *increased range of applicability* for the techniques and offered a *set of guidelines for organizing the body of knowledge about representations*. It also suggested that the acquisition of new instances be viewed as a process of *descent through the schema hierarchy*, and that the acquisition of new kinds of knowledge representations be viewed as a process of *adding new branches to the hierarchy.*

6–16.2   Current Capabilities

The schemata and associated structures offer a language and framework in which representations can be described. This language strongly emphasizes making explicit the many different kinds of knowledge about representations and offers a framework for organizing that information. The schema hierarchy, individual schemata, and slotnames each support their own variety of that knowledge. The result can be a useful global overview of the organization and design of all the representations in the system.

For both the system engineer and the applications domain expert, the knowledge acquisition capabilities of the schemata offer a very organized and thorough assistant that can:

Attend to many routine details.   Some of these are details of data structure management, and having the system attend to them means the expert need know nothing about programming. Others are details of organization and format, and with these out of the way, the task of specifying large amounts of knowledge becomes a good deal easier. The emphasis can then be placed on specifying its content rather than attending to details of format.

Show how knowledge should be specified.   In terms of the three systems pictured earlier, the assistant's intelligence always lies at the level above that of the knowledge being specified. While it cannot choose a representation for an organism, it can indicate how the representation should be specified. Similarly it cannot suggest what the gramstain of a new organism might be, but it can indicate that every organism must have one, and can describe exactly how it should be specified. It is this ability to structure the task and lead the user through it that is most useful.

Make sure that the user is reminded of all the items he has to supply.   Since knowledge base construction is viewed as a process of knowledge transfer, the assistant's thoroughness offers some assurance that the transfer operations will not inadvertently be left incomplete.

In summary, the assistant cannot supply answers, but it does know what all the proper questions are and what constitutes a syntactically valid answer for each. The application domain expert will rely on the assistant to show him how to transfer his knowledge to the program, while the system designer can use the assistant as an aid in knowledge base management, using it to help him keep track of the large number of representations that may accumulate during the construction of any sizable program.

All of this should make plausible the suggestion that the tools discussed above, when combined with a simple core of representation-independent information, offer a basis for assembling a sizable collection of knowledge. They provide, as well, a useful perspective on the organization and representation of several levels of knowledge, making the transfer process straightforward and effective.

Chapter 7

Strategies

Know that I have gone many ways wandering in thought.

Sophocles
Oedipus the King, lines 66–67

7-1 INTRODUCTION

In most existing performance programs, the largest number of knowledge sources relevant to any one goal is small enough that exhaustive invocation is still computationally feasible.[1] In current (June 1978) versions of MYCIN, for example, the largest number of rules relevant to a particular goal is on the order of 50, and all are invoked. It seems clear, however, that since the knowledge bases in such performance programs may eventually grow quite large, exhaustive invocation will

---

[1] Any piece of the system that contributes some task-specific bit of intelligence will be referred to as a knowledge source (KS). That intelligence may be at the level of the programming language (*e.g.*, LISP functions) might be some piece of domain-specific information, or information at any other level on which we care to focus. The primary concern here will be with KSs at the level of problem solving; in particular, inference rules of the sort shown in Figure 2–4. As is common, the "bit" of intelligence will be referred to as a *chunk*. (Since strategies contribute intelligence to the system, they are KSs as well. For the sake of clarity, however, we use the term only in the context of object-level KSs.)

in time prove too slow. It was in response to this that meta-rules were developed, to embody strategic knowledge about reasoning and to supply a mechanism for guiding the reasoning process.

Meta-rules are the third[2] major form of meta-level knowledge to be considered. They provide a way of expressing knowledge about the use of knowledge and are discussed here as a framework for knowledge organization. This chapter is divided into four main parts. The first, Section 7–3, gives a fairly general introduction to the concept of strategies and considers their place in guiding program operation. The second part, Section 7–4, discusses the specifics of meta-rule structure and function and examines their contribution to problem solving performance. The third, Section 7–5, explores possible implications that the current meta-rule implementation might have on programming in general. The final part, Section 7–6, then offers a very general view of strategies, describing a taxonomy of strategy types and discussing the impact of each on the organization of knowledge in a program.

7–2   THE MAIN IDEAS

Much of the utility and impact of meta-rules derives from a few basic ideas. These are listed and described below, then developed more fully in the remainder of this chapter.

> Almost all current problem-solving control structures are susceptible to *saturation*, the situation in which so many applicable knowledge sources are retrieved that it is unrealistic to consider nonselective, exhaustive invocation.

The issue of invocation, considered in the most general terms, is a central theme for much of the work described in this chapter. Over the years many different approaches to invocation have been developed, including standard sub-routine calling, varieties of pattern-directed invocation, etc. An important characteristic of all but the most basic scheme (subroutine calling) is that more than one knowledge source may be retrieved for invocation. All invocation schemes with this property share an important potential weakness, which we call *saturation*. That is, given a sufficiently large knowledge base, so many knowledge sources may be retrieved that it becomes impossible to invoke them all. In that case some decision must be made about how to order and choose from that set.

It was this issue that motivated the development of strategies described here, and it is this issue of strategies as a source of guidance in the face of control structure saturation that will provide much of the focus for this chapter.

We also consider some extensions of this view and describe, first, how strategies can provide useful guidance even when a program is not immobilized by saturation. In this case, strategic knowledge allows a program to proceed "more

---

[2] The others were the rule models and data structure schemata.

logically," without necessarily affecting the program's final result. Second, we show how the mechanism used to define strategies has interesting consequences, in terms of allowing more than just invocation control; it allows a definition of new invocation criteria as well.

We define a strategy to be information about which knowledge source(s) to invoke when more than one is potentially useful.

Strategies are thus one form of meta-level knowledge; specifically, information about the use of object-level knowledge. This view provides a useful perspective on the organization and use of knowledge in a program and suggests an important site for embedding knowledge to improve performance. We also show how this view can be generalized and consider strategies as any information about how or when to apply the various sources of object-level knowledge in a program.

Strategies can control invocation by "tuning" a control structure.

Our initial application of strategies is in the context of a single control structure and shows how to deal with potential saturation by "tuning" the existing knowledge source invocation scheme.

Meta-rules are implemented by a technique called *content-directed invocation*, which has interesting implications as a knowledge source retrieval mechanism.

By *content-directed invocation*, we mean that meta-rules refer to object-level rules by direct examination of the content of the object-level rules. We compare this to more traditional retrieval mechanisms and demonstrate its advantages with respect to ease of modification of the program.

Problem-solving control structures can be viewed as use of different retrieval criteria.

For example, goal-directed invocation involves retrieving knowledge sources by the goal they accomplish; data-directed invocation selects on the basis of the data available; while means-ends analysis retrieves on the basis of differences between the current state and the goal state.

Content-directed invocation provides an explicit, functional definition of retrieval criteria and offers a mechanism for defining new criteria.

TEIRESIAS thus provides an environment in which the retrieval criteria are not predefined and embedded in the interpreter (as in most programming languages) but are, instead, available to the programmer. We will see this idea applied primarily in the context of tuning an existing control structure. The idea is also considered briefly as the basis for a program that adaptively selects its own control structures.

7–3   WHAT IS A STRATEGY?

The word "strategy" has been used in many contexts and senses, and seems to be a somewhat elusive concept. We are concerned here mainly with its impact in the context of problem solving and offer a definition in these terms. To help set the context, we consider first a broadly construed view of problem solving and examine the notion of ill structured problems.

7–3.1   Ill Structured Problems

To characterize the class of problems most relevant to the framework presented below, we consider the distinction between a *well structured* and an *ill structured* problem. The former is described in [Newell69] as a problem:

(a)   Which can be stated in terms of numerical variables,
(b)   whose goals can be specified in terms of a well-defined objective function, and
(c)   for which there exists an algorithmic solution.

Ill structured problems are those which do not meet one or more of the above conditions. [3] The most general such case would lack even a definition of the initial state and a specification of the goal. Most problems attacked by AI, however, have well-defined initial and goal states; the third condition is the one most often not met. Note that the domain of clinical medicine is more ill structured than most since in many cases it is not certain what constitutes the "correct" diagnosis (and hence therapy).

To illustrate this distinction between well structured and ill structured problems, consider the task of the STUDENT program [Bobrow68], which dealt with the domain of simple algebra word problems. It first created equations that corresponded to the natural language text, then solved those equations. The problem of turning the natural language into a set of equations is highly ill structured. Once the equations are determined, however, the process of solving them is perfectly straightforward.

For purposes of this discussion we focus on the behavior displayed by programs that attempt to solve ill structured problems. We examine, in particular, the degree of nondeterminacy in the process of selecting a KS to invoke, and

---

[3] Simon has argued [Simon73] that the division between well structured and ill structured problems is less precise and that even problems meeting these criteria in principle may be ill structured in practice. This is due to the unrealistic amount of computation required to satisfy condition (c) above when a program's knowledge base is very large.

show that the nondeterminacy present in ill structured problems is a common source of saturation.

To see this, consider that well structured problems (like solving a set of linear equations) can (by definition) be solved algorithmically. Hence at each point of the problem solution there is no question about which knowledge source should be invoked next and no question of whether this invocation gets us closer to the solution. Since ill structured problems lack algorithmic solutions, the choice of a KS to invoke is at best a good guess. In such a case, we may be faced with a problem for which

(a)   It may be useful to make explicit in the program the process by which a KS is selected (as opposed to the situation in algorithmic programs, where only the end result of the selection process is evident, in the predefined sequence of KS invocations);

(b)   the result of the selection process may be a number of KSs, all of which are potentially useful (as opposed to the single KS [pre]selected for invocation at each step of an algorithmic program); and

(c)   the process of selecting a KS for invocation needs to be carried out often (*i.e.*, invocation of a particular KS does not carry the computation very far, and many such invocations are needed before reaching a solution).

As will become clear in the remainder of this chapter, all of these were important considerations in the concept and design of meta-rules. At the moment, however, it is useful to focus on the second, since it leads us back to the idea of saturation. That is, one important cause of saturation is the nondeterminism present in ill structured problems.

When ill structured problems are attacked with the production system methodology, the concept of "degree of nondeterminacy" has a well-specified instantiation: It is called the *conflict set*. This is the set of all rules that, at any given moment, meet the tests for applicability and, hence, could justifiably be used. Depending on the nature of the problem, the conflict set may range from a single rule to every rule in the system.

It will be useful to generalize this concept slightly so that it will be applicable to additional programming methodologies. Rather than the conflict set, we will speak of the *plausible knowledge source set* (PKS set) and mean by that the set of all KSs that, at some given moment, are plausibly useful and appropriate to invoke. This will also serve to emphasize that saturation is independent of any specific knowledge representation or control structure. Any system, faced with a sufficiently ill structured problem and a large enough knowledge base, may be unable to select out few enough KSs to make exhaustive invocation feasible.

By defining two averages on this set, we can construct a more quantitative interpretation of the concept of well structured and ill structured problems. The "average size" of the PKS set will be defined as a time average of its size over the course of the entire problem solution. The "average power" will be defined as the average of the power of each of its members. [4]

The "degree of ill-structuredness" of a problem should then be directly proportional to the average size of the PKS set and inversely proportional to its average power. (This is of course a relative rather than absolute scale, whose utility lies in making broad comparisons rather than independent measurements.) If this number is relatively small, the problem is more likely to be well structured and not the type of problem we will be considering here. The larger this number gets, the more relevant the remainder of this analysis becomes.

7–3.2 Strategies

With this background we can now examine the notion of strategy in more detail. We present three successively more general views, beginning with a definition in terms of coping with saturation.

7–3.2.1 Strategies as a Response to Saturation

Faced with a PKS set of nontrivial size and a desire to avoid blind, exhaustive invocation, some decision must be made about which KS should be the next to be invoked. It is our contention that this decision point is an important site for the embedding of knowledge, because system performance will be strongly influenced by the intelligence with which the decision is made. We claim also that it is a decision which in many systems is made on the basis of knowledge that is neither explicit, nor well organized, nor considered in appropriate generality.

We take this as a starting point and offer our initial definition of strategy in terms of it: We suggest that a strategy can profitably be viewed as *information concerning which chunk of knowledge might be invoked next, when more than one chunk may be applicable.*

The utility of this view of strategies arises from its applicability both to problem solving (in particular, for ill structured problems) and to current developments in programming languages. Invocation in traditional (*i.e.*, ALGOL-like) programs, for example, is "well specified," in the sense that only one procedure is considered for invocation at any given moment. Many of the programming paradigms developed more recently, however, admit (or even encourage) the possibility of retrieving several chunks of knowledge, all of which are plausibly useful in a single situation (*e.g.*, this is true for production rules, PLANNER-like languages, as well as other languages with choice-point and backtracking mechanisms). Typically, in these paradigms, the KSs are retrieved unordered and are invoked exhaustively, each considered in turn, until some stopping criterion is met or until all have been tried. However, faced with a set of alternatives large enough (or varied enough) that blind, exhaustive invocation would

---

[4] "Power" is the concept defined by Newell [Newell69] as "the ability to deliver solutions." He describes it as composed of (among other things): a KS's probability of finding a solution, the quality of the solution (optimal, or how suboptimal), and the computational expense incurred in invoking the KS.

be infeasible, some decision must be made about which should be chosen. [5] The concept of strategy thus appears to have a natural place in considering questions of programming language design as well as problem solving.

7–3.2.2   Strategies as Meta-Level Knowledge

Considered in more general terms, strategies are a third example of meta-level knowledge, in particular, knowledge about how (and when) to use the various sources of object-level knowledge.

To illustrate this concept and emphasize that it is widely applicable, three common approaches to problem solving are listed below, along with examples of object-level and meta-level knowledge for each. In each case, the meta-level knowledge consists of advice about how and when to use the various sources of object-level knowledge.

(a)   Problem decomposition:

Object level   Knowing how to decompose the problem (*i.e.*, knowing what the necessary and sufficient subgoals are),

Meta level   Knowing how to order the attack on the subgoals for efficiency (*i.e.*, knowing which of several possible decompositions to try);

(b)   Cooperating knowledge sources:

Object level   The domain knowledge contained in the various sources,

Meta level   Knowing which knowledge source to use at each point in solving the problem;

(c)   Heuristic search:

Object level   Knowledge of the search space (*e.g.*, for game playing, a legal move generator and other operations on the domain primitives),

Meta level   The various search strategies (alpha-beta, branch and bound, hill climbing, etc.).

To emphasize the generality issue, consider the concept of the PKS set, defined as all KSs that are "plausibly useful." What in fact constitutes "plausibly useful"? For the vast majority of systems, the answer is assumed to be obvious—in production systems and PLANNER-like languages, for instance, it is based on pattern matching and, after all, it's "obvious" when a pattern matches. Such knowledge is thus often buried deep within a system (if it is represented explicitly at all), and indeed the PLANNER pattern matcher operates at a very low level, compared with other features of the language. We claim, however, that even this chunk of knowledge should be regarded as a strategy and should be made explicit in the system.

---

[5] A few of the paradigms offer mechanisms for doing this. For example, the concept of *conflict resolution* used with production rules offers a limited means of ordering the KSs retrieved, but its use thus far has been purely syntactic. It may, for instance, order rules based on which of those retrieved was used least recently. As we will see, PLANNER's THUSE and THTBF mechanisms are somewhat more sophisticated.

Among the advantages would be flexibility. For example, in an event-driven system using pattern-directed invocation of KSs (*e.g.*, PLANNER antecedent theorems), only a certain subset of the KSs are considered—those with patterns containing obvious discrepancies with current information are ignored. Consider, however, the utility of checking for misinterpreted or missing data in a noisy domain in the following way: If several strategies indicated strongly that a certain KS would be useful, but its pattern doesn't currently match, it may be useful to retrieve that KS nevertheless. The discrepancies between this KS and the current data base might in fact be a useful hint about where to check for missing or misinterpreted data. Thus, by turning this "obvious" chunk of knowledge—defining what it means to "match"—into an explicit strategy, we obtain a highly flexible system, one that can be "tuned" to account for the degree of noise in the domain with relatively little trouble. Fundamental changes in system performance can therefore be controlled at a fairly high level.

Note that this view makes few assumptions concerning the underlying methodology. It appears to be a useful perspective over a range of representation techniques. It describes equally well, for example, the organization of knowledge for systems that are event driven as well as those that are goal directed. In the former case, the question is how to select the most relevant subset from all the potential implications of a new event; in the latter it becomes the intelligent choice of a KS that helps achieve the current goal.

7–3.2.3 Strategies as a Means of Defining and Choosing Invocation Criteria

Finally, strategies are also traditionally viewed as a kind of "fine-tuning" of a general method; as, for example, set-of-support is used to improve the performance of resolution theorem proving. As will become clear below, however, we need not restrict ourselves to this view. In the most general terms, we can view strategic knowledge as any decision concerning how or which knowledge to use. Adopting this view will make it clear that strategies need not be set in the context of tuning a single method but can more generally be used to choose (or even define) the method itself. This view is developed further in Section 7–5.

7–3.3 Levels of Knowledge

The discussion thus far has suggested the existence of only two levels of knowledge, the object and meta levels. It seems plausible, however, to continue this sequence through an arbitrary number of levels. Where strategies direct the use of object-level knowledge, second order strategies direct the use of strategies (*e.g.*, when is hill climbing better than branch and bound), third order strategies suggest the criteria for choosing strategies (*e.g.*, how do I go about deciding which search technique is the best), and so forth. Note that the process is the same at all levels; each level directs the use of the knowledge at the next lower level. [6]

Part of the intuitive appeal of the higher levels of strategy lies in the belief that the invocation of a useful piece of strategy knowledge at a high level offers advantages similar to choosing an appropriate branch early in the search of a large tree. That is, since the strategy at level N selects the relevant strategies at level $N - 1$, and since this carefully chosen subset of strategies does the same for the strategies at level $N - 2$, etc., the strategy at level N can exert a powerful focusing influence on the whole process.

Two global considerations are relevant here. First, the domain must allow successive levels of strategies. It is not obvious, for instance, what some of the fourth and higher level strategies would look like, even for familiar methodologies like heuristic search. The domain should thus be sufficiently formalized that it is possible to determine the conceptual primitives of each level of knowledge.

Second, these strategies must be effective, that is, the result of invoking any one level of strategy must be a useful selection of knowledge at the next lower level. This means that some fairly specific statements can be made about useful choices at each level.

In what follows, for the sake of exposition, most issues are discussed as if there were only two levels, but they can be generalized to an arbitrary number of levels.

By combining the concept of multiple levels with the view of the nature of strategic knowledge suggested earlier, we see the beginning of a general framework for the organization and explication of strategy knowledge. The selection of a methodology (like the ones in Section 7–3.2.2) might for instance be accomplished by a hierarchical set of strategies which decide, first, *how to choose* a methodology (second order strategy) and then *which methodology* to choose (first-order). As before, the selection of a particular methodology may then imply further decisions to be made that would once again be the task of strategic knowledge.

While writing strategies can involve a significant amount of effort, even a moderate investment appears to pay off quite well. Certain aspects of the organization of the HEARSAY II system, for example, can be viewed in light of successive levels of knowledge, demonstrating the power of the technique. That system is built around a large number of demons, each waiting to fire and contribute its chunk of knowledge. Each demon has a set of arbitrarily complex preconditions which specify the circumstances necessary for it to be relevant. But it would be prohibitively expensive to evaluate all implicated preconditions every time a new datum enters the data base. In order to avoid this, the precondition of each demon has its own precondition (the "pre-precondition"), which specifies the general conditions under which the system should bother to evaluate the whole precondition. Apparently even these two levels of knowledge are sufficiently

---

[6] This hierarchy is analogous to the one in chapter 6 labeled "levels of generality." In both cases, each higher level describes knowledge at the next lower level. Each level of the hierarchy discussed in chapter 6 (instance, schema, schema-schema) describes the *representation* of knowledge at the next lower level; here, each level of strategy describes the *use* of knowledge at the next lower level. However, while the hierarchy of chapter 6 appears to end at the third level, here there appears to be no a priori limit to the number of levels.

powerful to support acceptable performance.

7–3.4   Building Blocks: Conceptual Primitives, Language

Object-level knowledge is built from conceptual primitives specific to the domain of application. In MYCIN, for instance, the notions of organism gramstain, morphology, and identity are relevant concepts. Object-level primitives thus characterize the domain, and it is the search for an appropriate set of them, and a language in which to express and use them, that is a large part of the traditional representation problem of AI.

Strategies, on the other hand, require conceptual primitives that describe characteristics of knowledge rather than characteristics of the domain. Some of those primitives might deal with general attributes of a KS like:

(a)   preconditions for its use—to assure its utility,

(b)   any side effects—to make clear all the implications of using it,

(c)   its main effect—so that it can be used when relevant, and

(d)   the main factors on which it is based—a finer degree of characterization than main effect.

Others might be suggested by the structure of the object-level primitives. For instance, as noted earlier, the current performance program uses both consequent and antecedent rules; each rule is composed of a premise and an action; these, in turn, are made up of clauses; and the clauses are built from predicate functions, attributes, objects, values, certainty factors, etc. Each of these suggests several possible meta-level primitives: Is the rule an antecedent or consequent rule? How many premise clauses are there? Which functions, attributes, etc., does the rule employ? Is the certainty factor positive or negative? etc. In the same way, the components of any sort of KS could provide hints about potentially useful primitives for characterizing it.

A suitably large set of such primitives would form the basis for a useful *strategy language*. More is of course needed: It is not enough just to choose the primitives; there must be a way of expressing, combining, and using them, so as to effectively direct the use of object-level knowledge. Since there are many advantages to be gained by a uniform encoding of knowledge, it is useful if the object-level syntax can simply be augmented with the new meta-level primitives to provide the strategy language. A demonstration of this technique and a discussion of its advantages is given below.

While this view has indicated where to find a useful subset of meta-level primitives, the question of determining the entire collection may be a good deal harder. We claim below that the set is at least very large, and perhaps open-ended. These claims are, in turn, important considerations for the design of a strategy representation and are discussed in Section 7–5.3.3.

7–4 META-RULES

As noted, the initial motivation for meta-rules was to provide a mechanism to guide the performance program faced with saturation. This section discusses issues of meta-rule design and representation primarily in that light. It also considers additional applications for meta-rules and demonstrates their utility in a variety of contexts. Shortcomings of the current implementation are also reviewed.

7–4.1 Format

Two examples of meta-rules are shown below, in both the internal format and the English translation that results.[7] The strategic impact of the first rule arises from the fact that an old infection which has been cured only temporarily may recur, perhaps as much as a month later. Thus, one of the possible ways to deduce the identity of a current organism is by reference to previous infections. However, this line of reasoning is not valid if the current infection was cultured in a fashion that caused the sample to be nonsterile (*e.g.*, taken from a nonsterile site). Thus the rule, in effect, says *if the current culture is not from a sterile source, don't bother trying to deduce the current organism identity from the identity of previous organisms.* As should be clear, this is a global statement about how to reason in a given situation and as such offers a useful piece of strategic advice.

The second rule indicates that since enterobacteriaceae are commonly associated with a pelvic abscess, it is a good idea to try rules concluding about them first, before the less likely grampositive rods.

The syntax for meta-rules is identical to object-rule syntax, extended to include two new predicate functions (MENTIONS and its complement, DOESNT-MENTION), and two new attributes (which concern a rule's UTILITY and its place in the sequence of rules to .be invoked (DOBEFORE)). Two important benefits accrue from using a single syntax: First, meta-rules may employ all the existing machinery of certainty factors to make inexact statements, and, second, the system has a uniform encoding of all levels of knowledge. Implications of these are discussed below.

The current implementation has a very simple syntax but offers a useful range of expression. Meta-rules can indicate:

```
(a) the utility of object-level rules (as in METARULE001):
        under conditions A and B,
        rules which do {not} mention X in their {premise
                                                 action}
    will {definitely be useless
          probably be useless
```

```
            probably be especially useful
            definitely be especially useful}
(b) a partial ordering of the object—level rules (as in METARULEOO
      under conditions A and B,
      rules which do {not} mention X in their {premise
                                                action}

    should {definitely      be used {first.
            probably                 last.
            ...                      before
         possibly}                   after}
    rules which do {not} mention Y in their {premise
                                                action}
```

METARULE001

```
If      1) the culture was not obtained from a sterile source, and
        2) there are rules which mention in their premise a previous
           organism which may be the same as the current organism
Then it is definite (1.0) that each of them is not going to be useful.


PREMISE:    ($AND (NOTSAME CNTXT STERILESOURCE)
                  (THEREARE OBJRULES(MENTIONS CNTXT PREMISE 'SAMEBUG) SET1))
ACTION:     (CONCLIST SET1 UTILITY NO TALLY 1.0)
```

METARULE002

```
If      1) the infection is a pelvic-abscess, and
        2) there are rules which mention in their premise
           enterobacteriaceae, and
        3) there are rules which mention in their premise grampos-rods,
There is suggestive evidence (.4) that the former should be done before
        the latter.


PREMISE:    ($AND (SAME CNTXT PELVIC-ABSCESS)
                  (THEREARE OBJRULES(MENTIONS CNTXT PREMISE
                                     ENTEROBACTERIACEAE) SET1)
                  (THEREARE OBJRULES(MENTIONS CNTXT PREMISE GRAMPOS-RODS) SET2))
ACTION:     (CONCLIST SET1 DOBEFORE SET2 TALLY .4)
```

Figure 7–1   Meta-rule examples.

Note that the primitives that have been added to the syntax deal, as expected, with characteristics of knowledge. For example, the new predicate functions are based on the fact that the knowledge representation is a composite structure whose components are accessible; hence, it makes sense to refer to the content of a rule. The new attributes are based on the recognition, first, that a rule invocation is a discrete event, so it makes sense to indicate order; and, second, that one rule may be more useful than another, so we can talk meaningfully about utility. These simple additions allow the statement of the fairly broad range of strategies indicated above and have so far met all current needs.

7–4.2   Function

We present first a simplified picture of meta-rule function and elaborate on it in several stages. In the simplest case, meta-rules (like object-level rules) are associated with an attribute. As explained in chapter 2, during the course of attempting to establish the value of any attribute, the system retrieves the list of rules relevant to that attribute. Before any of these rules is invoked, however, the system checks for meta-rules associated with the same attribute. If there are any, these are executed first and act to reorder or prune the list of object-level rules (thereby guiding the system's search through the goal tree). The modified list is then passed to the standard rule interpreter described in chapter 2.

There is no reason to constrain this process to a single level of strategies, and the current implementation is general is this respect. If first-order meta-rules are present, the process recurs, and second-order rules are sought, which would then be used to reorder or select from the first-order list, and so on. [8] Recursion stops when there is no rule set of the next higher order, and the process unwinds, allowing each level of knowledge to direct the use of the next lower level.

Meta-rules may also be written to control the invocation of object-level antecedent rules. When a conclusion is made, the system retrieves the list of antecedent rules associated with that conclusion. If the list is not empty, the system checks for the existence of applicable meta-rules (*i.e.*, meta-rules associated with the antecedent rules dealing with that conclusion) and allows them to reorder or prune the list of conclusions to be made. This provides a mechanism for writing strategies to control the depth and breadth of implications drawn from any new fact or conclusion.

7–4.2.1   Details

Meta-rules operate by making conclusions about the utility and relative ordering for each object-level rule. To see how this is done, consider the invocation of the two meta-rules shown earlier in Figure 7–1.

Assume the system is attempting to determine the identity of an organism. It will retrieve the list of all object-level rules concluding about identity (call the list L) and then the list of meta-rules associated with identity. Assume the process ends here because there are no second-order meta-rules and that the first meta-rule in the list is METARULE001. If the culture under consideration is not from a sterile source, the first clause succeeds. Evaluation of the second clause

```
(THEREARE OBJRULES(MENTIONS CNTXT PREMISE SAMEBUG) SET1))
```

---

[8] We have not as yet uncovered any second or higher order meta-rules, but then neither have we actively looked for them. In general, meta-rules have offered more expressive power than we have yet been able to use.

results in assigning to SET1 the subset of rules that mention "a previous organism with possibly the same identity as the current organism" (SAMEBUG).

Note that determining the appropriate subset of object-level rules is accomplished by direct examination of the code of the object-level rules. That is, each of the rules in L is tested by the function MENTIONS, which examines the source code of the rule to see (in this case) if that rule mentions the attribute SAMEBUG in its PREMISE. (Implications of this direct examination of source code—which we call *content-directed invocation*—are explored below in Section 7–5.)

The action part of METARULE001 then concludes that each is definitely not useful.

Evaluating METARULE002 proceeds analogously: If the patient is a compromised host, SET1 is assigned the list of all rules mentioning the identity pseudomonas, SET2 is assigned all rules mentioning klebsiella. The conclusion would then indicate that there is "suggestive evidence" that each rule in SET1 should be done before any of those in SET2. This employs all the pre-existing certainty factor machinery, allowing the curious ability to make inexact statements about the order of a sequence of events. [9]

When all the meta-rules have been applied, they will have made a number of conclusions about the utility and relative order of the rules in L. The task now is to sort and perhaps prune L, based on those conclusions. Since the transitivity of the order relation often introduces constraints that are not explicitly mentioned by a meta-rule, [10] it is first necessary to compute the transitive closure of the set of ordering constraints. A straightforward implementation of Warshall's algorithm [Warshall62] supplies this.

The pruning of L is prompted by conclusions like those in Figure 7–1, which indicate that some rules will definitely be useless and hence can be deleted. For the remainder, the most useful rules should be tried first.

The final step is thus a sort-and-delete pass through L using the following criteria:

```
If the utility of a rule is −1, delete it from L, otherwise
rule X goes before rule Y if
        it is required by ordering constraints, or
        the utility of X is higher than the utility of Y
```

The result is a reordered and possibly shortened list.

Note that with exhaustive search of the goal tree, order will make a difference in the final answer only if the system happens to encounter a rule with CF = 1.0 that executes successfully, since in that case search is terminated. Even if

---

[9] By phrasing the rule correctly, DOBEFORE can be used to state four different relationships: "Do list X before list Y" and "do list X after list Y" are handled in the obvious way; "do X last" means "do complement-X before X," and "do X first" means "do X before complement-X."

[10] For instance, if "do X before Y" and "do Y before Z" are indicated by rules, often there is no rule that indicates the necessary condition of "do X before Z."

the final answer is unchanged, however, the program's performance may appear more rational as a result of reordering the rules, since it will then try the more "appropriate" lines of reasoning first. Section 7–4.6 considers the potential impact of this form of meta-rule if search is not exhaustive.

Note also that even though utility and rule order are both eventually used to sort the list, they are maintained as independent factors, since they represent two different kinds of judgments. To see this, consider that it might, for example, be possible to conclude that two rules are definitely (CF = 1) going to be especially useful; yet independent considerations might still indicate that one of them should be invoked before the other.

The entire process is summarized below (simplified by assuming that there is only one level of meta-rules):

```
To deduce the value of an attribute A:
  1) L  ← the list of rules which conclude about A
  2) L' ← the list of meta-rules associated with A
  3) Evaluate each of the rules in L'; this may result in some
conclusions about the rules in L
  4) Sort and prune L according to the criteria shown above
  5) Evaluate each of the rules in L; this may result in
        conclusions about the value of A
```

7–4.3   Implications of Meta-Rules as a Strategy Encoding

There are several advantages to this approach to encoding strategies. To make these advantages clear, recall that the basic control structure of the performance program is a depth-first search of the and/or goal tree sprouted by unwinding rules.

The first advantage arises from the significant leverage apparently available from the addition of a store of (meta-level) knowledge describing which chunk of object-level knowledge to invoke next. Considered again in tree search terms, we are talking about the difference between "blind" search of the tree and one guided by heuristics. The advantage of even a few good heuristics in cutting down the combinatorial explosion of tree search is well known.

Consider, too, that part of the definition of intelligence includes appropriate use of information. Even if a store of (object-level) information is not large, it is important to be able to use it properly. Meta-rules provide a mechanism for encoding strategies that can offer additional guidance to the system.

Third, the presence of meta-rules associated with individual attributes (as the rule in Figure 7–1 is associated with the attribute IDENTity) means that this goal tree has an interesting characteristic: At each node, when the system has to choose a path, there may be information stored advising about the best path to take. There may therefore be available an extensive body of knowledge to guide the search, but this knowledge is not embedded in the code of a clever search algorithm. It is instead organized around the specific objects that form the nodes in the tree; that is, instead of a smart algorithm, we have a "smart tree."

The power in using rules to guide rules applies at multiple levels as well: There is leverage in encoding heuristics that guide the use of heuristics. Thus, rather than adding more heuristics to improve performance, we might add more information at the next higher level concerning the effective use of existing heuristics.

Fourth, note that the rules can be judgmental. This makes it possible to write rules which make different conclusions about the best strategy to use, and then allows the underlying model of confirmation to weigh the evidence. That is, the strategies can "argue" about the best rule to use, and the strategy that presents the best case (as judged by the confirmation model) will win out.

The judgmental character also allows the novel possibility of both inexact and conflicting statements concerning relative order. We might, for instance, have two meta-rules that offer different opinions about the order of two sorts of object-level rules, indicating that there is evidence that "subset X should probably (.6) be done before subset Y" and that "subset Y should probably (.4) be done before subset X." Once again, the underlying model of confirmation will weigh the evidence and produce an answer. [11]

Next, there are several advantages associated with the use of strategies that are goal-specific and are embedded in a representation that is the same as that of the object-level knowledge. The fact that strategies are *goal-specific*, for instance, makes it possible to specify quite precise heuristics for a given goal, without imposing any overhead in the search for any other goals. That is, there may be a number of complex heuristics describing the best rules to use for a particular goal, but these will cause no computational overhead except in the search for that goal.

Finally, the use of a *uniform encoding of knowledge* makes the treatment of all levels of knowledge the same, and this offers several advantages. For example, our work on explanation (chapter 3) and knowledge acquisition (chapter 5) for object-level rules can, as a result of the uniform encoding, easily be extended to meta-rules as well. The first of these (explanation) has been done and makes possible an interesting capability: In addition to being able to display the object-level rules used during a consultation, the system can similarly display the meta-rules, thereby making visible the criteria it used in "deciding how to do what it did" (see Section 7–4.5). Knowledge in the strategies has become accessible to the rest of the system and can be displayed in the same fashion.

Additional advantages associated with making strategies explicit are described in Section 7–5.3.2.

7–4.4   Advanced Issues

For the sake of clarity, the description of meta-rule operation given above omitted

---

[11] Note that there is, in general, no logical contradiction in the concurrent existence of evidence suggesting both orderings. Only one case is contradictory: In the current model it would be contradictory to have definite evidence ($CF = 1$) for both the "before" and "after" orderings. The implementation of meta-rules does not now check for this case, but it should someday be upgraded to do so.

some details of knowledge organization. These details and their implications are examined below.

Experience with the meta-rule construct has also indicated that it is a convenient mechanism for encoding forms of knowledge in addition to those described above. Two such uses are discussed below, demonstrating that it is possible to embody in meta-rules a limited subset of the knowledge formerly embedded (sometimes quite subtly) in the performance program. These two types of rules either capture aspects of the control structure or make explicit what we refer to as "design decisions."

Some of the material presented here relies on some fairly specific (and occasionally subtle) aspects of the present performance program's organization. It is thus not as widely relevant as preceding material and is susceptible to change as experience with it increases.

7–4.4.1   Meta-Rule Organization: Static

It was indicated earlier that meta-rules, like object-level rules, are associated with specific attributes. It is also possible to associate a meta-rule with any of the objects (*e.g.*, an infection, culture, organism, etc.). In that case, the rule is used as a strategy for all attributes of that object and for all attributes of any object that gets sprouted below it. [12] This offers the opportunity to state strategies whose range of applicability runs from a single object (if associated with a leaf of the object tree) to the entire domain (if associated with the root of the tree—domain-independent strategies are stored there). The specificity of application of a strategy is thus controllable by choosing the proper node in the object tree.

7–4.4.2   Meta-Rule Organization: Dynamic

Previous examples have illustrated two different forms of meta-rules. The first meta-rule in Figure 7–1 concluded about the *individual* utility of a single object-level rule, while the second meta-rule described the *comparative* utility of two classes of rules. In terms of the tree search process that meta-rules guide, these two examples deal with different criteria for ordering the paths to be explored, based on a "look ahead" one level deep. It is also possible to express some very simple strategies that use a look-ahead several levels deep, to select a particular "line of reasoning."

A standard problem in doing this is the question of how deep in the line of reasoning to explore or, in our terms, how long a sequence of rules to consider. The longer the sequence, the more effective the choice may be; but more work is involved in simulating the rule retrieval mechanism to effect the look-ahead.

We have sidestepped the issue of how deep to look (and settled for a weaker solution) by implementing a "line-of-reasoning" type meta-rule that functions in a somewhat backward fashion. Each time the system tries to establish the value

---

[12] Recall that objects are organized into a tree of the sort shown in Figure 2–6.

of an attribute, it retrieves not only the meta-rules associated with that attribute but any associated with any attribute higher in the current chain of goals. Thus, instead of looking deeper from a node, each node "looks up." The combined set of meta-rules is used to reorder or prune the current list of object rules.

In simpler terms: The current implementation is functionally equivalent to (but more efficient than) taking each line-of-reasoning type meta-rule and putting copies at each node of the subtree to which it applies. Thus, instead of having the system actively search ahead more than one level, the relevant strategy is "brought down" the tree during the normal search process.

The solution is weaker because it is "hardwired" into the depth-first search used by the performance program and because it only searches one level ahead. A true line-of-reasoning strategy would require the ability to do its own examination of the search tree to an arbitrary number of levels.

There are thus several potential sources of meta-rules for any given attribute. They may be associated with:

(a)   the attribute itself,
(b)   the object to which that attribute applies,
(c)   any ancestor of that object, or
(d)   any other attribute higher in the current chain of goals.

Note that the scope of the first three of these is fixed but that the last is established dynamically as the consultation proceeds.

7–4.4.3 Encoding Control Structure Information

There are object-level rules in the system that mention the same attribute in their premise as they do in their actions. For example (paraphrasing): *If you think the identity of the organism is pseudomonas, and the patient has skin lesions, then that's strong additional evidence that the identity is in fact pseudomonas.* Such rules are referred to as "self-referencing." The current certainty factor model requires that all the non-self-referencing rules be invoked before those which are self-referencing. (Failure to do so would eliminate the commutative property of certainty factors, and the final result might be dependent on the order in which rules were invoked.)

In very early versions of the system, the mechanism that insured this partial ordering was a heavily recursive, rather obscure piece of code. It was not at all obvious what its purpose was, nor that this restriction on rule order existed. A later version included a separate function that did a straightforward reordering of the rule list just before it was invoked. This at least made fairly obvious what was happening and indicated explicitly what the ordering constraint was. Embedding this constraint in a meta-rule (Figure 7–2) represents a step toward a totally explicit, accessible chunk of knowledge. The constraint is now quite clear, can be explained to the user by the system itself (using the explanation capabilities outlined in chapter 3), and can be modified (if necessary) by editing the rule. [13]

METARULE003

If   1) there are rules which do not mention the current goal in their
            premise
        2) there are rules which mention the current goal in their premise
Then it is definite that the former should be done before the latter.

PREMISE   ($AND(THEREARE OBJRULES ($AND (DOESNTMENTION FREEVAR ACTION CURGOAL))
                            SET1)
                   (THEREARE OBJRULES ($AND (MENTIONS FREEVAR PREMISE CURGOAL)
                            SET2))
ACTION   (CONCLIST SET1 DOBEFORE SET2 1000)

Figure 7–2   Example of a control structure meta-rule.

A part of the rule interpreter has itself been encoded in rule form. It may prove
possible to express additional parts of the control structure in meta-rules. Each
time this is accomplished it means that some additional element of the system's
behavior becomes accessible and, hence, can be explained or modified using the
existing facilities.

7–4.4.4   Encoding Design Decision Information

For the sake of human engineering, it makes good sense during an infectious
disease consultation to ask about positive cultures (those which displayed bacterial
growth) before those that turned up negative. Originally, this decision was
embedded quite subtly in the ordering of a list internal to the system code. It
can be stated easily in a meta-rule, however, as shown in Figure 7–3.

Such decisions, based on human engineering, are common in user-oriented
systems. Expressing this information in a rule renders it explicit and accessible,
making possible its explanation and modification.

In summary, since meta-rules act by pruning or reordering the list of rules
to be invoked, they can be used to express any part of the control structure or
the design decisions that can be understood in those terms.

7–4.5   Explanation and Acquisition

One important advantage of a uniform encoding of different levels of knowledge is
the ability to use a single set of facilities for all levels. In the case of explanation,
for instance, all the machinery described earlier that deals with object-level rules
can be employed to deal with meta-rules. To do this, it proved necessary to make

---

[13] There was actually an intermediate solution which illustrates the standard conflict
between efficiency and comprehensibility. When it was agreed that changes to the knowledge
base would not be made while a consultation was in progress, it became possible to meet the
constraint by pre-setting the order of each internal list of rules by hand and keeping them
stored in that order. This eliminates all execution time overhead, but also means that all
representation of the constraint has disappeared from the system.

METARULE004

If   1) there are rules which are relevant to positive cultures, and
          2) there are rules which are relevant to negative cultures
Then it is definite that the former should be done before the latter.


```
PREMISE        ($AND(THEREARE OBJRULES ($AND (APPLIESTO FREEVAR POSCUL))
                            SET1)
                    (THEREARE OBJRULES ($AND (APPLIESTO FREEVAR NEGCUL))
                            SET2))
ACTION        (CONCLIST SET1 DOBEFORE SET2 1000)
```

Figure 7-3   Example of a design decision meta-rule.

only two small extensions, augmenting the existing record of rule invocations to include meta-rules and providing the natural language facilities for explaining the meta-rule's contribution to program performance. An example of the capability that resulted is shown in a consultation segment below. (Because METARULE001 refers to culture source, which is already known when the rule is invoked, it does not normally generate any questions and is thus transparent to the user. For the sake of illustration, the first clause has been changed to one that does generate a question, giving the user an opportunity to request an explanation.)

```
---------ORGANISM-1---------
10) Enter the identity of ORGANISM-1:
** UNK
11) Is ORGANISM-1 a rod or coccus (etc.):
** ROD
12) The gram stain of ORGANISM-1:
** NEG
13) Do you consider George Filbert to be a compromised host
    (alcoholic, immunosuppressed, etc.)?
** WHY
[i.e. WHY is it important to determine whether or not PATIENT-
4
 is a compromised host?]
[1.0] This will help determine a strategy for deducing the
      identity of ORGANISM-1.
      If
 [1.1] the patient is a compromised host, and
 [1.2] there are rules which mention in their premise a
      previous organism which may be the same as the current
      organism,
      then
It is definite (1.0) that each of them is not going to be
```

```
useful.
[METARULEOO1]
```

** HOW [1.0]

```
[i.e. HOW was the strategy for deducing the identity of
ORGANISM-1 determined?]
At that point METARULEOO1 was being used.
    In addition, the following were also used:
    [1.3] METARULEOO3 indicated it is definite that the former
            should be done before the latter
```

{*Due to the primitive approach to natural language, rule translation can be a bit cryptic at times. However, see below, where the full rule text makes things a little clearer.* }

** HOW [1.3]

```
[i.e. HOW was METARULEOO3 used?]
If [2.1] there are rules which do not mention the current goal
            in their premise, and
    [2.2] there are rules which mention the current goal in
            their premise
Then it is definite that the former should be done before the
latter.
[METARULEOO3]
```

We have not yet attempted the interactive acquisition of meta-rules—their slightly more complex syntax requires generalizing some of the details of the acquisition routines. It does not appear to be a difficult problem, however, and beyond it lie some interesting issues. Given the success with acquisition of object-level rules in the context of a bug, can the same be done with meta-rules? What are the superficial manifestations of a bug that suggest the need for a change in the way established knowledge is used (rather than a change in the content of the knowledge itself)? We have considered this briefly and the most obvious case seems to be one analogous to human behavior. When someone inexperienced in a domain takes a plausible, but (to the expert) inappropriate approach to a problem, the expert can often spot it and inquire why the novice took that approach. Similar situations may be encountered in which the program starts off on a plausible, but incorrect track; the appropriate remedy may be a new meta-rule. This appears to be one interesting direction for future work.

7-4.6 Limitations of the Current Implementation, Future Work

There are several shortcomings in the present implementation. Some are due to fundamental issues of system organization, while others are the result of limited experience with these constructs and, thus, may change in time.

One limitation arises from the way meta-rules augment the performance program's control structure. In the present implementation, their effect is constrained to the reordering or pruning of rule lists. While this is useful, examples above demonstrate that it offers a limited capability for encoding aspects of the control structure. More important, it provides no means of effecting the more interesting capability of switching methodologies. Since medical diagnosis is known to be a complex set of behaviors (see, e.g., [Miller75]), it might prove useful to be able to shift back and forth between, say, a goal-directed and a data-directed invocation of rules as the consultation progresses. (See Section 7–4.6 for some thoughts on how this might be accomplished.)

A second limitation is the restriction on circumstances under which meta-rules are invoked. As illustrated, they are invoked when a goal is sought or when a conclusion is made. There are many other events that could quite usefully trigger them. In particular, the *failure* of one of the object-level rules might be very informative and could suggest a useful reordering or pruning of the remainder of the list. The basic problem is that meta-rules are simply not a general demon-like mechanism. This may eventually be changed if a reasonably efficient scheme can be found which will avoid some of the overhead typically associated with demons.

One particularly useful application of such a scheme would be its use in conjunction with non-exhaustive application of the object-level rules. We noted above that, due to the exhaustive search currently used by the performance program, meta-rules typically do not change the final result reached by the program but can, instead, make the program appear more rational as it works to determine the answer. Non-exhaustive search might be implemented by adding "after-the-fact" meta-rules to the system: These would be meta-rules executed after an attempt had been made to determine the value of a specific attribute. In this case meta-rules executed before the search might indicate that only one or two reasoning paths should be tried. Meta-rules executed after the search could test the strength of the conclusions made so far and could perhaps indicate that the system should "go back and try again," this time exploring additional paths. This would permit the creation of strategies that decide when the result is "good enough" to make further search unprofitable and may prove quite useful when the rule base becomes very large.

The present implementation of meta-rules also has a problem of comprehensibility: The translations of the meta-rules shown earlier are not particularly lucid. This is due primarily to the primitive approach to natural language used in the system, especially the clause-by-clause approach to translation of rules. As the meta-rules begin to play a larger part in controlling the system's behavior, it will become important to provide a more sophisticated translation, one which yields more comprehensible results.

There are also limitations that arise out of the decision to encode strategies in the same production rule format as the object-level rules. While this offers the important advantage of a uniform encoding of knowledge, production rules are not well suited to the expression of complex control structures. In particular, they are not a particularly transparent medium for expressing a "chunk" of behavior that requires more than a single rule (see [Davis77a] for a discussion of this point). More generally, the issue of an appropriate strategy language is still an open question.

Problems also arise from the restricted syntax available in MYCIN and adopted, for the sake of uniformity, in TEIRESIAS. In particular, the fact that the only "action" currently available is to make a conclusion means that meta-rules can be used to perform only a limited "direction" of the use of object-level rules, reordering or pruning the list before it is invoked.

Finally, there is the subtlety of the distinction in the implementation of the "statement-of-utility" and "line-of-reasoning" types of strategy. As indicated earlier, at each goal the system retrieves all the meta-rules for the current attribute, as well as for any attributes above it in the current goal chain. It is necessary to distinguish between rules that are intended to be applicable at only a single level (*i.e.*, "statement of utility" types) and those that apply to an arbitrary number of levels (*i.e.*, anywhere along the line of reasoning leading to the goal). This is handled currently by a somewhat obscure solution to what is really a much larger, nontrivial issue: the problem of implicit context, described in Section 2–4. The difference in effect of associating a meta-rule with an attribute as opposed to an object is another aspect of this same issue and suffers from a similar obscurity.

7–5   BROADER IMPLICATIONS

The discussion thus far has centered on the concept of saturation and our method for dealing with it, namely, the use of meta-level knowledge as a site for embedding strategies to guide the program. As previous examples have shown, this technique is also useful for guiding program performance even when the system is not saturated.

At this point the discussion broadens to consider some interesting additional issues that arise from examining the mechanisms used to implement meta-rules. We consider in particular the implications that follow from two features: (a) meta-rules' ability to select object-level rules by direct examination of object-level rule code and (b) meta-rules' use of an explicit functional specification of retrieval criteria. The focus here is on these techniques as they apply to programming in general, not just the encoding of strategy information. We begin by examining in some detail the difference between various approaches to referencing knowledge sources.

7–5.1   Reference by Name vs. Reference by Description

Since strategies (in any form) are used to direct the invocation of object-level KSs, they must have some way of referencing them. Two fundamentally different approaches have typically been employed; we term them *reference by name* and *reference by description*. The former lists all KSs explicitly, while the latter offers a predicate indicating required characteristics. The THUSE construct of PLANNER uses reference by name, allowing the programmer to name one or more theorems that are likely to be especially useful. The effect of a statement like

```
(THGOAL (WIN POKER HAND) (THUSE BLUFF DRAW3 CHEAT))
```

is to specify the order in which some of the plausibly useful theorems will be applied. The GOALCLASS statement in QA4 is quite similar.

Meta-rules, on the other hand, effect reference by description. As previous examples have illustrated, they make conclusions about a class of rules that is specified by describing relevant characteristics. METARULE002, for instance, refers to *rules which mention pseudomonas in their conclusion.* PLANNER's theorem base filter (THTBF) construct is another example of this general sort of capability: It allows the specification of an arbitrary predicate to filter the selection of theorems to be applied to a goal.

There are numerous advantages to reference by description, primarily in terms of the ability of the knowledge base to accommodate changes. These are explored later in Section 7–5.3.3. Here we examine a more detailed point: the implications involved in two different ways of accomplishing reference by description.

7–5.2   External Descriptors vs. Content Reference

One way to accomplish reference by description is via a set of external descriptors. That is, a number of different characteristics could be chosen and each KS described in terms of them. For an ordinary procedure, for instance, the descriptor set might include elements describing the procedure's main effect, any side effects, preconditions for its use, etc. Strategies would then describe the relevant class of procedures in these terms.

The second implementation is by direct examination of KS content and is illustrated by meta-rules. For instance, when METARULE002 refers to *rules that mention pseudomonas in their premise,* the relevant set is determined by retrieving the premise of each of the rules in question and examining it directly to see if it contains the desired item.[14] That is, the meta-rules examine the code of the object-level rules to detect or infer the presence of any relevant characteristic.

This general notion of allowing one part of the system to examine the rules (code) executed by other parts is based on three main ideas. First, there is the concept of the unity of code and data structure, first suggested in the notion of a stored program computer and later made convenient by the LISP language. Second, the rules must be stored in a comprehensible form. In this case that means interpreted LISP code, written in a stylized form; but in general any relatively high-level language will do. Finally, the syntax and some of the semantics of that high-level language must be represented within the system, to be used as a guide in examining the code. In the current example, the syntax is represented by the template for each predicate function (allowing each function to describe its own

---

[14] This is accomplished via the template mechanism described in chapter 2.

calls) and the stylized form of rules. Semantics are supplied in part by internal data structures, which indicate, for example, that SAMEBUG is an attribute.

7–5.3   Benefits of Content Reference as an Invocation Mechanism

There are a number of interesting implications that follow from the use of content-reference as an invocation mechanism. The technique makes possible a system in which invocation has a greater degree of *reliability* and *expressiveness* (defined below), a system that makes it easier for a user to define his own *generalized invocation criteria*, and a system with a higher degree of *flexibility* in responding to changes. We consider each of these in turn, then review the limitations of our approach and the difficulties that remain before the benefits noted can be fully realized.

7–5.3.1   Reliability and Expressiveness

Effecting reference by description through direct examination of KS content can be seen as another step in the development of KS invocation mechanisms. To clarify this, consider breaking down the invocation process into two phases: determining the *relevance* and determining the *applicability* of a KS. The first involves the retrieval of one or more KSs that may plausibly be useful; the second concerns the actual determination of applicability. In the STRIPS system [Fikes71], for instance, relevance of an operator is determined by the contents of the add list, while its applicability is indicated by its preconditions.

The determination of relevance for a KS will be based on some link to it, a *handle* by which it can be referenced and retrieved (*e.g.*, in STRIPS, the add list).[15] We will be concerned here primarily with the various types of handles which have been used and, in particular, with their *reliability* and *expressiveness* (defined below). Table 7–1 sums up the discussion that follows.

Consider, first, the types of handles that have been used. In a historical perspective, the concept of a subroutine (procedure) can be viewed as the introduction of the notion of a distinct, nontrivial KS. The only handle on it was its name, assigned by the programmer.

The first major departure from this came in GPS [Newell72], and GPS-like systems such as STRIPS. In the latter, as noted, the handle on each KS is provided by the contents of its add list. Note that part of the *definition* of the KS itself (the add list) provides the handle and the name of the KS has become inconsequential.

Production rules are similar, since they are retrieved on the basis of symbols appearing in either their left- or right-hand sides, symbols which are part of the definition of the KS itself.

---

[15] We distinguish between the *handle* and *body* of a KS: The body is the part actually executed [or interpreted], while the handle is anything that is used as a way of accessing the body. Thus, for a subroutine, the name is the handle and its code is the body; while for a PLANNER theorem, the pattern is the handle and the theorem code is the body. As will become clear, the handle and the body are not necessarily distinct.

With the advent of PLANNER-like languages (PLANNER, QA4, etc.), the important concepts of pattern-directed and goal-directed invocation were firmly established as standard programming language tools. These languages provided links to KSs via patterns that were used to describe either the goal which the KS could achieve (consequent theorems) or the event to which it was relevant (antecedent and erasing theorems). Once again, the KS name is irrelevant.

Consider now the expressiveness and the reliability of the handles provided by current programming techniques (see Figure 7–4) and the impact of using each of them. We define *expressiveness* as the richness of the language that can be used in a handle. One crude measure is: Does it make any difference to program performance if every occurrence of a KS handle in the program text is uniformly replaced by some arbitrary string? That is, is the handle merely a token or does its structure convey information?

The *reliability* of a handle is determined by the nature of the relationship between the handle and the KS body. A crude measure might be seen in the effect of editing the KS: If I retrieve a KS because it supposedly has some property (*e.g.*, it supposedly accomplishes a particular goal), then can I change the KS in such a way as to remove that property, yet leave unchanged the invocation pattern based on that feature?

For example, the *name* of a subroutine is purely a token and is devoid of semantics (except of course in the programmer's mind). There is only one way to express which subroutine you want (by naming it); hence this technique has minimal expressiveness. Since there is no formal connection between the name and contents, arbitrary changes can be made to the code without affecting whether or not the subroutine is invoked. In this case, the handle has minimal reliability. As a result, the programmer himself must know exactly what each subroutine contains and select, by name, the proper one at the proper point in his program.

With the advent of pattern-directed invocation, the subroutine acquired a *pattern* which is used as the handle. There is a limited but useful sort of expressiveness here, in a syntax that typically permits a broad range of patterns. The structure of the pattern conveys information and, hence, can not in general be replaced by an arbitrary string without affecting program performance. Consider, however, the reliability of the link. Note that it is the programmer who writes both the body and the pattern for the KS, hence there is no guaranteed correspondence. Arbitrary changes can be made to the body of a PLANNER theorem, for instance, without changing whether or not it is invoked.

Goal-directed invocation was another step toward increased expressiveness as the pattern acquired an interpretation, which added further richness to the language. In PLANNER, for instance, there are three classes of patterns (goal, assertion event, and erasing event), while QA4 offers an extensive set of categories in a general demon mechanism. But the reliability remains the same (*i.e.*, minimal). Indeed, there is the potential for much deviousness in allowing the programmer to cause the invocation of an arbitrary body of code based on a pattern which may or may not describe what the theorem actually achieves:[16]

> The subroutines are not referenced by their names. Instead they are called because they accept arguments with a certain structure, and because *the programmer claimed* that they will solve goals of a certain class.[17]

As the final step in this dimension we have the use of a set of descriptors, the "external descriptor" approach described earlier. Note that this is a generalization of goal-directed invocation, since the "purpose" of a KS is only one description of it. Any number of other facts about it may prove relevant and could, equally well, be supplied. A suitably large set of such descriptors would make possible a useful language for referencing a KS. As *external* descriptors, however, they have no formal relationship to the KS body, and their reliability remains minimal— arbitrary changes to the body may render those descriptions inaccurate, yet the invocation pattern of the KS would remain unchanged.

The link in GPS and STRIPS is, as noted, based on part of the definition of the KS itself (the add list) and thus has a stronger degree of reliability. Consider that we cannot, for instance, changed the effect of the operator (say by changing one of the terms of the add list) without also seeing a change in its invocation pattern.[18] However, all of the retrieval mechanism is contained in the means-ends analysis that is embedded in the system interpreter and the programmer has no control over which KS is invoked. Thus, while the handle on the KS is reliable, the user has no means of expressing his preferences for which should be retrieved. Production rules are similar: The link is reliable because it is based on the content of the KS (the symbols appearing on the left or right hand side), but there is the same sort of single, "hardwired" mechanism that effects the retrieval, leaving the user no opportunity to express a preference.[19]

Traditional invocation mechanisms thus offer varying degrees of expressiveness and reliability. Is it possible to obtain both of these at once? The current implementation of meta-rules uses a technique that takes one step in this direction; we term it *content-directed invocation* to suggest its place in the ongoing

---

[16] And herein lies a seductive trap. The KS handle is no longer a token but conveys information. When that information is advertised as a "purpose," it is easy to start believing that every KS is sure to achieve its advertised "purpose." Consider the psychological difference between asking for "any KS whose pattern matches the following" and asking for "any KS that achieves the following goal." Note that the computational mechanism for both is identical and the difference (the interpretation of the pattern as a goal) exists purely in the programmer's mind. The first asks the proper question, in that it assumes nothing more than it can deliver; the latter is fraught with easily misinterpreted connotations. It is easy to forget that it is the programmer's responsibility to make sure each KS achieves its advertised effect.

[17] From the QA4 manual [Rulifson72], (emphasis added).

[18] Note that such a change in the add list may make the operator semantically incorrect (*i.e.*, it may no longer describe a valid operator in the domain). Content-directed invocation does not guarantee that the operator is semantically meaningful, only that it does in fact have the property for which it is being retrieved.

[19] It is possible to force specified interactions by anticipating the operation of the retrieval mechanism, but this is often difficult for a large system and is, in any case, contrary to the "spirit" of the formalism. See [Davis77a], especially Section 5, for a discussion of the issue.

development of KS invocation methods.[20]

It has a high degree of reliability because, like production rules and GPS-like systems, it references the KS code directly. Recall that by "reliability" we mean that the KS retrieved will in fact achieve the desired effect. That is, METARULE002, for example (Figure 7–1), will retrieve an object-level rule not because of the rule name, the rule number, or other external descriptor, but because examination of the code of that object-level rule reveals that it does in fact conclude about enterobacteriaceae. Content-directed invocation cannot of course assure that the object-level rule makes this conclusion with the appropriate justification—it would be far more difficult for the system to determine that a KS not only achieves a desired effect but does so based on reasoning (or actions) appropriate to and justifiable in the domain. Thus whether the object-level rule deduces enterobacteriaceae for valid medical reasons is a different issue that would require a great deal more inference on the part of the system. We claim to have taken only a first step (from external descriptors to content-reference) but submit that it can be a useful advance, especially in a knowledge base undergoing frequent revision.

Content-directed invocation is also expressive, since it offers a way of using any computable predicate (*e.g.*, MENTIONS in Figure 7–1). The link thus inherits its expressiveness from the programming language in which the system is written.

To see the potential impact of this, consider once again the historical perspective. The programmer using procedures effectively says "give me that KS next," indicating it by name. In GPS-STRIPS and traditional production systems, the user has little or no control over which KS is invoked next. PLANNER made it possible to say "give me any KS whose pattern matches this one"; in using that pattern as a designator of a goal, the request becomes "give me any KS that (supposedly) achieves the goal designated." Finally, content-directed invocation makes it possible to say "give me any KS that fits the following description." By writing the proper sort of description, we can have invocation that is goal-directed, side-effect-directed, speed-directed—in short, directed by any one or a combination of factors. Because direct reference is made to the content of the KSs being retrieved, we have a high degree of reliability as well.

Consider pursuing this one step further. The second clause of the premise of the meta-rule in Figure 7–1

(THEREARE OBJRULES(MENTIONS CNTXT PREMISE SAMEBUG) SET1))

is one very simple example of content-directed invocation. It determines whether or not an object-level rule mentions the attribute SAMEBUG. Consider then the impact of second order meta-rules—they can be used to select the criteria by which the KSs will be characterized. Thus we not only allow the user to specify arbitrary criteria to control retrieval, but make it possible for him to encode

[20] There has been a parallel evolution in access to memory locations, from absolute binary, to symbolic addressing in assemblers, to relocatable core images, on up to content addressable memories (*e.g.*, LEAP [Feldman72]). Content-directed invocation can thus be seen as the procedural analogue of content addressable memory.

knowledge that decides dynamically which are the most appropriate criteria to use.

Note that a plausible alternative to content-directed invocation would be the formalization of the link between the external descriptors and the body of the KS. There are at least two ways this mapping might be provided. The first is a "descriptor verifier" approach. This would involve submitting to a deductive system both the code for a KS and some descriptors for it, then allowing the deductive system to attempt to prove the correctness of the descriptors (much like current work in program verification). Another scheme would be to use a "descriptor generator," which, provided with the KS code and a characterization of the descriptors desired, would automatically generate them. A simple version of this was done some time ago: GPS was capable of constructing its own table of connections when supplied with operators in the form of rewrite rules (*e.g.*, symbolic logic transformation rules) and a set of routines for defining differences ([Newell59], [Newell61]). It matched the left- and right-hand sides of the rules and applied each difference detector to the result. This was feasible because the KS "code" had a very simple form, and because the "characterization of descriptors" was a procedure for finding the relevant features.

More powerful versions of either of these, however, would require substantial advances in the state of the art. It seems more reasonable for the time being to use content-directed invocation, which employs a procedural definition of the characteristic desired and allows the procedure to access the KS code, as the function MENTIONS does.

7–5.3.2 Generalized Invocation Criteria

All of the development thus far has been in the context of "tuning" a single control structure, in this case, goal-directed invocation. We noted above that the expressiveness of content-directed invocation made possible tuning based on a very wide range of criteria: any criterion that could be expressed in a computable predicate that examined the KS code. This is one interesting ability that arises from the use in meta-rules of an explicit, functional specification of desired KSs. That is, the meta-rule premise is, in effect, an executable procedure for selecting the appropriate KSs.

The ability to specify retrieval criteria can be turned to another use, which we term *generalized invocation criteria*. The point is simply to apply this criteria-defining capability to the specification of the basic control regime, rather than limiting its use to tuning an established control structure. To see how this might work, consider that, for example, goal-directed invocation might be specified as

```
Use rules that mention the current goal in their action.
```

while data-directed invocation might be phrased as

```
Use rules mentioning the current conclusion in their premise.
```

Table 7–1   KS Invocation Mechanisms.

KS Invocation Mechanisms

KS TYPE	TYPE OF HANDLE	VALIDITY	EXPRESSIVENESS
subroutine	name	minimal	minimal
GPS - STRIPS	add list	strong	very limited, hardwired
production rule	symbols in rule	strong	very limited, hardwired
PLANNER theorem	pattern + recommendation list advice	minimal	3 categories (goal assertion, erasing) and limited syntax
QA4 operator	pattern + GOALCLASS advice	minimal	syntax similar to PLANNER, but wider set of categories in a general demon mechanism
content directed invocation	arbitrary predicate on KS contents	explicit, formalized, testable	extensive, extensible, softwired

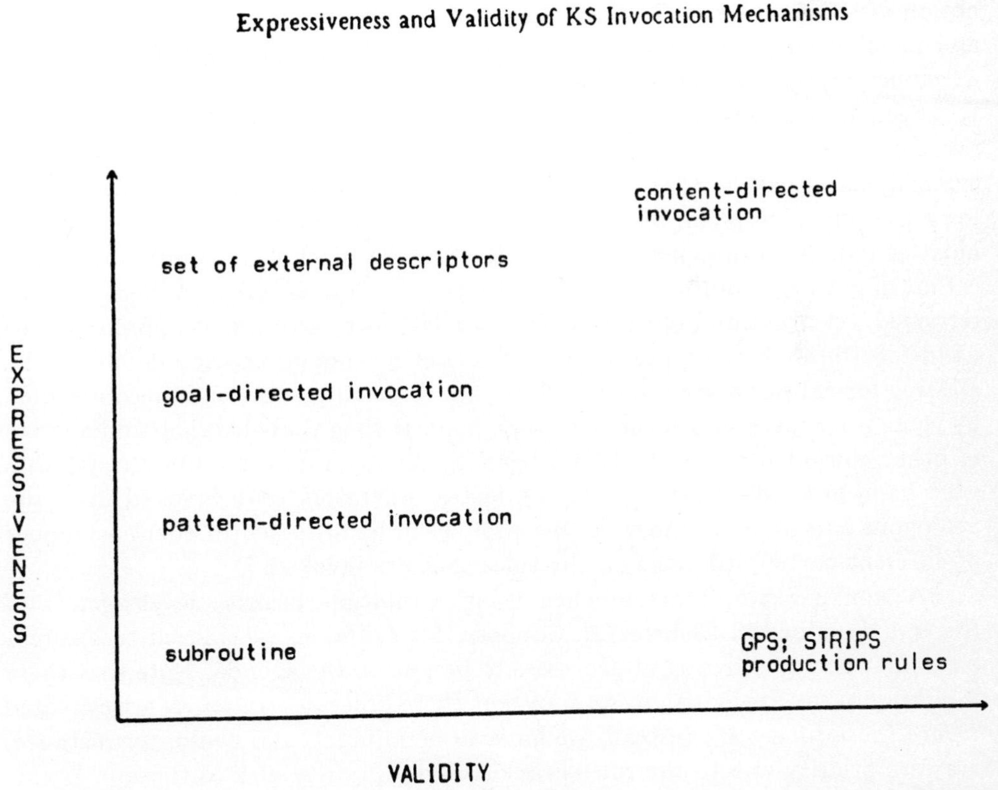

Expressiveness and Validity of KS Invocation Mechanisms

E
X
P
R
E
S
S
I
V
E
N
E
S
S

content-directed
invocation

set of external descriptors

goal-directed invocation

pattern-directed invocation

subroutine

GPS; STRIPS
production rules

VALIDITY

Figure 7-4   Expressiveness and Reliability of KS Invocation Mechanisms.

We might similarly specify new kinds of control regimes, as, for instance, the "speed-directed" retrieval criterion mentioned above. While accomplishing such sophisticated retrieval in its most precise and general form would be very difficult (since it would require automating part of analysis of algorithms), such a general solution is not required. Within the context of MYCIN, for example, the speed of a rule is dependent on a small number of well-known factors (including the number of premise clauses, number of new [unexamined] attributes mentioned, etc.). Similar analyses of other representations may yield analogous formulations, and even a good approximation would still be very effective in guiding KS retrieval. Hence as long as we are willing to work with a given representation (or set of representations), we need not solve the problem in complete generality in order to make use of the idea of generalized invocation criteria.

The ability to specify such generalized criteria appears to offer at least three advantages. First, it frees the programmer from the limitation of using only those control regimes (*e.g.*, goal-directed or data-directed) already hardwired into the programming language in use. That is, we have offered the programmer the notion of retrieval itself: The criteria for KS retrieval are no longer predefined and embedded in the language interpreter, but can be specified and changed (even dynamically) by the user himself.

Second, it makes possible an added degree of explicitness in program representation. To see the benefits that accrue from such explicitness, consider what typically happens when the available set of invocation mechanisms is incomplete for a particular problem: The programmer often resorts to various devious implicit or indirect techniques to achieve the desired effect. One popular approach is that of getting a multitude of effects from a single mechanism. Where KSs are retrieved via pre-computed index lists, for instance, a common approach is to hand-tool the ordering of these lists to achieve effects not otherwise available in the existing formalism. For example, where goal-directed invocation is accomplished by using pre-computed lists of operators, hand-tooling these lists can add a range of other control regimes. In [Waldinger74], for instance, the GOALCLASS lists were hand-ordered to insure that the fastest operators were invoked first; the analogous lists in MYCIN have, in the past, been hand-tooled to effect a number of different partial orderings on the rules that are invoked.

A similar example arises when using a multiple priority level agenda of the sort described in [Bobrow77]. Suppose, for example, we wanted to insure a particular partial ordering of processes to be put on the agenda. Note that there is no way to say explicitly, *make sure that these processes (in set A) are executed before those (in set B)*. Instead, we have to be indirect, and could, for instance, assign a priority of 6 to the rules in set A and a priority of 5 to those in B.

There are a number of problems associated with trying to do these sorts of indirect encodings, all of which seem to arise from the fact that information is unavoidably lost by the indirection involved. Note that in all the cases above, the intent of the hand-tooling and indirect priority setting is nowhere recorded.

The resulting system is both opaque and prone to bugs. To see the opacity of the system, consider, for instance, the agenda example where, after the priorities have been set, it will not be apparent *why* the processes in A were given higher priority than those in B. Were they more likely to be useful or was it desirable that those in A precede those in B no matter how useful each might be? After a while, even the programmer who set these priorities may forget what motivated the particular priorities chosen.

Bugs can arise in this setting due both to execution-time events and events in the long-term development of the program. Consider for instance what happens if, during a run, before any of the processes in A are invoked, an event occurs which makes it clear that the priority of processes in A ought to be reduced (for reasons unrelated to the desired partial ordering). If we adjust only the priority of those in A, an execution-time bug arises, since the desired relative ordering may be lost. Yet there is no record of the necessary interconnection of priorities to remind us to adjust all of them. A similar problem can arise during the long-term development of the program if we attempt to introduce another indirect effect by juggling priorities and end up modifying those in set A without making the necessary adjustments to those in B.

The problem with this approach is that it tries to use a single invocation mechanism to accomplish a number of effects. It does this by reducing a number of different, incommensurate factors to a single number, *with no record of how that number was reached.* Meta-rules, on the other hand, offer a mechanism for making these sorts of considerations explicit and for leaving a record of why a set of processes was queued in a particular order.

Third, meta-rules offer the advantage of *localizing* all of the control information. Note that juggling priorities means trying to achieve a global effect via a number of scattered local adjustments. This is often quite difficult and can be very hard to change or update. Localizing each such invocation criterion in a single meta-rule makes subsequent modifications easier. Since all of the information is in one place, changing a criterion can be accomplished by editing the relevant meta-rule rather than searching through a program for all the places in which priorities have been set to effect that criterion.

Our historical overview provides one further observation. Consider viewing the progress from standard procedure-calling to techniques like goal-directed invocation as making it possible to be less precise, and therefore less restrictive, about the role of a given procedure in a program. Where invocation by name (*i.e.*, procedures) requires that we decide exactly *where* and *when* the code is to be invoked, goal-directed invocation requires only that we specify *how* a procedure is to be used. The perspective suggested here moves us another step along that line, by considering retrieval separately from the writing of a KS. The programmer can, if he desires, write a KS without specifying how it is to be used and can leave this up to the invocation criteria to decide.

The point here is not that the programmer should not specify such information, since it can be very useful for cutting down combinatorics. For inference rules, for instance, it is important to know which are more useful in the goal-directed mode and which are more useful in the data-directed mode. Such information can cut down search or control the number of forward inferences drawn from a new assertion. The point is that if the programmer does want to specify such things, it is better if he is not limited to making that information synonymous with the handle used to retrieve the code. (This occurred in PLANNER, for instance, where the indication that a theorem ought to be used in a goal-directed mode for a particular pattern became the sole way of indexing it [by the single goal pattern].) If we keep these two things separate, we allow information about appropriate use to become a piece of advice rather than a constraint.

7–5.3.3   Flexibility

The choice of a KS reference technique (name, external descriptor, or content reference) can have a significant impact on the difficulty of making changes to a program. As we will see, content reference offers a number of advantages in this respect.

This consideration becomes particularly important for the applications we have described: Since much of our effort has involved making it possible for the expert to augment the knowledge base, we should take advantage of any means of minimizing the difficulty involved in propagating the effects of a change. Such flexibility will also become increasingly important as knowledge base construction proceeds, since as a program gets larger it becomes increasingly difficult to cope with the effects of changes.

For the sake of discussion, we identify two classes of such flexibility: *Compile time flexibility* is the ability to make changes in the knowledge base between performance runs and then have those changes integrated throughout the system; *execution time flexibility* refers to the ability to switch strategies during execution, under program control. This section deals with the former. Comments in Section 7–5.5 below deal with the latter.

To judge the impact of selecting one or another of the reference techniques, we examine two types of changes: editing or adding a (object-level) KS to the system, and editing or adding a strategy (meta-rule). [21] See Table 7–2 for an overview.

Consider, for example, the effect of editing (or adding) a KS and imagine that strategies used the reference-by-name approach. First, after editing a KS in such a system, all strategies that mention it must be retrieved and examined to see if they still apply, and then must be edited accordingly. Next, since it is also possible that the revised KS should now be mentioned in other strategies, the rest of the strategies must also be examined. Using the external-descriptor approach, we need only update the appropriate descriptors, which would be stored with the KS. In addition, the updating required should be evident from the sort of editing done on the KS itself. All relevant strategies will then automatically adjust to these changes. With content reference there is no additional effort of even updating descriptors since the strategies will adjust to the changes found

---

[21] While the impact is illustrated in the context of meta-rules and object-level rules, the point is more generally applicable to any kind of KS in a system invoking any other KS, regardless of the level of each.

in the edited KS.

Adding a new strategy to the system (or revising an old one) also causes problems for the reference-by-name approach: It is necessary to review all the KSs to determine which the new or revised strategy should mention. [22] Using external descriptors, it is possible that no additional effort is required, if the description in the new strategy uses the available "vocabulary" of descriptors. If, however, it requires a descriptor not yet in that vocabulary, we have the formidable task of reviewing all existing KSs and adding to each the appropriate entry for the new descriptor.

Thus there is a fundamental shortcoming in the external descriptor approach because it uses a fixed number of descriptive terms. Since adding a new term to this set can involve a lot of work, it becomes a task that should not be undertaken very often. Avoiding this updating problem is one important advantage of content reference: It gives meta-rules the ability to "go in and look" for any characteristic deemed significant. As a result, the addition of a new strategy with a new meta-level conceptual primitive is a transparent operation.

To make this clear, consider the following simple example. The performance program's backward chaining of rules produces a depth-first search of an and/or goal tree, where each clause of a rule may possibly sprout a new sub-tree. It might be useful, then, to try rules with the fewest clauses first. This approach would require a strategy that said something like *try those rules with three or fewer premise clauses first*, and might require a new meta-level primitive. In the external descriptor case, a property indicating the relevant information would have to be added to every rule. [23] Content reference makes the task much easier: We can write a new function that counts the number of premise clauses found in an object-level rule and use the function in a meta-rule. Nothing at all need be done to any object-level rule.

We claim, in addition, that the set of useful meta-level primitives is potentially large and therefore difficult to define a priori. Thus, over the course of most program development periods, it is effectively an open set, to which new members are continually being added. It is thus important to make this task as easy as possible. Where the external descriptor approach requires analyzing each new KS with reference to each of the descriptors, content reference requires simply that the new KS be "added to the pot." It will subsequently be referenced by any strategy that describes it appropriately.

---

[22] There is a plausible objection to this: It may be claimed that a new strategy is often written with some specific circumstance and purpose in mind and that this clearly restricts the number of KSs that need be considered to a small subset of the total. This is entirely correct. And it is on just such grounds that we would start to build the set of descriptors to be used in the reference by description approach. In part, then, the technique is simply a step toward greater formalization of knowledge already used in informal and ad hoc ways.

[23] This may not be a very difficult task if it is possible to write a bit of code that computes the relevant information and then apply it to every rule. This is, in fact, what we are suggesting, with two small but important differences. First, we don't bother to compute all properties of all object rules, so a considerable amount of space may be saved. Second, if this bit of code is kept around in a meta-rule, the addition of a new object-level rule later on is much easier.

To summarize, consider the difference between the first and third rows of Table 7–2. Note in particular how much easier it is to accomplish a number of standard knowledge base modifications. This can offer a substantive advantage when the knowledge base becomes appreciably large.

7–5.4 Limitations

The previous sections noted a number of the implications of using content-directed invocation: increased reliability and expressiveness of the handle used to retrieve a KS, the ability to specify generalized invocation criteria, and the flexibility of the system in responding to changes. There are, of course, a number of substantive difficulties in realizing all these benefits and a number of limitations to the techniques we have suggested. These are reviewed here to help outline the range of applicability of the work.

7–5.4.1 Reliability

The reliability of the "handle" provided by content reference arises from the ability to examine the code of a KS, yet we have dealt somewhat blithely in previous sections with this difficult problem. There are at least two sources of difficulty. First, even for a programmer, reading and understanding an arbitrary chunk of code can be difficult. Second, even if we could read it, it is not always clear what to look for: Try to specify for instance how to detect by reading its code what goal a procedure achieves.

TEIRESIAS currently has only the simplest form of code-examining ability, made possible by several useful shortcuts. We rely first on the nature of the representation in use. The organization of information in rules makes it possible to say that, for example, "rules which mention IDENTity in their conclusion" is an example of goal-directed retrieval. Second, the rules are viewed as a task-specific high-level language: The primitive terms they use are both domain-specific and reasonably abstract (e.g., "the culture was obtained from a STERILE SOURCE"). This makes their code much easier to decipher than, say, an assembly code version of the same thing. Finally, the code is strongly stylized (the predicates and associative triples), allowing us to use the template associated with each predicate function as a guide to deciphering code. As noted in chapter 2, the template describes the format of a call to the function (the order and generic type of its arguments), much like a simplified procedure declaration. Each predicate function thus carries a description of its own calls, and by referring to that description (i.e., retrieving the template associated with the CAR of a LISP form), we can dissect the call into its components (see Section 2–4.4).

We have, of course, thus far used this ability in only the most basic, syntactic ways. We have not yet developed means for deriving more interesting semantic content by examining code, and this is clearly a difficult problem. While the shortcuts described can be used with representations other than rules, they are not universally applicable. But while this whole problem is difficult, it is also a separable issue. That is, the extent of the current capability to examine code

Table 7–2   Flexibility benchmarks.

The Strategy Taxonomy

DIMENSION	SAMPLE POINTS	EXAMPLE
Generality	representation independent domain independent domain specific goal specific	Polya Green, Sacerdoti Gelernter PLANNER
Explicitness	conceptually implicit implementationally implicit explicit	Howe Green, Sacerdoti meta rules
Organization	KS-centered non-KS-centered, referral by name non-KS-centered, referral by description	HEARSAY II PLANNER: THUSE PLANNER: THTBF, meta rules
Character	individual, breadth comparative, breadth individual, depth comparative, depth	HEARSAY II PLANNER, QA4 STRIPS macro ops - - - - -

is extremely elementary, but even the simplest form of it makes available the interesting capabilities displayed above.

A more subtle point arises out of the possible suggestion that the scheme proposed here appears to be susceptible to the same criticism made of PLANNER: In our case, the user writes both the KS code and the predicates that examine it. There would seem to be room for chicanery in writing predicates specially tailored to the body of a particular KS. It is possible, for instance, to write a predicate that tests for the appearance of a uniquely named local variable in a program body, or that perhaps checks the time of day or phase of the moon.

Our claim, however, was not that the invocation criteria would always be meaningful, but only that they would be made explicit and precise. Thus, while it is curious to ask for a KS that contains the variable ZZ$XX, the user can in fact do this. The criterion may appear bizarre and may in fact be achieving some other effect indirectly via that variable name. But note that the criterion must be encoded explicitly in the predicate defined by the user, and hence there will at least be an explicit specification of the criterion used. This is an improvement over the situation where a list is hand-ordered, with no record left behind. We have supplied a means of specifying invocation criteria and a technique that can, if used correctly, insure that KSs are accurately described (i.e., by referencing the code directly). There are no constraints on how the user may choose to apply that capability, but any deviousness will at least be more explicit.

A further objection to our approach might claim that allowing arbitrary predicates to examine and characterize a KS may result in odd or unanticipated characterizations. This may in fact be an advantage and raises an interesting point. The use of knowledge in odd or unexpected ways is one aspect of that elusive quality, creativity. With this scheme, we have taken one small step toward making it possible for the system to discover that a particular KS has a characteristic that may not have occurred to the programmer who wrote the KS code. As a result, the system may find unexpected applications for its knowledge.

Even with the best of intentions, however, there remains the question of the correctness of the code that implements the content examination. That is, what the programmer intends to say in this invocation criteria "language" and what he actually writes may be slightly different. Have we, then, only pushed the problem back one level? No, because it has been formalized as well. Note that the "language" supplies a precise and explicit expression of the invocation criteria. Correctness is at least a well-specified and testable question.

7–5.4.2 Expressiveness and Generalized Invocation Criteria

One of the weaker claims made above concerned the expressiveness of content-directed invocation (and, by extension, the expressiveness of generalized invocation criteria). The weakness lies in our suggesting that the programmer use the programming language itself to express retrieval criteria, without having supplied any guidance or hints about how to do this effectively.

The combination of the meta-rules and LISP is, at best, adequate (in the sense of being able to express any computable predicate) and extensible only because, for example, new predicate functions can be added to the rule language by writing them in LISP. It would be better, of course, if the meta-rule language already included a set of primitives that provided a foundation for expressing invocation criteria. Then we could suggest not only that "it's useful to be able to define your own, generalized invocation criteria" but might also say, "and here's a well-designed language that will help get you started, without restricting you since it's also extensible." We have not as yet developed such a language; this is a focus for continued work.

The problem is difficult for many reasons, including the fact that the task of assembling the "vocabulary" of descriptors may appear quite imposing, and perhaps endless. What guarantee have we that there are in fact a finite number of descriptors (*i.e.*, a finite number of conceptual primitives for describing knowledge), rather than an infinite number of special characteristics? There may be no guarantee, but the benefits are in any case incremental—it is useful to write any of the system strategies in this form, so even a subset of the entire collection is useful.

7–5.4.3 Flexibility

We have emphasized the benefits of flexibility, but it is important to consider these benefits in the appropriate context. While it may be obvious, it is worth noting that the task at hand must somehow require this kind of flexibility. In our particular application it arises from the emphasis on the necessity of incremental construction of large performance programs. The central point is that there will be a large number of knowledge sources and strategies, with frequent changes to both over an extended period of time. In this case there is a premium on the ability to organize and manipulate knowledge. This is not necessarily true for smaller, well-established systems whose knowledge base has stabilized.

7–5.4.4 Speed

All of the advantages claimed for content-directed invocation depend on the indirection inherent in content reference. Yet examining KS code to find some property can be a time-consuming affair, even when looking for the presence of a particular token. The potential for loss of speed becomes acute when we consider the time taken in inferring the presence of some more subtle property, which requires invocation of several meta-rules for each object-level rule.

However, like many similar constructs, most of the computational cost can be paid in a background computation between performance runs. During that time the system could compute the sets of KSs determined by the various descriptions. The results might either be saved for execution time use, or, in a form of "pre-compiling," the source code might be rewritten, replacing the descriptions with the sets they define. This offers both the flexibility of reference by description

```
... source^i^i
          =compiler^i^i=>
                  source^i
                      =compiler^i=>
                             source
                                 =compiler=>
                                     machine language
```

Figure 7–5   Levels of code.

and the speed of reference by name. [24]

Other constructs (*e.g.*, LISP record structures) offer similar advantages, in providing a level of insulation from the effects of changes, without imposing execution time overhead. This particular example, however, effects a very standard compiler-style transformation: replacing a constant with its value. Since (by our definitions) the total KS set is fixed at compile time, the descriptions in a strategy are really constants and can be replaced by their values. This offers the symbolic analogue of the ability to write (SQRT(PI)/7), with the compiler doing the work to replace it with .253207683. The benefits of flexibility and clarity are identical.

It may be useful, then, to picture this process as a generalization of the usual view that there are two levels of code (source and machine language) and work with multiple source codes, each with its own compiler. This is indicated in Figure 7–5, with appropriate numbers to indicate level.

Each source further to the left is typically easier to read and understand, and more flexible, but also slower. It seems plausible to suggest that many of the techniques accepted for compilation and optimization of arithmetic expressions may have analogues in symbolic computation as well. (Related ideas are found in [Low74] and [Samet75].)

The generalized view of Figure 7–5 also demonstrates another point: The distinction we have drawn between compile time and execution time is one the user can determine on his own. The decision of what level of code to execute is entirely open—the higher level versions are more flexible, the lower level versions

---

[24] There are nontrivial problems associated with the appearance of free variables in the description parts, as in:

if conditions A and B hold, use any KS which deals with white cell counts at least as high as that of the current patient.

It is still possible, however, to turn this into a list of specific KS names. Consider the total range of the white cell count. Each KS in the system which deals with it will be relevant to a specific value or range of values. Thus, we can divide up the total range into, say, m different segments, and in each segment a specified set of KSs will be relevant. The single strategy above would have to be replaced with m strategies of the form,

if conditions A and B hold, and the white cell count is in range$_i$ then use $\{KS_{i1}, KS_{i2}, ...\}$

where range$_i$ is a segment of the total range and the descriptions have been replaced with the sets of relevant KSs. The same technique works for any continuous variable, of course; discrete valued variables are a degenerate case in which all the KSs are relevant to one or more single values rather than a range.

are faster. There is currently no way to have both at once, but given good compilers, the transformation is relatively painless. [25]

In general, then, the dividing line can be drawn at any point. Whatever is relegated to being a compile time transformation can be done in background mode and hence costs nothing at execution time.

Note that this also has some impact on the issue of complexity. It uses a succession of high-level languages, each of which suppresses more implementation detail and concentrates instead on the more important issue of knowledge organization and use.

7–5.4.5 Limitations: Summary

The point then is not that content-directed invocation ought to be used exclusively, nor that it replace concepts like goals, patterns, etc. We are concerned with the reliability of the connection between KS handles and KS code, how expressive the handles are, and what they contribute to the flexibility of the system in the face of changes to the knowledge base. Where possible, then, the approach of content-directed invocation provides a way of assuring a degree of reliability, can offer a more expressive syntax, and provides a flexibility that can be very useful.

7–5.5 Future Applications: Choosing Control Regimes

We described the use of strategies as a means of "tuning" a control structure and suggested in addition that content reference offered a means of defining generalized invocation criteria. While it has not as yet been implemented, we can imagine pushing this one step further. By adding another layer of rules above the invocation criteria, we might gain the ability to choose from among the set of criteria, that is, to choose the control regime to use. There would be a number of rules defining various retrieval criteria (goal, event, etc.) and a number of (meta-)rules which selected from among these rules and hence chose a control structure. This would make it possible for the program to dynamically change control structures as a problem progressed (an ability lacking in the current implementation, as noted in Section 7–4.6).

Such "execution time flexibility" would make possible a number of interesting abilities. Consider, for example, a program designed to do heuristic search. For domains in which a single search procedure does not provide effective performance, it would prove very useful for the program to be able to decide from moment to moment what form of search would most likely be successful. It might thus use branch and bound at one point, hill climbing at another, and so on. Note that we are not speaking of a pre-programmed succession of techniques, but an ability to choose each in response to changes in the problem state.

A more relevant example would be a system that attempted to simulate

---

[25] Work in this vein is described in [Mitchell70], which explores a programming language that makes possible the execution of different levels of code in a manner that is transparent to the user. See also [Hansen74], which describes a compiler that incrementally compiles and optimizes code according to the patterns of use and modification of the code.

the diagnostic behavior of an experienced clinician. Such behavior has been found ([Rubin75], [Miller75]) to be a complex shifting back and forth between processes of collecting data (event-driven implication), establishing causal chains (heuristic search), verifying (goal-directed search), and others. This is reminiscent of the general perspective on knowledge organization described earlier, since the physician is quite clearly changing his entire approach under the control of strategies ("clinical experience") that choose the most appropriate response.

Few computational systems have offered very much of this sort of flexibility, however. Typically, this results from three interrelated causes. The problem is that often an extensive amount of knowledge is (a) embedded in the control structure, (b) represented there only implicitly, and (c) treated on a special-case basis. In fact, much of what is typically described as clever coding or implementation technique often represents important insights into useful strategies. For example, [Green69], in describing modifications to resolution to allow his system to deal with program construction, mentions in passing several interesting domain-specific strategies. Expressing such chunks of knowledge as distinct strategies has in the past been inhibited by the lack of a convenient formalism and the difficulty of generalizing what may have been seen initially as simply a special-case coding trick.

Yet the desire for increased flexibility has a long history. Much of the early speculation about programs that could learn centered on the ability to shift strategies dynamically as the situation required. Gelernter mentioned it explicitly in 1959 [Gelernter59]; ten years later Green ([Green69]) discussed somewhat more concrete proposals centered around the possibility of expressing strategies in the same first-order predicate calculus that the rest of his system used. Meta-rules of the sort described in Section 7–4.4.3 make possible a limited form of execution time flexibility. They make part of the system's control structure explicit and accessible, and hence manipulable by other meta-rules.

What we are looking for, then, are "softwired" strategies. Achieving this objective is predicated on overcoming the three problems mentioned, yet this is often not difficult to do. First, the knowledge should be isolated as a distinct chunk, rather than embedded in the system code (*e.g.*, by putting it in a single meta-rule). Second, the knowledge should be made explicit, identifying exactly what it is that the system should know (*e.g.*, the criteria for deciding between control structures).

Finally, this well-defined chunk should be generalized as far as possible, to provide maximal power. By "generalize," we mean that it should be considered not as a special case or clever trick but, as far as possible, as a fundamental principle of knowledge organization.

If all of this is really so useful, why isn't it common practice? The primary reason is that new problem-solving methods are still being uncovered and explored—their power, potential, and applicability are yet to be totally defined. We are proposing a framework for integrating a number of methods, based on the belief that there are now a sufficient number of techniques understood well enough that we can begin examining the problem of integrating many of them into a cohesive system.

But why consider the whole tool set, with all the associated cost? The answer may lie in the nature of the problems currently being explored. Chapter 1 noted the trend toward real world problems of significant size. Where a single methodology may prove powerful enough to handle well-isolated tasks in selected domains, the broader scope of real world problems appears to require a correspondingly broader collection of abilities. Strategic knowledge may provide a facility for directing their use.

Thus, the primary advantage of increased execution time flexibility is the potential for building more flexible programs. Systems equipped with a single "hardwired" strategy, hence a single approach to the problem, would appear to suffer the same shortcomings as the general problem solver type programs. The latter proved unable to deal with difficult problems because of their single, domain-independent methodology, which could not be modified by important and useful domain-specific knowledge. Similarly, current task-specific programs, with their domain-specific methods, cannot dynamically shift the way they function and have an analogous limitation.

7-5.6 Review

The central aim of this section has been to consider the broader implications that follow from the techniques used in implementing meta-rules. The discussion focused on two techniques—content-directed invocation and generalized invocation criteria—and considered their implications as programming techniques in general, independent of the issue of encoding strategy knowledge.

We began by examining different approaches to referring to KSs and defined the idea of content reference. The use of this form of reference as a basis for KS retrieval and invocation was termed content-directed invocation and was compared to previous approaches to invocation. This historical overview suggested that content-directed invocation offers an added degree of reliability and expressiveness in invocation. The technique also offers a way of making the criteria for KS retrieval accessible and, hence, more easily modifiable, rather than predetermined and hardwired into the language interpreter, as is the case for most programming languages. Content-directed invocation was also seen to offer a number of advantages in terms of the flexibility of the resulting system: It is easier to introduce changes into the knowledge base in systems using this technique.

Generalized invocation criteria arose from making the invocation criteria accessible and from specifying them explicitly and functionally. This technique was seen to offer significant advantages in terms of effecting control structures explicitly rather than via a range of indirect effects.

Content-directed invocation and generalized invocation criteria appear to be programming techniques that offer potential increases in both the reliability and expressiveness of the invocation process, that offer increases in the flexibility of the system in response to changes in the knowledge base, and that permit explicit specification of invocation criteria.

We also examined several limitations of the current implementations and explored difficulties that have to be overcome before the full benefits of these techniques can be realized.

Finally, we speculated about the possible use of meta-rules in creating a system capable of adaptively changing its control structure as the problem solution proceeds.

7–6 A TAXONOMY, OF SORTS

In this section the discussion broadens beyond the specific implementation of strategies demonstrated by meta-rules. We examine the kinds of strategies that have been used in a variety of systems, with the aim of developing a rough taxonomy of strategy types. This, in turn, will help provide a better understanding of the range of possible strategy types and set in perspective the work on meta-rules.

The dimensions of the taxonomy are:

(a) generality,
(b) degree of explicitness,
(c) organization, and
(d) character.

While the set is not necessarily comprehensive, these four appear to capture a number of interesting distinctions and help characterize the range of possibilities. Examples of real systems are used to illustrate sample points in each dimension. [26]

7–6.1 Generality

The most general strategies are those we will term *representation independent*, since they describe problem-solving approaches which can be used no matter what underlying representation is chosen. As an example, the general idea of a goal-directed ("working backward") vs. a data-directed ("working forward") approach is relevant over a wide range of problem organizations and representations. Polya [Polya54] describes several such techniques; a recent book by Wickelgren [Wickelgren74] deals with the subject in more general terms. An interesting and very abstract approach is taken in *Strategy Notebook* [Interaction72], which explores six categories of strategies and offers analyses of the strengths and weaknesses of each. (The last category is labeled "metaheuristics" and describes several very general second-order strategies.)

The work in [Green69] is a good example of the use of *domain-independent* techniques. That system used first-order predicate calculus and resolution theorem proving. Strategies employed included unit preference, set of support, a

---

[26] Note that many of the references cited used a range of techniques so that at times only selected aspects of each may be relevant.

bound on the number of levels explored, and the deletion of subsumed clauses. Since these techniques are meaningless outside the context of theorem proving, they are not independent of the representation. The domain independence of the underlying methodology, however, indicates the applicability of the techniques to the theorem-proving process in any domain.

A second example of domain independence is the concept of planning in abstraction spaces, as described in [Sacerdoti73]. This system was based on the means-ends analysis methodology of STRIPS and used a powerful strategy of planning at multiple levels of detail. Since the basic task in STRIPS is the choice of an operator whose application moves the system closer to the goal, the use of repeated planning at successively lower levels of detail becomes a way of directing the choice of operators and is thus a domain-independent strategy.

By contrast, Gelernter's early work on a geometry theorem prover [Gelernter59] has some interesting examples of *domain-specific* strategies. It takes a problem reduction approach, setting up an exhaustive list of possible subgoals on the basis of available axioms and theorems. Subgoals are ordered, however, on the basis of several domain-specific criteria: For example, goals involving vertical angles are chosen first because they often turn out to have one-step proofs.

Finally, as illustrated earlier, meta-rules have been used to express strategies that are *goal specific*. The THUSE construct in PLANNER and the GOALCLASS statement of QA4 are programming language constructs that offer the facility for writing similar sorts of goal-specific strategies.

7–6.2 Degree of Explicitness

A second dimension concerns the degree of explicitness with which strategies are represented. *Explicit* strategies are those that are embodied in their own distinct constructs and that can be identified as separate entities in the system. *Implicit strategies* come in two varieties. Those that are bound up in some other aspect of the system (typically the control structure) we refer to as *implementationally implicit*. In this case the essential idea of the strategy has been coded explicitly in the system, but that code is embedded (perhaps quite subtly) in other constructs. *Conceptually implicit* strategies are those for which there is no distinct encoding mechanism anywhere in the system. Typically, their effect is realized via some side-effect of a process that other parts of the system are tuned to detect. Since one of the global themes in this work concerns the virtues of making all knowledge in a system explicit, we will make the case below that the first of these three approaches is the most advantageous and that the last presents problems.

The work reported in [Howe73] is a good example of a conceptually implicit strategy. That system used a production rule style representation of chemical reactions to solve chemical synthesis problems. Certain reactions (which were capable of supplying major structural features) were chosen as sufficiently desirable that they were considered important to use, if at all possible. This strategy was effected by leaving part of the precondition side of these rules incompletely specified. That is, the "details" of the preconditions were suppressed, a technique that can be seen as a special-case implementation of Sacerdoti's levels of abstraction idea. The rules thus appeared applicable in contexts that were, in fact, not exactly correct. The remainder of the rule was tailored to check for these mismatches and attempted to take care of all the necessary details before the rule was invoked. Since the rules were hand-coded to provide for this suppression of detail, the strategy is effected indirectly and has no explicit representation anywhere in the system.

The work of [Green69] and [Sacerdoti73] are examples of implementationally implicit strategies. In both, the strategies are realized as distinct sections of code, but the code is embedded in the control structure. Green notes that while there is a certain range of control available over strategy if the user understands program parameters (*e.g.*, the level bound on resolution), more extensive changes require knowledge of LISP and an ability to recode parts of the system.

Finally, meta-rules are an example of explicit representation of strategies, since they are constructs independent of the control structure and represent strategies in much the same way that object-level knowledge is represented by object-level rules.

7–6.3   Knowledge Organization

The next dimension concerns the organization of strategic knowledge and considers the indexing scheme around which the strategies are organized. A number of different approaches have been used, among them are strategies organized around:

KSs: In HEARSAY II, for instance, each KS carries with it a description of the circumstances under which it is most relevant.

Goals: As illustrated, meta-rules are associated with specific goals.

Goals in context: Since PLANNER's "advice list" of likely theorems to try (supplied by the THUSE and theorem base filter constructs) is part of a specific goal statement, the advice can be organized by both goal and context. That is, two THGOAL statements may have the same goal pattern but different advice lists because they are in two different theorems.

Events: The WHEN statement in QA4, for example, offers a rich syntax for describing events, along with associated specified responses. In general, "event" can be interpreted broadly to refer to any configuration of the data base allowing strategies to be organized around "situations" (data base configurations) of varying levels of specificity.

For the purposes of this discussion, it will be useful to make the simple distinction between strategies that are organized around individual KSs (the first example; they will be referred to as *KS-centered*) and those that are organized around anything else (all the rest; *non-KS-centered*). Note that those in the first class are *indexed* by KS and *refer* to goals or events in which the KS is useful; the latter are *indexed* around goals or events and *refer* to KSs.

7–6.4 Character

The final dimension offers four classifications for describing the "character" of strategy content. These four arise from two independent distinctions (Figure 7–6) that provide a framework for understanding the different types of meta-rules explored earlier. They are described initially in the paradigm of tree search and then generalized to demonstrate applicability for a range of problem-solving paradigms. Specific examples illustrate each classification.

A modified breadth-first tree search might involve collecting all the nodes that are descendants of the current node and attempting to decide which is the best to pursue. Information concerning the utility of each node might be of two forms. By *individual utility* we mean the sort typically found in heuristic search evaluation functions. For our purposes, its essential characteristic is that it gives a utility figure for a node based solely on knowledge about that single node and about the current state of the world. It does not refer to any of the other nodes.

A *comparative utility*, on the other hand, specifically refers to more than a single node so that it can offer statements about their relative utility. [27]

Now take a depth-first view of the tree and imagine that the nodes represent potential invocations of backward-chained rules. As we saw earlier, a sequence of several of them a few levels deep can be viewed as a "line of reasoning." We can thus have strategies which indicate either "this line of reasoning is useful" (individual utility) or "this line of reasoning is more useful than that one" (comparative).

The primary advantage of the line-of-reasoning type strategy is its ability to direct the system through local minima of evaluation functions. Since one intuitive aspect of intelligence is the ability to perform actions that may superficially appear counterproductive (but which are in fact useful), this seems to be an important source of knowledge.

By making a few simple replacements, this scheme can be generalized to fit many forms of problem solving: For "node", read KS; for "descendants of the current node," read plausible knowledge source set; and, finally, replace "depth" with time. Thus, instead of speaking of evaluating the nodes at a given level of the tree, we speak of choosing a KS from the PKS set; instead of thinking of search more than one level deep, we think ahead to the invocation of more than one KS.

With these substitutions, we can also take another look at each strategy type and consider examples from current systems. There are meta-rules illustrating two of these categories: METARULE001 is of the individual utility type, and METARULE002 indicates comparative utility.

There are numerous examples in other systems as well. The preconditions of the operators in HEARSAY II can be viewed as individual utility statements, since they are associated with an individual KS and describe the circumstances under which that KS is appropriate, without referring to other KSs.

---

[27] Note that while it is possible to arrive at such a comparison by examining individual utilities, this refers to strategies that compare two nodes explicitly.

Strategy Character

	breadth	depth
individual	individual utility	line of reasoning
comparative	comparative utility	comparison of lines of reasoning

Figure 7-6   Strategy characteristics.

In [Waldinger74] there are comparative utility strategies embodied in the GOALCLASS statements which specify an order for the use of applicable theorems. The PLANNER example above is another instance of a comparative utility strategy; it makes explicit reference to more than one KS in order to specify a relative ordering.

One early example of a line-of-reasoning type strategy is mentioned in Samuel's discussion of his checker program [Samuel67], where he terms it a "principle line." The macro operators in STRIPS described in [Fikes72] provide another example, as do meta-rules (although we have not as yet uncovered any examples specific to the medical domain).

7-7   LIMITATIONS OF THE GENERAL FORMALISM

There are several fundamental problems associated with a fully general implementation of the meta-rule framework: First, it is not always possible to organize a program as a collection of discrete knowledge sources; second, there is a considerable intellectual effort required to assemble all the elements necessary for the general implementation; third, the scheme will not work well if rules are created dynamically (*i.e.*, during a performance run); and finally, not all of the overhead required for execution time flexibility can be restricted to the background and may impose a significant reduction in speed.

7-7.1   Program Organization

The need to organize the program as a collection of discrete KSs is perhaps the most fundamental limitation encountered. While it may be possible to construe the definition broadly enough to fit almost any program, it is not always an informative view. There seem to be two important factors in deciding whether, and how, to decompose a program into distinct KSs: (a) The proposed KSs should be self-contained, in that each can by itself make some contribution to the problem solution, and (b) the problem should be sufficiently ill-specified (in the sense discussed in Section 7-3.1) that there is no predetermined sequence of KS invocations that will solve the problem; instead there is, at each point, some indeterminacy about which KS to invoke.

Table 7–3   The Strategy Taxonomy.

Flexibility Benchmarks

STRATEGY ORGANIZATION	BENCHMARKS			
	edit a KS	edit strategy	add a KS	add a strategy
KS centered	easy, as long as knowledge expressed is strictly "local"			
situation centered, reference by name	check all strategies that name it	make sure all KSs named are relevant; any to be added?	check all strategies to see where new KS belongs	check all KSs to see which it should name
situation centered, reference by description; via external descriptors	update descriptors associated with the KS	make sure all descriptions are still relevant; any to be added?	no additional effort	no additional effort
situation centered, reference by description; via content examination	no additional effort	make sure all descriptions are still relevant; any to be added?	no additional effort	no additional effort

If there is but a single KS in the program or (what amounts to the same thing) if the various sources of knowledge are so intertwined that separating them is impossible, then we clearly can't meet condition (a). Similarly, if there is an algorithmic solution to the problem, then we have none of the indeterminacy suggested in (b) and don't need all the machinery outlined above.

7–7.2 Intellectual Difficulty

The intellectual difficulty of implementing this approach arises out of several factors. It is not often easy, for example, to describe rather than name a KS. Consider the segment of code in Section 7–5 that might appear in a PLANNER version of a poker game. The strategy there is to try bluffing, if that doesn't work draw three cards, and if all else fails, cheat. To replace that with a description-oriented approach requires a more basic understanding of the domain and of the strategy being expressed. A rewritten version might say something like "first use any psychological ploys to discourage the competition, then try something that will improve your hand, and finally do anything that will make sure you win." Each of these is a more general description of the entire class of theorems from which each of the ones named might have been drawn. This is not often easy to produce and makes certain assumptions about the nature of the application domain. In particular, the domain must be sufficiently formalized (or formalizable) that it is a reasonable task to look for meta-level primitives. There are clearly domains for which this is not true.

Despite these difficulties, the direct benefits are considerable. The resulting flexibility can be an important tool in the construction of a very large system. There are, as well, indirect benefits. We have noted that this approach requires a more basic understanding of the domain and strategy. This in itself can be beneficial and lead to further insights. More important, however, the resulting strategy offers a more complete statement of the relevant knowledge. It makes more evident what it is the strategy expresses and why the system performs as it does. It is thus another example of one of our recurring themes—the benefits of the explicit representation of knowledge.

7–7.3 Dynamic Rule Creation

The compile-time vs. execution-time distinction and the "pre-compilation" of descriptions into corresponding sets of rule names offer efficiency only if the addition of rules to the system is restricted to the time between performance runs. The approach we have been describing imposes a significant cost on the attempt to add rules to the knowledge base while the program is in the midst of a performance run. At worst, it means all descriptions in strategies have to be run "interpreted," constantly recomputing the applicable set of rules. A slightly more efficient solution might employ an incremental compilation, which recomputed all the strategy descriptions with reference to the single new rule. Which of these is more desirable depends on the individual system, but in either case the computational cost is significant.

7–7.4 Overhead

The final problem is the cost in speed of great execution time flexibility. If, at every point where a KS must be chosen, the system performs a full-blown re-analysis—one that includes deciding once again on a methodology, deciding how to decide, and so on—nothing would ever get accomplished. Such continual complete reappraisal is in most cases a waste of time and should not be done. The question is, thus, how to invoke all (or any) of this "deciding-how-to-decide" procedure only when necessary. There are several possibilities.

The first, and perhaps the most effective, technique becomes clear if we recall our definition of ill structured problems. If a problem is completely ill structured, then the use of the fully general machinery is warranted. To the extent that it is well structured, the machinery is inappropriate. The point then is to combine both of these and to allow each to help answer the fundamental question of which KS to invoke next. The answer may then come from either the fully general "deciding-how-to-decide" mechanism or from one of the structures that expresses the known connections between KSs.

The result may be pictured as a construction in which the fully general re-analysis mechanisms play the role of mortar, occasionally holding together bricks (structured subproblems), at other times filling in molds (the super-structure). The size of the molds and bricks may vary widely, corresponding to the extent of understanding of different aspects of the problem. The issue thus becomes where and how the problem is cut up. As much of it as possible should be embodied in structures that reflect known interrelationships, leaving the most general technique as a mechanism available either to direct the use of those structures or to fill in if none are available.

To make this abstract picture more concrete, consider the place of the meta-rules in MYCIN's problem-solving formalism. The major superstructure there is the backward chaining of individual production rules producing an and/or goal tree. Within this framework, meta-rules are used to help guide the search through the tree. This arrangement constrains the general (and expensive) decision mechanism to a collection of well-specified locations. It can thus prove useful even when applied in only a part of the overall system.

At the beginning of this chapter we claimed that the framework of knowledge organization suggested by a fairly general conception of strategies offered a useful and illuminating device for knowledge explication. This point can be illustrated by this same issue of problem structure. It was noted, above, that the unrestricted use of the most general formalism is in most cases a waste of time. If the reader agrees, then the question is *how do you know?* Or more precisely, *what* is it that you know that suggests that the complete re-analysis is unwarranted? What kind of (or how many) failures would it take before you began to change your mind? This is just the sort of knowledge that can be formalized to provide direction for the problem-solving process. It may possibly be embedded in one of the conventional approaches, or perhaps in a line-of-reasoning style second-order strategy: "Don't reconsider the methodology until the next three KSs have been invoked using the current scheme."

There is one additional approach to all of this that may prove useful. In an analogy to human behavior, we might organize the system to allow it to fail "upward" through different levels of generality in its attempts to solve the problem. [28] Consider the problem of turning on a lamp and noticing that the light does not come on. We might try a sequence of solutions that looked like:

(a)   see if the lamp is plugged in,
(b)   try replacing the bulb,
(c)   see if the lamp switch is o.k.,
(d)   see if there is a fuse blown, or
(e)   find out if there has been a power failure.

Each failure causes successively fewer assumptions about the state of the world to be taken for granted and causes a more general approach to the solution. Analogously, a program failing in its heuristic search via hill climbing might first re-evaluate its distance metric, then the use of hill climbing, and finally the use of heuristic search. In this case the general re-evaluation mechanism is invoked only where necessary.

We can comment, too, on the investment needed for implementation of this methodology. Since the benefits (and costs) are all incremental, we need not implement the entire formalism to get any payoff. Even the smallest steps toward it are useful.

But is all this really necessary? That is, is all of this always relevant? Clearly not. There surely are times when systems are written to achieve a very well-specified purpose and will not necessarily profit from considering the task in its full generality, as suggested here. It must therefore be desirable to have such generality as a part of the system being constructed.

There are, however, two points to be considered. First, even a system that is not designed for extensive generality may be structured somewhat more cleanly if the knowledge is viewed along the lines we have suggested (*e.g.*, in Green's system). Second, it is rare that all the necessary capabilities of a system can be foreseen in advance, and redesign is a well-known occupational hazard. Note that the design and construction of any program (even for a well-understood task domain) is itself an ill structured problem. Thus, it may still prove useful to attempt to be general, even in the context of a well-defined task area.

7–8   SUMMARY

This chapter has proposed a general framework for understanding strategies as a form of meta-level knowledge and has suggested that any decision concerning the use of knowledge in problem solving should be viewed as a strategic choice. It

---

[28] A similar concept of successive levels of failure is found in [Winograd75]. The basic idea is also inherent in the view of AI as the "science of weak methods" [Newell69].

explored how this framework can help make clear the body of knowledge contained in a program and showed how it can contribute to both representation design and organization.

Meta-rules were described in detail as one instance of the general ideas outlined in the framework. We have seen how they help to guide problem-solving performance and have explored the range of knowledge that they can be used to represent. Explanation of meta-rules was shown to be possible with a straightforward extension of the facilities for object-level rules; steps toward interactive acquisition of meta-rules were also considered.

We saw that meta-rules refer to object-level rules by describing (rather than naming) them and that they effect this reference by examining their content directly. This led to a consideration of the different approaches to invoking a knowledge source and offered a perspective on the relevant factors involved. Content-directed invocation was shown to offer a handle on KSs that provides reliability, expressiveness, and an explicit specification of invocation criteria. While it requires a significant initial investment of effort, it can provide a useful level of flexibility for systems with large knowledge bases subject to frequent changes.

Finally, a taxonomy of strategy types was reviewed, offering a basis for comparing meta-rules to other forms of strategy encoding. An examination of the impact of the different forms of encoding led to some observations about organizing knowledge in ways that help make systems both easier to construct and more flexible in the face of changes.

Chapter 8

Conclusions

Alas, how terrible is wisdom when it brings no profit to the man that's wise! This I knew well, but had forgotten it; else I would not have come here.

Sophocles
Oedipus the King, lines 312–313

8–1 INTRODUCTION

The last five chapters have explored a number of different problems encountered in building TEIRESIAS, a program intended to establish a link between a human expert and a computer consultant. Those problems and solutions are reviewed briefly here and considered in the light of meta-level knowledge as a tool for knowledge base construction, maintenance, and use. This is followed by a discussion of some of the global limitations and shortcomings that arise from the attempt to link the expert and program. Finally, we return to the alternative set of themes listed in chapter 1, reconsidering some of this work in those terms and using them as a basis for speculation about future directions.

8–2   REVIEW OF MAJOR ISSUES

8–2.1   Forms of Meta-Level Knowledge

Figure 8–1 reviews the three major forms of meta-level knowledge developed in previous chapters. The rule models describe the *content* of inference rules in the knowledge base, making clear the global trends in those rules and providing useful assistance in acquiring new rules. The data structure schemata describe the *structure* of the conceptual primitives used in expressing rules and offer a basis for the acquisition of new primitives. Finally, the meta-rules describe how to *use* object-level rules and function as strategies to guide invocation of those rules.

One additional, less developed source of meta-level knowledge is the function templates (chapter 2), which describe part of the structure of inference rules and, like the rule models, are used in acquiring new rules.

FORM	DESCRIBES	USE
Rule models	CONTENT of inference rules	Acquisition of new inference rules
Data structure schemata	STRUCTURE of conceptual primitives	Acquisition of new conceptual primitives
Meta-rules	USE of object-level rules	Guide use of object-level knowl.

Figure 8–1   The three forms of meta-level knowledge.

8–2.2   Explanation

Chapter 3 discussed efforts to enable TEIRESIAS to explain the reasoning of a performance program to audiences that range from an expert acquainted with the program to a student with minimal experience in the field. The basic steps in building the explanation facility involved (a) determining the program operation that was to be considered primitive, (b) augmenting the performance program to leave behind a trace of behavior in terms of this operation, (c) finding a framework in which that trace could be understood, and (d) designing a program that would allow the user to examine the behavior trace in terms of the framework. This supplied a mechanism for exploring past actions; future actions of the system were explored by means of code in the explanation system which simulated the control structure of the performance program.

This approach to explanation relies on the assumption that a recap of program operations can be a reasonable basis for generating explanations. This was seen to suggest the areas of greatest applicability as well as imply a number of limitations. In particular, it seems best suited to programs whose primary mode of computation is symbolic reasoning rather than numeric operations.

The primary shortcomings in the current implementation were a failure to factor in the state of the viewer's knowledge, a lack of a general notion of what an explanation is, and a lack of ability to represent control structures. The latter becomes particularly evident when changes are made to the control structure of the performance program, since this often requires significant changes to the explanation program. We speculated about the possibility of a representation of control structures that emphasized intentional information, which, combined with a formalization of the concept of explanation, might make the system far more flexible and general. It might, ideally, be possible for the system to examine its own code, generating explanations on the basis of what it found there.

8–2.3 Knowledge Acquisition

Knowledge acquisition was described as a process of interactive transfer of expertise from an expert to a performance program, in which TEIRESIAS's task was to "listen" as attentively and intelligently as possible. The process was set in the context of a shortcoming in the knowledge base, as an aid to both the expert and the system. This context provides the expert with a useful organization and focus. He is not simply asked to describe all he knows about a domain. He is instead faced with a specific consultation whose results he finds incorrect and has available to him a set of tools that will allow him to uncover the extent of the system's knowledge and the rationale behind its performance. His task is then to specify the particular difference between the system's knowledge and his own that accounts for the discrepancy in results. The system relies on the context of the error to form a set of expectations about the character of the information that will be forthcoming. This leads to better comprehension of the expert's statement of that information and provides a number of checks on its content that insure it will in fact repair the problem discovered. In a single phrase, *interactive transfer of expertise in the context of a shortcoming in the knowledge base* characterizes our approach to the problem and suggests the source of many of the system's abilities.

8–2.3.1 Acquiring New Rules

New rule acquisition was seen in terms of model-directed understanding and a recognition-oriented approach to comprehension. This means that the system has some model of the content of the signal it is trying to interpret and uses this to help constrain the set of interpretations it will consider. In our case, the model took the form of rule models, constructs which offer a picture of a "typical" rule of a given type. These models are assembled by the system itself, using a primitive, statistically oriented form of concept formation to produce abstract descriptions of syntactic regularities in subsets of rules.

As noted, the context provided by the process of tracking down the error in the knowledge base makes it possible for TEIRESIAS to form expectations about the character of the new rule. These expectations are expressed by selecting a specific rule model. The text of the new rule is then allowed to suggest interpretations (a bottom-up, data-directed process), but these are constrained and evaluated for likely validity by reference to the rule model (a top-down, hypothesis-driven process). It is the intersection of these two information sources, approaching the task from different directions, that is responsible for much of the system's performance.

Further application of the model-directed formalism is seen in TEIRESIAS's ability to "second guess" the expert. Since it has a model of the knowledge base—the rule models—it can tell when something "fits" in the knowledge base. It is the occurrence of a partial match between the new rule and the selected rule model that prompts TEIRESIAS to make suggestions to the expert. This idea of an unmet expectation is not specific to the current organization or structure of the rule models and can be generalized to cover any aspects of a representation about which expectations can be formed.

Several implications were seen to follow from the fact that TEIRESIAS constructs the rule models from current contents of the knowledge base. Since the process is automated, the expert never has to enter models by hand; he may even be unaware of their existence. Moreover, unlike most other model-based systems, new models are constructed on the basis of past experience, since rules learned previously are used in forming new models. Since the models are updated as each new rule enters the knowledge base, the model set is kept current, evolving with the growing knowledge base and reflecting the shifting patterns it contains.

Other implications follow from the fact that these models give the system an abstract picture of its own knowledge base. It means that, in a rudimentary way, the system "knows what it knows, and knows where it is ignorant." It can answer questions about the content of its knowledge base by "reading" a rule model, giving a picture of global structure of its knowledge about a topic. Since the models are ordered on the basis of an empirically defined "strength," the system can also give some indications about possible gaps in its knowledge.

Finally, the coupling of model formation with the model-directed understanding process offers a novel form of closed-loop behavior. Existing rule models are used to guide the acquisition process, the new rule is added to the knowledge base, and the relevant rule models are recomputed. Performance of the acquisition routines may thus conceivably be improved on the very next rule.

In summary, TEIRESIAS constructs models of the knowledge base; it updates those models in response to changes, keeping them an accurate reflection of the current knowledge base; and it then uses them to aid in the acquisition of new knowledge.

8–2.3.2 Acquiring New Conceptual Primitives

The primary issue here is the representation and use of knowledge about representations. The schemata and associated structures offer a language for the expression of the knowledge and a framework for its organization. There are three levels to that organization: (*i*) the individual schema is the fundamental unit of organization and is a record-like structure that provides the basis for assembling a variety of information about a particular representation; (*ii*) the schema network is a generalization hierarchy that indicates the existing categories of data structures and relationships between them; and (*iii*) the slotnames and slotexperts that make up a schema deal with specific representation conventions at the programming language level.

Unlike standard records, however, the schemata and all associated structures are a part of the system itself and are available for examination and reference. They also have the ability to describe a certain amount of variability in structure description.

The process of acquiring a new conceptual primitive strongly resembles the creation of a new instance of a record, but has been extended in several ways. It has been made interactive, to allow the expert to supply information about the domain; the dialog is couched in high-level terms, to make it comprehensible to a nonprogrammer; and the whole process has been made as easy and "intelligent" as possible, to ease the task of assembling large amounts of knowledge.

This approach involves viewing representational primitives as extended data types and constructing the appropriate schema for each of them. That is, the language for describing representations was used to formalize a range of information about the performance program's representations.

The generality of this approach results from a stratification and isolation of different varieties of knowledge at different levels: Instances of individual schemata form the collection of domain-specific knowledge; the schemata themselves define a base of representation-specific information; while the schema-schema supplies a small foundation of representation-independent knowledge. This stratification makes it possible for the system to acquire both new instances of existing representations (as in learning about a new organism) and new types of representation (as in the acquisition of a new schema), using a single formalism and a single body of code.

Finally, it was noted that the same motivation was responsible for both the schemata and the recursive application of the idea to produce the schema-schema. The schemata were designed to automate the handling of the large number of details involved in the creation and management of data structures. But they themselves were sufficiently complex, detailed data structures that it was useful to have a similar device for their construction and management. This resulted in the creation of the schema-schema, and it, along with a small body of associated structures, forms a body of representation-independent knowledge from which a knowledge base can be constructed.

8–2.4   Strategies

The final form of meta-level knowledge explored was the concept of a strategy, defined as knowledge about the use of knowledge. This definition was extended to include the possibility of an arbitrary number of levels of strategies, each of which can direct the use of the information at the next lower level. We considered the possible building blocks for a strategy language and speculated about the source of the conceptual primitives from which such a language might be built. The resulting framework was seen to offer a reasonably general view, one that can help to organize and make explicit strategy knowledge that is otherwise often embedded subtly in program code.

We explored the character of problems for which this approach is useful, noted that it is most applicable to what are called ill structured problems and found that it offers the greatest advantage for programs with large knowledge bases subject to frequent change.

Meta-rules were described as one example of these ideas. They were seen to offer a convenient mechanism for the expression of strategies and proved capable of guiding program performance without introducing unreasonable overhead. The organization of knowledge they provide appears novel, in guiding heuristic search without being part of a search algorithm. The search routine itself is very simple; the "intelligence" is organized around and stored in the goal tree itself. This means that at any point where the system has to choose a path through the tree, there may possibly be information stored at that branch point available to guide it.

Meta-rules illustrated several interesting issues when considered as an invocation mechanism. First, the fact that meta-rules refer to object-level rules by reference to their content rather than by name was termed content-directed invocation and found to be a generalization of some of the traditional mechanisms of knowledge source invocation. This technique offers a greater degree of expressiveness and validity than is typically available and was seen to provide a high level of flexibility. Second, meta-rules offer a framework in which the user can define his own invocation criteria, leading to the idea of generalized invocation criteria. This frees the programmer from the restriction of using only those invocation criteria that are predefined and embedded in the programming language in use. He can instead define the set of criteria he wishes to use and can, as well, write programs capable of choosing from among that set at execution time. Third, the presence of multiple levels of meta-rules means that the invocation criteria (meta-rules at one level) are also treated as data objects (by meta-rules at the next higher level). This means that the system has a primitive capability to reason about the control structure it should use.

The limitations of this approach and its costs were also considered. While it is possible at present to implement it in simple ways, sophisticated use requires advances in the field of program understanding. It also imposes a computational overhead. While some of this can be relegated to a background pre-compilation phase, the system cannot then create rules dynamically during execution of the performance program. As noted above, the approach seems to offer the most substantive advantages when dealing with large knowledge bases with numerous strategies, in systems subject to frequent change. It is thus appropriate for programs where the size of the knowledge base and the necessity of an incremental approach to competence require the ability to assemble large amounts of knowledge and the ability to make numerous alterations to it.

8–3   GLOBAL LIMITATIONS

The fundamental problem we started out to consider was the creation of an intelligent link between a domain expert and a high-performance program. This provided a large collection of topics for discussion, and previous sections have noted the shortcomings and limitations of each of the individual solutions proposed. But what of this basic notion of linking the expert and program? What limitations might there be in that whole approach, and what limitations may arise from the particular solutions proposed and implementations described?

First, the current version of TEIRESIAS is still quite rough. It has not yet been given to any users for rigorous testing. It needs a good deal of polish and more attention to user convenience before it becomes a truly useful tool. Some suggestions along these lines were noted in earlier chapters, but there is a more basic question concerning the nature of the tools we have assembled. Some are conceptually neat, but are they what an expert building a large knowledge base would really find most useful?

For instance, is TEIRESIAS's ability to second guess an expert's new rule going to help, or will it only get in the way? Can it be made "smarter"? Could the system learn, for example, to recognize the fact that the expert is entering a whole new sequence of rules and that none of its current expectations are likely to be met?[1] In more general terms, we have stressed the advantages of debugging in context, but are there ways of increasing the range of that context? Acquisition is currently a rule-by-rule process, when it really ought to be day-by-day or instructor-by-instructor.

Experience with a number of experts may provide answers to these questions and indicate where tools may be needed for the more mundane, but more immediate, problems that arise in dealing with large amounts of knowledge.

The use of production rules also poses certain problems, one of which arises from the impact of rules on the organization of knowledge and the style of program writing, especially as compared to a procedural view. Rules are a reasonably natural and convenient form of knowledge encoding for what may be termed "single-level" phenomena—it is easy to think of single decisions or actions in terms of a rule. Experience has demonstrated, however, that even experts acquainted with the production rule encoding tend to think of a sequence of operations in procedural terms and find flowcharts a convenient medium of expression. While flowcharts can always be converted to an equivalent set of rules, the conversion is nontrivial and sometimes requires reconsidering the knowledge being expressed, since the two methodologies offer different perspectives on knowledge organization and use.

We may as well bow to the inevitable, then, and consider ways of formalizing this translation process. How might an expert describe a whole *sequence* of decisions, and how might the system then translate this into an equivalent

---

[1] In this sense the system is currently a bit like an overly eager student who is always trying to out-guess the instructor. There really ought to be a way to tell it to "keep quiet and listen."

(unordered) *set* of rules?[2] This appears to be an interesting prospect for further work.

We have also begun to encounter a standard technical problem, as the combination of TEIRESIAS and MYCIN has grown beyond the resources available in present PDP-10 based TENEX INTERLISP systems. The combination is already large enough that many data structures have to be retrieved from the disk during execution rather than kept in core. While this is accomplished with a very efficient hashing routine[3] the program is already too slow with normal machine loading—it is caught on both ends of the speed-space trade-off. Possible solutions lie both in increases in hardware resources and the use of faster programming languages.

Finally, this report started with the suggestion that it would be advantageous to replace the assistant indicated in Figure 1–1 by a program that allows the expert to educate the performance program directly. This offers many advantages from the point of view of speed, manpower, and ease of knowledge base construction. But what kinds of problems might it produce? Experience has demonstrated that a certain period of acclimatization is necessary before new experts are familiar enough with the *weltanschauung* implicit in the performance program to be able to view the domain and its challenges in those terms. During that period, the task of the assistant becomes more than simply translating the clinician's statements into LISP rules; it includes re-interpreting them as well. If the expert is put in direct contact with the program, what problems might arise from (unrecognized) differences in their models of the world? How much of what the assistant typically does in mediating between the expert and system involves a shift in representations and a resolution of such conflicts? Can this ability be formalized and made a part of the system itself? It appears to be difficult, requiring, as it does, solutions to problems known to be difficult, and will require a good deal of further work.

8–4 THE OTHER THEMES; SOME SPECULATIONS

Here we return at last to the list of themes given in chapter 1. Each is described in terms of three topics: (a) meaning—the substantive concept behind the catchphrase is explained and its utility made clear; (b) examples—several examples are given of how the idea has been employed in TEIRESIAS; and (c) evaluation and prognosis—the examples are evaluated in terms of the goals suggested by the phrases, and an indication is given of what difficult problems remain.

First, a word of warning. Despite attempts to linearize this discussion, it remains a network of interrelated ideas. The network is densely interconnected, and most of the ideas will lead to most of the others if followed far enough.

---

[2] Or a set of rules, plus a meta-rule for ordering. This approach assumes that, when feasible, it is more profitable in the long run to use a single representation (in this case, rules) and provide ways to translate all knowledge into this form, than to introduce new representations, each tailored to a specific task. Experience with TEIRESIAS so far suggests that this is true, but the issue is still far from settled.

[3] The routine was provided by Larry Masinter of Xerox PARC and Bill van Melle of the MYCIN group.

To make the discussion comprehensible, many of those connections have been ignored, except where truly necessary. Even so, the discussion occasionally loops back on itself.

It also tends to raise a good many more questions than it answers. After pointing out how these ideas have been used throughout the program, it looks forward and speculates about where some of this might eventually lead.

8–4.1   Why Write a Program: Two Views

The first five themes are grouped together because they represent different techniques involved in a certain style of programming. To make that style clear, consider two different, very broad characterizations of situations in which computer programs might be written.

Traditionally, programs have been written to solve specific problems and obtain "an answer." The answer may be of many types, including numeric (as in business and scientific computation), symbolic (*e.g.*, information retrieval), or others of a more abstract form. The main issue here is that these programs are applied to tasks with two important characteristics: (1) There is "an answer" to the problem, and (2) it is possible to speak of a "final," debugged version of a program that is to be used extensively as it is, with relatively long periods between changes to it. This view encourages a style of programming in which the programmer spends a long time thinking about the problem first, tries to solve as much of it as possible by hand, and then abstracts out only the very end-product of all that thought to be embodied in the program. That is, the program can become simply a way of manipulating symbols to provide "the answer," with little indication of what the original problem was or, more important, what knowledge was required to solve it.

Large, knowledge-based programs appear to have a fundamentally different character. As noted earlier, the construction of large knowledge bases is a long-term operation that is never really "finished." Not only is the approach to competence incremental (and occasionally asymptotic), but the fields to which such programs are applied are typically those which are still under active development. The knowledge base is thus inherently a dynamic structure. The aim here is thus not simply to build a program that exhibits a certain specified behavior,[4] but *to use the program construction process itself as a way of explicating knowledge in the field, and to use the program text as a medium of expression of many forms of knowledge about the task and its solution.* That is, the program becomes more than a collection of symbol manipulation instructions. It is used as an environment in which to elicit, collect, and store large amounts of diverse forms

---

[4] Indeed, it is not even clear whether a behavioral definition of such programs makes sense. In other cases behavioral definitions have been proposed and used (*e.g.*, for automatic programming as in [Shaw75]). They make sense in that case because they are a more compact expression than the program that produces the behavior. It is not clear that this would be true of large knowledge based programs—it appears difficult to give a complete specification for their behavior in any terms that produce a definition smaller than the actual knowledge base.

of knowledge.

To sum up these two long statements in a single phrase: In one case it is reasonable to think in terms of a program that represents a complete solution to a problem, and hence encode only the minimally necessary symbol manipulation steps in that solution; in the other, the process is a continuing one of codifying and accumulating information.

This second view has been adopted in building the knowledge bases needed for several performance programs over the years and has made it possible to organize and represent the large amounts of knowledge required. Question: Is it possible to turn the idea in on itself and apply it to the internal world, the world of representations and data structures inside the program? Will it be as useful at the meta-level as it was at the object level? Can it help to assemble, organize, and maintain the large amount of knowledge about representations and data structures that is necessary for knowledge base construction and maintenance? Other efforts in this vein have revolved around the use of more formal methods (*e.g.*, [Suzuki76], [Spitzen75]). Will the essentially informal, heuristic techniques we want to employ offer sufficient power?

The attempt to answer these questions affirmatively has been one of the central themes of this work.

The immediate application of these ideas has been to provide a basis for the tools described in earlier chapters. More fundamentally, however, they offer the possibility of getting a step closer to that seductive promise of the stored program computer: introspection. As we have seen, the most useful forms of meta-level knowledge are those that make it possible for the system to examine its own knowledge directly. Every step removed from direct examination represents a level of defeat and loses some of the advantages. Thus the rule models are derived from rules directly and adjust to changes in the knowledge base, while the explanation routines require rewriting whenever the control structure changes, because they do not directly reference the code of the system they are trying to explain.

With this overview, let's consider some of the specifics and see how the first five themes suggest steps in the direction of these goals.

Theme 1: Task-specific high-level languages make code easier to read.   "Task-specific high-level language" refers, simply enough, to a language in which the conceptual primitives are task specific. The primary example of this that we have seen is the set of rules, composed of primitives like *attribute* and *value*, whose instances in MYCIN include culture SITE and BLOOD. The rules were discussed in these terms in Section 2–4.4, where it was noted that they are in effect a domain-specific high-level language with a rule as the sole statement type.

There are several other examples, many of them found in the schemata described in chapter 6. Included are the "language" of data structure RELATIONS, the set of *slotnames* of which the schemata are composed, and the several types of *advice* found in slots.

The foremost reason for designing and using "languages" like these is to make possible what we might label "top-down code understanding." Previous efforts at building program understanding systems have been aimed at several goals, including proving programs correct (as in [Waldinger74] and [Manna69]) and for use in automatic programming (as in [Green74]). Most of these systems attempt to assign meaning to the code of some standard (domain independent) programming language like LISP or ALGOL.

Since the problems encountered in doing this are known to be difficult, we have used the high-level "languages" as a convenient shortcut. Rather than attempting to assign formal semantics to ordinary code, a "meaning" is assigned to each of the primitives in the language and represented in one or more informal ways. For example, part of the meaning of the concept *attribute* is represented by the routine associated with it that is invoked during new rule acquisition (see Section 4–4.2). Another part is represented by the code in the explanation routines that checks the attribute in a premise clause when dividing a rule premise into known and unknown clauses. The inequality described in Section 3–7 is another example; it is part of the "meaning" of a predicate function.

Since this technique has been employed extensively here, it is important to consider its limitations. While it does make program understanding easier, it approaches the task at a higher conceptual level, which makes the result correspondingly less powerful. We cannot, for instance, prove that the implementation of SAME is correct, but we can use its indicated "meaning" in the ways illustrated. More fundamentally, the entire approach depends on the existence of a finite number of "mostly independent" primitives. This means a set of primitives with only a few, well-specified interactions between them. The number of interactions should be far less than the total that is possible and interactions that do occur should be uncomplicated. In the case of the rule language, for instance, the concepts of certainty factor and attribute are independent, while attributes and values have a well-specified relation that is reasonably simple to represent.

This is an important limitation, one that we have encountered earlier. Recall the discussion in Section 3–9 on the deficiencies of the explanation routines that arise from the inability to represent control structures. We pointed out there the utility of a language of "intentions" in making it possible for the system to explain its actions, yet were unable to propose one.

When it is possible to find such a language, however, it can be applied in a variety of ways. In the simplest case, the "meaning" of each of the primitives is considered and used individually. A slightly more sophisticated use allows combinations of primitives to describe other structures. Consider, for example, the templates associated with each predicate function. The ability to dissect a given function call could have been based on individual, hand-tailored routines associated with each function. Instead, a lower level of detail was used. This makes it possible for each function to carry information describing its own calls and makes the system extensible: As long as calls to a new function can be described in terms of the available primitives, the function can be added to the system without any change to existing facilities.

This idea of "top-down code understanding" is the primary technique we have used to provide a degree of introspection. The system can examine parts of its own structure and can "understand" them in terms of the primitives of the high-level languages used.

Theme 2: Knowledge in programs should be explicit and accessible.   Consider the following two lists, taken from the current MYCIN system:

(BLOOD BONE BRAIN CSF JOINT LIVER LUNG MUSCLE TENDON-SHEATH)

(RULE012 RULE146 RULE087 RULE234 RULE043 RULE101)

The first appears to be ordered alphabetically; the ordering, if any, of the second is unclear. To avoid introducing bugs when adding a new element to either of them, two things are important: (a) If the list is ordered, what is the ordering criterion? and (b) What is the significance of the ordering (*i.e.*, who depends on it)?

The answer to the first question is required in order to determine where in the list the new element is to be placed. The second is important if we wish to consider violating the established order: It gives a clear picture of the consequences and indicates where changes may have to be made if serious problems result.

In the case of the first list, the ordering is in fact alphabetic, but this has no significance whatever to the rest of the system. The second list has a partial ordering of its elements that is crucial to system performance. Until recently, neither piece of information was represented anywhere in the system (nor in fact in any documentation). The same phenomenon manifests itself in many forms in almost all large systems. There is typically a large share of folklore about all kinds of structures that resides only in the minds of the system designers, yet such information is often crucial to the process of changing anything in the system.

This is the kind of information we have tried to capture with a variety of mechanisms. The first list above, for example, is classified internally as an alphabetically ordered linear list, and its ordering information is embodied in the updating function associated with the schema for that data type. The ordering of the second list can be expressed with meta-rules and, as noted in chapter 5, this makes the problem of updating disappear. The list can be stored unordered, new rules can simply be added to the front, and the meta-rules will take care of reordering the list.

There are other examples as well. The schema network, for instance, makes explicit the interrelationships of the data types in the system. Note that the point is not that this particular approach with its generalization hierarchy is necessarily the way the information should be represented. We claim only that information about the internal organization of data types should in some fashion be organized, formalized, and represented in program-accessible terms.

The meta-rules offer a more general example of the theme. One of their primary contributions was to provide a way of making explicit what most programming languages leave implicit—the criteria for selecting the next knowledge source to be invoked.

A final example worth recalling is the restriction on rule ordering required for the "self-referencing" rules described in Section 7–4.4. To maintain the commutativity of certainty factors, all non-self-referencing rules must be invoked before any that are self-referencing. This important piece of information was represented first in an obscure piece of recursive code buried in the control structure, later in a separate function, and finally was captured by a meta-rule which expresses the necessary ordering in a simple and straightforward form. It can be explained using the explanation facilities and changed, if necessary, using the existing rule editor. It has thus progressed from being implicit and inaccessible to being more explicit and more easily retrieved.

Many problems remain, however. The basic issue here is the standard difficult problem of representation of knowledge. One indication of a shortcoming in our solution is hinted at by the comment above that we have used a "variety of mechanisms." Our informal approach is too ad hoc and needs to be more rigorous before it can claim to be a substantive solution. A far better solution would provide a single representation formalism that could express all the different forms of information required. Some work (*e.g.*, [Suzuki76]) has examined the applicability of predicate calculus to similar problems, but that approach has not yet developed techniques capable of dealing with the size and complexity of the axiomatization and proof procedures required.

Theme 3: Programs can be given access to and an understanding of their own representations. One of the oldest and most fundamental issues in AI is that of representation. Different approaches have come and gone and generated innumerable discussions of respective power and virtue. But in all these arguments, one entity intimately concerned with the outcome has been left uninformed: the program itself.

Several capabilities follow from giving a program the ability to examine its own representations. The one we have employed most heavily is the ability to make multiple uses of the knowledge in a single representation. Rules, for example, are:

(a) viewed as code and executed to drive the consultation,
(b) viewed as data structures, and dissected and abstracted to form the rule models,
(c) dissected and examined to produce explanations,
(d) constructed during rule acquisition, and
(e) examined and reasoned about by the meta-rules.

As another example, the schemata provide a basis for accessing and "understanding" many of the other representations used in the system and support acquisition, as well as storage and retrieval. Each of these alternate uses requires knowledge in addition to that found in the representation, but if the knowledge stored there can be decoded, it need not be represented in more than one form.

It is important to note here that the feasibility of such multiplicity of uses is based less on the notion of production rules per se, than on the availability of a representation with a *small grain size* and a *simple syntax and semantics.* "Small," modular chunks of code written in a simple, heavily stylized form (though not necessarily a situation-action form) would have done as well, as would any representation with simple enough internal structure and of manageable size. The introduction of greater complexity in the representation, or the use of a representation that encoded significantly larger "chunks" of knowledge, would require more sophisticated techniques for dissecting and manipulating representations than we have developed thus far. But the key limitations are size and complexity of structure, rather than a specific style of knowledge encoding.

It is interesting to consider this view in the light of historical developments. When computers were programmed with plugboards, program and data were clearly distinct. With the advent of the stored program computer to make it possible and LISP to make it easy, the idea arose that *programs could be considered data.* In these terms, the view proposed here adds to this the ideas that

(a)   data structure architecture (*i.e.*, the schemata) can also be data, and
(b)   control architecture (invocation criteria, the meta-rules) can also be data.

As a result, the system gains access to two more of its fundamental components.

This perspective underlies much of our work in knowledge acquisition and knowledge base management and seems to have potential for future application. For example, the schemata can be viewed as definitions of data structures, and that set of definitions might be examined for inconsistencies. Do two different structures make conflicting assumptions about the organization of a third structure? Are there loops, or other illegal topological forms in the schema hierarchy? This problem is difficult because it means, first, defining what "inconsistent" means for our informal knowledge representation and then devising effective procedures for discovering it.

More speculatively, might the system be able to discover or conclude any "interesting things" in examining its own representations? Two primitive forms of this exist currently in TEIRESIAS: The rule models indicate statistical regularities found in the knowledge base, and the schema network editor is able to suggest possible interconnections for a new schema, based on its examination of the existing network. Can more sophisticated forms be developed? Can TEIRESIAS conceivably make useful suggestions about representation design, by noticing, perhaps, that (a) two representations are very "similar," (b) there are relatively "few" instances of either, and (c) combining the two might make the schema network "simpler." While this would have great utility in dealing with the organization and structure of large programs, the difficulty starts with attempts to give precise definitions to the words in quotes, and multiplies quickly. But let us speculate just a little further. Is it possible that some of those suggestions from TEIRESIAS about data structures might in fact have implications for understanding the domain itself? Can the regularities discovered by the rule models, for instance, ever suggest new and interesting things about the structure of reasoning in the domain? Or can the system's ability to discover useful things about data structures be made sophisticated enough that its suggestions offer some help in forming theories about the domain?

These are difficult issues. They address the problem of pattern detection and theory formation applied to a slightly different domain—the domain of representations. Chapter 5 considered this issue briefly and examined the rule models as an example of concept formation. All of the hard problems noted there are yet to be solved, as are the more complex issues involved in theory formation. The examples found in the present TEIRESIAS system serve basically as demonstrations of feasibility.

Theme 4: Programs can be self-understanding. One aspect of the idea of "self-understanding" has been illustrated in the previous section and concerns a program's ability to understand itself in terms of representations and data structures. Here we consider how it might understand its own behavior.

To make the discussion more concrete, consider the following criteria for "understanding":

Can the program

- explain its behavior?
- explain what it knows?
- change its behavior?
- change the content of its knowledge?

These criteria can be met with varying levels of success with respect to completeness (*i.e.*, how much of the system can be explained or changed) and generality (*i.e.*, are the techniques specific to the current implementation or are they more broadly applicable).

Consider the issue of generality first, and examine the combined TEIRESIAS-MYCIN system as one example. Chapter 3 noted the variety of techniques that has been used to generate explanations. These ranged from one program written specifically to explain part of another, to the system's ability to use the templates to examine the same rules it was executing. This latter form of introspection is the most powerful of the solutions we have explored, since it adjusts automatically to changes in the program's knowledge base and control structure (at least the part of the control structure that can be captured in meta-rules).

The question of completeness for the first three of the criteria above is answered currently by considering how much knowledge is in rules. The system can explain behavior that results from rule invocation, can refer to knowledge embedded in rules, and can change its behavior by the acquisition of new rules.

Where knowledge or behavior is not rule based, it cannot currently be explained. (The ability to acquire new conceptual primitives via the schemata offers another foundation for acquisition of new knowledge, so the system is currently more complete with regard to changing the content of its knowledge.)

There appears to be a fundamental limit on the completeness with which program behavior and knowledge might plausibly be explained or modified. It is characterized in the introduction to [Minksy68] as the distinction between "compiled" and "interpreted" behavior, where it is suggested that some behavior, some knowledge, may reasonably be considered "compiled" and, hence, inaccessible to further decomposition. The issue is more than just choosing a convenient level at which to view system behavior, as we did in chapter 3. Some behavior and knowledge is simply going to be inexplicable. For TEIRESIAS-MYCIN, for example, this might mean that the system would not and, indeed, need not ever be able to explain things like the mechanism of rule retrieval.

In line with our emphasis on making knowledge explicit, we might add another possibility: In addition to being compiled or interpreted, knowledge might also simply be absent. A program clearly cannot explain what it doesn't know, and before the use of meta-rules, MYCIN had no way of explaining why certain rules were executed in a particular order. It was in a position roughly analogous to someone who can recall a list from rote memorization, but never learned the rationale behind its order. [5]

As noted earlier, our efforts toward explanation, and this larger goal of self-understanding, have really only begun. The issue is again one of representation: How can knowledge be represented in forms that allow it to be both used and dissected? Our use of rules as a high-level language has provided a certain level of performance, but as previous sections have noted, there are many problems yet to be solved.

Theme 5: A representation can usefully be more than a densely encoded string of bits.   There is an obvious corollary to the belief that a program can be more than the minimum set of symbol manipulation operations necessary for solving a problem. Analogously, a representation can be viewed in terms other than the minimum number of bits that will carry the information required. This becomes necessary if we want a program to modify its knowledge base without introducing errors: If the program is to manipulate its representations in intelligent ways, then it needs to know a good deal more about each than standard declarations typically supply.

Some of the additional information about representations we used includes: its structure, the set of legal values for each component of the structure, its interrelations with other representations (as indicated by the RELATIONS), and its place in the whole collection of data structures (as indicated by the schema hierarchy). All of this information is necessary to perform even the simple and

---

[5] See [Parnas75] for some further thoughts on "compiled" and "interpreted" knowledge and its use in system design.

straightforward "clerical" kinds of tasks involved in knowledge base maintenance.

In addition, it makes possible much of the "intelligence" displayed by the acquisition system. As noted above, the representations used in the knowledge base are both data structures and a model of the domain of application. Part of an "intelligent" process of acquisition involves being able both to use this information and to insure that it is properly maintained. Chapter 5, for example, noted that one of the consistency constraints used in generating interpretations of a new rule relied on this world model to insure that an attribute in a clause was paired with an appropriate value. The integrity of the model is maintained by devices like the RELATIONS list, which insures that new structures are properly integrated and that existing dependencies are maintained.

All of this means an emphasis on the careful representation and organization of this information. The schema language is one attempt to provide a framework for organizing and accessing this information and may help to make its expression easier.

These first five themes have explored how TEIRESIAS supplies a base of meta-level knowledge—information about the organization, structure, and use of knowledge in the performance program. The ultimate goal is to make possible a useful level of introspection, one that will support "intelligent" behavior for the acquisition, explanation, and effective use of object-level knowledge. *Task-specific high-level languages* are the primary mechanism used to make this feasible, since they avoid the difficult problems involved in having a program read ordinary code or examine standard data structures. The emphasis on *making knowledge in programs explicit and accessible* follows from the desire to have the program modify its own knowledge base and behavior. To avoid introducing errors in doing this, it needs a large store of *information about its own representations*, information of the sort that is typically left either informally specified or omitted entirely. The concept of a *program that "understands" itself* concerns its ability to account for, and modify, its behavior and knowledge; this is introspection at the behavioral level. Finally, the suggestion was made that a *representation can be viewed in a broad context*, both as a data structure in the program and as part of the program's model of the world. This context is used as the basis for a language and framework in which to organize and express much of the required knowledge.

Theme 6: A program can have some grasp on its own complexity. The thought has been around for some time that a program ought to be able to help out in dealing with its own complexities (a recent collection of suggestions along this line is in [Winograd74]). There are at least two ways in which it should be possible to enlist a program's help.

The first involves simply coping with the complexity that inevitably arises. It is, as we have seen, difficult to make a single small change to any large system. There are typically a number of related changes that have to be made and constraints that must be met. Rather than relying on memory (or documentation) to keep track of all the details, why not have the system do it? Whatever knowledge there is concerning those details ought to be made explicit and then made accessible to and comprehensible by the system. Several examples of this have been explored in earlier chapters. The use of the schemata for acquisition of new conceptual primitives is a primary example. The schemata were designed to confront exactly this problem of the complexity and detail of structure and interrelationships typically encountered in any large set of data structures. Another example is found in the suggestion that it ought to be possible to edit the schemata and have TEIRESIAS edit all the instances similarly. The use of a "totally typed" language during acquisition is still another example. As illustrated, this makes it possible for the system to specify to the expert the legal form of the answer to any of its questions and to check the responses for syntactic validity. Finally, even the simple recap provided by the explanation routines can help the user cope with the wealth of detail that arises in a long consultation.

The second form of aid might arise from the capability of the system to simplify itself for the benefit of the viewer. Introspection may mean little if a program is very large and its behavior complex. If the system "explains" itself at a level that leaves the viewer drowning in a wealth of detail, little has been accomplished. Is it possible, then, for a program to abstract that detail and present a comprehensible picture? Can the "magnification" be varied to provide accounts which offer different levels of details?

Some very basic steps in this direction were described in chapters 3 and 5. The "higher level explanations" available with the WHY <n> command, for instance, offer a very simple form of simplification and variable magnification. The rule models are another example: As abstract descriptions of the content of the knowledge base they help to make clear the general trends in the reasoning while suppressing less important detail.

But these are only first steps. A more sophisticated solution would make it possible to base different explanations on different models of the underlying processes. It might even be able to choose a model tailored to both the current sequence of events and the current viewer. There is clearly much work that remains to be done.

Theme 7: Programs can be self-adjusting.   As the previous discussion suggests, dealing with complexity is difficult. One approach to the problem views it as an issue of design and asks: Rather than creating tools to recapture programs whose complexity has gotten out of hand, is it instead possible to design programs in ways that avoid complexity from the outset? That is, can we try to partition problems and design representations in ways that make them simple and self-contained. A few relevant ideas have been in the air for some time. Simon's *Sciences of the Artificial* contains some very general observations on system decomposition, while *Structured Programming* [Dijkstra72] offers some thoughts on control structure design.

There are also some well-established techniques of programming which confront this problem. One approach emphasizes dealing with change by *insulating* one part of the program from another. A number of techniques have been used, and a somewhat larger number of names have been invented for them.

   1   *Indirection*. Indirection insulates the program from referential changes. Thus, indirection in code (indirect addressing) makes possible compile time (or even execution time) assignment of addresses. Indirection in data (*e.g.*, use of a pointer to a set rather than an explicit list of its members) offers a similar flexibility.
   2   *Records*. One level of record structures will insulate a program from changes in data structure implementation ("dataless [representation-free] programming" [Balzer67]). Two levels of record structures can be used to insulate a program from certain kinds of changes in data structure design ("data independence," [Bachman75]).
   3   *Data abstraction*. Where records define a representation by its structure, data abstraction defines it by its behavior. It offers a similar form of insulation, allowing code to refer to data structure behavior without regard to details of the implementation of that behavior ("abstract data types" [Liskov74]).
   4   *Decomposition*. By choosing the proper boundaries, systems can be decomposed into modules that are insulated from changes in one another ("information hiding" [Parnas72]). (Consider the discussion about "traffic directors" in Section 6–9.1 in these terms.)
   5   *Content-directed invocation*. By describing (rather than naming) knowledge sources (KSs) and by effecting that reference via direct examination of KS content, system behavior is insulated from changes to the code of any of its KSs. Thus a KS can be edited and its pattern of invocation will change accordingly, without the necessity of making changes elsewhere in the system (see the discussion in Section 7–5.3.3).

   There may quite plausibly, however, be problems with elements that are inherently tightly connected and complex. It may be impossible to deal with these without a corresponding degree of complexity in the program that solves them. Rather than attempting to avoid complexity, therefore, can we, in this case, design systems which are *self-adjusting*? That is, is it possible to design a system to be inherently flexible, rather than as drastically fragile as most programs typically are?
   Achieving such flexibility would require systems that are inherently stable, in which the effects of changes are easily accommodated. Many large programs are currently similar to a house of cards, in that changes or additions must be made with utmost care, lest the entire structure collapse. There are simply too many unknown, unstable, and critical interdependencies. What we would like is something more akin to a pond—throw in a rock or add a lot of water and there is a commotion initially, but eventually, the ripples subside, the "system" adjusts to the new conditions by expanding or reconfiguring itself and remains as "competent" a pond as before.
   One established programming technique that confronts the problem of adjusting to changes is the idea of a *transform*. It expresses and automatically takes care of necessary interrelationships by propagating the effects of changes.

Consider a compiler in this light. To see the point most clearly, imagine in its absence the difficulty of maintaining both source code and machine code for a program. After any editing in the source, it would still be necessary to edit the machine code analogously. But given the subtlety, complexity, and amount of work involved in just understanding the mapping from source to machine language, the transform has been specified precisely and turned over to the system.

An analogous situation exists with respect to data structures. There are programs with established, complex interrelationships of data structures, and, at very best, the relationships are only documented somewhere. The programmer still does multiple edits of data structures to maintain those interrelationships, when he should be able to edit just one structure and "recompile the data structures" to have the system take care of the "ripples." It is true that compilers are both better understood and far more stable as transforms. Data structure interrelationships are both invented anew for each program and subject to constant change as programs evolve. Even so, we claim that there are interesting and important results that may follow from specifying the interrelationships. First, it can conceivably make possible larger systems than might otherwise be maintainable, and second, the task of being precise about those relationships can help insure that the design is free from obvious inconsistencies.

Our system has something of this sort in the RELATIONS associated with each schema. They specify data structure interrelationships and offer one level óf self-adjusting character: The effects of adding a new instance of a schema are propagated through the rest of the system. Recall, for example, the extensive interaction triggered by adding a new culture site to the knowledge base of the performance program. To push this one level further, however, consider a more fundamental change. What if it were necessary to change the definition of a data structure? Part of this might include writing a whole new set of RELATIONS specifications for it and making modifications to the RELATIONS for other structures.

But is there an easier way to do this? Would it be possible to write a definition of the data structure and "compile" it into the appropriate set of RELATIONS. Recall, for example, the three categories of culture sites mentioned in chapter 6. It should be possible to say that every culture site is either *sterile, non-sterile,* or *indeterminant,* that is, that there are three mutually exclusive and exhaustive classifications for it. If, later, it were discovered that yet another classification were necessary, rather than rewriting all the RELATIONS by hand, it should be possible to edit just the definition of a SITE, and have the "data structure compiler" recompute all the new RELATIONS.

This would be a useful capability, since representation redesign is an occupational hazard of programming and one that typically has far-reaching effects for even small modifications. Logical errors in design also occur, and with more formal definitions it might be possible to check for inconsistencies during the "compilation."

Note that it also extends the concept of a self-adjusting system. One level of change propagation was accomplished by the precise specification of the data structure interrelationships. Another level would be made possible by deriving the interrelationships themselves from more basic elements, making it possible to propagate the effects of changes in definitions.

But all this is only speculation that raises more questions than it answers. What constitutes a "definition" of a data structure? What information should it contain? The discussion above indicates that both structural and behavioral definitions have been proposed; there may be yet other possibilities. How is the information to be represented? Much work has been directed toward the use of formal languages, and has demonstrated the complexity that lies beneath apparently simple structures when their properties are described precisely (see, for instance, [Spitzen75]).

One further speculation to set all this in the broadest terms: Some elements of the techniques that have been employed in dealing with change seem general enough to be widely applicable. Can this set of principles be extended and made large enough to provide useful guidance? Might there someday be a "science" of representation design?

8–5 PROJECTIONS

The past seven chapters have explored some preliminary solutions to the myriad of problems encountered in the attempt to facilitate the construction of expert systems. This is only a beginning, for much remains to be done. But what might be the eventual impact of success? What might be gained by solving the problems? Two simple but significant possibilities come to mind.

One result might be the realization of a different form of generality in problem solving. This report began with the observation that the search for generality in AI programs has traditionally focused on broadly applicable problem-solving methods and has so far proved unsuccessful. An alternative form of generality was suggested, one that took its breadth not from general problem-solving methods, but from powerful knowledge acquisition techniques.

> The appropriate place for an attack on the problem of generality may be at the meta-levels of learning, knowledge transformation, and representation, not at the level of performance programs. Perhaps for the designer of intelligent systems what is most significant about human problem solving behavior is the ability to learn specialties as needed—to learn expertise in problem areas by learning problem-specific heuristics, by acquiring problem-specific information, and by transforming general knowledge and general processes into specialized forms. [6]

We have taken a step in this direction by making possible a limited form of communication between an expert in an application domain and a high-performance program. The program is capable of explaining significant portions

[6] From [Feigenbaum71].

of its behavior and is prepared to accept new knowledge and integrate it into its knowledge base.

Finally, if it were truly easy to construct large knowledge-based systems, then might they eventually become an important medium of expression? Might they provide a medium for the formalization of knowledge in domains where it is as yet highly informal, and could they provide a useful framework for its expression and organization? Such systems might help to collect and organize knowledge on a scale large enough to become useful tools in the attempts to understand and develop theories for domains where no cohesive theories yet exist.

I will say nothing further.
Against this answer let your temper rage as wildly as you will.

Sophocles
Oedipus the King, lines 343–344

Appendix One

References

Several abbreviations are used for readability:

3IJCAI *Proceedings of the Third International Joint Conference on Artificial Intelligence,* [available from SRI International, Publications, 330 Ravenswood Ave, Menlo Park, CA 94025].

4IJCAI *Proceedings of the Fourth International Joint Conference on Artificial Intelligence,* [available from MIT A.I. Lab, 545 Technology Square, Cambridge, MA 02138].

AIM # A. I. Memo #, Computer Science Department, Stanford, California.

MIT Massachusetts Institute of Technology, Cambridge, MA.

CMU Carnegie Mellon University, Pittsburgh, Pennsylvania.

1 Aristotle, *Rhetoric,* J. H. Freese (trans.), G. P. Putnam, New York, 1926. [Aristotle26]
2 Bachman, C. W., Trends in data base management–1975, *National Computer Conference,* 1975, pp. 569-576. [Bachman75]
3 Balzer, R. M., Dataless programming, *Proc. AFIPS Conf.,* 1967, pp. 535-544. [Balzer67]
4 Barrow, H. G., and J. M. Tannenbaum, Representation and use of knowledge in vision, *SIGART Newsletter,* June 1975, pp. 2-8. (Also see the articles following it.)

[Barrow75]

5   Baumgart, B. G., Geometric models for computer vision, AIM 249, October 1974. [Baumgart74]

6   Bobrow, D. N., Natural language input for a computer problem solving system, in M. Minsky (Ed.), *Semantic Information Processing*, The MIT Press, MIT, 1968, pp. 146-226. [Bobrow68]

7   Bobrow, D. N., and A. Collins (Eds.), *Representation and Understanding*, Academic Press, New York, 1975. [Bobrow75]

8   Bobrow, D. N., and T. Winograd, Overview of KRL, *Cognitive Science*, vol. 1, January 1977, pp. 3-47. [Bobrow77]

9   Brachman, R. J., Structural knowledge in a document information consulting system, TR 6-75, Center for Research in Computing Technology, Harvard University, Cambridge, 1975. [Brachman75]

10   Brown, J. S., Uses of AI and advanced computer technology in education, Bolt, Beranek, & Newman, Cambridge, December 1975. [Brown75]

11   Brown, J. S., and R. R. Burton, Diagnostic models for procedural bugs in mathematical skills, *Cognitive Science*, volume 2, April-June 1978, pp. 155-192. [Brown78]

12   Buchanan, B. G., and J. Lederberg, The heuristic DENDRAL program for explaining empirical data, *IFIP*, 1971, pp. 179-188. [Buchanan71]

13   Buchanan, B. G., E. A. Feigenbaum, and N. S. Sridharan, Heuristic theory formation: Data interpretation and rule formation, in B. Meltzer and D. Michie (Eds.), *Machine Intelligence 7*, Edinburgh University Press, Edinburgh, 1972, pp. 267-292. [Buchanan72]

14   Buchanan, B. G. and T. Mitchell, Model-directed learning of production rules, in *Pattern-Directed Inference Systems*, (Waterman and Hayes-Roth, eds.), pp 297-312, Academic Press, NY, 1978. [Buchanan78]

15   Carbonell, J. R., and A. M. Collins, Natural semantics in AI, *3IJCAI*, 1973, pp. 344-351. [Carbonell73]

16   Carroll, L., Alice's Adventures in Wonderland, in M. Gardner (Ed.), *The Annotated Alice*, World Publishing Company, 1960. [Carroll60]

17   Dahl, O. J., B. Myhrhaug, and K. Nygaard, Common base language, *Norwegian Computing Center Technical Report*, 1970. [Dahl70]

18   Davis, R., and J. King, An overview of production systems, in E. W. Elcock and D. Michie (Eds.), *Machine Intelligence 8*, John Wiley & Sons, New York, 1977 (also AIM 271). [Davis77a]

19   Davis, R., B. G. Buchanan, and E. Shortliffe, Production rules as a representation for a knowledge-based consultation program, *Artificial Intelligence*, vol. 8, no. 1, February 1977, pp. 15-45 (also AIM 266). [Davis77b]

20   Dijkstra, E., O. J. Dahl, and C. A. R. Hoare, *Structured Programming*, Academic Press, New York, 1972. [Dijkstra72]

21   Eswaran, K. P., and D. D. Chamberlain, Functional specification of a subsystem for data base integrity, *Proceedings of International Conference on Very Large Data Bases*, September 1975. [Eswaran75]

22   Falk, G., Computer interpretation of imperfect line data, AIM 132, August 1970. [Falk70]

23   Faught, W., K. Colby, and R. Parkison, The interaction of affects, intentions and desires, AIM 253, December 1974. [Faught74]

24 Feigenbaum, E. A., B. Buchanan, and J. Lederberg, On generality and problem solving, in B. Meltzer and D. Michie (Eds.), *Machine Intelligence 6*, Edinburgh University Press, Edinburgh, 1971, pp. 165-190. [Feigenbaum71]

25 Feldman, J., J. R. Low, D. C. Swinehart, and R. H. Taylor, Recent developments in SAIL, an ALGOL-based language for artificial intelligence, AIM 176, November 1972. [Feldman72]

26 Fikes, R. J., and N. J. Nilsson, STRIPS—A new approach to the application of theorem proving to problem solving, *Artificial Intelligence*, vol. 2, Winter 1971, pp. 189-208. [Fikes71]

27 Fikes R. J., P. E. Hart, and N. J. Nilsson, Learning and executing generalized robot plans, *Artificial Intelligence*, vol. 3, Winter 1972, pp. 251-288. [Fikes72]

28 Finkel, R., R. Taylor, R. Bolles, R. Paul, and J. Feldman, AL, a programming system for automation, AIM 243, June 1975. [Finkel74]

29 Gelernter, H., Realization of a geometry-theorem proving machine, in E. A. Feigenbaum and J. Feldman (Eds.), *Computers and Thought*, McGraw-Hill, New York, 1963, pp. 134-152. [Gelernter59]

30 Goldstein, I., Understanding simple picture programs, AI-TR-294, MIT, September 1974. [Goldstein74]

31 Green, C. C., The application of theorem proving to question answering systems, AIM 96, August 1969. [Green69]

32 Green, C. C., R. J. Waldinger, D. R. Barstow, R. Elschlager, D. B. Lenat, B. P. McCune, D. E. Shaw, and L. I. Steinberg, Progress report on program-understanding systems, AIM 240, August 1974. [Green74]

33 Gregory, R. L., *Eye and Brain*, McGraw-Hill, New York, 1966. [Gregory66]

34 Guzman, A., Computer recognition of 3-D objects in a visual scene, MAC-TR-59, MIT, December 1968. [Guzman68]

35 Hansen, G., Adaptive systems for dynamic run-time optimization of programs, doctoral dissertation, CMU, March 1974. [Hansen74]

36 Harre, R., *The Principles of Scientific Thinking*, University of Chicago Press, Chicago, 1970. [Harre70]

37 Hart, P. E., Progress on a computer-based consultant, *4IJCAI*, 1975, pp. 831-841. [Hart75]

38 Hayes-Roth, F., and J. McDermott, Knowledge acquisition from structural descriptions, Tech. Rep., Computer Science Department, CMU, February 1976. [Hayes-Roth76]

39 Hewitt, C., Procedural semantics—models of procedures and the teaching of procedures, *Natural Language Processing* (Courant Computer Science Symposium), vol. 8, 1971, pp. 331-350. [Hewitt71]

40 Hewitt, C., Description and theoretical analysis of PLANNER, doctoral dissertation, Department of Mathematics, MIT, 1972. [Hewitt72]

41 Hewitt, C., and B. Smith, Toward a programmer's apprentice, *IEEE Transactions on Software Engineering*, SE-1, March 1975, pp. 26-45. [Hewitt75]

42 Howe, W. J., Computer-assisted design of complex organic syntheses, doctoral dissertation, Harvard University, Cambridge, 1973 (*Dissertation Abstracts*, P5207 B, 33/11). [Howe73]

43 Interaction Associates, *Strategy Notebook*, Interaction Associates, Inc., San Francisco, 1972. [Interaction72]

44 Johnson, H. R., A schema report facility for a CODASYL-based data definition language, in B. C. M. Dougue and G. M. Nijssen (Eds.), *Data Base Description*, American Elsevier, New York, 1975, pp. 299-328. [Johnson75]

45 Kulikowski, C. A., S. Weiss, and A. Saifr, Glaucoma diagnosis and therapy by computer, *Proceedings of Annual Meeting of Assoc. for Research in Vision and Opthamology*, May 1973. [Kulikowski73]

46 Learning Research Group, Personal dynamic media, Xerox PARC, Palo Alto, Calif., 1976. [Learning76]

47 Lesser, V. R., R. D. Fennell, L. D. Erman, and D. R. Reddy, Organization of the HEARSAY II speech understanding system, *IEEE Transactions on Acoustics, Speech, and Signal Processing*, ASSP-23, February 1975, pp. 11-23. [Lesser74]

48 Liskov, B., and S. Zilles, Programming with abstract data types, *SIGPLAN Notices*, April 1974. [Liskov74]

49 Low J., Automatic coding: Choice of data structures, AIM 242, August 1974. [Low74]

50 Lukasiewicz, J., A numerical interpretation of the theory of propositions, in L. Borkowski (Ed.), *Jan Lukasiewicz: Selected Works*, 1970. [Lukasiewisz70]

51 The MACSYMA reference manual, The MATHLAB Group, MIT, September 1974. [MACSYMA74]

52 Manna, Z., Correctness of programs, *Journal of Computer Systems Sciences*, May 1969. [Manna69]

53 McDermott, D., Assimilation of new information, AI-TR-291, MIT, February 1974. [McDermott74]

54 McLeod, D. J., High level domain definition in a relational data base system, *SIGPLAN Notices*, no. 1, April 1976, pp. 47-57. [McLeod76]

55 Miller, P. B., Strategy selection in medical diagnosis, Project MAC TR-153, MIT, September 1975. [Miller75]

56 Minsky, M. (Ed.), *Semantic Information Processing*, MIT Press, MIT, 1968. [Minsky68]

57 Minsky, M., A framework for representing knowledge, MIT AI Memo 306, June 1974. [Minsky74]

58 Mitchell, J. G., The design and construction of flexible and efficient interactive programming systems, doctoral dissertation, Department of Computer Science, CMU, June 1970. [Mitchell70]

59 Newell, A., J. C. Shaw, and H. A. Simon, A variety of intelligent learning in a general problem-solver, in M. Yovitts and S. Cameron (Eds.), *Self-organizing Systems*, Pergamon, New York, pp. 153-189. [Newell59]

60 Newell, A., and H. A. Simon, GPS, a program that simulates human thought, in E. A. Feigenbaum and J. Feldman (Eds.), *Computers and Thought*, McGraw-Hill, New York, pp. 279-296. [Newell61]

61 Newell, A., Heuristic programming; ill-structured problems, in Aronofsky (Ed.), *Progress in Operations Research*, vol. 3, 1969, pp. 362-414. [Newell69]

62 Newell, A., and H. Simon, *Human Problem Solving*, Prentice-Hall, Englewood Cliffs, New Jersey, 1972. [Newell72]

63 Norman, D. A., and D. E. Rumelhart, *Explorations in Cognition*, W. H. Freeman, San Francisco, 1975. [Norman75]

64 Parnas, D. L., On the criteria to be used in decomposing systems into modules, *CACM*, vol. 15, December 1972, pp. 1053-1058. [Parnas72]

65   Parnas, D. L., and D. P. Siewiorek, Use of the concept of transparency in the design of hierarchically structured systems, *CACM*, vol. 18, July 1975, pp. 401-408. [Parnas75]

66   Polya, G., *How to Solve It*, McGraw-Hill, Princeton, New Jersey, 1954. [Polya54]

67   Pople, H., J. Meyers, and R. Miller, DIALOG, a model of diagnostic logic for internal medicine, *4IJCAI*, 1975, pp. 848-855. (The system has since been renamed INTERNIST.) [Pople75]

68   Post, E.: Formal reductions of the general combinatorial problem, *American Journal of Math*, vol. 65, 1943, pp. 197-268. [Post43] For an introduction to the general principles involved, see M. Minksy, *Computation: Finite and infinite machines*, Prentice Hall, Englewood Cliffs, New Jersey, 1967, chap. 12.

69   Reddy, R., The HEARSAY speech understanding system, *3IJCAI*, 1973, pp. 185-199. [Reddy73]

70   Reiger, C. J., Conceptual memory: A theory and computer program, AIM 233, July 1974. [Reiger74]

71   Resier, J. F., BAIL - A debugger for SAIL, AIM 270, October 1975. [Resier75]

72   Roberts, L. G., Machine perception of 3-D solids, Tech. Rep. 315, Lincoln Labs, MIT, May 1963. [Roberts63]

73   Rubin, A. D., Hypothesis formation and evaluation in medical diagnosis, AI-TR-316, MIT, January 1975. [Rubin75]

74   Rulifson, J. F., J. A. Derksen, and R. J. Waldinger, QA4: A procedural calculus for intuitive reasoning, Tech. Note 73, SRI International, Palo Alto, Calif., November 1972. [Rulifson72]

75   Rumelhart, D. E., and D. A. Norman, Active semantic networks as a model of human memory, *3IJCAI*, 1973, pp. 450-458. [Rumelhart73]

76   Sacerdoti, E., Planning in a hierarchy of abstraction spaces, *3IJCAI*, 1973, pp. 412-422. [Sacerdoti73]

77   Sacerdoti, E., *A Structure for Plans and Behavior*, American Elsevier, New York, 1977. [Sacerdoti77]

78   Samet, H., Automatically proving the correctness of translations involving optimized code, AIM 259, May 1975. [Samet75]

79   Samuel, A. L., Some studies in machine learning using the game of checkers II—recent progress, *IBM Journal of Research and Development*, vol. 11, 1967, pp. 601-617. [Samuel67]

80   Sandewall, E., Ideas about managment of LISP data bases, *4IJCAI*, 1975, pp. 585-592. [Sandewall75]

81   Shaw, D., W. Swartout, and C. Green, Inferring LISP programs from examples, *4IJCAI*, 1975, pp. 260-267. [Shaw75]

82   Shortliffe, E. H., R. Davis, B. G. Buchanan, S. G. Axline, C. C. Green, and S. N. Cohen, Computer-based consultations in clinical therapeutics—explanation and rule acquisition capabilities of the MYCIN system, *Computers and Biomedical Research*, vol. 8, 1975, pp. 303-320. [Shortliffe75a]

83   Shortliffe, E. H., and B. G. Buchanan, A model of inexact reasoning in medicine, *Mathematical Biosciences*, vol. 23, 1975, pp. 351-379. [Shortliffe75b]

84   Shortliffe, E. H., *MYCIN: Computer-based Medical Consultations*, American Elsevier, New York, 1976. [Shortliffe76]

85   Simon, H., The structure of ill-structured problems, *Artificial Intelligence*, vol. 4, 1973, pp.181-201. [Simon73]

86 Sophocles, Oedipus the King (427 B.C.), in Greene and Lattimore (Eds.), *Greek Tragedies*, vol. 1, University of Chicago Press, Chicago, 1960. [Sophocles27]

87 Spitzen, J., and B. Wegbreit, The verification and synthesis of data structures, *Acta Informatica*, vol. 4, 1975, pp. 127-144. [Spitzen75]

88 Stonebreaker, M., Implementation of integrity constraints and views by modification, *Proc. SIGMOD Conf.*, 1975, pp. 65-78. [Stonebreaker75]

89 Sussman, G., *A Computational Model of Skill Acquisition*, American Elsevier, New York, 1975. [Sussman75]

90 Suzuki, N., Automatic verification of programs with complex data structures, AIM 279, February 1976. [Suzuki76]

91 Tversky, A., and D. Kahneman, Judgment under uncertainty: Heuristics and biases, *Science*, vol. 185, September 18 1974, pp. 1129-1131. [Tversky74]

92 van Melle, W., Would you like advice on another horn, MYCIN project internal working paper, Stanford University, Stanford, Calif., December 1974. [van Melle74]

93 Waldinger, R., and K. N. Levitt, Reasoning about programs, *Artificial Intelligence*, vol. 5, Fall 1974, pp. 235-316. [Waldinger74]

94 Waltz, D., Generating semantic descriptions from drawings of scenes with shadows, AI-TR-271, MIT, November 1972. [Waltz72]

95 Warshall, S., A theorem on Boolean matrices, *JACM*, vol. 9, January 1962, pp. 11-12. [Warshall62]

96 Waterman, D. A., Generalization learning techniques for automating the learning of heuristics, *Artificial Intelligence*, vol. 1, 1970, pp. 121-170. [Waterman70]

97 Waterman, D. A., Exemplary programming, in D. Waterman and R. Hayes-Roth (Eds.), *Pattern-directed Inference Systems*, Academic Press, 1977. [Waterman77]

98 Wickelgren, W. A., *How to Solve Problems*, W. H. Freeman, San Francisco, 1974. [Wickelgren74]

99 Winograd, T., *Understanding Natural Language*, Academic Press, New York, 1972. [Winograd72]

100 Winograd, T., Breaking the complexity barrier, again, *SIGPLAN Notices*, no. 1, January 1974. [Winograd74]

101 Winograd, T., Frame representations and the procedural/declarative controversy, in D. N. Bobrow and A. Collins (Eds.), *Representation and Understanding*, Academic Press, New York, 1975. [Winograd75]

102 Winston, P. H., Learning structural descriptions from examples, MAC TR-76, MIT, September 1970. [Winston70]